1996 Capital Access

Derivatives Desk Reference

Buyside & Sellside Profiles

Table of Contents

1996 Capital Access
Derivatives Desk Reference
Buyside & Sellside Profiles

Capital Access Corporation
Mountain Heights Center • 430 Mountain Avenue • Murray Hill, NJ 07974
Tel: 908 771-0800 • Tel: 800 866-5987 • Fax: 908 771-0330 • E-mail: cac@planet.net

PUBLISHER
David D. Farrington

SENIOR EDITOR
Carrie Thomas

EDITORS
Karen Ardington
Carrie Diehl
Darren Duffy
Norrie Kurtz

DATA RESEARCH
Najma Carey
Sussie DeAngelis
Jeannette Quinton
Stephanie Snedeker
Kim Crouch
Lisa Meyers
Joanne Russak
Sue Turner

MARKETING
Courtney Kole
Paula Siwczak

SALES
Steve Miller
Matt Zanelli

CLIENT SERVICE
Michael Ruvo
Jen Weiss

SYSTEMS
Jim Sample
Mary Schneider
Joe Walkowich

DESIGN
Chris Badgley, RCI Group Inc.

PUBLICATIONS ADMINISTRATION
Regina Longo

ISBN 1-888815-00-0 ISBN 1-888815-01-9 ISSN 1088-0674

A Note from the Publisher

Worldwide, investing in derivatives has attracted the concern of many people, market observers and investors alike. As a firm which specializes in tracking institutional investment in fixed-income securities, Capital Access has had a unique vantage point from which to observe derivatives investment and related controversy.

In our day-to-day business, we monitor evolving practices in derivatives use and investment among knowledgeable professionals on both the buy and sell sides of the financial securities marketplace. According to our intelligence, it's clear that the vast majority of investment professionals relying on derivatives are using them in a concerted effort to responsibly manage risk.

In addition to the insight we have gained into investment activity in both the U.S. and European derivatives marketplaces, we have become acutely aware that there is no readily accessible, comprehensive resource for identifying the key buyside institutions and top sellside firms participating in the derivatives marketplace. Nor, is there any resource for identifying the professionals who actively participate in the structuring, sale, trading and purchasing of the myriad types of derivative instruments and transactions.

Our goal in publishing this edition of the ***Derivatives Desk Reference*** is to provide such a resource for the U.S. securities marketplace. The ***Derivatives Desk Reference*** is one in a series of buyside and sellside directories which Capital Access is publishing on different segments of the fixed-income securities markets. These references will be available in both hard copy and CD-ROM.

For those who are looking for more in-depth information on the fixed-income markets, we invite you to discover the FINCOM ***Encyclopedia of Investor Profiles*** and MAXX, the securities industry's leading contact management software. Both are produced by Capital Access.

We would be pleased to provide you with information on these and other products and services. We are grateful to you for purchasing this ***Derivatives Desk Reference*** and wholeheartedly hope that it will become, for you, a valued resource. Please let us know how we might improve upon this edition so that we may strive to meet your expectations for future publications.

— David D. Farrington
Publisher

PETE WHISENANT
JOHNNY KLIPPSTEIN
PITCHER
LOS ANGELES DODGERS
CASEY WISE
MATCHBOX
75
WHOEVER HAS
THE BEST STUFF
TO TRADE
STILL WINS.
Products that have shaped the market. Customer service that sets industry standards. The resources that maintain the most productive exchange in the world. Considering the advantages of the Chicago Board of Trade, there really is no competition.
CHICAGO BOARD OF TRADE
http://www.cbot.com
Major League Baseball trademarks used with permission of MLB Properties, Inc.
Matchbox is a registered trademark of Matchbox International Limited. Used with permission.

Foreword

The revolution that has taken place in the world financial markets was aptly described by a noted economist, Henry Kaufman, in the 1985 Annual Report of Phibro-Salomon:

> If a modern-day Rip Van Winkle had fallen asleep twenty years ago, or for that matter even ten years back, on awakening today, he would be astonished as to what has happened in the financial markets. Instead of a world of isolated national capital markets and a preponderance of fixed-rate financing, he would discover a world of highly integrated capital markets, an extensive array of financing instruments and new methods of addressing market risk.

By 1996, an even more extensive array of instruments has been developed for managing not only market risk but credit risk. Derivatives are the instruments that have been used to address market risk. Derivatives include futures, forwards, swaps, swaptions, options, caps, and floors.

The derivatives market is an integral part of the global capital market. Derivatives are not—as often categorized by the popular press and some of our less informed congressional representatives and regulators—"exotic" instruments. Derivatives provide a vehicle by which market participants can control risk, borrowers can control borrowing costs and institutional investors can control the market risk of their portfolios. It is safe to say that without the derivative markets, there would not be an efficient global capital market. Regrettably, what the financial press fails to identify are cases where derivatives have prevented a major financial debacle. That news simply doesn't sell newspapers and magazines.

To participate in this market, it is not only necessary to understand how derivatives are valued and their application in controlling risk, but it is essential to know who the players are who have the information. The ***Capital Access Derivatives Desk Reference*** fills this critical role.

— Frank J. Fabozzi

In America, you are not required
to offer food to the hungry.
Or shelter to the homeless.
There is no ordinance forcing
you to visit the lonely, or comfort
the infirm. Nowhere in the
Constitution does it say you have
to provide clothing for the poo
In fact, one of the nicest things
about living here in Americ
is that you really don't have
to do anything for anybod
To the 80 million of you who volunteered time and money last year, thanks
for all you've given. Imagine what more could do. Call
1-800-55-GIVE 5. It's what in the world you can do.
INDEPENDENT SECTOR
Ad Council

Introduction

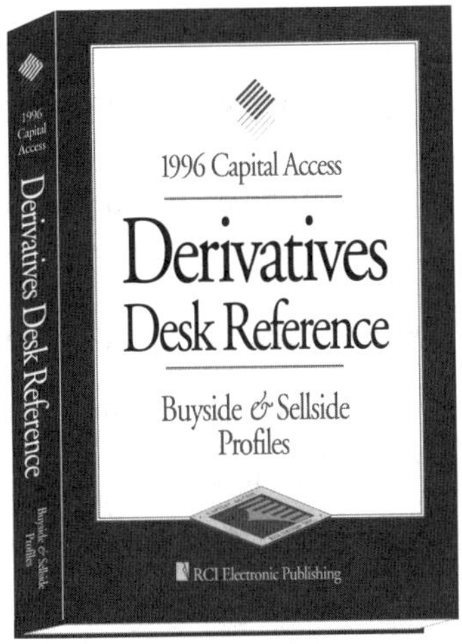

We welcome you to the inaugural edition of the ***Capital Access Derivatives Desk Reference***, an easy-to-use compendium of key decision-makers at the leading U.S. buyside institutions and sellside firms involved in the fixed-income derivatives industry.

Scope

The *DDR*, as it has been affectionately dubbed by those closest to it, provides essential data derived from public documents, such as annual and quarterly reports, insurance company filings, SEC filings, as well as directly from firms monitored by Capital Access Corporation.

To keep the *DDR* to a practical and functional size, we have concentrated on leading corporations and on investment firms which manage fixed-income assets of $500 million or more. The *DDR* profiles nearly 800 institutional investors and corporations which use derivatives for investment and/or risk management purposes.

The *DDR* is not an exhaustive volume on the ever-expanding array of derivatives types. Rather, it is designed to provide basic insight to a firm's involvement in several broad categories of derivatives activities, namely: exchange-traded options and futures, OTC swaps and derivatives, and structured notes.

Buyside Firm Profiles

The buyside profiles in the *DDR* comprise firms which identified themselves as *permitted and active* in the use of derivatives, as well as firms which are *permitted, but currently inactive* in derivatives. Firms in the latter category are denoted by the **CAC Class** designation "Inactive." (See the **Terminology** section later in this Introduction.)

Collectively, the firms listed in the *DDR* manage $8.3 trillion in total assets and $4.3 trillion in fixed-income assets. The aggregate total notional amount of their derivatives contracts is $5.3 trillion.

Each buyside entry provides the firm name, address, telephone and fax numbers; type of firm; total assets and investment profile (for investment firms); uses of derivatives; currencies; regions of activity, as well as a denotation of the specific types of permitted derivatives transactions. Each firm's entry also identifies key managers and derivatives specialists featuring title, job function, and direct telephone and fax numbers, where provided.

Market Sector information appears to the right of the phone and fax numbers. If the key managers and derivatives specialists cover all market sectors, "all" is implicit. Otherwise specific market sectors are indicated. Insight is also offered on each listed firm's involvement in other alternative investments such as repos, reverse repos, stripped securities, and mortgage-backed derivatives.

Buyside Derivatives

AAA Derivatives Group Inc. Insurance Co/Management

Sub of Corporate Derivatives Company Inc.

Location: 1234 Main Street, 10th Floor
Anytown, USA 10000
Fax: 212/555-5500 **Phone:** 212/555-5500

Profile: Spread investor
Investment Portfolio: $4.3 billion

Use:

Balance Sheet/Risk Management	Investment Purposes
Alter portfolio weighting	Hedge balance sheet
Asset allocation	Hedge commercial paper
Capture extra yield	Hedge currency risk
Diversify portfolio	Hedge interest rate risk
Expand international investments	Hedge overseas investments
Hedge bond portfolio risk	Protect currency gains
Hedge currency risk	Strategic liability management
Hedge equity risk	
Hedge interest rate risk	
Protect currency gains	
Provide incremental return	
Reduce variability of returns	

Currencies: Australian $, Belgian franc, Canadian $, ECU, French franc, German mark, Italian lira, Japanese yen, Spanish peseta, Swiss franc, U.K. pound

Regions: United States, UK & Europe, Emerging markets, Canada, Latin America, Pacific rim

DERIVATIVES ACTIVITIES: **CAC Class:** 1

Exchange-traded Options & Futures	**Bond, Currency, Interest rate**	
U.S. Treasury futures	U.S. Treasury options	
OTC Derivatives	**Bond, Currency, Interest rate**	
Plain Vanilla Derivatives	Swaps Forwards Swaptions	Caps Floors Collars
Exotic Derivatives	Bond index swaps CMT swaps CMT options Detached Calls	Index amortizing swaps Index extendible swaps Periodic caps/floors
Structured Notes	Corporate MTNs Govt. agency MTNs Bond Index notes Index amortizing notes Constant maturity Tres notes	Floaters Inverse floaters Periodic capped floaters Tender options bonds Multi-step-up callable bonds
Counterparty Rating Requirement:	AAA	

OTHER ALTERNATIVE INVESTMENTS:

CMOs/REMICs - Govt	Strips
CMOs/REMICs - Private	Repros/reverse repros
GICs	
MOPs/TOPs	

KEY MANAGERS & DERIVATIVES SPECIALISTS:	Direct Phone/Fax	Job Function
Mr. John Q. Arbitrage Assistant Vice President	212/555-5500 212/555-5555	Portfolio Mgr - Derivatives *Taxable*
Mr. William A. Bond Vice President - Securities	212/555-5500 212/555-5555	Chief Investment Officer *Corp*
Mr. Andrew A. Collars Vice President	212/555-5500 212/555-5555	Portfolio Mgr - Structured Notes *Govt, Muni*
Mr. Michael S. Fund Assistant Vice President	212/555-5500 212/555-5555	Portfolio Mgr - Options *Govt, Muni*
Mrs. Donna F. Swaps Assistant Vice President	212/555-5500 212/555-5555	Portfolio Mgr - Futures *Govt, Muni*

1996 Capital Access - Derivatives Desk Reference 3

Sample Buyside Profile

Sellside Firm Profiles

The sellside firms highlighted in the *DDR* are the leading broker/dealer and bank/dealer firms involved in the structuring, sale and trading of fixed-income derivative securities and contracts.

The sellside firm profiles include the firm name, address, telephone and fax numbers, along with a listing of key managers and derivatives specialists, titles, job functions, and direct telephone and fax numbers, where provided.

TERMINOLOGY

Most of the terms used throughout this directory will be very familiar to you. However, we thought the following details about various headings used in the *DDR* might be useful:

Investment Profile:
To provide a concise snapshot of each firm's investment profile, derivatives users are classified according to one of the following categories which describes their *primary* investment goal:

Spread	Total return
Current yield	Hold to maturity
Stable asset	Volatility
Directional	Net asset value

Types of Derivatives:
Here are the types of derivatives covered by this directory:

Exchange-traded Options & Futures

U.S. Treasury futures
U.S. Treasury options
U.S. municipal futures
U.S. municipal options

OTC Derivatives

Plain Vanilla Derivatives

Caps	Floors
Collars	Swaps
Forwards	Swaptions

Exotic Derivatives

Bond index swaps	Index amortizing swaps
CMT swaps	Index extendible swaps
CMT options	Periodic caps/floors
Detached calls	

Structured Notes

Bond index notes	Inverse floaters
Constant maturity Treas notes	Multi-step-up callable bonds
Corporate MTNs	Periodic capped floaters
Floaters	Govt. agency MTNs
Tender option bonds	Index amortizing notes

CAC Class

Based on public filings and direct input from firms, we have characterized each firm's involvement in derivatives through a dollar **range** which most closely depicts its typical contract total, expressed as a notional amount. These ranges have been synthesized into a family of **CAC Class** codes as defined below. There is no indication of **CAC Class** for firms for which this information was not provided.

CAC CLASS	Average Total Contracts (NOTIONAL AMOUNT)
Inactive	Firm is permitted to use derivatives contracts, but is presently inactive.
1	$ 1 - 10 million
2	$ 11 - 99 million
3	$100 - 249 million
4	$250 - 499 million
5	$500 - 999 million
6	$ 1 - 3 billion
7	$ 4 - 10 billion
8	More than $10 billion

CROSS REFERENCES

As noted in the Table of Contents, the ***Derivatives Desk Reference*** provides 11 cross-references to assist you in directly reaching the firms and decision-makers of greatest interest to you. Buyside firms are listed as appropriate in each of the following alphabetical cross-references:

Derivatives Use: Investment Purposes
Derivatives Use: Balance Sheet/Risk Management
Exchange-traded Options & Futures
OTC Derivatives
Currency Swaps & Options
Interest Rate Swaps & Options
Structured Notes
Non-dollar Transactions

A combined buyside/sellside geographical cross-reference, arranged alphabetically by state, is included to help you identify firms in a particular city or state. The *DDR's* rapid reference alphabetical listings for firms and professionals provide instant contact information.

We thank you for choosing the ***1996 Capital Access Derivatives Desk Reference.*** As you incorporate the *DDR* into your daily derivatives activities, please let us know about any suggestions you may have for future enhancements.

The Publisher and editors of this endeavor hope you will count the *DDR* among your most valuable business assets.

Buyside Derivatives

The Acacia Group

Insurance Co/P & C

Location: 51 Louisiana Avenue N.W.
Washington, DC 20001-2176

Fax: 202/638-0345 **Phone:** 202/628-4506

Profile: Spread investor

Investment Portfolio: $ 1.3 billion

Use: **Investment Purposes**
Capture extra yield

Currencies: US dollar

Regions: United States

DERIVATIVES ACTIVITIES: **CAC Class: 1**

Structured Notes	Corporate MTNs	Inverse floaters

OTHER ALTERNATIVE INVESTMENTS:

	CMOs/REMICs – Govt.	CMOs/REMICs – Private

KEY MANAGERS & DERIVATIVES SPECIALISTS:	**Direct Phone/Fax**	**Job Function**
Mr. Stephen B. Couch Vice President	Ext. 362	Chief Investment Officer Portfolio Mgr – Structured Notes
Mr. Andrew S. White Vice President – Securities	Ext. 415	Bond Department Head *Taxable* Trader – Structured Investments *Corp*

Acorn Derivatives Management Corp.

Corporation

Location: One Water Street
White Plains, NY 10601

Fax: 914/949-3521 **Phone:** 914/949-3516

Use: **Balance Sheet/Risk Management**

Currencies: US dollar

Regions: United States

DERIVATIVES ACTIVITIES:

Exchange-traded Options & Futures

OTC Derivatives
Plain Vanilla Derivatives

KEY MANAGERS & DERIVATIVES SPECIALISTS:	**Direct Phone/Fax**	**Job Function**
Mr. William J. Kamperman President & C.E.O.		President Chief Investment Officer Portfolio Mgr – Derivatives Portfolio Mgr – Futures

Adams, Viner & Mosler

Investment Manager

Location: 250 Australian Avenue South
One Clearlake Center Suite 600
West Palm Beach, FL 33401-5012

Fax: 407/655-3059 **Phone:** 407/655-4900

Profile: Spread investor

Investment Portfolio: $ 4.5 billion

Use: **Investment Purposes**
Capture extra yield

Currencies: US dollar, Australian dollar, Belgian franc, Canadian dollar, ECU, French franc, German mark, Italian lira, Indonesian rupiah, Japanese yen, Mexican peso, Spanish peseta, Swiss franc, Thai baht, UK pound

Regions: United States, Canada, Europe, Latin America, Pacific Rim, Emerging mkts

DERIVATIVES ACTIVITIES: **CAC Class: 8**

Exchange-traded Options & Futures
U.S. Treasury futures

OTC Derivatives
Plain Vanilla Derivatives

Bond, Interest rate
Swaps
Forwards
Swaptions
Caps
Floors
Collars

Structured Notes

Govt. agency MTNs
CMT notes
Floaters
Inverse floaters
Periodic capped floaters
Tender options bonds
Multi-step-up callable bonds

OTHER ALTERNATIVE INVESTMENTS:

CMOs/REMICs – Govt.
CMOs/REMICs – Private
Strips
Repos/reverse repos

KEY MANAGERS & DERIVATIVES SPECIALISTS:	Direct Phone/Fax	Job Function
Mr. Warren B. Mosler President & C.E.O.		President Chief Investment Officer Portfolio Mgr – Derivatives Portfolio Mgr – Structured Notes
Mr. Michael Reger General Partner		Portfolio Mgr – Derivatives Portfolio Mgr – Futures Portfolio Mgr – Structured Notes
Mr. Clifford Viner General Partner		Chief Investment Officer Portfolio Mgr – Derivatives

Advanced Micro Devices, Inc.

Corporation

Location: One AMD Place
Sunnyvale, CA 94088

Fax: 408/982-6161 **Phone:** 408/732-2400

Use: **Balance Sheet/Risk Management**
Create synthetic fixed/floating rate
Hedge currency risk
Hedge interest rate risk
Hedge overseas investments
Strategic liability management

Currencies: US dollar, French franc, German mark, Italian lira, Japanese yen, UK pound

Regions: United States, Pacific Rim

DERIVATIVES ACTIVITIES: **CAC Class: 2**

Exchange-traded Options & Futures	**Currency**	
OTC Derivatives	**Currency, Interest rate**	
Plain Vanilla Derivatives	Swaps	Forwards
Counterparty Rating Requirement:	AA	

KEY MANAGERS & DERIVATIVES SPECIALISTS:	**Direct Phone/Fax**	**Job Function**
Mr. Marvin Burkett S.V.P., C.F.O. & Treasurer		Chief Financial Officer Treasurer Portfolio Mgr – Derivatives Portfolio Mgr – Options
Mr. Richard Previte President & C.O.O.		President

Advisers Capital Management Inc.

Investment Manager

Location: 58 Pine Street
Fifth Floor
New York, NY 10005

Fax: 212/514-5780 **Phone:** 212/514-5110

Profile: Total return investor

Investment Portfolio: $ 2.1 billion

Use: **Investment Purposes**

Currencies: US dollar

Regions: United States, Europe

DERIVATIVES ACTIVITIES:

Exchange-traded Options & Futures	**Bond**
U.S. Treasury futures	U.S. Treasury options

OTHER ALTERNATIVE INVESTMENTS:

CMOs/REMICs – Govt.
CMOs/REMICs – Private
Repos/reverse repos

Advisers Capital Management Inc. – continued

KEY MANAGERS & DERIVATIVES SPECIALISTS:	**Direct Phone/Fax**	**Job Function**
Ms. Lauren Best Vice President		Portfolio Mgr – Futures *Govt* Portfolio Mgr – Options *Govt*
Ms. Patricia Klink President		President Chief Investment Officer

AEGON U.S.A. Investment Management (Cedar Rapids)

Insurance Co/Management

Sub of Aegon U.S.A., Inc.

Location: 4333 Edgewood Road N.E.
Cedar Rapids, IA 52499

Fax: 319/369-2009 **Phone:** 319/363-5400

Profile: Current yield investor

Investment Portfolio: $ 11.0 - 20.0 billion

Use: **Balance Sheet/Risk Management**
Create synthetic fixed/floating rate
Strategic liability management

Investment Purposes
Alter portfolio weighting
Capture extra yield

Currencies: US dollar

Regions: United States

DERIVATIVES ACTIVITIES:		**CAC Class: 6**
Exchange-traded Options & Futures U.S. Treasury futures	U.S. Treasury options	
OTC Derivatives **Plain Vanilla Derivatives**	**Interest rate** Swaps	Caps
Structured Notes	Corporate MTNs	Bond index notes
Counterparty Rating Requirement:	AA	

OTHER ALTERNATIVE INVESTMENTS:		
	CMOs/REMICs – Govt. CMOs/REMICs – Private GICs	Strips Repos/reverse repos

AEGON U.S.A. Investment Management (Cedar Rapids) – continued

KEY MANAGERS & DERIVATIVES SPECIALISTS:	Direct Phone/Fax	Job Function
Mr. Peter Birkey	319/369-2399	Trader – Derivatives Trader – Futures Trader – Options Trader – Structured Investments
Mr. Patrick Falconio Executive Vice President	319/398-8660	Chief Investment Officer Bond Department Head
Mr. Ralph M. O'Brien Senior Vice President	319/398-8529	Bond Department Head *MBS* Fixed-Income Strategist
Mr. James Ross Executive Vice President	319/398-7821	Portfolio Mgr – Derivatives Portfolio Mgr – Futures Portfolio Mgr – Options Portfolio Mgr – Structured Notes
Mr. Clifford A. Sheets Executive Vice President	319/369-2351	Bond Department Head *Corp.*

Aetna Life & Casualty (Portfolio Management Group)

Insurance Co/Management

Sub of Aetna Life & Casualty Co.

Location: 242 Trumbull Street
Hartford, CT 06103-1212

Fax: 203/275-4846 **Phone:** 203/273-0123

Profile: Total return investor

Investment Portfolio: $ 28.0 billion

Use: **Balance Sheet/Risk Management**
Access global mkts
Create synthetic fixed/floating rate
Hedge balance sheet

Investment Purposes
Alter portfolio weighting
Adjust portfolio duration
Asset allocation
Diversify portfolio
Enter new mkts/lower risk
Expand international investments
Hedge bond portfolio risk
Hedge interest rate risk
Reduce variability of returns

Currencies: US dollar

Regions: United States

DERIVATIVES ACTIVITIES:		CAC Class: 6
Exchange-traded Options & Futures U.S. Treasury futures	**Bond, Currency, Interest rate**	
OTC Derivatives **Plain Vanilla Derivatives**	**Bond** Swaps	Forwards
Exotic Derivatives	Detached calls	Periodic caps/floors
Structured Notes	Corporate MTNs Govt. agency MTNs Bond index notes Index amortizing notes	Floaters Inverse floaters Periodic capped floaters Multi-step-up callable bonds
Counterparty Rating Requirement:	AAA	

Aetna Life & Casualty (Portfolio Management Group) – continued

OTHER ALTERNATIVE INVESTMENTS:

	CMOs/REMICs – Govt.	Strips
	CMOs/REMICs – Private	Repos/reverse repos

KEY MANAGERS & DERIVATIVES SPECIALISTS:	**Direct Phone/Fax**	**Job Function**
Mr. M. Timothy Corbett Senior Portfolio Manager	203/275-3407 203/275-4496	Portfolio Mgr – Derivatives Portfolio Mgr – Futures Portfolio Mgr – Structured Notes
Mr. Timothy A. Holt Vice President	203/275-2585 203/275-4798	Bond Department Head
Mr. John Y. Kim Managing Director	203/273-4936	Chief Investment Officer
Mr. Mitchell S. Penn Portfolio Manager	203/275-3405 203/275-4496	Portfolio Mgr – Derivatives Portfolio Mgr – Futures Portfolio Mgr – Structured Notes
Mr. Paul Selian	203/275-3410	Portfolio Mgr – Derivatives Portfolio Mgr – Futures Portfolio Mgr – Structured Notes

AgriBank, FCB

Bank/Government

Location: 375 Jackson Street
St. Paul, MN 55164-0949

Fax: 612/282-8666 **Phone:** 612/282-8800

Profile: Net asset value investor

Investment Portfolio: $ 1.6 billion

Use: **Balance Sheet/Risk Management**
Create synthetic fixed/floating rate
Hedge balance sheet
Hedge interest rate risk

Currencies: US dollar

Regions: United States

DERIVATIVES ACTIVITIES: **CAC Class: 6**

OTC Derivatives	**Interest rate**	
Plain Vanilla Derivatives	Swaps Forwards Swaptions	Caps Floors
Exotic Derivatives	CMT swaps	Index amortizing swaps
Structured Notes	Corporate MTNs Govt. agency MTNs Index amortizing notes CMT notes	Floaters Inverse floaters Multi-step-up callable bonds
Counterparty Rating Requirement:	AA	

AgriBank, FCB – continued

KEY MANAGERS & DERIVATIVES SPECIALISTS:	Direct Phone/Fax	Job Function
Mr. Larry Ryan Manager-Investments & Funding	612/282-8472	Trader – Derivatives Trader – Structured Investments
Mr. William Wolfe Treasurer	612/282-8734	Chief Investment Officer Treasurer Portfolio Mgr – Derivatives Portfolio Mgr – Structured Notes

H.F. Ahmanson & Company

Corporation

Location: 4900 Rivergrade Road
Irwindale, CA 91706

Fax: 818/962-9679 **Phone:** 818/960-6311

Use: **Balance Sheet/Risk Management**
Hedge interest rate risk
Strategic liability management

Currencies: US dollar

Regions: United States

DERIVATIVES ACTIVITIES: **CAC Class: 3**

OTC Derivatives	**Interest rate**
Plain Vanilla Derivatives	Swaps
Exotic Derivatives	Index amortizing swaps

OTHER ALTERNATIVE INVESTMENTS:

Repos/reverse repos

KEY MANAGERS & DERIVATIVES SPECIALISTS:	Direct Phone/Fax	Job Function
Ms. Anne-Drue M. Anderson E.V.P. & Treasurer		Treasurer Portfolio Mgr – Derivatives
Mr. Charles R. Rinehart Chairman, President & C.E.O.		President
Mr. Kevin M. Twomey Exec. Vice President & C.F.O.		Chief Financial Officer

Aid Association for Lutherans (AAL)

Insurance Co/Life

Location: 4321 North Ballard Road
Appleton, WI 54919-0001

Fax: 414/730-3752 **Phone:** 414/734-5721

Profile: Hold to maturity investor

Investment Portfolio: $ 11.0 - 20.0 billion

Use: **Investment Purposes**

Currencies: US dollar

Regions: United States

Aid Association for Lutherans (AAL) – continued

DERIVATIVES ACTIVITIES: **CAC Class: Inactive**

OTHER ALTERNATIVE INVESTMENTS:

CMOs/REMICs – Govt. CMOs/REMICs – Private

KEY MANAGERS & DERIVATIVES SPECIALISTS:	Direct Phone/Fax	Job Function
Mr. James Abitz Vice President – Securities	414/730-3788	Bond Department Head *Taxable*
Mr. John Gilbert President & C.O.O.		President
Mr. John Pender	414/730-2606	Chief Investment Officer

AIM Advisors, Inc.

Mutual Fund Manager

Sub of AIM Management Group of Companies

Location: 11 Greenway Plaza
Suite 1919
Houston, TX 77046-1173

Fax: 713/626-0642 **Phone:** 713/626-1919

Profile: Total return investor

Investment Portfolio: $ 28.0 billion

Use: **Investment Purposes**
Adjust portfolio duration
Asset allocation
Capture extra yield
Hedge bond portfolio risk
Hedge currency risk
Hedge equity portfolio risk
Hedge interest rate risk

Currencies: US dollar, Australian dollar, Belgian franc, Canadian dollar, French franc, German mark, Italian lira, Japanese yen, Swiss franc

Regions: United States

DERIVATIVES ACTIVITIES:

Exchange-traded Options & Futures	**Bond, Interest rate**	
OTC Derivatives **Plain Vanilla Derivatives**	**Currency** Forwards	
Structured Notes	Floaters	Multi-step-up callable bonds

OTHER ALTERNATIVE INVESTMENTS:

Repos/reverse repos

AIM Advisors, Inc. – continued

KEY MANAGERS & DERIVATIVES SPECIALISTS:	Direct Phone/Fax	Job Function
Mr. Robert G. Alley Senior Vice President	713/626-1919 713/622-7350	Portfolio Mgr – Derivatives Portfolio Mgr – Futures Portfolio Mgr – Options Portfolio Mgr – Structured Notes
Mr. Stuart Coco Vice President	713/214-1302	Research Analyst – Derivatives
Mr. Gary T. Crum President	713/214-1125	President Chief Investment Officer
Ms. Karen Dunn-Kelly Senior Vice President	713/214-1188	Trader – Derivatives Trader – Futures Trader – Structured Investments
Mr. Craig A. Smith Vice President		Trader – Derivatives Trader – Options

Alaska Permanent Capital Management Company

Investment Manager

Location: 900 West Fifth Avenue
Suite 601
Anchorage, AK 99501

Fax: 907/272-7574 **Phone:** 907/272-7575

Profile: Total return investor

Investment Portfolio: $ 650.0 million

Use: **Investment Purposes**
Capture extra yield

Currencies: US dollar

Regions: United States

DERIVATIVES ACTIVITIES:		CAC Class: 1
Structured Notes	Corporate MTNs Govt. agency MTNs	Multi-step-up callable bonds

OTHER ALTERNATIVE INVESTMENTS:		
	Strips	Repos/reverse repos

KEY MANAGERS & DERIVATIVES SPECIALISTS:	Direct Phone/Fax	Job Function
Ms. Jane Cuddy Senior Vice President		Bond Department Head
Mr. Petter Jahnsen Vice President		Portfolio Mgr – Structured Notes Trader – Structured Investments
Mr. David A. Rose Chairman & C.E.O.		Chief Investment Officer
Mr. Bert Wagnon Vice President-Investments		Portfolio Mgr – Structured Notes

Alaska Retirement Systems

Government Pension Fund

Location: 333 Willoughby Avenue
11th Floor
Juneau, AK 99811

Fax: 907/465-4397 **Phone:** 907/465-4399

Profile: Hold to maturity investor

Investment Portfolio: $ 7.6 billion

Use: **Investment Purposes**

Currencies: US dollar

Regions: United States

DERIVATIVES ACTIVITIES: **CAC Class: 4**

Structured Notes	Corporate MTNs Govt. agency MTNs	Floaters

OTHER ALTERNATIVE INVESTMENTS:

	CMOs/REMICs – Govt.	Repos/reverse repos

KEY MANAGERS & DERIVATIVES SPECIALISTS:	Direct Phone/Fax	Job Function
Mr. Michael S. Cheung State Investment Officer	907/465-3702 907/463-3565	Portfolio Mgr – Structured Notes
Mr. John R. Jenks State Investment Officer		Portfolio Mgr – Structured Notes
Mr. Christopher Phillips State Investment Officer		Portfolio Mgr – Structured Notes
Mr. Robert D. Storer		Chief Investment Officer

Alcoa

Corporation

Location: 425 Sixth Avenue
Pittsburgh, PA 15219-1850

Fax: 412/553-4498 **Phone:** 412/553-4545

Use: **Balance Sheet/Risk Management**
Hedge currency risk
Hedge interest rate risk

Currencies: US dollar, Australian dollar, German mark, UK pound

Regions: United States, Europe

DERIVATIVES ACTIVITIES: **CAC Class: 6**

Exchange-traded Options & Futures	**Currency**	
OTC Derivatives	**Currency, Interest rate**	
Plain Vanilla Derivatives	Swaps Forwards	Caps
Counterparty Rating Requirement:	AAA	

Alcoa – continued

KEY MANAGERS & DERIVATIVES SPECIALISTS:	Direct Phone/Fax	Job Function
Mr. Howard W. Burdett Vice President & Treasurer		Treasurer Portfolio Mgr – Derivatives
Mr. Jan H. M. Hommen Exec. Vice President & C.F.O.		Chief Financial Officer
Mr. Joseph C. Pellegrino V.P. – Pension Fund Invts.		Chief Investment Officer

Alfa Corporation

Corporation

Location: 2108 East South Boulevard
Montgomery, AL 36116

Fax: 334/288-0905 **Phone:** 334/288-3900

Use: **Balance Sheet/Risk Management**

Currencies: US dollar

Regions: United States

DERIVATIVES ACTIVITIES:	
Exchange-traded Options & Futures	**Bond, Currency, Interest rate**
OTC Derivatives **Plain Vanilla Derivatives**	**Bond, Currency, Interest rate**

KEY MANAGERS & DERIVATIVES SPECIALISTS:	Direct Phone/Fax	Job Function
Mr. Goodwin L. Myrick Chairman, President & C.E.O.		President
Mr. Donald Price Sr. Vice President – Finance		Chief Financial Officer
Mr. B. Phil Richardson Vice President & Treasurer		Treasurer Portfolio Mgr – Derivatives

Alfa Group

Insurance Co/Management

Sub of Alfa Corporation

Location: 2108 East South Boulevard
Montgomery, AL 36116-2015

Fax: 334/288-0905 **Phone:** 334/288-3900

Profile: Total return investor

Investment Portfolio: $ 2.0 billion

Use: **Investment Purposes**

Currencies: US dollar

Regions: United States

Alfa Group – continued

DERIVATIVES ACTIVITIES: **CAC Class: Inactive**

OTHER ALTERNATIVE INVESTMENTS:

	CMOs/REMICs – Govt.	Strips
	CMOs/REMICs – Private	Repos/reverse repos

KEY MANAGERS & DERIVATIVES SPECIALISTS:	Direct Phone/Fax	Job Function
Mr. C. Lee Ellis III Executive Vice President	334/613-4326	Chief Investment Officer

Allendale Mutual Insurance Company

Insurance Co/P & C

Location: 1301 Atwood Avenue
Johnston, RI 02919-4908

Fax: 401/275-3022 **Phone:** 401/275-3000

Profile: Total return investor

Investment Portfolio: $ 1.0 - 3.0 billion

Use: **Investment Purposes**

Currencies: US dollar

Regions: United States

DERIVATIVES ACTIVITIES: **CAC Class: Inactive**

OTHER ALTERNATIVE INVESTMENTS:

	CMOs/REMICs – Govt.	Repos/reverse repos
	CMOs/REMICs – Private	

KEY MANAGERS & DERIVATIVES SPECIALISTS:	Direct Phone/Fax	Job Function
Mr. Norman D. Baker, Jr. Senior Vice President	Ext. 1570	Chief Investment Officer

Alliance Capital Management L.P.

Insurance Co/Management

Sub of The Equitable Companies Incorporated

Location: 1345 Avenue of the Americas
New York, NY 10105-0096

Fax: 212/969-2284 **Phone:** 212/969-1000

Profile: Total return investor

Investment Portfolio: $ 66.4 billion

Use: **Balance Sheet/Risk Management**
Strategic liability management

Investment Purposes
Alter portfolio weighting
Adjust portfolio duration
Asset allocation
Hedge bond portfolio risk
Hedge currency risk
Hedge equity portfolio risk
Hedge interest rate risk
Protect currency gains
Reduce variability of returns

Currencies: US dollar, Australian dollar, Canadian dollar, French franc, German mark, Japanese yen, Swiss franc, UK Pound

Regions: United States, Canada, Europe, Latin America, Pacific Rim, Emerging mkts

DERIVATIVES ACTIVITIES: **CAC Class: 7**

Exchange-traded Options & Futures	**Currency, Interest rate**	
U.S. Treasury futures	U.S. Treasury options	
OTC Derivatives	**Bond, Currency**	
Plain Vanilla Derivatives	Swaps	Forwards
Structured Notes	Corporate MTNs	Floaters
	Govt. agency MTNs	Multi-step-up callable bonds
	Bond index notes	
Counterparty Rating Requirement:	AA	

OTHER ALTERNATIVE INVESTMENTS:

CMOs/REMICs – Govt.	Strips
CMOs/REMICs – Private	Repos/reverse repos
GICs	

KEY MANAGERS & DERIVATIVES SPECIALISTS:	**Direct Phone/Fax**	**Job Function**
Mr. Andrew M. Aran Senior Vice President	212/969-1237 212/969-1356	Portfolio Mgr – Derivatives Portfolio Mgr – Futures Portfolio Mgr – Structured Notes
Mr. Bruce W. Calvert Vice Chairman & C.I.O.	212/969-1070	Chief Investment Officer
Mr. John Carifa President & C.E.O.	212/969-1080	President

Alliance Capital Management L.P. – continued

KEY MANAGERS & DERIVATIVES SPECIALISTS:	Direct Phone/Fax	Job Function
Ms. Kathleen Corbet Senior Vice President	212/969-2468	Bond Department Head Portfolio Mgr – Derivatives Portfolio Mgr – Futures Portfolio Mgr – Options Portfolio Mgr – Structured Notes
Ms. Anne S. Drennan Vice President & Treasurer	212/969-6443	Treasurer
Mr. Mark N. Gordon Vice President	212/969-2487 212/969-1162	Fixed-Income Strategist *MBS*
Mr. Robert H. Joseph, Jr. Sr. Vice President & C.F.O.	212/969-2384	Chief Financial Officer
Mr. Paul D. Knudsvig Vice President	212/969-2496 212/969-1162	Portfolio Mgr – Derivatives Portfolio Mgr – Futures Portfolio Mgr – Options Portfolio Mgr – Structured Notes Trader – Derivatives Trader – Futures Trader – Options
Mr. Jonathan H. Nye Vice President	212/969-2483 212/969-2285	Research Analyst – Derivatives

Alliance Capital Management (Minneapolis)

Mutual Fund Manager

Sub of The Equitable Companies Incorporated

Location: 601 Second Avenue South
Suite 5000
Minneapolis, MN 55402

Fax: 612/342-2149 **Phone:** 612/332-1544

Profile: Total return investor

Investment Portfolio: $ 65.0 billion

Use: **Investment Purposes**

Currencies: US dollar, Australian dollar, Canadian dollar, French franc, German mark, Japanese yen, Swiss franc, UK pound

Regions: United States

DERIVATIVES ACTIVITIES:

OTC Derivatives **Plain Vanilla Derivatives**	**Currency, Interest rate**

OTHER ALTERNATIVE INVESTMENTS:

CMOs/REMICs – Govt. CMOs/REMICs – Private

Alliance Capital Management (Minneapolis) – continued

KEY MANAGERS & DERIVATIVES SPECIALISTS:	Direct Phone/Fax	Job Function
Mr. Alfred Harrison		Chief Investment Officer
Ms. Susan Peterson Assistant Vice President	612/332-1544	Trader – Derivatives

Allianz Investment Corporation

Insurance Co/Management

Sub of Allianz Versicherungs-Aktiengesellschaft

Location: 55 Greens Farms Road
Westport, CT 06881

Fax: 203/221-8529 **Phone:** 203/221-8500

Profile: Total return investor

Investment Portfolio: $ 15.8 billion

Use: **Balance Sheet/Risk Management**

Currencies: US dollar

Regions: United States

DERIVATIVES ACTIVITIES: **CAC Class: Inactive**

OTHER ALTERNATIVE INVESTMENTS:

CMOs/REMICs – Govt. CMOs/REMICs – Private

KEY MANAGERS & DERIVATIVES SPECIALISTS:	Direct Phone/Fax	Job Function
Mr. Gary Brown Managing Director	203/221-8553	Bond Department Head
Mr. David P. Marks President	203/221-8525	President Chief Investment Officer

Allied-Signal Inc.

Corporation

Location: 101 Columbia Road
Morristown, NJ 07962

Fax: 201/455-4807 **Phone:** 201/455-2000

Profile: Total return investor

Investment Portfolio: $ 8.0 billion

Use: **Investment Purposes**
Hedge bond portfolio risk
Hedge interest rate risk

Currencies: US dollar

Regions: United States

DERIVATIVES ACTIVITIES: **CAC Class: 3**

Exchange-traded Options & Futures U.S. Treasury futures	**Bond, Interest rate** U.S. Treasury options
Structured Notes	Govt. agency MTNs

Allied-Signal Inc. – continued

OTHER ALTERNATIVE INVESTMENTS:

	CMOs/REMICs – Govt.	Strips
	CMOs/REMICs – Private	

KEY MANAGERS & DERIVATIVES SPECIALISTS:	**Direct Phone/Fax**	**Job Function**
Mr. Jay W. Burden Senior Portfolio Manager	201/455-4861 201/455-6761	Portfolio Mgr – Futures Portfolio Mgr – Options Portfolio Mgr – Structured Notes
Mr. Edward T. Tokar Vice President – Investments		Chief Investment Officer

Allmerica Asset Management, Inc.

Insurance Co/Management

Sub of Allmerica Financial

Location: 440 Lincoln Street
Worcester, MA 01653-1959

Fax: 508/852-6935 **Phone:** 508/855-1000

Profile: Total return investor

Investment Portfolio: $ 11.0 billion

Use: **Balance Sheet/Risk Management**
Hedge interest rate risk
Incremental return

Currencies: US dollar

Regions: United States

DERIVATIVES ACTIVITIES: **CAC Class: 2**

Exchange-traded Options & Futures U.S. Treasury futures	**Bond, Interest rate**	
OTC Derivatives **Plain Vanilla Derivatives**	**Bond, Interest rate** Swaps Swaptions	 Caps Floors
Exotic Derivatives	CMT options	
Structured Notes	Corporate MTNs Govt. agency MTNs Index amortizing notes	Floaters Inverse floaters Periodic capped floaters
Counterparty Rating Requirement:	AA	

OTHER ALTERNATIVE INVESTMENTS:

	CMOs/REMICs – Govt.	CMOs/REMICs – Private

KEY MANAGERS & DERIVATIVES SPECIALISTS:	**Direct Phone/Fax**	**Job Function**
Mr. Jonathan E. Austad Vice President	508/855-2427	Portfolio Mgr – Derivatives
Mr. Ras Boateng Assistant Vice President	508/855-3476	Research Analyst – Derivatives

Allmerica Asset Management, Inc. – continued

KEY MANAGERS & DERIVATIVES SPECIALISTS:	Direct Phone/Fax	Job Function
Ms. Lisa M. Coleman Vice President	508/855-2393 508/855-6508	Portfolio Mgr – Derivatives
Mr. John C. Donohue Assistant Vice President	508/855-2159	Portfolio Mgr – Derivatives
Mr. William Fain Vice President	508/855-4104	Portfolio Mgr – Derivatives
Mr. Richard J. Litchfield Assistant Vice President	508/855-2461 508/855-6508	Portfolio Mgr – Derivatives
Mr. John Nunley Senior Vice President	508/855-2170	Portfolio Mgr – Derivatives
Ms. Ann K. Tripp Vice President	508/855-3856 508/853-6332	Portfolio Mgr – Derivatives Portfolio Mgr – Futures Portfolio Mgr – Options Portfolio Mgr – Structured Notes Trader – Derivatives Trader – Futures Trader – Options Trader – Structured Investments
Ms. Diane E. Wood Executive Vice President	508/855-3593 508/853-6332	Chief Investment Officer Fixed-Income Strategist

Allstate Insurance Company

Insurance Co/Life

Sub of The Allstate Corporation

Location: 3075 Sanders Road
Northbrook, IL 60062-7127

Fax: 708/402-4347 **Phone:** 708/402-5000

Profile: Current yield investor

Investment Portfolio: $ 48.2 billion

Use:

Balance Sheet/Risk Management
- Access global mkts
- Create synthetic fixed/floating rate
- Hedge balance sheet
- Hedge currency risk
- Hedge interest rate risk
- Lower transaction costs
- Meet cash flow target
- Strategic liability management

Investment Purposes
- Alter portfolio weighting
- Adjust portfolio duration
- Asset allocation
- Beat conventional rates
- Capture extra yield
- Convexity objectives
- Discretionary situations
- Diversify portfolio
- Expand international investments
- Hedge bond portfolio risk
- Hedge currency risk
- Hedge equity portfolio risk
- Hedge interest rate risk
- Immunize from volatility
- Lower transactions costs

Currencies: US dollar

Regions: United States

Allstate Insurance Company – continued

DERIVATIVES ACTIVITIES:		CAC Class: 6
Exchange-traded Options & Futures U.S. Treasury futures	**Interest rate** U.S. Treasury options	
OTC Derivatives **Plain Vanilla Derivatives**	**Interest rate** Swaps Swaptions Caps	 Floors Collars
Structured Notes	Corporate MTNs Govt. agency MTNs Bond index notes	Floaters Inverse floaters
Counterparty Rating Requirement:	AAA	

OTHER ALTERNATIVE INVESTMENTS:		
	CMOs/REMICs – Govt. CMOs/REMICs – Private GICs	Strips Repos/reverse repos

KEY MANAGERS & DERIVATIVES SPECIALISTS:	Direct Phone/Fax	Job Function
Mr. Matthew C. Halperin Derivatives Manager	708/402-7309 708/402-0164	Portfolio Mgr – Derivatives *Govt, MBS* Portfolio Mgr – Structured Notes Research Analyst – Derivatives *Govt, MBS* Trader – Derivatives *Govt, MBS*
Mr. Vincent Hitchcock Associate Investment Analyst	708/402-8256 708/402-0164	Portfolio Mgr – Derivatives
Mr. Robert Jostes Director	708/402-5294 708/402-0164	Bond Department Head *ABS, MBS* Fixed-Income Strategist
Mr. Louis G. Lower II President		President
Mr. Casey J. Sylla Senior Vice President		Chief Investment Officer
Mr. Thomas J. Wilson Chief Financial Officer		Chief Financial Officer

Amalgamated Bank of New York (Investment Management Group)

Bank/Trust

Location: 11–15 Union Square
3rd Floor
New York, NY 10003

Fax: 212/675-6926 **Phone:** 212/255-6200

Profile: Total return investor

Investment Portfolio: $ 2.1 billion

Use: **Investment Purposes**

Currencies: US dollar

Regions: United States

Amalgamated Bank of New York (Investment Management Group) – continued

DERIVATIVES ACTIVITIES:		**CAC Class: Inactive**

OTHER ALTERNATIVE INVESTMENTS:		
	CMOs/REMICs – Govt.	Strips

KEY MANAGERS & DERIVATIVES SPECIALISTS:	**Direct Phone/Fax**	**Job Function**
Mr. Richard Cohen Senior Vice President	212/620-8679	Chief Investment Officer

AMBAC Inc.

Corporation

Location: One State Street Plaza
New York, NY 10004

Fax: 212/509-9190 **Phone:** 212/668-0340

Use: **Balance Sheet/Risk Management**
Create synthetic fixed/floating rate
Hedge interest rate risk
Meet interest rate target
Strategic liability management

Currencies: US dollar **Regions:** United States

DERIVATIVES ACTIVITIES:		**CAC Class: 6**
Exchange-traded Options & Futures	**Interest rate**	
OTC Derivatives	**Interest rate**	
Plain Vanilla Derivatives	Swaps	Forwards
Counterparty Rating Requirement:	AA	

KEY MANAGERS & DERIVATIVES SPECIALISTS:	**Direct Phone/Fax**	**Job Function**
Mr. Frank J. Bivona Senior Vice President & C.F.O.	212/208-3236	Chief Financial Officer
Mr. Phillip B. Lassiter Chairman, President & C.E.O.	212/208-2297	President

AMBAC Financial Services, L.P.

Corporation

Sub of AMBAC Inc.

Location: 300 Nyala Farms Road
Westport, CT 06880

Fax: 203/341-2351 **Phone:** 203/222-9691

Use: **Balance Sheet/Risk Management**
Hedge interest rate risk
Incremental return

Currencies: US dollar **Regions:** United States

AMBAC Financial Services, L.P. – continued

DERIVATIVES ACTIVITIES: **CAC Class: 5**

OTC Derivatives	**Interest rate**	
Plain Vanilla Derivatives	Swaps	Forwards
Counterparty Rating Requirement:	AA	

KEY MANAGERS & DERIVATIVES SPECIALISTS:	Direct Phone/Fax	Job Function
Mr. Steve Dymant Managing Director		Portfolio Mgr – Derivatives Trader – Derivatives
Mr. Michael W. Kelly Managing Director	203/341-2303	Research Analyst – Derivatives *Muni* Trader – Derivatives *Muni*
Mr. W. Dayle Nattress President & C.E.O.		President Chief Investment Officer Portfolio Mgr – Derivatives

AMCORE Bank, N.A. Rockford

Bank/Trust

Sub of AMCORE Financial, Inc.

Location: 501 Seventh Street
Rockford, IL 61114-1200

Fax: 815/961-7746 **Phone:** 815/968-2241

Profile: Current yield investor

Investment Portfolio: $ 2.2 billion

Use: **Balance Sheet/Risk Management**
Create synthetic fixed/floating rate
Hedge balance sheet
Hedge interest rate risk
Lower transaction costs
Reduce cost of capital
Strategic liability management

Investment Purposes
Adjust portfolio duration
Beat conventional rates
Capture extra yield
Convexity objectives
Hedge bond portfolio risk
Hedge interest rate risk
Provide incremental return
Reduce variability of returns

Currencies: US dollar

Regions: United States

DERIVATIVES ACTIVITIES: **CAC Class: 4**

Exchange-traded Options & Futures U.S. Treasury options	**Bond**	
OTC Derivatives	**Bond, Interest rate**	
Plain Vanilla Derivatives	Swaps Forwards	Floors
Exotic Derivatives	Index amortizing swaps	Periodic caps/floors
Structured Notes	Govt. agency MTNs CMT notes	Floaters Multi-step-up callable bonds
Counterparty Rating Requirement:	None	

AMCORE Bank, N.A. Rockford – continued

OTHER ALTERNATIVE INVESTMENTS:

	CMOs/REMICs – Govt.	Repos/reverse repos

KEY MANAGERS & DERIVATIVES SPECIALISTS:	Direct Phone/Fax	Job Function
Mr. Jay H. Evans	815/961-7120	Chief Investment Officer Portfolio Mgr – Derivatives Portfolio Mgr – Structured Notes
Mr. Charles E. Gagnier President & C.E.O.	815/961-7500	President
Ms. Elizabeth S. Pierson Vice President	815/961-7126	Bond Department Head Portfolio Mgr – Derivatives Portfolio Mgr – Structured Notes

AMCORE Financial, Inc.

Bank Holding Company

Location: 501 Seventh Street
Rockford, IL 61104

Fax: 815/961-7749 **Phone:** 815/968-2241

Use: **Balance Sheet/Risk Management**
Create synthetic fixed/floating rate
Hedge balance sheet
Hedge interest rate risk
Incremental return
Meet interest rate target
Strategic liability management

Currencies: US dollar **Regions:** United States

DERIVATIVES ACTIVITIES: **CAC Class: 2**

Exchange-traded Options & Futures
U.S. Treasury options

OTC Derivatives	**Interest rate**	
Plain Vanilla Derivatives	Swaps Forwards	Caps
Exotic Derivatives	Index amortizing swaps	Periodic caps/floors

Counterparty Rating Requirement: A

KEY MANAGERS & DERIVATIVES SPECIALISTS:	Direct Phone/Fax	Job Function
Mr. Carl J. Dargene Chairman, President & C.E.O.		President
Mr. John R. Hecht Sr. Vice President & C.F.O.		Chief Financial Officer Treasurer Portfolio Mgr – Derivatives

American Agricultural Insurance Company

Insurance Co/P & C

Sub of American Farm Bureau

Location: 225 Touhy Avenue
Park Ridge, IL 60068

Fax: 312/399-5896 **Phone:** 312/399-5700

Profile: Total return investor

Investment Portfolio: $ 882.0 million

Use: **Investment Purposes**

Currencies: US dollar

Regions: United States

DERIVATIVES ACTIVITIES: **CAC Class: Inactive**

OTHER ALTERNATIVE INVESTMENTS:

CMOs/REMICs – Govt.

KEY MANAGERS & DERIVATIVES SPECIALISTS:	**Direct Phone/Fax**	**Job Function**
Mr. Fred Baechle	312/399-5718	Chief Investment Officer

American Express Company

Corporation

Location: American Express Tower
World Financial Center
New York, NY 10285

Fax: 212/611-9802 **Phone:** 212/640-2000

Use: **Balance Sheet/Risk Management**
Create synthetic fixed/floating rate
Hedge currency risk
Hedge interest rate risk
Hedge overseas investments
Incremental return
Lower transaction costs
Protect currency gains
Reduce cost of capital
Strategic liability management

Currencies: US dollar

Regions: United States

DERIVATIVES ACTIVITIES: **CAC Class: 8**

Exchange-traded Options & Futures	**Currency**	
OTC Derivatives **Plain Vanilla Derivatives**	**Interest rate** Swaps Forwards	 Caps
Counterparty Rating Requirement:	AA	

KEY MANAGERS & DERIVATIVES SPECIALISTS:	**Direct Phone/Fax**	**Job Function**
Mr. Michael P. Monaco E.V.P., Treasurer & C.F.O.		Chief Financial Officer Treasurer Portfolio Mgr – Derivatives
Mr. Jeffrey E. Stiefler President		President

American Express Bank Ltd.

Bank Holding Company

Sub of American Express Company

Location: American Express Tower
23rd Floor
New York, NY 10285-2300

Fax: 212/619-9872 **Phone:** 212/306-9000

Use: **Balance Sheet/Risk Management**
Hedge balance sheet
Hedge currency risk
Hedge interest rate risk

Currencies: US dollar

Regions: United States

DERIVATIVES ACTIVITIES:		**CAC Class: 8**
Exchange-traded Options & Futures	**Currency, Interest rate**	
OTC Derivatives	**Currency, Interest rate**	
Plain Vanilla Derivatives	Swaps	Forwards
Counterparty Rating Requirement:	AA	

KEY MANAGERS & DERIVATIVES SPECIALISTS:	**Direct Phone/Fax**	**Job Function**
Mr. James Hohorst Treasurer	212/640-1834	Treasurer Portfolio Mgr – Derivatives Portfolio Mgr – Futures Portfolio Mgr – Options

American Express Financial Advisors

Mutual Fund Manager

Sub of American Express Company

Location: 80 South Eighth Street
IDS Tower Ten
Minneapolis, MN 55440

Fax: 612/671-2733 **Phone:** 612/671-3131

Profile: Current yield investor

Investment Portfolio: $ 100.0 billion

Use: **Balance Sheet/Risk Management**
Hedge balance sheet
Hedge interest rate risk
Strategic liability management

Currencies: US dollar

Regions: United States

DERIVATIVES ACTIVITIES:		**CAC Class: 6**
Exchange-traded Options & Futures	**Currency, Interest rate**	
OTC Derivatives	**Currency, Interest rate**	
Plain Vanilla Derivatives	Forwards Caps	Collars
Exotic Derivatives	CMT options	Periodic caps/floors
Structured Notes	Corporate MTNs Govt. agency MTNs Index amortizing notes	Floaters Inverse floaters Multi-step-up callable bonds
Counterparty Rating Requirement:	A	

American Express Financial Advisors – continued

OTHER ALTERNATIVE INVESTMENTS:

CMOs/REMICs – Govt.
CMOs/REMICs – Private
GICs
Strips
Repos/reverse repos

KEY MANAGERS & DERIVATIVES SPECIALISTS:	**Direct Phone/Fax**	**Job Function**
Mr. John Bredemus	612/671-1853	Research Analyst – Derivatives
Mr. William H. Dudley Executive Vice President	612/671-3243	Chief Investment Officer
Mr. David M. Kuplic	612/671-2227 612/671-6314	Portfolio Mgr – Derivatives Portfolio Mgr – Options Portfolio Mgr – Structured Notes
Mr. William Lee	612/671-2169 612/671-6314	Research Analyst – Derivatives
Ms. Mary McQuillen	612/671-2998	Portfolio Mgr – Derivatives Portfolio Mgr – Futures Portfolio Mgr – Structured Notes
Mr. James W. Snyder	612/671-3701 612/671-5514	Portfolio Mgr – Derivatives Portfolio Mgr – Futures
Mr. Richard H. Warden		Portfolio Mgr – Futures

American Family Insurance Group

Insurance Co/P & C

Location: 6000 American Parkway
Madison, WI 53783-0001

Fax: 608/243-4923 **Phone:** 608/242-4100

Profile: Total return investor

Investment Portfolio: $ 4.5 billion

Use: **Balance Sheet/Risk Management**

Investment Purposes

Currencies: US dollar

Regions: United States

DERIVATIVES ACTIVITIES:

CAC Class: Inactive

OTHER ALTERNATIVE INVESTMENTS:

CMOs/REMICs – Govt.

KEY MANAGERS & DERIVATIVES SPECIALISTS:	**Direct Phone/Fax**	**Job Function**
Mr. Philip S. Hannifan Director – Fixed Income	Ext. 30954	Bond Department Head *Corp, Govt, MBS, Muni*
Mr. Thomas S. King Vice President	Ext. 30373	Chief Investment Officer

American Family Life Assurance Company (AFLAC)

Insurance Co/Life

Sub of AFLAC Incorporated

Location: 1932 Wynnton Road
Columbus, GA 31999

Fax: 706/323-1838 **Phone:** 706/323-3431

Profile: Total return investor

Investment Portfolio: $ 16.0 billion

Use: **Balance Sheet/Risk Management**
Create synthetic fixed/floating rate
Hedge interest rate risk

Currencies: US dollar, Japanese yen

Regions: United States, Pacific Rim

DERIVATIVES ACTIVITIES: **CAC Class: 3**

OTC Derivatives	**Currency, Interest rate**	
Plain Vanilla Derivatives	Swaps	Forwards
Counterparty Rating Requirement:	AA	

OTHER ALTERNATIVE INVESTMENTS:

CMOs/REMICs – Govt.

KEY MANAGERS & DERIVATIVES SPECIALISTS:	**Direct Phone/Fax**	**Job Function**
Mr. Daniel P. Amos President & C.E.O.		President
Mr. Kriss Cloninger III Exec. Vice President & C.F.O.		Chief Financial Officer Portfolio Mgr – Derivatives
Mr. Joseph W. Smith, Jr. Sr. Vice President & C.I.O.		Chief Investment Officer Bond Department Head *Muni* Fixed-Income Strategist Portfolio Mgr – Derivatives
Mr. Gary L. Stegman S.V.P. & Assistant C.F.O.		Treasurer Portfolio Mgr – Derivatives

American General Corporation

Insurance Co/Management

Location: 2929 Allen Parkway
37th Floor
Houston, TX 77019-2155

Fax: 713/831-6218 **Phone:** 713/522-1111

Profile: Spread investor

Investment Portfolio: $ 30.7 billion

Use: **Balance Sheet/Risk Management**
Access global mkts
Create synthetic fixed/floating rate
Hedge balance sheet
Hedge commercial paper
Hedge currency risk
Hedge interest rate risk
Hedge overseas investments

Currencies: US dollar, Canadian dollar

Regions: United States, Canada

American General Corporation – continued

DERIVATIVES ACTIVITIES: **CAC Class: 3**

OTC Derivatives	**Interest rate**	
Plain Vanilla Derivatives	Swaps	Forwards
Counterparty Rating Requirement:	AAA	

OTHER ALTERNATIVE INVESTMENTS:

	CMOs/REMICs – Govt.	Strips
	CMOs/REMICs – Private	

KEY MANAGERS & DERIVATIVES SPECIALISTS:	Direct Phone/Fax	Job Function
Mr. John A. Cobb	713/831-6209	Portfolio Mgr – Derivatives
Mr. Robert M. Devlin President & C.E.O.	713/831-2001	President
Mr. James L. Gleaves Vice President & Treasurer	713/831-1222	Treasurer
Mr. Michael McEachern V.P. – Fixed-Income Trading	713/831-6232	Trader – Derivatives
Mr. Calvin D. Slater Manager	713/831-1317	Fixed-Income Strategist
Mr. Peter V. Tuters Sr. Vice President & C.I.O.	713/831-1935 713/831-1366	Chief Investment Officer
Mr. Austin P. Young Sr. Vice President & C.F.O.	713/831-1094	Chief Financial Officer

American Money Management Corporation

Insurance Co/Management

Sub of American Financial Corporation

Location: One East Fourth Street
Cincinnati, OH 45202-3701

Fax: 513/579-2580 **Phone:** 513/579-2192

Profile: Total return investor

Investment Portfolio: $ 10.0 billion

Use: **Investment Purposes**

Currencies: US dollar

Regions: United States

DERIVATIVES ACTIVITIES: **CAC Class: 4**

Structured Notes	CMT notes	Floaters

American Money Management Corporation – continued

OTHER ALTERNATIVE INVESTMENTS:

	CMOs/REMICs – Govt.	Repos/reverse repos
	CMOs/REMICs – Private	

KEY MANAGERS & DERIVATIVES SPECIALISTS:	**Direct Phone/Fax**	**Job Function**
Mr. William A. Effler Vice President	513/579-2515 513/579-0323	Portfolio Mgr – Structured Notes
Mr. S. Craig Lindner President	513/579-2529 513/579-2915	President Chief Investment Officer

American Mutual Life Insurance Company

Insurance Co/Life

Location: 611 Fifth Avenue
Des Moines, IA 50309

Fax: 515/242-4670 **Phone:** 515/283-2371

Profile: Spread investor

Investment Portfolio: $ 5.0 billion

Use: **Balance Sheet/Risk Management**
Hedge interest rate risk
Incremental return
Meet interest rate target

Investment Purposes
Adjust portfolio duration
Beat conventional rates
Hedge bond portfolio risk
Hedge interest rate risk
Immunize from volatility

Currencies: US dollar

Regions: United States

DERIVATIVES ACTIVITIES: **CAC Class: 3**

Exchange-traded Options & Futures	**Interest rate**	
OTC Derivatives **Plain Vanilla Derivatives**	Swaps Forwards	Caps
Structured Notes	Corporate MTNs CMT notes	Floaters Periodic capped floaters
Counterparty Rating Requirement:	None	

OTHER ALTERNATIVE INVESTMENTS:

	CMOs/REMICs – Govt.	CMOs/REMICs – Private

KEY MANAGERS & DERIVATIVES SPECIALISTS:	**Direct Phone/Fax**	**Job Function**
Mr. David Bulin	515/283-3442	Portfolio Mgr – Derivatives Portfolio Mgr – Futures Portfolio Mgr – Options Portfolio Mgr – Structured Notes
Mr. Thomas Godlasky		Chief Investment Officer

American National Corporation

Corporation

Sub of First Chicago/NBD Corporation

Location: 33 North La Salle Street
Chicago, IL 60602-2607

Fax: 312/661-6417 **Phone:** 312/661-5000

Use:

Balance Sheet/Risk Management
Create synthetic fixed/floating rate
Hedge interest rate risk
Incremental return
Strategic liability management

Investment Purposes
Discretionary situations
Hedge interest rate risk
Provide incremental return

Currencies: US dollar, Australian dollar, German mark, Japanese yen, UK pound

Regions: United States

DERIVATIVES ACTIVITIES: **CAC Class: 5**

OTC Derivatives
Plain Vanilla Derivatives

Currency, Interest rate
Swaps
Forwards
Caps
Floors
Collars

KEY MANAGERS & DERIVATIVES SPECIALISTS:	**Direct Phone/Fax**	**Job Function**
Mr. Alan F. Delp President & C.E.O.		President
Ms. Ruth M. Gillis Sr. Vice President & C.F.O.		Chief Financial Officer
Mr. Robert S. Marjan S.V.P. & Treasurer		Treasurer Portfolio Mgr – Derivatives

American National Bank & Trust (Chicago) (Trust)

Bank/Trust

Sub of American National Corporation

Location: 33 North LaSalle Street
Chicago, IL 60690

Fax: 312/661-5341 **Phone:** 312/661-5000

Profile: Total return investor

Investment Portfolio: $ 1.6 billion

Use: **Investment Purposes**

Currencies: US dollar

Regions: United States

American National Bank & Trust (Chicago) (Trust) – continued

DERIVATIVES ACTIVITIES: **CAC Class: Inactive**

OTHER ALTERNATIVE INVESTMENTS:

CMOs/REMICs – Govt. CMOs/REMICs – Private

KEY MANAGERS & DERIVATIVES SPECIALISTS:	Direct Phone/Fax	Job Function
Mr. Christopher S. Page Vice President	312/661-5282	Chief Investment Officer

American President Companies, Ltd.

Corporation

Location: 1111 Broadway
Oakland, CA 94607

Fax: 510/272-7941 **Phone:** 510/272-7000

Use: **Balance Sheet/Risk Management**
Hedge currency risk
Hedge overseas investments
Incremental return
Protect currency gains
Strategic liability management

Currencies: US dollar German mark **Regions:** United States

DERIVATIVES ACTIVITIES: **CAC Class: 3**

OTC Derivatives
Plain Vanilla Derivatives — **Currency**: Swaps, Forwards

KEY MANAGERS & DERIVATIVES SPECIALISTS:	Direct Phone/Fax	Job Function
Mr. Will M. Storey E.V.P., Treasurer & C.F.O.		Chief Financial Officer Treasurer Portfolio Mgr – Derivatives

American Savings Bank, F.A.

Savings Bank/Bldg Society

Location: 17877 Von Karman Avenue
Irvine, CA 92714

Fax: 714/252-6884 **Phone:** 714/252-4300

Profile: Total return investor

Investment Portfolio: $ 4.0 - 10.0 billion

Use: **Balance Sheet/Risk Management**
Hedge interest rate risk

Investment Purposes
Hedge interest rate risk
Provide incremental return

Currencies: US dollar

Regions: United States

American Savings Bank, F.A. – continued

DERIVATIVES ACTIVITIES:

OTC Derivatives	**Interest rate**	
Plain Vanilla Derivatives	Swaps	Floors
	Caps	
Structured Notes		

OTHER ALTERNATIVE INVESTMENTS:

	CMOs/REMICs – Govt.	CMOs/REMICs – Private

KEY MANAGERS & DERIVATIVES SPECIALISTS:	Direct Phone/Fax	Job Function
Mr. Timothy Maimone	714/252-6858	Bond Department Head Portfolio Mgr – Derivatives Portfolio Mgr – Structured Notes

American United Life Insurance Company

Insurance Co/Life

Location: One American Square
Indianapolis, IN 46204-0002

Fax: 317/263-1225 **Phone:** 317/263-1877

Profile: Total return investor

Investment Portfolio: $ 6.0 billion

Use: **Balance Sheet/Risk Management**

Currencies: US dollar

Regions: United States

DERIVATIVES ACTIVITIES: **CAC Class: Inactive**

OTHER ALTERNATIVE INVESTMENTS:

	CMOs/REMICs – Govt.	CMOs/REMICs – Private

KEY MANAGERS & DERIVATIVES SPECIALISTS:	Direct Phone/Fax	Job Function
Mr. George D. Sapp Senior Vice President – Invsts.	317/263-1823	Chief Investment Officer

Ameritas Investment Advisors Inc.

Insurance Co/Management

Sub of Ameritas Life Insurance Corporation

Location: 5900 O Street
Lincoln, NE 68510-2234

Fax: 402/467-6970 **Phone:** 402/467-6980

Profile: Total return investor

Investment Portfolio: $ 1.6 billion

Use: **Investment Purposes**

Currencies: US dollar

Regions: United States

Ameritas Investment Advisors Inc. – continued

DERIVATIVES ACTIVITIES:		**CAC Class: Inactive**

OTHER ALTERNATIVE INVESTMENTS:		
	CMOs/REMICs – Govt.	CMOs/REMICs – Private

KEY MANAGERS & DERIVATIVES SPECIALISTS:	Direct Phone/Fax	Job Function
Mr. Jonathan C. Headrick Executive Vice President	402/467-6957	Chief Investment Officer

Amoco Corporation

Corporation

Location: 200 East Randolph Drive
Chicago, IL 60601

Fax: 312/856-2454 **Phone:** 312/856-6111

Use: **Balance Sheet/Risk Management** **Investment Purposes**

Currencies: US dollar, German mark, French franc, Japanese yen

Regions: United States

DERIVATIVES ACTIVITIES:	
Exchange-traded Options & Futures	**Currency**
OTC Derivatives	**Currency, Interest rate**
Plain Vanilla Derivatives	Swaps

KEY MANAGERS & DERIVATIVES SPECIALISTS:	Direct Phone/Fax	Job Function
Mr. John L. Carl Exec. Vice President & C.F.O.		Chief Financial Officer
Mr. William G. Lowrie President		President
Ms. Marsha C. Williams Treasurer		Treasurer Portfolio Mgr – Derivatives

AMR Investment Services, Inc.

Investment Manager

Sub of AMR Corp.

Location: 4333 Amon Carter Boulevard
Fort Worth, TX 76155

Fax: 817/967-9721 **Phone:** 817/967-3509

Profile: Spread investor

Investment Portfolio: $ 13.0 billion

Use:

Balance Sheet/Risk Management
Create synthetic fixed/floating rate
Hedge currency risk
Hedge interest rate risk
Protect currency gains

Investment Purposes
Adjust portfolio duration
Capture extra yield
Hedge currency risk
Provide incremental return

Currencies: US dollar, Belgian franc, French franc, German mark, Italian lira, Japanese yen, Spanish peseta, UK pound

Regions: United States, Europe, Pacific Rim

DERIVATIVES ACTIVITIES: **CAC Class: 6**

Exchange-traded Options & Futures
U.S. Treasury futures

Structured Notes
Corporate MTNs
Index amortizing notes
Floaters
Periodic capped floaters

OTHER ALTERNATIVE INVESTMENTS:

CMOs/REMICs – Govt.
CMOs/REMICs – Private
Repos/reverse repos

KEY MANAGERS & DERIVATIVES SPECIALISTS:	Direct Phone/Fax	Job Function
Mr. Michael W. Fields Vice President	817/967-1537 817/931-3797	Bond Department Head
Mr. Benjamin Mayer Senior Portfolio Manager	817/967-0824	Portfolio Mgr – Structured Notes
Mr. William F. Quinn President	817/967-1525	President Chief Investment Officer

AmSouth Bank N.A. (Portfolio)

Bank/Portfolio

Sub of AmSouth Bancorporation

Location: 1900 Fifth Avenue North
Birmingham, AL 35203

Fax: 205/326-5572 **Phone:** 205/326-5120

Profile: Total return investor

Investment Portfolio: $ 4.6 billion

Use: **Balance Sheet/Risk Management**
Create synthetic fixed/floating rate
Hedge interest rate risk
Strategic liability management

Currencies: US dollar

Regions: United States

DERIVATIVES ACTIVITIES: **CAC Class: 5**

Exchange-traded Options & Futures U.S. Treasury options	**Bond**	
OTC Derivatives **Plain Vanilla Derivatives**	**Interest rate** Swaps Caps	 Floors
Structured Notes		

OTHER ALTERNATIVE INVESTMENTS:

	CMOs/REMICs – Govt.	CMOs/REMICs – Private

KEY MANAGERS & DERIVATIVES SPECIALISTS:	**Direct Phone/Fax**	**Job Function**
Mr. James Bridges Assistant Vice President	205/581-7749	Portfolio Mgr – Derivatives Portfolio Mgr – Options Trader – Derivatives Trader – Options Trader – Structured Investments
Ms. Kristen M. Hudak Senior E.V.P. & C.F.O.		Chief Financial Officer
Mr. John Kottmeyer Treasurer		Treasurer
Mr. William C. Rice Senior Vice President	205/326-5645 205/801-0109	Chief Investment Officer Fixed-Income Strategist Portfolio Mgr – Derivatives Portfolio Mgr – Options Portfolio Mgr – Structured Notes Trader – Derivatives Trader – Options Trader – Structured Investments

AmSouth Bank N.A. (Trust)

Bank/Trust

Sub of AmSouth Bancorporation

Location: 1901 Sixth Avenue North
Fourth Floor
Birmingham, AL 35203

Fax: 205/581-7433 **Phone:** 205/326-5120

Profile: Total return investor

Investment Portfolio: $ 6.0 billion

Use: **Investment Purposes**

Currencies: US dollar

Regions: United States

DERIVATIVES ACTIVITIES: **CAC Class: Inactive**

OTHER ALTERNATIVE INVESTMENTS:

CMOs/REMICs – Govt.
CMOs/REMICs – Private
Strips
Repos/reverse repos

KEY MANAGERS & DERIVATIVES SPECIALISTS:	Direct Phone/Fax	Job Function
Mr. John H. Goff, Jr. Senior Vice President	205/326-5434	Chief Investment Officer

ANB Investment Management & Trust Co. of Chicago

Bank/Management Division

Sub of American National Bank & Trust (Chicago) (Trust)

Location: One North LaSalle Street
Suite 600
Chicago, IL 60690

Fax: 312/661-5054 **Phone:** 312/661-5866

Profile: Total return investor

Investment Portfolio: $ 18.5 billion

Use: **Investment Purposes**
Hedge bond portfolio risk
Hedge currency risk
Hedge interest rate risk

Currencies: US dollar

Regions: United States Europe

DERIVATIVES ACTIVITIES: **CAC Class: 6**

Exchange-traded Options & Futures **Bond, Currency**

OTHER ALTERNATIVE INVESTMENTS:

CMOs/REMICs – Govt.

ANB Investment Management & Trust Co. of Chicago – continued

KEY MANAGERS & DERIVATIVES SPECIALISTS:	Direct Phone/Fax	Job Function
Mr. Steven Manus President	312/661-6192	President
Mr. John Stodden	312/661-6840	Portfolio Mgr – Futures Portfolio Mgr – Options
Mr. Neil Wright	312/661-6009	Chief Investment Officer

Anhalt/O'Connell, Inc.

Investment Manager

Location: 345 South Figueroa Street
Suite 303
Los Angeles, CA 90071-1002

Fax: 213/613-0805 **Phone:** 213/622-0066

Profile: Total return investor

Investment Portfolio: $ 797.9 million

Use: **Investment Purposes**
Hedge bond portfolio risk

Currencies: US dollar

Regions: United States

DERIVATIVES ACTIVITIES:

Exchange-traded Options & Futures
U.S. Treasury futures
U.S. Treasury options

OTHER ALTERNATIVE INVESTMENTS:

CMOs/REMICs – Govt.

KEY MANAGERS & DERIVATIVES SPECIALISTS:	Direct Phone/Fax	Job Function
Mr. Michael F. O'Connell Managing Director		Chief Investment Officer Portfolio Mgr – Futures Portfolio Mgr – Options
Mr. Paul D. Werts Vice President		Derivatives Specialist

AON Advisors Incorporated

Insurance Co/Management

Sub of AON Corporation

Location: 123 North Wacker Drive
Chicago, IL 60606-9611

Fax: 312/701-3900 **Phone:** 312/701-3000

Profile: Spread investor

Investment Portfolio: $ 10.0 billion

Use: **Balance Sheet/Risk Management**
Create synthetic fixed/floating rate
Hedge balance sheet
Hedge commercial paper
Hedge currency risk
Hedge interest rate risk
Strategic liability management

Currencies: US dollar, Canadian dollar, Australian dollar, UK pound

Regions: United States, Europe, Canada, Pacific Rim

DERIVATIVES ACTIVITIES: **CAC Class: 6**

Exchange-traded Options & Futures	**Bond, Interest rate**	
U.S. Treasury futures	U.S. Treasury options	
OTC Derivatives	**Bond, Currency, Interest rate**	
Plain Vanilla Derivatives	Swaps	Floors
	Forwards	Collars
	Caps	
Exotic Derivatives	CMT swaps	
Structured Notes	CMT notes	
Counterparty Rating Requirement:	None	

OTHER ALTERNATIVE INVESTMENTS:

CMOs/REMICs – Govt.	Repos/reverse repos
CMOs/REMICs – Private	

KEY MANAGERS & DERIVATIVES SPECIALISTS:	**Direct Phone/Fax**	**Job Function**
Mr. Robert Dunn		Portfolio Mgr – Derivatives Portfolio Mgr – Futures Portfolio Mgr – Options Portfolio Mgr – Structured Notes
Mr. Lawrence R. Miller Senior Executive Director	312/701-3918	Bond Department Head
Mr. Anthony Rettino S.V.P./Financial Risk Manager	312/701-3909	Portfolio Mgr – Derivatives Portfolio Mgr – Futures Portfolio Mgr – Options Portfolio Mgr – Structured Notes
Mr. Patrick G. Ryan President & C.I.O.		President Chief Investment Officer

Ark Asset Management Company, Inc.

Investment Manager

Location: One New York Plaza
29th Floor
New York, NY 10004

Fax: 212/668-6198 **Phone:** 212/668-4800

Profile: Total return investor

Investment Portfolio: $ 19.2 billion

Use: **Investment Purposes**
Alter portfolio weighting
Adjust portfolio duration
Asset allocation
Capture extra yield
Provide incremental return

Currencies: US dollar

Regions: United States

DERIVATIVES ACTIVITIES: **CAC Class: 6**

Exchange-traded Options & Futures	**Bond, Interest rate**	
U.S. Treasury futures	U.S. Treasury options	
Structured Notes	Corporate MTNs CMT notes	Floaters Inverse floaters

OTHER ALTERNATIVE INVESTMENTS:

	CMOs/REMICs – Govt. CMOs/REMICs – Private	Strips Repos/reverse repos

KEY MANAGERS & DERIVATIVES SPECIALISTS:	Direct Phone/Fax	Job Function
Mr. Coleman Brandt Co-Chairman/Managing Director	212/668-4870	Chief Investment Officer
Mr. James R. Marbach Director – Fixed Income	212/668-5640	Bond Department Head
Mr. Bruce Phelps Portfolio Manager	212/668-5672	Portfolio Mgr – Futures Portfolio Mgr – Options Portfolio Mgr – Structured Notes
Mr. Stephen D. Wood Managing Director	212/668-7611 212/668-6196	Trader – Futures Trader – Options

Arvin Industries, Inc.

Corporation

Location: 1531 13th Street
Columbus, IN 47201

Fax: 812/379-3688 **Phone:** 812/379-3000

Use: **Balance Sheet/Risk Management**
Hedge currency risk
Hedge interest rate risk
Protect currency gains

Currencies: US dollar
French franc
German mark
Italian lira
UK pound

Regions: United States

Arvin Industries, Inc. – continued

DERIVATIVES ACTIVITIES:		CAC Class: 3
Exchange-traded Options & Futures		
OTC Derivatives	**Interest rate**	
Plain Vanilla Derivatives	Swaps	Forwards
Counterparty Rating Requirement:	AA	

KEY MANAGERS & DERIVATIVES SPECIALISTS:	Direct Phone/Fax	Job Function
Mr. Byron O. Pond President & C.E.O.		President
Mr. A. R. Sales Treasurer		Treasurer Portfolio Mgr – Derivatives
Mr. Richard A. Smith Vice President & C.F.O.		Chief Financial Officer

ASB Capital Management, Inc.

Bank/Management Division

Sub of NationsBank Corporation

Location: 1101 Pennsylvania Avenue N.W.
Third Floor
Washington, DC 20004-2504

Fax: 202/347-8389 **Phone:** 202/383-6300

Profile: Total return investor

Investment Portfolio: $ 8.8 billion

Use: **Investment Purposes**

Currencies: US dollar

Regions: United States

DERIVATIVES ACTIVITIES: **CAC Class: Inactive**

OTHER ALTERNATIVE INVESTMENTS:

CMOs/REMICs – Govt.	Strips
CMOs/REMICs – Private	Repos/reverse repos

KEY MANAGERS & DERIVATIVES SPECIALISTS:	Direct Phone/Fax	Job Function
Mr. Robert Phillips President	202/383-6379	President Chief Investment Officer
Mr. Robert A. Wasilewski Managing Director	202/383-6286	Bond Department Head

Asset Allocation & Management Company

Investment Manager

Location: 30 North LaSalle Street
Suite 3600
Chicago, IL 60602

Fax: 312/263-1193 **Phone:** 312/263-2900

Profile: Total return investor

Investment Portfolio: $ 4.0 - 10.0 billion

Use: **Investment Purposes**

Currencies: US dollar

Regions: United States

DERIVATIVES ACTIVITIES: **CAC Class: Inactive**

OTHER ALTERNATIVE INVESTMENTS:

	CMOs/REMICs – Govt.	Strips
	CMOs/REMICs – Private	Repos/reverse repos

KEY MANAGERS & DERIVATIVES SPECIALISTS:	Direct Phone/Fax	Job Function
Mr. Barry G. Hoyt Partner & C.I.O.		Chief Investment Officer

Associated Bank Green Bay, N.A.

Bank/Trust

Sub of Associated Banc-Corp

Location: 200 North Adams Street
Green Bay, WI 54301-5074

Fax: 414/433-4381 **Phone:** 414/433-3200

Profile: Directional investor

Investment Portfolio: $ 2.0 billion

Use: **Investment Purposes**
Capture extra yield

Currencies: US dollar

Regions: United States

DERIVATIVES ACTIVITIES: **CAC Class: 4**

Structured Notes	Corporate MTNs	Govt. agency MTNs
Counterparty Rating Requirement:	None	

OTHER ALTERNATIVE INVESTMENTS:

	CMOs/REMICs – Govt.	CMOs/REMICs – Private

KEY MANAGERS & DERIVATIVES SPECIALISTS:	Direct Phone/Fax	Job Function
Mr. Robert C. Gallagher President & Regional C.E.O.	414/433-3100	President
Mr. Kevin Jaklin	414/433-7737	Portfolio Mgr – Structured Notes
Mr. Kenneth F. Nimmer Vice President & Manager	414/433-3105	Chief Investment Officer Portfolio Mgr – Structured Notes

Associates Corporation of North America

Finance/Credit Company

Location: 250 East John Carpenter Freeway
Irving, TX 75062

Fax: 214/541-4032 **Phone:** 214/541-4000

Profile: Stable asset investor

Investment Portfolio: $ 1.1 billion

Use: **Balance Sheet/Risk Management**

Currencies: US dollar

Regions: United States

DERIVATIVES ACTIVITIES: **CAC Class: Inactive**

OTHER ALTERNATIVE INVESTMENTS:

CMOs/REMICs – Govt.

KEY MANAGERS & DERIVATIVES SPECIALISTS:	**Direct Phone/Fax**	**Job Function**
Mr. James E. Jack Exec. Vice President & C.F.O.	214/541-4566 214/541-4629	Chief Investment Officer Chief Financial Officer
Mr. Richard W. Ulrich Senior Vice President	214/541-6307 214/541-4629	Bond Department Head *Corp, Govt, MBS*

Atlantic Asset Management Partners Inc.

Investment Manager

Location: 40 Signal Road
Stamford, CT 06902-7983

Fax: 203/363-5110 **Phone:** 203/363-5100

Profile: Total return investor

Investment Portfolio: $ 1.0 - 3.0 billion

Use: **Investment Purposes**
Adjust portfolio duration
Asset allocation
Capture extra yield
Diversify portfolio
Hedge bond portfolio risk
Hedge currency risk

Currencies: US dollar

Regions: United States

DERIVATIVES ACTIVITIES: **CAC Class: 2**

Exchange-traded Options & Futures	**Interest rate**	
Structured Notes	Corporate MTNs	Govt. agency MTNs
Counterparty Rating Requirement:	A	

OTHER ALTERNATIVE INVESTMENTS:

CMOs/REMICs – Govt. | Strips
CMOs/REMICs – Private | Repos/reverse repos

Atlantic Asset Management Partners Inc. – continued

KEY MANAGERS & DERIVATIVES SPECIALISTS:	Direct Phone/Fax	Job Function
Ms. Connie Bavely Senior Vice President	203/425-3515	Fixed-Income Strategist
Ms. Elaine Hunt Senior Vice President	203/425-3519	Portfolio Mgr – Structured Notes *Govt*
Ms. Janet Kappenberg Senior Vice President	203/425-3517 203/425-3542	Fixed-Income Strategist Portfolio Mgr – Futures Portfolio Mgr – Structured Notes *Corp*
Mr. Ronald W. Sellers President & C.E.O.		President Chief Investment Officer

AT&T

Corporation

Location: 32 Avenue of the Americas
Room 2430E
New York, NY 10013-2412

Fax: 212/226-4935 **Phone:** 212/387-5400

Use: **Balance Sheet/Risk Management**
Create synthetic fixed/floating rate
Hedge currency risk
Hedge interest rate risk
Hedge overseas investments
Lower transaction costs
Protect currency gains
Reduce cost of capital
Strategic liability management

Currencies: US dollar, Canadian dollar, German mark, Japanese yen, UK pound

Regions: United States, Europe

DERIVATIVES ACTIVITIES:		CAC Class: 7
Exchange-traded Options & Futures	**Currency**	
OTC Derivatives	**Currency, Interest rate**	
Plain Vanilla Derivatives	Swaps Forwards	Caps
Counterparty Rating Requirement:	AA	

KEY MANAGERS & DERIVATIVES SPECIALISTS:	Direct Phone/Fax	Job Function
Mr. Brian Fluck Assistant Treasurer		Portfolio Mgr – Derivatives
Mr. Richard W. Miller Sr. E.V.P. & C.F.O.		Chief Financial Officer
Mr. S. Lawrence Prendergast Vice President & Treasurer		Treasurer Portfolio Mgr – Derivatives

Auto Club Insurance Association

Insurance Co/P & C

Location: 17380 North Laurel Park Drive
Livonia, MI 48152

Fax: 313/462-8061 **Phone:** 313/336-1234

Profile: Total return investor

Investment Portfolio: $ 2.0 billion

Use: **Investment Purposes**

Currencies: US dollar

Regions: United States

DERIVATIVES ACTIVITIES: **CAC Class: Inactive**

OTHER ALTERNATIVE INVESTMENTS:

CMOs/REMICs – Govt.

KEY MANAGERS & DERIVATIVES SPECIALISTS:	Direct Phone/Fax	Job Function
Ms. Paula Downey A.V.P. & Treasurer	313/462-7008	Chief Investment Officer Treasurer

Auto-Owners Insurance Company

Insurance Co/P & C

Location: 6101 AnaCapri Boulevard
Lansing, MI 48917

Fax: 517/323-8796 **Phone:** 517/323-1200

Profile: Spread investor

Investment Portfolio: $ 4.8 billion

Use: **Investment Purposes**

Currencies: US dollar

Regions: United States

DERIVATIVES ACTIVITIES: **CAC Class: Inactive**

Structured Notes Corporate MTNs Govt. agency MTNs

OTHER ALTERNATIVE INVESTMENTS:

CMOs/REMICs – Govt.

KEY MANAGERS & DERIVATIVES SPECIALISTS:	Direct Phone/Fax	Job Function
Mr. Greg Cornell Treasurer		Chief Investment Officer Treasurer
Mr. Ian R. Ward Vice President	517/323-1487	Bond Department Head Portfolio Mgr – Structured Notes

Avatar Investors Associates

Investment Manager

Location: 900 Third Avenue
33rd Floor
New York, NY 10022-4793

Fax: 212/644-0332 **Phone:** 212/753-7710

Profile: Total return investor

Investment Portfolio: $ 726.6 million

Use: **Investment Purposes**

Currencies: US dollar

Regions: United States

DERIVATIVES ACTIVITIES: **CAC Class: Inactive**

OTHER ALTERNATIVE INVESTMENTS:

CMOs/REMICs – Govt. CMOs/REMICs – Private

KEY MANAGERS & DERIVATIVES SPECIALISTS:	**Direct Phone/Fax**	**Job Function**
Mr. Edward S. Babbitt, Jr. President		President Chief Investment Officer
Mr. Charles M. White Managing Director		Bond Department Head

Back Bay Advisors, L.P.

Insurance Co/Management

Sub of New England Investment Companies, L.P.

Location: 399 Boylston Street
Boston, MA 02116-3300

Fax: 617/424-8665 **Phone:** 617/578-1500

Profile: Current yield investor

Investment Portfolio: $ 6.2 billion

Use:

Balance Sheet/Risk Management
- Access global mkts
- Hedge currency risk
- Hedge interest rate risk
- Hedge overseas investments
- Incremental return
- Protect currency gains

Investment Purposes
- Alter portfolio weighting
- Adjust portfolio duration
- Asset allocation
- Capture extra yield
- Diversify portfolio
- Hedge bond portfolio risk
- Hedge currency risk
- Hedge equity portfolio risk
- Hedge interest rate risk
- Immunize from volatility
- Protect currency gains
- Provide incremental return
- Reduce variability of returns

Currencies: US dollar, Canadian dollar, French franc, German mark, Italian lira, Japanese yen, Swiss franc, UK pound

Regions: United States, Canada, Europe, Latin America, Pacific Rim

Back Bay Advisors, L.P. – continued

DERIVATIVES ACTIVITIES:		CAC Class: 4
Exchange-traded Options & Futures U.S. Treasury futures U.S. Treasury options	**Bond, Interest rate** Municipal futures	
OTC Derivatives **Plain Vanilla Derivatives**	**Currency** Forwards	
Structured Notes	Govt. agency MTNs Floaters	Inverse floaters Periodic capped floaters
Counterparty Rating Requirement:	AA	

OTHER ALTERNATIVE INVESTMENTS:		
	CMOs/REMICs – Govt. CMOs/REMICs – Private GICs	Strips Repos/reverse repos

KEY MANAGERS & DERIVATIVES SPECIALISTS:	Direct Phone/Fax	Job Function
Ms. Catherine L. Bunting Senior Vice President	617/578-1743	Portfolio Mgr – Structured Notes *Corp* Trader – Structured Investments *Corp*
Ms. Kimberly P. Forsyth Senior Vice President	617/578-1751	Bond Department Head *Muni*
Mr. Eric N. Gutterson Vice President	617/578-1725	Portfolio Mgr – Futures Portfolio Mgr – Options
Mr. John Maloney	617/578-1770	Trader – Derivatives Trader – Futures Trader – Options
Mr. Scott Millimet Executive Vice President	617/578-1767	OTC Deriv/Swaps – Head Portfolio Mgr – Futures Portfolio Mgr – Options Structured Notes – Head
Mr. Edgar M. Reed Executive Vice President	617/578-1748	Chief Investment Officer
Ms. Jennifer Sheppard Investment Officer	617/578-1627	Portfolio Mgr – Structured Notes *Corp*
Mr. James S. Welch Vice President	617/578-1755	Portfolio Mgr – Derivatives Portfolio Mgr – Futures Portfolio Mgr – Options

Back Bay Advisors, L.P. – continued

KEY MANAGERS & DERIVATIVES SPECIALISTS:	Direct Phone/Fax	Job Function
Mr. Nathaniel R. Wentworth Vice President	617/578-1703	Portfolio Mgr – Derivatives *Muni* Portfolio Mgr – Futures *Muni* Portfolio Mgr – Options *Muni*

BANC ONE Corporation

Bank Holding Company

Location: 100 East Broad Street
Columbus, OH 43271

Fax: 614/248-9344 **Phone:** 614/248-5944

Use: **Balance Sheet/Risk Management**
Create synthetic fixed/floating rate
Hedge interest rate risk
Strategic liability management

Currencies: US dollar

Regions: United States

DERIVATIVES ACTIVITIES: **CAC Class: 7**

OTC Derivatives	**Interest rate**	
Plain Vanilla Derivatives	Swaps Caps	Floors

KEY MANAGERS & DERIVATIVES SPECIALISTS:	Direct Phone/Fax	Job Function
Mr. Frederick Cullen President & C.O.O.		President
Mr. Michael McMennamin Exec. Vice President-Finance		Chief Financial Officer
Mr. George R. Meiling Treasurer		Treasurer Portfolio Mgr – Derivatives

Banco Popular of Puerto Rico (Portfolio)

Bank/Portfolio

Location: 209 Ponce de Leon Avenue
Hato Rey, PR 00919

Fax: 809/754-9290 **Phone:** 809/765-9800

Profile: Total return investor

Investment Portfolio: $ 2.3 billion

Use: **Balance Sheet/Risk Management**
Hedge interest rate risk

Investment Purposes
Asset allocation
Beat conventional rates
Capture extra yield
Diversify portfolio
Hedge interest rate risk
Lower transactions costs

Currencies: US dollar

Regions: United States

Banco Popular of Puerto Rico (Portfolio) – continued

DERIVATIVES ACTIVITIES: **CAC Class: 5**

Exchange-traded Options & Futures	**Bond, Interest rate**	
U.S. Treasury futures	U.S. Treasury options	
OTC Derivatives	**Bond, Interest rate**	
Plain Vanilla Derivatives	Swaps	Caps
	Swaptions	Floors
Structured Notes	Govt. agency MTNs	Inverse floaters
	Bond index notes	Periodic capped floaters
	Index amortizing notes	Multi-step-up callable bonds
	Floaters	
Counterparty Rating Requirement:	A	

OTHER ALTERNATIVE INVESTMENTS:

CMOs/REMICs – Govt.	Strips
CMOs/REMICs – Private	Repos/reverse repos

KEY MANAGERS & DERIVATIVES SPECIALISTS:	**Direct Phone/Fax**	**Job Function**
Mr. Juan Guerrero Senior Vice President	809/753-9240	Chief Investment Officer Portfolio Mgr – Derivatives
Mr. Francisco J. Maldonado Officer Investment Division	809/753-1400	Portfolio Mgr – Derivatives Portfolio Mgr – Options Portfolio Mgr – Structured Notes

BancOklahoma Trust Company

Bank/Trust

Sub of BOK Financial Corporation

Location: One Williams Center
Tenth Floor Northeast
Tulsa, OK 74102

Fax: 918/588-6939 **Phone:** 918/588-6000

Profile: Total return investor

Investment Portfolio: $ 2.2 billion

Use: **Investment Purposes**

Currencies: US dollar

Regions: United States

DERIVATIVES ACTIVITIES: **CAC Class: Inactive**

OTHER ALTERNATIVE INVESTMENTS:

CMOs/REMICs – Govt.	Strips
CMOs/REMICs – Private	Repos/reverse repos
GICs	

KEY MANAGERS & DERIVATIVES SPECIALISTS:	**Direct Phone/Fax**	**Job Function**
Mr. James L. Huntzinger Senior Vice President	918/588-6317	Chief Investment Officer

Bank of America Illinois (Institutional Trust)

Bank/Trust

Sub of BankAmerica Corporation

Location: 231 South LaSalle Street
20th Floor
Chicago, IL 60697-0001

Fax: 312/987-0500 **Phone:** 312/828-7574

Profile: Net asset value investor

Investment Portfolio: $ 10.0 billion

Use: **Investment Purposes**
Alter portfolio weighting
Adjust portfolio duration
Reduce variability of returns

Currencies: US dollar

Regions: United States

DERIVATIVES ACTIVITIES: **CAC Class: 6**

Structured Notes	Corporate MTNs Govt. agency MTNs	CMT notes Floaters

OTHER ALTERNATIVE INVESTMENTS:

CMOs/REMICs – Govt. CMOs/REMICs – Private	Strips Repos/reverse repos

KEY MANAGERS & DERIVATIVES SPECIALISTS:	**Direct Phone/Fax**	**Job Function**
Mr. Anthony Pertile Senior Vice President	312/828-7530	Bond Department Head *ABS, Corp, MBS* Portfolio Mgr – Structured Notes

Bank of America NT & SA (Portfolio)

Bank/Portfolio

Sub of BankAmerica Corporation

Location: 100 West Liberty Street
Suite 650
Reno, NV 89501

Fax: 702/688-8787 **Phone:** 702/688-8600

Profile: Total return investor

Investment Portfolio: $ 17.1 billion

Use: **Balance Sheet/Risk Management**
Hedge balance sheet
Hedge currency risk
Hedge interest rate risk
Protect currency gains
Strategic liability management

Investment Purposes
Adjust portfolio duration
Discretionary situations
Expand international investments
Hedge bond portfolio risk
Hedge interest rate risk
Protect currency gains
Provide incremental return
Reduce variability of returns

Currencies: US dollar
Canadian dollar
French franc
German mark
Italian lira
Japanese yen
Swiss franc
UK pound

Regions: United States

Bank of America NT & SA (Portfolio) – continued

DERIVATIVES ACTIVITIES:		**CAC Class: 8**
Exchange-traded Options & Futures		
OTC Derivatives	**Currency, Interest rate**	
Plain Vanilla Derivatives	Swaps	Caps
	Forwards	Floors
	Swaptions	Collars
Exotic Derivatives		
Counterparty Rating Requirement:	A	

OTHER ALTERNATIVE INVESTMENTS:

	CMOs/REMICs – Govt.	Strips
	CMOs/REMICs – Private	Repos/reverse repos

KEY MANAGERS & DERIVATIVES SPECIALISTS:	**Direct Phone/Fax**	**Job Function**
Mr. Chris Ballinger Vice President	702/688-8820	Portfolio Mgr – Derivatives
Mr. Steven J. Dixon Senior Vice President	702/688-8888	Chief Investment Officer Portfolio Mgr – Derivatives Portfolio Mgr – Futures Portfolio Mgr – Options

Bank of America Texas, N.A.

Savings Bank/Bldg Society

Sub of BankAmerica Corporation

Location: 1925 West John Carpenter Freeway
Irving, TX 75063

Fax: 214/444-5460 **Phone:** 214/444-5555

Use: **Balance Sheet/Risk Management**
Hedge balance sheet
Hedge interest rate risk

Investment Portfolio: $ 4.0 - 10.0 billion

Currencies: US dollar

Regions: United States

DERIVATIVES ACTIVITIES:		**CAC Class: 6**
OTC Derivatives	**Interest rate**	
Plain Vanilla Derivatives	Swaps	
Counterparty Rating Requirement:	AA	

OTHER ALTERNATIVE INVESTMENTS:

	CMOs/REMICs – Govt.	CMOs/REMICs – Private

Bank of America Texas, N.A. – continued

KEY MANAGERS & DERIVATIVES SPECIALISTS:	Direct Phone/Fax	Job Function
Mr. David J. Berry President		President
Mr. Barry Hagan Treasurer	214/444-5437	Chief Investment Officer Treasurer Portfolio Mgr – Derivatives

Bank of Boston (Treasury)

Bank/Portfolio

Sub of Bank of Boston Corporation

Location: 100 Federal Street
Boston, MA 02110-1898

Fax: 617/434-6795 **Phone:** 617/434-2200

Profile: Total return investor

Investment Portfolio: $ 4.0 billion

Use: **Balance Sheet/Risk Management**
Create synthetic fixed/floating rate
Hedge interest rate risk
Strategic liability management

Currencies: US dollar

Regions: United States

DERIVATIVES ACTIVITIES:

Exchange-traded Options & Futures		
U.S. Treasury futures	U.S. Treasury options	
OTC Derivatives		
Plain Vanilla Derivatives	Swaps Swaptions	Caps Floors
Structured Notes	Govt. agency MTNs	Floaters

OTHER ALTERNATIVE INVESTMENTS:

	CMOs/REMICs – Govt. CMOs/REMICs – Private	Repos/reverse repos

KEY MANAGERS & DERIVATIVES SPECIALISTS:	Direct Phone/Fax	Job Function
Mr. Brian Shannahan	617/434-6851	Portfolio Mgr – Derivatives Portfolio Mgr – Futures Portfolio Mgr – Options Portfolio Mgr – Structured Notes
Mr. Bradford H. Warner Treasurer		Chief Investment Officer

The Bank of California, N.A.

Corporation

Sub of BanCal Tri-State Corporation

Location: 400 California Street
San Francisco, CA 94104

Fax: 415/765-2788 **Phone:** 415/765-0400

Use:

Balance Sheet/Risk Management
Hedge currency risk
Hedge interest rate risk
Incremental return
Protect currency gains
Strategic liability management

Investment Purposes
Capture extra yield
Discretionary situations
Hedge bond portfolio risk
Hedge currency risk
Hedge interest rate risk
Provide incremental return

Currencies: US dollar, French franc, German mark, Japanese yen, Swiss franc

Regions: United States

DERIVATIVES ACTIVITIES: **CAC Class: 6**

Exchange-traded Options & Futures	**Currency, Interest rate**	
OTC Derivatives	**Interest rate**	
Plain Vanilla Derivatives	Swaps	Forwards

KEY MANAGERS & DERIVATIVES SPECIALISTS:	**Direct Phone/Fax**	**Job Function**
Mr. David W. Ehlers Exec. Vice President & C.F.O.		Chief Financial Officer Treasurer Portfolio Mgr – Derivatives
Mr. Yoichi Kambara S.V.P. & General Manager		Portfolio Mgr – Derivatives
Mr. Hiroo Nozawa Chairman, President & C.E.O.		President
Mr. Ralph J. Rasmussen General Manager-Invt. Services		Portfolio Mgr – Derivatives

Bank of Hawaii (Investments)

Bank/Portfolio

Sub of Bancorp Hawaii Inc.

Location: 130 Merchant Street
12th Floor
Honolulu, HI 96813

Fax: 808/538-4471 **Phone:** 808/847-8888

Profile: Spread investor

Investment Portfolio: $ 4.4 billion

Use:

Balance Sheet/Risk Management
Hedge balance sheet
Hedge interest rate risk
Strategic liability management

Currencies: US dollar

Regions: United States

Bank of Hawaii (Investments) – continued

DERIVATIVES ACTIVITIES:		CAC Class: 6
OTC Derivatives **Plain Vanilla Derivatives**	**Interest rate** Swaps	
Structured Notes	Govt. agency MTNs	Inverse floaters

OTHER ALTERNATIVE INVESTMENTS:		
	CMOs/REMICs – Private	Repos/reverse repos

KEY MANAGERS & DERIVATIVES SPECIALISTS:	Direct Phone/Fax	Job Function
Mr. Robert Crowell Senior Vice President	808/537-8313	Chief Investment Officer Portfolio Mgr – Derivatives Portfolio Mgr – Structured Notes
Mr. Lee Moriwaki	808/537-8347	Trader – Derivatives
Mr. David Todani	808/538-4637 808/538-4007	Portfolio Mgr – Derivatives Portfolio Mgr – Structured Notes

The Bank of New York Company, Inc.

Bank Holding Company

Location: 48 Wall Street, New York, NY 10038
Fax: 212/815-4023 **Phone:** 212/495-1784

Use:

Balance Sheet/Risk Management
Create synthetic fixed/floating rate
Hedge balance sheet
Hedge currency risk
Hedge interest rate risk
Hedge overseas investments
Protect currency gains
Incremental return
Strategic liability management

Investment Purposes

Currencies: US dollar, Canadian dollar, French franc, German mark, Japanese yen, Mexican peso, UK pound

Regions: United States, Europe, Pacific Rim

DERIVATIVES ACTIVITIES:		CAC Class: 8
Exchange-traded Options & Futures U.S. Treasury futures	U.S. Treasury options	
OTC Derivatives **Plain Vanilla Derivatives**	**Currency, Interest rate** Swaps Forwards	 Swaptions Floors

KEY MANAGERS & DERIVATIVES SPECIALISTS:	Direct Phone/Fax	Job Function
Mr. Thomas P. Gibbons Senior Vice President	212/804-2006	Portfolio Mgr – Derivatives
Mr. Deno D. Papageorge Sr. Exec. Vice President & CFO	212/495-1427	Chief Financial Officer Portfolio Mgr – Derivatives

The Bank of New York Company, Inc. – continued

KEY MANAGERS & DERIVATIVES SPECIALISTS:	Direct Phone/Fax	Job Function
Mr. Thomas A. Renyi President & C.E.O.	212/495-3007 212/495-2413	President
Ms. Roseanne M. Witmer Senior Vice President		Portfolio Mgr – Derivatives

The Bank of North Dakota

Bank/Management Division

Location: 700 East Main Avenue
Bismarck, ND 58501

Fax: 701/328-5632 **Phone:** 701/328-5600

Profile: Hold to maturity investor

Investment Portfolio: $ 500.0 - 999.0 million

Use: **Balance Sheet/Risk Management**
Hedge interest rate risk

Currencies: US dollar

Regions: United States

DERIVATIVES ACTIVITIES: **CAC Class: 1**

OTC Derivatives	**Interest rate**	
Plain Vanilla Derivatives	Swaps	Caps
Structured Notes	Index amortizing notes	Multi-step-up callable bonds
Counterparty Rating Requirement:	A	

OTHER ALTERNATIVE INVESTMENTS:

	CMOs/REMICs – Govt.	Repos/reverse repos

KEY MANAGERS & DERIVATIVES SPECIALISTS:	Direct Phone/Fax	Job Function
Mr. John Hoeven President		President
Mr. Timothy Porter	701/328-5820	Trader – Derivatives Trader – Structured Investments
Mr. Allen F. Weisbeck Investment Department Manager	701/328-5678	Chief Investment Officer Portfolio Mgr – Derivatives Portfolio Mgr – Structured Notes Trader – Derivatives Trader – Structured Investments

Bank of Oklahoma, N.A. (Portfolio)

Bank/Portfolio

Sub of BOK Financial Corporation

Location: One Williams Center
Tulsa, OK 74103

Fax: 918/588-6510 **Phone:** 918/588-6000

Profile: Total return investor

Investment Portfolio: $ 1.0 - 3.0 billion

Use: **Balance Sheet/Risk Management**
Hedge interest rate risk

Currencies: US dollar

Regions: United States

Bank of Oklahoma, N.A. (Portfolio) – continued

DERIVATIVES ACTIVITIES: **CAC Class: 3**

OTC Derivatives **Plain Vanilla Derivatives**	**Interest rate** Swaps
Counterparty Rating Requirement:	A

OTHER ALTERNATIVE INVESTMENTS:

Repos/reverse repos

KEY MANAGERS & DERIVATIVES SPECIALISTS:	Direct Phone/Fax	Job Function
Mr. Lee C. Allen Vice President	918/588-6856	Trader – Derivatives
Mr. Stanley A. Lybarger President & C.E.O.		President
Mr. John Marow		Portfolio Mgr – Derivatives
Mr. James A. White Exec. Vice President & C.F.O.	918/588-6416	Chief Financial Officer
Mr. Charles Williamson		Chief Investment Officer

Bank One, Dayton, N.A.

Bank/Trust

Sub of BANC ONE Corporation

Location: 40 North Main Street
Sixth Floor
Dayton, OH 45401

Fax: 513/449-7199 **Phone:** 513/449-8600

Profile: Total return investor

Investment Portfolio: $ 2.6 billion

Use: **Investment Purposes**

Currencies: US dollar

Regions: United States

DERIVATIVES ACTIVITIES: **CAC Class: Inactive**

OTHER ALTERNATIVE INVESTMENTS:

CMOs/REMICs – Govt. CMOs/REMICs – Private

KEY MANAGERS & DERIVATIVES SPECIALISTS:	Direct Phone/Fax	Job Function
Mr. Peter Sorrentino Vice President	513/449-4820	Chief Investment Officer

The Bank of Tokyo Trust Company (Pension & Investments)

Bank/Trust

Sub of The Bank of Tokyo Ltd. (Japan)

Location: 100 Broadway
New York, NY 10005

Fax: 212/571-5150 **Phone:** 212/782-4000

Profile: Total return investor

Investment Portfolio: $ 1.0 - 3.0 billion

Use: **Investment Purposes**
Hedge interest rate risk

Currencies: US dollar

Regions: United States

DERIVATIVES ACTIVITIES:

Exchange-traded Options & Futures

KEY MANAGERS & DERIVATIVES SPECIALISTS:	**Direct Phone/Fax**	**Job Function**
Mr. Stephen W. Blocklin Vice President		Bond Department Head Portfolio Mgr – Futures
Mr. Harold C. Elliot	212/766-8494	Chief Investment Officer
Mr. Charles E. Ryan Vice President	212/766-8683	Chief Investment Officer

The Bank of Tokyo Trust Company (Securities & Investments)

Bank/Trust

Sub of The Bank of Tokyo Ltd. (Japan)

Location: 1251 Avenue of the Americas
11th Floor Securities & Inv. Dept.
New York, NY 10116-3138

Fax: 212/782-6426 **Phone:** 212/782-6705

Profile: Total return investor

Investment Portfolio: $ 8.0 billion

Use: **Balance Sheet/Risk Management**
Create synthetic fixed/floating rate
Hedge interest rate risk
Strategic liability management

Currencies: US dollar

Regions: United States

DERIVATIVES ACTIVITIES: **CAC Class: 6**

OTC Derivatives
Plain Vanilla Derivatives

Currency, Interest rate
Swaps
Swaptions
Caps
Floors

OTHER ALTERNATIVE INVESTMENTS:

CMOs/REMICs – Govt.
CMOs/REMICs – Private

The Bank of Tokyo Trust Company (Securities & Investments) – continued

KEY MANAGERS & DERIVATIVES SPECIALISTS:	Direct Phone/Fax	Job Function
Mr. Yosuke Aoyagi Vice President & Manager	212/782-6706	Bond Department Head Portfolio Mgr – Derivatives
Mr. Hideo Kazusa		Trader – Derivatives *Taxable*
Mr. Sachio Kohjima President	212/782-4030	President
Mr. Ichiro Tago		Portfolio Mgr – Derivatives *Taxable*

Bank United of Texas, FSB

Savings Bank/Bldg Society

Location: 3200 Southwest Freeway
19th Floor
Houston, TX 77027

Fax: 713/543-7927 **Phone:** 713/543-6500

Profile: Spread investor

Investment Portfolio: $ 4.0 - 10.0 billion

Use: **Balance Sheet/Risk Management**
Create synthetic fixed/floating rate
Hedge balance sheet
Hedge interest rate risk
Incremental return
Reduce cost of capital
Strategic liability management

Currencies: US dollar

Regions: United States

DERIVATIVES ACTIVITIES:		**CAC Class: 6**
Exchange-traded Options & Futures U.S. Treasury futures	**Interest rate**	
OTC Derivatives **Plain Vanilla Derivatives**	**Interest rate** Swaps Forwards Swaptions	 Caps Floors Collars
Exotic Derivatives	Index amortizing swaps	Periodic caps/floors
Counterparty Rating Requirement:	A	

OTHER ALTERNATIVE INVESTMENTS:		
	CMOs/REMICs – Govt. CMOs/REMICs – Private	Repos/reverse repos

Bank United of Texas, FSB – continued

KEY MANAGERS & DERIVATIVES SPECIALISTS:	Direct Phone/Fax	Job Function
Mr. Steven Champagne	713/543-6996	Portfolio Mgr – Derivatives Portfolio Mgr – Futures
Mr. Mario Chiodetti		Bond Department Head Portfolio Mgr – Derivatives Portfolio Mgr – Futures
Mr. Frank Elliott		Portfolio Mgr – Derivatives Portfolio Mgr – Futures
Mr. Karl Weiss Managing Director		Chief Investment Officer Portfolio Mgr – Derivatives Portfolio Mgr – Futures

Bank of the West (Portfolio)

Bank/Portfolio

Location: 1450 Treat Boulevard
Walnut Creek, CA 94596

Fax: 510/256-7202 **Phone:** 510/942-8400

Profile: Hold to maturity investor

Investment Portfolio: $ 944.0 million

Use: **Balance Sheet/Risk Management**
Hedge balance sheet
Hedge currency risk
Hedge interest rate risk
Strategic liability management

Currencies: US dollar, French franc, German mark, Japanese yen

Regions: United States

DERIVATIVES ACTIVITIES:

CAC Class: 2

Exchange-traded Options & Futures	**Bond, Currency, Interest rate**	
U.S. Treasury futures	U.S. Treasury options	
OTC Derivatives		
Plain Vanilla Derivatives	**Bond, Currency, Interest rate**	
	Swaps	Caps
Exotic Derivatives	Periodic caps/floors	
Counterparty Rating Requirement:	A	

OTHER ALTERNATIVE INVESTMENTS:

CMOs/REMICs – Govt.
CMOs/REMICs – Private
Repos/reverse repos

KEY MANAGERS & DERIVATIVES SPECIALISTS:	Direct Phone/Fax	Job Function
Mr. Richard W. Aubrey	510/942-8475	Chief Investment Officer Portfolio Mgr – Derivatives Portfolio Mgr – Futures

Bankers Trust Global Investment Management

Bank/Management Division

Sub of Bankers Trust – New York Corporation

Location: 130 Liberty Street
35th Floor
New York, NY 10006-1012

Fax: 212/250-9857 **Phone:** 212/250-2500

Profile: Total return investor

Investment Portfolio: $ 170.0 billion

Use: **Investment Purposes**
Alter portfolio weighting
Adjust portfolio duration
Asset allocation
Capture extra yield
Diversify portfolio
Enter new mkts/lower risk
Expand international investments
Hedge bond portfolio risk
Hedge currency risk
Hedge interest rate risk
Protect currency gains
Provide incremental return
Reduce variability of returns

Currencies: US dollar, Australian dollar, Belgian franc, Canadian dollar, French franc, German mark, Italian lira, Japanese yen, Spanish peseta, Swiss franc, UK pound

Regions: United States, Canada, Europe, Pacific Rim

DERIVATIVES ACTIVITIES: **CAC Class: 5**

Exchange-traded Options & Futures
U.S. Treasury futures
U.S. Treasury options

OTC Derivatives
Plain Vanilla Derivatives

Currency
Swaps
Forwards
Swaptions

Caps
Floors
Collars

Structured Notes
Corporate MTNs
Govt. agency MTNs
Bond index notes
Floaters
Inverse floaters
Periodic capped floaters

Counterparty Rating Requirement: None

OTHER ALTERNATIVE INVESTMENTS:

CMOs/REMICs – Govt.
CMOs/REMICs – Private
Strips

Bankers Trust Global Investment Management – continued

KEY MANAGERS & DERIVATIVES SPECIALISTS:	Direct Phone/Fax	Job Function
Mr. Vernon R. Barback Managing Director	212/250-9205	Bond Department Head
Mr. Ralph Langenbourg Vice President	212/250-6087	Portfolio Mgr – Derivatives
Mr. Frank Minard Managing Director	212/250-3870	Chief Investment Officer
Mr. Gary R. Pollack Vice President	212/250-9640	Bond Department Head *Muni*
Mr. David W. Rossmiller Vice President	212/250-8521	Bond Department Head Portfolio Mgr – Derivatives Portfolio Mgr – Options Portfolio Mgr – Structured Notes

Bankers Trust – New York Corporation (Portfolio)

Bank/Portfolio

Sub of Bankers Trust – New York Corporation

Location: 130 Liberty Street
New York, NY 10006

Fax: 212/775-2487 **Phone:** 212/250-2500

Profile: Total return investor

Investment Portfolio: $ 6.3 billion

Use: **Investment Purposes**
Hedge interest rate risk

Currencies: US dollar

Regions: United States

DERIVATIVES ACTIVITIES:

Exchange-traded Options & Futures
U.S. Treasury futures

OTHER ALTERNATIVE INVESTMENTS:

CMOs/REMICs – Govt. Repos/reverse repos

KEY MANAGERS & DERIVATIVES SPECIALISTS:	Direct Phone/Fax	Job Function
Mr. Richard Daniel Chief Financial Officer		Chief Financial Officer
Mr. Paul Gibson	212/250-5754	Trader – Futures
Mr. Frank Newman President & C.E.O.		President Chief Investment Officer

Baring Asset Management Company

Investment Manager

Sub of Internationale Nederlanden Group (ING) NV

Location: 125 High Street
Suite 2700
Boston, MA 02110-2723

Fax: 617/951-1432 **Phone:** 617/951-0052

Profile: Total return investor

Investment Portfolio: $ 1.2 billion

Use: **Investment Purposes**
Hedge currency risk

Currencies: US dollar, Australian dollar, Belgian franc, Canadian dollar, ECU, French franc, German mark, Italian lira, Japanese yen, Spanish peseta, UK pound

Regions: Europe

DERIVATIVES ACTIVITIES: **CAC Class: 5**

OTC Derivatives **Plain Vanilla Derivatives**	**Currency** Forwards	
Structured Notes	Floaters	Multi-step-up callable bonds
Counterparty Rating Requirement:	A	

OTHER ALTERNATIVE INVESTMENTS:

	CMOs/REMICs – Govt.	Strips

KEY MANAGERS & DERIVATIVES SPECIALISTS:	Direct Phone/Fax	Job Function
Mr. John Power Senior Vice President		Bond Department Head Portfolio Mgr – Derivatives

Barnett Banks, Inc.

Bank/Portfolio

Location: 50 Laura Street
11th Floor
Jacksonville, FL 32202-3638

Fax: 904/791-7185 **Phone:** 904/791-7500

Profile: Stable asset investor

Investment Portfolio: $ 8.1 billion

Use:

Balance Sheet/Risk Management
Access global mkts
Create synthetic fixed/floating rate
Hedge balance sheet
Hedge commercial paper
Hedge interest rate risk
Incremental return
Reduce cost of capital
Strategic liability management

Investment Purposes
Alter portfolio weighting
Adjust portfolio duration
Asset allocation
Capture extra yield
Hedge bond portfolio risk
Protect currency gains
Provide incremental return
Reduce variability of returns

Currencies: US dollar

Regions: United States

Barnett Banks, Inc. – continued

DERIVATIVES ACTIVITIES: **CAC Class: 6**

Exchange-traded Options & Futures
U.S. Treasury futures | U.S. Treasury options

OTC Derivatives
Plain Vanilla Derivatives

	Interest rate	
	Swaps	Caps
	Forwards	Floors
	Swaptions	Collars

Counterparty Rating Requirement: AA

OTHER ALTERNATIVE INVESTMENTS:

CMOs/REMICs – Govt. | CMOs/REMICs – Private

KEY MANAGERS & DERIVATIVES SPECIALISTS:	**Direct Phone/Fax**	**Job Function**
Mr. Allen L. Lastinger, Jr. President & C.O.O.		President
Mr. Charles W. Newman Chief Financial Officer		Chief Financial Officer
Mr. Richard J. Redick Director – Finance		Portfolio Mgr – Derivatives
Mr. Randy B. Robertson Director – Investments	904/791-7621	Chief Investment Officer Portfolio Mgr – Derivatives Portfolio Mgr – Futures Portfolio Mgr – Options

Barrow, Hanley, Mewhinney & Strauss, Inc.

Investment Manager

Sub of United Asset Management Corporation

Location: 200 Crescent Court
Suite 1900
Dallas, TX 75201-1870

Fax: 214/665-1965 **Phone:** 214/665-1900

Profile: Total return investor

Investment Portfolio: $ 14.4 billion

Use: **Investment Purposes**

Currencies: US dollar

Regions: United States

DERIVATIVES ACTIVITIES: **CAC Class: Inactive**

OTHER ALTERNATIVE INVESTMENTS:

CMOs/REMICs – Govt. | Repos/reverse repos

Barrow, Hanley, Mewhinney & Strauss, Inc. – continued

KEY MANAGERS & DERIVATIVES SPECIALISTS:	**Direct Phone/Fax**	**Job Function**
Mr. Bryant M. Hanley, Jr. President, Secretary/Treasurer		President Treasurer
Mr. John S. Williams Principal	214/871-5309	Bond Department Head *Taxable*

Bartlett & Co.

Investment Manager

Sub of Legg Mason, Inc.

Location: 36 East Fourth Street
Second Floor
Cincinnati, OH 45202-3896

Fax: 513/621-6462 **Phone:** 513/621-4612

Profile: Total return investor

Investment Portfolio: $ 2.1 billion

Use: **Investment Purposes**
Capture extra yield
Hedge currency risk

Currencies: US dollar

Regions: United States

DERIVATIVES ACTIVITIES: **CAC Class: 2**

Structured Notes	Govt. agency MTNs	Inverse floaters

OTHER ALTERNATIVE INVESTMENTS:

	CMOs/REMICs – Govt.	Strips
	CMOs/REMICs – Private	Repos/reverse repos
	GICs	

KEY MANAGERS & DERIVATIVES SPECIALISTS:	**Direct Phone/Fax**	**Job Function**
Mr. James A. Miller President		President
Mr. Dale H. Rabiner Director – Fixed Income		Chief Investment Officer Portfolio Mgr – Structured Notes
Mr. Troy R. Snider Analyst	Ext. 698	Fixed-Income Strategist

Bausch & Lomb Incorporated

Corporation

Location: One Chase Square
Rochester, NY 14601-0054

Fax: 716/338-6007 **Phone:** 716/338-6000

Use: **Balance Sheet/Risk Management**
Create synthetic fixed/floating rate
Hedge balance sheet
Hedge commercial paper
Hedge currency risk
Hedge interest rate risk
Lower transaction costs
Strategic liability management

Currencies: US dollar
Australian dollar
Belgian franc
Canadian dollar
French franc
German mark
Italian lira
Japanese yen
Mexican peso
Spanish peseta
Swiss franc
UK pound

Regions: United States

DERIVATIVES ACTIVITIES:

OTC Derivatives	**Bond, Currency, Interest rate**	
Plain Vanilla Derivatives	Swaps	Caps
	Forwards	Floors
	Swaptions	Collars
Counterparty Rating Requirement:	BBB	

KEY MANAGERS & DERIVATIVES SPECIALISTS:	**Direct Phone/Fax**	**Job Function**
Mr. Alan H. Resnick Vice President & Treasurer	716/338-6045	Treasurer Portfolio Mgr – Derivatives
Mr. Peter Stephenson S.V.P. – Finance		Chief Financial Officer
Mr. Ronald L. Zarrella President & C.O.O.	716/338-5079	President

Baxter International Inc.

Corporation

Location: One Baxter Parkway
Deerfield, IL 60015-4633

Fax: 847/948-3948 **Phone:** 847/948-2000

Use: **Balance Sheet/Risk Management**
Create synthetic fixed/floating rate
Hedge balance sheet
Hedge interest rate risk
Hedge overseas investments
Incremental return
Lower transaction costs
Reduce cost of capital

Currencies: US dollar
Belgian franc
Canadian dollar
French franc
Japanese yen

Regions: United States

Baxter International Inc.– continued

DERIVATIVES ACTIVITIES:		CAC Class: 6
Exchange-traded Options & Futures	**Interest rate**	
OTC Derivatives	**Bond, Currency, Interest rate**	
Plain Vanilla Derivatives	Swaps	Caps
	Swaptions	Floors
Counterparty Rating Requirement:	AA	

KEY MANAGERS & DERIVATIVES SPECIALISTS:	Direct Phone/Fax	Job Function
Mr. Lawrence D. Damon Treasurer		Treasurer Portfolio Mgr – Derivatives
Mr. Harry M. Jansen Kraemer, Jr. Sr. Vice President & C.F.O.		Chief Financial Officer

Bay View Federal Bank, A Federal Savings Bank

Savings Bank/Bldg Society

Sub of Bay View Capital Corporation

Location: 2121 South El Camino Real
San Mateo, CA 94403

Fax: 415/573-1028 **Phone:** 415/312-7268

Profile: Spread investor

Investment Portfolio: $ 1.0 billion

Use: **Balance Sheet/Risk Management**
Hedge interest rate risk

Currencies: US dollar

Regions: United States

DERIVATIVES ACTIVITIES:		CAC Class: 3
OTC Derivatives	**Interest rate**	
Plain Vanilla Derivatives	Swaps	Floors
	Caps	Collars
Counterparty Rating Requirement:	AA	

OTHER ALTERNATIVE INVESTMENTS:		
	CMOs/REMICs – Govt.	Repos/reverse repos
	CMOs/REMICs – Private	

KEY MANAGERS & DERIVATIVES SPECIALISTS:	Direct Phone/Fax	Job Function
Ms. Susan Lansel Vice President	415/312-7268	Chief Investment Officer Portfolio Mgr – Derivatives

BayBank Boston, N.A. (Portfolio)

Bank/Portfolio

Location: 155 Federal Street
Seventh Floor
Boston, MA 02110

Fax: 617/556-6650 **Phone:** 617/556-6717

Profile: Hold to maturity investor

Investment Portfolio: $ 3.0 billion

Use: **Balance Sheet/Risk Management**
Create synthetic fixed/floating rate
Hedge balance sheet
Hedge currency risk
Hedge interest rate risk
Lower transaction costs

Currencies: US dollar

Regions: United States

DERIVATIVES ACTIVITIES: **CAC Class: 2**

OTC Derivatives	**Currency, Interest rate**	
Plain Vanilla Derivatives	Swaps	Swaptions
	Forwards	
Counterparty Rating Requirement:	None	

OTHER ALTERNATIVE INVESTMENTS:

CMOs/REMICs – Govt. Repos/reverse repos

KEY MANAGERS & DERIVATIVES SPECIALISTS:	**Direct Phone/Fax**	**Job Function**
Mr. Brian D. Stewart Vice President		Chief Investment Officer Portfolio Mgr – Derivatives

BEA Associates

Investment Manager

Location: 153 East 53rd Street
58th Floor
New York, NY 10022

Fax: 212/355-1545 **Phone:** 212/832-2626

Profile: Spread investor

Investment Portfolio: $ 17.8 billion

Use: **Investment Purposes**
Asset allocation
Capture extra yield
Hedge bond portfolio risk
Hedge currency risk
Hedge equity portfolio risk
Provide incremental return
Reduce variability of returns

Currencies: US dollar

Regions: United States

BEA Associates – continued

DERIVATIVES ACTIVITIES:		CAC Class: 7
Exchange-traded Options & Futures U.S. Treasury futures	**Bond, Currency, Interest rate** U.S. Treasury options	
OTC Derivatives **Plain Vanilla Derivatives**	**Bond, Currency, Interest rate** Swaps Forwards Caps	 Floors Collars
Structured Notes	Corporate MTNs Govt. agency MTNs	Bond index notes
Counterparty Rating Requirement:	A	

OTHER ALTERNATIVE INVESTMENTS:		
	CMOs/REMICs – Govt. Strips	Repos/reverse repos

KEY MANAGERS & DERIVATIVES SPECIALISTS:	Direct Phone/Fax	Job Function
Mr. Jeffrey Geller Managing Director		Portfolio Mgr – Derivatives *Corp* Portfolio Mgr – Futures *Corp*
Mr. Robert J. Moore Managing Director	Ext. 204 212/355-1662	Bond Department Head Portfolio Mgr – Derivatives Portfolio Mgr – Futures Portfolio Mgr – Options
Mr. Mark K. Silverstein Senior Vice President	212/310-0305	Portfolio Mgr – Derivatives Portfolio Mgr – Futures Portfolio Mgr – Options Portfolio Mgr – Structured Notes

Bear, Stearns Asset Management Inc.

Broker/Management Sub

Sub of Bear, Stearns & Company Inc.

Location: 575 Lexington Avenue
Tenth Floor
New York, NY 10022

Fax: 212/272-3107 **Phone:** 212/272-2814

Profile: Total return investor

Investment Portfolio: $ 7.7 billion

Use: **Investment Purposes**

Currencies: US dollar

Regions: United States

Bear, Stearns Asset Management Inc. – continued

DERIVATIVES ACTIVITIES:		CAC Class: 2
Structured Notes	Corporate MTNs Govt. agency MTNs Floaters	Inverse floaters Periodic capped floaters

OTHER ALTERNATIVE INVESTMENTS:		
	CMOs/REMICs – Govt. CMOs/REMICs – Private	Strips

KEY MANAGERS & DERIVATIVES SPECIALISTS:	Direct Phone/Fax	Job Function
Mr. Neil Eigen		Chief Investment Officer
Mr. Peter Mahoney Director – Fixed Income	212/272-6027	Bond Department Head Portfolio Mgr – Structured Notes

Bear, Stearns & Co. Inc. (Unit Trust)

Unit Investment Trust

Sub of Bear, Stearns & Company Inc.

Location: 245 Park Avenue, New York, NY 10167 **Fax:** 212/272-3104 **Phone:** 212/272-2500

Profile: Hold to maturity investor **Investment Portfolio:** $ 3.8 billion

Use: **Investment Purposes**

Currencies: US dollar **Regions:** United States

DERIVATIVES ACTIVITIES:		CAC Class: Inactive

OTHER ALTERNATIVE INVESTMENTS:		
	CMOs/REMICs – Govt.	CMOs/REMICs – Private

KEY MANAGERS & DERIVATIVES SPECIALISTS:	Direct Phone/Fax	Job Function
Mr. Peter J. DeMarco Managing Director	212/272-5500	Bond Department Head

BellSouth Corporation

Corporation

Location: 1155 Peachtree Street N.E.
Atlanta, GA 30309

Fax: 404/249-5597 **Phone:** 404/249-2000

Profile: Stable asset investor

Investment Portfolio: $ 1.0 - 3.0 billion

Use: **Balance Sheet/Risk Management**
Hedge currency risk
Hedge interest rate risk
Lower transaction costs
Reduce cost of capital

Currencies: US dollar, Australian dollar, ECU, French franc, UK pound

Regions: United States

DERIVATIVES ACTIVITIES:

OTC Derivatives **Plain Vanilla Derivatives**	**Bond**	
Structured Notes	Corporate MTNs	Govt. agency MTNs
Counterparty Rating Requirement:	AA	

OTHER ALTERNATIVE INVESTMENTS:

CMOs/REMICs – Govt.
CMOs/REMICs – Private
Repos/reverse repos

KEY MANAGERS & DERIVATIVES SPECIALISTS:	**Direct Phone/Fax**	**Job Function**
Mr. Jerry Guthrie Assistant Treasurer	404/249-3300	Chief Investment Officer
Mr. Earle Mauldin Exec. Vice President & C.F.O.	404/249-4030	Chief Financial Officer
Mr. Arlen G. Yokley Vice President & Treasurer	404/249-3400	Treasurer Portfolio Mgr – Derivatives

Beneficial Insurance Group, Inc.

Insurance Co/P & C

Sub of Beneficial Corporation

Location: 400 Beneficial Center
Peapack, NJ 07977

Fax: 908/781-4479 **Phone:** 908/781-4246

Profile: Total return investor

Investment Portfolio: $ 1.3 billion

Use: **Balance Sheet/Risk Management**
Create synthetic fixed/floating rate
Hedge balance sheet
Hedge currency risk
Hedge interest rate risk
Hedge overseas investments
Strategic liability management

Currencies: US dollar, Canadian dollar, German mark, UK pound

Regions: United States

Beneficial Insurance Group, Inc. – continued

DERIVATIVES ACTIVITIES: **CAC Class: Inactive**

Counterparty Rating Requirement: AA

OTHER ALTERNATIVE INVESTMENTS:

CMOs/REMICs – Govt. CMOs/REMICs – Private

KEY MANAGERS & DERIVATIVES SPECIALISTS:	Direct Phone/Fax	Job Function
Mr. Daniel R. O'Brien President & C.E.O.		President
Mr. Lavern R. Wolfanger Vice President		Bond Department Head

Beneficial Life Insurance Company

Insurance Co/Life

Location: 36 South State Street
Salt Lake City, UT 84136

Fax: 801/531-3315 **Phone:** 801/531-7979

Profile: Total return investor

Investment Portfolio: $ 1.0 - 3.0 billion

Use: **Investment Purposes**

Currencies: US dollar

Regions: United States

DERIVATIVES ACTIVITIES: **CAC Class: Inactive**

OTHER ALTERNATIVE INVESTMENTS:

CMOs/REMICs – Govt. Repos/reverse repos

KEY MANAGERS & DERIVATIVES SPECIALISTS:	Direct Phone/Fax	Job Function
Mr. Bruce H. Cundick		Chief Investment Officer

Benefit Capital Management Corporation

Investment Manager

Sub of Union Carbide Corporation

Location: 39 Old Ridgebury Road
Danbury, CT 06817

Fax: 203/794-2693 **Phone:** 203/794-4762

Profile: Total return investor

Investment Portfolio: $ 3.2 billion

Use: **Investment Purposes**

Currencies: US dollar

Regions: United States

Benefit Capital Management Corporation – continued

DERIVATIVES ACTIVITIES:		**CAC Class: Inactive**

OTHER ALTERNATIVE INVESTMENTS:

CMOs/REMICs – Govt.

KEY MANAGERS & DERIVATIVES SPECIALISTS:	**Direct Phone/Fax**	**Job Function**
Mr. Michael F. Hoben President	203/794-7337	President
Mr. James E. McCabe Vice President-Fixed Income	203/794-5938	Chief Investment Officer

Benham Capital Management Group

Mutual Fund Manager

Sub of Twentieth Century Companies

Location: 1665 Charleston Road
Mountain View, CA 94043-1212

Fax: 415/965-4902 **Phone:** 415/965-8300

Profile: Total return investor

Investment Portfolio: $ 10.0 billion

Use: **Investment Purposes**
- Alter portfolio weighting
- Adjust portfolio duration
- Asset allocation
- Capture extra yield
- Convexity objectives
- Hedge bond portfolio risk
- Lower transactions costs

Currencies: US dollar

Regions: United States, Europe

DERIVATIVES ACTIVITIES:		**CAC Class: 2**
Exchange-traded Options & Futures Municipal futures	**Bond, Interest rate**	
Structured Notes	Floaters	Inverse floaters

OTHER ALTERNATIVE INVESTMENTS:

	CMOs/REMICs – Govt.	Strips
	CMOs/REMICs – Private	Repos/reverse repos
	MOPs/TOPs	

KEY MANAGERS & DERIVATIVES SPECIALISTS:	**Direct Phone/Fax**	**Job Function**
Mr. Steven Colton	415/967-9790	Portfolio Mgr – Futures *Corp*
Mr. G. David MacEwen	415/967-9787	Bond Department Head *Muni* Portfolio Mgr – Futures *Muni*

Benham Capital Management Group – continued

KEY MANAGERS & DERIVATIVES SPECIALISTS:	Direct Phone/Fax	Job Function
Mr. Randall Merk Vice President	415/967-9792 415/965-1446	Chief Investment Officer Portfolio Mgr – Structured Notes

Berkeley Capital Management

Investment Manager

Sub of London-Pacific Group, Ltd

Location: 650 California Street
Suite 2800
San Francisco, CA 94108

Fax: 415/393-0392 **Phone:** 415/393-0300

Profile: Total return investor

Investment Portfolio: $ 2.0 billion

Use: **Investment Purposes**
Alter portfolio weighting

Currencies: US dollar

Regions: United States

DERIVATIVES ACTIVITIES: **CAC Class: 1**

Exchange-traded Options & Futures
U.S. Treasury futures

Bond

OTHER ALTERNATIVE INVESTMENTS:

CMOs/REMICs – Govt.
CMOs/REMICs – Private

Strips

KEY MANAGERS & DERIVATIVES SPECIALISTS:	Direct Phone/Fax	Job Function
Mr. William F. Cox Senior Vice President	415/393-0346	Portfolio Mgr – Futures
Mr. Timothy Warner President		President Chief Investment Officer
Mr. Richard B. Woodbury Principal	415/393-0354 415/393-0391	Portfolio Mgr – Futures

Berkley Dean & Co.

Insurance Co/Management

Sub of W.R. Berkley Corporation

Location: 165 Mason Street
Greenwich, CT 06836

Fax: 203/629-4359 **Phone:** 203/629-2880

Profile: Total return investor

Investment Portfolio: $ 4.0 - 10.0 billion

Use: **Investment Purposes**

Currencies: US dollar

Regions: United States

Berkley Dean & Co. – continued

DERIVATIVES ACTIVITIES: **CAC Class: Inactive**

OTHER ALTERNATIVE INVESTMENTS:

CMOs/REMICs – Govt.
CMOs/REMICs – Private
Repos/reverse repos

KEY MANAGERS & DERIVATIVES SPECIALISTS:	**Direct Phone/Fax**	**Job Function**
Mr. James Shiel President – Investments		President Bond Department Head

Berkshire Life Insurance Co.

Insurance Co/Life

Location: 700 South Street
Pittsfield, MA 01201

Fax: 413/443-9397 **Phone:** 413/499-4321

Profile: Hold to maturity investor

Investment Portfolio: $ 1.8 billion

Use: **Investment Purposes**

Currencies: US dollar

Regions: United States

DERIVATIVES ACTIVITIES: **CAC Class: Inactive**

OTHER ALTERNATIVE INVESTMENTS:

CMOs/REMICs – Govt.

KEY MANAGERS & DERIVATIVES SPECIALISTS:	**Direct Phone/Fax**	**Job Function**
Mr. David O'Clair Vice President	Ext. 468	Chief Investment Officer

Sanford C. Bernstein & Co., Inc.

Investment Manager

Location: 767 Fifth Avenue
22nd Floor
New York, NY 10153-0185

Fax: 212/756-4550 **Phone:** 212/486-5800

Profile: Total return investor

Investment Portfolio: $ 26.0 billion

Use: **Investment Purposes**
Alter portfolio weighting
Adjust portfolio duration
Asset allocation
Capture extra yield
Hedge bond portfolio risk
Hedge currency risk
Hedge interest rate risk

Currencies: US dollar
Belgian franc
Canadian dollar
French franc
German mark
Italian lira
Japanese yen
Swiss franc
UK pound

Regions: United States
Europe

Sanford C. Bernstein & Co., Inc. – continued

DERIVATIVES ACTIVITIES:

Exchange-traded Options & Futures	**Bond, Currency, Interest rate**	
OTC Derivatives		
Plain Vanilla Derivatives	Swaps	Forwards
Exotic Derivatives	CMT swaps	CMT options

OTHER ALTERNATIVE INVESTMENTS:

	CMOs/REMICs – Govt.	Strips

KEY MANAGERS & DERIVATIVES SPECIALISTS:	**Direct Phone/Fax**	**Job Function**
Mr. Robert Guy Davidson III Director – Municipal Bonds	212/756-4150	Bond Department Head *Muni*
Ms. Marilyn G. Fedak	212/756-4489	Chief Investment Officer
Mr. Mark Hamilton	212/756-4623	Portfolio Mgr – Derivatives Portfolio Mgr – Futures Portfolio Mgr – Options
Mr. Richard J. Kaye	212/756-4127	Portfolio Mgr – Derivatives Portfolio Mgr – Futures Portfolio Mgr – Options
Ms. Elaine Mintzer	212/756-4131 212/486-8329	Trader – Derivatives Trader – Futures Trader – Options
Ms. Elizabeth Ruskin Senior Portfolio Manager	212/756-4135	Portfolio Mgr – Derivatives Portfolio Mgr – Futures Portfolio Mgr – Options
Mr. Francis H. Trainer, Jr. Director – Fixed Income Taxable	212/756-4138	Bond Department Head *Taxable* Portfolio Mgr – Derivatives Portfolio Mgr – Futures Portfolio Mgr – Structured Notes

Bessemer Trust Company, N.A.

Bank/Trust

Sub of The Bessemer Group, Inc.

Location: 630 Fifth Avenue
New York, NY 10111

Fax: 212/265-5826 **Phone:** 212/708-9100

Profile: Total return investor

Investment Portfolio: $ 8.5 billion

Use: **Balance Sheet/Risk Management**
Access global mkts
Hedge currency risk
Strategic liability management

Investment Purposes
Hedge currency risk

Currencies: US dollar, ECU, French franc, German mark, Swiss franc, UK pound

Regions: United States, Europe

Bessemer Trust Company, N.A. – continued

DERIVATIVES ACTIVITIES:		**CAC Class: 2**
OTC Derivatives	**Currency, Interest rate**	
Plain Vanilla Derivatives	Swaps	Forwards

OTHER ALTERNATIVE INVESTMENTS:	
	CMOs/REMICs – Govt.

KEY MANAGERS & DERIVATIVES SPECIALISTS:	**Direct Phone/Fax**	**Job Function**
Mr. Timothy J. Morris Sr. E.V.P. & Chief Inv. Officer		Chief Investment Officer
Mr. John Whitmore President & C.E.O.		President
Mr. Harold S. Woolley Senior Vice President	212/708-9293 212/586-2806	Bond Department Head Portfolio Mgr – Derivatives

BlackRock Financial Management L.P.

Investment Manager

Sub of PNC Bank Corporation

Location: 345 Park Avenue
30th Floor
New York, NY 10154-0126

Fax: 212/754-8790 **Phone:** 212/754-5560

Profile: Total return investor

Investment Portfolio: $ 36.6 billion

Use: **Balance Sheet/Risk Management**
Hedge interest rate risk

Investment Purposes
Alter portfolio weighting
Adjust portfolio duration
Asset allocation
Capture extra yield
Hedge bond portfolio risk
Hedge interest rate risk
Reduce variability of returns

Currencies: US dollar

Regions: United States

DERIVATIVES ACTIVITIES:		
Exchange-traded Options & Futures	**Bond, Interest rate**	
OTC Derivatives	**Bond, Interest rate**	
Plain Vanilla Derivatives	Forwards	Floors
	Caps	Collars
Structured Notes	Corporate MTNs	Floaters
	Govt. agency MTNs	Inverse floaters
	CMT notes	Periodic capped floaters

OTHER ALTERNATIVE INVESTMENTS:		
	CMOs/REMICs – Govt.	Strips
	CMOs/REMICs – Private	Repos/reverse repos

BlackRock Financial Management L.P. – continued

KEY MANAGERS & DERIVATIVES SPECIALISTS:	Direct Phone/Fax	Job Function
Mr. Scott M. Amero Vice President & Partner	212/754-5330	Fixed-Income Strategist Portfolio Mgr – Derivatives Portfolio Mgr – Options Portfolio Mgr – Structured Notes
Mr. Laurence D. Fink Chairman & C.E.O.	212/754-5546	Chief Investment Officer
Mr. Ben Golub Managing Director		Derivatives Specialist
Mr. Robert S. Kapito Vice Chairman	212/754-5330	Bond Department Head
Mr. Scott Peng		Derivatives Specialist
Mr. Ralph L. Schlosstein President		President
Mr. Joel Shaiman	212/754-5540 212/754-8777	Portfolio Mgr – Futures

Bluebonnet Savings Bank Fsb

Savings Bank/Bldg Society

Location: 3100 Monticello
Dallas, TX 75205

Fax: 214/443-4376 **Phone:** 214/443-9000

Profile: Total return investor

Investment Portfolio: $ 3.1 billion

Use: **Balance Sheet/Risk Management**
Hedge interest rate risk

Currencies: US dollar

Regions: United States

DERIVATIVES ACTIVITIES: **CAC Class: 2**

Exchange-traded Options & Futures	**Interest rate**	
OTC Derivatives **Plain Vanilla Derivatives**	**Interest rate** Swaps Caps	 Floors
Structured Notes	Index amortizing notes	
Counterparty Rating Requirement:	A	

OTHER ALTERNATIVE INVESTMENTS:

	CMOs/REMICs – Govt. Strips	Repos/reverse repos

KEY MANAGERS & DERIVATIVES SPECIALISTS:	Direct Phone/Fax	Job Function
Mr. Bryce Fowler	Ext. 3320	Chief Investment Officer
Mr. Joseph Simanek Treasurer	Ext. 3336	Treasurer Portfolio Mgr – Derivatives

The Boatmen's National Bank of St. Louis (Portfolio)

Bank/Portfolio

Sub of Boatmen's Bancshares, Inc.

Location: 800 Market Street
One Boatmen's Plaza
8th Floor
St. Louis, MO 63101

Fax: 314/466-8480 **Phone:** 314/466-6000

Investment Portfolio: $ 6.4 - 10.0 billion

Use:

Balance Sheet/Risk Management
Create synthetic fixed/floating rate
Hedge balance sheet
Hedge interest rate risk
Incremental return
Lower transaction costs
Meet interest rate target
Reduce cost of capital
Strategic liability management

Investment Purposes
Adjust portfolio duration
Capture extra yield
Discretionary situations
Diversify portfolio
Hedge bond portfolio risk
Hedge interest rate risk
Lower transactions costs
Provide incremental return
Reduce variability of returns

Currencies: US dollar

Regions: United States

DERIVATIVES ACTIVITIES: **CAC Class: 2**

Exchange-traded Options & Futures	**Bond, Interest rate**	
U.S. Treasury futures	U.S. Treasury options	
OTC Derivatives	**Bond, Interest rate**	
Plain Vanilla Derivatives	Swaps	
Exotic Derivatives	Index amortizing swaps	
Structured Notes	Govt. agency MTNs	Periodic capped floaters
	CMT notes	Multi-step-up callable bonds
	Floaters	

OTHER ALTERNATIVE INVESTMENTS:

	CMOs/REMICs – Govt.	Repos/reverse repos
	CMOs/REMICs – Private	

KEY MANAGERS & DERIVATIVES SPECIALISTS:	**Direct Phone/Fax**	**Job Function**
Mr. Bradley Cunningham Vice President	314/466-8321	Portfolio Mgr – Derivatives Portfolio Mgr – Futures *Govt* Portfolio Mgr – Options *Govt* Portfolio Mgr – Structured Notes
Mr. David W. Jacus Vice President	314/466-8318	Portfolio Mgr – Derivatives *MBS*
Mr. John Morton III President & C.E.O.		President
Mr. Phillip E. Peters E.V.P. & Managing Director		Chief Investment Officer
Mr. Keith Welden Vice President	314/466-8317	Portfolio Mgr – Structured Notes

Boatmen's Trust (St. Louis) (Fixed Income)

Bank/Trust

Sub of Boatmen's Bancshares, Inc.

Location: 100 North Broadway
Fifth Floor
St. Louis, MO 63102-2728

Fax: 314/466-4098 **Phone:** 314/466-4086

Profile: Total return investor

Investment Portfolio: $ 27.1 billion

Use: **Investment Purposes**

Currencies: US dollar

Regions: United States

DERIVATIVES ACTIVITIES: **CAC Class: 2**

Structured Notes	Floaters

OTHER ALTERNATIVE INVESTMENTS:

CMOs/REMICs – Govt. CMOs/REMICs – Private

KEY MANAGERS & DERIVATIVES SPECIALISTS:	Direct Phone/Fax	Job Function
Mr. Frank J. Aten Senior Vice President	314/466-4087	Bond Department Head Portfolio Mgr – Structured Notes
Mr. J.J. Landers Carnal Senior Vice President	314/466-4088	Chief Investment Officer

Boatmen's Trust Company of Texas

Bank/Trust

Sub of Boatmen's Bancshares, Inc.

Location: 5847 San Felipe Drive
Suite 4600
Houston, TX 77057

Fax: 713/952-9141 **Phone:** 713/952-9100

Profile: Total return investor

Investment Portfolio: $ 1.4 billion

Use: **Investment Purposes**

Currencies: US dollar

Regions: United States

DERIVATIVES ACTIVITIES:

Structured Notes	Corporate MTNs

OTHER ALTERNATIVE INVESTMENTS:

CMOs/REMICs – Govt. CMOs/REMICs – Private

KEY MANAGERS & DERIVATIVES SPECIALISTS:	Direct Phone/Fax	Job Function
Mr. Joseph Bybee		Portfolio Mgr – Structured Notes
Mr. George E. Crosby Vice President		Fixed-Income Strategist Portfolio Mgr – Structured Notes
Mr. Thomas Hunt Assistant Vice President		Portfolio Mgr – Structured Notes

Boatmen's Trust Company of Texas – continued

KEY MANAGERS & DERIVATIVES SPECIALISTS:	Direct Phone/Fax	Job Function
Mr. Joe Ince President		President Portfolio Mgr – Structured Notes

The Boeing Company

Corporation

Location: 7755 East Marginal Way South
Seattle, WA 98108

Fax: 206/655-1177 **Phone:** 206/655-2121

Use: **Balance Sheet/Risk Management**
Create synthetic fixed/floating rate
Hedge interest rate risk

Currencies: US dollar **Regions:** United States

DERIVATIVES ACTIVITIES:

OTC Derivatives
Plain Vanilla Derivatives Swaps

Counterparty Rating Requirement: AA

OTHER ALTERNATIVE INVESTMENTS:

Repos/reverse repos

KEY MANAGERS & DERIVATIVES SPECIALISTS:	Direct Phone/Fax	Job Function
Mr. Philip M. Condit President		President
Mr. Boyd E. Givan Senior Vice President & C.F.O.		Chief Financial Officer
Mr. David A. Jaeger Vice President & Treasurer		Treasurer Portfolio Mgr – Derivatives

Boeing Employee Credit Union

Credit Union

Location: 12770 Gateway Drive
Tukwila, WA 98168

Fax: 206/439-5806 **Phone:** 206/439-5700

Profile: Total return investor **Investment Portfolio:** $ 2.0 billion

Use: **Investment Purposes**

Currencies: US dollar **Regions:** United States

DERIVATIVES ACTIVITIES: **CAC Class: Inactive**

OTHER ALTERNATIVE INVESTMENTS:

Strips Repos/reverse repos

Boeing Employee Credit Union – continued

KEY MANAGERS & DERIVATIVES SPECIALISTS:	Direct Phone/Fax	Job Function
Mr. Gary J. Oakland President & C.E.O.		President
Mr. Timothy Perman	206/439-5952	Chief Investment Officer

BofA Capital Management Inc. (Los Angeles)

Bank/Management Division

Sub of BankAmerica Corporation

Location: 300 South Grand Avenue
Suite 2200/2500
Los Angeles, CA 90071-3157

Fax: 213/626-2162 **Phone:** 213/229-1400

Profile: Total return investor

Investment Portfolio: $ 20.0 billion

Use: **Investment Purposes**

Currencies: US dollar

Regions: United States

DERIVATIVES ACTIVITIES: **CAC Class: Inactive**

OTHER ALTERNATIVE INVESTMENTS:

	CMOs/REMICs – Govt. Strips	Repos/reverse repos

KEY MANAGERS & DERIVATIVES SPECIALISTS:	Direct Phone/Fax	Job Function
Ms. Kim I. Michalski V.P./Director-T/E Fixed Income	213/229-1404	Bond Department Head *Muni*
Mr. Keith Wirtz Senior Vice President	213/229-1928	Chief Investment Officer

The Boston Company Asset Management

Investment Manager

Sub of Mellon Bank Corporation

Location: One Boston Place
13th Floor
Boston, MA 02108

Fax: 617/722-7250 **Phone:** 617/722-7000

Profile: Total return investor

Investment Portfolio: $ 22.0 billion

Use: **Investment Purposes**
Hedge bond portfolio risk
Hedge interest rate risk

Currencies: US dollar

Regions: United States

DERIVATIVES ACTIVITIES: **CAC Class: 3**

Exchange-traded Options & Futures

Structured Notes	Corporate MTNs Floaters	Inverse floaters

The Boston Company Asset Management – continued

OTHER ALTERNATIVE INVESTMENTS:

CMOs/REMICs – Govt.	Strips
CMOs/REMICs – Private	Repos/reverse repos
GICs	

KEY MANAGERS & DERIVATIVES SPECIALISTS:	**Direct Phone/Fax**	**Job Function**
Mr. Almond G. Goduti, Jr. Vice President	617/722-7822	Portfolio Mgr – Futures Portfolio Mgr – Structured Notes
Mr. John F. Poole Senior Vice President	617/722-7713	Fixed-Income Strategist
Mr. Alexander Webb III Vice Chairman	617/722-7779	Chief Investment Officer
Mr. Andrew S. Windmueller Vice President	617/722-7233	Fixed-Income Strategist

Boston Safe Deposit and Trust Company

Bank/Trust

Sub of Mellon Bank Corporation

Location: One Boston Place
Boston, MA 02108

Fax: 617/722-7807 **Phone:** 617/722-7000

Profile: Total return investor

Investment Portfolio: $ 4.0 - 10.0 billion

Use: **Investment Purposes**

Currencies: US dollar

Regions: United States

DERIVATIVES ACTIVITIES: **CAC Class: Inactive**

OTHER ALTERNATIVE INVESTMENTS:

CMOs/REMICs – Govt.	Repos/reverse repos
Strips	

KEY MANAGERS & DERIVATIVES SPECIALISTS:	**Direct Phone/Fax**	**Job Function**
Mr. H. Vernon Winters		Chief Investment Officer

BPS Associates, Inc.

Investment Manager

Location: 7831 Glenroy Road
Suite 218
Bloomington, MN 55439

Fax: 612/893-0909 **Phone:** 612/893-0177

Profile: Total return investor

Investment Portfolio: $ 1.3 billion

Use: **Investment Purposes**

Currencies: US dollar

Regions: United States

BPS Associates, Inc. – continued

DERIVATIVES ACTIVITIES: **CAC Class: Inactive**

OTHER ALTERNATIVE INVESTMENTS:

	CMOs/REMICs – Govt.	CMOs/REMICs – Private

KEY MANAGERS & DERIVATIVES SPECIALISTS:	Direct Phone/Fax	Job Function
Mr. Lewis Coffey President		President Chief Investment Officer

BR Investment Associates

Investment Manager

Location: 867 River Road
Chatham, NJ 07928

Fax: 908/771-7452 **Phone:** 908/771-7452

Profile: Total return investor

Investment Portfolio: $ 588.0 million

Use: **Investment Purposes**
Hedge bond portfolio risk
Hedge interest rate risk
Provide incremental return

Currencies: US dollar

Regions: United States

DERIVATIVES ACTIVITIES: **CAC Class: 3**

Exchange-traded Options & Futures Municipal futures	**Bond, Interest rate**	
OTC Derivatives **Plain Vanilla Derivatives**	**Interest rate** Swaps Forwards Swaptions	 Caps Floors Collars
Exotic Derivatives	Bond index swaps	Index amortizing swaps
Structured Notes	Corporate MTNs Govt. agency MTNs Index amortizing notes	Floaters Inverse floaters Multi-step-up callable bonds
Counterparty Rating Requirement:	A	

OTHER ALTERNATIVE INVESTMENTS:

	CMOs/REMICs – Govt. CMOs/REMICs – Private GICs	Strips Repos/reverse repos

BR Investment Associates – continued

KEY MANAGERS & DERIVATIVES SPECIALISTS:	Direct Phone/Fax	Job Function
Mr. Canfield Ardington		Portfolio Mgr – Options Portfolio Mgr – Structured Notes
Mr. Oscar Jensen		Trader – Derivatives Head Trader – Derivatives
Mr. E. T. Kingford Vice President		Chief Investment Officer
Ms. Kim B. Kurtz		Portfolio Mgr – Derivatives Portfolio Mgr – Futures
Mr. Howard G. Orelek		Research Analyst – Derivatives

Bradford & Marzec, Inc.

Investment Manager

Location: 333 South Hope Street
Suite 4050
Los Angeles, CA 90071

Fax: 213/687-9189 **Phone:** 213/687-9170

Profile: Hold to maturity investor

Investment Portfolio: $ 2.2 billion

Use: **Investment Purposes**

Currencies: US dollar

Regions: United States

DERIVATIVES ACTIVITIES: **CAC Class: Inactive**

OTHER ALTERNATIVE INVESTMENTS:

CMOs/REMICs – Govt.
CMOs/REMICs – Private
Strips

KEY MANAGERS & DERIVATIVES SPECIALISTS:	Direct Phone/Fax	Job Function
Mr. Edward T. Bradford Managing Director & C.E.O.		Chief Investment Officer
Ms. Zelda Marzec President & C.E.O.		President Chief Investment Officer

Branch Banking & Trust Company (BB&T-NC) (Portfolio)

Bank/Portfolio

Sub of Southern National Corporation

Location: 200 West Second Street
Southern National Financial Center
Winston-Salem, NC 27101

Fax: 910/733-2238 **Phone:** 910/733-2000

Profile: Total return investor

Investment Portfolio: $ 4.5 billion

Use: **Balance Sheet/Risk Management**
Hedge balance sheet
Hedge commercial paper
Hedge currency risk
Hedge interest rate risk
Hedge overseas investments

Currencies: US dollar

Regions: United States

DERIVATIVES ACTIVITIES:

CAC Class: 6

Exchange-traded Options & Futures U.S. Treasury futures U.S. Treasury options	**Bond, Interest rate** Municipal futures Municipal options	
OTC Derivatives **Plain Vanilla Derivatives**	**Interest rate** Swaps Forwards Caps	 Floors Collars
Structured Notes	Govt. agency MTNs	Bond index notes
Counterparty Rating Requirement:	AAA	

OTHER ALTERNATIVE INVESTMENTS:

CMOs/REMICs – Govt.
Repos/reverse repos

KEY MANAGERS & DERIVATIVES SPECIALISTS:	**Direct Phone/Fax**	**Job Function**
Mr. Jeff Cook	910/733-2174	Portfolio Mgr – Derivatives Portfolio Mgr – Futures *Govt* Portfolio Mgr – Options *Govt* Portfolio Mgr – Structured Notes
Mr. Robert E. Greene President	910/733-2304	President
Mr. Brian Hodgson Vice President	910/733-2146	Portfolio Mgr – Derivatives
Mr. Rodney Hughes	910/733-2147	Portfolio Mgr – Derivatives
Mr. Morris D. Marley Treasurer	910/733-2288	Chief Investment Officer Treasurer Portfolio Mgr – Derivatives
Ms. Gypsy A. McKenzie	910/733-2143	Portfolio Mgr – Derivatives Trader – Derivatives
Mr. Scott E. Reed Sr. Exec. V.P. & C.F.O.	910/733-3088	Chief Financial Officer

Branch Banking & Trust Company (Trust)

Bank/Trust

Sub of Southern National Corporation

Location: 434 Fayetteville Street Mall
Raleigh, NC 27611

Fax: 919/831-4397 **Phone:** 919/831-3990

Profile: Hold to maturity investor

Investment Portfolio: $ 2.6 billion

Use: **Investment Purposes**

Currencies: US dollar

Regions: United States

DERIVATIVES ACTIVITIES: **CAC Class: Inactive**

OTHER ALTERNATIVE INVESTMENTS:

CMOs/REMICs – Govt.
CMOs/REMICs – Private
Strips
Repos/reverse repos

KEY MANAGERS & DERIVATIVES SPECIALISTS:	**Direct Phone/Fax**	**Job Function**
Mr. David McMahon	919/831-4350	Chief Investment Officer

Stacey Braun Associates Incorporated

Investment Manager

Location: 377 Broadway
Eighth Floor
New York, NY 10013

Fax: 212/941-0759 **Phone:** 212/226-7707

Profile: Total return investor

Investment Portfolio: $ 2.3 billion

Use: **Investment Purposes**

Currencies: US dollar

Regions: United States

DERIVATIVES ACTIVITIES: **CAC Class: Inactive**

OTHER ALTERNATIVE INVESTMENTS:

CMOs/REMICs – Govt.
CMOs/REMICs – Private
Strips

KEY MANAGERS & DERIVATIVES SPECIALISTS:	**Direct Phone/Fax**	**Job Function**
Mr. Martin H. Wexler President		President Chief Investment Officer

Bridgewater Associates Inc.

Investment Manager

Location: 372 Danbury Road
Wilton, CT 06897

Fax: 203/762-2615 **Phone:** 203/762-8511

Profile: Total return investor

Investment Portfolio: $ 4.8 billion

Use: **Investment Purposes**
Hedge bond portfolio risk
Hedge currency risk
Hedge equity portfolio risk
Protect currency gains
Provide incremental return

Currencies: US dollar
Australian dollar
German mark
Italian lira
Swiss franc

Regions: United States

DERIVATIVES ACTIVITIES:

Exchange-traded Options & Futures	**Bond**	
OTC Derivatives	**Bond, Currency, Interest rate**	
Plain Vanilla Derivatives	Swaps	Forwards

OTHER ALTERNATIVE INVESTMENTS:

CMOs/REMICs – Govt.

KEY MANAGERS & DERIVATIVES SPECIALISTS:	**Direct Phone/Fax**	**Job Function**
Mr. Daniel Bernstein		Portfolio Mgr – Derivatives Portfolio Mgr – Futures
Mr. Raymond Dalio President		President Chief Investment Officer Portfolio Mgr – Derivatives Portfolio Mgr – Futures
Mr. Ronald E. Madey		Portfolio Mgr – Derivatives Portfolio Mgr – Futures

Brinson Partners, Inc.

Investment Manager

Sub of Schweizerischer Bankverein (Basel)

Location: 209 South LaSalle Street
Suite 1100
Chicago, IL 60604-1295

Fax: 312/220-7199 **Phone:** 312/220-7100

Profile: Total return investor

Investment Portfolio: $ 43.0 billion

Use: **Investment Purposes**
- Adjust portfolio duration
- Asset allocation
- Capture extra yield
- Expand international investments
- Hedge bond portfolio risk
- Hedge currency risk
- Hedge interest rate risk

Currencies: US dollar, Australian dollar, Belgian franc, Canadian dollar, ECU, French franc, German mark, Italian lira, Japanese yen, Mexican peso, Spanish peseta, Swiss franc, UK pound

Regions: United States, Canada, Europe

DERIVATIVES ACTIVITIES:

Exchange-traded Options & Futures U.S. Treasury futures	**Bond, Currency, Interest rate**
OTC Derivatives **Plain Vanilla Derivatives**	**Currency, Interest rate** Swaps
Structured Notes	

OTHER ALTERNATIVE INVESTMENTS:

CMOs/REMICs – Govt.   CMOs/REMICs – Private

KEY MANAGERS & DERIVATIVES SPECIALISTS:	Direct Phone/Fax	Job Function
Mr. Christopher J. Brightman Partner	312/220-7266	Portfolio Mgr – Derivatives Portfolio Mgr – Futures
Mr. Gary P. Brinson President		President Chief Investment Officer Portfolio Mgr – Futures
Mr. Thomas D. Clarkson Partner	312/220-7263 312/220-7266	Portfolio Mgr – Derivatives Portfolio Mgr – Futures Portfolio Mgr – Structured Notes

Brinson Partners, Inc. – continued

KEY MANAGERS & DERIVATIVES SPECIALISTS:	Direct Phone/Fax	Job Function
Mr. Dennis L. Hesse Managing Partner		Bond Department Head *Corp, Govt, MBS* Portfolio Mgr – Derivatives Portfolio Mgr – Futures Portfolio Mgr – Structured Notes
Mr. B. Craig Hutson Partner	312/220-7808	Portfolio Mgr – Derivatives Portfolio Mgr – Futures
Ms. Debra J. Johnson Partner		Portfolio Mgr – Derivatives Portfolio Mgr – Futures Portfolio Mgr – Structured Notes
Dr. Denis S. Karnosky Partner		Fixed-Income Strategist Portfolio Mgr – Derivatives Portfolio Mgr – Futures Portfolio Mgr – Structured Notes
Ms. Linda A. Kent Partner		Portfolio Mgr – Derivatives Portfolio Mgr – Futures
Ms. Catherine A. Nowinski Partner & Invt. Strategist		Fixed-Income Strategist
Mr. Gregory P. Smith Partner	312/220-7253 312/220-7266	Portfolio Mgr – Derivatives Portfolio Mgr – Futures Portfolio Mgr – Structured Notes
Mr. David Strouse Partner		Portfolio Mgr – Derivatives Portfolio Mgr – Futures Portfolio Mgr – Structured Notes
Ms. Anne M. Tremmel Partner		Research Analyst – Derivatives
Ms. Mary M. Wilson Partner		Portfolio Mgr – Derivatives Portfolio Mgr – Futures Portfolio Mgr – Structured Notes
Mr. Glenn G. Wozniak Partner	312/220-7266	Portfolio Mgr – Futures *Govt*

Alex. Brown Investment Management

Broker/Management Sub

Sub of Alex. Brown & Sons, Inc.

Location: 217 East Redwood Street
14th Floor
Baltimore, MD 21202

Fax: 410/837-8338 **Phone:** 410/727-1700

Profile: Total return investor

Investment Portfolio: $ 2.5 - 3.0 billion

Use: **Investment Purposes**

Currencies: US dollar

Regions: United States

Alex. Brown Investment Management – continued

DERIVATIVES ACTIVITIES: **CAC Class: Inactive**

OTHER ALTERNATIVE INVESTMENTS:

CMOs/REMICs – Govt.
CMOs/REMICs – Private

KEY MANAGERS & DERIVATIVES SPECIALISTS:	**Direct Phone/Fax**	**Job Function**
Mr. J. Dorsey Brown III Managing Director & C.E.O.		Chief Investment Officer

Brown Brothers Harriman & Co. (Investments)

Bank/Management Division

Location: 59 Wall Street
New York, NY 10005

Fax: 212/493-8526 **Phone:** 212/483-1818

Profile: Total return investor

Investment Portfolio: $ 20.0 billion

Use: **Investment Purposes**
Hedge bond portfolio risk
Hedge currency risk

Currencies: US dollar, Canadian dollar, French franc, German mark, Italian lira, Japanese yen, UK pound

Regions: United States

DERIVATIVES ACTIVITIES:

Exchange-traded Options & Futures	**Currency**
OTC Derivatives **Plain Vanilla Derivatives**	**Currency** Swaps

OTHER ALTERNATIVE INVESTMENTS:

CMOs/REMICs – Govt.
CMOs/REMICs – Private
Repos/reverse repos

KEY MANAGERS & DERIVATIVES SPECIALISTS:	**Direct Phone/Fax**	**Job Function**
Mr. Elbridge T. Gerry Partner	212/826-1571	Chief Investment Officer
Ms. Maureen McFarland	212/493-8017	Portfolio Mgr – Derivatives Portfolio Mgr – Options
Mr. Donald B. Murphy Partner		Bond Department Head
Mr. Eugene C. Rainis Partner & Director	212/493-7830	Bond Department Head
Mr. John M. Wetherhold	212/493-8828	Fixed-Income Strategist

Brown Brothers Harriman & Co. (Investments) (Chicago)

Bank/Management Division

Location: 125 South Wacker Drive
Suite 2150
Chicago, IL 60606-4402

Fax: 312/368-1287 **Phone:** 312/781-7111

Profile: Total return investor

Investment Portfolio: $ 1.9 billion

Use: **Investment Purposes**
Hedge interest rate risk

Currencies: US dollar

Regions: United States

DERIVATIVES ACTIVITIES: **CAC Class: 2**

Structured Notes Corporate MTNs

OTHER ALTERNATIVE INVESTMENTS:

CMOs/REMICs – Govt.
CMOs/REMICs – Private
Repos/reverse repos

KEY MANAGERS & DERIVATIVES SPECIALISTS:	Direct Phone/Fax	Job Function
Mr. John Borland		Chief Investment Officer
Ms. Cherie Jeffries		Portfolio Mgr – Structured Notes
Mr. Kelly Walters Deputy Manager/Head-Fixed Inc.	312/781-7118	Bond Department Head Portfolio Mgr – Derivatives

Brundage, Story and Rose

Investment Manager

Location: One Broadway
5th Floor
New York, NY 10004

Fax: 212/425-4286 **Phone:** 212/269-3050

Profile: Total return investor

Investment Portfolio: $ 4.0 - 10.0 billion

Use: **Investment Purposes**

Currencies: US dollar

Regions: United States

DERIVATIVES ACTIVITIES: **CAC Class: Inactive**

OTHER ALTERNATIVE INVESTMENTS:

CMOs/REMICs – Govt.
CMOs/REMICs – Private
Repos/reverse repos

KEY MANAGERS & DERIVATIVES SPECIALISTS:	Direct Phone/Fax	Job Function
Mr. H. Dean Benner Managing Director		Bond Department Head
Mr. Malcolm D. Clarke, Jr.		Chief Investment Officer
Mr. Charles Watson		Chief Investment Officer

BZW Barclays Global Investors

Investment Manager

Sub of Barclays de Zoete Wedd Limited Holdings

Location: 45 Fremont Street
17th Floor
San Francisco, CA 94105-2228

Fax: 415/597-2011 **Phone:** 415/597-2000

Profile: Total return investor

Investment Portfolio: $ 171.2 billion

Use: **Balance Sheet/Risk Management**
Hedge currency risk
Hedge interest rate risk

Investment Purposes
Hedge bond portfolio risk
Hedge currency risk
Hedge equity portfolio risk
Hedge interest rate risk

Currencies: US dollar, Canadian dollar, French franc, German mark, Italian lira, Japanese yen, UK pound

Regions: United States

DERIVATIVES ACTIVITIES:

Exchange-traded Options & Futures	**Bond**	
U.S. Treasury futures		
OTC Derivatives	**Currency, Interest rate**	
Plain Vanilla Derivatives	Swaps	Forwards
Structured Notes	Floaters	Inverse floaters
Counterparty Rating Requirement:	A	

OTHER ALTERNATIVE INVESTMENTS:

	CMOs/REMICs – Govt.	Repos/reverse repos

KEY MANAGERS & DERIVATIVES SPECIALISTS:	**Direct Phone/Fax**	**Job Function**
Mr. Eric Clothier		Chief Investment Officer
Ms. Patricia C. Dunn President & C.E.O.	415/597-2002 415/597-2010	President
Mr. Blake Grossman Sr. Vice President & Manager	415/597-2138	Chief Investment Officer
Mr. David Lahorgue C.I.O.-Investment Strategy	415/597-2106	Chief Investment Officer Portfolio Mgr – Derivatives
Mr. Lawrence Tint		Chief Investment Officer

Calamos Asset Management, Inc.

Investment Manager

Location: 1111 East Warrenville Road
Naperville, IL 60563-1493

Fax: 708/245-7531 **Phone:** 708/245-7200

Profile: Total return investor

Investment Portfolio: $ 1.2 billion

Use: **Investment Purposes**
Hedge currency risk
Hedge equity portfolio risk

Currencies: US dollar, ECU, German mark, UK pound

Regions: United States

DERIVATIVES ACTIVITIES: **CAC Class: 2**

Exchange-traded Options & Futures	**Currency**	
OTC Derivatives	**Currency**	
Plain Vanilla Derivatives	Swaps	Forwards

OTHER ALTERNATIVE INVESTMENTS:

CMOs/REMICs – Govt. CMOs/REMICs – Private

KEY MANAGERS & DERIVATIVES SPECIALISTS:	**Direct Phone/Fax**	**Job Function**
Mr. John P. Calamos President		President Chief Investment Officer Portfolio Mgr – Derivatives Portfolio Mgr – Futures *Corp* Portfolio Mgr – Options
Mr. Nicholas P. Calamos Senior Vice President		Portfolio Mgr – Derivatives Portfolio Mgr – Futures Portfolio Mgr – Options
Ms. Denise LeMay		Trader – Derivatives Trader – Futures Trader – Options

California Federal Bank, A Federal Savings Bank

Savings Bank/Bldg Society

Sub of Cal Fed Bancorp Inc.

Location: 5700 Wilshire Boulevard
Suite 327A
Los Angeles, CA 90036

Fax: 213/930-6272 **Phone:** 213/932-4321

Profile: Hold to maturity investor

Investment Portfolio: $ 1.0 - 3.0 billion

Use: **Balance Sheet/Risk Management**
Hedge balance sheet
Hedge interest rate risk
Incremental return

Investment Purposes
Capture extra yield
Hedge interest rate risk
Provide incremental return

Currencies: US dollar

Regions: United States

California Federal Bank, A Federal Savings Bank – continued

DERIVATIVES ACTIVITIES:		CAC Class: 5
Exchange-traded Options & Futures	**Bond, Interest rate**	
U.S. Treasury futures	Municipal futures	
U.S. Treasury options	Municipal options	
OTC Derivatives	**Bond, Interest rate**	
Plain Vanilla Derivatives	Swaps	Caps
	Forwards	Floors
	Swaptions	
Exotic Derivatives	Index extendible swaps	
Structured Notes	Corporate MTNs	Periodic capped floaters
	Floaters	
Counterparty Rating Requirement:	None	

OTHER ALTERNATIVE INVESTMENTS:

	CMOs/REMICs – Govt.	Repos/reverse repos
	CMOs/REMICs – Private	

KEY MANAGERS & DERIVATIVES SPECIALISTS:	Direct Phone/Fax	Job Function
Mr. Gary W. Brummett E.V.P., Controller & Co-C.F.O		Chief Financial Officer Portfolio Mgr – Derivatives
Mr. Dale E. Cohen E.V.P., Treasurer & Co-C.F.O.		Chief Financial Officer Treasurer Portfolio Mgr – Derivatives
Mr. Edward G. Harshfield President & C.E.O.		President
Mr. Bruce Hitchman Vice President	213/932-2070	Chief Investment Officer Portfolio Mgr – Derivatives Portfolio Mgr – Structured Notes

California Public Employees' Retirement System

Government Pension Fund

Location: 400 P Street
Suite 3492
Sacramento, CA 95814

Fax: 916/326-3363 **Phone:** 916/326-3400

Profile: Total return investor

Investment Portfolio: $ 77.0 billion

Use: **Investment Purposes**
Adjust portfolio duration
Hedge interest rate risk

Currencies: US dollar, Australian dollar, French franc, German mark, Japanese yen, Swiss franc, UK pound

Regions: United States

California Public Employees' Retirement System – continued

DERIVATIVES ACTIVITIES: **CAC Class: 6**

Exchange-traded Options & Futures	**Currency, Interest rate**	
OTC Derivatives **Plain Vanilla Derivatives**	Swaps	
Structured Notes	Corporate MTNs Govt. agency MTNs	Floaters
Counterparty Rating Requirement:	AAA	

OTHER ALTERNATIVE INVESTMENTS:

CMOs/REMICs – Govt. CMOs/REMICs – Private	Strips

KEY MANAGERS & DERIVATIVES SPECIALISTS:	Direct Phone/Fax	Job Function
Mr. Curtis D. Ishii Principal Investment Officer	916/326-3425	Portfolio Mgr – Derivatives Portfolio Mgr – Structured Notes
Ms. Sheryl Pressler Chief Investment Officer		Chief Investment Officer
Mr. Kevin Winter Investment Officer	916/326-3394	Portfolio Mgr – Structured Notes Trader – Derivatives

California State Teachers' Retirement System

Government Pension Fund

Location: 7667 Folsom Boulevard
Suite 250
Sacramento, CA 95826

Fax: 916/387-9585 **Phone:** 916/229-3870

Profile: Total return investor

Investment Portfolio: $ 55.0 billion

Use: **Balance Sheet/Risk Management**
Hedge currency risk
Hedge overseas investments
Protect currency gains

Currencies: US dollar, French franc, Japanese yen, Swiss franc

Regions: United States

DERIVATIVES ACTIVITIES: **CAC Class: 4**

Exchange-traded Options & Futures	**Currency**

OTHER ALTERNATIVE INVESTMENTS:

CMOs/REMICs – Govt. CMOs/REMICs – Private	Repos/reverse repos

KEY MANAGERS & DERIVATIVES SPECIALISTS:	Direct Phone/Fax	Job Function
Ms. Michelle Cunningham Investment Officer	916/229-3743	Trader – Derivatives

California State Teachers' Retirement System – continued

KEY MANAGERS & DERIVATIVES SPECIALISTS:	Direct Phone/Fax	Job Function
Mr. Thomas E. Flanigan	916/229-3736	Chief Investment Officer Portfolio Mgr – Derivatives Portfolio Mgr – Structured Notes
Mr. Patrick Mitchell Chief-Fixed Income & Equities	916/229-3723	Portfolio Mgr – Futures

Calvert Asset Management Company, Inc.

Mutual Fund Manager

Sub of The Acacia Group

Location: 4550 Montgomery Avenue
Suite 1000-N
Bethesda, MD 20814

Fax: 301/657-1982 **Phone:** 301/951-4800

Profile: Total return investor

Investment Portfolio: $ 5.1 billion

Use: **Balance Sheet/Risk Management**
Hedge interest rate risk
Meet interest rate target

Investment Purposes
Provide incremental return

Currencies: US dollar

Regions: United States

DERIVATIVES ACTIVITIES:

Exchange-traded Options & Futures
U.S. Treasury futures
U.S. Treasury options
Municipal futures
Municipal options

Structured Notes
Govt. agency MTNs
Inverse floaters

OTHER ALTERNATIVE INVESTMENTS:

CMOs/REMICs – Govt.
CMOs/REMICs – Private
Repos/reverse repos

KEY MANAGERS & DERIVATIVES SPECIALISTS:	Direct Phone/Fax	Job Function
Mr. Daniel K. Hayes Vice President – Research		Portfolio Mgr – Futures Portfolio Mgr – Options Portfolio Mgr – Structured Notes
Mr. Reno Martini Chief Investment Officer		Chief Investment Officer Bond Department Head
Mr. Stephen N. VanOrder Asst. Mgr-Portfolio Investment		Portfolio Mgr – Derivatives *Muni*

Campbell Soup Company

Corporation

Location: Campbell Place
Camden, NJ 08103-1799

Fax: 609/342-3878 **Phone:** 609/342-4800

Use: **Balance Sheet/Risk Management**
Create synthetic fixed/floating rate
Hedge commercial paper
Hedge currency risk
Hedge interest rate risk

Currencies: US dollar, Canadian dollar, Australian dollar

Regions: United States, Canada

DERIVATIVES ACTIVITIES:

Exchange-traded Options & Futures	**Currency, Interest rate**	
OTC Derivatives		
Plain Vanilla Derivatives	Swaps	Forwards
Structured Notes	Corporate MTNs	
Counterparty Rating Requirement:	None	

KEY MANAGERS & DERIVATIVES SPECIALISTS:	**Direct Phone/Fax**	**Job Function**
Ms. Brenda E. Edgerton Vice President & Treasurer		Treasurer Portfolio Mgr – Derivatives
Mr. David W. Johnson Chairman, President & C.E.O.	609/342-5252	President
Mr. Frank E. Weise III Senior Vice President & C.F.O.		Chief Financial Officer

Capital Guardian Trust Company

Investment Manager

Sub of The Capital Group, Inc.

Location: 11100 Santa Monica Boulevard
Los Angeles, CA 90025-3302

Fax: 310/996-6200 **Phone:** 310/996-6000

Profile: Total return investor

Investment Portfolio: $ 39.4 billion

Use: **Investment Purposes**
Capture extra yield
Diversify portfolio
Hedge currency risk
Provide incremental return

Currencies: US dollar, Canadian dollar, French franc, German mark, Italian lira, Japanese yen, Mexican peso, Spanish peseta, UK pound

Regions: Canada, Europe, Latin America, Pacific Rim

Capital Guardian Trust Company – continued

DERIVATIVES ACTIVITIES:		CAC Class: 4
Exchange-traded Options & Futures	**Bond**	
OTC Derivatives **Plain Vanilla Derivatives**	Forwards	
Structured Notes	Corporate MTNs Govt. agency MTNs	Inverse floaters
Counterparty Rating Requirement:	A	

OTHER ALTERNATIVE INVESTMENTS:		
	CMOs/REMICs – Govt. CMOs/REMICs – Private	Strips

KEY MANAGERS & DERIVATIVES SPECIALISTS:	Direct Phone/Fax	Job Function
Mr. James R. Mulally Senior Vice President	310/996-6109	Portfolio Mgr – Derivatives Portfolio Mgr – Futures Portfolio Mgr – Structured Notes
Mr. Glen Payne	310/996-6113	Trader – Derivatives Trader – Futures Trader – Structured Investments

Capital One Financial Corporation

Bank Holding Company

Location: 2980 Fairview Park Drive
Suite 1300
Falls Church, VA 22042

Fax: 703/205-1755 **Phone:** 703/205-1000

Use: **Balance Sheet/Risk Management**
Create synthetic fixed/floating rate
Hedge interest rate risk
Incremental return
Meet interest rate target
Strategic liability management

Currencies: US dollar **Regions:** United States

DERIVATIVES ACTIVITIES:		CAC Class: 5
OTC Derivatives **Plain Vanilla Derivatives**	**Interest rate** Swaps	

KEY MANAGERS & DERIVATIVES SPECIALISTS:	Direct Phone/Fax	Job Function
Mr. Nigel W. Morris President & C.O.O.		President
Mr. David M. Willey Sr. Vice President & Treasurer		Treasurer Portfolio Mgr – Derivatives
Mr. James M. Zinn Sr. Vice President & C.F.O.		Chief Financial Officer

Capital Research & Management Company

Mutual Fund Manager

Sub of The Capital Group, Inc.

Location: 11100 Santa Monica Boulevard
15th Floor
Los Angeles, CA 90025-3302

Fax: 310/996-6200 **Phone:** 310/996-6000

Profile: Total return investor

Investment Portfolio: $ 132.0 billion

Use: **Investment Purposes**

Currencies: US dollar, Canadian dollar, French franc, German mark, Italian lira, Japanese yen, Mexican peso, Spanish peseta, UK pound

Regions: United States

DERIVATIVES ACTIVITIES: **CAC Class: Inactive**

OTHER ALTERNATIVE INVESTMENTS:

CMOs/REMICs – Govt.
CMOs/REMICs – Private
Strips
Repos/reverse repos

KEY MANAGERS & DERIVATIVES SPECIALISTS:	**Direct Phone/Fax**	**Job Function**
Mr. Abner D. Goldstine Senior Vice President	310/996-6118	Chief Investment Officer

Capital Research & Management Company (New York)

Mutual Fund Manager

Sub of The Capital Group, Inc.

Location: 630 Fifth Avenue
36th Floor
New York, NY 10111

Fax: 212/582-7878 **Phone:** 212/581-5000

Profile: Total return investor

Investment Portfolio: $ 132.0 billion

Use: **Investment Purposes**
Hedge currency risk

Currencies: US dollar, UK pound

Regions: United States

DERIVATIVES ACTIVITIES:

Exchange-traded Options & Futures **Currency**

OTHER ALTERNATIVE INVESTMENTS:

CMOs/REMICs – Govt.
CMOs/REMICs – Private

KEY MANAGERS & DERIVATIVES SPECIALISTS:	**Direct Phone/Fax**	**Job Function**
Mr. Stephen Bepler Senior Vice President		Portfolio Mgr – Futures
Mr. John W. Ressner Vice President	212/649-1577 212/649-1533	Bond Department Head

Capitol Federal Savings & Loan Association

Savings Bank/Bldg Society

Location: 700 South Kansas Avenue
Topeka, KS 66603-3894

Fax: 913/231-6361 **Phone:** 913/235-1341

Profile: Hold to maturity investor

Investment Portfolio: $ 4.3 billion

Use: **Investment Purposes**
Adjust portfolio duration
Asset allocation
Beat conventional rates
Capture extra yield
Convexity objectives
Discretionary situations
Diversify portfolio
Provide incremental return

Currencies: US dollar

Regions: United States

DERIVATIVES ACTIVITIES: **CAC Class: 3**

Structured Notes
Corporate MTNs
Govt. agency MTNs
Bond index notes
Index amortizing notes
CMT notes
Multi-step-up callable bonds

OTHER ALTERNATIVE INVESTMENTS:

CMOs/REMICs – Govt.
Repos/reverse repos

KEY MANAGERS & DERIVATIVES SPECIALISTS:	Direct Phone/Fax	Job Function
Mr. Neil F. McKay Executive Vice President		Chief Investment Officer Chief Financial Officer Portfolio Mgr – Structured Notes

Capitoline Investment Services, Inc. (Richmond)

Bank/Management Division

Sub of Crestar Financial Corporation

Location: 919 East Main Street
Richmond, VA 23219

Fax: 804/782-5839 **Phone:** 804/782-7242

Profile: Total return investor

Investment Portfolio: $ 7.9 billion

Use: **Investment Purposes**

Currencies: US dollar

Regions: United States

DERIVATIVES ACTIVITIES: **CAC Class: 2**

Structured Notes
Floaters

OTHER ALTERNATIVE INVESTMENTS:

CMOs/REMICs – Govt.
Repos/reverse repos

KEY MANAGERS & DERIVATIVES SPECIALISTS:	Direct Phone/Fax	Job Function
Mr. Boyce G. Reid Director	804/782-7921	Portfolio Mgr – Structured Notes *MBS*

Capitoline Investment Services, Inc. (Washington, DC)

Bank/Management Division

Sub of Crestar Financial Corporation

Location: 1445 New York Avenue N.W.
Washington, DC 20005

Fax: 202/879-6333 **Phone:** 202/879-6277

Profile: Total return investor

Investment Portfolio: $ 1.0 billion

Use: **Investment Purposes**
Capture extra yield

Currencies: US dollar

Regions: United States

DERIVATIVES ACTIVITIES: **CAC Class: 2**

Structured Notes Floaters

OTHER ALTERNATIVE INVESTMENTS:

CMOs/REMICs – Govt.

KEY MANAGERS & DERIVATIVES SPECIALISTS:	**Direct Phone/Fax**	**Job Function**
Mr. Alan Gayle Sr. Vice President & Director	202/879-6075 202/879-6073	Portfolio Mgr – Structured Notes
Mr. James M. MacIver Vice President	202/879-6284	Chief Investment Officer

Cardinal Management Corporation

Mutual Fund Manager

Sub of The Ohio Company

Location: 155 East Broad Street
11th Floor
Columbus, OH 43215

Fax: 614/464-8713 **Phone:** 614/464-6811

Profile: Total return investor

Investment Portfolio: $ 1.6 billion

Use: **Investment Purposes**
Hedge bond portfolio risk
Hedge interest rate risk

Currencies: US dollar

Regions: United States

DERIVATIVES ACTIVITIES:

Exchange-traded Options & Futures
U.S. Treasury futures

Bond, Interest rate
U.S. Treasury options

OTHER ALTERNATIVE INVESTMENTS:

CMOs/REMICs – Govt.
CMOs/REMICs – Private
Repos/reverse repos

Cardinal Management Corporation – continued

KEY MANAGERS & DERIVATIVES SPECIALISTS:	Direct Phone/Fax	Job Function
Mr. John R. Carle Vice President	614/464-8797	Portfolio Mgr – Futures *Govt* Portfolio Mgr – Options *Govt* Trader – Futures *Govt* Trader – Options *Govt*
Mr. Frank Siegel President	614/464-8652	President

Caremark International Inc.

Corporation

Location: 2215 Sanders Road
Northbrook, IL 60062

Fax: 708/559-4648 **Phone:** 708/559-4700

Use: **Balance Sheet/Risk Management**
Hedge currency risk
Protect currency gains

Currencies: US dollar, German mark, Japanese yen

Regions: United States

DERIVATIVES ACTIVITIES: **CAC Class: 1**

OTC Derivatives	Currency
Plain Vanilla Derivatives	Forwards
Counterparty Rating Requirement:	AA

KEY MANAGERS & DERIVATIVES SPECIALISTS:	Direct Phone/Fax	Job Function
Mr. James G. Connelly III President & C.O.O.		President
Mr. Thomas W. Hodson Sr. Vice President & C.F.O.		Chief Financial Officer
Mr. Dennis Owczarski Treasurer		Treasurer Portfolio Mgr – Derivatives

Carillon Advisers, Inc.

Insurance Co/Management

Sub of The Union Central Life Insurance Company

Location: 1876 Waycross Road
Cincinnati, OH 45240

Fax: 513/595-2843 **Phone:** 513/595-2900

Profile: Total return investor

Investment Portfolio: $ 4.9 billion

Use: **Balance Sheet/Risk Management**
Hedge balance sheet
Strategic liability management

Investment Purposes
Asset allocation
Hedge equity portfolio risk
Hedge interest rate risk
Provide incremental return

Currencies: US dollar

Regions: United States

Carillon Advisers, Inc. – continued

DERIVATIVES ACTIVITIES:

Exchange-traded Options & Futures		
OTC Derivatives	**Interest rate**	
Plain Vanilla Derivatives	Swaps Forwards	Collars
Structured Notes	Govt. agency MTNs Bond index notes CMT notes	Floaters Inverse floaters Multi-step-up callable bonds
Counterparty Rating Requirement:	AAA	

OTHER ALTERNATIVE INVESTMENTS:

CMOs/REMICs – Govt.	Strips
CMOs/REMICs – Private	Repos/reverse repos

KEY MANAGERS & DERIVATIVES SPECIALISTS:	Direct Phone/Fax	Job Function
Mr. George L. Clucas President & C.E.O.	513/595-2476	President Chief Investment Officer
Mr. Steven R. Sutermeister Vice President	513/595-2745	Bond Department Head *Taxable* Portfolio Mgr – Derivatives

Cashman, Farrell and Associates

Investment Manager

Location: 1235 Westlakes Drive
Suite 370
Berwyn, PA 19312

Fax: 610/889-1665 **Phone:** 610/889-1500

Profile: Total return investor

Investment Portfolio: $ 3.0 billion

Use: **Investment Purposes**

Currencies: US dollar

Regions: United States

DERIVATIVES ACTIVITIES: **CAC Class: Inactive**

OTHER ALTERNATIVE INVESTMENTS:

CMOs/REMICs – Govt.	CMOs/REMICs – Private

KEY MANAGERS & DERIVATIVES SPECIALISTS:	Direct Phone/Fax	Job Function
Mr. Anthony J. Basile Partner & Director		Bond Department Head
Mr. Daniel V. Cashman Senior Partner		Chief Investment Officer
Mr. James H. Farrell, Jr. Senior Partner		Chief Investment Officer
Mr. Richard Zackroff Fixed-Income Co-Dept. Head		Bond Department Head

CDC Investment Management Corp. (CIMCO)

Investment Manager

Sub of Caisse des Dépôts et Consignations (DADF)

Location: Nine West 57th Street
36th Floor
New York, NY 10019

Fax: 212/891-6294 **Phone:** 212/891-6100

Profile: Total return investor

Investment Portfolio: $ 4.0 - 10.0 billion

Use: **Balance Sheet/Risk Management**
Hedge balance sheet
Hedge commercial paper
Hedge currency risk
Hedge interest rate risk
Hedge overseas investments

Currencies: US dollar, Australian dollar, Belgian franc, Canadian dollar, French franc, German mark, Italian lira, Japanese yen, Spanish peseta, Swiss franc, UK pound

Regions: United States

DERIVATIVES ACTIVITIES: **CAC Class: 2**

Exchange-traded Options & Futures	**Bond, Currency, Interest rate**	
U.S. Treasury futures	U.S. Treasury options	
OTC Derivatives	**Bond, Currency, Interest rate**	
Plain Vanilla Derivatives	Swaps	Caps
	Forwards	Floors
	Swaptions	Collars
Structured Notes	Corporate MTNs	Floaters
	Index amortizing notes	Inverse floaters
	CMT notes	Periodic capped floaters
Counterparty Rating Requirement:	AA	

OTHER ALTERNATIVE INVESTMENTS:

CMOs/REMICs – Govt.	Strips
CMOs/REMICs – Private	Repos/reverse repos

KEY MANAGERS & DERIVATIVES SPECIALISTS:	**Direct Phone/Fax**	**Job Function**
Mr. Nicholas Demonico	212/891-6136 212/891-6116	Bond Department Head *ABS, Corp, MBS*
Mr. Ramine Rouhani	212/891-6170	Portfolio Mgr – Derivatives Portfolio Mgr – Futures Portfolio Mgr – Options Portfolio Mgr – Structured Notes
Mr. Charles Schoenig Vice President	212/891-6169	Portfolio Mgr – Derivatives Portfolio Mgr – Futures Portfolio Mgr – Options Portfolio Mgr – Structured Notes Trader – Derivatives Trader – Futures Trader – Structured Investments
Mr. Mark Turner Managing Director		Portfolio Mgr – Derivatives

Central Carolina Bank & Trust Co. (Portfolio)

Bank/Portfolio

Sub of CCB Financial Corporation

Location: 111 Corcoran Street
Durham, NC 27701-3231

Fax: 919/682-3870 **Phone:** 919/683-7777

Profile: Current yield investor

Investment Portfolio: $ 621.0 million

Use:

Balance Sheet/Risk Management
Create synthetic fixed/floating rate
Hedge balance sheet
Hedge interest rate risk
Strategic liability management

Investment Purposes
Alter portfolio weighting
Adjust portfolio duration
Capture extra yield
Hedge bond portfolio risk
Hedge interest rate risk
Immunize from volatility
Reduce variability of returns

Currencies: US dollar

Regions: United States Europe

DERIVATIVES ACTIVITIES: **CAC Class: 5**

Exchange-traded Options & Futures	**Bond, Interest rate**	
U.S. Treasury futures	U.S. Treasury options	
OTC Derivatives	**Bond, Interest rate**	
Plain Vanilla Derivatives	Swaps Forwards Caps	Floors Collars
Exotic Derivatives	Bond index swaps CMT swaps	CMT options Periodic caps/floors
Structured Notes	Bond index notes Floaters	Multi-step-up callable bonds
Counterparty Rating Requirement:	AAA	

OTHER ALTERNATIVE INVESTMENTS:

	CMOs/REMICs – Govt.	Repos/reverse repos

KEY MANAGERS & DERIVATIVES SPECIALISTS:	**Direct Phone/Fax**	**Job Function**
Mr. W. Harold Parker, Jr. S.V.P. & Controller		Chief Financial Officer Portfolio Mgr – Derivatives Portfolio Mgr – Structured Notes
Mr. Ernest C. Roessler President & C.E.O.		President
Mr. David P. Shaw	919/683-7608 919/682-1191	Chief Investment Officer Portfolio Mgr – Derivatives Portfolio Mgr – Structured Notes

Central Fidelity National Bank (Richmond) (Portfolio)

Bank/Portfolio

Sub of Central Fidelity Banks, Inc.

Location: 1021 East Cary Street
3rd Floor
Richmond, VA 23219

Fax: 804/783-8335 **Phone:** 804/782-4000

Profile: Total return investor

Investment Portfolio: $ 5.1 billion

Use:

Balance Sheet/Risk Management
Create synthetic fixed/floating rate
Hedge interest rate risk
Strategic liability management

Investment Purposes
Adjust portfolio duration
Capture extra yield
Hedge interest rate risk

Currencies: US dollar

Regions: United States

DERIVATIVES ACTIVITIES: **CAC Class: 5**

OTC Derivatives	**Interest rate**
Plain Vanilla Derivatives	Swaps
Exotic Derivatives	Index amortizing swaps
Counterparty Rating Requirement:	A

OTHER ALTERNATIVE INVESTMENTS:

CMOs/REMICs – Govt.
CMOs/REMICs – Private
Repos/reverse repos

KEY MANAGERS & DERIVATIVES SPECIALISTS:	**Direct Phone/Fax**	**Job Function**
Mr. Joseph A. Jennings III	804/697-6921	Portfolio Mgr – Derivatives
Mr. John T. Percy, Jr. Corporate Exec. Vice President	804/697-6766	Chief Investment Officer Portfolio Mgr – Derivatives

The Central Trust Bank

Bank/Management Division

Location: 238 Madison Street
Jefferson City, MO 65101-3249

Fax: 314/634-7813 **Phone:** 314/634-1234

Profile: Total return investor

Investment Portfolio: $ 1.0 - 3.0 billion

Use: **Investment Purposes**

Currencies: US dollar

Regions: United States

DERIVATIVES ACTIVITIES: **CAC Class: Inactive**

OTHER ALTERNATIVE INVESTMENTS:

Repos/reverse repos

KEY MANAGERS & DERIVATIVES SPECIALISTS:	**Direct Phone/Fax**	**Job Function**
Mr. Donald Perdue		Chief Investment Officer

Century Investment Management Co. (CIMCO)

Insurance Co/P & C

Location: 5910 Mineral Point Road, Madison, WI 53705

Fax: 608/238-2316 **Phone:** 608/232-6111

Profile: Spread investor

Investment Portfolio: $ 5.3 billion

Use:

Balance Sheet/Risk Management
Hedge balance sheet
Hedge interest rate risk

Investment Purposes
Asset allocation
Hedge interest rate risk

Currencies: US dollar

Regions: United States

DERIVATIVES ACTIVITIES: **CAC Class: 3**

OTC Derivatives	**Bond**
Exotic Derivatives	CMT swaps
Counterparty Rating Requirement:	AA

OTHER ALTERNATIVE INVESTMENTS:

CMOs/REMICs – Govt. CMOs/REMICs – Private

KEY MANAGERS & DERIVATIVES SPECIALISTS:	**Direct Phone/Fax**	**Job Function**
Mr. Michael S. Daubs	608/231-7500	Chief Investment Officer
Mr. Joseph L. Gogola Senior Investment Officer	608/231-7104	Portfolio Mgr – Derivatives
Mr. Thomas Merfeld Director – Asset Liability	608/231-8597	Portfolio Mgr – Derivatives

Charter One Bank, F.S.B.

Savings Bank/Bldg Society

Sub of Charter One Financial Inc.

Location: 1215 Superior Avenue, Cleveland, OH 44114

Fax: 216/566-5308 **Phone:** 216/566-5300

Profile: Hold to maturity investor

Investment Portfolio: $ 1.0 - 3.0 billion

Use:

Balance Sheet/Risk Management
Hedge interest rate risk
Strategic liability management

Investment Purposes
Hedge bond portfolio risk
Hedge equity portfolio risk

Currencies: US dollar

Regions: United States

DERIVATIVES ACTIVITIES:

OTC Derivatives	**Interest rate**
Plain Vanilla Derivatives	Swaps

Charter One Bank, F.S.B. – continued

OTHER ALTERNATIVE INVESTMENTS:

	CMOs/REMICs – Govt. CMOs/REMICs – Private	Repos/reverse repos

KEY MANAGERS & DERIVATIVES SPECIALISTS:	**Direct Phone/Fax**	**Job Function**
Ms. Darlene A. Fernald Vice President		Portfolio Mgr – Derivatives
Mr. Michael Grudzien Vice President		Bond Department Head
Mr. Richard W. Neu Exec. Vice President & C.F.O.	216/566-5337	Chief Financial Officer Treasurer

Charter One Bank, F.S.B. (Michigan)

Savings Bank/Bldg Society

Sub of Charter One Financial Inc.

Location: 1001 Woodward Avenue
Detroit, MI 48226-1967

Fax: 313/965-5936 **Phone:** 313/965-1400

Profile: Current yield investor

Investment Portfolio: $ 5.0 billion

Use: **Balance Sheet/Risk Management**
Hedge interest rate risk

Currencies: US dollar

Regions: United States

DERIVATIVES ACTIVITIES: **CAC Class: 6**

OTC Derivatives **Plain Vanilla Derivatives**	**Interest rate** Swaps	 Caps
Counterparty Rating Requirement:	AAA	

OTHER ALTERNATIVE INVESTMENTS:

	CMOs/REMICs – Govt.	Repos/reverse repos

KEY MANAGERS & DERIVATIVES SPECIALISTS:	**Direct Phone/Fax**	**Job Function**
Mr. Bernard Pawloski Vice President	313/965-5902	Portfolio Mgr – Derivatives

Chase Manhattan Private Bank Investment Management

Bank/Management Division

Sub of The Chase Manhattan Corporation

Location: 1211 Avenue of the Americas
32nd Floor
New York, NY 10036

Fax: 212/398-1872 **Phone:** 212/789-4000

Profile: Total return investor

Investment Portfolio: $ 66.7 billion

Use: **Investment Purposes**
Alter portfolio weighting
Adjust portfolio duration
Asset allocation
Capture extra yield
Enter new mkts/lower risk
Expand international investments
Hedge bond portfolio risk
Hedge currency risk
Hedge interest rate risk
Protect currency gains
Provide incremental return
Reduce variability of returns

Currencies: US dollar, Canadian dollar, French franc, German mark, Italian lira, Japanese yen, UK pound

Regions: United States

DERIVATIVES ACTIVITIES: **CAC Class: 3**

Exchange-traded Options & Futures	**Bond**	
U.S. Treasury futures	U.S. Treasury options	
OTC Derivatives	**Bond**	
Plain Vanilla Derivatives	Swaps	Forwards
Structured Notes	Corporate MTNs	CMT notes
	Govt. agency MTNs	Floaters
	Bond index notes	Inverse floaters
Counterparty Rating Requirement:	A	

OTHER ALTERNATIVE INVESTMENTS:

	CMOs/REMICs – Govt.	Strips
	CMOs/REMICs – Private	Repos/reverse repos

KEY MANAGERS & DERIVATIVES SPECIALISTS:	**Direct Phone/Fax**	**Job Function**
Ms. Susan Huang Vice President	212/789-5846	Bond Department Head Fixed-Income Strategist
Mr. Mark R. Richardson Senior Vice President	212/789-5193	Chief Investment Officer
Mr. Bruce A. Whiteford Vice President	212/789-5569 212/789-5589	Fixed-Income Strategist Research Analyst – Derivatives

Chemical Bank (Portfolio)

Bank/Portfolio

Sub of Chemical Banking Corporation

Location: 270 Park Avenue
New York, NY 10172

Fax: 212/834-6550 **Phone:** 212/834-5000

Profile: Directional investor

Investment Portfolio: $ 53.0 billion

Use:

Balance Sheet/Risk Management
Hedge commercial paper
Hedge currency risk
Hedge interest rate risk
Hedge overseas investments
Protect currency gains

Investment Purposes
Hedge equity portfolio risk
Hedge interest rate risk

Currencies: US dollar, Australian dollar, Belgian franc, Canadian dollar, French franc, Indonesian rupiah, Japanese yen, Spanish peseta, UK pound

Regions: United States, Canada, Europe, Pacific Rim

DERIVATIVES ACTIVITIES:

Exchange-traded Options & Futures	**Bond, Interest rate**	
U.S. Treasury futures	U.S. Treasury options	
OTC Derivatives	**Bond, Interest rate**	
Plain Vanilla Derivatives	Swaps	Caps
	Forwards	Floors
	Swaptions	Collars
Structured Notes		
Counterparty Rating Requirement:	AA	

OTHER ALTERNATIVE INVESTMENTS:

CMOs/REMICs – Govt.
Strips

KEY MANAGERS & DERIVATIVES SPECIALISTS:	**Direct Phone/Fax**	**Job Function**
Ms. Ina Drew Senior Managing Director		Chief Investment Officer Portfolio Mgr – Derivatives Portfolio Mgr – Futures

Chevy Chase Federal Savings Bank

Savings Bank/Bldg Society

Sub of B.F. Saul Real Estate Investment Trust

Location: 8401 Connecticut Avenue
Chevy Chase, MD 20815-5803

Fax: 301/986-7002 **Phone:** 301/986-7000

Profile: Total return investor

Investment Portfolio: $ 2.0 billion

Use: **Investment Purposes**

Currencies: US dollar

Regions: United States

DERIVATIVES ACTIVITIES: **CAC Class: Inactive**

OTHER ALTERNATIVE INVESTMENTS:

CMOs/REMICs – Govt.
CMOs/REMICs – Private

Chevy Chase Federal Savings Bank – continued

KEY MANAGERS & DERIVATIVES SPECIALISTS:	**Direct Phone/Fax**	**Job Function**
Mr. Mark A. Holles Vice President	301/986-7222	Chief Investment Officer

The Chicago Corporation – Asset Management Group

Broker/Management Sub

Location: 208 South LaSalle Street, 4th Floor, Chicago, IL 60604

Fax: 312/855-4066 **Phone:** 312/855-7600

Profile: Total return investor

Investment Portfolio: $ 2.5 billion

Use: **Investment Purposes**

Currencies: US dollar

Regions: United States

DERIVATIVES ACTIVITIES: **CAC Class: Inactive**

OTHER ALTERNATIVE INVESTMENTS:

CMOs/REMICs – Govt.

KEY MANAGERS & DERIVATIVES SPECIALISTS:	**Direct Phone/Fax**	**Job Function**
Mr. Robert T. Brehm President	312/855-7703	President
Mr. Jonathan T. Ender Senior Vice President	312/855-7738	Chief Investment Officer

The Chubb Corporation

Insurance Co/P & C

Sub of The Chubb Group of Insurance Companies

Location: 15 Mountain View Road, Warren, NJ 07059

Fax: 908/580-3775 **Phone:** 908/903-2000

Profile: Total return investor

Investment Portfolio: $ 4.0 - 10.0 billion

Use: **Investment Purposes**
- Adjust portfolio duration
- Hedge bond portfolio risk
- Hedge currency risk
- Hedge interest rate risk
- Protect currency gains

Currencies: US dollar, Belgian franc, Canadian dollar, French franc, German mark, Italian lira, Japanese yen, Swiss franc, UK pound

Regions: United States, Canada, Europe, Latin America, Pacific Rim

The Chubb Corporation – continued

DERIVATIVES ACTIVITIES:		CAC Class: 3
Exchange-traded Options & Futures U.S. Treasury futures	**Bond, Interest rate**	
OTC Derivatives **Plain Vanilla Derivatives**	**Interest rate** Swaps	
Structured Notes		
Counterparty Rating Requirement:	AA	

OTHER ALTERNATIVE INVESTMENTS:

	CMOs/REMICs – Govt.	Strips
	CMOs/REMICs – Private	Repos/reverse repos

KEY MANAGERS & DERIVATIVES SPECIALISTS:	Direct Phone/Fax	Job Function
Mr. Frederick W. Gaertner Vice President	908/580-3752	Bond Department Head
Mr. Michael O'Reilly Chief Investment Officer	908/903-3764	Chief Investment Officer Portfolio Mgr – Derivatives Portfolio Mgr – Futures Portfolio Mgr – Structured Notes

CIGNA Investment Management (U.S.A.)

Investment Manager

Sub of CIGNA Corporation

Location: 900 Cottage Grove Road
Hartford, CT 06152-2116

Fax: 203/726-8530 **Phone:** 203/726-6000

Profile: Total return investor

Investment Portfolio: $ 5.8 billion

Use: **Investment Purposes**
Hedge bond portfolio risk
Hedge currency risk
Hedge equity portfolio risk
Hedge interest rate risk

Currencies: US dollar, Australian dollar, Belgian franc, Canadian dollar, ECU, French franc, German mark, Italian lira, Indonesian rupiah, Japanese yen, Mexican peso, Spanish peseta, Swiss franc, Thai baht, UK pound

Regions: United States, Canada, Pacific Rim

CIGNA Investment Management (U.S.A.) – continued

DERIVATIVES ACTIVITIES:		**CAC Class: 3**
Exchange-traded Options & Futures	**Bond, Currency, Interest rate**	
U.S. Treasury futures	U.S. Treasury options	
OTC Derivatives	**Bond, Currency, Interest rate**	
Plain Vanilla Derivatives	Swaps	Caps
	Forwards	Floors
	Swaptions	Collars
Structured Notes	Index amortizing notes	Multi-step-up callable bonds
	Floaters	
Counterparty Rating Requirement:	AAA	

OTHER ALTERNATIVE INVESTMENTS:

	CMOs/REMICs – Govt.	Repos/reverse repos
	Strips	

KEY MANAGERS & DERIVATIVES SPECIALISTS:	Direct Phone/Fax	Job Function
Mr. Richard H. Forde President	203/726-6686	President Chief Investment Officer
Mr. Joseph Mazon	203/726-7423	Trader – Derivatives
Mr. Suresh Raghavan Vice President	203/726-5757	Portfolio Mgr – Derivatives

CIGNA Investments, Inc.

Insurance Co/P & C

Sub of CIGNA Corporation

Location: 900 Cottage Grove Road
Hartford, CT 06152-2116

Fax: 203/726-8137 **Phone:** 203/726-6000

Profile: Hold to maturity investor

Investment Portfolio: $ 59.0 billion

Use:

Balance Sheet/Risk Management
Hedge currency risk
Hedge interest rate risk

Investment Purposes
Alter portfolio weighting
Diversify portfolio
Hedge bond portfolio risk
Hedge currency risk
Hedge interest rate risk

Currencies: US dollar, UK pound

Regions: United States, Europe

CIGNA Investments, Inc. – continued

DERIVATIVES ACTIVITIES: **CAC Class: 5**

Exchange-traded Options & Futures	**Bond, Currency, Interest rate**	
U.S. Treasury futures	Municipal futures	
OTC Derivatives	**Bond, Currency, Interest rate**	
Plain Vanilla Derivatives	Swaps	Floors
	Forwards	Collars
	Caps	
Structured Notes	Corporate MTNs	Inverse floaters
	Govt. agency MTNs	Tender options bonds
	Floaters	
Counterparty Rating Requirement:	AAA	

OTHER ALTERNATIVE INVESTMENTS:

	CMOs/REMICs – Govt.	CMOs/REMICs – Private

KEY MANAGERS & DERIVATIVES SPECIALISTS:	Direct Phone/Fax	Job Function
Ms. Mary Lou Casey Senior Managing Director	203/726-3444	Portfolio Mgr – Structured Notes
Mr. Robert W. Eccles Vice President		Portfolio Mgr – Structured Notes *Corp*
Mr. Lawrence S. Harris Senior Managing Director	203/726-7722	Bond Department Head
Mr. Cris W. Jacobs Managing Director	203/726-7591	Bond Department Head
Mr. Arthur C. Reeds III President	203/726-7559	President Chief Investment Officer
Mr. Henry C. Wagner III	203/726-2793	Portfolio Mgr – Derivatives Portfolio Mgr – Futures *Corp, Govt* Portfolio Mgr – Structured Notes

Circus Circus Enterprises, Inc.

Corporation

Location: 2880 Las Vegas Boulevard South
Las Vegas, NV 89109-1102

Fax: 702/794-3831 **Phone:** 702/734-0410

Use: **Balance Sheet/Risk Management**
Hedge interest rate risk

Currencies: US dollar

Regions: United States Europe

DERIVATIVES ACTIVITIES: **CAC Class: 4**

Exchange-traded Options & Futures	**Interest rate**	
OTC Derivatives	**Interest rate**	
Plain Vanilla Derivatives	Swaps	Caps
Counterparty Rating Requirement:	AA	

Circus Circus Enterprises, Inc. – continued

KEY MANAGERS & DERIVATIVES SPECIALISTS:	Direct Phone/Fax	Job Function
Mr. Daniel N. Copp E.V.P., C.F.O. & Treasurer		Chief Financial Officer Treasurer Portfolio Mgr – Derivatives Portfolio Mgr – Futures Portfolio Mgr – Options
Mr. Clyde T. Turner Chairman, President & C.E.O.		President

Citibank, N.A. (Portfolio)

Bank/Portfolio

Sub of Citicorp

Location: 153 East 53rd Street
Corporate Finance Office
6th Floor
New York, NY 10043

Fax: 212/527-2737 **Phone:** 212/559-1000

Investment Portfolio: $ 7.6 billion

Use:

Balance Sheet/Risk Management
Create synthetic fixed/floating rate
Hedge balance sheet
Hedge currency risk
Hedge interest rate risk
Incremental return

Investment Purposes
Alter portfolio weighting
Adjust portfolio duration
Asset allocation
Hedge bond portfolio risk
Hedge currency risk
Hedge equity portfolio risk
Hedge interest rate risk

Currencies: US dollar, French franc, German mark, Italian lira, Japanese yen, Swiss franc, UK pound

Regions: United States

DERIVATIVES ACTIVITIES:

Exchange-traded Options & Futures	**Currency, Interest rate**
OTC Derivatives **Plain Vanilla Derivatives**	**Currency, Interest rate** Forwards

OTHER ALTERNATIVE INVESTMENTS:

CMOs/REMICs – Govt. Repos/reverse repos

KEY MANAGERS & DERIVATIVES SPECIALISTS:	Direct Phone/Fax	Job Function
Mr. Ronald Walter Director – Investments	212/559-4393	Chief Investment Officer Portfolio Mgr – Derivatives Portfolio Mgr – Options

Citibank Private Banking Investment Division

Bank/Management Division

Sub of Citicorp

Location: 153 East 53rd Street
21st Floor
New York, NY 10043

Fax: 212/527-2099 **Phone:** 212/559-2838

Profile: Total return investor

Investment Portfolio: $ 36.0 billion

Use: **Investment Purposes**
Alter portfolio weighting
Adjust portfolio duration
Asset allocation
Hedge bond portfolio risk
Hedge interest rate risk

Currencies: US dollar

Regions: United States

DERIVATIVES ACTIVITIES: **CAC Class: 4**

Exchange-traded Options & Futures U.S. Treasury futures	**Bond, Interest rate**
Structured Notes	Floaters

OTHER ALTERNATIVE INVESTMENTS:

CMOs/REMICs – Govt.
CMOs/REMICs – Private
Repos/reverse repos

KEY MANAGERS & DERIVATIVES SPECIALISTS:	Direct Phone/Fax	Job Function
Mr. Farhan Sharaff Vice President and C.I.O.	212/559-4478	Chief Investment Officer
Mr. Robert Stricker Vice President	212/559-5029	Bond Department Head Portfolio Mgr – Futures

Citicorp

Bank Holding Company

Location: 399 Park Avenue
New York, NY 10043

Fax: 212/291-4007 **Phone:** 212/291-2542

Use: **Balance Sheet/Risk Management**
Create synthetic fixed/floating rate
Hedge balance sheet
Hedge currency risk
Hedge interest rate risk
Hedge overseas investments
Protect currency gains

Investment Purposes
Capture extra yield
Discretionary situations
Hedge bond portfolio risk
Hedge currency risk
Hedge equity portfolio risk
Hedge interest rate risk

Currencies: US dollar
Canadian dollar
French franc
German mark
Italian lira
Japanese yen
Swiss franc
UK pound

Regions: United States
Europe

Citicorp – continued

DERIVATIVES ACTIVITIES: **CAC Class: 6**

Exchange-traded Options & Futures	**Currency, Interest rate**	
OTC Derivatives	**Currency, Interest rate**	
Plain Vanilla Derivatives	Swaps	Forwards

KEY MANAGERS & DERIVATIVES SPECIALISTS:	**Direct Phone/Fax**	**Job Function**
Mr. Thomas E. Jones E.V.P. – Financial Control		Chief Financial Officer
Ms. Nancy S. Newcomb Senior Officer – Treasury		Treasurer Portfolio Mgr – Derivatives Portfolio Mgr – Futures Portfolio Mgr – Options

Citizens Federal Bank, F.S.B.

Savings Bank/Bldg Society

Sub of CitFed Bancorp, Inc.

Location: One Citizens Federal Center
Dayton, OH 45402

Fax: 513/228-5510 **Phone:** 513/223-4234

Profile: Hold to maturity investor

Investment Portfolio: $ 656.6 million

Use: **Balance Sheet/Risk Management**
Hedge interest rate risk

Currencies: US dollar

Regions: United States

DERIVATIVES ACTIVITIES: **CAC Class: 2**

OTC Derivatives	**Interest rate**	
Plain Vanilla Derivatives	Swaps	Forwards
Counterparty Rating Requirement:	AA	

OTHER ALTERNATIVE INVESTMENTS:

Repos/reverse repos

KEY MANAGERS & DERIVATIVES SPECIALISTS:	**Direct Phone/Fax**	**Job Function**
Mr. Jerry L. Kirby Chairman & President		President Chief Investment Officer
Mr. Michael T. Sauer Vice President	513/229-8352	Portfolio Mgr – Derivatives

Citizens National Bank of Evansville (Portfolio)

Bank/Portfolio

Location: 20 Northwest Third Street
Evansville, IN 47739-0001

Fax: 812/464-3496 **Phone:** 812/464-3400

Profile: Current yield investor

Investment Portfolio: $ 1.0 billion

Use: **Balance Sheet/Risk Management**
Create synthetic fixed/floating rate
Hedge interest rate risk

Currencies: US dollar

Regions: United States

DERIVATIVES ACTIVITIES: **CAC Class: 3**

OTC Derivatives
Plain Vanilla Derivatives

Interest rate
Swaps
Caps

OTHER ALTERNATIVE INVESTMENTS:

CMOs/REMICs – Govt.
CMOs/REMICs – Private
Repos/reverse repos

KEY MANAGERS & DERIVATIVES SPECIALISTS:	Direct Phone/Fax	Job Function
Mr. Stephen R. Bowman	812/464-3446	Portfolio Mgr – Derivatives
Mr. David Viar		Chief Investment Officer Portfolio Mgr – Derivatives

Citizens Trust Company & Savings Bank (Trust)

Bank/Trust

Sub of Citizens Financial Group Incorporated

Location: One Citizens Plaza
3rd Floor
Providence, RI 02903-1339

Fax: 401/455-5310 **Phone:** 401/456-7000

Profile: Total return investor

Investment Portfolio: $ 2.8 billion

Use: **Investment Purposes**

Currencies: US dollar

Regions: United States

DERIVATIVES ACTIVITIES: **CAC Class: Inactive**

OTHER ALTERNATIVE INVESTMENTS:

CMOs/REMICs – Govt.
CMOs/REMICs – Private

KEY MANAGERS & DERIVATIVES SPECIALISTS:	Direct Phone/Fax	Job Function
Mr. Salvatore C. DiSanto Senior Vice President	401/456-7330	Fixed-Income Strategist
Mr. William F. Dwyer		Chief Investment Officer

Coast Federal Bank, Federal Savings Bank (Administration)

Savings Bank/Bldg Society

Location: 8433 Fallbrook Avenue
West Hills, CA 91304

Fax: 818/316-3228 **Phone:** 818/316-8000

Profile: Current yield investor

Investment Portfolio: $ 8.1 billion

Use: **Balance Sheet/Risk Management**
Hedge balance sheet
Hedge interest rate risk

Currencies: US dollar

Regions: United States

DERIVATIVES ACTIVITIES: **CAC Class: 2**

OTC Derivatives	**Bond, Interest rate**	
Plain Vanilla Derivatives	Swaps	Caps
Structured Notes	CMT notes	
Counterparty Rating Requirement:	AAA	

OTHER ALTERNATIVE INVESTMENTS:

CMOs/REMICs – Govt. Repos/reverse repos

KEY MANAGERS & DERIVATIVES SPECIALISTS:	**Direct Phone/Fax**	**Job Function**
Ms. Sara Mason	Ext. 8635 818/368-4767	Chief Investment Officer Portfolio Mgr – Derivatives Portfolio Mgr – Structured Notes

Coastal Banc ssb

Savings Bank/Bldg Society

Sub of Coastal Bancorp, Inc.

Location: Eight Greenway Plaza
Suite 1500
Houston, TX 77046

Fax: 713/960-9864 **Phone:** 713/623-2600

Profile: Spread investor

Investment Portfolio: $ 2.2 billion

Use: **Balance Sheet/Risk Management**
Bypass regulations
Create synthetic fixed/floating rate
Hedge balance sheet
Hedge interest rate risk
Meet interest rate target
Strategic liability management

Investment Purposes
Adjust portfolio duration
Asset allocation
Beat conventional rates
Capture extra yield
Convexity objectives
Hedge bond portfolio risk
Hedge interest rate risk
Immunize from volatility
Provide incremental return
Reduce variability of returns

Currencies: US dollar

Regions: United States

Coastal Banc ssb – continued

DERIVATIVES ACTIVITIES:		CAC Class: 5
OTC Derivatives	**Interest rate**	
Plain Vanilla Derivatives	Swaps	Caps
Counterparty Rating Requirement:	None	

OTHER ALTERNATIVE INVESTMENTS:		
	CMOs/REMICs – Govt.	Strips
	CMOs/REMICs – Private	Repos/reverse repos

KEY MANAGERS & DERIVATIVES SPECIALISTS:	Direct Phone/Fax	Job Function
Ms. Sandy Orr Executive Vice President		Chief Investment Officer Portfolio Mgr – Derivatives

Collective Bank

Savings Bank/Bldg Society

Sub of Collective Bancorp

Location: 158 Philadelphia Avenue
Egg Harbor City, NJ 08215

Fax: 609/625-9149 **Phone:** 609/965-1235

Profile: Total return investor

Investment Portfolio: $ 2.3 billion

Use: **Investment Purposes**

Currencies: US dollar

Regions: United States

DERIVATIVES ACTIVITIES:		CAC Class: 1
Structured Notes	Govt. agency MTNs	

OTHER ALTERNATIVE INVESTMENTS:		
	CMOs/REMICs – Govt.	Repos/reverse repos
	CMOs/REMICs – Private	

KEY MANAGERS & DERIVATIVES SPECIALISTS:	Direct Phone/Fax	Job Function
Mr. Arthur Foster E.V.P. – Finance		Chief Investment Officer Portfolio Mgr – Structured Notes
Mr. Russell Graves	609/625-6103	Bond Department Head *Govt, MBS, Muni* Portfolio Mgr – Structured Notes

Colonial Management Associates

Mutual Fund Manager

Location:	One Financial Center 12th Floor Boston, MA 02111-2621	**Fax:** 617/737-0358	**Phone:** 617/426-3750
Profile:	Total return investor	**Investment Portfolio:** $ 11.0 - 20.0 billion	
Use:	**Balance Sheet/Risk Management** Strategic liability management	**Investment Purposes** Hedge bond portfolio risk Hedge interest rate risk	
Currencies:	US dollar	**Regions:** United States, Canada	Europe

DERIVATIVES ACTIVITIES: **CAC Class: 6**

Exchange-traded Options & Futures Municipal futures	**Bond, Currency, Interest rate** Municipal options
OTC Derivatives **Plain Vanilla Derivatives**	**Currency**
Exotic Derivatives	
Structured Notes	Inverse floaters

OTHER ALTERNATIVE INVESTMENTS:

CMOs/REMICs – Govt.	Strips
CMOs/REMICs – Private	Repos/reverse repos
MOPs/TOPs	

KEY MANAGERS & DERIVATIVES SPECIALISTS:	**Direct Phone/Fax**	**Job Function**
Mr. Carl C. Ericson Vice President	617/772-3735	Portfolio Mgr – Futures *Corp, Govt* Research Analyst – Futures/Options *Corp, Govt*
Ms. Helen F. Peters S.V.P. & Director	617/772-3730	Chief Investment Officer Portfolio Mgr – Derivatives Portfolio Mgr – Options
Ms. Ann T. Peterson Research Associate	617/772-3773	Research Analyst – Futures/Options *Govt*
Mr. Robert S. Waas	617/772-3191	Portfolio Mgr – Futures *Muni* Portfolio Mgr – Options *Muni*

Columbia Management Company

Mutual Fund Manager

Location: 1300 Southwest Sixth Avenue
Portland, OR 97201

Fax: 503/243-2928 **Phone:** 503/222-3600

Profile: Total return investor

Investment Portfolio: $ 15.6 billion

Use: **Investment Purposes**

Currencies: US dollar

Regions: United States

DERIVATIVES ACTIVITIES: **CAC Class: Inactive**

OTHER ALTERNATIVE INVESTMENTS:

CMOs/REMICs – Govt. CMOs/REMICs – Private

KEY MANAGERS & DERIVATIVES SPECIALISTS:	Direct Phone/Fax	Job Function
Mr. James F. Rippey President	503/243-5052	President Chief Investment Officer
Mr. Thomas L. Thomsen Vice President – Bonds		Bond Department Head

Columbus Circle Investors

Investment Manager

Sub of Pacific Investment Management Co. (PIMCO)

Location: One Station Place
Metro Center 8th Floor South
Stamford, CT 06902

Fax: 203/353-6041 **Phone:** 203/353-6000

Profile: Total return investor

Investment Portfolio: $ 12.5 billion

Use: **Investment Purposes**
Hedge bond portfolio risk
Hedge equity portfolio risk
Hedge interest rate risk

Currencies: US dollar

Regions: United States

DERIVATIVES ACTIVITIES:

Exchange-traded Options & Futures **Bond, Interest rate**

OTHER ALTERNATIVE INVESTMENTS:

CMOs/REMICs – Govt. GICs
CMOs/REMICs – Private Repos/reverse repos

KEY MANAGERS & DERIVATIVES SPECIALISTS:	Direct Phone/Fax	Job Function
Mr. Donald A. Chiboucas President	203/353-6015	President
Mr. Jacob Navon	203/353-5776	Bond Department Head Portfolio Mgr – Futures Portfolio Mgr – Options

Columbus Circle Investors – continued

KEY MANAGERS & DERIVATIVES SPECIALISTS:	Direct Phone/Fax	Job Function
Mr. Andrew Serotta Vice President	203/353-5693	Portfolio Mgr – Futures Portfolio Mgr – Options Trader – Futures Trader – Options
Mr. Irwin F. Smith Chairman & C.E.O.	203/353-6010	Chief Investment Officer

Comerica Bank (Funds Management)

Bank/Portfolio

Location: 100 Renaissance Center
Comerica Bank Tower
Detroit, MI 48243

Fax: 313/222-9825 **Phone:** 313/222-4000

Profile: Hold to maturity investor

Investment Portfolio: $ 32.0 billion

Use: **Balance Sheet/Risk Management**
Hedge balance sheet
Hedge interest rate risk

Investment Purposes
Beat conventional rates

Currencies: US dollar

Regions: United States

DERIVATIVES ACTIVITIES: **CAC Class: 7**

Exchange-traded Options & Futures
U.S. Treasury futures
U.S. Treasury options

OTC Derivatives
Plain Vanilla Derivatives — **Interest rate**: Swaps, Caps

Exotic Derivatives — Index amortizing swaps

OTHER ALTERNATIVE INVESTMENTS:

CMOs/REMICs – Govt.
CMOs/REMICs – Private
Repos/reverse repos

KEY MANAGERS & DERIVATIVES SPECIALISTS:	Direct Phone/Fax	Job Function
Mr. Alan R. Goldman Senior Vice President	313/222-7200	Chief Investment Officer
Mr. Anthony Magdowski	313/222-0058	Portfolio Mgr – Derivatives Portfolio Mgr – Futures Portfolio Mgr – Options
Mr. Lawrence Sharley	313/222-7201	Bond Department Head *Govt, MBS* Portfolio Mgr – Derivatives
Mr. Gregory A. Yovan Vice President	313/222-7202	Portfolio Mgr – Derivatives Portfolio Mgr – Futures Portfolio Mgr – Options

Commander Investment Corporation

Investment Manager

Location: 738 Chestnut Street, Meadville, PA 16335

Fax: No fax **Phone:** 814/724-5078

Profile: Total return investor

Investment Portfolio: $ 500.0 - 999.0 million

Use: **Investment Purposes**
Capture extra yield
Hedge currency risk
Hedge interest rate risk

Currencies: US dollar, Canadian dollar, French franc, German mark, Italian lira, Japanese yen, UK pound

Regions: United States, Europe, Pacific Rim

DERIVATIVES ACTIVITIES:

CAC Class: 3

Exchange-traded Options & Futures	**Bond, Currency, Interest rate**	
U.S. Treasury futures	U.S. Treasury options	
Structured Notes	Corporate MTNs Govt. agency MTNs Bond index notes	Floaters Inverse floaters Periodic capped floaters

OTHER ALTERNATIVE INVESTMENTS:

CMOs/REMICs – Govt.	MOPs/TOPs
CMOs/REMICs – Private	Strips
GICs	Repos/reverse repos

KEY MANAGERS & DERIVATIVES SPECIALISTS:

	Direct Phone/Fax	Job Function
Mr. Clive Beck		Portfolio Mgr – Futures *Govt* Portfolio Mgr – Options *Govt*
Mr. David Daniel		Portfolio Mgr – Structured Notes Trader – Structured Investments
Mr. Matt Lagman		Trader – Currency Options Head Trader – Currency Futures Trader – Currency Options Trader – Currency Swaps
Ms. Marian Rogers		Research Analyst – Futures/Options
Mr. E. T. Zappia		Chief Investment Officer Bond Department Head Fixed-Income Strategist Portfolio Mgr – Derivatives Trader – Derivatives

Commerce Bancshares Inc.

Bank/Portfolio

Location: 8000 Forsythe Boulevard
Clayton, MO 63105-1797

Fax: 314/746-7432 **Phone:** 314/726-2255

Profile: Total return investor

Investment Portfolio: $ 2.5 billion

Use: **Investment Purposes**
Adjust portfolio duration
Hedge interest rate risk

Currencies: US dollar

Regions: United States

DERIVATIVES ACTIVITIES: **CAC Class: 4**

Exchange-traded Options & Futures

OTC Derivatives
Plain Vanilla Derivatives — **Interest rate**: Swaps, Forwards

OTHER ALTERNATIVE INVESTMENTS:

Strips
Repos/reverse repos

KEY MANAGERS & DERIVATIVES SPECIALISTS:	**Direct Phone/Fax**	**Job Function**
Mr. Gary D. Campbell Senior Vice President	314/746-7254	Chief Investment Officer
Mr. A. Bayard Clark Chief Financial Officer		Chief Financial Officer
Mr. Scott Colbert Vice President	314/746-8557	Portfolio Mgr – Derivatives

Commerce Bank Investment Management Group

Bank/Management Division

Sub of Commerce Bancshares Inc.

Location: 922 Walnut Street
Kansas City, MO 64106

Fax: 816/234-2545 **Phone:** 816/234-2000

Profile: Total return investor

Investment Portfolio: $ 2.2 billion

Use: **Investment Purposes**
Hedge bond portfolio risk
Hedge interest rate risk

Currencies: US dollar

Regions: United States

DERIVATIVES ACTIVITIES:

Exchange-traded Options & Futures — **Bond, Interest rate**

OTHER ALTERNATIVE INVESTMENTS:

CMOs/REMICs – Govt.
CMOs/REMICs – Private
Strips
Repos/reverse repos

Commerce Bank Investment Management Group – continued

KEY MANAGERS & DERIVATIVES SPECIALISTS:	Direct Phone/Fax	Job Function
Mr. Craig A. MacPherson Vice President	816/234-2415	Bond Department Head *Corp, Govt, Muni* Fixed-Income Strategist
Mr. Thomas E. Weiford Senior Vice President	816/234-2579	Chief Investment Officer

Commercial Federal Corporation

Savings Bank/Bldg Society

Location: 2120 South 72nd Street
Omaha, NE 68124

Fax: 402/390-5143 **Phone:** 402/554-9200

Profile: Hold to maturity investor

Investment Portfolio: $ 1.3 billion

Use: **Investment Purposes**

Currencies: US dollar

Regions: United States

DERIVATIVES ACTIVITIES: **CAC Class: Inactive**

OTHER ALTERNATIVE INVESTMENTS:

CMOs/REMICs – Govt.
CMOs/REMICs – Private
Repos/reverse repos

KEY MANAGERS & DERIVATIVES SPECIALISTS:	Direct Phone/Fax	Job Function
Mr. James A. Laphen President & C.O.O.		President Chief Investment Officer
Ms. Joy J. Narzisi Treasurer	402/390-5132	Treasurer Bond Department Head

Commercial Union Investment Management

Insurance Co/Management

Sub of Commercial Union Insurance Companies

Location: One Beacon Street
17th Floor
Boston, MA 02108-3100

Fax: 617/725-6702 **Phone:** 617/725-6000

Profile: Total return investor

Investment Portfolio: $ 5.3 billion

Use: **Balance Sheet/Risk Management**

Investment Purposes

Currencies: US dollar

Regions: United States

Commercial Union Investment Management – continued

DERIVATIVES ACTIVITIES:		**CAC Class: Inactive**

OTHER ALTERNATIVE INVESTMENTS:		
	CMOs/REMICs – Govt.	CMOs/REMICs – Private

KEY MANAGERS & DERIVATIVES SPECIALISTS:	**Direct Phone/Fax**	**Job Function**
Mr. Robert C. Pickett Chairman & President	617/725-6445	President Chief Investment Officer

Commonwealth Investment Counsel

Broker/Management Sub

Sub of Wheat First Butcher Singer, Inc.

Location: 901 East Byrd Street
6th Floor
Richmond, VA 23219-4069

Fax: 804/782-3629 **Phone:** 804/782-3207

Profile: Total return investor

Investment Portfolio: $ 3.9 billion

Use: **Balance Sheet/Risk Management**
Hedge interest rate risk

Investment Purposes
Hedge interest rate risk

Currencies: US dollar

Regions: United States

DERIVATIVES ACTIVITIES:		
Exchange-traded Options & Futures U.S. Treasury futures	**Bond** U.S. Treasury options	
OTC Derivatives **Plain Vanilla Derivatives**	**Interest rate** Swaps	Caps

OTHER ALTERNATIVE INVESTMENTS:		
	CMOs/REMICs – Govt. Strips	Repos/reverse repos

KEY MANAGERS & DERIVATIVES SPECIALISTS:	**Direct Phone/Fax**	**Job Function**
Mr. John Davenport President		President Chief Investment Officer
Mr. Michael Jones	804/782-3759	Bond Department Head Portfolio Mgr – Derivatives Portfolio Mgr – Futures Portfolio Mgr – Options
Mr. Hance West Jr.	804/782-3742	Bond Department Head Portfolio Mgr – Derivatives

Compass Bank (Portfolio)

Bank/Portfolio

Sub of Compass Bancshares, Inc.

Location: 701 South 20th Street
Birmingham, AL 35233

Fax: 205/715-7997 **Phone:** 205/933-3000

Profile: Total return investor

Investment Portfolio: $ 4.5 billion

Use:

Balance Sheet/Risk Management
Create synthetic fixed/floating rate
Hedge balance sheet
Hedge interest rate risk
Incremental return
Reduce cost of capital
Strategic liability management

Investment Purposes
Alter portfolio weighting
Adjust portfolio duration
Asset allocation
Capture extra yield
Diversify portfolio
Enter new mkts/lower risk
Hedge bond portfolio risk
Hedge interest rate risk
Provide incremental return
Reduce variability of returns

Currencies: US dollar

Regions: United States

DERIVATIVES ACTIVITIES: **CAC Class: 6**

Exchange-traded Options & Futures	**Interest rate**	
U.S. Treasury futures	Municipal futures	
U.S. Treasury options		
OTC Derivatives	**Interest rate**	
Plain Vanilla Derivatives	Swaps	Caps
	Forwards	Floors
	Swaptions	Collars
Exotic Derivatives	CMT swaps	Periodic caps/floors
	Index amortizing swaps	
Structured Notes	Govt. agency MTNs	Inverse floaters
	Index amortizing notes	Periodic capped floaters
	Floaters	Multi-step-up callable bonds
Counterparty Rating Requirement:	A	

OTHER ALTERNATIVE INVESTMENTS:

	CMOs/REMICs – Govt.	Strips
	CMOs/REMICs – Private	Repos/reverse repos

KEY MANAGERS & DERIVATIVES SPECIALISTS:	**Direct Phone/Fax**	**Job Function**
Ms. Christina L. Boles	205/933-3881	Chief Investment Officer
Senior Vice President		Portfolio Mgr – Derivatives
		Portfolio Mgr – Structured Notes

Compass Bank (Trust)

Bank/Trust

Sub of Compass Bancshares, Inc.

Location: 701 South 32nd Street, Birmingham, AL 35233

Fax: 205/558-6754 **Phone:** 205/558-6785

Profile: Total return investor

Investment Portfolio: $ 1.0 - 3.0 billion

Use: **Investment Purposes**

Currencies: US dollar

Regions: United States

DERIVATIVES ACTIVITIES: **CAC Class: Inactive**

OTHER ALTERNATIVE INVESTMENTS:

CMOs/REMICs – Govt.

KEY MANAGERS & DERIVATIVES SPECIALISTS:	**Direct Phone/Fax**	**Job Function**
Ms. Dea Woodham V.P. & Sr. Trust Officer	205/558-6308	Chief Investment Officer Bond Department Head

Conseco Capital Management

Insurance Co/Management

Sub of Conseco Inc.

Location: 11825 North Pennsylvania Street, Carmel, IN 46032

Fax: 317/817-2763 **Phone:** 317/817-6100

Profile: Spread investor

Investment Portfolio: $ 26.2 billion

Use: **Investment Purposes**
Adjust portfolio duration
Provide incremental return

Currencies: US dollar

Regions: United States

DERIVATIVES ACTIVITIES: **CAC Class: 5**

Exchange-traded Options & Futures U.S. Treasury futures	U.S. Treasury options	
OTC Derivatives **Plain Vanilla Derivatives**	**Bond** Swaps	
Structured Notes	Corporate MTNs Govt. agency MTNs Floaters	Periodic capped floaters Multi-step-up callable bonds
Counterparty Rating Requirement:	AA	

OTHER ALTERNATIVE INVESTMENTS:

CMOs/REMICs – Govt.
CMOs/REMICs – Private
Strips
Repos/reverse repos

Conseco Capital Management – continued

KEY MANAGERS & DERIVATIVES SPECIALISTS:	**Direct Phone/Fax**	**Job Function**
Mr. Maxwell E. Bublitz Senior Vice President	 317/817-6161	President Chief Investment Officer
Mr. Andrew S. Chow Second Vice President	317/817-2602 317/817-6419	Portfolio Mgr – Derivatives Portfolio Mgr – Structured Notes Trader – Derivatives Trader – Futures Trader – Structured Investments
Mr. Albert J. Gutierrez Senior Vice President	317/817-2741 317/817-6161	Bond Department Head Portfolio Mgr – Derivatives Portfolio Mgr – Structured Notes
Mr. See Yeng Quek Second Vice President	317/817-6725 317/817-6347	Portfolio Mgr – Derivatives *MBS* Research Analyst – Derivatives *MBS* Trader – Derivatives *MBS*

Consistent Asset Management Company

Investment Manager

Location: 116 Commons Court
The Commons at Chadds Ford
Chadds Ford, PA 19317

Fax: 610/558-3002 **Phone:** 610/558-3000

Profile: Total return investor

Investment Portfolio: $ 595.0 million

Use: **Investment Purposes**

Currencies: US dollar

Regions: United States

DERIVATIVES ACTIVITIES: **CAC Class: Inactive**

OTHER ALTERNATIVE INVESTMENTS:

CMOs/REMICs – Govt. CMOs/REMICs – Private

KEY MANAGERS & DERIVATIVES SPECIALISTS:	**Direct Phone/Fax**	**Job Function**
Mr. Daryl L. Hudson Chairman		Chief Investment Officer
Mr. David W. Umbs President		President

Continental Asset Management

Insurance Co/Management

Sub of Trust Company of the West (TCW)

Location: 180 Maiden Lane
10th Floor
New York, NY 10038

Fax: 212/440-7518 **Phone:** 212/440-7526

Profile: Total return investor

Investment Portfolio: $ 4.0 - 10.0 billion

Use: **Investment Purposes**
Hedge bond portfolio risk
Hedge currency risk
Hedge interest rate risk
Protect currency gains

Currencies: US dollar, Canadian dollar, French franc, German mark, UK pound

Regions: United States

DERIVATIVES ACTIVITIES:

Exchange-traded Options & Futures U.S. Treasury futures	**Bond**	
OTC Derivatives **Plain Vanilla Derivatives**	**Currency, Interest rate** Swaps	 Forwards
Structured Notes	Corporate MTNs	Govt. agency MTNs
Counterparty Rating Requirement:	A	

OTHER ALTERNATIVE INVESTMENTS:

	CMOs/REMICs – Govt. CMOs/REMICs – Private	GICs

KEY MANAGERS & DERIVATIVES SPECIALISTS:	**Direct Phone/Fax**	**Job Function**
Mr. Walter J. Blasberg President	212/440-7525	President Chief Investment Officer
Mr. Mitchell Brownstein	212/440-3613	Portfolio Mgr – Derivatives Portfolio Mgr – Futures
Ms. Virginia Fagan	212/440-7511	Portfolio Mgr – Derivatives *Corp* Portfolio Mgr – Futures *Corp* Portfolio Mgr – Structured Notes *Corp*
Mr. Robert J. Martin III Vice President	212/440-7544	Bond Department Head *Muni*
Mr. Stephen Santangelo Assistant Vice President	212/440-7515	Portfolio Mgr – Derivatives Portfolio Mgr – Futures

Continental Asset Management – continued

KEY MANAGERS & DERIVATIVES SPECIALISTS:	Direct Phone/Fax	Job Function
Ms. Catherine Waterworth Managing Director	212/440-7753	Portfolio Mgr – Derivatives Portfolio Mgr – Futures
Mr. Gregory Whiteley	212/440-7522	Portfolio Mgr – Derivatives *MBS*

CoreStates Investment Advisers, Inc.

Bank/Management Division

Location: 1500 Market Street
Center Square Upper Mezzanine
Philadelphia, PA 19102

Fax: 215/973-3460 **Phone:** 215/973-3350

Profile: Total return investor

Investment Portfolio: $ 9.5 billion

Use: **Investment Purposes**

Currencies: US dollar

Regions: United States

DERIVATIVES ACTIVITIES: **CAC Class: Inactive**

OTHER ALTERNATIVE INVESTMENTS:

CMOs/REMICs – Govt. Strips

KEY MANAGERS & DERIVATIVES SPECIALISTS:	Direct Phone/Fax	Job Function
Mr. Mark E. Stalnecker Chief Investment Officer	215/786-7566	Chief Investment Officer
Mr. Dung Vukhas Senior Vice President	215/973-3745 215/973-3589	Bond Department Head

Corning Incorporated

Corporation

Location: One Riverfront Plaza
Corning, NY 14831

Fax: 607/974-8150 **Phone:** 607/974-9000

Use: **Balance Sheet/Risk Management**

Currencies: US dollar, Australian dollar, Belgian franc, German mark, Japanese yen, UK pound

Regions: United States

DERIVATIVES ACTIVITIES:

Exchange-traded Options & Futures	**Currency**
OTC Derivatives **Plain Vanilla Derivatives**	**Currency** Swaps
Counterparty Rating Requirement:	AA

Corning Incorporated – continued

KEY MANAGERS & DERIVATIVES SPECIALISTS:	Direct Phone/Fax	Job Function
Mr. Roger G. Ackerman President & C.O.O.		President
Mr. Van C. Campbell Vice Chairman & C.F.O.		Chief Financial Officer
Ms. Sandra L. Helton S.V.P. & Treasurer		Treasurer Portfolio Mgr – Derivatives

The Crabbe-Huson Group, Inc.

Investment Manager

Location: 121 Southwest Morrison
Suite 1400
Portland, OR 97204

Fax: 503/295-2939 **Phone:** 503/295-0111

Profile: Total return investor

Investment Portfolio: $ 3.0 billion

Use: **Investment Purposes**

Currencies: US dollar

Regions: United States

DERIVATIVES ACTIVITIES: **CAC Class: Inactive**

OTHER ALTERNATIVE INVESTMENTS:

CMOs/REMICs – Govt.

KEY MANAGERS & DERIVATIVES SPECIALISTS:	Direct Phone/Fax	Job Function
Mr. Richard S. Huson		Chief Investment Officer

Crestar Bank (Portfolio)

Bank/Portfolio

Location: 919 East Main Street
Richmond, VA 23219

Fax: 804/782-5100 **Phone:** 804/782-5000

Profile: Total return investor

Investment Portfolio: $ 2.3 billion

Use: **Balance Sheet/Risk Management**
Create synthetic fixed/floating rate
Hedge interest rate risk
Strategic liability management

Currencies: US dollar

Regions: United States

DERIVATIVES ACTIVITIES: **CAC Class: 6**

OTC Derivatives	**Interest rate**	
Plain Vanilla Derivatives	Swaps	Caps
	Forwards	Floors

Counterparty Rating Requirement: A

OTHER ALTERNATIVE INVESTMENTS:

Repos/reverse repos

Crestar Bank (Portfolio) – continued

KEY MANAGERS & DERIVATIVES SPECIALISTS:	Direct Phone/Fax	Job Function
Mr. Robert Hunter Vice President	804/782-7837	Portfolio Mgr – Structured Notes *MBS*
Ms. Margo Miller Vice President	804/782-7391	Portfolio Mgr – Derivatives
Mr. Alexander K. Scott Senior Vice President	804/782-5697	Portfolio Mgr – Derivatives
Mr. Douglas Wallace Senior Vice President	804/782-5696	Bond Department Head

CTT Investment Management Group

Insurance Co/Management

Sub of Chicago Title & Trust

Location: 171 North Clark Street
Chicago, IL 60602

Fax: 312/223-5170 **Phone:** 312/223-2000

Profile: Total return investor

Investment Portfolio: $ 4.1 billion

Use: **Investment Purposes**
Capture extra yield

Currencies: US dollar

Regions: United States

DERIVATIVES ACTIVITIES: **CAC Class: 2**

Structured Notes	Corporate MTNs CMT notes	Floaters

OTHER ALTERNATIVE INVESTMENTS:

	CMOs/REMICs – Govt. Strips	Repos/reverse repos

KEY MANAGERS & DERIVATIVES SPECIALISTS:	Direct Phone/Fax	Job Function
Mr. Frederick W. Engimann	312/223-3403	Bond Department Head
Mr. Charles F. Henderson	312/223-2735	Chief Investment Officer
Mr. Thomas Marthaler Vice President	312/223-2612	Portfolio Mgr – Structured Notes
Ms. Lois A. Pasquale	312/223-2767	Portfolio Mgr – Structured Notes

Dana Investment Advisors, Inc.

Investment Manager

Location: 330 South Executive Drive
Suite 301
Brookfield, WI 53005

Fax: 414/782-0581 **Phone:** 414/782-3631

Profile: Total return investor

Investment Portfolio: $ 1.1 billion

Use: **Investment Purposes**

Currencies: US dollar

Regions: United States

DERIVATIVES ACTIVITIES: **CAC Class: Inactive**

OTHER ALTERNATIVE INVESTMENTS:

CMOs/REMICs – Govt.

KEY MANAGERS & DERIVATIVES SPECIALISTS:	**Direct Phone/Fax**	**Job Function**
Mr. James Ivey Sr. Vice President-Investments	414/782-2907	Chief Investment Officer Bond Department Head

Dauphin Deposit Bank & Trust Company (Portfolio)

Bank/Portfolio

Sub of Dauphin Deposit Corporation

Location: 213 Market Street
Harrisburg, PA 17101

Fax: 717/255-2073 **Phone:** 717/255-2121

Profile: Total return investor

Investment Portfolio: $ 1.8 billion

Use: **Investment Purposes**
Asset allocation

Currencies: US dollar

Regions: United States

DERIVATIVES ACTIVITIES: **CAC Class: 2**

Structured Notes Govt. agency MTNs

OTHER ALTERNATIVE INVESTMENTS:

CMOs/REMICs – Govt. Repos/reverse repos

KEY MANAGERS & DERIVATIVES SPECIALISTS:	**Direct Phone/Fax**	**Job Function**
Mr. Kenneth Sallade Executive Vice President	717/255-2131 717/255-2135	Chief Investment Officer

Dauphin Deposit Bank & Trust Company (Trust)

Bank/Trust

Sub of Dauphin Deposit Corporation

Location: 213 Market Street
Harrisburg, PA 17101

Fax: 717/255-2073 **Phone:** 717/255-2121

Profile: Total return investor

Investment Portfolio: $ 2.0 billion

Use: **Investment Purposes**
Capture extra yield

Currencies: US dollar

Regions: United States

DERIVATIVES ACTIVITIES: **CAC Class: 1**

Structured Notes	CMT notes Floaters	Multi-step-up callable bonds

OTHER ALTERNATIVE INVESTMENTS:

CMOs/REMICs – Govt.

KEY MANAGERS & DERIVATIVES SPECIALISTS:	**Direct Phone/Fax**	**Job Function**
Mr. Darrell Girton Vice President	717/255-2317	Portfolio Mgr – Structured Notes
Ms. Cathleen Saylor Vice President-Fixed Income	717/255-2318	Portfolio Mgr – Structured Notes
Mr. Paul B. Shannon President	717/231-2644	President
Mr. Robert Spicer Senior Vice President	717/255-2315	Chief Investment Officer

Davis Selected Advisers, L.P.

Mutual Fund Manager

Location: 124 East Marcy Street
Santa Fe, NM 87501

Fax: 505/820-1222 **Phone:** 505/820-1000

Profile: Total return investor

Investment Portfolio: $ 500.0 - 999.0 million

Use: **Investment Purposes**
Hedge equity portfolio risk

Currencies: US dollar

Regions: United States

DERIVATIVES ACTIVITIES: **CAC Class: 1**

Structured Notes	Govt. agency MTNs CMT notes	Floaters Inverse floaters
Counterparty Rating Requirement:	<BBB	

OTHER ALTERNATIVE INVESTMENTS:

CMOs/REMICs – Govt. Repos/reverse repos

Davis Selected Advisers, L.P. – continued

KEY MANAGERS & DERIVATIVES SPECIALISTS:	**Direct Phone/Fax**	**Job Function**
Mr. Andrew A. Davis President	505/982-7116	President Portfolio Mgr – Structured Notes
Mr. B. Clark Stamper Executive Vice President		Chief Investment Officer

C.H. Dean Investment Associates

Investment Manager

Location: 2480 Kettering Tower
Dayton, OH 45423

Fax: 513/227-9313 **Phone:** 513/222-9531

Profile: Total return investor

Investment Portfolio: $ 5.9 billion

Use: **Investment Purposes**
Adjust portfolio duration
Hedge bond portfolio risk
Hedge interest rate risk

Currencies: US dollar

Regions: United States

DERIVATIVES ACTIVITIES: **CAC Class: 2**

Structured Notes	Corporate MTNs Govt. agency MTNs	Floaters Multi-step-up callable bonds

OTHER ALTERNATIVE INVESTMENTS:

	CMOs/REMICs – Govt.	CMOs/REMICs – Private

KEY MANAGERS & DERIVATIVES SPECIALISTS:	**Direct Phone/Fax**	**Job Function**
Mr. Dennis D. Dean President		President Chief Investment Officer
Mr. David Oda	Ext. 394	Fixed-Income Strategist Portfolio Mgr – Structured Notes

Dean Witter, Discover & Co.

Corporation

Location: Two World Trade Center
New York, NY 10048

Fax: 212/392-8405 **Phone:** 212/392-2222

Use: **Balance Sheet/Risk Management**
Hedge interest rate risk

Investment Purposes
Discretionary situations
Provide incremental return
Reduce variability of returns

Currencies: US dollar
French franc
German mark
Italian lira
Japanese yen
Swiss franc
UK pound

Regions: United States

Dean Witter, Discover & Co. – continued

DERIVATIVES ACTIVITIES:		**CAC Class: 8**
Exchange-traded Options & Futures	**Currency**	
OTC Derivatives	**Interest rate**	
Plain Vanilla Derivatives	Swaps	Forwards

KEY MANAGERS & DERIVATIVES SPECIALISTS:	**Direct Phone/Fax**	**Job Function**
Mr. Birenda Kumar S.V.P. & Treasurer		Treasurer
Mr. Thomas C. Schneider Exec. Vice President & C.F.O.		Chief Financial Officer Portfolio Mgr – Derivatives
Mr. Robert P. Seass S.V.P. & Controller		Treasurer

Dean Witter InterCapital Inc.

Mutual Fund Manager

Sub of Dean Witter, Discover & Co.

Location: Two World Trade Center
72nd Floor
New York, NY 10048

Fax: 212/392-4282 **Phone:** 212/392-1600

Profile: Current yield investor

Investment Portfolio: $ 70.0 billion

Use: **Investment Purposes**
Hedge currency risk

Currencies: Australian dollar, Belgian franc, Canadian dollar, ECU, French franc, German mark, Italian lira, Indonesian rupiah, Japanese yen, Mexican peso, Spanish peseta, Swiss franc, Thai baht, UK pound

Regions: United States, Canada, Europe, Latin America, Pacific Rim, Emerging mkts

DERIVATIVES ACTIVITIES:		**CAC Class: 5**
Exchange-traded Options & Futures	**Currency**	
Structured Notes	Floaters	Inverse floaters

OTHER ALTERNATIVE INVESTMENTS:		
	CMOs/REMICs – Govt.	Strips
	CMOs/REMICs – Private	Repos/reverse repos

KEY MANAGERS & DERIVATIVES SPECIALISTS:	**Direct Phone/Fax**	**Job Function**
Mr. Rajesh K. Gupta	212/392-1655 212/392-3836	Portfolio Mgr – Futures *Govt*
Mr. Konrad Krill	212/392-1818	Portfolio Mgr – Futures *Govt*
Mr. Joseph J. McAlinden Managing Director	212/392-0770	Chief Investment Officer Fixed-Income Strategist
Mr. James F. Willison Senior Vice President	212/392-1659	Bond Department Head

Delaware Management Company Inc.

Mutual Fund Manager

Sub of Lincoln National Corporation

Location: 2005 Market Street
One Commerce Square
Philadelphia, PA 19103

Fax: 215/988-1005 **Phone:** 215/988-1200

Profile: Total return investor

Investment Portfolio: $ 27.0 billion

Use: **Investment Purposes**
Alter portfolio weighting
Adjust portfolio duration
Asset allocation
Capture extra yield

Currencies: US dollar

Regions: United States

DERIVATIVES ACTIVITIES: **CAC Class: 3**

OTC Derivatives	**Bond**	
Plain Vanilla Derivatives	Swaps	
Structured Notes	Corporate MTNs Govt. agency MTNs	Floaters

OTHER ALTERNATIVE INVESTMENTS:

	CMOs/REMICs – Govt. CMOs/REMICs – Private	GICs Repos/reverse repos

KEY MANAGERS & DERIVATIVES SPECIALISTS:	**Direct Phone/Fax**	**Job Function**
Mr. Joseph Soprani	215/255-2984	Portfolio Mgr – Derivatives Portfolio Mgr – Options Portfolio Mgr – Structured Notes
Mr. Paul E. Suckow Senior Vice President	215/255-2310 215/988-1325	Chief Investment Officer Bond Department Head
Mr. Brian F. Wruble President & C.O.O.		President

Delphi Capital Management, Inc.

Insurance Co/Management

Sub of Delphi Financial Group

Location: 650 Madison Avenue
26th Floor
New York, NY 10022

Fax: 212/838-7598 **Phone:** 212/838-7000

Profile: Total return investor

Investment Portfolio: $ 2.0 billion

Use: **Investment Purposes**
Adjust portfolio duration
Hedge interest rate risk

Currencies: US dollar

Regions: United States

DERIVATIVES ACTIVITIES: **CAC Class: 5**

Exchange-traded Options & Futures U.S. Treasury futures	**Bond, Interest rate** U.S. Treasury options
OTC Derivatives **Plain Vanilla Derivatives**	**Bond, Interest rate** Swaps
Structured Notes	Govt agency MTNs

OTHER ALTERNATIVE INVESTMENTS:

Repos/reverse repos

KEY MANAGERS & DERIVATIVES SPECIALISTS:	**Direct Phone/Fax**	**Job Function**
Ms. Jane R. Dunlap Vice President & Treasurer	215/787-3942	Treasurer
Mr. Robert Ryan Manager of Trading		Trader – Derivatives Head Trader – Interest Rate Options *Govt* Trader – Interest Rate Futures *Govt*
Mr. Thomas A. Sullivan President		President Bond Department Head

Denver Investment Advisors Inc.

Investment Manager

Location: 1225 17th Street
26th Floor
Denver, CO 80202

Fax: 303/312-4900 **Phone:** 303/312-5000

Profile: Total return investor

Investment Portfolio: $9.0 billion

Use: **Investment Purposes**

Currencies: US dollar

Regions: United States

DERIVATIVES ACTIVITIES: **CAC Class: 5**

Structured Notes	Corporate MTNs	

OTHER ALTERNATIVE INVESTMENTS:

	CMOs/REMICs – Govt. GICs	Strips

KEY MANAGERS & DERIVATIVES SPECIALISTS:	**Direct Phone/Fax**	**Job Function**
Mr. Charles Anderson President	303/312-5050	President Chief Investment Officer
Mr. John R. Cormey Vice President	303/312-5060	Bond Department Head *Taxable*
Mr. Thomas B. Stevens Vice President	303/312-5062	Portfolio Mgr – Structured Notes

Deposit Guaranty Corp.

Bank Holding Company

Location: 210 East Capitol Street
Jackson, MS 39205

Fax: 601/354-8329 **Phone:** 601/354-8211

Use: **Balance Sheet/Risk Management**
Hedge balance sheet
Hedge interest rate risk

Investment Purposes

Currencies: US dollar

Regions: United States

DERIVATIVES ACTIVITIES: **CAC Class: 5**

OTC Derivatives **Plain Vanilla Derivatives**	**Interest rate** Swaps Forwards	 Caps
Counterparty Rating Requirement:	AAA	

KEY MANAGERS & DERIVATIVES SPECIALISTS:	**Direct Phone/Fax**	**Job Function**
Mr. Arlen L. McDonald E.V.P. & C.F.O.		Chief Financial Officer
Mr. Howard L. McMillan, Jr. President & C.O.O.		President

Deposit Guaranty National Bank (Portfolio)

Bank/Portfolio

Sub of Deposit Guaranty Corp.

Location: 210 East Capitol Street
Jackson, MS 39201

Fax: 601/354-8361 **Phone:** 601/354-8486

Profile: Total return investor

Investment Portfolio: $ 1.0 - 3.0 billion

Use:

Balance Sheet/Risk Management
Create synthetic fixed/floating rate
Hedge balance sheet
Hedge interest rate risk

Investment Purposes
Capture extra yield
Hedge bond portfolio risk
Hedge interest rate risk

Currencies: US dollar

Regions: United States

DERIVATIVES ACTIVITIES: **CAC Class: 4**

Exchange-traded Options & Futures	**Interest rate**	
U.S. Treasury futures		
OTC Derivatives	**Bond**	
Plain Vanilla Derivatives	Swaps	Floors
	Caps	
Structured Notes	Govt. agency MTNs	Multi-step-up callable bonds

OTHER ALTERNATIVE INVESTMENTS:

	CMOs/REMICs – Govt.	
	CMOs/REMICs – Private	Repos/reverse repos

KEY MANAGERS & DERIVATIVES SPECIALISTS:	**Direct Phone/Fax**	**Job Function**
Mr. Steve Blackwood A.V.P.-Derivatives	601/354-8016	Portfolio Mgr – Derivatives Portfolio Mgr – Futures
Mr. Joseph Powell Treasurer	601/354-8018	Portfolio Mgr – Derivatives
Mr. Timothy Stokes Assistant Vice President	601/354-8517	Portfolio Mgr – Derivatives Portfolio Mgr – Structured Notes
Mr. Raymond Thompson Senior Vice President	601/354-8494	Chief Investment Officer

Deposit Guaranty National Bank (Trust)

Bank/Trust

Sub of Deposit Guaranty Corp.

Location: 210 East Capitol Street
8th Floor
Jackson, MS 39201

Fax: 601/354-8143 **Phone:** 601/354-8128

Profile: Total return investor

Investment Portfolio: $ 1.3 billion

Use: **Investment Purposes**

Currencies: US dollar

Regions: United States

Deposit Guaranty National Bank (Trust) – continued

DERIVATIVES ACTIVITIES:		**CAC Class: Inactive**

OTHER ALTERNATIVE INVESTMENTS:		
	CMOs/REMICs – Govt. Strips	Repos/Reverse repos

KEY MANAGERS & DERIVATIVES SPECIALISTS:	Direct Phone/Fax	Job Function
Mr. Gerald L. White Senior Vice President	601/354-8129	Chief Investment Officer

Dewey Square Investors Corporation

Investment Manager

Sub of United Asset Management Corporation

Location: One Financial Center
24th Floor
Boston, MA 02111

Fax: 617/526-1337 **Phone:** 617/526-1300

Profile: Total return investor

Investment Portfolio: $ 3.4 billion

Use: **Investment Purposes**

Currencies: US dollar

Regions: United States

DERIVATIVES ACTIVITIES:		**CAC Class: Inactive**

OTHER ALTERNATIVE INVESTMENTS:		
	CMOs/REMICs – Govt.	Repos/reverse repos

KEY MANAGERS & DERIVATIVES SPECIALISTS:	Direct Phone/Fax	Job Function
Mr. Peter M. Whitman, Jr. President	617/434-6229	President Chief Investment Officer

The Dime Savings Bank of New York, FSB

Savings Bank/Bldg Society

Sub of Dime Bancorp

Location: 589 Fifth Avenue
2nd Floor
New York, NY 10017

Fax: 212/326-6907 **Phone:** 212/326-6912

Profile: Spread investor

Investment Portfolio: $ 4.0 - 10.0 billion

Use: **Balance Sheet/Risk Management**
Create synthetic fixed/floating rate
Hedge interest rate risk

Currencies: US dollar

Regions: United States

DERIVATIVES ACTIVITIES: **CAC Class: 7**

Exchange-traded Options & Futures	**Interest rate**	
U.S. Treasury futures	U.S. Treasury options	
OTC Derivatives	**Interest rate**	
Plain Vanilla Derivatives	Swaps	Floors
	Caps	
Counterparty Rating Requirement:	AA	

OTHER ALTERNATIVE INVESTMENTS:

CMOs/REMICs – Govt.	Strips
CMOs/REMICs – Private	Repos/reverse repos

KEY MANAGERS & DERIVATIVES SPECIALISTS:	**Direct Phone/Fax**	**Job Function**
Mr. James Daras Treasurer	212/326-6912	Chief Investment Officer Treasurer Portfolio Mgr – Derivatives Portfolio Mgr – Futures Portfolio Mgr – Options
Mr. Ken Schmidt V.P. & Senior Trader	212/326-6951	Trader – Derivatives Trader – Futures

Dimensional Fund Advisors, Inc.

Investment Manager

Location: 1299 Ocean Avenue
11th Floor
Santa Monica, CA 90401-1038

Fax: 310/395-6140 **Phone:** 310/395-8005

Profile: Total return investor

Investment Portfolio: $ 12.0 billion

Use: **Balance Sheet/Risk Management**
Hedge currency risk
Hedge overseas investments

Currencies: US dollar, Australian dollar, Japanese yen, UK pound

Regions: United States, Europe, Pacific Rim

Dimensional Fund Advisors, Inc. – continued

DERIVATIVES ACTIVITIES:

OTC Derivatives **Plain Vanilla Derivatives**	**Currency** Forwards
Structured Notes	Corporate MTNs
Counterparty Rating Requirement:	AA

OTHER ALTERNATIVE INVESTMENTS:

CMOs/REMICs – Govt. CMOs/REMICs – Private	Repos/reverse repos

KEY MANAGERS & DERIVATIVES SPECIALISTS:	**Direct Phone/Fax**	**Job Function**
Ms. Judith Jonas	310/395-7603	Portfolio Mgr – Derivatives Portfolio Mgr – Structured Notes
Mr. Rex A. Sinquefield Chairman & C.I.O.		Chief Investment Officer

Dodge & Cox Inc.

Investment Manager

Location: One Sansome Street
35th Floor
San Francisco, CA 94104

Fax: 415/986-5471 **Phone:** 415/981-1710

Profile: Total return investor

Investment Portfolio: $ 14.9 billion

Use: **Investment Purposes**

Currencies: US dollar

Regions: United States

DERIVATIVES ACTIVITIES: **CAC Class: Inactive**

OTHER ALTERNATIVE INVESTMENTS:

CMOs/REMICs – Govt.

KEY MANAGERS & DERIVATIVES SPECIALISTS:	**Direct Phone/Fax**	**Job Function**
Mr. John A. Gunn President		President Chief Investment Officer

Dominion Resources, Inc.

Corporation

Location: Riverfront Plaza West
901 East Byrd Street Suite 1700
Richmond, VA 23219

Fax: 804/775-5819 **Phone:** 804/775-5700

Use: **Balance Sheet/Risk Management**
Create synthetic fixed/floating rate
Hedge interest rate risk
Lower transaction costs

Currencies: US dollar

Regions: United States

DERIVATIVES ACTIVITIES:

OTC Derivatives	**Interest rate**	
Plain Vanilla Derivatives	Swaps	Caps
Counterparty Rating Requirement:	A	

KEY MANAGERS & DERIVATIVES SPECIALISTS:	**Direct Phone/Fax**	**Job Function**
Mr. Thomas E. Capps Chairman, President & C.E.O.	804/775-5811	President
Mr. Linwood R. Robertson Vice President & Treasurer	804/775-5895	Treasurer Portfolio Mgr – Derivatives

Dow Jones & Company, Inc.

Corporation

Location: World Financial Center
200 Liberty Street
New York, NY 10281

Fax: 212/416-2655 **Phone:** 212/416-2000

Use: **Balance Sheet/Risk Management**
Hedge currency risk
Protect currency gains

Currencies: US dollar, Canadian dollar, Japanese yen, UK pound

Regions: United States

DERIVATIVES ACTIVITIES: **CAC Class: 3**

OTC Derivatives	**Currency**	
Plain Vanilla Derivatives	Swaps	Forwards
Counterparty Rating Requirement:	AAA	

KEY MANAGERS & DERIVATIVES SPECIALISTS:	**Direct Phone/Fax**	**Job Function**
Mr. Kenneth L. Burenga President & C.O.O.		President
Mr. Leonard E. Doherty Treasurer & Asst. Secretary		Treasurer Portfolio Mgr – Derivatives
Mr. Kevin J. Roche V.P. - Finance & C.F.O.		Chief Financial Officer

The Dreyfus Corporation

Mutual Fund Manager

Sub of Mellon Bank Corporation

Location: 200 Park Avenue
55th Floor
New York, NY 10166

Fax: 212/922-6076 **Phone:** 212/922-6000

Profile: Total return investor

Investment Portfolio: $ 73.0 billion

Use: **Balance Sheet/Risk Management**
Hedge currency risk

Investment Purposes
Asset allocation
Hedge bond portfolio risk
Hedge currency risk
Hedge equity portfolio risk
Hedge interest rate risk

Currencies: US dollar
Japanese yen

Regions: United States

DERIVATIVES ACTIVITIES: **CAC Class: 7**

Exchange-traded Options & Futures U.S. Treasury futures	**Bond, Currency**	
OTC Derivatives **Plain Vanilla Derivatives**	**Currency, Interest rate** Swaps	Forwards
Exotic Derivatives	Bond index swaps	
Structured Notes	Inverse floaters	
Counterparty Rating Requirement:	AA	

OTHER ALTERNATIVE INVESTMENTS:

	CMOs/REMICs – Govt. Strips	Repos/reverse repos

KEY MANAGERS & DERIVATIVES SPECIALISTS:	**Direct Phone/Fax**	**Job Function**
Mr. Stephen E. Canter Chairman	212/922-6360	Chief Investment Officer
Mr. Christopher M. Condron Chairman & President		President
Mr. Kevin M. McClintock Managing Director		Bond Department Head
Mr. Gerald E. Thunelius Portfolio Manager	212/922-6496	Portfolio Mgr – Derivatives
Mr. David Zagorski Portfolio Manager	212/922-6207	Portfolio Mgr – Derivatives

Dreyfus Management

Investment Manager

Sub of Mellon Bank Corporation

Location: 200 Park Avenue
New York, NY 10166

Fax: 212/715-6014 **Phone:** 212/922-6000

Profile: Total return investor

Investment Portfolio: $ 1.3 billion

Use: **Investment Purposes**

Currencies: US dollar

Regions: United States

DERIVATIVES ACTIVITIES: **CAC Class: Inactive**

OTHER ALTERNATIVE INVESTMENTS:

CMOs/REMICs – Govt. CMOs/REMICs – Private

KEY MANAGERS & DERIVATIVES SPECIALISTS:	**Direct Phone/Fax**	**Job Function**
Mr. Dean Lewallen	212/922-6239	Chief Investment Officer

Duke Power Company

Corporation

Location: 422 South Church Street
Charlotte, NC 28242-0001

Fax: 704/382-7363 **Phone:** 704/594-9400

Use: **Balance Sheet/Risk Management**
Create synthetic fixed/floating rate
Hedge balance sheet
Hedge interest rate risk
Lower transaction costs
Strategic liability management

Currencies: US dollar

Regions: United States

DERIVATIVES ACTIVITIES:

OTC Derivatives
Plain Vanilla Derivatives

Interest rate
Swaps
Caps
Floors
Collars

Counterparty Rating Requirement: A

KEY MANAGERS & DERIVATIVES SPECIALISTS:	**Direct Phone/Fax**	**Job Function**
Ms. Sue A. Becht Treasurer	704/382-8695	Treasurer Portfolio Mgr – Derivatives
Mr. Stephen G. DeMay Financial Analyst	704/382-2620	Portfolio Mgr – Derivatives
Mr. William H. Grigg Chairman, President & C.E.O.	704/382-7535	President
Mr. Richard J. Osborne Vice President & C.F.O.	704/382-5159	Chief Financial Officer

Eagle Asset Management, Inc.

Broker/Management Sub

Sub of Raymond James Financial Inc.

Location: 880 Carillon Parkway
St. Petersburg, FL 33716

Fax: 813/573-8325 **Phone:** 813/573-2453

Profile: Total return investor

Investment Portfolio: $ 4.3 billion

Use: **Investment Purposes**

Currencies: US dollar

Regions: United States

DERIVATIVES ACTIVITIES: **CAC Class: Inactive**

OTHER ALTERNATIVE INVESTMENTS:

CMOs/REMICs – Govt. Strips

KEY MANAGERS & DERIVATIVES SPECIALISTS:	**Direct Phone/Fax**	**Job Function**
Mr. Kenneth Corba		Chief Investment Officer

Eastbridge Capital, Inc.

Investment Manager

Sub of Nippon Credit Bank of Japan

Location: 135 East 57th Street
14th Floor
New York, NY 10022

Fax: 212/756-7270 **Phone:** 212/756-7200

Profile: Total return investor

Investment Portfolio: $ 1.0 - 3.0 billion

Use: **Investment Purposes**
Hedge bond portfolio risk
Hedge currency risk
Hedge interest rate risk

Currencies: US dollar, Canadian dollar, French franc, German mark, Italian lira, Japanese yen, UK pound

Regions: United States

DERIVATIVES ACTIVITIES: **CAC Class: 5**

Exchange-traded Options & Futures
U.S. Treasury futures

Bond, Currency, Interest rate
U.S. Treasury options

OTHER ALTERNATIVE INVESTMENTS:

CMOs/REMICs – Govt. Repos/reverse repos
GICs

Eastbridge Capital, Inc. – continued

KEY MANAGERS & DERIVATIVES SPECIALISTS:	Direct Phone/Fax	Job Function
Mr. Paul R. DeRosa Managing Director		Chief Investment Officer
Mr. Arthur E. Gandolfi		Chief Investment Officer
Mr. Walter G. Kirkland Vice President	212/756-7263	Portfolio Mgr – Futures Portfolio Mgr – Options
Mr. Michael Zazzarino	212/756-7264 212/756-7160	Portfolio Mgr – Futures Portfolio Mgr – Options

Eaton Corporation

Corporation

Location: Eaton Center
Cleveland, OH 44114-2584

Fax: 216/523-4787 **Phone:** 216/523-5000

Use:

Balance Sheet/Risk Management
Hedge currency risk
Hedge interest rate risk
Hedge overseas investments
Protect currency gains
Strategic liability management

Investment Purposes
Provide incremental return

Currencies: US dollar, Canadian dollar, French franc, German mark, Italian lira, Japanese yen, Mexican peso, Spanish peseta, Swiss franc, UK pound

Regions: United States, Canada, Europe, Latin America, Pacific Rim

DERIVATIVES ACTIVITIES:

Exchange-traded Options & Futures	**Currency**	
OTC Derivatives **Plain Vanilla Derivatives**	**Currency, Interest rate** Swaps Forwards	 Caps
Counterparty Rating Requirement:	A	

KEY MANAGERS & DERIVATIVES SPECIALISTS:	Direct Phone/Fax	Job Function
Mr. John M. Carmont Vice President & Treasurer		Treasurer Portfolio Mgr – Derivatives Portfolio Mgr – Options
Mr. Stephen R. Hardis Vice Chairman & C.F.O.		Chief Financial Officer
Mr. John S. Rodewig President		President

Eaton Vance Management, Inc.

Mutual Fund Manager

Sub of Eaton Vance Corporation

Location: 24 Federal Street
Boston, MA 02110

Fax: 617/451-0642 **Phone:** 617/482-8260

Profile: Total return investor

Investment Portfolio: $ 16.7 billion

Use: **Investment Purposes**
Hedge bond portfolio risk
Hedge interest rate risk

Currencies: US dollar

Regions: United States

DERIVATIVES ACTIVITIES:

Exchange-traded Options & Futures U.S. Treasury futures	**Bond, Currency, Interest rate**	
Structured Notes	Inverse floaters	Tender options bonds

OTHER ALTERNATIVE INVESTMENTS:

	CMOs/REMICs – Govt. GICs	Repos/reverse repos

KEY MANAGERS & DERIVATIVES SPECIALISTS:	**Direct Phone/Fax**	**Job Function**
Mr. M. Dozier Gardner President		President
Mr. Peter Kiely Director - Research		Chief Investment Officer
Mr. Mark S. Venezia Vice President	Ext. 563 617/482-1572	Portfolio Mgr – Futures

Ecolab Inc.

Corporation

Location: Ecolab Center
St. Paul, MN 55102-1390

Fax: 612/293-2471 **Phone:** 612/293-2233

Use: **Balance Sheet/Risk Management**
Hedge currency risk

Currencies: US dollar German mark

Regions: United States
Europe

DERIVATIVES ACTIVITIES: **CAC Class: 3**

OTC Derivatives **Plain Vanilla Derivatives**	**Currency** Forwards

Ecolab Inc. – continued

KEY MANAGERS & DERIVATIVES SPECIALISTS:	Direct Phone/Fax	Job Function
Mr. Steven L. Fritze Vice President & Treasurer		Treasurer Portfolio Mgr – Derivatives
Mr. Allan L. Schuman President & C.E.O.		President
Mr. Michael E. Shannon Vice Chairman, C.F.O. & C.A.O.		Chief Financial Officer

Employers Reinsurance Corporation

Insurance Co/P & C

Sub of General Electric Company

Location: 5200 Metcalf Avenue
4th Floor
Overland Park, KS 66202

Fax: 913/676-5221 **Phone:** 913/676-5200

Profile: Total return investor

Investment Portfolio: $ 4.9 billion

Use: **Balance Sheet/Risk Management**
Incremental return
Strategic liability management

Investment Purposes
Alter portfolio weighting
Adjust portfolio duration
Hedge equity portfolio risk
Provide incremental return

Currencies: US dollar

Regions: United States

DERIVATIVES ACTIVITIES: **CAC Class: 2**

Structured Notes	Floaters	Inverse floaters

OTHER ALTERNATIVE INVESTMENTS:

	CMOs/REMICs – Govt. Strips	Repos/reverse repos

KEY MANAGERS & DERIVATIVES SPECIALISTS:	Direct Phone/Fax	Job Function
Mr. Charles E. Heath Vice President	913/676-5445	Chief Investment Officer
Mr. Bradley Smith Assistant Vice President		Portfolio Mgr – Futures Portfolio Mgr – Structured Notes

Enhance Financial Services Group Inc.

Insurance Co/Management

Sub of GE Capital Company

Location: 335 Madison Avenue
25th Floor
New York, NY 10017-4605

Fax: 212/682-5377 **Phone:** 212/983-3100

Profile: Total return investor

Investment Portfolio: $ 655.2 million

Use: **Balance Sheet/Risk Management**
Create synthetic fixed/floating rate
Strategic liability management

Currencies: US dollar

Regions: United States

DERIVATIVES ACTIVITIES:

CAC Class: 2

OTC Derivatives **Plain Vanilla Derivatives**	**Interest rate** Swaps
Counterparty Rating Requirement:	AAA

OTHER ALTERNATIVE INVESTMENTS:

CMOs/REMICs – Govt.

KEY MANAGERS & DERIVATIVES SPECIALISTS:	**Direct Phone/Fax**	**Job Function**
Mr. Daniel Gross President & C.E.O.		President
Mr. Richard S. O'Connell, Jr. Senior Vice President		Chief Investment Officer Portfolio Mgr – Derivatives
Mr. Robert M. Rosenberg Exec. Vice President & C.F.O.		Chief Financial Officer

Equifax, Inc.

Corporation

Location: 1600 Peachtree Street, N.W.
Atlanta, GA 30309

Fax: 404/885-5452 **Phone:** 404/885-8000

Use: **Balance Sheet/Risk Management**
Hedge currency risk
Hedge interest rate risk

Currencies: US dollar, Canadian dollar, UK pound

Regions: United States, Europe

DERIVATIVES ACTIVITIES:

OTC Derivatives **Plain Vanilla Derivatives**	**Currency, Interest rate** Swaps
Counterparty Rating Requirement:	None

Equifax, Inc. – continued

KEY MANAGERS & DERIVATIVES SPECIALISTS:	Direct Phone/Fax	Job Function
Mr. Donald U. Hallman Senior Vice President & C.F.O.		Chief Financial Officer
Mr. R. F. Haygood Treasurer		Treasurer Portfolio Mgr – Derivatives
Mr. Daniel W. McGlaughlin President & C.O.O.		President
Mr. Wayne P. Weitz Director - Corporate Finance	404/885-8575 404/885-8121	Portfolio Mgr – Derivatives

The Equitable Companies Incorporated

Corporation

Sub of AXA S.A.

Location: 787 Seventh Avenue
New York, NY 10019-1743

Fax: 212/554-2320 **Phone:** 212/554-1234

Use:

Balance Sheet/Risk Management
Hedge balance sheet
Hedge currency risk
Hedge interest rate risk
Incremental return
Strategic liability management

Investment Purposes
Hedge bond portfolio risk
Hedge currency risk
Hedge equity portfolio risk
Hedge interest rate risk
Provide incremental return

Currencies: US dollar, Canadian dollar, French franc, German mark, UK pound

Regions: United States

DERIVATIVES ACTIVITIES: **CAC Class: 6**

OTC Derivatives **Plain Vanilla Derivatives**	**Interest rate** Swaps
Counterparty Rating Requirement:	AA

KEY MANAGERS & DERIVATIVES SPECIALISTS:	Direct Phone/Fax	Job Function
Mr. Jerry M. de St. Paer Exec. Vice President & C.F.O.		Chief Financial Officer
Mr. Joseph J. Melone President & C.E.O.		President
Mr. Peter D. Norris Executive Vice President		Chief Investment Officer
Mr. Brian S. O'Neil Exec. Vice President & C.I.O.		Portfolio Mgr – Derivatives

Equitable Investment Services, Inc.

Insurance Co/P & C

Sub of Equitable of Iowa Companies

Location: 699 Walnut Street
Hub Tower 20th Floor
Des Moines, IA 50309

Fax: 515/282-9538 **Phone:** 515/282-0323

Profile: Total return investor

Investment Portfolio: $ 6.0 billion

Use: **Investment Purposes**

Currencies: US dollar

Regions: United States

DERIVATIVES ACTIVITIES: **CAC Class: Inactive**

OTHER ALTERNATIVE INVESTMENTS:

CMOs/REMICs – Govt. CMOs/REMICs – Private

KEY MANAGERS & DERIVATIVES SPECIALISTS:	**Direct Phone/Fax**	**Job Function**
Mr. Paul R. Schlaack President & C.E.O.		President Chief Investment Officer

Erie Insurance Group

Insurance Co/P & C

Location: 100 Erie Insurance Place
Erie, PA 16530

Fax: 814/870-3126 **Phone:** 814/870-2000

Profile: Hold to maturity investor

Investment Portfolio: $ 4.1 billion

Use: **Investment Purposes**

Currencies: US dollar

Regions: United States

DERIVATIVES ACTIVITIES: **CAC Class: 2**

Structured Notes

Corporate MTNs
Govt. agency MTNs

Index amortizing notes

OTHER ALTERNATIVE INVESTMENTS:

CMOs/REMICs – Govt. CMOs/REMICs – Private

KEY MANAGERS & DERIVATIVES SPECIALISTS:	**Direct Phone/Fax**	**Job Function**
Mr. Mark Borowy	814/870-3197	Portfolio Mgr – Structured Notes
Ms. Laurie Hirt	814/870-2098	Research Analyst - Derivatives
Mr. Douglas F. Ziegler Sr. Vice President & Treasurer	814/870-2038	Chief Investment Officer

Evangelical Lutheran Church-Board of Pensions

Foundation/Endowment

Location: 800 Marquette Avenue
Suite 1050
Minneapolis, MN 55402

Fax: 612/334-5307 **Phone:** 612/333-7651

Profile: Total return investor

Investment Portfolio: $ 2.0 billion

Use:

Balance Sheet/Risk Management
Hedge commercial paper
Hedge interest rate risk
Incremental return
Strategic liability management

Investment Purposes
Alter portfolio weighting
Adjust portfolio duration
Capture extra yield
Diversify portfolio
Enter new mkts/lower risk
Hedge bond portfolio risk
Hedge interest rate risk
Provide incremental return
Reduce variability of returns

Currencies: US dollar

Regions: United States

DERIVATIVES ACTIVITIES: **CAC Class: 3**

OTC Derivatives **Plain Vanilla Derivatives**	**Bond** Forwards	
Structured Notes	Corporate MTNs Govt. agency MTNs	Floaters Inverse floaters
Counterparty Rating Requirement:	AAA	

OTHER ALTERNATIVE INVESTMENTS:

CMOs/REMICs – Govt.	Strips
CMOs/REMICs – Private	Repos/reverse repos

KEY MANAGERS & DERIVATIVES SPECIALISTS:	**Direct Phone/Fax**	**Job Function**
Ms. Lynne Gehling	612/334-5358	Portfolio Mgr – Structured Notes
Mr. Mark Haney		Portfolio Mgr – Derivatives Portfolio Mgr – Structured Notes
Mr. John Kapanke President		President Chief Investment Officer

Evergreen Asset Management Corp. (New York)

Mutual Fund Manager

Sub of First Union National Bank of North Carolina - Funds Mgmt.

Location: 2500 Westchester Avenue
4th Floor
Purchase, NY 10577-2555

Fax: 914/641-2279 **Phone:** 914/694-2020

Profile: Total return investor

Investment Portfolio: $ 3.6 billion

Use: **Investment Purposes**

Currencies: US dollar

Regions: United States

Evergreen Asset Management Corp. (New York) – continued

DERIVATIVES ACTIVITIES: **CAC Class: Inactive**

OTHER ALTERNATIVE INVESTMENTS:

CMOs/REMICs – Govt. CMOs/REMICs – Private

KEY MANAGERS & DERIVATIVES SPECIALISTS:	Direct Phone/Fax	Job Function
Ms. Nola M. Falcone President & Co-C.E.O.		President
Mr. Stephen A. Lieber Chairman & Co-C.E.O.		Chief Investment Officer

Evergreen Asset Management, Inc. (Washington)

Investment Manager

Location: 1301 Fifth Avenue
Suite 3634
Seattle, WA 98101

Fax: 206/382-0950 **Phone:** 206/224-9914

Profile: Total return investor

Investment Portfolio: $ 500.0 - 999.0 million

Use: **Investment Purposes**

Currencies: US dollar

Regions: United States

DERIVATIVES ACTIVITIES: **CAC Class: Inactive**

OTHER ALTERNATIVE INVESTMENTS:

CMOs/REMICs – Govt.

KEY MANAGERS & DERIVATIVES SPECIALISTS:	Direct Phone/Fax	Job Function
Ms. Elana D. Russell Chief Executive Officer		Chief Investment Officer

Exxon Corporation

Corporation

Location: 5959 Las Colinas Boulevard
Irving, TX 75039-2298

Fax: 214/444-1348 **Phone:** 214/444-1000

Profile: Hold to maturity investor

Investment Portfolio: $ 500.0 - 999.0 million

Use:

Balance Sheet/Risk Management
Hedge balance sheet
Hedge currency risk
Hedge interest rate risk
Protect currency gains

Investment Purposes
Capture extra yield
Hedge bond portfolio risk
Hedge currency risk
Hedge interest rate risk
Protect currency gains

Currencies: US dollar
French franc
German mark
Japanese yen
Swiss franc

Regions: United States

Exxon Corporation – continued

DERIVATIVES ACTIVITIES:		**CAC Class: 7**
OTC Derivatives	**Currency, Interest rate**	
Plain Vanilla Derivatives	Swaps	
Counterparty Rating Requirement:	AA	

OTHER ALTERNATIVE INVESTMENTS:

CMOs/REMICs – Govt.

KEY MANAGERS & DERIVATIVES SPECIALISTS:	Direct Phone/Fax	Job Function
Mr. James E. Bayne Manager-Benefits, Fin. & Invt.	214/444-1574	Chief Investment Officer Portfolio Mgr – Derivatives Portfolio Mgr – Futures Portfolio Mgr – Options
Mr. E.A. Robinson Vice President & Treasurer		Treasurer

Falcon Asset Management, Inc.

Insurance Co/Management

Sub of USF&G Corp.

Location: 100 Light Street
22nd Floor
Baltimore, MD 21202

Fax: 410/547-3582 **Phone:** 410/547-3660

Profile: Current yield investor

Investment Portfolio: $ 11.0 - 20.0 billion

Use: **Investment Purposes**
Diversify portfolio

Currencies: US dollar

Regions: United States

DERIVATIVES ACTIVITIES:	
Structured Notes	Corporate MTNs

OTHER ALTERNATIVE INVESTMENTS:

CMOs/REMICs – Govt.

KEY MANAGERS & DERIVATIVES SPECIALISTS:	Direct Phone/Fax	Job Function
Mr. Joseph Carwile Assistant Vice President	410/547-3542	Portfolio Mgr – Structured Notes
Mr. Geoffrey C. Getman Senior Vice President	410/547-3398 410/234-2365	Bond Department Head Portfolio Mgr – Structured Notes
Mr. Michael Sollott	410/547-3545	Portfolio Mgr – Structured Notes
Mr. John Sweeney Senior Vice President	410/547-3662	Chief Investment Officer

Farmers Insurance Group of Companies

Insurance Co/P & C

Sub of BAT Industries p.l.c.

Location: 4680 Wilshire Boulevard
Los Angeles, CA 90010

Fax: 213/930-3101 **Phone:** 213/932-3200

Profile: Total return investor

Investment Portfolio: $ 11.0 - 20.0 billion

Use: **Balance Sheet/Risk Management**
Access global mkts
Create synthetic fixed/floating rate
Hedge balance sheet
Hedge currency risk
Protect currency gains

Currencies: US dollar, French franc, German mark, Italian lira, Japanese yen, Spanish peseta, Swiss franc, UK pound

Regions: United States, Canada, Europe, Pacific Rim

DERIVATIVES ACTIVITIES: **CAC Class: 2**

Exchange-traded Options & Futures	**Currency**	
OTC Derivatives	**Currency**	
Plain Vanilla Derivatives	Swaps	Forwards
Structured Notes	Corporate MTNs Bond index notes Index amortizing notes	CMT notes Floaters Multi-step-up callable bonds
Counterparty Rating Requirement:	AAA	

OTHER ALTERNATIVE INVESTMENTS:

CMOs/REMICs – Govt.	Strips
CMOs/REMICs – Private	

KEY MANAGERS & DERIVATIVES SPECIALISTS:	**Direct Phone/Fax**	**Job Function**
Mr. Michael A. Hart	213/932-3565 213/549-4410	Portfolio Mgr – Derivatives Portfolio Mgr – Futures Portfolio Mgr – Structured Notes
Mr. Laszlo Heredy Vice President	213/932-3061	Chief Investment Officer
Mr. Reed Nuttall Securities Analyst	213/932-3213	Portfolio Mgr – Derivatives Portfolio Mgr – Options Portfolio Mgr – Structured Notes
Mr. Paul Secord		Chief Investment Officer

Federal Home Loan Bank of Atlanta

Bank/Government

Location: 1475 Peachtree Street, N.E.
Atlanta, GA 30309

Fax: 404/897-1846 **Phone:** 404/888-8000

Profile: Spread investor

Investment Portfolio: $ 8.6 billion

Use: **Balance Sheet/Risk Management**
Create synthetic fixed/floating rate
Hedge balance sheet
Hedge interest rate risk

Currencies: US dollar, Canadian dollar, French franc, German mark, Swiss franc, UK pound

Regions: United States, Canada, Europe

DERIVATIVES ACTIVITIES: **CAC Class: 7**

OTC Derivatives **Plain Vanilla Derivatives**	**Interest rate** Swaps Forwards Swaptions	 Caps Floors
Structured Notes	Govt. agency MTNs Bond index notes Index amortizing notes	Inverse floaters Multi-step-up callable bonds
Counterparty Rating Requirement:	AA	

OTHER ALTERNATIVE INVESTMENTS:

Repos/reverse repos

KEY MANAGERS & DERIVATIVES SPECIALISTS:	**Direct Phone/Fax**	**Job Function**
Mr. D. Haddon Foster II V.P. & Mgr-Invest. Portfolio	404/888-8183	Portfolio Mgr – Derivatives Portfolio Mgr – Structured Notes Trader – Derivatives Trader – Structured Investments
Mr. Gary A. Glass S.V.P. & Treasurer	404/888-8181	Treasurer Portfolio Mgr – Derivatives Portfolio Mgr – Structured Notes
Mr. Andrew B. Mills V.P.-Investment Svcs & Systems	404/888-8187	Portfolio Mgr – Derivatives Portfolio Mgr – Structured Notes Trader – Derivatives Trader – Structured Investments

Federal Home Loan Bank of Boston

Bank/Government

Location: One Financial Center
Boston, MA 02111

Fax: 617/292-9645 **Phone:** 617/542-0150

Profile: Total return investor

Investment Portfolio: $ 4.0 - 10.0 billion

Use: **Balance Sheet/Risk Management**
Hedge balance sheet
Hedge interest rate risk
Strategic liability management

Currencies: US dollar

Regions: United States

DERIVATIVES ACTIVITIES: **CAC Class: 6**

Exchange-traded Options & Futures U.S. Treasury futures	**Bond** U.S. Treasury options	
OTC Derivatives **Plain Vanilla Derivatives**	**Bond, Interest rate** Swaps Forwards	 Caps
Structured Notes	Govt. agency MTNs Bond index notes Index amortizing notes CMT notes	Floaters Inverse floaters Periodic capped floaters Multi-step-up callable bonds
Counterparty Rating Requirement:	None	

OTHER ALTERNATIVE INVESTMENTS:

CMOs/REMICs – Govt. Repos/reverse repos

KEY MANAGERS & DERIVATIVES SPECIALISTS:	**Direct Phone/Fax**	**Job Function**
Mr. Nicholas Lang Investments Officer		Portfolio Mgr – Derivatives Portfolio Mgr – Futures Portfolio Mgr – Options Portfolio Mgr – Structured Notes
Mr. Robert C. Simmons		Chief Investment Officer

Federal Home Loan Bank of Chicago

Bank/Government

Location: 111 East Wacker Drive
Suite 700
Chicago, IL 60601

Fax: 312/565-5823 **Phone:** 312/565-5700

Profile: Hold to maturity investor

Investment Portfolio: $ 10.0 billion

Use: **Balance Sheet/Risk Management**
Create synthetic fixed/floating rate
Hedge balance sheet
Hedge interest rate risk
Strategic liability management

Investment Purposes
Hedge interest rate risk

Currencies: US dollar

Regions: United States, Europe, Pacific Rim

Federal Home Loan Bank of Chicago – continued

DERIVATIVES ACTIVITIES:		CAC Class: 8
OTC Derivatives	**Interest rate**	
Plain Vanilla Derivatives	Swaps Caps	Floors
Structured Notes	Govt. agency MTNs Bond index notes Index amortizing notes CMT notes	Floaters Inverse floaters Periodic capped floaters Multi-step-up callable bonds
Counterparty Rating Requirement:	A	

OTHER ALTERNATIVE INVESTMENTS:		
	CMOs/REMICs – Govt. CMOs/REMICs – Private	Repos/reverse repos

KEY MANAGERS & DERIVATIVES SPECIALISTS:	Direct Phone/Fax	Job Function
Mr. William D. Miller Vice President-Capital Markets	312/565-6924	Trader – Derivatives
Mr. Michael Moore	312/565-5797	Chief Investment Officer Bond Department Head *Govt, MBS*

Federal Home Loan Bank of San Francisco

Bank/Government

Location: 600 California Street
San Francisco, CA 94108

Fax: 415/616-2626 **Phone:** 415/616-1000

Profile: Spread investor

Investment Portfolio: $ 5.0 billion

Use: **Balance Sheet/Risk Management**
Create synthetic fixed/floating rate
Hedge balance sheet
Hedge interest rate risk

Currencies: US dollar

Regions: United States

DERIVATIVES ACTIVITIES:		CAC Class: 8
Exchange-traded Options & Futures	**Interest rate**	
U.S. Treasury futures	U.S. Treasury options	
OTC Derivatives	**Interest rate**	
Plain Vanilla Derivatives	Swaps Caps	Floors
Structured Notes	Govt. agency MTNs Bond index notes	Inverse floaters
Counterparty Rating Requirement:	AA	

OTHER ALTERNATIVE INVESTMENTS:		
	Repos/reverse repos	

Federal Home Loan Bank of San Francisco – continued

KEY MANAGERS & DERIVATIVES SPECIALISTS:	**Direct Phone/Fax**	**Job Function**
Mr. Steven T. Honda S.V.P. & C.F.O.		Chief Financial Officer
Mr. David A. O'Brien Vice President & Treasurer	415/616-2570	Treasurer Portfolio Mgr – Derivatives Portfolio Mgr – Futures Portfolio Mgr – Options Portfolio Mgr – Structured Notes
Mr. Stephen Traynor Assistant Treasurer		Trader – Derivatives Trader – Futures Trader – Options

Federal Home Loan Bank of Seattle

Bank/Government

Location: 1501 Fourth Avenue
Seattle, WA 98101

Fax: 206/340-2485 **Phone:** 206/340-2300

Profile: Hold to maturity investor

Investment Portfolio: $ 18.2 billion

Use: **Balance Sheet/Risk Management**
Create synthetic fixed/floating rate
Hedge interest rate risk
Strategic liability management

Currencies: US dollar

Regions: United States

DERIVATIVES ACTIVITIES:		**CAC Class: 7**
Exchange-traded Options & Futures U.S. Treasury futures	**Interest rate** U.S. Treasury options	
OTC Derivatives **Plain Vanilla Derivatives**	**Interest rate** Swaps Swaptions Caps	 Floors Collars
Exotic Derivatives	CMT swaps Index amortizing swaps	Index extendible swaps Periodic caps/floors
Structured Notes	Govt. agency MTNs Bond index notes Index amortizing notes CMT notes	Floaters Inverse floaters Periodic capped floaters Multi-step-up callable bonds
Counterparty Rating Requirement:	A	

OTHER ALTERNATIVE INVESTMENTS:

Repos/reverse repos

Federal Home Loan Bank of Seattle – continued

KEY MANAGERS & DERIVATIVES SPECIALISTS:	Direct Phone/Fax	Job Function
Ms. Kelli L. Bono Vice President & Treasurer		Treasurer
Ms. Margarita M. Seeley Assistant Vice President		Chief Investment Officer Portfolio Mgr – Derivatives Portfolio Mgr – Futures Portfolio Mgr – Structured Notes

Federal Home Loan Bank of Topeka

Bank/Government

Location: Two Townsite Plaza
2nd Floor
Topeka, KS 66603

Fax: 913/234-1796 **Phone:** 913/233-0507

Profile: Hold to maturity investor

Investment Portfolio: $ 6.7 billion

Use:

Balance Sheet/Risk Management
Hedge balance sheet
Hedge commercial paper
Hedge currency risk
Hedge interest rate risk

Investment Purposes
Hedge bond portfolio risk
Hedge currency risk
Hedge interest rate risk

Currencies: US dollar, German mark, Japanese yen

Regions: United States

DERIVATIVES ACTIVITIES: **CAC Class: 7**

Exchange-traded Options & Futures U.S. Treasury futures	**Bond, Interest rate** U.S. Treasury options	
OTC Derivatives **Plain Vanilla Derivatives**	**Bond, Interest rate** Swaps Forwards Swaptions	 Caps Floors Collars
Structured Notes	Govt. agency MTNs Bond index notes Index amortizing notes CMT notes Floaters	Inverse floaters Periodic capped floaters Tender options bonds Multi-step-up callable bonds
Counterparty Rating Requirement:	A	

OTHER ALTERNATIVE INVESTMENTS:

CMOs/REMICs – Govt.
CMOs/REMICs – Private
Repos/reverse repos

KEY MANAGERS & DERIVATIVES SPECIALISTS:	Direct Phone/Fax	Job Function
Mr. Matthew Boatwright Assistant Vice President	Ext. 557	Portfolio Mgr – Derivatives Portfolio Mgr – Futures Portfolio Mgr – Options Portfolio Mgr – Structured Notes

Federal Home Loan Bank of Topeka – continued

KEY MANAGERS & DERIVATIVES SPECIALISTS:	Direct Phone/Fax	Job Function
Mr. Greg McClaren Assistant Vice President	Ext. 552	Portfolio Mgr – Derivatives Portfolio Mgr – Futures Portfolio Mgr – Options Portfolio Mgr – Structured Notes
Mr. Frank Tiernan Vice President & C.F.O.	Ext. 224	Chief Investment Officer Chief Financial Officer Portfolio Mgr – Derivatives

Federal National Mortgage Association

Corporation

Location: 3900 Wisconsin Avenue N.W.
Washington, DC 20016

Fax: 202/752-4447 **Phone:** 202/752-7000

Profile: Hold to maturity investor

Investment Portfolio: $ 21.0 - 49.0 billion

Use: **Balance Sheet/Risk Management**
Hedge interest rate risk

Currencies: US dollar

Regions: United States

DERIVATIVES ACTIVITIES:

OTC Derivatives	**Interest rate**	
Plain Vanilla Derivatives	Swaps	Caps
	Forwards	Floors
	Swaptions	Collars
Structured Notes		

OTHER ALTERNATIVE INVESTMENTS:

	CMOs/REMICs - Govt.	Repos/reverse repos
	Strips	

KEY MANAGERS & DERIVATIVES SPECIALISTS:	Direct Phone/Fax	Job Function
Mr. Joseph Amato V.P. - Portfolio Strategy	202/752-5013	Portfolio Mgr – Derivatives
Mr. Timothy Howard Exec. Vice President & C.F.O.	202/752-7140	Chief Investment Officer Chief Financial Officer
Ms. Linda K. Knight S.V.P. & Treasurer	202/752-6113	Treasurer Fixed-Income Strategist
Mr. Thomas Lawler Senior Vice President	202/752-6785	Portfolio Mgr – Derivatives
Mr. Lawrence M. Small President & C.O.O.	202/752-7790	President

Federated Group

Insurance Co./Diversified

Location: 121 East Park Square
Owatonna, MN 55060

Fax: 507/455-5199 **Phone:** 507/455-5200

Profile: Hold to maturity investor

Investment Portfolio: $ 2.2 billion

Use: **Investment Purposes**
Capture extra yield

Currencies: US dollar

Regions: United States

DERIVATIVES ACTIVITIES: **CAC Class: 2**

Structured Notes	Corporate MTNs

OTHER ALTERNATIVE INVESTMENTS:

CMOs/REMICs – Govt.	Repos/reverse repos
CMOs/REMICs – Private	

KEY MANAGERS & DERIVATIVES SPECIALISTS:	Direct Phone/Fax	Job Function
Mr. Joel Drube Second Vice President	Ext. 5301	Portfolio Mgr – Structured Notes
Mr. Mark Hood Bond Portfolio Manager	Ext. 8460	Portfolio Mgr – Structured Notes
Mr. Gregory Stroik Vice President/Asst. Treasurer	Ext. 5229	Chief Investment Officer

Federated Investors

Mutual Fund Manager

Location: 1001 Liberty Avenue
Federated Investors Tower
Pittsburgh, PA 15222-3779

Fax: 412/288-1982 **Phone:** 412/288-1900

Profile: Total return investor

Investment Portfolio: $ 56.0 billion

Use: **Investment Purposes**
Adjust portfolio duration
Asset allocation
Capture extra yield
Convexity objectives
Discretionary situations
Hedge bond portfolio risk
Hedge interest rate risk
Immunize from volatility
Provide incremental return
Reduce variability of returns

Currencies: US dollar

Regions: United States

Federated Investors – continued

DERIVATIVES ACTIVITIES:		CAC Class: 8
Exchange-traded Options & Futures	**Bond, Interest rate**	
U.S. Treasury futures	U.S. Treasury options	
OTC Derivatives	**Bond, Interest rate**	
Plain Vanilla Derivatives	Forwards	
Exotic Derivatives	CMT options	
Structured Notes	Corporate MTNs CMT notes Floaters	Inverse floaters Periodic capped floaters
Counterparty Rating Requirement:	AAA	

OTHER ALTERNATIVE INVESTMENTS:		
	CMOs/REMICs - Govt. Strips	Repos/reverse repos

KEY MANAGERS & DERIVATIVES SPECIALISTS:	Direct Phone/Fax	Job Function
Ms. Deborah A. Cunningham V.P. & Senior Portfolio Mgr	412/288-8481 412/288-8690	Portfolio Mgr – Derivatives Portfolio Mgr – Futures Portfolio Mgr – Options Portfolio Mgr – Structured Notes
Mr. William D. Dawson Senior Vice President	412/288-1990	Bond Department Head *Muni*
Mr. J. Christopher Donahue President & C.O.O.		President
Dr. Henry J. Galliot	412/288-1931	Chief Investment Officer
Mr. J. Thomas Madden Senior Vice President	412/288-1932 412/288-7560	Portfolio Mgr – Derivatives Portfolio Mgr – Options Portfolio Mgr – Structured Notes
Ms. Diane Tolby	412/288-1925 412/288-6425	Portfolio Mgr – Structured Notes Trader – Derivatives Trader – Futures Trader – Options

Ferguson, Wellman, Rudd, Purdy & Van Winkle, Inc.

Investment Manager

Location: 888 Southwest Fifth Avenue
Suite 1200
Portland, OR 97204-2026

Fax: 503/226-3647 **Phone:** 503/226-1444

Profile: Total return investor

Investment Portfolio: $ 944.0 million

Use: **Investment Purposes**
Discretionary situations
Provide incremental return

Currencies: US dollar

Regions: United States

DERIVATIVES ACTIVITIES:		CAC Class: 2
Structured Notes	Corporate MTNs	Govt. agency MTNs
Counterparty Rating Requirement:	A	

Ferguson, Wellman, Rudd, Purdy & Van Winkle, Inc. – continued

OTHER ALTERNATIVE INVESTMENTS:

CMOs/REMICs – Govt.

KEY MANAGERS & DERIVATIVES SPECIALISTS:	**Direct Phone/Fax**	**Job Function**
Mr. Marc Fovinci		Bond Department Head
Mr. L. Wayne Purdy		Bond Department Head Portfolio Mgr – Structured Notes
Mr. James Rudd Chief Executive Officer		Chief Investment Officer

Fidelity Management & Research Company

Mutual Fund Manager

Sub of FMR Corp.

Location: One Boston Place
40th Floor
Boston, MA 02109

Fax: 617/723-9637 **Phone:** 617/563-2500

Profile: Total return investor

Investment Portfolio: $ 290.0 billion

Use: **Investment Purposes**
Asset allocation
Capture extra yield
Hedge bond portfolio risk
Hedge currency risk
Hedge interest rate risk
Provide incremental return
Reduce variability of returns

Currencies:
US dollar
Australian dollar
Belgian franc
Canadian dollar
ECU
French franc
German mark
Italian lira
Indonesian rupiah
Japanese yen
Mexican peso
Spanish peseta
Swiss franc
UK pound

Regions:
United States
Canada
Europe
Latin America
Pacific Rim

DERIVATIVES ACTIVITIES:

Exchange-traded Options & Futures U.S. Treasury futures U.S. Treasury options	**Bond, Currency, Interest rate** Municipal futures	
OTC Derivatives **Plain Vanilla Derivatives**	**Bond, Interest rate** Forwards	
Structured Notes	Corporate MTNs Govt. agency MTNs Bond index notes Index amortizing notes Floaters	Inverse floaters Periodic capped floaters Tender options bonds Multi-step-up callable bonds
Counterparty Rating Requirement:	A	

Fidelity Management & Research Company – continued

OTHER ALTERNATIVE INVESTMENTS:

CMOs/REMICs - Govt.	Strips
CMOs/REMICs - Private	Repos/reverse repos
GICs	

KEY MANAGERS & DERIVATIVES SPECIALISTS:	**Direct Phone/Fax**	**Job Function**
Mr. Robert Beckwitt	617/563-2537	Portfolio Mgr – Derivatives *Corp, Govt, MBS* Portfolio Mgr – Futures *Corp, Govt*
Mr. Michael S. Gray Vice President	617/563-2520 617/476-9743	Portfolio Mgr – Derivatives Portfolio Mgr – Futures Portfolio Mgr – Options Portfolio Mgr – Structured Notes
Mr. Boyce I. Greer Senior Vice President	617/563-2552	Chief Investment Officer Bond Department Head *Muni* Portfolio Mgr – Derivatives Portfolio Mgr – Options Portfolio Mgr – Structured Notes
Mr. Frederick L. Henning, Jr. Managing Director	617/563-2122	Bond Department Head
Mr. Christopher Mahabir Director-Derivative Strategies	617/563-2512 617/479-9743	Trader – Derivatives *Taxable*

Fidelity Management Trust Company

Bank/Trust

Sub of FMR Corp.

Location: 82 Devonshire Street
Boston, MA 02109

Fax: 617/476-9858 **Phone:** 617/563-8700

Profile: Total return investor

Investment Portfolio: $ 20.0 billion

Use: **Investment Purposes**

Currencies:

US dollar	Italian lira
Belgian franc	Japanese yen
ECU	Spanish peseta
French franc	Swiss franc
German mark	UK pound

Regions: United States

Fidelity Management Trust Company – continued

DERIVATIVES ACTIVITIES:		**CAC Class: 3**
Exchange-traded Options & Futures	**Bond, Currency, Interest rate**	

OTHER ALTERNATIVE INVESTMENTS:		
	CMOs/REMICs - Govt.	Strips
	CMOs/REMICs - Private	Repos/reverse repos

KEY MANAGERS & DERIVATIVES SPECIALISTS:	Direct Phone/Fax	Job Function
Mr. Scott Stewart	617/563-7706 617/476-3834	Bond Department Head Portfolio Mgr – Futures

Fiduciary Asset Management

Investment Manager

Location: 8112 Maryland Avenue
Suite 310
Clayton, MO 63105

Fax: 314/863-4360 **Phone:** 314/726-5533

Profile: Total return investor

Investment Portfolio: $ 2.5 billion

Use: **Investment Purposes**

Currencies: US dollar

Regions: United States

DERIVATIVES ACTIVITIES:	
Exchange-traded Options & Futures	**Interest rate**

KEY MANAGERS & DERIVATIVES SPECIALISTS:	Direct Phone/Fax	Job Function
Mr. Wiley D. Angell Senior Vice President	314/863-4488	Portfolio Mgr – Futures
Mr. John P. Maguire Vice President		Chief Investment Officer
Mr. Charles Walbrandt President		President

Fiduciary Trust Company International

Bank/Trust

Location: Two World Trade Center
Suite 9400
New York, NY 10048-0772

Fax: 212/839-6403 **Phone:** 212/466-4100

Profile: Stable asset investor

Investment Portfolio: $ 27.0 billion

Use: **Investment Purposes**
Alter portfolio weighting
Adjust portfolio duration
Asset allocation
Capture extra yield
Diversify portfolio
Enter new mkts/lower risk
Hedge bond portfolio risk
Hedge currency risk
Hedge interest rate risk
Protect currency gains
Provide incremental return
Reduce variability of returns

Currencies: US dollar, Australian dollar, Belgian franc, Canadian dollar, ECU, French franc, German mark, Italian lira, Japanese yen, Spanish peseta, Swiss franc, UK pound

Regions: United States, Canada, Europe

DERIVATIVES ACTIVITIES: **CAC Class: 8**

Exchange-traded Options & Futures	**Bond, Currency, Interest rate**
Counterparty Rating Requirement:	None

OTHER ALTERNATIVE INVESTMENTS:

CMOs/REMICs – Govt.
CMOs/REMICs – Private
Strips

KEY MANAGERS & DERIVATIVES SPECIALISTS:	**Direct Phone/Fax**	**Job Function**
Mr. Jeremy H. Biggs Vice Chairman	Ext. 2693	Chief Investment Officer
Mr. Stuart C. Hochberger Senior Vice President	Ext. 2430	Bond Department Head Portfolio Mgr – Futures Portfolio Mgr – Options

Fiduciary Trust Company of Massachusetts

Bank/Trust

Location: 175 Federal Street
Boston, MA 02110-2289

Fax: 617/482-3774 **Phone:** 617/482-5270

Profile: Total return investor

Investment Portfolio: $ 2.0 billion

Use: **Investment Purposes**

Currencies: US dollar

Regions: United States

DERIVATIVES ACTIVITIES: **CAC Class: Inactive**

OTHER ALTERNATIVE INVESTMENTS:

CMOs/REMICs – Govt. CMOs/REMICs – Private

KEY MANAGERS & DERIVATIVES SPECIALISTS:	**Direct Phone/Fax**	**Job Function**
Mr. Douglas Smith-Petersen		Chief Investment Officer

Fielding Management Company, Inc.

Mutual Fund Manager

Location: 350 Linden Oaks
Rochester, NY 14625-2804

Fax: 716/383-0914 **Phone:** 716/383-1300

Profile: Total return investor

Investment Portfolio: $ 1.0 - 3.0 billion

Use: **Investment Purposes**
Hedge bond portfolio risk
Hedge interest rate risk

Currencies: US dollar

Regions: United States

DERIVATIVES ACTIVITIES:

Exchange-traded Options & Futures Municipal options	**Bond, Interest rate**
Structured Notes	Inverse floaters

OTHER ALTERNATIVE INVESTMENTS:

CMOs/REMICs – Govt.
CMOs/REMICs – Private
Repos/reverse repos

KEY MANAGERS & DERIVATIVES SPECIALISTS:	**Direct Phone/Fax**	**Job Function**
Mr. Ronald H. Fielding President		President Chief Investment Officer Portfolio Mgr – Options *Muni*
Mr. Michael S. Rosen Vice President		Portfolio Mgr – Options *Muni*

Fifth Third Bank

Bank/Trust

Sub of Fifth Third Bancorp

Location: 38 Fountain Square Plaza
Cincinnati, OH 45263

Fax: 513/579-4312 **Phone:** 513/579-5300

Profile: Total return investor

Investment Portfolio: $ 7.0 billion

Use: **Investment Purposes**

Currencies: US dollar

Regions: United States

DERIVATIVES ACTIVITIES: **CAC Class: Inactive**

OTHER ALTERNATIVE INVESTMENTS:

CMOs/REMICs – Govt.	Strips
CMOs/REMICs – Private	Repos/reverse repos

KEY MANAGERS & DERIVATIVES SPECIALISTS:	Direct Phone/Fax	Job Function
Mr. Thomas H. Atteberry V.P. & Senior Trust Officer	513/579-6100	Bond Department Head Fixed-Income Strategist
Mr. James D. Berghausen	513/744-7545	Chief Investment Officer

The Fifth Third Bank of Northwestern Ohio

Bank/Trust

Sub of Fifth Third Bancorp

Location: 606 Madison Avenue
8th Floor
Toledo, OH 43604

Fax: 419/259-7869 **Phone:** 419/259-7890

Profile: Hold to maturity investor

Investment Portfolio: $ 1.6 billion

Use: **Investment Purposes**
Hedge bond portfolio risk
Hedge interest rate risk

Currencies: US dollar

Regions: United States

DERIVATIVES ACTIVITIES: **CAC Class: 2**

Structured Notes	Multi-step-up callable bonds
Counterparty Rating Requirement:	A

OTHER ALTERNATIVE INVESTMENTS:

CMOs/REMICs – Govt.	Repos/reverse repos

KEY MANAGERS & DERIVATIVES SPECIALISTS:	Direct Phone/Fax	Job Function
Mr. Jeffrey H. MacArthur Vice President	419/259-6951 419/259-6939	Chief Investment Officer Portfolio Mgr – Structured Notes

Financial Counselors, Inc.

Broker/Management Sub

Sub of Mitchell Hutchins Asset Management, Inc.

Location: 700 West 47th Street
Suite 500
Kansas City, MO 64112

Fax: 816/751-5265 **Phone:** 816/751-5258

Profile: Total return investor

Investment Portfolio: $ 1.3 billion

Use: **Investment Purposes**
Adjust portfolio duration
Asset allocation
Capture extra yield
Diversify portfolio
Provide incremental return

Currencies: US dollar

Regions: United States

DERIVATIVES ACTIVITIES: **CAC Class: 2**

Structured Notes	Govt. agency MTNs	CMT notes
Counterparty Rating Requirement:	A	

OTHER ALTERNATIVE INVESTMENTS:

CMOs/REMICs – Govt.

KEY MANAGERS & DERIVATIVES SPECIALISTS:	**Direct Phone/Fax**	**Job Function**
Mr. Bryant P. Barnes President & C.F.O.	816/751-5268	President Chief Investment Officer Chief Financial Officer Bond Department Head *Corp, Govt, MBS*
Mr. Peter G. Greig Vice President	816/751-5215	Portfolio Mgr – Structured Notes

Financial Holding Corporation

Insurance Co/Life

Location: 300 West 11th Street
Kansas City, MO 64105

Fax: 816/391-2165 **Phone:** 816/391-2000

Profile: Total return investor

Investment Portfolio: $ 1.3 billion

Use: **Investment Purposes**

Currencies: US dollar

Regions: United States

DERIVATIVES ACTIVITIES: **CAC Class: Inactive**

OTHER ALTERNATIVE INVESTMENTS:

CMOs/REMICs – Govt. Strips

KEY MANAGERS & DERIVATIVES SPECIALISTS:	**Direct Phone/Fax**	**Job Function**
Mr. Mark Fallon	816/391-2037	Chief Investment Officer

The FINOVA Group Inc.

Corporation

Location: 1850 North Central Avenue
Phoenix, AZ 85002-2209

Fax: 602/207-5543 **Phone:** 602/207-4900

Use: **Balance Sheet/Risk Management**
Hedge interest rate risk

Currencies: US dollar **Regions:** United States

DERIVATIVES ACTIVITIES:		**CAC Class: 6**
OTC Derivatives	**Interest rate**	
Plain Vanilla Derivatives	Swaps	
Exotic Derivatives	Index amortizing swaps	

KEY MANAGERS & DERIVATIVES SPECIALISTS:	**Direct Phone/Fax**	**Job Function**
Mr. Samuel L. Eichenfield Chairman, President & C.E.O.		President
Mr. Robert J. Fitzsimmons S.V.P. - Treasurer		Treasurer
Mr. Gregory C. Smalis Group Vice President		Portfolio Mgr – Derivatives

First of America Bank Corporation

Bank/Portfolio

Location: 211 South Rose Street
Kalamazoo, MI 49007-5264

Fax: 616/376-7484 **Phone:** 616/376-7460

Profile: Total return investor

Investment Portfolio: $ 4.0 - 10.0 billion

Use: **Balance Sheet/Risk Management**
Hedge interest rate risk
Strategic liability management

Currencies: US dollar **Regions:** United States

DERIVATIVES ACTIVITIES:			**CAC Class: 4**
OTC Derivatives	**Interest rate**		
Plain Vanilla Derivatives	Swaps	Caps	
Counterparty Rating Requirement:	BBB		

OTHER ALTERNATIVE INVESTMENTS:		
	CMOs/REMICs – Govt. CMOs/REMICs – Private	Repos/reverse repos

First of America Bank Corporation – continued

KEY MANAGERS & DERIVATIVES SPECIALISTS:	Direct Phone/Fax	Job Function
Mr. Richard F. Chormann President & C.O.O.	616/376-7004	President
Mr. David S. Fisher Director	616/376-7464	Chief Investment Officer Portfolio Mgr – Derivatives
Ms. Leslie Khosravani	616/376-7463	Trader – Derivatives
Mr. Thomas W. Lambert Exec. Vice President & C.F.O.	616/376-7004	Chief Financial Officer
Ms. Kim Lee Derivatives Manager	616/376-7460	Portfolio Mgr – Derivatives Trader – Derivatives
Mr. Samuel G. Stone Sr. Vice President & Treasurer	616/376-7008	Treasurer
Mr. James Yealin		Trader – Derivatives

First of America Investment Corporation

Bank/Management Division

Sub of First of America Bank Corporation

Location: 303 North Rose Street
Suite 500
Kalamazoo, MI 49007

Fax: 616/385-0227 **Phone:** 616/385-0200

Profile: Total return investor

Investment Portfolio: $ 10.1 billion

Use: **Investment Purposes**
Capture extra yield
Hedge bond portfolio risk
Hedge equity portfolio risk
Hedge interest rate risk

Currencies: US dollar

Regions: United States

DERIVATIVES ACTIVITIES: **CAC Class: 3**

OTC Derivatives **Plain Vanilla Derivatives**	**Interest rate** Swaps
Structured Notes	Govt. agency MTNs

OTHER ALTERNATIVE INVESTMENTS:

CMOs/REMICs – Govt.
CMOs/REMICs – Private
Repos/reverse repos

First of America Investment Corporation – continued

KEY MANAGERS & DERIVATIVES SPECIALISTS:	Direct Phone/Fax	Job Function
Mr. Dennis Clary Vice President	616/385-0203	Portfolio Mgr – Derivatives Portfolio Mgr – Structured Notes
Mr. George Delaney Vice President	616/385-0203	Portfolio Mgr – Derivatives Portfolio Mgr – Structured Notes
Mr. Timothy Eisel	616/385-0224	Trader – Derivatives Trader – Structured Investments
Mr. Derek Rummel	616/385-0222	Portfolio Mgr – Derivatives Portfolio Mgr – Structured Notes
Mr. Roger Stamper Managing Director		Portfolio Mgr – Derivatives
Mr. Christian Swantek Vice President	616/385-0297	Portfolio Mgr – Derivatives Portfolio Mgr – Structured Notes
Mr. Marc Tourangeau Vice President	616/385-0221	Portfolio Mgr – Derivatives Portfolio Mgr – Structured Notes
Mr. Michael Vandenboffshe	616/385-0206	Trader – Derivatives Trader – Structured Investments
Mr. Richard A. Wolf President	616/385-0202	President Chief Investment Officer

First American Corporation

Bank Holding Company

Location: First American Center
Nashville, TN 37237-0814

Fax: 615/541-6372 **Phone:** 615/748-2000

Use: **Balance Sheet/Risk Management**
Hedge interest rate risk
Strategic liability management

Investment Purposes

Currencies: US dollar

Regions: United States

DERIVATIVES ACTIVITIES: **CAC Class: 6**

OTC Derivatives	**Interest rate**	
Plain Vanilla Derivatives	Swaps	Forwards

KEY MANAGERS & DERIVATIVES SPECIALISTS:	Direct Phone/Fax	Job Function
Mr. Dale W. Polley Vice Chairman & President		President Chief Financial Officer Treasurer

First Asset Management

Bank/Management Division

Sub of First Bank System

Location: 601 Second Avenue South
First Bank Place
16th Floor
Minneapolis, MN 55402

Fax: 612/973-0200 **Phone:** 612/973-0999

Profile: Total return investor

Investment Portfolio: $ 30.0 billion

Use: **Investment Purposes**
Alter portfolio weighting
Adjust portfolio duration
Asset allocation
Capture extra yield
Diversify portfolio
Provide incremental return

Currencies: US dollar

Regions: United States

DERIVATIVES ACTIVITIES: **CAC Class: 3**

Structured Notes	Corporate MTNs	Floaters

OTHER ALTERNATIVE INVESTMENTS:

CMOs/REMICs – Govt.	Strips
CMOs/REMICs – Private	Repos/reverse repos

KEY MANAGERS & DERIVATIVES SPECIALISTS:	**Direct Phone/Fax**	**Job Function**
Mr. Martin L. Jones Managing Director-Fixed Income	612/973-0174	Bond Department Head Portfolio Mgr – Structured Notes
Mr. John W. Murphy, Jr. Managing Director	612/973-0180	Chief Investment Officer
Mr. Richard W. Stanley Manager - Investment Research	612/973-0027	Chief Investment Officer
Mr. Joseph M. Ulrey	612/973-0196	Portfolio Mgr – Structured Notes

First Bank, N.A. (Omaha) (Trust)

Bank/Trust

Sub of First Bank System

Location: 17th & Farnam Street
Omaha, NE 68102-2183

Fax: 402/348-7819 **Phone:** 402/348-6000

Profile: Total return investor

Investment Portfolio: $ 2.0 billion

Use: **Investment Purposes**

Currencies: US dollar

Regions: United States

First Bank, N.A. (Omaha) (Trust) – continued

DERIVATIVES ACTIVITIES:		CAC Class: 2
Structured Notes	Corporate MTNs	Govt. agency MTNs

OTHER ALTERNATIVE INVESTMENTS:		
	CMOs/REMICs – Govt.	Strips
	CMOs/REMICs – Private	Repos/reverse repos

KEY MANAGERS & DERIVATIVES SPECIALISTS:	Direct Phone/Fax	Job Function
Mr. Robert Campbell Fixed-Income Strategist	402/348-6388	Fixed-Income Strategist
Mr. William Giovanni		Bond Department Head *Muni*
Ms. Terrie Ringwalt Vice President	402/348-6042	Chief Investment Officer Portfolio Mgr – Structured Notes

First Bank Puerto Rico

Savings Bank/Bldg Society

Location: 1519 Ponce de Leon Avenue
(PH) Investment Department STOP 23
Santurce, PR 00908

Fax: 809/724-5965 **Phone:** 809/729-8200

Profile: Total return investor

Investment Portfolio: $ 729.0 million

Use:

Balance Sheet/Risk Management
Create synthetic fixed/floating rate
Hedge balance sheet
Hedge interest rate risk
Meet interest rate target
Reduce cost of capital
Strategic liability management

Investment Purposes
Hedge bond portfolio risk
Hedge interest rate risk
Reduce variability of returns

Currencies: US dollar

Regions: United States

DERIVATIVES ACTIVITIES:		CAC Class: 2
Exchange-traded Options & Futures U.S. Treasury options	**Bond**	
OTC Derivatives **Plain Vanilla Derivatives**	**Interest rate** Swaps	
Exotic Derivatives	Detached calls	
Structured Notes	Govt. agency MTNs	Floaters
Counterparty Rating Requirement:	None	

OTHER ALTERNATIVE INVESTMENTS:		
	CMOs/REMICs – Govt.	Strips
	CMOs/REMICs – Private	Repos/reverse repos

First Bank Puerto Rico – continued

KEY MANAGERS & DERIVATIVES SPECIALISTS:	Direct Phone/Fax	Job Function
Ms. Annie Astor de Carbonell Exec. Vice President & C.F.O.	809/729-8110	Chief Financial Officer Portfolio Mgr – Derivatives Portfolio Mgr – Options Portfolio Mgr – Structured Notes
Mr. Fernando L. Batlle Senior Vice President	809/729-8110	Chief Investment Officer Portfolio Mgr – Derivatives Portfolio Mgr – Structured Notes

First Bank System (Portfolio)

Bank/Portfolio

Sub of First Bank System

Location: 601 Second Avenue South
Minneapolis, MN 55402-4302

Fax: 612/973-0965 **Phone:** 612/973-1111

Profile: Total return investor

Investment Portfolio: $ 4.6 billion

Use: **Balance Sheet/Risk Management**
Hedge balance sheet
Hedge interest rate risk

Currencies: US dollar

Regions: United States

DERIVATIVES ACTIVITIES: **CAC Class: 7**

OTC Derivatives
Plain Vanilla Derivatives

Interest rate
Swaps
Forwards
Caps
Floors

OTHER ALTERNATIVE INVESTMENTS:

CMOs/REMICs – Govt.

KEY MANAGERS & DERIVATIVES SPECIALISTS:	Direct Phone/Fax	Job Function
Mr. David R. Edstam S.V.P. & Treasurer	612/973-2278	Treasurer
Mr. David Prochaska	612/973-2297	Chief Investment Officer

First Chicago/NBD Corporation

Bank Holding Company

Location: One First National Plaza
Chicago, IL 60670

Fax: 312/732-3366 **Phone:** 312/732-4000

Profile: Spread investor

Use: **Balance Sheet/Risk Management**
Create synthetic fixed/floating rate
Hedge balance sheet
Hedge currency risk
Hedge interest rate risk
Incremental return
Strategic liability management

Investment Purposes
Capture extra yield
Discretionary situations
Hedge bond portfolio risk
Hedge currency risk
Hedge equity portfolio risk
Hedge interest rate risk
Provide incremental return

First Chicago/NBD Corporation – continued

Currencies: US dollar, Australian dollar, Belgian franc, Canadian dollar, French franc, German mark, Italian lira, Japanese yen, Swiss franc, UK pound

Regions: United States, Europe

DERIVATIVES ACTIVITIES: **CAC Class: 7**

Exchange-traded Options & Futures	**Bond, Currency, Interest rate**	
U.S. Treasury futures	U.S. Treasury options	
OTC Derivatives	**Bond, Currency, Interest rate**	
Plain Vanilla Derivatives	Swaps Forwards Swaptions	Caps Floors Collars
Exotic Derivatives	Periodic caps/floors	
Structured Notes		

KEY MANAGERS & DERIVATIVES SPECIALISTS:	**Direct Phone/Fax**	**Job Function**
Mr. Verne G. Istock President and C.E.O.	312/732-9532	President
Ms. Mary Eileen Kennedy Sr. Vice President & Treasurer	312/732-1581 312/732-3366	Treasurer Portfolio Mgr – Derivatives
Mr. Robert A. Rosholt Exec. Vice President & C.F.O.	312/732-3209	Chief Financial Officer Portfolio Mgr – Derivatives

First Citizens Bank & Trust Co.

Bank/Portfolio

Location: 3128 Smoketree Court
Raleigh, NC 27604

Fax: 919/755-7545 **Phone:** 919/755-7285

Profile: Total return investor

Investment Portfolio: $ 2.0 billion

Use: **Investment Purposes**
- Beat conventional rates
- Capture extra yield
- Convexity objectives
- Provide incremental return

Currencies: US dollar

Regions: United States

DERIVATIVES ACTIVITIES: **CAC Class: 5**

Exchange-traded Options & Futures	**Bond**	
Structured Notes	Floaters Inverse floaters	Periodic capped floaters
Counterparty Rating Requirement:	BBB	

OTHER ALTERNATIVE INVESTMENTS:

CMOs/REMICs – Govt.	GICs
CMOs/REMICs – Private	Repos/reverse repos

First Citizens Bank & Trust Co. – continued

KEY MANAGERS & DERIVATIVES SPECIALISTS:	**Direct Phone/Fax**	**Job Function**
Mr. Gregory D. Boal	919/755-7265	Portfolio Mgr – Futures *Corp, Govt* Portfolio Mgr – Structured Notes Research Analyst – Futures/Options *Corp, Govt*
Mr. John R. Noles	919/755-7324	Chief Investment Officer

First Commercial Corporation

Bank/Portfolio

Location: 400 West Capitol Avenue
Little Rock, AR 72201

Fax: 501/371-7413 **Phone:** 501/371-7000

Profile: Total return investor

Investment Portfolio: $ 1.5 billion

Use: **Investment Purposes**
Hedge interest rate risk
Provide incremental return

Currencies: US dollar

Regions: United States

DERIVATIVES ACTIVITIES: **CAC Class: 2**

OTC Derivatives **Plain Vanilla Derivatives**	**Interest rate** Swaps	
Structured Notes	Index amortizing notes Floaters	Multi-step-up callable bonds

OTHER ALTERNATIVE INVESTMENTS:

	CMOs/REMICs – Govt. Strips	Repos/reverse repos

KEY MANAGERS & DERIVATIVES SPECIALISTS:	**Direct Phone/Fax**	**Job Function**
Mr. Doug Barber	501/371-3387	Portfolio Mgr – Structured Notes
Mr. William Suliburk Vice President	501/371-7108	Chief Investment Officer Portfolio Mgr – Derivatives

First Commercial Capital Management

Bank/Management Division

Sub of First Commercial Corporation

Location: 400 West Capitol Avenue
Little Rock, AR 72201-1471

Fax: 501/371-7487 **Phone:** 501/371-6756

Profile: Total return investor

Investment Portfolio: $ 1.6 billion

First Commercial Capital Management – continued

Use: **Investment Purposes**
Alter portfolio weighting
Adjust portfolio duration
Capture extra yield
Diversify portfolio

Currencies: US dollar

Regions: United States

DERIVATIVES ACTIVITIES: **CAC Class: 2**

Structured Notes	Corporate MTNs	Govt. agency MTNs

OTHER ALTERNATIVE INVESTMENTS:

	CMOs/REMICs – Govt.	CMOs/REMICs – Private

KEY MANAGERS & DERIVATIVES SPECIALISTS:	**Direct Phone/Fax**	**Job Function**
Ms. Susan Gammill	501/371-6755	Trader – Derivatives
Ms. Lisa McDaniel Investment Officer		Portfolio Mgr – Structured Notes

First Federal Savings and Loan Association of Rochester

Savings Bank/Bldg Society

Location: One First Federal Plaza
Rochester, NY 14614-7160

Fax: 716/238-2056 **Phone:** 716/238-2119

Profile: Total return investor

Investment Portfolio: $ 1.2 billion

Use: **Balance Sheet/Risk Management**
Bypass regulations
Create synthetic fixed/floating rate
Hedge balance sheet
Hedge interest rate risk
Lower transaction costs
Meet interest rate target
Reduce cost of capital
Strategic liability management

Currencies: US dollar

Regions: United States

DERIVATIVES ACTIVITIES: **CAC Class: 7**

Exchange-traded Options & Futures U.S. Treasury futures	**Bond, Interest rate** U.S. Treasury options	
OTC Derivatives **Plain Vanilla Derivatives**	**Bond, Interest rate** Swaps Forwards	 Caps Floors
Counterparty Rating Requirement:	None	

OTHER ALTERNATIVE INVESTMENTS:

	CMOs/REMICs – Govt.	Repos/reverse repos

First Federal Savings and Loan Association of Rochester – continued

KEY MANAGERS & DERIVATIVES SPECIALISTS:	Direct Phone/Fax	Job Function
Mr. Thomas N. Borshoff President & C.E.O.		President
Mr. George H. Collins Vice President & Treasurer	716/238-2574	Treasurer
Mr. Sadakichi B. Robbins Assistant Vice President	716/238-2119	Chief Investment Officer Portfolio Mgr – Derivatives Portfolio Mgr – Futures *Govt* Portfolio Mgr – Options *Govt*
Mr. Clay Simmons Chief Financial Officer	716/238-2426	Chief Financial Officer

First Interstate Bank of California (Trust)

Bank/Trust

Location: 707 Wilshire Boulevard
Los Angeles, CA 90017-3500

Fax: 213/614-2468 **Phone:** 213/614-4111

Profile: Total return investor

Investment Portfolio: $ 8.0 billion

Use: **Investment Purposes**

Currencies: US dollar

Regions: United States

DERIVATIVES ACTIVITIES: **CAC Class: Inactive**

OTHER ALTERNATIVE INVESTMENTS:

CMOs/REMICs – Govt. CMOs/REMICs – Private

KEY MANAGERS & DERIVATIVES SPECIALISTS:	Direct Phone/Fax	Job Function
Ms. Susan Riechel Vice President	213/614-2990	Bond Department Head

First Interstate Bank of Denver (Trust)

Bank/Trust

Location: 633 17th Street
North Tower 18th Floor
Denver, CO 80202

Fax: 303/293-5163 **Phone:** 303/293-2211

Profile: Total return investor

Investment Portfolio: $ 3.5 billion

Use: **Investment Purposes**

Currencies: US dollar

Regions: United States

First Interstate Bank of Denver (Trust) – continued

DERIVATIVES ACTIVITIES: **CAC Class: Inactive**

OTHER ALTERNATIVE INVESTMENTS:

CMOs/REMICs – Govt. Repos/reverse repos
CMOs/REMICs – Private

KEY MANAGERS & DERIVATIVES SPECIALISTS:	Direct Phone/Fax	Job Function
Mr. Edward Clanuch Senior Vice President	303/293-5527	Chief Investment Officer

First Interstate Bank of Nevada

Bank/Trust

Location: 3800 Howard Hughes Parkway
Las Vegas, NV 89109

Fax: 702/791-6131 **Phone:** 702/791-6150

Profile: Total return investor

Investment Portfolio: $ 1.2 billion

Use: **Investment Purposes**

Currencies: US dollar

Regions: United States

DERIVATIVES ACTIVITIES: **CAC Class: Inactive**

OTHER ALTERNATIVE INVESTMENTS:

CMOs/REMICs – Govt. Strips
CMOs/REMICs – Private Repos/reverse repos

KEY MANAGERS & DERIVATIVES SPECIALISTS:	Direct Phone/Fax	Job Function
Mr. Randall Campanale Capital Management Manager	702/791-6151	Chief Investment Officer

First Interstate Bank of Oregon (Trust)

Bank/Trust

Location: 1300 Southwest Fifth Avenue
First Interstate Tower 11th Floor
Portland, OR 97208

Fax: 503/225-4066 **Phone:** 503/225-2376

Profile: Total return investor

Investment Portfolio: $ 2.4 billion

Use: **Investment Purposes**

Currencies: US dollar

Regions: United States

DERIVATIVES ACTIVITIES: **CAC Class: Inactive**

OTHER ALTERNATIVE INVESTMENTS:

CMOs/REMICs – Govt. GICs

First Interstate Bank of Oregon (Trust) – continued

KEY MANAGERS & DERIVATIVES SPECIALISTS:	**Direct Phone/Fax**	**Job Function**
Mr. Dale Annis Vice President	503/225-2472	Chief Investment Officer

The First Interstate Bank of Texas (Portfolio)

Bank/Portfolio

Sub of First Interstate Bancorporation

Location: 1000 Louisiana Street
Houston, TX 77002

Fax: 713/226-1958 **Phone:** 713/224-6611

Profile: Total return investor

Investment Portfolio: $ 1.0 - 3.0 billion

Use: **Balance Sheet/Risk Management**

Investment Purposes

Currencies: US dollar

Regions: United States

DERIVATIVES ACTIVITIES: **CAC Class: Inactive**

OTHER ALTERNATIVE INVESTMENTS:

CMOs/REMICs – Govt. Repos/reverse repos

KEY MANAGERS & DERIVATIVES SPECIALISTS:	**Direct Phone/Fax**	**Job Function**
Ms. Pamela Dawson		Chief Investment Officer

First Investors Management Co., Inc.

Mutual Fund Manager

Sub of First Investors Corporation

Location: 95 Wall Street
23rd Floor
New York, NY 10005-4297

Fax: 212/858-8078 **Phone:** 212/858-8000

Profile: Current yield investor

Investment Portfolio: $ 4.0 - 10.0 billion

Use: **Balance Sheet/Risk Management**
Hedge balance sheet

Currencies: US dollar

Regions: United States

DERIVATIVES ACTIVITIES:

Structured Notes		
	Corporate MTNs	CMT notes
	Bond index notes	Floaters

OTHER ALTERNATIVE INVESTMENTS:

CMOs/REMICs – Govt. CMOs/REMICs – Private

First Investors Management Co., Inc. – continued

KEY MANAGERS & DERIVATIVES SPECIALISTS:	Direct Phone/Fax	Job Function
Mr. Thomas Caton	212/858-8062	Portfolio Mgr – Structured Notes
Mr. Clark D. Wagner Vice President	212/858-8094	Chief Investment Officer

First Manhattan Capital Management

Broker/Management Sub

Location: 437 Madison Avenue
New York, NY 10022

Fax: 212/223-4175 **Phone:** 212/756-3300

Profile: Total return investor

Investment Portfolio: $ 6.0 billion

Use: **Investment Purposes**

Currencies: US dollar

Regions: United States

DERIVATIVES ACTIVITIES: **CAC Class: Inactive**

OTHER ALTERNATIVE INVESTMENTS:

CMOs/REMICs – Govt. CMOs/REMICs – Private

KEY MANAGERS & DERIVATIVES SPECIALISTS:	Direct Phone/Fax	Job Function
Mr. David S. Gottesman Managing Director		Chief Investment Officer

First National Bank of Commerce (Investment)

Bank/Portfolio

Sub of First Commerce Corporation

Location: 210 Baronne Street
4th Floor
New Orleans, LA 70112-1753

Fax: 504/561-1923 **Phone:** 504/561-1380

Profile: Net asset value investor

Investment Portfolio: $ 3.0 billion

Use: **Balance Sheet/Risk Management**
Hedge balance sheet

Investment Purposes
Hedge interest rate risk

Currencies: US dollar

Regions: United States

DERIVATIVES ACTIVITIES: **CAC Class: 4**

OTC Derivatives	**Interest rate**	
Plain Vanilla Derivatives	Swaps	Caps
Exotic Derivatives	Index amortizing swaps	
Counterparty Rating Requirement:	A	

OTHER ALTERNATIVE INVESTMENTS:

CMOs/REMICs – Govt. Repos/reverse repos

First National Bank of Commerce (Investment) – continued

KEY MANAGERS & DERIVATIVES SPECIALISTS:	Direct Phone/Fax	Job Function
Mr. Gary Hickerson	504/561-1351	Chief Investment Officer
Mr. Michael Middleton Vice President	504/561-1388	Portfolio Mgr – Derivatives

First National Bank Evergreen Park (Portfolio)

Bank/Portfolio

Location: 3101 West 95th Street
Evergreen Park, IL 60642

Fax: 708/422-6827 **Phone:** 708/422-6700

Profile: Total return investor

Investment Portfolio: $ 1.0 - 3.0 billion

Use: **Balance Sheet/Risk Management**

Currencies: US dollar

Regions: United States

DERIVATIVES ACTIVITIES: **CAC Class: Inactive**

OTHER ALTERNATIVE INVESTMENTS:

CMOs/REMICs – Govt.

KEY MANAGERS & DERIVATIVES SPECIALISTS:	Direct Phone/Fax	Job Function
Mr. H. Richard Brown Vice President		Chief Investment Officer

First National Bank Gainesville (Portfolio)

Bank/Portfolio

Location: 111 Green Street
Gainesville, GA 30501

Fax: 770/503-2706 **Phone:** 770/503-2000

Profile: Hold to maturity investor

Investment Portfolio: $ 2.4 billion

Use: **Investment Purposes**
Hedge interest rate risk

Currencies: US dollar

Regions: United States

DERIVATIVES ACTIVITIES: **CAC Class: 2**

Structured Notes Multi-step-up callable bonds

OTHER ALTERNATIVE INVESTMENTS:

CMOs/REMICs – Govt. Repos/reverse repos

KEY MANAGERS & DERIVATIVES SPECIALISTS:	Direct Phone/Fax	Job Function
Mr. Laurence O. Howard, Jr. Group V.P. & Sr. Inv. Officer	770/503-2150	Bond Department Head Portfolio Mgr – Structured Notes

First National Bank of Maryland (Portfolio)

Bank/Portfolio

Sub of First Maryland Bancorp

Location: 25 South Charles Street
12th Floor
Baltimore, MD 21201-3330

Fax: 410/244-4477 **Phone:** 410/244-4000

Profile: Hold to maturity investor

Investment Portfolio: $ 4.0 - 10.0 billion

Use:

Balance Sheet/Risk Management
Create synthetic fixed/floating rate
Hedge balance sheet
Hedge interest rate risk
Lower transaction costs
Strategic liability management

Investment Purposes
Adjust portfolio duration
Convexity objectives
Hedge bond portfolio risk
Hedge interest rate risk

Currencies: US dollar, German mark, Japanese yen

Regions: United States

DERIVATIVES ACTIVITIES:

CAC Class: 7

Exchange-traded Options & Futures	**Bond, Currency, Interest rate**	
U.S. Treasury futures	U.S. Treasury options	
OTC Derivatives	**Bond, Currency, Interest rate**	
Plain Vanilla Derivatives	Swaps	Caps
	Forwards	Floors
	Swaptions	Collars
Exotic Derivatives	Index amortizing swaps	
Structured Notes	Index amortizing notes	Floaters
	CMT notes	
Counterparty Rating Requirement:	None	

OTHER ALTERNATIVE INVESTMENTS:

CMOs/REMICs – Govt.	Repos/reverse repos
CMOs/REMICs – Private	

KEY MANAGERS & DERIVATIVES SPECIALISTS:	**Direct Phone/Fax**	**Job Function**
Mr. Robert Ray Senior Vice President	410/244-4676	Chief Investment Officer Portfolio Mgr – Derivatives Portfolio Mgr – Options Portfolio Mgr – Structured Notes

First National Bank of Ohio

Bank/Trust

Sub of FirstMerit Corporation

Location: 121 South Main Street
Suite 200
Akron, OH 44308

Fax: 216/253-1849 **Phone:** 216/384-8000

Profile: Total return investor

Investment Portfolio: $ 1.0 billion

Use: **Investment Purposes**

Currencies: US dollar

Regions: United States

DERIVATIVES ACTIVITIES: **CAC Class: Inactive**

OTHER ALTERNATIVE INVESTMENTS:

CMOs/REMICs – Govt. Repos/reverse repos

KEY MANAGERS & DERIVATIVES SPECIALISTS:	**Direct Phone/Fax**	**Job Function**
Mr. Randall Thornton Vice President	216/384-7354	Chief Investment Officer

The First National Bank of Omaha (Trust)

Bank/Trust

Sub of First National Bank of Nebraska Inc.

Location: 1620 Dodge Street
One First National Center
Omaha, NE 68102

Fax: 402/341-6556 **Phone:** 402/633-3434

Profile: Total return investor

Investment Portfolio: $ 1.4 billion

Use: **Investment Purposes**

Currencies: US dollar

Regions: United States

DERIVATIVES ACTIVITIES: **CAC Class: Inactive**

OTHER ALTERNATIVE INVESTMENTS:

CMOs/REMICs – Govt. Repos/reverse repos
Strips

KEY MANAGERS & DERIVATIVES SPECIALISTS:	**Direct Phone/Fax**	**Job Function**
Mr. Thomas W. Allen Trust Officer	402/633-3414	Chief Investment Officer Bond Department Head

First Nationwide Bank, A Federal Savings Bank

Savings Bank/Bldg Society

Sub of First Nationwide Financial Corp.

Location: 135 Main Street
San Francisco, CA 94105-1817

Fax: 415/904-1325 **Phone:** 415/904-1100

Profile: Total return investor

Investment Portfolio: $ 2.9 billion

Use: **Balance Sheet/Risk Management**
Create synthetic fixed/floating rate
Hedge balance sheet
Hedge interest rate risk
Strategic liability management

Currencies: US dollar

Regions: United States

DERIVATIVES ACTIVITIES: **CAC Class: 5**

OTC Derivatives **Plain Vanilla Derivatives**	**Interest rate** Swaps	
Structured Notes	Floaters Periodic capped floaters	Multi-step-up callable bonds
Counterparty Rating Requirement:	AAA	

OTHER ALTERNATIVE INVESTMENTS:

	CMOs/REMICs – Govt. CMOs/REMICs – Private	Repos/reverse repos

KEY MANAGERS & DERIVATIVES SPECIALISTS:	**Direct Phone/Fax**	**Job Function**
Mr. Lawrence Reed Treasurer	415/904-1348 415/904-0149	Chief Investment Officer Treasurer
Mr. Craig Sosey	415/904-1349	Portfolio Mgr – Derivatives Portfolio Mgr – Structured Notes

First NH Bank

Savings Bank/Bldg Society

Sub of The Bank of Ireland

Location: 1000 Elm Street
Manchester, NH 03101

Fax: 603/634-7189 **Phone:** 603/634-7145

Profile: Total return investor

Investment Portfolio: $ 1.0 - 3.0 billion

Use: **Balance Sheet/Risk Management**
Hedge balance sheet
Hedge currency risk
Hedge interest rate risk
Incremental return

Investment Purposes
Adjust portfolio duration
Capture extra yield
Diversify portfolio
Hedge interest rate risk
Provide incremental return
Reduce variability of returns

Currencies: US dollar, Italian lira, UK pound

Regions: United States, Europe

First NH Bank – continued

DERIVATIVES ACTIVITIES:		CAC Class: 4
OTC Derivatives **Plain Vanilla Derivatives**	**Currency** Forwards	
Structured Notes	Govt. agency MTNs Index amortizing notes CMT notes	Floaters Periodic capped floaters Multi-step-up callable bonds
Counterparty Rating Requirement:	AA	

OTHER ALTERNATIVE INVESTMENTS:

CMOs/REMICs – Govt.
Repos/reverse repos

KEY MANAGERS & DERIVATIVES SPECIALISTS:	Direct Phone/Fax	Job Function
Mr. John C. Baity		Treasurer Portfolio Mgr – Derivatives Portfolio Mgr – Structured Notes
Mr. Patrick Murphy Chairman & C.E.O.		Chief Investment Officer

First NH Investment Services

Bank/Management Division

Sub of The Bank of Ireland

Location: 1000 Elm Street
Manchester, NH 03105-1900

Fax: 603/224-9405 **Phone:** 603/634-6165

Profile: Total return investor

Investment Portfolio: $ 1.0 - 3.0 billion

Use: **Balance Sheet/Risk Management**

Investment Purposes

Currencies: US dollar

Regions: United States

DERIVATIVES ACTIVITIES:		CAC Class: 2
Structured Notes	Corporate MTNs Govt. agency MTNs	Bond index notes

OTHER ALTERNATIVE INVESTMENTS:

CMOs/REMICs – Govt.
Strips

KEY MANAGERS & DERIVATIVES SPECIALISTS:	Direct Phone/Fax	Job Function
Mr. Phillip Boehmke Vice President	603/634-6156	Bond Department Head Portfolio Mgr – Structured Notes
Mr. Paul J. Mangus	603/634-6160	Chief Investment Officer

First Tennessee Bank

Bank/Portfolio

Location: 165 Madison Avenue
Memphis, TN 38103-2723

Fax: 901/523-4266 **Phone:** 901/523-4444

Profile: Current yield investor

Investment Portfolio: $ 3.0 billion

Use: **Balance Sheet/Risk Management**
Hedge interest rate risk

Investment Purposes
Alter portfolio weighting
Asset allocation
Capture extra yield
Hedge interest rate risk

Currencies: US dollar

Regions: United States

DERIVATIVES ACTIVITIES: **CAC Class: 6**

OTC Derivatives	**Interest rate**	
Plain Vanilla Derivatives	Swaps	
Exotic Derivatives	Index amortizing swaps	
Counterparty Rating Requirement:	A	

OTHER ALTERNATIVE INVESTMENTS:

CMOs/REMICs – Govt. Repos/reverse repos

KEY MANAGERS & DERIVATIVES SPECIALISTS:	**Direct Phone/Fax**	**Job Function**
Mr. Thomas Adams Senior Vice President		Chief Investment Officer Portfolio Mgr – Derivatives

First Union Corporation

Bank Holding Company

Location: Two First Union Plaza
Charlotte, NC 28288-0570

Fax: 704/374-4609 **Phone:** 704/374-6161

Profile: Spread investor

Use: **Balance Sheet/Risk Management**
Create synthetic fixed/floating rate
Hedge interest rate risk
Strategic liability management

Investment Purposes
Capture extra yield
Discretionary situations
Hedge interest rate risk
Provide incremental return

Currencies: US dollar

Regions: United States

DERIVATIVES ACTIVITIES: **CAC Class: 8**

Exchange-traded Options & Futures	**Interest rate**	
OTC Derivatives	**Currency, Interest rate**	
Plain Vanilla Derivatives	Swaps Forwards Swaptions	Caps Floors Collars

First Union Corporation – continued

OTHER ALTERNATIVE INVESTMENTS:

Repos/reverse repos

KEY MANAGERS & DERIVATIVES SPECIALISTS:	Direct Phone/Fax	Job Function
Mr. Robert T. Atwood Exec. Vice President & C.F.O.		Chief Financial Officer
Mr. Kenneth R. Stancliff S.V.P. & Treasurer		Treasurer Portfolio Mgr – Derivatives

First Union National Bank of Florida

Savings Bank/Bldg Society

Sub of First Union Corporation

Location: 2511 Ponce de Leon Boulevard
Coral Gables, FL 33134

Fax: 305/569-1938 **Phone:** 305/569-1904

Profile: Hold to maturity investor

Investment Portfolio: $ 500.0 - 999.0 million

Use: **Investment Purposes**
Beat conventional rates
Diversify portfolio
Reduce variability of returns

Currencies: US dollar

Regions: United States

DERIVATIVES ACTIVITIES: **CAC Class: 3**

OTC Derivatives **Plain Vanilla Derivatives**	**Bond** Swaps	
Structured Notes	Govt. agency MTNs Floaters	Multi-step-up callable bonds
Counterparty Rating Requirement:	BBB	

OTHER ALTERNATIVE INVESTMENTS:

CMOs/REMICs – Govt. Repos/reverse repos

KEY MANAGERS & DERIVATIVES SPECIALISTS:	Direct Phone/Fax	Job Function
Mr. George Chain	305/569-1963	Chief Investment Officer Portfolio Mgr – Derivatives Portfolio Mgr – Structured Notes

First Union National Bank (New Jersey)

Bank/Management Division

Sub of First Union Corporation

Location: 765 Broad Street
Newark, NJ 07102

Fax: 201/430-4821 **Phone:** 201/565-3200

Profile: Total return investor

Investment Portfolio: $ 9.0 billion

Use: **Investment Purposes**

Currencies: US dollar

Regions: United States

DERIVATIVES ACTIVITIES:

Structured Notes	Floaters

OTHER ALTERNATIVE INVESTMENTS:

CMOs/REMICs – Govt. Strips	Repos/reverse repos

KEY MANAGERS & DERIVATIVES SPECIALISTS:	**Direct Phone/Fax**	**Job Function**
Mr. Ed Apelian Assistant Vice President	201/430-4412	Portfolio Mgr – Structured Notes
Mr. L. Robert Cheshire	201/430-4392	Bond Department Head Portfolio Mgr – Structured Notes
Mr. David Crimmins Vice President	201/430-4407	Portfolio Mgr – Structured Notes

First Union National Bank of North Carolina - Funds Mgmt.

Bank/Management Division

Sub of First Union Corporation

Location: 301 South Tryon Street
Two First Union Plaza
Charlotte, NC 28288

Fax: 704/374-6902 **Phone:** 704/374-6161

Profile: Total return investor

Investment Portfolio: $ 17.0 billion

Use: **Balance Sheet/Risk Management**
Create synthetic fixed/floating rate
Hedge currency risk
Hedge interest rate risk
Hedge overseas investments
Strategic liability management

Currencies: US dollar, Australian dollar, Canadian dollar, French franc, German mark, Japanese yen, Mexican peso, Swiss franc, UK pound

Regions: United States, Canada, Europe, Latin America, Pacific Rim

First Union National Bank of North Carolina - Funds Mgmt. – continued

DERIVATIVES ACTIVITIES:		CAC Class: 8
Exchange-traded Options & Futures	**Currency, Interest rate**	
U.S. Treasury futures	Municipal futures	
U.S. Treasury options		
OTC Derivatives	**Currency, Interest rate**	
Plain Vanilla Derivatives	Swaps	Floors
	Forwards	Collars
	Caps	

OTHER ALTERNATIVE INVESTMENTS:		
	CMOs/REMICs – Govt.	Strips
	CMOs/REMICs – Private	Repos/reverse repos

KEY MANAGERS & DERIVATIVES SPECIALISTS:	Direct Phone/Fax	Job Function
Mr. Malcolm E. Everett III President		President
Mr. Glen T. Insley S.V.P. & Director	704/383-7682	Bond Department Head
Mr. Terry Turner S.V.P.-Risk Management	704/383-1815	Portfolio Mgr – Derivatives Trader – Derivatives Trader – Futures
Mr. Richard K. Wagoner Executive Vice President	704-374-4549	Chief Investment Officer

First Union National Bank (Pennsylvania) (Instl. Trust)

Bank/Trust

Sub of First Union Corporation

Location: 123 South Broad Street
13th Floor
Philadelphia, PA 19109

Fax: 215/985-6441 **Phone:** 215/985-6423

Profile: Total return investor

Investment Portfolio: $ 4.0 - 10.0 billion

Use: **Investment Purposes**

Currencies: US dollar

Regions: United States

DERIVATIVES ACTIVITIES:		CAC Class: 3
Structured Notes	Floaters	Multi-step-up callable bonds

OTHER ALTERNATIVE INVESTMENTS:		
	CMOs/REMICs – Govt.	CMOs/REMICs – Private

First Union National Bank (Pennsylvania) (Instl. Trust) – continued

KEY MANAGERS & DERIVATIVES SPECIALISTS:	Direct Phone/Fax	Job Function
Mr. Bruce J. Besecker Vice President	215/985-6423	Portfolio Mgr – Structured Notes
Mr. James M. Stark Vice President	215/985-6424	Portfolio Mgr – Structured Notes

Fischer, Francis, Trees and Watts, Inc.

Investment Manager

Location: 200 Park Avenue
46th Floor
New York, NY 10166-0005

Fax: 212/681-3250 **Phone:** 212/681-3000

Profile: Total return investor

Investment Portfolio: $ 16.3 billion

Use: **Investment Purposes**

Currencies: US dollar

Regions: United States

DERIVATIVES ACTIVITIES: **CAC Class: Inactive**

OTHER ALTERNATIVE INVESTMENTS:

CMOs/REMICs – Govt.
CMOs/REMICs – Private
Strips
Repos/reverse repos

KEY MANAGERS & DERIVATIVES SPECIALISTS:	Direct Phone/Fax	Job Function
Mr. Richard G. Fischer President		President
Mr. Carl C. Hamann		Bond Department Head
Mr. John H. Watts Chairman		Chief Investment Officer

Flaherty & Crumrine, Inc.

Equity Manager

Location: 301 East Colorado Boulevard
Suite 720
Pasadena, CA 91101

Fax: 818/795-0269 **Phone:** 818/795-7300

Profile: Total return investor

Investment Portfolio: $ 1.1 billion

Use: **Balance Sheet/Risk Management**
Hedge interest rate risk

Currencies: US dollar

Regions: United States

Flaherty & Crumrine, Inc. – continued

DERIVATIVES ACTIVITIES: **CAC Class: 5**

Exchange-traded Options & Futures U.S. Treasury futures	**Interest rate** U.S. Treasury options
Structured Notes	Inverse floaters

OTHER ALTERNATIVE INVESTMENTS:

CMOs/REMICs – Govt. Repos/reverse repos

KEY MANAGERS & DERIVATIVES SPECIALISTS:	Direct Phone/Fax	Job Function
Mr. Donald F. Crumrine Vice President		Portfolio Mgr – Futures Portfolio Mgr – Options Portfolio Mgr – Structured Notes *Corp*
Mr. Robert Ettinger Vice President		Portfolio Mgr – Futures Portfolio Mgr – Options Portfolio Mgr – Structured Notes *Corp*
Mr. Robert Flaherty President		President Chief Investment Officer Portfolio Mgr – Futures Portfolio Mgr – Options Portfolio Mgr – Structured Notes *Corp*
Mr. Peter Stimes Vice President		Portfolio Mgr – Futures Portfolio Mgr – Options Portfolio Mgr – Structured Notes *Corp*

Fleet Bank of Maine (Portland)

Bank/Trust

Sub of Fleet Financial Group

Location: One City Center
7th Floor
Portland, ME 04101

Fax: 207/874-5230 **Phone:** 207/874-5000

Profile: Hold to maturity investor

Investment Portfolio: $ 2.0 billion

Use: **Investment Purposes**

Currencies: US dollar

Regions: United States

DERIVATIVES ACTIVITIES: **CAC Class: Inactive**

OTHER ALTERNATIVE INVESTMENTS:

CMOs/REMICs – Govt.

Fleet Bank of Maine (Portland) – continued

KEY MANAGERS & DERIVATIVES SPECIALISTS:	Direct Phone/Fax	Job Function
Mr. Robert Cyr Vice President	207/874-5016	Chief Investment Officer

Fleet Financial Group

Bank Holding Company

Location: One Federal Street
Boston, MA 02211

Fax: 617/346-0130 **Phone:** 617/346-2000

Profile: Spread investor

Use:

Balance Sheet/Risk Management
Create synthetic fixed/floating rate
Hedge currency risk
Hedge interest rate risk
Incremental return
Strategic liability management

Investment Purposes
Adjust portfolio duration
Capture extra yield
Discretionary situations
Hedge bond portfolio risk
Hedge currency risk
Hedge interest rate risk
Protect currency gains
Provide incremental return

Currencies: US dollar, Australian dollar, Canadian dollar, German mark

Regions: United States

DERIVATIVES ACTIVITIES: **CAC Class: 8**

Exchange-traded Options & Futures

OTC Derivatives

Plain Vanilla Derivatives — **Currency, Interest rate**
Swaps
Forwards
Caps
Floors
Collars

Exotic Derivatives — Index amortizing swaps

Counterparty Rating Requirement: A

KEY MANAGERS & DERIVATIVES SPECIALISTS:	Direct Phone/Fax	Job Function
Mr. Douglas L. Jacobs Exec. V.P. & Treasurer	617/346-1165	Treasurer Portfolio Mgr – Derivatives
Mr. Eugene M. McQuade Exec. Vice President & C.F.O.		Chief Financial Officer
Mr. Terrence Murray Chairman, President & C.E.O.		President

Fleet Investment Advisors (Boston)

Bank/Management Division

Sub of Fleet Financial Group

Location: One Federal Street
30th Floor
Boston, MA 02211-2003

Fax: 617/292-2061 **Phone:** 617/346-5686

Profile: Total return investor

Investment Portfolio: $ 13.0 billion

Use:

Balance Sheet/Risk Management
Hedge balance sheet
Hedge interest rate risk
Lower transaction costs
Strategic liability management

Investment Purposes
Alter portfolio weighting
Adjust portfolio duration
Asset allocation
Convexity objectives
Hedge bond portfolio risk
Hedge currency risk
Hedge equity portfolio risk
Hedge interest rate risk
Lower transactions costs
Provide incremental return

Currencies: US dollar

Regions: United States

DERIVATIVES ACTIVITIES: **CAC Class: 5**

Exchange-traded Options & Futures U.S. Treasury futures	**Bond** U.S. Treasury options	
OTC Derivatives **Plain Vanilla Derivatives**	Swaps	Forwards
Structured Notes	Corporate MTNs CMT notes	Floaters
Counterparty Rating Requirement:	AAA	

OTHER ALTERNATIVE INVESTMENTS:

	CMOs/REMICs – Govt. CMOs/REMICs – Private	Strips Repos/reverse repos

KEY MANAGERS & DERIVATIVES SPECIALISTS:	**Direct Phone/Fax**	**Job Function**
Mr. Glenn Migliozzi Managing Director-Fixed Income	617/346-2221	Bond Department Head
Mr. Thomas M. O'Neill Chief Investment Officer	617/346-2201	Chief Investment Officer
Mr. Gunnar S. Overstrom Vice Chairman		Chief Financial Officer
Mr. Perry J. Vieth	617/346-5709	Portfolio Mgr – Derivatives Portfolio Mgr – Futures Portfolio Mgr – Options Portfolio Mgr – Structured Notes

Fleming Companies, Inc.

Corporation

Location: 6301 Waterford Boulevard
Oklahoma City, OK 73126-0647

Fax: 405/841-8149 **Phone:** 405/840-7200

Use: **Balance Sheet/Risk Management**
Create synthetic fixed/floating rate
Hedge balance sheet
Hedge commercial paper
Hedge interest rate risk
Meet interest rate target

Currencies: US dollar

Regions: United States, Canada, Europe

DERIVATIVES ACTIVITIES:

OTC Derivatives	**Interest rate**	
Plain Vanilla Derivatives	Swaps Forwards	Caps
Counterparty Rating Requirement:	None	

KEY MANAGERS & DERIVATIVES SPECIALISTS:	**Direct Phone/Fax**	**Job Function**
Mr. R. Randolph Devening Vice Chairman & C.F.O.		Chief Financial Officer
Mr. Robert E. Stauth Chairman, President & C.E.O.		President
Mr. John M. Thompson Vice President & Treasurer	405/841-8170	Treasurer Portfolio Mgr – Derivatives

Florida State Board of Administration

Government Pension Fund

Location: 1801 Hermitage Boulevard
Tallahassee, FL 32308

Fax: 904/921-2131 **Phone:** 904/488-4406

Profile: Total return investor

Investment Portfolio: $ 41.2 billion

Use: **Investment Purposes**
Alter portfolio weighting
Adjust portfolio duration
Asset allocation
Capture extra yield
Hedge bond portfolio risk
Hedge currency risk
Hedge interest rate risk
Protect currency gains

Currencies: US dollar, Australian dollar, Belgian franc, Canadian dollar, ECU, French franc, German mark, Italian lira, Japanese yen, Spanish peseta, Swiss franc, UK pound

Regions: United States, Canada, Europe, Pacific Rim

DERIVATIVES ACTIVITIES: **CAC Class: 7**

Exchange-traded Options & Futures U.S. Treasury futures	**Bond** U.S. Treasury options	
OTC Derivatives **Plain Vanilla Derivatives**	**Bond, Currency** Forwards	
Structured Notes	Corporate MTNs	Floaters
Counterparty Rating Requirement:	AA	

OTHER ALTERNATIVE INVESTMENTS:

CMOs/REMICs – Govt.
CMOs/REMICs – Private
GICs
Strips
Repos/reverse repos

KEY MANAGERS & DERIVATIVES SPECIALISTS:	Direct Phone/Fax	Job Function
Ms. Barbara L. Jarriel Chief Investment Officer	904/488-3061	Chief Investment Officer Portfolio Mgr – Futures Portfolio Mgr – Options
Ms. Deborah McCoy	904/488-3061	Portfolio Mgr – Derivatives Portfolio Mgr – Futures Portfolio Mgr – Options Portfolio Mgr – Structured Notes
Mr. Timothy Parker Senior Portfolio Manager	904/488-3061	Portfolio Mgr – Derivatives Portfolio Mgr – Futures Portfolio Mgr – Options Portfolio Mgr – Structured Notes

Florida State Board of Administration – continued

KEY MANAGERS & DERIVATIVES SPECIALISTS:	Direct Phone/Fax	Job Function
Ms. Sheilah R. Smith	904/488-3061	Portfolio Mgr – Derivatives Portfolio Mgr – Futures Portfolio Mgr – Options Portfolio Mgr – Structured Notes
Ms. Lynn H. Thompson Senior Portfolio Manager	904/488-4061	Portfolio Mgr – Derivatives Portfolio Mgr – Futures Portfolio Mgr – Options Portfolio Mgr – Structured Notes

The Ford Foundation

Foundation/Endowment

Location: 320 East 43rd Street
New York, NY 10017-4816

Fax: 212/599-4584 **Phone:** 212/573-5000

Profile: Total return investor

Investment Portfolio: $ 6.6 billion

Use: **Investment Purposes**
Hedge bond portfolio risk
Hedge currency risk
Protect currency gains

Currencies: US dollar, Japanese yen, UK pound

Regions: United States

DERIVATIVES ACTIVITIES: **CAC Class: 4**

OTC Derivatives **Plain Vanilla Derivatives**	**Currency** Forwards
Counterparty Rating Requirement:	AAA

OTHER ALTERNATIVE INVESTMENTS:

CMOs/REMICs – Govt.

KEY MANAGERS & DERIVATIVES SPECIALISTS:	Direct Phone/Fax	Job Function
Mr. Nicholas Gabriel Treasurer	212/573-4613	Treasurer
Mr. Walter Giles	212/573-4737	Fixed-Income Strategist *Corp, Govt, MBS* Research Analyst - Derivatives
Ms. Susan A. Ollila Director - Fixed-Income	212/573-4757	Bond Department Head *Corp, Govt, MBS* Portfolio Mgr – Derivatives
Ms. Linda B. Strumpf Vice President	212/573-5052	Chief Investment Officer
Mr. Franklin A. Thomas President	212/573-5383	President

Ford Motor Company

Corporation

Location:	The American Road Room 1040 Dearborn, MI 48121	**Fax:** 313/390-2106	**Phone:** 313/322-3000
Profile:	Total return investor	**Investment Portfolio:** $ 21.0 - 49.0 billion	
Use:	**Balance Sheet/Risk Management** Hedge currency risk Hedge interest rate risk Hedge overseas investments		

Currencies:	US dollar Australian dollar Canadian dollar German mark	Japanese yen Mexican peso Spanish peseta UK pound	**Regions:**	United States

DERIVATIVES ACTIVITIES: **CAC Class: 8**

Exchange-traded Options & Futures	**Currency**	
OTC Derivatives **Plain Vanilla Derivatives**	**Currency, Interest rate** Swaps Forwards	 Caps Floors

OTHER ALTERNATIVE INVESTMENTS:

	CMOs/REMICs – Govt.	Repos/reverse repos

KEY MANAGERS & DERIVATIVES SPECIALISTS:	Direct Phone/Fax	Job Function
Mr. John M. Devine V.P. & Chief Financial Officer		Chief Financial Officer
Mr. James Keefer	313/322-1480	Chief Investment Officer Portfolio Mgr – Derivatives
Mr. Malcolm S. Macdonald Treasurer		Treasurer
Mr. Alex Trotman Chairman, President & C.E.O.		President

Fort Washington Investment Advisors Inc.

Insurance Co/Management

Sub of The Western-Southern Life Insurance Company

Location: 400 Broadway
Cincinnati, OH 45202

Fax: 513/629-1047 **Phone:** 513/421-1800

Profile: Total return investor

Investment Portfolio: $ 7.0 billion

Use: **Investment Purposes**

Currencies: US dollar

Regions: United States

DERIVATIVES ACTIVITIES: **CAC Class: Inactive**

OTHER ALTERNATIVE INVESTMENTS:

CMOs/REMICs – Govt. CMOs/REMICs – Private

KEY MANAGERS & DERIVATIVES SPECIALISTS:	**Direct Phone/Fax**	**Job Function**
Mr. William F. Ledwin President	513/629-1170	President Chief Investment Officer Portfolio Mgr – Derivatives

Fort Washington Investment Advisors Inc. (Cincinnati)

Insurance Co/Management

Sub of The Western-Southern Life Insurance Company

Location: 420 East Fourth Street
Cincinnati, OH 45202

Fax: 513/361-7699 **Phone:** 513/361-7600

Profile: Total return investor

Investment Portfolio: $ 7.0 billion

Use: **Investment Purposes**

Currencies: US dollar

Regions: United States

DERIVATIVES ACTIVITIES: **CAC Class: Inactive**

OTHER ALTERNATIVE INVESTMENTS:

CMOs/REMICs – Govt. CMOs/REMICs – Private

KEY MANAGERS & DERIVATIVES SPECIALISTS:	**Direct Phone/Fax**	**Job Function**
Mr. James B. McGuire Vice President		Bond Department Head

Fort Wayne National Bank (Trust)

Bank/Trust

Sub of Fort Wayne National Corporation

Location: 110 West Berry Street
Fort Wayne, IN 46801-2311

Fax: 219/461-6214 **Phone:** 219/426-0555

Profile: Total return investor

Investment Portfolio: $ 1.4 billion

Use: **Investment Purposes**

Currencies: US dollar

Regions: United States

DERIVATIVES ACTIVITIES: **CAC Class: Inactive**

OTHER ALTERNATIVE INVESTMENTS:

CMOs/REMICs – Govt. Strips

KEY MANAGERS & DERIVATIVES SPECIALISTS:	**Direct Phone/Fax**	**Job Function**
Mr. George Donner Vice President		Chief Investment Officer

Fortis Advisers, Inc.

Mutual Fund Manager

Location: 5500 Wayzata Boulevard
Suite 1150
Golden Valley, MN 55416-1269

Fax: 612/544-6363 **Phone:** 612/544-1531

Profile: Total return investor

Investment Portfolio: $ 1.0 - 3.0 billion

Use: **Investment Purposes**
Hedge bond portfolio risk
Hedge currency risk
Hedge equity portfolio risk
Hedge interest rate risk

Currencies: US dollar

Regions: United States

DERIVATIVES ACTIVITIES:

Exchange-traded Options & Futures **Bond, Currency, Interest rate**

Fortis Advisers, Inc. – continued

OTHER ALTERNATIVE INVESTMENTS:

	CMOs/REMICs – Govt. CMOs/REMICs – Private	Repos/reverse repos

KEY MANAGERS & DERIVATIVES SPECIALISTS:	**Direct Phone/Fax**	**Job Function**
Mr. Dennis M. Ott S.V.P. - Fixed Income		Fixed-Income Strategist
Mr. Steven Poling Chief Financial Officer		Chief Investment Officer

Fortis Asset Management

Insurance Co/Management

Location: One Chase Manhattan Plaza
41st Floor
New York, NY 10005

Fax: 212/859-7202 **Phone:** 212/859-7000

Profile: Total return investor

Investment Portfolio: $ 5.4 billion

Use: **Investment Purposes**

Currencies: US dollar

Regions: United States

DERIVATIVES ACTIVITIES: **CAC Class: Inactive**

OTHER ALTERNATIVE INVESTMENTS:

CMOs/REMICs – Govt.

KEY MANAGERS & DERIVATIVES SPECIALISTS:	**Direct Phone/Fax**	**Job Function**
Mr. Howard Hudson Senior Vice President	212/859-7084 212/775-9773	Bond Department Head
Mr. Gary Yalen President	212/859-7062	President Chief Investment Officer

Franklin Federal Bancorp, A Federal Savings Bank

Savings Bank/Bldg Society

Sub of First Federal Financial Corp.

Location: 111 Congress Avenue
Austin, TX 78701-3217

Fax: 512/479-3498 **Phone:** 512/477-5000

Profile: Total return investor

Investment Portfolio: $ 1.0 - 3.0 billion

Use: **Investment Purposes**

Currencies: US dollar

Regions: United States

DERIVATIVES ACTIVITIES: **CAC Class: Inactive**

OTHER ALTERNATIVE INVESTMENTS:

CMOs/REMICs – Govt.
CMOs/REMICs – Private
Repos/reverse repos

KEY MANAGERS & DERIVATIVES SPECIALISTS:	Direct Phone/Fax	Job Function
Mr. Raymond Starrett S.V.P. & Treasurer		Treasurer Bond Department Head

Franklin Resources, Inc.

Mutual Fund Manager

Location: 16 South Main Street
Suite 303
Norwalk, CT 06854

Fax: 203/866-9961 **Phone:** 203/866-8575

Profile: Hold to maturity investor

Investment Portfolio: $ 3.0 billion

Use: **Investment Purposes**

Currencies: US dollar

Regions: United States

DERIVATIVES ACTIVITIES: **CAC Class: Inactive**

OTHER ALTERNATIVE INVESTMENTS:

CMOs/REMICs – Govt.
CMOs/REMICs – Private

KEY MANAGERS & DERIVATIVES SPECIALISTS:	Direct Phone/Fax	Job Function
Mr. John B. Pinkham V.P. – Franklin Group of Funds		Chief Investment Officer

Freeport-McMoRan Inc.

Corporation

Location: 1615 Poydras Street
New Orleans, LA 70112

Fax: 504/582-4936 **Phone:** 504/582-4000

Use: **Balance Sheet/Risk Management**
Create synthetic fixed/floating rate
Hedge currency risk
Hedge interest rate risk
Strategic liability management

Currencies: US dollar, German mark, Spanish peseta

Regions: United States, Europe

DERIVATIVES ACTIVITIES: **CAC Class: 8**

OTC Derivatives	**Currency, Interest rate**
Plain Vanilla Derivatives	

KEY MANAGERS & DERIVATIVES SPECIALISTS:	**Direct Phone/Fax**	**Job Function**
Mr. Richard C. Adkerson Senior Vice President & C.F.O.		Chief Financial Officer
Mr. William L. Arnold Director – Risk Management		Portfolio Mgr – Derivatives
Mr. R. Foster Duncan Treasurer		Treasurer

Fremont General Corporation

Insurance Co/Management

Location: 2020 Santa Monica Boulevard
6th Floor
Santa Monica, CA 90404

Fax: 310/315-5599 **Phone:** 310/315-5500

Profile: Spread investor

Investment Portfolio: $ 1.0 - 3.0 billion

Use: **Balance Sheet/Risk Management**
Hedge interest rate risk

Currencies: US dollar

Regions: United States

DERIVATIVES ACTIVITIES: **CAC Class: 2**

OTC Derivatives	**Interest rate**
Plain Vanilla Derivatives	Swaps

Counterparty Rating Requirement: A

OTHER ALTERNATIVE INVESTMENTS:

CMOs/REMICs – Govt.
CMOs/REMICs – Private
Strips
Repos/reverse repos

KEY MANAGERS & DERIVATIVES SPECIALISTS:	**Direct Phone/Fax**	**Job Function**
Mr. Wayne Bailey		Chief Investment Officer
Mr. Troy Grande Assistant Treasurer	310/315-5520 310/315-5593	Portfolio Mgr – Derivatives

Fremont Investment Advisors Inc.

Investment Manager

Location: 50 Fremont Street
Suite 3600
San Francisco, CA 94105

Fax: 415/284-8122 **Phone:** 415/768-4258

Profile: Total return investor

Investment Portfolio: $ 1.9 billion

Use: **Investment Purposes**

Currencies: US dollar

Regions: United States

DERIVATIVES ACTIVITIES: **CAC Class: Inactive**

OTHER ALTERNATIVE INVESTMENTS:

CMOs/REMICs – Govt. GICs

KEY MANAGERS & DERIVATIVES SPECIALISTS:	**Direct Phone/Fax**	**Job Function**
Mr. William Feeney	415/768-0521	Bond Department Head *Muni*
Mr. David L. Redo President & C.E.O.	415/768-6959	President Chief Investment Officer

The Frost National Bank (Portfolio)

Bank/Portfolio

Sub of Cullen/Frost Bankers, Inc.

Location: 100 West Houston Street
T-7
San Antonio, TX 78205-1457

Fax: 210/220-4614 **Phone:** 210/220-4011

Profile: Hold to maturity investor

Investment Portfolio: $ 1.0 - 3.0 billion

Use: **Balance Sheet/Risk Management**
Hedge interest rate risk

Currencies: US dollar

Regions: United States

DERIVATIVES ACTIVITIES:

OTC Derivatives	**Interest rate**
Plain Vanilla Derivatives	Swaps

Counterparty Rating Requirement: A

OTHER ALTERNATIVE INVESTMENTS:

CMOs/REMICs – Govt.
CMOs/REMICs – Private
Repos/reverse repos

The Frost National Bank (Portfolio) – continued

KEY MANAGERS & DERIVATIVES SPECIALISTS:	**Direct Phone/Fax**	**Job Function**
Mr. Samuel L. Bright Vice President	210/220-4859	Portfolio Mgr – Derivatives
Mr. George Mead Executive Vice President	210/220-4936 210/220-4619	Chief Investment Officer

Fulton Bank (Trust)

Bank/Trust

Location: One Penn Square
Lancaster, PA 17602

Fax: 717/291-2695 **Phone:** 717/291-2411

Profile: Total return investor

Investment Portfolio: $ 1.0 billion

Use: **Investment Purposes**

Currencies: US dollar

Regions: United States

DERIVATIVES ACTIVITIES: **CAC Class: Inactive**

OTHER ALTERNATIVE INVESTMENTS:

CMOs/REMICs – Govt.
CMOs/REMICs – Private
Strips

KEY MANAGERS & DERIVATIVES SPECIALISTS:	**Direct Phone/Fax**	**Job Function**
Mr. Thomas Webber Vice President	717/291-2556	Chief Investment Officer

Gabelli-O'Connor Fixed Income Management Co.

Investment Manager

Location: 19 Old Kings Highway South
Darien, CT 06820-4526

Fax: 203/655-7719 **Phone:** 203/655-1999

Profile: Total return investor

Investment Portfolio: $ 4.0 billion

Use: **Investment Purposes**

Currencies: US dollar

Regions: United States

DERIVATIVES ACTIVITIES: **CAC Class: Inactive**

OTHER ALTERNATIVE INVESTMENTS:

CMOs/REMICs – Govt.

KEY MANAGERS & DERIVATIVES SPECIALISTS:	**Direct Phone/Fax**	**Job Function**
Mr. Thomas E. O'Connor Managing General Partner		Bond Department Head
Mr. Henley L. Smith Sr. Portfolio Mgr-Money Mkt.		Chief Investment Officer

GEM Capital Management, Inc.

Investment Manager

Location: 70 East 55th Street
12th Floor
New York, NY 10022

Fax: 212/753-0735 **Phone:** 212/753-0700

Profile: Total return investor

Investment Portfolio: $ 1.1 billion

Use: **Investment Purposes**

Currencies: US dollar

Regions: United States

DERIVATIVES ACTIVITIES: **CAC Class: Inactive**

OTHER ALTERNATIVE INVESTMENTS:

CMOs/REMICs – Govt.

KEY MANAGERS & DERIVATIVES SPECIALISTS:	**Direct Phone/Fax**	**Job Function**
Mr. Gerald Untermann President		President Chief Investment Officer

General Accident Group

Insurance Co/P & C

Sub of General Accident Insurance

Location: 436 Walnut Street
Philadelphia, PA 19105

Fax: 215/625-2103 **Phone:** 215/625-1000

Profile: Hold to maturity investor

Investment Portfolio: $ 5.5 billion

Use: **Balance Sheet/Risk Management**

Currencies: US dollar

Regions: United States

DERIVATIVES ACTIVITIES: **CAC Class: Inactive**

OTHER ALTERNATIVE INVESTMENTS:

CMOs/REMICs – Govt.

KEY MANAGERS & DERIVATIVES SPECIALISTS:	**Direct Phone/Fax**	**Job Function**
Mr. George Morris Vice Chairman	215/625-1021	Chief Investment Officer
Mr. Kevin Schildt Vice President	215/625-2064	Bond Department Head

General American Investment Management Company (GAIMCO)

Insurance Co/Life

Sub of General American Life Insurance Co.

Location: 700 Market Street
St. Louis, MO 63101

Fax: 314/444-0486 **Phone:** 314/231-1700

Profile: Total return investor

Investment Portfolio: $ 7.0 billion

Use: **Balance Sheet/Risk Management**

Currencies: US dollar

Regions: United States

DERIVATIVES ACTIVITIES: **CAC Class: Inactive**

OTHER ALTERNATIVE INVESTMENTS:

CMOs/REMICs – Govt.
CMOs/REMICs – Private
Strips
Repos/reverse repos

KEY MANAGERS & DERIVATIVES SPECIALISTS:	**Direct Phone/Fax**	**Job Function**
Mr. Richard A. Liddy President & C.E.O.	314/444-0655	President
Mr. Leonard M. Rubenstein Executive Vice President	314/444-0624	Chief Investment Officer
Ms. Terri Tanaka Vice President	314/444-0781 314/444-0726	Bond Department Head *Corp, Govt, MBS*

General Electric Company

Corporation

Location: 3135 Easton Turnpike
Fairfield, CT 06431

Fax: 203/373-3131 **Phone:** 203/373-2211

Use: **Balance Sheet/Risk Management**
Hedge currency risk
Hedge interest rate risk
Hedge overseas investments
Strategic liability management

Currencies: US dollar
Australian dollar
Belgian franc
Canadian dollar
ECU
French franc
German mark
Italian lira
Indonesian rupiah
Japanese yen
Mexican peso
Spanish peseta
Swiss franc
Thai baht
UK pound

Regions: United States
Canada
Europe
Latin America
Pacific Rim
Emerging mkts

DERIVATIVES ACTIVITIES: **CAC Class: 6**

OTC Derivatives — **Bond, Currency, Interest rate**

Plain Vanilla Derivatives
Swaps
Forwards

Exotic Derivatives
CMT options

General Electric Company – continued

KEY MANAGERS & DERIVATIVES SPECIALISTS:	Direct Phone/Fax	Job Function
Mr. James R. Bunt Vice President & Treasurer		Treasurer Portfolio Mgr – Derivatives
Mr. Dennis D. Dammerman Senior Vice President-Finance		Chief Financial Officer

General Electric Capital Corporation

Corporation

Sub of General Electric Company

Location: 260 Long Ridge Road
Stamford, CT 06927

Fax: 203/357-6791 **Phone:** 203/357-4000

Use: **Balance Sheet/Risk Management**
Access global mkts
Hedge balance sheet
Hedge currency risk
Hedge interest rate risk
Hedge overseas investments
Strategic liability management

Currencies: US dollar, Australian dollar, Belgian franc, Canadian dollar, ECU, French franc, German mark, Italian lira, Japanese yen, Spanish peseta, Swiss franc, Thai baht, UK pound

Regions: United States, Canada, Europe, Latin America, Pacific Rim, Emerging mkts

DERIVATIVES ACTIVITIES: **CAC Class: 8**

OTC Derivatives	**Bond, Currency, Interest rate**	
Plain Vanilla Derivatives	Swaps	Forwards

Counterparty Rating Requirement: AA

KEY MANAGERS & DERIVATIVES SPECIALISTS:	Direct Phone/Fax	Job Function
Mr. James A. Colica S.V.P. – Risk Management	203/357-4244	Portfolio Mgr – Derivatives
Mr. James A. Parke Sr. Vice President – Finance	203/357-4304	Chief Financial Officer
Mr. Jeffrey S. Werner Vice President & Treasurer	203/357-4963	Treasurer Portfolio Mgr – Derivatives

General Electric Investment Corporation

Corporate Pension Fund

Sub of General Electric Company

Location: 3003 Summer Street
Stamford, CT 06905

Fax: 203/326-4215 **Phone:** 203/326-2300

Profile: Total return investor

Investment Portfolio: $ 41.0 billion

Use: **Investment Purposes**

Currencies: US dollar

Regions: United States

DERIVATIVES ACTIVITIES: **CAC Class: Inactive**

OTHER ALTERNATIVE INVESTMENTS:

CMOs/REMICs – Govt.

KEY MANAGERS & DERIVATIVES SPECIALISTS:	Direct Phone/Fax	Job Function
Mr. Dale F. Frey Chairman & President	203/326-2310	President Chief Investment Officer

General Motors Acceptance Corporation

Finance/Credit Company

Sub of General Motors Corporation

Location: 3031 West Grand Boulevard
New Center One Suite 695
Detroit, MI 48202

Fax: 313/974-1244 **Phone:** 313/974-1222

Profile: Total return investor

Investment Portfolio: $ 4.0 - 10.0 billion

Use: **Balance Sheet/Risk Management**
Hedge currency risk
Hedge interest rate risk
Meet interest rate target

Currencies: US dollar, Australian dollar, Canadian dollar, UK pound

Regions: United States

DERIVATIVES ACTIVITIES: **CAC Class: 7**

Exchange-traded Options & Futures — **Interest rate**

OTC Derivatives — **Currency, Interest rate**
Plain Vanilla Derivatives: Swaps, Swaptions, Caps

OTHER ALTERNATIVE INVESTMENTS:

CMOs/REMICs – Govt. CMOs/REMICs – Private

KEY MANAGERS & DERIVATIVES SPECIALISTS:	Direct Phone/Fax	Job Function
Mr. John D. Finnegan Exec. Vice President & C.F.O.		Chief Financial Officer
Mr. John R. Rines President		President
Mr. David Walker Director-Liability Risk Mgmt.		Bond Department Head Portfolio Mgr – Derivatives

General Motors Investment Management Corp.

Corporation

Location: 767 Fifth Avenue
26th Floor
New York, NY 10153-0013

Fax: 212/418-3665 **Phone:** 212/418-6100

Profile: Total return investor

Investment Portfolio: $ 1.0 - 3.0 billion

Use: **Investment Purposes**

Currencies: US dollar

Regions: United States

DERIVATIVES ACTIVITIES:

Structured Notes	Corporate MTNs

OTHER ALTERNATIVE INVESTMENTS:

CMOs/REMICs – Govt. Strips

KEY MANAGERS & DERIVATIVES SPECIALISTS:	Direct Phone/Fax	Job Function
Mr. William P. Miller Director	212/418-6327	Portfolio Mgr – Structured Notes
Mr. William Noah Director – Asset Mix Management		Portfolio Mgr – Structured Notes
Mr. W. Allen Reed President & C.E.O.	212/418-3585	President Chief Investment Officer
Mr. Edgar Sullivan Director – Portfolio Strategy	212/418-6369	Fixed-Income Strategist

General Re Asset Management, Inc.

Insurance Co/Management

Sub of General Re Corporation

Location: 695 East Main Street
Financial Centre
Stamford, CT 06901

Fax: 203/328-6504 **Phone:** 203/328-5000

Profile: Spread investor

Investment Portfolio: $ 19.0 billion

Use: **Balance Sheet/Risk Management**
Create synthetic fixed/floating rate
Hedge balance sheet
Hedge currency risk
Hedge interest rate risk
Incremental return
Strategic liability management

Investment Purposes
Asset allocation
Convexity objectives
Discretionary situations
Diversify portfolio
Hedge bond portfolio risk
Provide incremental return

Currencies: US dollar

Regions: United States

General Re Asset Management, Inc. – continued

DERIVATIVES ACTIVITIES: **CAC Class: 4**

Exchange-traded Options & Futures	**Bond, Interest rate**	
U.S. Treasury futures	U.S. Treasury options	
OTC Derivatives	**Currency, Interest rate**	
Plain Vanilla Derivatives	Swaps	Caps
	Forwards	Floors
Exotic Derivatives		

OTHER ALTERNATIVE INVESTMENTS:

CMOs/REMICs – Govt.	Repos/reverse repos
CMOs/REMICs – Private	

KEY MANAGERS & DERIVATIVES SPECIALISTS:	**Direct Phone/Fax**	**Job Function**
Mr. Enrique Chang Director-Quantitative Strategy		Portfolio Mgr – Derivatives Portfolio Mgr – Futures Portfolio Mgr – Options
Mr. Stephen F. Fluegel President	203/328-6522 203/328-6423	President Portfolio Mgr – Derivatives Portfolio Mgr – Futures Portfolio Mgr – Options
Mr. Ernest C. Frohboese Sr. Vice President & C.E.O.	203/328-6506	Chief Investment Officer
Mr. Yifeng Yang Assistant Director		Portfolio Mgr – Derivatives Portfolio Mgr – Futures Portfolio Mgr – Options

Gibraltar Advisors

Broker/Management Sub

Location: Nine West 57th Street
40th Floor
New York, NY 10019

Fax: 212/415-5885 **Phone:** 212/415-5800

Profile: Total return investor

Investment Portfolio: $ 1.8 billion

Use: **Investment Purposes**

Currencies: US dollar

Regions: United States

DERIVATIVES ACTIVITIES: **CAC Class: Inactive**

OTHER ALTERNATIVE INVESTMENTS:

CMOs/REMICs – Govt.	Strips
CMOs/REMICs – Private	

KEY MANAGERS & DERIVATIVES SPECIALISTS:	**Direct Phone/Fax**	**Job Function**
Ms. Katherine Kreig	212/415-5833 212/415-5814	Bond Department Head

The Glenmede Trust Company

Bank/Trust

Sub of Glenmede Corporation

Location: 1650 Market Street
One Liberty Plaza Suite 1200
Philadelphia, PA 19103

Fax: 215/419-6197 **Phone:** 215/419-6000

Profile: Total return investor

Investment Portfolio: $ 7.3 billion

Use: **Investment Purposes**

Currencies: US dollar

Regions: United States

DERIVATIVES ACTIVITIES: **CAC Class: Inactive**

OTHER ALTERNATIVE INVESTMENTS:

CMOs/REMICs – Govt.
CMOs/REMICs – Private
Strips
Repos/reverse repos

KEY MANAGERS & DERIVATIVES SPECIALISTS:	**Direct Phone/Fax**	**Job Function**
Mr. John W. Church, Jr. Senior Vice President	215/419-6030	Chief Investment Officer
Mr. Thomas W. Langfitt President		President
Ms. Mary Ann B. Wirts V.P. & Director – Fixed Income	215/419-6037	Bond Department Head

Glickenhaus & Company (Investments)

Broker/Management Sub

Location: Six East 43rd Street
10th Floor
New York, NY 10017-4641

Fax: 212/599-2537 **Phone:** 212/953-7800

Profile: Total return investor

Investment Portfolio: $ 3.0 billion

Use: **Investment Purposes**

Currencies: US dollar

Regions: United States

DERIVATIVES ACTIVITIES: **CAC Class: Inactive**

OTHER ALTERNATIVE INVESTMENTS:

CMOs/REMICs – Govt.
CMOs/REMICs – Private
Repos/reverse repos

KEY MANAGERS & DERIVATIVES SPECIALISTS:	**Direct Phone/Fax**	**Job Function**
Mr. Seth M. Glickenhaus	212/953-7877	Chief Investment Officer
Mr. James R. Vaccacio Manager	212/953-7563	Bond Department Head

GMG/Seneca Capital Management

Investment Manager

Location: 909 Montgomery Street
Suite 600
San Francisco, CA 94133

Fax: 415/677-1692 **Phone:** 415/677-1550

Profile: Total return investor

Investment Portfolio: $ 2.4 billion

Use: **Balance Sheet/Risk Management**
Create synthetic fixed/floating rate
Hedge currency risk

Investment Purposes
Hedge bond portfolio risk
Hedge interest rate risk

Currencies: US dollar

Regions: United States, Canada, Europe, Latin America, Pacific Rim, Emerging mkts

DERIVATIVES ACTIVITIES: **CAC Class: 2**

Exchange-traded Options & Futures
U.S. Treasury futures
U.S. Treasury options
Municipal futures
Municipal options

OTC Derivatives
Plain Vanilla Derivatives — **Bond**: Swaps, Forwards

Structured Notes: Inverse floaters

Counterparty Rating Requirement: A

OTHER ALTERNATIVE INVESTMENTS:

CMOs/REMICs – Govt.
CMOs/REMICs – Private
Strips

KEY MANAGERS & DERIVATIVES SPECIALISTS:	Direct Phone/Fax	Job Function
Mr. Harold Nathan Senior Portfolio Manager		Portfolio Mgr – Derivatives Portfolio Mgr – Futures Portfolio Mgr – Options Portfolio Mgr – Structured Notes
Ms. Gail P. Seneca		Chief Investment Officer

GNA Capital Management Inc.

Insurance Co/Management

Sub of GE Capital Company

Location: 601 Union Street
Two Union Square Suite 5600
Seattle, WA 98101

Fax: 206/583-5606 **Phone:** 206/625-1755

Profile: Total return investor

Investment Portfolio: $ 11.0 - 20.0 billion

Use: **Balance Sheet/Risk Management**
Hedge balance sheet
Hedge interest rate risk
Strategic liability management

Investment Purposes
Adjust portfolio duration
Hedge bond portfolio risk
Hedge interest rate risk

Currencies: US dollar

Regions: United States

GNA Capital Management Inc. – continued

DERIVATIVES ACTIVITIES:		**CAC Class: 4**
Exchange-traded Options & Futures U.S. Treasury options	**Interest rate**	
OTC Derivatives **Plain Vanilla Derivatives**	**Currency, Interest rate** Swaptions	
Structured Notes	Govt. agency MTNs	
Counterparty Rating Requirement:	AA	

OTHER ALTERNATIVE INVESTMENTS:		
	CMOs/REMICs – Govt. CMOs/REMICs – Private	Strips

KEY MANAGERS & DERIVATIVES SPECIALISTS:	**Direct Phone/Fax**	**Job Function**
Mr. Charles A. Kaminski Vice President – Investments	206/516-4998	Portfolio Mgr – Derivatives Portfolio Mgr – Structured Notes
Mr. William Koski Vice President	206/625-2854	Chief Investment Officer Portfolio Mgr – Derivatives Portfolio Mgr – Futures Portfolio Mgr – Options Portfolio Mgr – Structured Notes
Mr. Jerome Powers	206/625-2799	Portfolio Mgr – Derivatives Portfolio Mgr – Futures Portfolio Mgr – Options Portfolio Mgr – Structured Notes
Mr. Geoffrey Stiff Chief Investment Officer		Chief Financial Officer

Golden Eagle Insurance Company

Insurance Co/P & C

Location: 7175 Navajo Road
San Diego, CA 92119-1642

Fax: 619/460-3820 **Phone:** 619/463-5800

Profile: Total return investor

Investment Portfolio: $ 1.2 billion

Use: **Investment Purposes**

Currencies: US dollar

Regions: United States

DERIVATIVES ACTIVITIES:	**CAC Class: Inactive**

OTHER ALTERNATIVE INVESTMENTS:		
	CMOs/REMICs – Govt.	CMOs/REMICs – Private

KEY MANAGERS & DERIVATIVES SPECIALISTS:	**Direct Phone/Fax**	**Job Function**
Mr. Daniel Ukkestad Vice President	Ext. 1315	Chief Investment Officer

Goldman Sachs Asset Management (U.S.A.)

Broker/Management Sub

Sub of Goldman, Sachs & Company

Location: One New York Plaza
41st Floor
New York, NY 10004

Fax: 212/902-9100 **Phone:** 212/902-0800

Profile: Total return investor

Investment Portfolio: $ 50.0 billion

Use: **Balance Sheet/Risk Management**
Hedge currency risk
Hedge interest rate risk
Incremental return

Currencies: US dollar

Regions: United States

DERIVATIVES ACTIVITIES:

Exchange-traded Options & Futures	**Bond, Interest rate**	
OTC Derivatives **Plain Vanilla Derivatives**	**Bond**	
Structured Notes	Corporate MTNs Govt. agency MTNs Floaters	Inverse floaters Periodic capped floaters

OTHER ALTERNATIVE INVESTMENTS:

CMOs/REMICs – Govt. CMOs/REMICs – Private GICs	Strips Repos/reverse repos

KEY MANAGERS & DERIVATIVES SPECIALISTS:	**Direct Phone/Fax**	**Job Function**
Ms. Sharmin Mossavar-Rahmani	212/902-2300	Chief Investment Officer Bond Department Head
Mr. Theodore T. Sotir	212/357-1221	Portfolio Mgr – Derivatives Portfolio Mgr – Structured Notes

W.R. Grace & Company

Corporation

Location: One Town Center Road
Boca Raton, FL 33486-1001

Fax: 407/362-2193 **Phone:** 407/362-2000

Profile: Directional investor

Use: **Balance Sheet/Risk Management**
Access global mkts
Bypass regulations
Create synthetic fixed/floating rate
Hedge balance sheet
Hedge commercial paper
Hedge currency risk
Hedge interest rate risk
Lower transaction costs
Meet interest rate target
Meet principal target
Meet cash flow target
Reduce cost of capital

Investment Purposes
Hedge currency risk
Provide incremental return

Currencies: US dollar

Regions: United States Europe

W.R. Grace & Company – continued

DERIVATIVES ACTIVITIES:

OTC Derivatives		
Plain Vanilla Derivatives	Swaps Corporate MTNs	Bond index notes
Counterparty Rating Requirement:	A	

KEY MANAGERS & DERIVATIVES SPECIALISTS:	**Direct Phone/Fax**	**Job Function**
Mr. Peter D. Houchin S.V.P., Treasurer & C.F.O.	407/362-1955	Chief Financial Officer Treasurer
Mr. Hartmut Liebel Director – Financial Risk Mgmt	407/362-1962	Portfolio Mgr – Derivatives

Gradison-McDonald Asset Management

Broker/Management Sub

Location: 580 Walnut Street
1st Floor
Cincinnati, OH 45202

Fax: 513/579-5080 **Phone:** 513/579-5000

Profile: Total return investor

Investment Portfolio: $ 2.5 billion

Use: **Balance Sheet/Risk Management**
Hedge interest rate risk

Investment Purposes
Alter portfolio weighting
Capture extra yield
Diversify portfolio
Provide incremental return
Reduce variability of returns

Currencies: US dollar

Regions: United States

DERIVATIVES ACTIVITIES: **CAC Class: 2**

Exchange-traded Options & Futures Municipal futures		
Structured Notes	Govt. agency MTNs	Floaters

OTHER ALTERNATIVE INVESTMENTS:

	CMOs/REMICs – Govt. CMOs/REMICs – Private	Repos/reverse repos

KEY MANAGERS & DERIVATIVES SPECIALISTS:	**Direct Phone/Fax**	**Job Function**
Mr. Stephen C. Dilbone Vice President	513/579-5966	Portfolio Mgr – Futures Portfolio Mgr – Structured Notes
Mr. William Leugers Executive Vice President	513/579-5098	Chief Investment Officer
Mr. Michael J. Link Senior Vice President	513/579-5860	Bond Department Head *Muni*
Mr. Steven Wesselkamper	513/579-5074 513/579-5947	Portfolio Mgr – Futures Portfolio Mgr – Structured Notes

Grantham, Mayo, Van Otterloo & Company

Investment Manager

Location: 40 Rowes Wharf
4th Floor
Boston, MA 02110

Fax: 617/439-0457 **Phone:** 617/346-7610

Profile: Total return investor

Investment Portfolio: $ 14.8 billion

Use: **Investment Purposes**
Hedge bond portfolio risk
Hedge currency risk
Hedge equity portfolio risk
Hedge interest rate risk

Currencies: US dollar

Regions: United States

DERIVATIVES ACTIVITIES:

Exchange-traded Options & Futures	**Bond, Currency, Interest rate**

OTHER ALTERNATIVE INVESTMENTS:

CMOs/REMICs – Govt.	Repos/reverse repos
CMOs/REMICs – Private	

KEY MANAGERS & DERIVATIVES SPECIALISTS:	**Direct Phone/Fax**	**Job Function**
Mr. Jeremy Grantham Senior Partner		Chief Investment Officer
Ms. Barbara Wall		Portfolio Mgr – Futures Portfolio Mgr – Options

Great Western Bank, a Federal Savings Bank (Treasury)

Savings Bank/Bldg Society

Sub of Great Western Financial Corporation

Location: 9200 Oakdale Avenue
Chatsworth, CA 91311

Fax: 818/775-2811 **Phone:** 818/775-2800

Profile: Hold to maturity investor

Investment Portfolio: $ 10.0 billion

Use: **Balance Sheet/Risk Management**
Create synthetic fixed/floating rate
Hedge balance sheet
Hedge interest rate risk
Strategic liability management

Currencies: US dollar

Regions: United States

DERIVATIVES ACTIVITIES: **CAC Class: 4**

OTC Derivatives **Plain Vanilla Derivatives**	**Interest rate** Swaps Forwards	 Caps Floors
Structured Notes	Corporate MTNs Govt. agency MTNs	Floaters Periodic capped floaters
Counterparty Rating Requirement:	A	

Great Western Bank, a Federal Savings Bank (Treasury) – continued

OTHER ALTERNATIVE INVESTMENTS:

	CMOs/REMICs – Govt.	Repos/reverse repos

KEY MANAGERS & DERIVATIVES SPECIALISTS:	Direct Phone/Fax	Job Function
Mr. Bruce Antenberg Treasurer		Treasurer
Mr. Michael Clawson First Vice President	818/775-3450	Chief Investment Officer
Mr. Carl Geuther Chief Financial Officer	818/775-3436 818/775-3333	Chief Financial Officer
Mr. Mark Javurek		Portfolio Mgr – Derivatives

The Greater New York Savings Bank

Savings Bank/Bldg Society

Location: One Penn Plaza
New York, NY 10019

Fax: 212/613-4117 **Phone:** 212/613-4000

Profile: Hold to maturity investor

Investment Portfolio: $ 2.5 billion

Use: **Balance Sheet/Risk Management**
Create synthetic fixed/floating rate
Hedge balance sheet
Hedge interest rate risk
Strategic liability management

Currencies: US dollar

Regions: United States

DERIVATIVES ACTIVITIES:

OTC Derivatives **Plain Vanilla Derivatives**	Caps	Floors
Structured Notes	Corporate MTNs CMT notes	Floaters Periodic capped floaters

OTHER ALTERNATIVE INVESTMENTS:

	CMOs/REMICs – Govt. CMOs/REMICs – Private	Repos/reverse repos

KEY MANAGERS & DERIVATIVES SPECIALISTS:	Direct Phone/Fax	Job Function
Mr. Philip A. Cimino		Chief Investment Officer
Mr. Matthew Connolly First Vice President		Portfolio Mgr – Derivatives Portfolio Mgr – Structured Notes
Mr. Gene Smolenski		Portfolio Mgr – Derivatives Portfolio Mgr – Structured Notes

Greenwich Street Advisors

Mutual Fund Manager

Sub of Smith Barney, Inc. (Greenwich Street)

Location: 388 Greenwich Street
22nd Floor
New York, NY 10013

Fax: 212/816-6006 **Phone:** 212/816-5700

Profile: Total return investor

Investment Portfolio: $ 50.1 billion

Use: **Investment Purposes**
Hedge bond portfolio risk

Currencies: US dollar

Regions: United States

DERIVATIVES ACTIVITIES: **CAC Class: 7**

Exchange-traded Options & Futures
U.S. Treasury futures
U.S. Treasury options

Bond
Municipal futures
Municipal options

OTC Derivatives
Plain Vanilla Derivatives

Counterparty Rating Requirement: AA

OTHER ALTERNATIVE INVESTMENTS:

CMOs/REMICs – Govt.
CMOs/REMICs – Private
GICs
Strips
Repos/reverse repos

KEY MANAGERS & DERIVATIVES SPECIALISTS:	**Direct Phone/Fax**	**Job Function**
Mr. James E. Conroy Managing Director	212/816-4117	Bond Department Head Portfolio Mgr – Futures *Corp, Govt*
Mr. Joseph P. Deane S.V.P. & Managing Director	212/816-4275	Portfolio Mgr – Futures Portfolio Mgr – Options
Mr. Peter Demirale Assistant Vice President		Bond Department Head *Govt*
Mr. Kenneth Egan Managing Director	212/816-4732	Portfolio Mgr – Derivatives Portfolio Mgr – Futures Portfolio Mgr – Options
Mr. Patrick Sheehan Vice President		Portfolio Mgr – Derivatives
Mr. Thomas B. Stiles Chairman	212/816-5723	Chief Investment Officer

Greenwich Street Advisors Municipal Management

Broker/Management Sub

Sub of Smith Barney, Inc.

Location: 388 Greenwich Street
23rd Floor
New York, NY 10013

Fax: 212/816-5117 **Phone:** 212/816-5711

Profile: Total return investor

Investment Portfolio: $ 1.0 - 3.0 billion

Use: **Investment Purposes**

Currencies: US dollar

Regions: United States

DERIVATIVES ACTIVITIES: **CAC Class: Inactive**

OTHER ALTERNATIVE INVESTMENTS:

CMOs/REMICs – Govt.
CMOs/REMICs – Private

KEY MANAGERS & DERIVATIVES SPECIALISTS:	**Direct Phone/Fax**	**Job Function**
Mr. Ronald E. Perry Managing Director		Chief Investment Officer Bond Department Head *Muni*

Guaranty Federal Bank, F.S.B.

Savings Bank/Bldg Society

Location: 8333 Douglas Avenue
Dallas, TX 75225

Fax: 214/360-8983 **Phone:** 214/360-3360

Profile: Hold to maturity investor

Investment Portfolio: $ 7.7 billion

Use: **Balance Sheet/Risk Management**
Hedge interest rate risk

Currencies: US dollar

Regions: United States

DERIVATIVES ACTIVITIES: **CAC Class: 4**

Exchange-traded Options & Futures

OTC Derivatives **Plain Vanilla Derivatives**	**Interest rate** Swaps
Counterparty Rating Requirement:	A

OTHER ALTERNATIVE INVESTMENTS:

CMOs/REMICs – Govt.
CMOs/REMICs – Private
Repos/reverse repos

KEY MANAGERS & DERIVATIVES SPECIALISTS:	**Direct Phone/Fax**	**Job Function**
Mr. Jack Falconi Director of Investments	Ext. 4865	Bond Department Head *Govt, MBS* Portfolio Mgr – Derivatives

Guardian Life Insurance Co. of America

Insurance Co/Life

Location: 201 Park Avenue South
7th Floor
New York, NY 10003

Fax: 212/777-6715 **Phone:** 212/598-8000

Profile: Total return investor

Investment Portfolio: $ 9.0 billion

Use: **Balance Sheet/Risk Management** **Investment Purposes**

Currencies: US dollar

Regions: United States

DERIVATIVES ACTIVITIES:

Structured Notes	Corporate MTNs	Govt. agency MTNs

OTHER ALTERNATIVE INVESTMENTS:

	CMOs/REMICs – Govt.	CMOs/REMICs – Private

KEY MANAGERS & DERIVATIVES SPECIALISTS:	**Direct Phone/Fax**	**Job Function**
Mr. Mark Dunetz Assistant Vice President	212/598-1961	Portfolio Mgr – Structured Notes
Dr. Frank J. Jones Exec. Vice President & C.I.O.	212/598-8232	Chief Investment Officer
Mr. Joseph D. Sargent President & C.E.O.		President

Guardian Savings & Loan Association

Savings Bank/Bldg Society

Location: 1220 Augusta Street
Houston, TX 77057

Fax: 713/787-3192 **Phone:** 713/787-3100

Profile: Total return investor

Investment Portfolio: $ 1.9 billion

Use: **Investment Purposes**

Currencies: US dollar

Regions: United States

DERIVATIVES ACTIVITIES: **CAC Class: Inactive**

OTHER ALTERNATIVE INVESTMENTS:

	CMOs/REMICs – Govt.	CMOs/REMICs – Private

KEY MANAGERS & DERIVATIVES SPECIALISTS:	**Direct Phone/Fax**	**Job Function**
Mr. James Day Executive Vice President		Chief Investment Officer

M.A. Hanna Company

Corporation

Location: 200 Public Square
Cleveland, OH 44114-2304

Fax: 216/589-4200 **Phone:** 216/589-4000

Use: **Balance Sheet/Risk Management**
Hedge balance sheet
Hedge currency risk
Protect currency gains
Strategic liability management

Currencies: US dollar, Canadian dollar, French franc, German mark, Japanese yen, UK pound

Regions: United States

DERIVATIVES ACTIVITIES: **CAC Class: 2**

Exchange-traded Options & Futures — **Currency**

OTC Derivatives
Plain Vanilla Derivatives — Swaps, Forwards

KEY MANAGERS & DERIVATIVES SPECIALISTS:	**Direct Phone/Fax**	**Job Function**
Mr. Michael S. Duffey Treasurer		Treasurer Portfolio Mgr – Derivatives
Mr. Douglas R. Schrank Vice President & C.F.O.		Chief Financial Officer

Harbor Capital Management Company, Inc.

Investment Manager

Location: 125 High Street
26th Floor
Boston, MA 02110

Fax: 617/439-9789 **Phone:** 617/478-7200

Profile: Total return investor

Investment Portfolio: $ 2.7 billion

Use: **Investment Purposes**

Currencies: US dollar

Regions: United States

DERIVATIVES ACTIVITIES: **CAC Class: Inactive**

OTHER ALTERNATIVE INVESTMENTS:

CMOs/REMICs – Govt. CMOs/REMICs – Private

KEY MANAGERS & DERIVATIVES SPECIALISTS:	**Direct Phone/Fax**	**Job Function**
Mr. Malcolm Pirnie President & C.E.O.	617/478-7213	President
Mr. Frederick G. Thorne Chairman	617/478-7216	Chief Investment Officer

Harleysville Mutual Insurance Company

Insurance Co/P & C

Sub of Harleysville Group Inc.

Location: 355 Maple Avenue
Harleysville, PA 19438-2297

Fax: 215/256-5601 **Phone:** 215/256-5000

Profile: Total return investor

Investment Portfolio: $ 1.9 billion

Use: **Investment Purposes**
Capture extra yield

Currencies: US dollar

Regions: United States

DERIVATIVES ACTIVITIES: **CAC Class: 4**

Structured Notes	Corporate MTNs	Govt. agency MTNs

OTHER ALTERNATIVE INVESTMENTS:

	CMOs/REMICs – Govt.	Strips

KEY MANAGERS & DERIVATIVES SPECIALISTS:	**Direct Phone/Fax**	**Job Function**
Ms. Josephine A. Baker	215/256-5027	Portfolio Mgr – Structured Notes
Mr. Mark R. Cummins S.V.P., C.I.O. & Treasurer	215/256-5036	Chief Investment Officer Treasurer
Mr. J. Gary Morris Senior Portfolio Manager	215/256-5029	Portfolio Mgr – Structured Notes

Harris Corporation

Corporation

Location: 1025 West NASA Boulevard
Melbourne, FL 32919

Fax: 407/727-9344 **Phone:** 407/727-9100

Use: **Balance Sheet/Risk Management**
Hedge currency risk
Hedge overseas investments
Protect currency gains
Strategic liability management

Currencies: US dollar, French franc, German mark

Regions: United States, Europe, Pacific Rim

DERIVATIVES ACTIVITIES: **CAC Class: 4**

OTC Derivatives **Plain Vanilla Derivatives**	**Currency**

KEY MANAGERS & DERIVATIVES SPECIALISTS:	**Direct Phone/Fax**	**Job Function**
Mr. Phillip W. Farmer President & C.O.O.		President
Mr. Bryan R. Roub Senior Vice President & C.F.O.		Chief Financial Officer
Mr. David S. Wasserman Vice President – Treasurer		Treasurer Portfolio Mgr – Derivatives Portfolio Mgr – Options

Harris Associates, L.P.

Investment Manager

Sub of New England Investment Companies, L.P.

Location: Two North LaSalle Street
Suite 500
Chicago, IL 60602

Fax: 312/621-0372 **Phone:** 312/621-0600

Profile: Total return investor

Investment Portfolio: $ 5.9 billion

Use: **Investment Purposes**

Currencies: US dollar

Regions: United States

DERIVATIVES ACTIVITIES: **CAC Class: Inactive**

OTHER ALTERNATIVE INVESTMENTS:

CMOs/REMICs – Govt.

KEY MANAGERS & DERIVATIVES SPECIALISTS:	Direct Phone/Fax	Job Function
Mr. Victor Morgenstern President	312/621-0666	President
Ms. Christine Pilat Fixed Income Specialist	312/621-0373	Chief Investment Officer

Harris Investment Management, Inc.

Bank/Management Division

Sub of Bank of Montréal

Location: 190 South LaSalle Street
4th Floor
Chicago, IL 60603

Fax: 312/765-8160 **Phone:** 312/461-7699

Profile: Total return investor

Investment Portfolio: $ 13.3 billion

Use: **Balance Sheet/Risk Management**
Strategic liability management

Currencies: US dollar

Regions: United States

DERIVATIVES ACTIVITIES: **CAC Class: 2**

Exchange-traded Options & Futures — **Interest rate**
U.S. Treasury futures

Structured Notes — Floaters

OTHER ALTERNATIVE INVESTMENTS:

CMOs/REMICs – Govt.
GICs
Strips
Repos/reverse repos

Harris Investment Management, Inc. – continued

KEY MANAGERS & DERIVATIVES SPECIALISTS:	Direct Phone/Fax	Job Function
Mr. William O. Leszinske President		President Chief Investment Officer
Mr. Jack Moswich Sr. Partner & Mgr-Analytics	312/461-3233	Portfolio Mgr – Futures Portfolio Mgr – Options
Mr. Mark E. Newlin Senior Partner & Manager	312/461-5521	Bond Department Head Portfolio Mgr – Futures Portfolio Mgr – Options Portfolio Mgr – Structured Notes

Harris Trust & Savings (Personal Trust)

Bank/Trust

Sub of Bank of Montréal

Location: 111 West Monroe Street
7th Floor
Chicago, IL 60603

Fax: 312/461-7142 **Phone:** 312/461-2121

Profile: Total return investor

Investment Portfolio: $ 7.6 billion

Use: **Investment Purposes**
Adjust portfolio duration
Hedge equity portfolio risk
Provide incremental return

Currencies: US dollar

Regions: United States

DERIVATIVES ACTIVITIES: **CAC Class: 2**

Structured Notes Corporate MTNs

OTHER ALTERNATIVE INVESTMENTS:

CMOs/REMICs – Private
GICs
Repos/reverse repos

KEY MANAGERS & DERIVATIVES SPECIALISTS:	Direct Phone/Fax	Job Function
Mr. Todd J. Barre Vice President	312/461-2773 312/394-8730	Portfolio Mgr – Structured Notes
Mr. David Mead	312/461-7756	Chief Investment Officer

Harsco Corporation

Corporation

Location: 350 Poplar Church Road
Wormleysburg, PA 17043

Fax: 717/763-6424 **Phone:** 717/763-7064

Use: **Balance Sheet/Risk Management**
Hedge balance sheet
Hedge commercial paper
Hedge currency risk
Hedge overseas investments
Protect currency gains

Currencies: US dollar
Belgian franc
French franc
German mark
Italian lira

Regions: United States
Europe

Harsco Corporation – continued

DERIVATIVES ACTIVITIES:		**CAC Class: 1**
OTC Derivatives **Plain Vanilla Derivatives**	**Currency** Forwards	
Counterparty Rating Requirement:	AA	

KEY MANAGERS & DERIVATIVES SPECIALISTS:	Direct Phone/Fax	Job Function
Mr. Leonard A. Campanaro Senior Vice President & C.F.O.		Chief Financial Officer
Mr. Derek C. Hathaway Chairman, President & C.E.O.		President
Mr. Barry M. Sullivan Vice President & Treasurer		Treasurer Portfolio Mgr – Derivatives

Harvard Management Company

Foundation/Endowment

Location: 600 Atlantic Avenue
16th Floor
Boston, MA 02210

Fax: 617/523-1283 **Phone:** 617/523-4400

Profile: Total return investor

Investment Portfolio: $ 6.0 billion

Use:

Balance Sheet/Risk Management
Create synthetic fixed/floating rate
Hedge currency risk
Hedge interest rate risk
Protect currency gains

Investment Purposes
Capture extra yield
Hedge interest rate risk

Currencies:
US dollar
Australian dollar
Belgian franc
Canadian dollar
ECU
French franc
German mark
Italian lira
Indonesian rupiah
Japanese yen
Mexican peso
Spanish peseta
Swiss franc
Thai baht
UK pound

Regions:
United States
Canada
Europe
Latin America
Pacific Rim
Emerging mkts

DERIVATIVES ACTIVITIES:		
Exchange-traded Options & Futures U.S. Treasury futures	U.S. Treasury options	
OTC Derivatives **Plain Vanilla Derivatives**	Swaps Forwards Swaptions	Caps Floors
Structured Notes		
Counterparty Rating Requirement:	AAA	

Harvard Management Company – continued

OTHER ALTERNATIVE INVESTMENTS:

	CMOs/REMICs – Govt. CMOs/REMICs – Private	Strips

KEY MANAGERS & DERIVATIVES SPECIALISTS:	Direct Phone/Fax	Job Function
Mr. Edward DeNoble	617/523-5308	Portfolio Mgr – Derivatives Portfolio Mgr – Futures Portfolio Mgr – Options Portfolio Mgr – Structured Notes
Mr. Jack R. Meyer President & C.E.O.		President Chief Investment Officer
Mr. David R. Mittelman S.V.P. & Director-Fixed Income	617/523-5308	Bond Department Head
Mr. Verne O. Sedlacek Exec. Vice President & C.F.O.		Chief Financial Officer

Hawaiian Electric Industries, Inc.

Corporation

Location: 900 Richards Street
Honolulu, HI 96808

Fax: 808/543-7966 **Phone:** 808/543-5662

Profile: Total return investor

Use: **Investment Purposes**
Hedge currency risk
Hedge equity portfolio risk
Hedge interest rate risk
Provide incremental return

Currencies: US dollar, Canadian dollar, French franc, German mark, Japanese yen, Mexican peso

Regions: United States, Canada, Europe, Latin America, Pacific Rim, Emerging mkts

DERIVATIVES ACTIVITIES:

Exchange-traded Options & Futures	**Currency**	
Structured Notes	Corporate MTNs	Govt. agency MTNs
Counterparty Rating Requirement:	None	

OTHER ALTERNATIVE INVESTMENTS:

	Strips	Repos/reverse repos

KEY MANAGERS & DERIVATIVES SPECIALISTS:	Direct Phone/Fax	Job Function
Mr. Robert F. Clarke President & C.E.O.	808/543-7600	President
Ms. Constance H. Lau Treasurer	808/543-7384	Treasurer Portfolio Mgr – Derivatives
Mr. Robert F. Mougeot Financial Vice Pres. & C.F.O.	808/543-7750	Chief Financial Officer

Hawaiian Trust Co., Ltd.

Bank/Trust

Sub of Bancorp Hawaii Inc.

Location: 111 South King Street
Fourth Floor
Honolulu, HI 96813

Fax: 808/538-1788 **Phone:** 808/538-4444

Profile: Total return investor

Investment Portfolio: $ 6.6 billion

Use: **Investment Purposes**

Currencies: US dollar

Regions: United States

DERIVATIVES ACTIVITIES: **CAC Class: Inactive**

OTHER ALTERNATIVE INVESTMENTS:

CMOs/REMICs – Govt.

KEY MANAGERS & DERIVATIVES SPECIALISTS:	**Direct Phone/Fax**	**Job Function**
Mr. William J. Barton Senior Vice President	808/538-4622	Chief Investment Officer

Heber Fuger Wendin Incorporated

Investment Manager

Location: 180 Oakland Avenue
Suite 200
Birmingham, MI 48009-3434

Fax: 810/258-9295 **Phone:** 810/258-6866

Profile: Spread investor

Investment Portfolio: $ 4.0 - 10.0 billion

Use: **Balance Sheet/Risk Management**
Hedge interest rate risk

Investment Purposes
Hedge interest rate risk
Provide incremental return

Currencies: US dollar

Regions: United States

DERIVATIVES ACTIVITIES: **CAC Class: 3**

OTC Derivatives	**Currency, Interest rate**	
Plain Vanilla Derivatives	Swaps	
Exotic Derivatives	Index amortizing swaps	
Structured Notes	Corporate MTNs Govt. agency MTNs Bond index notes Index amortizing notes	CMT notes Floaters Periodic capped floaters Multi-step-up callable bonds
Counterparty Rating Requirement:	None	

OTHER ALTERNATIVE INVESTMENTS:

CMOs/REMICs – Govt.
Strips
Repos/reverse repos

Heber Fuger Wendin Incorporated – continued

KEY MANAGERS & DERIVATIVES SPECIALISTS:	Direct Phone/Fax	Job Function
Mr. Mark Maissonneuf		Portfolio Mgr – Derivatives Portfolio Mgr – Structured Notes
Mr. Mark Williams President		President Chief Investment Officer Portfolio Mgr – Derivatives Portfolio Mgr – Structured Notes

Heine Securities Corporation

Investment Manager

Location: 51 John F. Kennedy Parkway
Short Hills, NJ 07078

Fax: 201/912-0147 **Phone:** 201/912-2000

Profile: Total return investor

Investment Portfolio: $ 8.5 billion

Use: **Investment Purposes**

Currencies: US dollar

Regions: United States

DERIVATIVES ACTIVITIES: **CAC Class: Inactive**

OTHER ALTERNATIVE INVESTMENTS:

CMOs/REMICs – Govt.

KEY MANAGERS & DERIVATIVES SPECIALISTS:	Direct Phone/Fax	Job Function
Mr. Michael F. Price President	201/912-2010	President Chief Investment Officer Portfolio Mgr – Futures *Corp*

Hercules Incorporated

Corporation

Location: Hercules Plaza
Wilmington, DE 19894-0001

Fax: 302/594-5405 **Phone:** 302/594-5000

Use: **Balance Sheet/Risk Management**
Access global mkts
Create synthetic fixed/floating rate
Hedge balance sheet
Hedge commercial paper
Hedge currency risk
Hedge interest rate risk
Hedge overseas investments
Meet interest rate target
Protect currency gains
Strategic liability management

Currencies: US dollar Belgian franc

Regions: United States

Hercules Incorporated – continued

DERIVATIVES ACTIVITIES:

Exchange-traded Options & Futures	**Currency, Interest rate**	
U.S. Treasury futures	Municipal futures	
U.S. Treasury options	Municipal options	
OTC Derivatives	**Currency, Interest rate**	
Plain Vanilla Derivatives	Swaps	Forwards
Exotic Derivatives		
Counterparty Rating Requirement:	None	

KEY MANAGERS & DERIVATIVES SPECIALISTS:	**Direct Phone/Fax**	**Job Function**
Mr. R. Keith Elliott Senior Vice President & C.F.O.	302/594-5250	Chief Financial Officer
Mr. Thomas L. Gossage Chairman, President & C.E.O.	302/594-5120	President
Mr. George MacKenzie Vice President & Treasurer	302/594-5175	Treasurer Portfolio Mgr – Derivatives
Mr. Daniel R. McFadden Manager – Foreign Exchange	302/594-5452 302/594-5371	Portfolio Mgr – Derivatives

Heritage Asset Management, Inc.

Mutual Fund Manager

Sub of Raymond James Financial Inc.

Location: 880 Carillon Parkway
St. Petersburg, FL 33716

Fax: 813/573-8334 **Phone:** 813/573-8320

Profile: Total return investor

Investment Portfolio: $ 1.8 billion

Use: **Balance Sheet/Risk Management**
Hedge balance sheet
Hedge interest rate risk

Currencies: US dollar

Regions: United States

DERIVATIVES ACTIVITIES:

Exchange-traded Options & Futures

OTHER ALTERNATIVE INVESTMENTS:

CMOs/REMICs – Govt.	Strips
CMOs/REMICs – Private	Repos/reverse repos
GICs	

KEY MANAGERS & DERIVATIVES SPECIALISTS:	**Direct Phone/Fax**	**Job Function**
Mr. H. Peter Wallace Director – Fixed Income		Bond Department Head *Taxable* Portfolio Mgr – Futures

Heritage House Asset Management

Investment Manager

Sub of Standard Chartered p.l.c.

Location: Ten Liberty Square
4th Floor
Boston, MA 02109

Fax: 617/451-0800 **Phone:** 617/482-8877

Profile: Total return investor

Investment Portfolio: $ 8.0 billion

Use: **Investment Purposes**

Currencies: US dollar

Regions: United States

DERIVATIVES ACTIVITIES: **CAC Class: Inactive**

OTHER ALTERNATIVE INVESTMENTS:

CMOs/REMICs – Govt.

KEY MANAGERS & DERIVATIVES SPECIALISTS:	**Direct Phone/Fax**	**Job Function**
Mr. Michael D. Aquilino Senior Vice President		Chief Investment Officer

Hibernia Corporation

Bank Holding Company

Location: 313 Carondelet Street
New Orleans, LA 70130

Fax: 504/586-5841 **Phone:** 504/586-5552

Use:

Balance Sheet/Risk Management
Hedge interest rate risk
Strategic liability management

Investment Purposes
Discretionary situations
Provide incremental return

Currencies: US dollar

Regions: United States

DERIVATIVES ACTIVITIES: **CAC Class: 4**

Exchange-traded Options & Futures

OTC Derivatives Interest rate

Plain Vanilla Derivatives	Swaps Caps	Floors
Exotic Derivatives	CMT options	

KEY MANAGERS & DERIVATIVES SPECIALISTS:	**Direct Phone/Fax**	**Job Function**
Mr. Stephen A. Hansel President & C.E.O.		President
Mr. Ronald E. Samford, Jr. E.V.P. & Controller		Chief Financial Officer Portfolio Mgr – Derivatives

Hibernia National Bank (Trust)

Bank/Trust

Sub of Hibernia Corporation

Location: 313 Carondelet Street
7th Floor
New Orleans, LA 70112

Fax: 504/533-0153 **Phone:** 504/533-5531

Profile: Total return investor

Investment Portfolio: $ 1.6 billion

Use: **Investment Purposes**

Currencies: US dollar

Regions: United States

DERIVATIVES ACTIVITIES: **CAC Class: Inactive**

OTHER ALTERNATIVE INVESTMENTS:

CMOs/REMICs – Govt.
CMOs/REMICs – Private
Repos/reverse repos

KEY MANAGERS & DERIVATIVES SPECIALISTS:	**Direct Phone/Fax**	**Job Function**
Mr. John S. Hall V.P. & Trust Invt. Officer	504/533-5638	Bond Department Head

Hoisington Investment Management Co.

Investment Manager

Location: 1250 Capital Texas Highway South
Building Three Suite 600
Austin, TX 78746

Fax: 512/327-8646 **Phone:** 512/327-7200

Profile: Total return investor

Investment Portfolio: $ 2.7 billion

Use: **Investment Purposes**

Currencies: US dollar

Regions: United States

DERIVATIVES ACTIVITIES: **CAC Class: Inactive**

OTHER ALTERNATIVE INVESTMENTS:

CMOs/REMICs – Govt.
CMOs/REMICs – Private

KEY MANAGERS & DERIVATIVES SPECIALISTS:	**Direct Phone/Fax**	**Job Function**
Mr. Van R. Hoisington, Sr. President		President Chief Investment Officer

Honeywell, Inc.

Corporation

Location: Honeywell Plaza
Minneapolis, MN 55408-1792

Fax: 612/951-3070 **Phone:** 612/951-1000

Use: **Balance Sheet/Risk Management**
Hedge currency risk
Hedge interest rate risk
Strategic liability management

Currencies: US dollar, German mark, Canadian dollar

Regions: United States, Canada

DERIVATIVES ACTIVITIES: **CAC Class: 6**

OTC Derivatives	**Currency, Interest rate**
Plain Vanilla Derivatives	Swaps
Counterparty Rating Requirement:	AAA

KEY MANAGERS & DERIVATIVES SPECIALISTS:	**Direct Phone/Fax**	**Job Function**
Mr. William M. Hjerpe Vice President & C.F.O.	612/951-0142	Chief Financial Officer
Mr. D. Larry Moore President & C.O.O.	612/951-0089	President
Mr. Paul N. Saleh Vice President & Treasurer		Treasurer Portfolio Mgr – Derivatives

Hotchkis and Wiley

Investment Manager

Location: 800 West Sixth Street
Fifth Floor
Los Angeles, CA 90017

Fax: 213/623-7880 **Phone:** 213/362-8888

Profile: Total return investor

Investment Portfolio: $ 7.3 billion

Use: **Balance Sheet/Risk Management**
Hedge balance sheet
Hedge interest rate risk

Investment Purposes
Capture extra yield

Currencies: US dollar

Regions: United States

DERIVATIVES ACTIVITIES: **CAC Class: 2**

Structured Notes	Corporate MTNs Govt. agency MTNs	Floaters Inverse floaters

OTHER ALTERNATIVE INVESTMENTS:

CMOs/REMICs – Govt. Strips

Hotchkis and Wiley – continued

KEY MANAGERS & DERIVATIVES SPECIALISTS:	Direct Phone/Fax	Job Function
Mr. John F. Hotchkis		Chief Investment Officer
Mr. Stephen M. Kane		Portfolio Mgr – Structured Notes
Mr. Laird Landmann		Portfolio Mgr – Structured Notes
Ms. Laura Mulpagano		Research Analyst – Derivatives
Mr. Tad Rivelle	213/623-8905	Portfolio Mgr – Structured Notes
Mr. George Wiley		Chief Investment Officer

Household International, Inc.

Corporation

Location: 2700 Sanders Road
Prospect Heights, IL 60070

Fax: 708/564-6110 **Phone:** 708/564-5000

Use: **Balance Sheet/Risk Management**
Create synthetic fixed/floating rate
Hedge balance sheet
Hedge commercial paper
Hedge currency risk
Hedge interest rate risk
Lower transaction costs
Meet interest rate target
Protect currency gains
Strategic liability management

Currencies: US dollar, Canadian dollar, Australian dollar, UK pound

Regions: United States, Europe, Canada

DERIVATIVES ACTIVITIES:

OTC Derivatives	**Bond, Currency, Interest rate**
Plain Vanilla Derivatives	Swaps
Counterparty Rating Requirement:	A

KEY MANAGERS & DERIVATIVES SPECIALISTS:	Direct Phone/Fax	Job Function
Mr. Joseph W. Hoff Vice President – Finance	708/564-7973	Chief Financial Officer
Mr. Daniel P. Simet		Portfolio Mgr – Derivatives
Mr. David D. Wesselimk Vice President & Treasurer		Treasurer Portfolio Mgr – Derivatives

Howard Hughes Medical Institute

Foundation/Endowment

Location: 4000 Jones Bridge Road
Investment Department
Chevy Chase, MD 20815-6789

Fax: 301/215-8691 **Phone:** 301/215-8687

Profile: Total return investor **Investment Portfolio:** $ 5.9 billion

Use: **Investment Purposes**

Currencies: US dollar **Regions:** United States

DERIVATIVES ACTIVITIES: **CAC Class: Inactive**

OTHER ALTERNATIVE INVESTMENTS:

CMOs/REMICs – Govt. CMOs/REMICs – Private

KEY MANAGERS & DERIVATIVES SPECIALISTS:	**Direct Phone/Fax**	**Job Function**
Ms. Ellen B. Safir Managing Director-Investments		Bond Department Head *Corp, Govt, MBS*
Mr. Carter Wolfe Vice President	301/215-8686	Chief Investment Officer

HSBC Asset Management Americas Inc.

Bank/Management Division

Sub of The HongKong and Shanghai Banking Corporation Limited

Location: 250 Park Avenue
Third Floor
New York, NY 10177

Fax: 212/503-6808 **Phone:** 212/503-6815

Profile: Total return investor **Investment Portfolio:** $ 5.0 billion

Use: **Investment Purposes**

Currencies: US dollar **Regions:** United States

DERIVATIVES ACTIVITIES: **CAC Class: 2**

Structured Notes

Corporate MTNs
Govt. agency MTNs
Index amortizing notes
Multi-step-up callable bonds

OTHER ALTERNATIVE INVESTMENTS:

CMOs/REMICs – Govt. CMOs/REMICs – Private

KEY MANAGERS & DERIVATIVES SPECIALISTS:	**Direct Phone/Fax**	**Job Function**
Mr. David Fox Managing Director	212/503-6848 212/503-6756	Bond Department Head Fixed-Income Strategist Portfolio Mgr – Structured Notes
Mr. Leo Grohowski Managing Director	212/503-6918	Chief Investment Officer

Humana Inc.

Corporation

Location: 500 West Main Street
11th Floor
Louisville, KY 40202

Fax: 502/580-4089 **Phone:** 502/580-1000

Profile: Current yield investor

Investment Portfolio: $ 1.0 - 3.0 billion

Use: **Balance Sheet/Risk Management**

Currencies: US dollar

Regions: United States

DERIVATIVES ACTIVITIES:		**CAC Class: 2**
Exchange-traded Options & Futures	**Currency, Interest rate**	

OTHER ALTERNATIVE INVESTMENTS:		
	CMOs/REMICs – Govt.	CMOs/REMICs – Private

KEY MANAGERS & DERIVATIVES SPECIALISTS:	**Direct Phone/Fax**	**Job Function**
Mr. James W. Doucette Vice President	502/580-1002	Chief Investment Officer
Mr. Michael C. Fosbury	502/580-1004	Portfolio Mgr – Futures

Huntington Bancshares, Incorporated

Bank Holding Company

Location: Huntington Center
41 South High Street
Columbus, OH 43287

Fax: 614/480-3761 **Phone:** 614/480-8300

Profile: Total return investor

Use: **Balance Sheet/Risk Management**
Create synthetic fixed/floating rate
Hedge balance sheet
Hedge interest rate risk

Investment Purposes
Hedge bond portfolio risk
Hedge interest rate risk

Currencies: US dollar

Regions: United States

DERIVATIVES ACTIVITIES:		**CAC Class: 7**
OTC Derivatives	**Interest rate**	
Plain Vanilla Derivatives	Swaps	Floors
	Forwards	Collars
	Caps	
Counterparty Rating Requirement:	A	

KEY MANAGERS & DERIVATIVES SPECIALISTS:	**Direct Phone/Fax**	**Job Function**
Mr. Zuheir Sofia President & C.O.O.		President
Mr. Gerald R. Williams Exec. Vice President & C.F.O.		Chief Financial Officer Portfolio Mgr – Derivatives

The Huntington Trust Company, N.A.

Bank/Management Division

Sub of Huntington Bancshares, Incorporated

Location: 41 South High Street
Huntington Center
Suite HC1113
Columbus, OH 43287

Fax: 614/480-5223 **Phone:** 614/463-5345

Profile: Total return investor

Investment Portfolio: $ 2.9 billion

Use: **Investment Purposes**

Currencies: US dollar

Regions: United States

DERIVATIVES ACTIVITIES: **CAC Class: Inactive**

OTHER ALTERNATIVE INVESTMENTS:

CMOs/REMICs – Govt.
CMOs/REMICs – Private
Repos/reverse repos

KEY MANAGERS & DERIVATIVES SPECIALISTS:	**Direct Phone/Fax**	**Job Function**
Mr. James Buskirk	614/480-5566	Chief Investment Officer
Mr. Stephen M. Geis Vice President	614/480-5205	Fixed-Income Strategist
Mr. Norman A. Jacobs President & C.E.O.		President

Hyperion Capital Management, Inc.

Investment Manager

Location: 520 Madison Avenue
Tenth Floor
New York, NY 10022

Fax: 212/753-5869 **Phone:** 212/980-8400

Profile: Total return investor

Investment Portfolio: $ 4.0 billion

Use: **Investment Purposes**

Currencies: US dollar

Regions: United States

DERIVATIVES ACTIVITIES: **CAC Class: Inactive**

OTHER ALTERNATIVE INVESTMENTS:

CMOs/REMICs – Govt.
CMOs/REMICs – Private

KEY MANAGERS & DERIVATIVES SPECIALISTS:	**Direct Phone/Fax**	**Job Function**
Mr. Clifford E. Lai Managing Director	212/593-4906	Chief Investment Officer
Mr. Kenneth Weiss President & C.E.O.		President

I.B.J.-Schroder Bank & Trust Co. (Trust)

Bank/Trust

Sub of Industrial Bank of Japan, Ltd. (Japan)

Location: One State Street Plaza
Second Floor
New York, NY 10004

Fax: 212/514-9279 **Phone:** 212/858-2000

Profile: Total return investor

Investment Portfolio: $ 1.0 billion

Use: **Balance Sheet/Risk Management**
Hedge interest rate risk

Currencies: US dollar

Regions: United States

DERIVATIVES ACTIVITIES: **CAC Class: 2**

Exchange-traded Options & Futures — **Interest rate**
U.S. Treasury options

OTHER ALTERNATIVE INVESTMENTS:

CMOs/REMICs – Govt. CMOs/REMICs – Private

KEY MANAGERS & DERIVATIVES SPECIALISTS:	Direct Phone/Fax	Job Function
Mr. Martin J. Liebgott Senior Vice President	212/858-2385	Portfolio Mgr – Options
Mr. Charles Porten Senior Vice President	212/858-2278	Chief Investment Officer
Mr. William Yost	212/858-2402	Trader – Options

IDS Fixed Income Advisors

Investment Manager

Sub of IDS Advisory Group

Location: 80 South Eighth Street
IDS Tower 10
Minneapolis, MN 55440

Fax: 612/671-2733 **Phone:** 612/671-3335

Profile: Total return investor

Investment Portfolio: $ 1.0 - 1.1 billion

Use: **Investment Purposes**
Capture extra yield
Hedge interest rate risk

Currencies: US dollar

Regions: United States

DERIVATIVES ACTIVITIES:

Exchange-traded Options & Futures

OTC Derivatives
Plain Vanilla Derivatives

Structured Notes

OTHER ALTERNATIVE INVESTMENTS:

CMOs/REMICs – Govt. CMOs/REMICs – Private

IDS Fixed Income Advisors – continued

KEY MANAGERS & DERIVATIVES SPECIALISTS:	Direct Phone/Fax	Job Function
Mr. Edward Labenski, Jr. President	612/671-3227	President Chief Investment Officer Bond Department Head Portfolio Mgr – Derivatives

Illinois State Board of Investment

Government Pension Fund

Location: 180 North LaSalle Street
Room 2015
Chicago, IL 60601

Fax: 312/793-2266 **Phone:** 312/793-5712

Profile: Hold to maturity investor

Investment Portfolio: $ 1.6 billion

Use: **Investment Purposes**

Currencies: US dollar

Regions: United States

DERIVATIVES ACTIVITIES: **CAC Class: Inactive**

OTHER ALTERNATIVE INVESTMENTS:

CMOs/REMICs – Govt.
CMOs/REMICs – Private
Strips

KEY MANAGERS & DERIVATIVES SPECIALISTS:	Direct Phone/Fax	Job Function
Mr. Lawrence G. Darlington Manager – Fixed Income		Bond Department Head *Taxable*

Independence One Capital Management Corp.

Bank/Management Division

Sub of Michigan National Corporation

Location: 27777 Inkster Road
Farmington Hills, MI 48334

Fax: 810/473-3094 **Phone:** 810/473-3300

Profile: Hold to maturity investor

Investment Portfolio: $ 2.2 billion

Use: **Balance Sheet/Risk Management**

Currencies: US dollar

Regions: United States

DERIVATIVES ACTIVITIES: **CAC Class: Inactive**

OTHER ALTERNATIVE INVESTMENTS:

CMOs/REMICs – Govt.

KEY MANAGERS & DERIVATIVES SPECIALISTS:	Direct Phone/Fax	Job Function
Mr. Robert Stapleton President & C.I.O.	810/473-2615	President Chief Investment Officer

Independent Bank Corp.

Bank Holding Company

Location: 288 Union Street
Rockland, MA 02370

Fax: 617/982-6591 **Phone:** 617/878-6100

Use: **Balance Sheet/Risk Management**
Hedge interest rate risk

Currencies: US dollar **Regions:** United States

DERIVATIVES ACTIVITIES:		**CAC Class: 3**
OTC Derivatives	**Interest rate**	
Plain Vanilla Derivatives	Swaps	

Counterparty Rating Requirement: AA

KEY MANAGERS & DERIVATIVES SPECIALISTS:	Direct Phone/Fax	Job Function
Mr. Douglas H. Philipsen President		President
Mr. Richard J. Seaman C.F.O.. & Treasurer		Chief Financial Officer Treasurer Portfolio Mgr – Derivatives

ING Investment Management Inc. – Americas Region

Insurance Co/Management

Sub of Internationale Nederlanden Group (ING) NV

Location: 300 Galleria Parkway N.W.
Suite 1200
Atlanta, GA 30339-3149

Fax: 770/850-4801 **Phone:** 770/850-4800

Profile: Total return investor

Investment Portfolio: $ 5.0 billion

Use: **Balance Sheet/Risk Management**
Hedge interest rate risk

Currencies: US dollar **Regions:** United States

DERIVATIVES ACTIVITIES:		**CAC Class: 6**
OTC Derivatives	**Interest rate**	
Plain Vanilla Derivatives	Swaps	Caps
	Swaptions	Floors

OTHER ALTERNATIVE INVESTMENTS:		
	CMOs/REMICs – Govt.	CMOs/REMICs – Private

KEY MANAGERS & DERIVATIVES SPECIALISTS:	Direct Phone/Fax	Job Function
Mr. Thomas Balachowski President		President Chief Investment Officer
Mr. Kirby Brown Vice President	770/850-4807	Portfolio Mgr – Derivatives

Integra Financial Corporation

Bank/Management Division

Location: 300 Fourth Avenue
Pittsburgh, PA 15222

Fax: 412/261-7279 **Phone:** 412/644-7669

Profile: Spread investor

Investment Portfolio: $ 11.1 billion

Use: **Balance Sheet/Risk Management**
Hedge balance sheet
Hedge interest rate risk
Incremental return
Reduce cost of capital

Investment Purposes
Adjust portfolio duration
Asset allocation
Beat conventional rates
Capture extra yield
Diversify portfolio
Hedge interest rate risk
Provide incremental return
Reduce variability of returns

Currencies: US dollar

Regions: United States

DERIVATIVES ACTIVITIES: **CAC Class: 6**

OTC Derivatives	**Interest rate**	
Plain Vanilla Derivatives	Swaps Swaptions	Caps
Exotic Derivatives	Index amortizing swaps	Periodic caps/floors
Structured Notes	Govt. agency MTNs Index amortizing notes	Floaters Multi-step-up callable bonds
Counterparty Rating Requirement:	A	

OTHER ALTERNATIVE INVESTMENTS:

CMOs/REMICs – Govt.

KEY MANAGERS & DERIVATIVES SPECIALISTS:	**Direct Phone/Fax**	**Job Function**
Mr. Leonard M. Carroll President & C.O.O.		President
Mr. Ross Dillon	412/644-8528	Portfolio Mgr – Derivatives Portfolio Mgr – Structured Notes
Mr. Raymond Egan	412/644-8557	Portfolio Mgr – Derivatives Portfolio Mgr – Structured Notes
Mr. Scott M. Elliot	412/644-8534	Portfolio Mgr – Derivatives Portfolio Mgr – Structured Notes
Mr. Donald Kenst Senior Portfolio Manager	412/644-7910	Portfolio Mgr – Derivatives Portfolio Mgr – Structured Notes
Mr. William Kistler	412/644-6032	Portfolio Mgr – Derivatives Portfolio Mgr – Structured Notes

Integra Financial Corporation – continued

KEY MANAGERS & DERIVATIVES SPECIALISTS:	Direct Phone/Fax	Job Function
Mr. Richard Mahany Senior Vice President	412/644-8116	Chief Investment Officer
Mr. Richard McLaughlin	412/644-8758	Portfolio Mgr – Derivatives Portfolio Mgr – Structured Notes
Mr. David G. Paulson	412/644-8210	Portfolio Mgr – Derivatives Portfolio Mgr – Structured Notes
Mr. James Schrott	412/644-8513	Portfolio Mgr – Derivatives Portfolio Mgr – Structured Notes
Mr. Thomas Sheehan	412/644-8469	Portfolio Mgr – Derivatives Portfolio Mgr – Structured Notes *Corp*

Intel Corporation

Corporation

Location: 2200 Mission College Boulevard
Santa Clara, CA 95052-8119

Fax: 408/765-1821 **Phone:** 408/765-8080

Use:

Balance Sheet/Risk Management
Create synthetic fixed/floating rate
Hedge currency risk
Hedge interest rate risk
Hedge overseas investments
Incremental return
Protect currency gains

Investment Purposes
Hedge equity portfolio risk

Currencies: US dollar, Belgian franc, French franc, German mark, Italian lira, Japanese yen, UK pound

Regions: United States, Europe, Pacific Rim

DERIVATIVES ACTIVITIES: **CAC Class: 6**

Exchange-traded Options & Futures	**Currency**	
OTC Derivatives **Plain Vanilla Derivatives**	**Bond, Currency, Interest rate** Swaps	 Forwards
Counterparty Rating Requirement:	A	

KEY MANAGERS & DERIVATIVES SPECIALISTS:	Direct Phone/Fax	Job Function
Mr. Andrew D. Bryant Vice President & C.F.O.		Chief Financial Officer
Mr. Andrew S. Grove President & C.E.O.		President
Mr. Arvind Sodhani Vice President – Treasurer		Treasurer Portfolio Mgr – Derivatives

Inter-American Development Bank

Bank/Government

Location: 1300 New York Avenue, N.W.
Washington, DC 20577

Fax: 202/623-3096 **Phone:** 202/623-1000

Profile: Total return investor

Investment Portfolio: $ 10.5 billion

Use: **Investment Purposes**
Hedge interest rate risk

Currencies: US dollar

Regions: United States

DERIVATIVES ACTIVITIES: **CAC Class: 3**

Exchange-traded Options & Futures	**Interest rate**	
U.S. Treasury futures		
OTC Derivatives		
Plain Vanilla Derivatives	Swaps Forwards Swaptions	Caps Floors Collars
Exotic Derivatives	Bond index swaps CMT swaps CMT options Detached calls	Index amortizing swaps Index extendible swaps Periodic caps/floors

KEY MANAGERS & DERIVATIVES SPECIALISTS:	**Direct Phone/Fax**	**Job Function**
Mr. Michael Mullan	202/623-2320	Chief Investment Officer Portfolio Mgr – Futures

Inter-Regional Financial Group, Inc.

Corporation

Location: Dain Bosworth Plaza
60 South Sixth Street
Minneapolis, MN 55402-4422

Fax: 612/371-7755 **Phone:** 612/371-7750

Use: **Balance Sheet/Risk Management**
Hedge balance sheet
Hedge interest rate risk
Incremental return

Currencies: US dollar

Regions: United States

DERIVATIVES ACTIVITIES: **CAC Class: 1**

Exchange-traded Options & Futures	**Interest rate**

OTHER ALTERNATIVE INVESTMENTS:

Repos/reverse repos

KEY MANAGERS & DERIVATIVES SPECIALISTS:	**Direct Phone/Fax**	**Job Function**
Mr. Louis C. Fornetti E.V.P., C.F.O. & Treasurer		Chief Financial Officer Treasurer
Mr. Irving Weiser Chairman, President & C.E.O.		President

Interstate/Johnson Lane, Inc.

Corporation

Location: 121 West Trade Tower
Charlotte, NC 28202

Fax: 704/379-9281 **Phone:** 704/379-9000

Use: **Balance Sheet/Risk Management**
Hedge interest rate risk

Investment Purposes
Discretionary situations
Hedge interest rate risk

Currencies: US dollar

Regions: United States

DERIVATIVES ACTIVITIES: **CAC Class: 4**

Exchange-traded Options & Futures U.S. Treasury futures	**Bond** U.S. Treasury options
OTC Derivatives **Plain Vanilla Derivatives**	**Interest rate** Swaps
Counterparty Rating Requirement:	A

KEY MANAGERS & DERIVATIVES SPECIALISTS:	**Direct Phone/Fax**	**Job Function**
Mr. Freeman Barber First Vice President	704/379-9135	Portfolio Mgr – Derivatives Portfolio Mgr – Futures *Govt* Portfolio Mgr – Options *Govt*
Mr. James H. Morgan President & C.E.O.	704/379-9295 704/379-9122	President
Mr. Edward C. Ruff Sr. Vice President & C.F.O.	704/379-9119 704/379-9122	Chief Financial Officer

INTRUST Bank (Trust)

Bank/Trust

Sub of INTRUST Financial Corporation

Location: 105 North Main Street
Wichita, KS 67202

Fax: 316/383-1140 **Phone:** 316/383-1111

Profile: Total return investor

Investment Portfolio: $ 1.2 billion

Use: **Investment Purposes**

Currencies: US dollar

Regions: United States

DERIVATIVES ACTIVITIES: **CAC Class: Inactive**

OTHER ALTERNATIVE INVESTMENTS:

CMOs/REMICs – Govt. Strips

KEY MANAGERS & DERIVATIVES SPECIALISTS:	**Direct Phone/Fax**	**Job Function**
Mr. Michael B. Colgan Vice President	316/383-1331	Chief Investment Officer

INVESCO Management and Research, Inc.

Investment Manager

Sub of INVESCO MIM p.l.c.

Location: 101 Federal Street
20th Floor
Boston, MA 02110-1800

Fax: 617/261-4560 **Phone:** 617/345-8200

Profile: Total return investor

Investment Portfolio: $ 2.2 billion

Use: **Investment Purposes**
Alter portfolio weighting
Hedge bond portfolio risk
Hedge interest rate risk

Currencies: US dollar

Regions: United States

DERIVATIVES ACTIVITIES: **CAC Class: 3**

Structured Notes	Corporate MTNs Floaters	Multi-step-up callable bonds

OTHER ALTERNATIVE INVESTMENTS:

	CMOs/REMICs – Govt. Strips	Repos/reverse repos

KEY MANAGERS & DERIVATIVES SPECIALISTS:	**Direct Phone/Fax**	**Job Function**
Mr. Edmund F. Ingalls, Jr. Vice President	617/345-8246	Portfolio Mgr – Structured Notes
Mr. William M. McCarthy Sr. Vice President & Manager	617/345-8536	Bond Department Head Fixed-Income Strategist

INVESCO MIM Inc.

Investment Manager

Sub of INVESCO MIM p.l.c.

Location: 1315 Peachtree Street N.E.
Suite 500
Atlanta, GA 30309

Fax: 404/892-3204 **Phone:** 404/892-0896

Profile: Total return investor

Investment Portfolio: $ 49.5 billion

Use: **Investment Purposes**

Currencies: US dollar

Regions: United States

DERIVATIVES ACTIVITIES: **CAC Class: Inactive**

OTHER ALTERNATIVE INVESTMENTS:

	CMOs/REMICs – Govt. Strips	Repos/reverse repos

INVESCO MIM Inc. – continued

KEY MANAGERS & DERIVATIVES SPECIALISTS:	**Direct Phone/Fax**	**Job Function**
Mr. Ralph H. Jenkins	404/607-2192	Bond Department Head
Mr. Wendell M. Starke President		President Chief Investment Officer

Investek Capital Management

Investment Manager

Location: 317 East Capitol Street
Suite 101
Jackson, MS 39201

Fax: 601/949-3177 **Phone:** 601/949-3105

Profile: Total return investor

Investment Portfolio: $ 1.6 billion

Use: **Investment Purposes**

Currencies: US dollar

Regions: United States

DERIVATIVES ACTIVITIES: **CAC Class: Inactive**

OTHER ALTERNATIVE INVESTMENTS:

CMOs/REMICs – Govt. CMOs/REMICs – Private

KEY MANAGERS & DERIVATIVES SPECIALISTS:	**Direct Phone/Fax**	**Job Function**
Mr. Michael T. McRee		Chief Investment Officer

Investment Advisers, Inc.

Investment Manager

Sub of TSB Group p.l.c.

Location: 601 Second Avenue South
37th Floor
Minneapolis, MN 55402

Fax: 612/376-2616 **Phone:** 612/376-2600

Profile: Total return investor

Investment Portfolio: $ 14.2 billion

Use: **Investment Purposes**
Capture extra yield
Hedge interest rate risk

Currencies: US dollar

Regions: United States

DERIVATIVES ACTIVITIES: **CAC Class: 3**

Exchange-traded Options & Futures **Bond**
U.S. Treasury futures

Investment Advisers, Inc. – continued

OTHER ALTERNATIVE INVESTMENTS:

	CMOs/REMICs – Govt. CMOs/REMICs – Private	Repos/reverse repos

KEY MANAGERS & DERIVATIVES SPECIALISTS:	**Direct Phone/Fax**	**Job Function**
Mr. Livingston G. Douglas Vice President	612/376-2768	Fixed-Income Strategist
Mr. Lawrence R. Hill Executive Vice President	612/376-2770	Chief Investment Officer
Mr. Timothy A. Palmer Senior Vice President	612/376-2773	Portfolio Mgr – Futures
Mr. Mark L. Simenstad Vice President	612/376-2667	Portfolio Mgr – Futures *Govt*

Investment Counselors of Maryland, Inc.

Investment Manager

Sub of United Asset Management Corporation

Location: 803 Cathedral Street, Baltimore, MD 21201

Fax: 410/783-7321 **Phone:** 410/539-3838

Profile: Total return investor

Investment Portfolio: $ 3.6 billion

Use: **Investment Purposes**
Hedge currency risk
Hedge interest rate risk

Currencies: US dollar

Regions: United States, Europe, Pacific Rim

DERIVATIVES ACTIVITIES:

Exchange-traded Options & Futures U.S. Treasury futures	**Bond, Currency, Interest rate** U.S. Treasury options	
OTC Derivatives **Plain Vanilla Derivatives**	Forwards	
Structured Notes	Corporate MTNs CMT notes	Floaters
Counterparty Rating Requirement:	AAA	

OTHER ALTERNATIVE INVESTMENTS:

	CMOs/REMICs – Govt. CMOs/REMICs – Private	Strips Repos/reverse repos

Investment Counselors of Maryland, Inc. – continued

KEY MANAGERS & DERIVATIVES SPECIALISTS:	Direct Phone/Fax	Job Function
Ms. Linda W. McCleary Senior Vice President		Bond Department Head Portfolio Mgr – Derivatives
Mr. Stephen Scott		Chief Investment Officer
Mr. Daniel Shackelford Vice President		Portfolio Mgr – Derivatives Portfolio Mgr – Futures *Govt* Portfolio Mgr – Options *Govt* Portfolio Mgr – Structured Notes

Investors Management Group, Ltd. (IMG)

Investment Manager

Location: 418 Sixth Avenue
Liberty Building Suite 720
Des Moines, IA 50309-2410

Fax: 515/244-2353 **Phone:** 515/244-5426

Profile: Total return investor

Investment Portfolio: $ 1.0 billion

Use: **Investment Purposes**

Currencies: US dollar

Regions: United States

DERIVATIVES ACTIVITIES: **CAC Class: Inactive**

OTHER ALTERNATIVE INVESTMENTS:

CMOs/REMICs – Govt.
Strips
Repos/reverse repos

KEY MANAGERS & DERIVATIVES SPECIALISTS:	Direct Phone/Fax	Job Function
Mr. James W. Paulsen Senior Managing Director		Chief Investment Officer

Investors Savings Bank

Savings Bank/Bldg Society

Location: 249 Millburn Avenue
Millburn, NJ 07041

Fax: 201/376-5243 **Phone:** 201/376-5100

Profile: Total return investor

Investment Portfolio: $ 1.0 - 3.0 billion

Use: **Investment Purposes**

Currencies: US dollar

Regions: United States

DERIVATIVES ACTIVITIES: **CAC Class: Inactive**

OTHER ALTERNATIVE INVESTMENTS:

CMOs/REMICs – Govt.

Investors Savings Bank – continued

KEY MANAGERS & DERIVATIVES SPECIALISTS:	Direct Phone/Fax	Job Function
Mr. Mathew F. Raftree Executive Vice President	Ext. 285	Chief Investment Officer

Israel Discount Bank of New York

Bank/Portfolio

Location: 511 Fifth Avenue, New York, NY 10017
Fax: 212/370-9623
Phone: 212/551-8500

Profile: Total return investor
Investment Portfolio: $ 3.5 billion

Use: **Investment Purposes**

Currencies: US dollar
Regions: United States

DERIVATIVES ACTIVITIES: **CAC Class: 2**

Structured Notes — Corporate MTNs

OTHER ALTERNATIVE INVESTMENTS:

Repos/reverse repos

KEY MANAGERS & DERIVATIVES SPECIALISTS:	Direct Phone/Fax	Job Function
Mr. Harry Feder Chief Investment Officer	212/551-8145	Chief Investment Officer
Mr. Kenneth E. Walters	212/551-8820	Portfolio Mgr – Structured Notes *Corp*

ITT Corporation

Corporation

Location: 1330 Avenue of the Americas, New York, NY 10019-5490
Fax: 212/258-1027
Phone: 212/258-1000

Use: **Balance Sheet/Risk Management**
Hedge currency risk
Hedge interest rate risk
Hedge overseas investments

Currencies: US dollar, Belgian franc, French franc, German mark, Italian lira, Swiss franc, UK pound
Regions: United States, Europe

DERIVATIVES ACTIVITIES: **CAC Class: 6**

OTC Derivatives
Plain Vanilla Derivatives — **Currency, Interest rate**: Swaps, Forwards, Caps, Collars

ITT Corporation – continued

KEY MANAGERS & DERIVATIVES SPECIALISTS:	Direct Phone/Fax	Job Function
Mr. Rand V. Araskog Chairman, President & C.E.O.		President
Mr. Robert A. Bowman Exec. Vice President & C.F.O.		Chief Financial Officer
Ms. Ann N. Reese S.V.P. & Treasurer	212/489-3596	Treasurer

ITT Hartford Life Insurance Company

Insurance Co/Life

Location: 200 Hopmeadow Street
Simsbury, CT 06089

Fax: 203/843-6457 **Phone:** 203/547-5000

Profile: Total return investor

Investment Portfolio: $ 21.0 - 49.0 billion

Use: **Balance Sheet/Risk Management**
Hedge overseas investments

Investment Purposes
Asset allocation
Hedge bond portfolio risk
Hedge currency risk
Hedge equity portfolio risk
Hedge interest rate risk

Currencies: US dollar

Regions: United States

DERIVATIVES ACTIVITIES:

Exchange-traded Options & Futures U.S. Treasury futures	U.S. Treasury options	
OTC Derivatives **Plain Vanilla Derivatives**	**Currency, Interest rate** Swaps Forwards Swaptions	 Caps Floors Collars
Structured Notes	Inverse floaters	
Counterparty Rating Requirement:	AA	

OTHER ALTERNATIVE INVESTMENTS:

CMOs/REMICs – Govt.
CMOs/REMICs – Private

KEY MANAGERS & DERIVATIVES SPECIALISTS:	Direct Phone/Fax	Job Function
Mr. Joseph H. Gareau Executive Vice President	203/843-3295	Chief Investment Officer Fixed-Income Strategist *Taxable*
Mr. David Hall Director-Portfolio Management	203/843-8003	Portfolio Mgr – Derivatives Portfolio Mgr – Futures *Govt* Portfolio Mgr – Options *Govt*

ITT Hartford Life Insurance Company – continued

KEY MANAGERS & DERIVATIVES SPECIALISTS:	Direct Phone/Fax	Job Function
Mr. Theodore Moran		Trader – Futures *Govt* Trader – Options *Govt*
Mr. Michael Piper		Trader – Futures *Govt* *Trader – Options* *Govt*

Jamaica Savings Bank, Fsb

Savings Bank/Bldg Society

Location: 303 Merrick Road
Lynbrook, NY 11563

Fax: 516/596-1205 **Phone:** 516/887-7000

Profile: Total return investor

Investment Portfolio: $ 1.6 billion

Use: **Investment Purposes**

Currencies: US dollar

Regions: United States

DERIVATIVES ACTIVITIES: **CAC Class: Inactive**

OTHER ALTERNATIVE INVESTMENTS:

CMOs/REMICs – Govt. CMOs/REMICs – Private

KEY MANAGERS & DERIVATIVES SPECIALISTS:	Direct Phone/Fax	Job Function
Mr. John F. Bennett S.V.P. – Investments	Ext. 304	Chief Investment Officer

John Alden Asset Management

Insurance Co/Management

Sub of John Alden Financial Corporation

Location: 7300 Corporate Center Drive
Seventh Floor
Miami, FL 33126-1208

Fax: 305/715-3914 **Phone:** 305/715-2000

Investment Portfolio: $ 4.0 - 10.0 billion

Use: **Investment Purposes**

Currencies: US dollar

Regions: United States

DERIVATIVES ACTIVITIES: **CAC Class: Inactive**

OTHER ALTERNATIVE INVESTMENTS:

CMOs/REMICs – Govt. CMOs/REMICs – Private

KEY MANAGERS & DERIVATIVES SPECIALISTS:	Direct Phone/Fax	Job Function
Mr. Marvin Assofsky	305/715-3190	Chief Investment Officer

John Hancock Advisers, Inc.

Mutual Fund Manager

Sub of John Hancock Mutual Life Insurance Company

Location: 101 Huntington Avenue
Seventh Floor
Boston, MA 02199-7603

Fax: 617/375-1831 **Phone:** 617/375-1500

Investment Portfolio: $ 6.8 billion

Use: **Investment Purposes**
Adjust portfolio duration
Diversify portfolio
Enter new mkts/lower risk
Hedge bond portfolio risk
Hedge currency risk
Hedge interest rate risk
Protect currency gains

Currencies: US dollar, Australian dollar, Canadian dollar, French franc, German mark, Italian lira, Spanish peseta, Swiss franc

Regions: United States, Canada, Europe, Latin America

DERIVATIVES ACTIVITIES:

Exchange-traded Options & Futures	**Bond, Currency**	
U.S. Treasury futures	Municipal futures	
U.S. Treasury options	Municipal options	
OTC Derivatives	**Bond, Currency**	
Plain Vanilla Derivatives	Forwards	
Structured Notes	Corporate MTNs	Floaters
	Govt. agency MTNs	
Counterparty Rating Requirement:	AA	

OTHER ALTERNATIVE INVESTMENTS:

CMOs/REMICs – Govt.
CMOs/REMICs – Private
GICs
Repos/reverse repos

KEY MANAGERS & DERIVATIVES SPECIALISTS:	**Direct Phone/Fax**	**Job Function**
Mr. Barry H. Evans Senior Vice President	617/375-1979	Bond Department Head *Govt* Portfolio Mgr – Futures *Govt* Portfolio Mgr – Options *Govt*
Mr. Robert G. Freedman President	617/375-1968	President Chief Investment Officer
Mr. Thomas C. Goggins Senior Vice President	617/375-1579	Bond Department Head *Muni*
Mr. James K. Ho Senior Vice President	617/375-1981	Bond Department Head
Ms. Anne M. McDonley Senior Vice President	617/375-6253	Portfolio Mgr – Derivatives Portfolio Mgr – Futures Portfolio Mgr – Structured Notes

John Hancock Mutual Life Insurance Company

Insurance Co/Life

Location: 200 Clarendon Street
Boston, MA 02116

Fax: 617/572-1605 **Phone:** 617/572-6000

Profile: Spread investor

Investment Portfolio: $ 41.2 billion

Use:

Balance Sheet/Risk Management
Hedge balance sheet
Strategic liability management

Investment Purposes
Alter portfolio weighting
Hedge bond portfolio risk
Hedge currency risk
Hedge interest rate risk

Currencies: US dollar, Canadian dollar, French franc, Swiss franc, UK Pound

Regions: United States

DERIVATIVES ACTIVITIES:

CAC Class: 6

Exchange-traded Options & Futures	**Bond**	
U.S. Treasury futures		
OTC Derivatives	**Bond, Currency, Interest rate**	
Plain Vanilla Derivatives	Swaps	Caps
Exotic Derivatives	CMT swaps	
Structured Notes	Floaters Inverse floaters	Periodic capped floaters
Counterparty Rating Requirement:	AA	

OTHER ALTERNATIVE INVESTMENTS:

CMOs/REMICs – Private
Repos/reverse repos

KEY MANAGERS & DERIVATIVES SPECIALISTS:	**Direct Phone/Fax**	**Job Function**
Mr. Foster L. Aborn Vice Chairman	617/572-6625	Chief Investment Officer
Mr. George H. Braun Vice President	617/572-9615	Portfolio Mgr – Derivatives Portfolio Mgr – Futures Portfolio Mgr – Options Portfolio Mgr – Structured Notes
Mr. Francis X. Felcon	617/572-9617	Portfolio Mgr – Derivatives Portfolio Mgr – Futures Portfolio Mgr – Options Portfolio Mgr – Structured Notes
Mr. Roger G. Nastou Vice President	617/572-9615	Portfolio Mgr – Derivatives Portfolio Mgr – Futures Portfolio Mgr – Structured Notes
Ms. Maryann E. Navin	617/572-4249 617/572-9560	Trader – Derivatives Trader – Futures Trader – Structured Investments

Johnson Controls, Inc.

Corporation

Location: 5757 North Green Bay Avenue
Milwaukee, WI 53202

Fax: 414/228-2302 **Phone:** 414/228-1200

Use: **Balance Sheet/Risk Management**
Hedge currency risk
Hedge overseas investments
Strategic liability management

Currencies: US dollar, Canadian dollar, French franc, German mark, Spanish peseta, UK pound

Regions: United States, Europe

DERIVATIVES ACTIVITIES: **CAC Class: 4**

OTC Derivatives	**Currency**
Plain Vanilla Derivatives	Swaps
Counterparty Rating Requirement:	AAA

KEY MANAGERS & DERIVATIVES SPECIALISTS:	**Direct Phone/Fax**	**Job Function**
Mr. Ben C. M. Bastianen Treasurer		Treasurer Portfolio Mgr – Derivatives
Mr. Stephen A. Roell Vice President & C.F.O.		Chief Financial Officer

Johnson Investment Counsel Incorporated

Investment Manager

Location: 5556 Cheviot Road
Cincinnati, OH 45247

Fax: 513/385-8947 **Phone:** 513/385-4001

Profile: Total return investor

Investment Portfolio: $ 1.4 billion

Use: **Investment Purposes**

Currencies: US dollar

Regions: United States

DERIVATIVES ACTIVITIES: **CAC Class: Inactive**

OTHER ALTERNATIVE INVESTMENTS:

CMOs/REMICs – Govt.

KEY MANAGERS & DERIVATIVES SPECIALISTS:	**Direct Phone/Fax**	**Job Function**
Dr. Timothy E. Johnson President		President Chief Investment Officer

Kansas City Life Insurance Company

Insurance Co/Life

Location: 3520 Broadway
Kansas City, MO 64111-2565

Fax: 816/753-1354 **Phone:** 816/753-7299

Profile: Total return investor

Investment Portfolio: $ 2.0 billion

Use: **Investment Purposes**

Currencies: US dollar

Regions: United States

DERIVATIVES ACTIVITIES: **CAC Class: Inactive**

OTHER ALTERNATIVE INVESTMENTS:

CMOs/REMICs – Govt.
CMOs/REMICs – Private
Repos/reverse repos

KEY MANAGERS & DERIVATIVES SPECIALISTS:	**Direct Phone/Fax**	**Job Function**
Mr. Richard Finn Senior Vice President-Finance	Ext. 8216	Chief Investment Officer

Henry Kaufman & Company, Inc.

Investment Manager

Location: 65 East 55th Street
26th Floor
New York, NY 10022

Fax: 212/755-4090 **Phone:** 212/755-3040

Profile: Total return investor

Investment Portfolio: $ 500.0 - 999.0 million

Use: **Investment Purposes**

Currencies: US dollar

Regions: United States

DERIVATIVES ACTIVITIES: **CAC Class: Inactive**

OTHER ALTERNATIVE INVESTMENTS:

CMOs/REMICs – Govt.

KEY MANAGERS & DERIVATIVES SPECIALISTS:	**Direct Phone/Fax**	**Job Function**
Mr. Henry Kaufman President		President Chief Investment Officer

Kennedy Associates Inc.

Investment Manager

Location: 2400 Financial Center Building
1215 Fourth Avenue
Seattle, WA 98161

Fax: 206/624-8515 **Phone:** 206/624-9640

Profile: Total return investor

Investment Portfolio: $ 2.8 billion

Use: **Investment Purposes**

Currencies: US dollar

Regions: United States

Kennedy Associates Inc. – continued

DERIVATIVES ACTIVITIES: **CAC Class: Inactive**

OTHER ALTERNATIVE INVESTMENTS:

CMOs/REMICs – Govt.
Strips

KEY MANAGERS & DERIVATIVES SPECIALISTS:	Direct Phone/Fax	Job Function
Mr. Robert E. Grady, Jr. Senior Vice President		Bond Department Head *ABS, Govt, MBS*
Mr. Duff Kennedy President & C.E.O.		President Chief Investment Officer

Kentucky National Insurance Co.

Insurance Co/Life

Location: 300 West Vine Street
Kincaid Towers 14th Floor
Lexington, KY 40507

Fax: 606/253-5203 **Phone:** 606/253-5200

Profile: Hold to maturity investor

Investment Portfolio: $ 1.0 billion

Use: **Investment Purposes**
Provide incremental return

Currencies: US dollar

Regions: United States

DERIVATIVES ACTIVITIES: **CAC Class: 1**

Exchange-traded Options & Futures

Structured Notes
Corporate MTNs
Govt. agency MTNs

OTHER ALTERNATIVE INVESTMENTS:

CMOs/REMICs – Govt.
CMOs/REMICs – Private
Repos/reverse repos

KEY MANAGERS & DERIVATIVES SPECIALISTS:	Direct Phone/Fax	Job Function
Mr. Joseph DeAlessandro President		President
Mr. Enoch G. Roberts Director of Administration		Chief Investment Officer Portfolio Mgr – Options Portfolio Mgr – Structured Notes

Key Trust Company (Albany)

Bank/Trust

Sub of KeyCorp

Location: 35 State Street
Fourth Floor
Albany, NY 12207

Fax: 518/488-5846 **Phone:** 518/488-5800

Profile: Total return investor

Investment Portfolio: $ 1.9 billion

Use: **Investment Purposes**

Currencies: US dollar

Regions: United States

DERIVATIVES ACTIVITIES:

CAC Class: Inactive

OTHER ALTERNATIVE INVESTMENTS:

CMOs/REMICs – Govt.
CMOs/REMICs – Private
Strips
Repos/reverse repos

KEY MANAGERS & DERIVATIVES SPECIALISTS:	Direct Phone/Fax	Job Function
Mr. Frederick Pitone	518/488-5841	Chief Investment Officer

Key Trust Company (Syracuse)

Bank/Trust

Sub of KeyCorp

Location: 221 South Warren Street
Suite 440
Syracuse, NY 13202

Fax: 315/470-5283 **Phone:** 315/470-5209

Profile: Total return investor

Investment Portfolio: $ 1.4 billion

Use: **Investment Purposes**

Currencies: US dollar

Regions: United States

DERIVATIVES ACTIVITIES:

CAC Class: Inactive

OTHER ALTERNATIVE INVESTMENTS:

CMOs/REMICs – Govt.
CMOs/REMICs – Private
Strips
Repos/reverse repos

KEY MANAGERS & DERIVATIVES SPECIALISTS:	Direct Phone/Fax	Job Function
Mr. Drayton Jones Senior Vice President	315/470-5213	Chief Investment Officer

KeyCorp

Bank Holding Company

Location: 127 Public Square
Cleveland, OH 44114-1306

Fax: 216/689-5115 **Phone:** 216/689-0234

Use:
Balance Sheet/Risk Management
Hedge currency risk
Hedge interest rate risk
Incremental return
Strategic liability management

Investment Purposes
Hedge currency risk
Protect currency gains
Provide incremental return

Currencies: US dollar, Canadian dollar, French franc, German mark, Japanese yen, UK pound

Regions: United States

DERIVATIVES ACTIVITIES: **CAC Class: 8**

Exchange-traded Options & Futures	**Interest rate**	
OTC Derivatives	**Currency, Interest rate**	
Plain Vanilla Derivatives	Swaps Forwards	Caps Floors
Exotic Derivatives	CMT swaps CMT options	Index amortizing swaps
Counterparty Rating Requirement:	AA	

KEY MANAGERS & DERIVATIVES SPECIALISTS:	**Direct Phone/Fax**	**Job Function**
Mr. Robert W. Gillespie President & C.E.O.		President
Mr. Lee Irving E.V.P. & Treasurer		Treasurer
Mr. K. Brent Somers Sr. Exec. V.P. & C.F.O.		Chief Financial Officer
Mr. Terry Taylor V.P. Inv. Products Risk Mgmt.	216/689-4875	Portfolio Mgr – Derivatives Portfolio Mgr – Futures Portfolio Mgr – Structured Notes
Mr. James W. Wert Chief Investment Officer	216/689-5850 216/689-7827	Chief Investment Officer

Keystone Custodian Funds, Inc.

Mutual Fund Manager

Location: 200 Berkeley Street
Boston, MA 02116-5034

Fax: 617/338-3351 **Phone:** 617/338-3200

Profile: Total return investor

Investment Portfolio: $ 12.0 billion

Use:
Investment Purposes
Provide incremental return

Currencies: US dollar

Regions: United States

Keystone Custodian Funds, Inc. – continued

DERIVATIVES ACTIVITIES:

Structured Notes	Inverse floaters	

OTHER ALTERNATIVE INVESTMENTS:

	CMOs/REMICs – Govt.	CMOs/REMICs – Private

KEY MANAGERS & DERIVATIVES SPECIALISTS:	**Direct Phone/Fax**	**Job Function**
Ms. Betsy A. Blacher Vice President	617/338-3458	Bond Department Head *Muni*
Mr. James R. McCall President	617/338-3462	President Chief Investment Officer

Keystone Investment Services

Bank/Management Division

Sub of Keystone Financial, Inc.

Location: Front & Market Streets
One Keystone Plaza
Harrisburg, PA 17105

Fax: 717/231-5758 **Phone:** 717/231-5724

Profile: Hold to maturity investor

Investment Portfolio: $ 1.2 billion

Use: **Balance Sheet/Risk Management**
Hedge interest rate risk

Investment Purposes
Beat conventional rates
Capture extra yield

Currencies: US dollar

Regions: United States

DERIVATIVES ACTIVITIES: **CAC Class: 2**

OTC Derivatives **Plain Vanilla Derivatives**	**Interest rate** Swaps	
Exotic Derivatives	Index amortizing swaps	
Structured Notes	Govt. agency MTNs Floaters	Multi-step-up callable bonds
Counterparty Rating Requirement:	A	

OTHER ALTERNATIVE INVESTMENTS:

	CMOs/REMICs – Govt.	CMOs/REMICs – Private

KEY MANAGERS & DERIVATIVES SPECIALISTS:	**Direct Phone/Fax**	**Job Function**
Mr. Thomas L. Downing Vice President		Portfolio Mgr – Derivatives *MBS* Portfolio Mgr – Structured Notes
Mr. A. James Durica Senior Vice President		Chief Investment Officer

Kiewit Investment Management

Corporation

Location: 1000 Kiewit Plaza
Omaha, NE 68131

Fax: 402/271-2918 **Phone:** 402/342-2052

Profile: Total return investor

Investment Portfolio: $ 1.0 - 3.0 billion

Use: **Investment Purposes**
Hedge bond portfolio risk

Currencies: US dollar

Regions: United States

DERIVATIVES ACTIVITIES:

Exchange-traded Options & Futures **Bond**

OTHER ALTERNATIVE INVESTMENTS:

CMOs/REMICs – Govt.
CMOs/REMICs – Private
Repos/reverse repos

KEY MANAGERS & DERIVATIVES SPECIALISTS:	**Direct Phone/Fax**	**Job Function**
Mr. Paul Strong	402/271-2896	Chief Investment Officer Portfolio Mgr – Futures Portfolio Mgr – Options
Mr. P. Greggory Williams	402/342-3665	Portfolio Mgr – Futures Portfolio Mgr – Options

Luther King Capital Management

Investment Manager

Location: 301 Commerce Street Suite 1600
Fort Worth, TX 76102

Fax: 817/332-4630 **Phone:** 817/332-3235

Profile: Total return investor

Investment Portfolio: $ 5.0 billion

Use: **Investment Purposes**

Currencies: US dollar

Regions: United States

DERIVATIVES ACTIVITIES: **CAC Class: Inactive**

OTHER ALTERNATIVE INVESTMENTS:

CMOs/REMICs – Govt.
CMOs/REMICs – Private

KEY MANAGERS & DERIVATIVES SPECIALISTS:	**Direct Phone/Fax**	**Job Function**
Mr. Robert M. Holt, Jr. Vice President		Bond Department Head *ABS, Corp, Govt, Muni*
Mr. J. Luther King President		President Chief Investment Officer

Knights of Columbus

Insurance Co/Life

Location: One Columbus Plaza
New Haven, CT 06507-3325

Fax: 203/772-0037 **Phone:** 203/865-1710

Profile: Total return investor

Investment Portfolio: $ 5.5 billion

Use: **Balance Sheet/Risk Management**

Currencies: US dollar

Regions: United States

DERIVATIVES ACTIVITIES: **CAC Class: Inactive**

OTHER ALTERNATIVE INVESTMENTS:

Repos/reverse repos

KEY MANAGERS & DERIVATIVES SPECIALISTS:	Direct Phone/Fax	Job Function
Mr. Charles C. Walden Senior Vice President	Ext. 331	Chief Investment Officer

Laidlaw Capital Management, Inc.

Investment Manager

Sub of W.R. Lazard, Laidlaw & Mead, Inc.

Location: 14 Wall Street
18th Floor
New York, NY 10005

Fax: 212/233-7784 **Phone:** 212/949-5400

Profile: Total return investor

Investment Portfolio: $ 1.2 billion

Use: **Investment Purposes**

Regions: United States

DERIVATIVES ACTIVITIES: **CAC Class: Inactive**

OTHER ALTERNATIVE INVESTMENTS:

CMOs/REMICs – Govt. CMOs/REMICs – Private

KEY MANAGERS & DERIVATIVES SPECIALISTS:	Direct Phone/Fax	Job Function
Mr. Thomas M. Meade		Bond Department Head

The Laredo National Bank

Bank/Portfolio

Location: 700 San Bernardo Avenue
Laredo, TX 78040-5025

Fax: 210/723-0260 **Phone:** 210/723-1151

Profile: Total return investor

Investment Portfolio: $ 500.0 - 999.0 million

Use: **Investment Purposes**

Currencies: US dollar

Regions: United States

The Laredo National Bank – continued

DERIVATIVES ACTIVITIES:		**CAC Class: 2**
Structured Notes	Govt. agency MTNs	

OTHER ALTERNATIVE INVESTMENTS:		
	CMOs/REMICs – Govt.	Repos/reverse repos

KEY MANAGERS & DERIVATIVES SPECIALISTS:	**Direct Phone/Fax**	**Job Function**
Mr. Joaquin G. Cigarroa III Executive Vice President		Chief Investment Officer
Mr. Nicholas Van Steenberg First Vice President		Portfolio Mgr – Structured Notes *Govt*

LaSalle National Bank (Portfolio)

Bank/Portfolio

Sub of ABN AMRO North America

Location: 181 West Madison Street
Treasury Building
Chicago, IL 60602

Fax: 312/750-6244 **Phone:** 312/781-8000

Profile: Total return investor

Investment Portfolio: $ 11.0 billion

Use: **Balance Sheet/Risk Management**
Create synthetic fixed/floating rate
Hedge balance sheet
Hedge interest rate risk
Incremental return
Strategic liability management

Currencies: US dollar

Regions: United States

DERIVATIVES ACTIVITIES:		**CAC Class: 6**
Exchange-traded Options & Futures U.S. Treasury futures	**Interest rate** U.S. Treasury options	
OTC Derivatives **Plain Vanilla Derivatives**	**Interest rate** Swaps Forwards Swaptions	 Caps Floors
Counterparty Rating Requirement:	AA	

OTHER ALTERNATIVE INVESTMENTS:		
	CMOs/REMICs – Govt. CMOs/REMICs – Private	Repos/reverse repos

LaSalle National Bank (Portfolio) – continued

KEY MANAGERS & DERIVATIVES SPECIALISTS:	Direct Phone/Fax	Job Function
Mr. Norman R. Bobins President	312/904-8400	President
Mr. James Curtin First Vice President	312/904-8648	Portfolio Mgr – Derivatives Portfolio Mgr – Futures Portfolio Mgr – Options
Mr. Walter Lazuka Senior Vice President	312/781-8349 312/781-8026	Portfolio Mgr – Derivatives
Mr. Martin Penstein Senior Vice President	312/904-7805	Chief Investment Officer

Lazard Freres Asset Management

Broker/Management Sub

Location: 30 Rockefeller Plaza
58th Floor
New York, NY 10020-2167

Fax: 212/632-6060 **Phone:** 212/632-6000

Profile: Total return investor

Investment Portfolio: $ 29.4 billion

Use: **Investment Purposes**
Hedge currency risk
Hedge equity portfolio risk
Hedge interest rate risk

Currencies: US dollar, Australian dollar, Belgian franc, Canadian dollar, ECU, French franc, German mark, Italian lira, Japanese yen, Spanish peseta, Swiss franc, UK pound

Regions: United States, Canada, Europe, Latin America

DERIVATIVES ACTIVITIES: **CAC Class: 6**

Exchange-traded Options & Futures	**Currency, Interest rate**	
OTC Derivatives **Plain Vanilla Derivatives**	**Currency, Interest rate** Forwards	
Structured Notes	Corporate MTNs	Govt. agency MTNs
Counterparty Rating Requirement:	AA	

OTHER ALTERNATIVE INVESTMENTS:

CMOs/REMICs – Govt. Strips

KEY MANAGERS & DERIVATIVES SPECIALISTS:	Direct Phone/Fax	Job Function
Mr. Thomas F. Dunn Vice President	212/632-8267	Portfolio Mgr – Derivatives Portfolio Mgr – Futures Portfolio Mgr – Structured Notes
Mr. Herbert Gullquist General Partner	212/632-6419	Chief Investment Officer

Leader Federal Bank for Savings

Savings Bank/Bldg Society

Sub of Leader Financial Corporation

Location: 158 Madison Avenue
Memphis, TN 38103

Fax: 901/524-5715 **Phone:** 901/578-2000

Profile: Hold to maturity investor

Investment Portfolio: $ 2.0 billion

Use: **Balance Sheet/Risk Management**
Create synthetic fixed/floating rate

Investment Purposes
Beat conventional rates
Diversify portfolio

Currencies: US dollar

Regions: United States

DERIVATIVES ACTIVITIES: **CAC Class: 2**

OTC Derivatives	**Bond, Interest rate**	
Plain Vanilla Derivatives	Swaps	Forwards
Structured Notes	Govt. agency MTNs	Multi-step-up callable bonds
Counterparty Rating Requirement:	None	

OTHER ALTERNATIVE INVESTMENTS:

	Strips	Repos/reverse repos

KEY MANAGERS & DERIVATIVES SPECIALISTS:	Direct Phone/Fax	Job Function
Mr. Warren East	901/578-2419	Portfolio Mgr – Derivatives Portfolio Mgr – Structured Notes
Mr. Mark S. Martini Vice President – Investments	901/578-2452	Portfolio Mgr – Derivatives Portfolio Mgr – Structured Notes
Mr. David Wadlington	901/578-2410	Chief Investment Officer Portfolio Mgr – Derivatives Portfolio Mgr – Structured Notes

Lehman Brothers Global Asset Management, Inc. (New York)

Broker/Management Sub

Location: Three World Financial Center
Seventh Floor
New York, NY 10285-0900

Fax: 212/528-6300 **Phone:** 212/526-0600

Profile: Total return investor

Investment Portfolio: $ 5.0 billion

Use: **Investment Purposes**

Currencies: US dollar

Regions: United States

DERIVATIVES ACTIVITIES: **CAC Class: Inactive**

OTHER ALTERNATIVE INVESTMENTS:

Repos/reverse repos

Lehman Brothers Global Asset Management, Inc. (New York) – continued

KEY MANAGERS & DERIVATIVES SPECIALISTS:	Direct Phone/Fax	Job Function
Mr. Jack Winters	212/526-7850	Chief Investment Officer

Leucadia National Corporation

Corporation

Location: 315 Park Avenue South
New York, NY 10010

Fax: 212/598-4869 **Phone:** 212/460-1900

Profile: Total return investor

Investment Portfolio: $ 4.0 - 10.0 billion

Use: **Balance Sheet/Risk Management**
Hedge interest rate risk

Currencies: US dollar

Regions: United States

DERIVATIVES ACTIVITIES: **CAC Class: 1**

Exchange-traded Options & Futures	**Interest rate**
OTC Derivatives	**Interest rate**
Plain Vanilla Derivatives	Swaps

OTHER ALTERNATIVE INVESTMENTS:

CMOs/REMICs – Govt.

KEY MANAGERS & DERIVATIVES SPECIALISTS:	Direct Phone/Fax	Job Function
Mr. Thomas E. Mara E.V.P. & Treasurer	212/460-1981	Chief Financial Officer Treasurer Portfolio Mgr – Derivatives Portfolio Mgr – Futures Portfolio Mgr – Options
Mr. David Sherman Vice President	212/460-1935	Chief Investment Officer
Mr. Joseph S. Steinberg President	212/460-1944	President

Lexington Management Corporation

Mutual Fund Manager

Sub of Piedmont Management Company, Inc.

Location: Park 80 West
Plaza Two – Eighth Floor
Saddle Brook, NJ 07663

Fax: 201/845-5121 **Phone:** 201/845-7300

Profile: Total return investor

Investment Portfolio: $ 3.5 billion

Use: **Investment Purposes**

Currencies: US dollar

Regions: United States

Lexington Management Corporation – continued

DERIVATIVES ACTIVITIES: **CAC Class: Inactive**

OTHER ALTERNATIVE INVESTMENTS:

CMOs/REMICs – Govt. CMOs/REMICs – Private

KEY MANAGERS & DERIVATIVES SPECIALISTS:	**Direct Phone/Fax**	**Job Function**
Mr. Robert M. DeMichele Chairman		Chief Investment Officer

LGT Asset Management

Investment Manager

Location: 50 California Street
27th Floor
San Francisco, CA 94111

Fax: 415/956-5617 **Phone:** 415/392-6181

Profile: Total return investor

Investment Portfolio: $ 22.0 billion

Use:

Balance Sheet/Risk Management
Protect currency gains
Strategic liability management

Investment Purposes
Alter portfolio weighting
Asset allocation
Capture extra yield
Diversify portfolio
Expand international investments
Hedge bond portfolio risk
Hedge currency risk
Hedge equity portfolio risk
Hedge interest rate risk
Protect currency gains
Provide incremental return
Reduce variability of returns

Currencies: US dollar, Australian dollar, Belgian franc, Canadian dollar, ECU, French franc, German mark, Italian lira, Japanese yen, Swiss franc, UK pound

Regions: United States, Canada, Europe, Latin America, Pacific Rim, Emerging mkts

DERIVATIVES ACTIVITIES:

Exchange-traded Options & Futures
U.S. Treasury futures

Bond

OTC Derivatives
Plain Vanilla Derivatives

Currency
Forwards
Caps
Floors
Collars

Structured Notes

Corporate MTNs
Govt. agency MTNs

OTHER ALTERNATIVE INVESTMENTS:

CMOs/REMICs – Govt.
CMOs/REMICs – Private
GICs
Repos/reverse repos

LGT Asset Management – continued

KEY MANAGERS & DERIVATIVES SPECIALISTS:	Direct Phone/Fax	Job Function
Mr. Ralf Lochmüller		Chief Investment Officer
Mr. Donald Mattersdorf Vice President	415/399-5444	Portfolio Mgr – Derivatives Portfolio Mgr – Futures Portfolio Mgr – Structured Notes
Mr. Wolfgang Seiler Chief Financial Officer		Chief Financial Officer Bond Department Head *Corp, Govt*
Mr. Malcolm Tulloch V.P.-International Strategies	415/399-5440	Fixed-Income Strategist
Mr. Christian Wignall		Chief Investment Officer

Libby, Inc.

Corporation

Location: 420 Madison Avenue
Toledo, OH 43699

Fax: 419/727-2585 **Phone:** 419/727-2100

Use: **Balance Sheet/Risk Management**
Hedge balance sheet
Hedge interest rate risk

Currencies: US dollar **Regions:** United States

DERIVATIVES ACTIVITIES: **CAC Class: 3**

OTC Derivatives	**Interest rate**
Plain Vanilla Derivatives	Swaps
Counterparty Rating Requirement:	AA

KEY MANAGERS & DERIVATIVES SPECIALISTS:	Direct Phone/Fax	Job Function
Mr. Richard I. Reynolds Vice President & C.F.O.		Chief Financial Officer
Mr. Kenneth G. Wilkes Vice President & Treasurer		Treasurer Portfolio Mgr – Derivatives

Liberty Bank and Trust Co. (Oklahoma City) (Portfolio)

Bank/Portfolio

Sub of Liberty Bancorp, Inc.

Location: 100 North Broadway Avenue
Oklahoma City, OK 73102-8625

Fax: 405/231-6758 **Phone:** 405/231-6000

Profile: Total return investor

Investment Portfolio: $ 2.7 billion

Use: **Balance Sheet/Risk Management**
Hedge interest rate risk

Currencies: US dollar

Regions: United States

DERIVATIVES ACTIVITIES:

OTC Derivatives	**Interest rate**
Plain Vanilla Derivatives	Swaps

OTHER ALTERNATIVE INVESTMENTS:

CMOs/REMICs – Govt. Repos/reverse repos

KEY MANAGERS & DERIVATIVES SPECIALISTS:	Direct Phone/Fax	Job Function
Mr. Kenneth R. Brown Senior Vice President	405/231-6454	Bond Department Head *Corp, Govt, MBS, Muni*
Mr. Mark Horrell		Portfolio Mgr – Derivatives
Mr. Charles E. Nelson Chairman, President & C.E.O.		President

Liberty Bank and Trust Co. (Oklahoma City) (Trust)

Bank/Trust

Sub of Liberty Bancorp, Inc.

Location: 100 North Broadway Avenue
Oklahoma City, OK 73102-8625

Fax: 405/231-6725 **Phone:** 405/231-6453

Profile: Directional investor

Investment Portfolio: $ 1.2 billion

Use: **Investment Purposes**
Discretionary situations

Currencies: US dollar

Regions: United States

DERIVATIVES ACTIVITIES: **CAC Class: 1**

Structured Notes	Corporate MTNs Govt. agency MTNs	Floaters
Counterparty Rating Requirement:	None	

Liberty Bank and Trust Co. (Oklahoma City) (Trust) – continued

OTHER ALTERNATIVE INVESTMENTS:

	CMOs/REMICs – Govt. Strips	Repos/reverse repos

KEY MANAGERS & DERIVATIVES SPECIALISTS:	**Direct Phone/Fax**	**Job Function**
Mr. Charles B. Johnson Senior Vice President	405/231-6453	Chief Investment Officer Portfolio Mgr – Structured Notes *Corp, Govt*

Liberty Capital Advisors, Inc.

Insurance Co/Management

Sub of The Liberty Corporation

Location: 2000 Wade Hampton Boulevard
Greenville, SC 29615-1037

Fax: 803/292-4097 **Phone:** 803/268-8303

Profile: Total return investor

Investment Portfolio: $ 1.3 billion

Use: **Investment Purposes**

Currencies: US dollar

Regions: United States

DERIVATIVES ACTIVITIES: **CAC Class: Inactive**

OTHER ALTERNATIVE INVESTMENTS:

	CMOs/REMICs – Govt.	CMOs/REMICs – Private

KEY MANAGERS & DERIVATIVES SPECIALISTS:	**Direct Phone/Fax**	**Job Function**
Mr. Douglas W. Kroske President		President Chief Investment Officer

Life Insurance Company of the Southwest

Insurance Co/Life

Location: 1300 West Mockingbird Lane
Dallas, TX 75247-4921

Fax: 214/638-9393 **Phone:** 214/638-7100

Profile: Hold to maturity investor

Investment Portfolio: $ 1.0 - 3.0 billion

Use: **Investment Purposes**

Currencies: US dollar

Regions: United States

DERIVATIVES ACTIVITIES: **CAC Class: 2**

Structured Notes	Corporate MTNs	Govt. agency MTNs

OTHER ALTERNATIVE INVESTMENTS:

	CMOs/REMICs – Govt.	CMOs/REMICs – Private

Life Insurance Company of the Southwest – continued

KEY MANAGERS & DERIVATIVES SPECIALISTS:	Direct Phone/Fax	Job Function
Mr. Robert C. Davis	214/638-9247	Chief Investment Officer
Ms. Roseann Sezcik	214/638-9243	Portfolio Mgr – Structured Notes

Life Partners Group

Insurance Co/Management

Location: 7887 East Belleview Avenue
Englewood, CO 80111-6015

Fax: 303/796-7576 **Phone:** 303/779-1111

Profile: Current yield investor

Investment Portfolio: $ 5.0 billion

Use: **Investment Purposes**
Adjust portfolio duration
Beat conventional rates
Capture extra yield

Currencies: US dollar

Regions: United States

DERIVATIVES ACTIVITIES: **CAC Class: 2**

OTC Derivatives **Plain Vanilla Derivatives**	**Interest rate** Swaps	
Structured Notes	Corporate MTNs Govt. agency MTNs Floaters	Inverse floaters Multi-step-up callable bonds

OTHER ALTERNATIVE INVESTMENTS:

CMOs/REMICs – Govt.	Strips
CMOs/REMICs – Private	Repos/reverse repos

KEY MANAGERS & DERIVATIVES SPECIALISTS:	Direct Phone/Fax	Job Function
Mr. George Councill Executive Vice President		Chief Investment Officer Portfolio Mgr – Derivatives Portfolio Mgr – Structured Notes
Mr. George Paz Treasurer		Treasurer

Lincoln National Corporation

Corporation

Location: 200 East Berry Street
Fort Wayne, IN 46802

Fax: 219/455-2301 **Phone:** 219/455-2000

Profile: Spread investor

Use: **Balance Sheet/Risk Management**
Create synthetic fixed/floating rate
Hedge currency risk
Hedge interest rate risk
Hedge overseas investments

Investment Purposes
Adjust portfolio duration
Capture extra yield
Hedge bond portfolio risk
Hedge currency risk
Hedge interest rate risk

Currencies: US dollar UK pound

Regions: United States

Lincoln National Corporation – continued

DERIVATIVES ACTIVITIES: **CAC Class: 7**

Exchange-traded Options & Futures	**Bond, Interest rate**	
OTC Derivatives **Plain Vanilla Derivatives**	**Currency, Interest rate** Swaps Forwards Caps	 Floors Collars
Counterparty Rating Requirement:	A	

KEY MANAGERS & DERIVATIVES SPECIALISTS:	**Direct Phone/Fax**	**Job Function**
Mr. Robert A. Anker President & C.O.O.		President
Mr. Richard S. Robertson E.V.P. – Risk Management		Portfolio Mgr – Derivatives
Mr. Max A. Roesler Treasurer		Treasurer
Mr. Richard C. Vaughan Exec. Vice President & C.F.O.		Chief Financial Officer

Lincoln National Investment Management Co.

Insurance Co/Management

Sub of Lincoln National Corporation

Location: 200 East Berry Street
Fort Wayne, IN 46802-2204

Fax: 219/455-1475 **Phone:** 219/455-2000

Profile: Total return investor

Investment Portfolio: $ 39.0 billion

Use: **Balance Sheet/Risk Management**
Create synthetic fixed/floating rate
Hedge balance sheet
Hedge currency risk
Hedge interest rate risk
Hedge overseas investments
Incremental return
Strategic liability management

Currencies: US dollar, Canadian dollar, French franc, German mark, Italian lira, Japanese yen, UK pound

Regions: United States, Canada, Europe, Pacific Rim

Lincoln National Investment Management Co. – continued

DERIVATIVES ACTIVITIES: **CAC Class: 4**

Exchange-traded Options & Futures U.S. Treasury futures	**Bond, Currency, Interest rate** U.S. Treasury options	
OTC Derivatives **Plain Vanilla Derivatives**	**Bond, Currency, Interest rate** Swaps Forwards Caps	 Floors Collars
Exotic Derivatives	CMT swaps	
Structured Notes	Corporate MTNs Govt. agency MTNs Bond index notes	CMT notes Floaters
Counterparty Rating Requirement:	None	

OTHER ALTERNATIVE INVESTMENTS:

CMOs/REMICs – Govt.	Strips
CMOs/REMICs – Private	Repos/reverse repos

KEY MANAGERS & DERIVATIVES SPECIALISTS:	**Direct Phone/Fax**	**Job Function**
Mr. Howard Lodge	219/455-6492	Portfolio Mgr – Derivatives Portfolio Mgr – Futures Portfolio Mgr – Options Portfolio Mgr – Structured Notes
Mr. Tom McAvity V.P.-Quantitative Research	219/455-5118	Portfolio Mgr – Derivatives Portfolio Mgr – Futures Portfolio Mgr – Options
Mr. H. Thomas McMeekin President & C.I.O.		President Chief Investment Officer Portfolio Mgr – Derivatives Portfolio Mgr – Options Portfolio Mgr – Structured Notes
Ms. Ann L. Warner Senior Vice President	219/455-3204 219/455-1441	Bond Department Head

Lipper & Company, L.P.

Investment Manager

Location: 101 Park Avenue
6th Floor
New York, NY 10178

Fax: 212/883-8701 **Phone:** 212/883-6333

Profile: Total return investor

Investment Portfolio: $ 2.5 billion

Use: **Investment Purposes**
Provide incremental return

Currencies: US dollar

Regions: United States

DERIVATIVES ACTIVITIES:

OTC Derivatives
Plain Vanilla Derivatives

Lipper & Company, L.P. – continued

KEY MANAGERS & DERIVATIVES SPECIALISTS:	Direct Phone/Fax	Job Function
Ms. Nancy Freedman	212/883-2215	Portfolio Mgr – Derivatives
Mr. Kenneth Lipper President & C.E.O.	212/883-6333	President
Mr. Edward J. Strafaci Managing Director	212/883-2301	Chief Investment Officer

Litton Industries, Inc.

Corporation

Location: 360 North Crestwood Drive
Beverly Hills, CA 90210-4867

Fax: 310/859-5940 **Phone:** 310/859-5000

Use: **Balance Sheet/Risk Management**
Hedge balance sheet
Hedge currency risk

Currencies: US dollar Canadian dollar **Regions:** United States

DERIVATIVES ACTIVITIES:

Exchange-traded Options & Futures	
OTC Derivatives **Plain Vanilla Derivatives**	Forwards
Structured Notes	Corporate MTNs
Counterparty Rating Requirement:	None

OTHER ALTERNATIVE INVESTMENTS:

Repos/reverse repos

KEY MANAGERS & DERIVATIVES SPECIALISTS:	Direct Phone/Fax	Job Function
Mr. Michael R. Brown President & C.O.O.		President
Mr. Rudolph E. Lang, Jr. Chief Financial Officer		Chief Financial Officer
Ms. Carol A. Weisner Vice President & Treasurer		Treasurer Portfolio Mgr – Derivatives

The Long Island Savings Bank, F.S.B.

Savings Bank/Bldg Society

Location: 201 Old Country Road
Melville, NY 11747-2724

Fax: 516/547-3029 **Phone:** 516/547-2265

Profile: Hold to maturity investor

Investment Portfolio: $ 2.1 billion

Use: **Balance Sheet/Risk Management**
Hedge interest rate risk

Currencies: US dollar

Regions: United States

DERIVATIVES ACTIVITIES: **CAC Class: 3**

OTC Derivatives		
Plain Vanilla Derivatives	Caps	Floors
Structured Notes	Corporate MTNs	
Counterparty Rating Requirement:	AA	

OTHER ALTERNATIVE INVESTMENTS:

CMOs/REMICs – Govt. Repos/reverse repos

KEY MANAGERS & DERIVATIVES SPECIALISTS:	**Direct Phone/Fax**	**Job Function**
Ms. Christine A. Quigley Vice President	516/547-3072	Portfolio Mgr – Derivatives Portfolio Mgr – Structured Notes
Mr. W. Douglas Singer Executive Vice President	516/547-3070	Chief Investment Officer Portfolio Mgr – Derivatives Portfolio Mgr – Structured Notes

Loomis, Sayles & Company L.P.

Investment Manager

Sub of New England Investment Companies, L.P.

Location: One Financial Center
33rd Floor
Boston, MA 02111-2660

Fax: 617/482-1985 **Phone:** 617/482-2450

Profile: Total return investor

Investment Portfolio: $ 17.7 billion

Use: **Investment Purposes**

Currencies: US dollar

Regions: United States

DERIVATIVES ACTIVITIES: **CAC Class: Inactive**

OTHER ALTERNATIVE INVESTMENTS:

CMOs/REMICs – Govt. CMOs/REMICs – Private

Loomis, Sayles & Company L.P. – continued

KEY MANAGERS & DERIVATIVES SPECIALISTS:	Direct Phone/Fax	Job Function
Mr. Daniel J. Fuss Executive Vice President	617/951-2747	Chief Investment Officer Bond Department Head
Mr. Patrick P. Hurley Director-Fixed Income Research	617/482-2828	Fixed-Income Strategist

Loomis, Sayles & Company L.P. (Bloomfield Hills)

Investment Manager

Sub of New England Investment Companies, L.P.

Location: 1533 North Woodward Avenue
Suite 300
Bloomfield Hills, MI 48304

Fax: 810/645-8608 **Phone:** 810/646-2100

Profile: Total return investor

Investment Portfolio: $ 5.8 billion

Use: **Investment Purposes**

Currencies: US dollar

Regions: United States

DERIVATIVES ACTIVITIES: **CAC Class: Inactive**

OTHER ALTERNATIVE INVESTMENTS:

CMOs/REMICs – Govt.
CMOs/REMICs – Private
Strips

KEY MANAGERS & DERIVATIVES SPECIALISTS:	Direct Phone/Fax	Job Function
Mr. Michael H. Harris	810/646-2592	Bond Department Head

Loomis, Sayles & Company L.P. (Milwaukee)

Investment Manager

Sub of New England Investment Companies, L.P.

Location: 111 East Kilbourn Avenue
Suite 2700
Milwaukee, WI 53202-6611

Fax: 414/272-1531 **Phone:** 414/272-4844

Profile: Total return investor

Investment Portfolio: $ 1.6 billion

Use: **Investment Purposes**

Currencies: US dollar

Regions: United States

DERIVATIVES ACTIVITIES: **CAC Class: Inactive**

OTHER ALTERNATIVE INVESTMENTS:

CMOs/REMICs – Govt.
CMOs/REMICs – Private

Loomis, Sayles & Company L.P. (Milwaukee) – continued

KEY MANAGERS & DERIVATIVES SPECIALISTS:	Direct Phone/Fax	Job Function
Mr. Richard R. Davidson Vice President		Chief Investment Officer

Loomis, Sayles & Company L.P. (Pasadena)

Investment Manager

Sub of New England Investment Companies, L.P.

Location: 155 North Lake Avenue
Suite 1030
Pasadena, CA 91101-1857

Fax: 818/584-1197 **Phone:** 818/793-8989

Profile: Total return investor

Investment Portfolio: $ 7.4 billion

Use: **Investment Purposes**

Currencies: US dollar

Regions: United States

DERIVATIVES ACTIVITIES: **CAC Class: Inactive**

OTHER ALTERNATIVE INVESTMENTS:

CMOs/REMICs – Govt. CMOs/REMICs – Private

KEY MANAGERS & DERIVATIVES SPECIALISTS:	Direct Phone/Fax	Job Function
Ms. Meri Anne Beck Senior Partner	818/584-9831	Bond Department Head
Ms. Carol C. McMurtrie Managing Partner		Chief Investment Officer

Loomis, Sayles & Company Inc. (San Francisco)

Investment Manager

Sub of New England Investment Companies, L.P.

Location: 555 California Street
Suite 2750
San Francisco, CA 94104-1603

Fax: 415/956-1052 **Phone:** 415/956-2424

Profile: Total return investor

Investment Portfolio: $ 3.6 billion

Use: **Investment Purposes**

Currencies: US dollar

Regions: United States

DERIVATIVES ACTIVITIES: **CAC Class: Inactive**

OTHER ALTERNATIVE INVESTMENTS:

CMOs/REMICs – Govt. Strips
CMOs/REMICs – Private

Loomis, Sayles & Company Inc. (San Francisco) – continued

KEY MANAGERS & DERIVATIVES SPECIALISTS:	**Direct Phone/Fax**	**Job Function**
Mr. Kent P. Newmark Managing Partner	415/956-1052	Chief Investment Officer

Loomis, Sayles & Company Inc. (Washington, D.C.)

Investment Manager

Sub of New England Investment Companies, L.P.

Location: 2001 Pennsylvania Avenue N.W.
Suite 200
Washington, DC 20006-1813

Fax: 202/293-8264 **Phone:** 202/463-6200

Profile: Total return investor

Investment Portfolio: $ 3.8 billion

Use: **Investment Purposes**
Capture extra yield
Discretionary situations
Hedge bond portfolio risk
Hedge currency risk
Hedge equity portfolio risk
Hedge interest rate risk

Currencies: US dollar

Regions: United States

DERIVATIVES ACTIVITIES:

Exchange-traded Options & Futures	**Bond, Currency, Interest Rate**	
OTC Derivatives **Plain Vanilla Derivatives**	**Bond, Currency, Interest rate** Swaps Caps	Floors
Structured Notes		

OTHER ALTERNATIVE INVESTMENTS:

	CMOs/REMICs – Govt.	CMOs/REMICs – Private

KEY MANAGERS & DERIVATIVES SPECIALISTS:	**Direct Phone/Fax**	**Job Function**
Mr. Daniel Ryczek Vice President		Bond Department Head Portfolio Mgr – Derivatives Portfolio Mgr – Options

Lord Abbett & Company

Mutual Fund Manager

Location: 767 Fifth Avenue
11th Floor
New York, NY 10153-0203

Fax: 212/888-4405 **Phone:** 212/848-1800

Profile: Total return investor

Investment Portfolio: $ 16.5 billion

Use: **Investment Purposes**

Currencies: US dollar

Regions: United States

Lord Abbett & Company – continued

DERIVATIVES ACTIVITIES:		CAC Class: Inactive

OTHER ALTERNATIVE INVESTMENTS:

	CMOs/REMICs – Govt.	GICs

KEY MANAGERS & DERIVATIVES SPECIALISTS:	**Direct Phone/Fax**	**Job Function**
Mr. Robert S. Dow Executive Vice President	212/848-1873	Chief Investment Officer Bond Department Head
Mr. Richard Szaro	212/848-1881 212/980-6835	Fixed-Income Strategist

Los Angeles County Treasurer

Government

Location: 500 West Temple Street
432 Hall of Administration
Los Angeles, CA 90012

Fax: 213/625-2249 **Phone:** 213/974-2191

Profile: Hold to maturity investor

Investment Portfolio: $ 6.0 billion

Use: **Balance Sheet/Risk Management**
Create synthetic fixed/floating rate
Hedge currency risk
Hedge interest rate risk
Strategic liability management

Currencies: US dollar

Regions: United States

DERIVATIVES ACTIVITIES:		CAC Class: 5
Exchange-traded Options & Futures U.S. Treasury futures	**Interest rate**	
OTC Derivatives **Plain Vanilla Derivatives**	**Interest rate** Swaps	
Structured Notes	Govt. agency MTNs Floaters	Periodic capped floaters Multi-step-up callable bonds
Counterparty Rating Requirement:	A	

OTHER ALTERNATIVE INVESTMENTS:

	CMOs/REMICs – Govt. CMOs/REMICs – Private	Strips Repos/reverse repos

KEY MANAGERS & DERIVATIVES SPECIALISTS:	**Direct Phone/Fax**	**Job Function**
Mr. Richard Davis		Chief Investment Officer Portfolio Mgr – Derivatives Portfolio Mgr – Structured Notes
Mr. Anthony Mason		Portfolio Mgr – Derivatives Portfolio Mgr – Futures

Lotsoff Capital Management

Investment Manager

Sub of ReliaStar Financial Corporation

Location: 20 North Wacker Drive
Suite 3200
Chicago, IL 60606-2801

Fax: 312/750-1131 **Phone:** 312/368-1442

Profile: Total return investor

Investment Portfolio: $ 1.4 billion

Use: **Investment Purposes**
Alter portfolio weighting
Adjust portfolio duration
Asset allocation
Capture extra yield
Diversify portfolio
Hedge bond portfolio risk
Hedge equity portfolio risk
Hedge interest rate risk
Provide incremental return
Reduce variability of returns

Currencies: US dollar

Regions: United States

DERIVATIVES ACTIVITIES: **CAC Class: 2**

Exchange-traded Options & Futures	**Bond, Interest rate**	
U.S. Treasury futures	U.S. Treasury options	
OTC Derivatives	**Bond, Interest rate**	
Plain Vanilla Derivatives	Forwards	Caps
Counterparty Rating Requirement:	A	

OTHER ALTERNATIVE INVESTMENTS:

	CMOs/REMICs – Govt.	CMOs/REMICs – Private

KEY MANAGERS & DERIVATIVES SPECIALISTS:	**Direct Phone/Fax**	**Job Function**
Mr. Stephen K. Bossu		Portfolio Mgr – Derivatives Portfolio Mgr – Options
Mr. David Hershey		Portfolio Mgr – Derivatives Portfolio Mgr – Options
Mr. Seymour N. Lotsoff		Chief Investment Officer
Mr. Matthew R. Smith		Portfolio Mgr – Derivatives Portfolio Mgr – Options

Lutheran Brotherhood

Insurance Co/Life

Location: 625 Fourth Avenue South
Tenth Floor
Minneapolis, MN 55415-1665

Fax: 612/340-8328 **Phone:** 612/340-7000

Profile: Total return investor

Investment Portfolio: $ 4.0 - 10.0 billion

Use: **Investment Purposes**
Provide incremental return

Currencies: US dollar

Regions: United States

DERIVATIVES ACTIVITIES:

Exchange-traded Options & Futures	**Interest rate**
Structured Notes	Inverse floaters

OTHER ALTERNATIVE INVESTMENTS:

CMOs/REMICs – Govt.
CMOs/REMICs – Private
GICs

KEY MANAGERS & DERIVATIVES SPECIALISTS:	**Direct Phone/Fax**	**Job Function**
Mr. Rolf F. Bjelland Executive Vice President	612/340-7274	Chief Investment Officer
Ms. Janet Grangaard	612/340-5779	Portfolio Mgr – Structured Notes *Muni*
Mr. Charles E. Heeren Vice President	612/340-7316 612/340-6497	Bond Department Head Portfolio Mgr – Futures *Govt*
Mr. Michael G. Landreville A.V.P.-Derivative Management	612/340-8505 612/340-6497	Portfolio Mgr – Futures

Madison Investment Advisors, Inc.

Investment Manager

Location: 6411 Mineral Point Road
Madison, WI 53705

Fax: 608/274-7905 **Phone:** 608/274-0300

Profile: Total return investor

Investment Portfolio: $ 2.2 billion

Use: **Investment Purposes**

Currencies: US dollar

Regions: United States

DERIVATIVES ACTIVITIES: **CAC Class: Inactive**

OTHER ALTERNATIVE INVESTMENTS:

CMOs/REMICs – Govt.

KEY MANAGERS & DERIVATIVES SPECIALISTS:	**Direct Phone/Fax**	**Job Function**
Mr. Frank E. Burgess President		President Chief Investment Officer

Madison Scottsdale

Investment Manager

Location: 8777 North Gainey Center Drive
Suite 152
Scottsdale, AZ 85258

Fax: 602/596-3303 **Phone:** 602/596-3338

Profile: Hold to maturity investor

Investment Portfolio: $ 2.2 billion

Use: **Investment Purposes**

Currencies: US dollar

Regions: United States

DERIVATIVES ACTIVITIES: **CAC Class: Inactive**

OTHER ALTERNATIVE INVESTMENTS:

CMOs/REMICs – Govt.

KEY MANAGERS & DERIVATIVES SPECIALISTS:	**Direct Phone/Fax**	**Job Function**
Mr. Louis LeGoullon President		President Chief Investment Officer

Magna Group, Inc.

Bank/Portfolio

Location: One Magna Place
1401 South Brentwood Boulevard
St. Louis, MO 63144-1401

Fax: 314/963-2691 **Phone:** 314/963-2500

Investment Portfolio: $ 4.9 billion

Use: **Balance Sheet/Risk Management**
Create synthetic fixed/floating rate
Hedge interest rate risk
Meet interest rate target
Strategic liability management

Currencies: US dollar

Regions: United States

DERIVATIVES ACTIVITIES: **CAC Class: 2**

OTC Derivatives	**Interest rate**
Plain Vanilla Derivatives	Swaps

OTHER ALTERNATIVE INVESTMENTS:

CMOs/REMICs – Govt. CMOs/REMICs – Private

KEY MANAGERS & DERIVATIVES SPECIALISTS:	**Direct Phone/Fax**	**Job Function**
Mr. Ronald Buerges	314/963-3030	Chief Financial Officer
Mr. Jon L. Henderson Senior Vice President	314/963-3014	Portfolio Mgr – Derivatives
Mr. James D. Jolley Executive Vice President	314/963-3012	Chief Investment Officer

Manning & Napier Advisors Inc.

Investment Manager

Location: 1100 Chase Square
Suite 1100
Rochester, NY 14604

Fax: 716/325-1992 **Phone:** 716/325-6880

Profile: Total return investor

Investment Portfolio: $ 5.0 billion

Use: **Investment Purposes**

Currencies: US dollar

Regions: United States

DERIVATIVES ACTIVITIES: **CAC Class: Inactive**

OTHER ALTERNATIVE INVESTMENTS:

CMOs/REMICs – Govt.

KEY MANAGERS & DERIVATIVES SPECIALISTS:	Direct Phone/Fax	Job Function
Mr. William Manning		Chief Investment Officer

Manufacturers & Traders Trust Company (Portfolio)

Bank/Portfolio

Sub of First Empire State Corporation

Location: 350 Park Avenue
New York, NY 10022

Fax: 212/350-2166 **Phone:** 212/350-2000

Profile: Total return investor

Investment Portfolio: $ 1.0 - 3.0 billion

Use: **Balance Sheet/Risk Management**
Hedge interest rate risk

Investment Purposes
Hedge interest rate risk

Currencies: US dollar

Regions: United States

DERIVATIVES ACTIVITIES:

Exchange-traded Options & Futures **Bond, Interest rate**

KEY MANAGERS & DERIVATIVES SPECIALISTS:	Direct Phone/Fax	Job Function
Mr. Spyro Degleris		Trader – Futures
Mr. Adam Kugler Senior Vice President	212/350-2486	Portfolio Mgr – Futures
Mr. William Rappolt Executive Vice President	212/350-2403	Chief Investment Officer

Manufacturers & Traders Trust Company (Treasury)

Corporation

Sub of First Empire State Corporation

Location: One M&T Plaza
Third Floor
Buffalo, NY 14240

Fax: 716/842-5823 **Phone:** 716/842-4200

Use: **Balance Sheet/Risk Management**
Hedge balance sheet
Hedge interest rate risk
Strategic liability management

Currencies: US dollar **Regions:** United States

DERIVATIVES ACTIVITIES:

OTC Derivatives	**Interest rate**
Plain Vanilla Derivatives	Swaps
Exotic Derivatives	Index amortizing swaps

OTHER ALTERNATIVE INVESTMENTS:

CMOs/REMICs – Govt.
CMOs/REMICs – Private
Repos/reverse repos

KEY MANAGERS & DERIVATIVES SPECIALISTS:	Direct Phone/Fax	Job Function
Mr. Scott Warman Vice President	716/842-5813	Portfolio Mgr – Derivatives

Marine Midland Bank, N.A. (Trust)

Bank/Trust

Sub of The HongKong and Shanghai Banking Corporation Limited

Location: One Marine Midland Center
Buffalo, NY 14203

Fax: 716/841-4244 **Phone:** 716/841-2424

Profile: Total return investor

Investment Portfolio: $ 17.0 billion

Use: **Investment Purposes**

Currencies: US dollar **Regions:** United States

DERIVATIVES ACTIVITIES: **CAC Class: Inactive**

OTHER ALTERNATIVE INVESTMENTS:

CMOs/REMICs – Govt.
CMOs/REMICs – Private

KEY MANAGERS & DERIVATIVES SPECIALISTS:	Direct Phone/Fax	Job Function
Mr. Bruce Kaz Vice President	716/841-7345	Bond Department Head *Corp, Govt, Muni*
Mr. John Reynolds S.V.P.-Investments	716/841-7800	Chief Investment Officer

Mark Twain Bank (Portfolio)

Bank/Portfolio

Sub of Mark Twain Bancshares, Inc.

Location: 8820 Ladue Road
St. Louis, MO 63124-2096

Fax: 314/746-2609 **Phone:** 314/727-1000

Profile: Hold to maturity investor

Investment Portfolio: $ 568.0 million

Use: **Balance Sheet/Risk Management**
Hedge currency risk

Currencies: US dollar

Regions: United States

DERIVATIVES ACTIVITIES: **CAC Class: Inactive**

OTC Derivatives		
Plain Vanilla Derivatives	Swaps	Forwards

OTHER ALTERNATIVE INVESTMENTS:

	CMOs/REMICs – Govt.	CMOs/REMICs – Private

KEY MANAGERS & DERIVATIVES SPECIALISTS:	Direct Phone/Fax	Job Function
Mr. Robert W. Holle Treasurer & Asst. Secretary		Treasurer Portfolio Mgr – Derivatives
Mr. Keith Miller S.V.P. – Finance & C.F.O.	314/889-0799 314/889-0784	Chief Investment Officer Chief Financial Officer

Marshall & Ilsley Corporation

Bank/Portfolio

Location: 770 North Water Street
Milwaukee, WI 53202

Fax: 414/765-7645 **Phone:** 414/765-7700

Profile: Total return investor

Investment Portfolio: $ 4.0 - 10.0 billion

Use: **Balance Sheet/Risk Management**
Hedge interest rate risk

Currencies: US dollar

Regions: United States

DERIVATIVES ACTIVITIES:

OTC Derivatives		
Plain Vanilla Derivatives	Swaps Caps	Floors Collars

KEY MANAGERS & DERIVATIVES SPECIALISTS:	Direct Phone/Fax	Job Function
Mr. Michael J. Flaherty Vice President		Chief Investment Officer
Mr. Donald Wilson Treasurer	414/765-8043	Treasurer Portfolio Mgr – Derivatives

Martin Marietta Corporation

Corporate Pension Fund

Location: 6801 Rockledge Drive, Bethesda, MD 20817

Fax: 301/897-6929 **Phone:** 301/897-6000

Profile: Total return investor

Investment Portfolio: $ 4.4 billion

Use: **Investment Purposes**

Currencies: US dollar

Regions: United States

DERIVATIVES ACTIVITIES: **CAC Class: Inactive**

OTHER ALTERNATIVE INVESTMENTS:

CMOs/REMICs – Govt.
Repos/reverse repos

KEY MANAGERS & DERIVATIVES SPECIALISTS:	Direct Phone/Fax	Job Function
Mr. Wayne H. Shaner Vice President		Chief Investment Officer

Maryland State Retirement & Pension System

Government Pension Fund

Location: 301 West Preston Street, Suite 901A, Baltimore, MD 21201

Fax: 410/523-8133 **Phone:** 410/225-1020

Profile: Hold to maturity investor

Investment Portfolio: $ 19.0 billion

Use: **Investment Purposes**

Currencies: US dollar

Regions: United States

DERIVATIVES ACTIVITIES: **CAC Class: 3**

Structured Notes

Govt. agency MTNs
Floaters
Multi-step-up callable bonds

OTHER ALTERNATIVE INVESTMENTS:

CMOs/REMICs – Govt.
CMOs/REMICs – Private
Strips
Repos/reverse repos

KEY MANAGERS & DERIVATIVES SPECIALISTS:	Direct Phone/Fax	Job Function
Ms. Carol Casey	410/225-1021	Chief Investment Officer
Ms. Victoria Willard Director – Fixed Income	410/225-1025	Bond Department Head Portfolio Mgr – Structured Notes

Masco Corporation

Corporate Pension Fund

Location: 21001 Van Born Road
Taylor, MI 48180

Fax: 313/374-6666 **Phone:** 313/274-7400

Profile: Hold to maturity investor

Investment Portfolio: $ 1.0 billion

Use: **Investment Purposes**
Hedge bond portfolio risk
Hedge currency risk

Currencies: US dollar, Japanese yen

Regions: United States

DERIVATIVES ACTIVITIES: **CAC Class: 1**

Exchange-traded Options & Futures	**Bond, Currency, Interest rate**
OTC Derivatives	**Bond, Currency, Interest rate**
Plain Vanilla Derivatives	Swaps

OTHER ALTERNATIVE INVESTMENTS:

CMOs/REMICs – Govt. CMOs/REMICs – Private

KEY MANAGERS & DERIVATIVES SPECIALISTS:	**Direct Phone/Fax**	**Job Function**
Mr. Andrew Greig		Portfolio Mgr – Derivatives Trader – Derivatives *Govt*
Mr. Samuel Valenti III Vice President – Investments		Chief Investment Officer

Massachusetts Financial Services Company

Mutual Fund Manager

Sub of Sun Life Assurance Company of Canada

Location: 500 Boylston Street
23rd Floor
Boston, MA 02116

Fax: 617/954-6603 **Phone:** 617/954-5000

Profile: Total return investor

Investment Portfolio: $ 33.0 billion

Use: **Balance Sheet/Risk Management**
Access global mkts
Hedge currency risk
Hedge interest rate risk
Hedge overseas investments
Incremental return
Protect currency gains

Investment Purposes
Alter portfolio weighting
Adjust portfolio duration
Capture extra yield
Diversify portfolio
Enter new mkts/lower risk
Expand international investments
Hedge bond portfolio risk
Hedge currency risk
Hedge interest rate risk
Protect currency gains
Provide incremental return
Reduce variability of returns

Currencies: US dollar, Canadian dollar, French franc, German mark, Japanese yen, UK pound

Regions: United States, Canada, Europe, Pacific Rim

Massachusetts Financial Services Company – continued

DERIVATIVES ACTIVITIES: **CAC Class: 7**

Exchange-traded Options & Futures	**Currency, Interest rate**	
U.S. Treasury futures	Municipal futures	
U.S. Treasury options	Municipal options	
OTC Derivatives	**Bond, Currency, Interest rate**	
Plain Vanilla Derivatives	Swaps	Floors
	Forwards	Collars
	Caps	
Structured Notes	Corporate MTNs	Floaters
	Govt. agency MTNs	Inverse floaters
	Index amortizing notes	
Counterparty Rating Requirement:	AA	

OTHER ALTERNATIVE INVESTMENTS:

CMOs/REMICs – Govt.	Strips
CMOs/REMICs – Private	Repos/reverse repos
GICs	

KEY MANAGERS & DERIVATIVES SPECIALISTS:	Direct Phone/Fax	Job Function
Mr. Leslie J. Nanberg Managing Director	617/954-5860	Bond Department Head
Mr. Daniel G. Scherman Assistant Vice President	617/954-5860	Trader – Derivatives
Mr. David Steck Investment Officer	617/954-5860	Portfolio Mgr – Derivatives Portfolio Mgr – Options Portfolio Mgr – Structured Notes Trader – Derivatives

Massachusetts Mutual Life Insurance Co.

Insurance Co/Life

Location: 1295 State Street
Springfield, MA 01111-0001

Fax: 413/744-6127 **Phone:** 413/788-8411

Profile: Net asset value investor

Investment Portfolio: $ 36.7 billion

Use: **Balance Sheet/Risk Management**
Hedge balance sheet
Hedge interest rate risk
Strategic liability management

Currencies: US dollar

Regions: United States Emerging mkts

Massachusetts Mutual Life Insurance Co. – continued

DERIVATIVES ACTIVITIES: **CAC Class: 7**

Exchange-traded Options & Futures

OTC Derivatives	**Currency, Interest rate**	
Plain Vanilla Derivatives	Swaps Forwards Swaptions	Caps Floors Collars
Structured Notes	Corporate MTNs Floaters	Inverse floaters
Counterparty Rating Requirement:	A	

OTHER ALTERNATIVE INVESTMENTS:

CMOs/REMICs – Govt. CMOs/REMICs – Private GICs	Strips Repos/reverse repos

KEY MANAGERS & DERIVATIVES SPECIALISTS:	**Direct Phone/Fax**	**Job Function**
Mr. Allen Compton Second Vice President	413/744-8491	Portfolio Mgr – Derivatives Portfolio Mgr – Futures Portfolio Mgr – Structured Notes
Mr. Ronald E. Desautels		Trader – Derivatives Trader – Futures
Mr. Stuart H. Reese Senior Vice President	413/744-7878	Fixed-Income Strategist *Taxable*
Mr. Gary E. Wendlandt Executive Vice President	413/744-6060	Chief Investment Officer
Ms. Mary E. Wilson Vice President	413/744-8798	Bond Department Head

MBIA Securities Corporation

Investment Manager

Sub of MBIA Inc.

Location: 113 King Street
Armonk, NY 10504

Fax: 914/765-3375 **Phone:** 914/273-4545

Profile: Total return investor

Investment Portfolio: $ 4.5 billion

Use: **Investment Purposes**

Currencies: US dollar

Regions: United States

MBIA Securities Corporation – continued

DERIVATIVES ACTIVITIES: **CAC Class: Inactive**

OTHER ALTERNATIVE INVESTMENTS:

	CMOs/REMICs – Govt.	Strips
	CMOs/REMICs – Private	Repos/reverse repos

KEY MANAGERS & DERIVATIVES SPECIALISTS:	**Direct Phone/Fax**	**Job Function**
Mr. Robert Ohanesian President	914/273-3370	President Bond Department Head

MBNA Corporation

Bank Holding Company

Location: 400 Christiana Road
Newark, DE 19713

Fax: 302/456-8541 **Phone:** 302/456-8588

Use: **Balance Sheet/Risk Management**
Create synthetic fixed/floating rate
Hedge currency risk
Hedge interest rate risk
Hedge overseas investments

Currencies: US dollar UK pound **Regions:** United States

DERIVATIVES ACTIVITIES: **CAC Class: 6**

OTC Derivatives	**Currency, Interest rate**	
Plain Vanilla Derivatives	Swaps	Forwards
Counterparty Rating Requirement:	A	

KEY MANAGERS & DERIVATIVES SPECIALISTS:	**Direct Phone/Fax**	**Job Function**
Mr. Kenneth F. Boehl General Auditor – Risk Mgmt.		Portfolio Mgr – Derivatives
Mr. Charles M. Cawley President		President
Mr. M. Scot Kaufman Chief Financial Officer		Chief Financial Officer Treasurer

McDonald's Corporation

Corporation

Location: McDonald's Plaza
Oak Brook, IL 60521

Fax: 708/575-6941 **Phone:** 708/575-3000

Use: **Balance Sheet/Risk Management**

Currencies: US dollar, Australian dollar, French franc, German mark, Japanese yen, UK pound

Regions: United States

DERIVATIVES ACTIVITIES:

OTC Derivatives	**Currency, Interest rate**	
Plain Vanilla Derivatives	Swaps	Forwards

KEY MANAGERS & DERIVATIVES SPECIALISTS:	**Direct Phone/Fax**	**Job Function**
Mr. Jack M. Greenberg Vice Chairman & C.F.O.		Chief Financial Officer Treasurer Portfolio Mgr – Derivatives
Mr. Edward H. Rensi President & C.E.O		President

McDonnell Douglas Corporation

Corporation

Location: World Headquarters Building
J.S. McDonnell & Airport Road
St. Louis, MO 63134

Fax: 314/234-3826 **Phone:** 314/232-0232

Use: **Balance Sheet/Risk Management**
Hedge currency risk
Protect currency gains

Currencies: US dollar, Canadian dollar, French franc, German mark, Japanese yen, UK pound

Regions: United States

DERIVATIVES ACTIVITIES: **CAC Class: 3**

OTC Derivatives	**Currency**	
Plain Vanilla Derivatives	Swaps	Forwards
Counterparty Rating Requirement:	AA	

KEY MANAGERS & DERIVATIVES SPECIALISTS:	**Direct Phone/Fax**	**Job Function**
Mr. Herbert J. Lanese Exec. Vice President & C.F.O.		Chief Financial Officer
Mr. James F. Palmer Vice President – Treasurer		Treasurer Portfolio Mgr – Derivatives
Mr. Harry C. Stonecipher President & C.E.O.		President

MCI Communications Corporation

Corporation

Location: 1801 Pennsylvania Avenue, N.W.
Washington, DC 20006

Fax: 202/887-2443 **Phone:** 202/872-1600

Use: **Balance Sheet/Risk Management**
Create synthetic fixed/floating rate
Hedge currency risk
Hedge interest rate risk
Protect currency gains

Currencies: US dollar **Regions:** United States

DERIVATIVES ACTIVITIES: **CAC Class: 3**

OTC Derivatives	**Currency, Interest rate**
Plain Vanilla Derivatives	Swaps

KEY MANAGERS & DERIVATIVES SPECIALISTS:	**Direct Phone/Fax**	**Job Function**
Mr. Douglas L. Maine Chief Financial Officer		Chief Financial Officer
Ms. Jonelle St. John Treasurer		Treasurer Portfolio Mgr – Derivatives
Mr. Gerald H. Taylor President & C.O.O.		President

C.S. McKee & Company, Inc.

Investment Manager

Sub of United Asset Management Corporation

Location: One Gateway Center
Eighth Floor
Pittsburgh, PA 15222

Fax: 412/566-1548 **Phone:** 412/566-1234

Profile: Total return investor **Investment Portfolio:** $ 2.5 billion

Use: **Investment Purposes**

Currencies: US dollar **Regions:** United States

DERIVATIVES ACTIVITIES: **CAC Class: Inactive**

OTHER ALTERNATIVE INVESTMENTS:

CMOs/REMICs – Govt.

KEY MANAGERS & DERIVATIVES SPECIALISTS:	**Direct Phone/Fax**	**Job Function**
Mr. Joseph F. Bonomo, Jr. Senior Vice President		Bond Department Head
Mr. James H. Hanes President		President
Mr. Charles E. Jacobs Chairman	Ext. 218	Chief Investment Officer

McKesson Corporation

Corporation

Location: One Post Street
San Francisco, CA 94101

Fax: 415/983-7160 **Phone:** 415/983-8300

Profile: Hold to maturity investor

Use: **Balance Sheet/Risk Management**
Create synthetic fixed/floating rate
Hedge balance sheet
Hedge currency risk
Hedge overseas investments
Reduce cost of capital
Strategic liability management

Currencies: US dollar **Regions:** United States

DERIVATIVES ACTIVITIES: **CAC Class: Inactive**

OTC Derivatives	**Bond, Currency, Interest rate**
Plain Vanilla Derivatives	Swaps
Counterparty Rating Requirement:	AA

OTHER ALTERNATIVE INVESTMENTS:

Repos/reverse repos

KEY MANAGERS & DERIVATIVES SPECIALISTS:	**Direct Phone/Fax**	**Job Function**
Mr. Jon W. d'Alessio Treasurer		Treasurer Portfolio Mgr – Derivatives
Mr. Garret A. Scholz Vice President – Finance	415/983-8639	Chief Financial Officer

MCN Corporation

Corporation

Location: 500 Griswold Street
Detroit, MI 48226

Fax: 313/256-5232 **Phone:** 313/256-5500

Use: **Balance Sheet/Risk Management**
Hedge balance sheet
Hedge interest rate risk
Meet interest rate target

Currencies: US dollar **Regions:** United States

DERIVATIVES ACTIVITIES: **CAC Class: 2**

OTC Derivatives	**Interest rate**	
Plain Vanilla Derivatives	Swaps Caps	Floors
Counterparty Rating Requirement:	A	

MCN Corporation – continued

KEY MANAGERS & DERIVATIVES SPECIALISTS:	Direct Phone/Fax	Job Function
Mr. Alfred R. Glancy III Chairman, President & C.E.O.		President
Mr. William K. McCrackin Vice Chairman & C.F.O.		Chief Financial Officer Portfolio Mgr – Derivatives

The Mead Corporation

Corporation

Location: Courthouse Plaza Northeast
Dayton, OH 45463

Fax: 513/461-2424 **Phone:** 513/495-6323

Use: **Balance Sheet/Risk Management**
Create synthetic fixed/floating rate
Hedge currency risk
Hedge interest rate risk
Strategic liability management

Currencies: US dollar, Australian dollar, Canadian dollar, French franc, German mark, Italian lira, Japanese yen, Swiss franc

Regions: United States

DERIVATIVES ACTIVITIES:

OTC Derivatives	**Currency, Interest rate**	
Plain Vanilla Derivatives	Swaps Forwards Swaptions	Caps Floors Collars
Exotic Derivatives	CMT options	
Counterparty Rating Requirement:	A	

KEY MANAGERS & DERIVATIVES SPECIALISTS:	Direct Phone/Fax	Job Function
Mr. Gregory T. Geswein Treasurer	513/495-5155	Treasurer
Mr. William R. Graber Vice President & C.F.O.	513/495-3996	Chief Financial Officer
Mr. Lester Hess Manager – Domestic Finance	513/495-3020 513/228-5555	Portfolio Mgr – Derivatives

The Medical Protective Company

Insurance Co/P & C

Location: 5814 Reed Road
Fort Wayne, IN 46835

Fax: 219/486-0415 **Phone:** 219/485-9622

Profile: Hold to maturity investor

Investment Portfolio: $ 1.1 billion

Use: **Investment Purposes**
Provide incremental return

Currencies: US dollar

Regions: United States

The Medical Protective Company – continued

DERIVATIVES ACTIVITIES:

Structured Notes	Corporate MTNs

OTHER ALTERNATIVE INVESTMENTS:

CMOs/REMICs – Govt.

KEY MANAGERS & DERIVATIVES SPECIALISTS:	**Direct Phone/Fax**	**Job Function**
Mr. Timothy P. Beck Senior Vice President & C.F.O.		Chief Investment Officer Chief Financial Officer
Mr. Kenneth L. Weddle		Portfolio Mgr – Structured Notes *Corp*

Mellon Bank, N.A. (Portfolio)

Bank/Portfolio

Sub of Mellon Bank Corporation

Location: 500 Grant Street
One Mellon Bank Center
Pittsburgh, PA 15258-0001

Fax: 412/234-8913 **Phone:** 412/234-4100

Investment Portfolio: $ 4.0 - 10.0 billion

Use: **Balance Sheet/Risk Management**
Hedge balance sheet
Hedge interest rate risk
Incremental return
Reduce cost of capital

Currencies: US dollar

Regions: United States

DERIVATIVES ACTIVITIES: **CAC Class: 7**

Exchange-traded Options & Futures Municipal futures	**Interest rate**	
OTC Derivatives **Plain Vanilla Derivatives**	**Interest rate** Swaps Forwards	Caps Floors
Exotic Derivatives	Index amortizing swaps	

OTHER ALTERNATIVE INVESTMENTS:

CMOs/REMICs – Govt. Repos/reverse repos

KEY MANAGERS & DERIVATIVES SPECIALISTS:	**Direct Phone/Fax**	**Job Function**
Mr. Donald Ellenberger	412/234-8604	Portfolio Mgr – Derivatives Portfolio Mgr – Futures Portfolio Mgr – Options
Mr. Johnson Moore Vice President	412/234-8604 412/234-7834	Bond Department Head *Corp, Govt, MBS, Muni* Portfolio Mgr – Derivatives Portfolio Mgr – Options

Mellon Bank, N.A. (Trust)

Bank/Trust

Sub of Mellon Bank Corporation

Location: 500 Grant Street
One Mellon Bank Center
Pittsburgh, PA 15258-0001

Fax: 412/236-0648 **Phone:** 412/234-4100

Investment Portfolio: $ 13.0 billion

Use: **Investment Purposes**
Hedge currency risk

Currencies: US dollar, Canadian dollar, French franc, German mark, Japanese yen, UK pound

Regions: United States, Canada, Europe, Latin America, Pacific Rim

DERIVATIVES ACTIVITIES: **CAC Class: 6**

Exchange-traded Options & Futures U.S. Treasury futures	**Bond** U.S. Treasury options	
OTC Derivatives **Plain Vanilla Derivatives**	**Currency** Swaps Forwards Swaptions	Caps Floors Collars
Structured Notes	Corporate MTNs Govt. agency MTNs Bond index notes	Floaters Inverse floaters Tender options bonds

OTHER ALTERNATIVE INVESTMENTS:

CMOs/REMICs – Govt.	Strips
CMOs/REMICs – Private	Repos/reverse repos

KEY MANAGERS & DERIVATIVES SPECIALISTS:	**Direct Phone/Fax**	**Job Function**
Mr. Thomas P. Burrows Vice President	412/234-4697	Bond Department Head
Mr. Philip R. Roberts Executive Vice President	412/234-1685	Chief Investment Officer Portfolio Mgr – Derivatives Portfolio Mgr – Futures Portfolio Mgr – Structured Notes

Mellon Private Asset Management Group

Bank/Management Division

Sub of Mellon Bank Corporation

Location: One Boston Place
13th Floor
Boston, MA 02108

Fax: 617/722-7250 **Phone:** 617/722-7000

Profile: Total return investor

Investment Portfolio: $ 4.0 - 10.0 billion

Use: **Investment Purposes**

Currencies: US dollar

Regions: United States

Mellon Private Asset Management Group – continued

DERIVATIVES ACTIVITIES: **CAC Class: Inactive**

OTHER ALTERNATIVE INVESTMENTS:

CMOs/REMICs – Govt.

KEY MANAGERS & DERIVATIVES SPECIALISTS:	**Direct Phone/Fax**	**Job Function**
Mr. Arthur J. MacBride III Senior Vice President	617/722-7151	Fixed-Income Strategist
Mr. Richard Noone	617/722-7619	Chief Investment Officer

Mercantile Banks of St. Louis, N.A.

Bank/Portfolio

Sub of Mercantile Bancorporation Inc.

Location: 721 Locust Street
19th Floor
St. Louis, MO 63101

Fax: 314/425-2727 **Phone:** 314/425-2525

Profile: Total return investor

Investment Portfolio: $ 4.2 billion

Use: **Balance Sheet/Risk Management**
Hedge interest rate risk

Currencies: US dollar

Regions: United States

DERIVATIVES ACTIVITIES: **CAC Class: 3**

Structured Notes

OTHER ALTERNATIVE INVESTMENTS:

CMOs/REMICs – Govt.
CMOs/REMICs – Private
Repos/reverse repos

KEY MANAGERS & DERIVATIVES SPECIALISTS:	**Direct Phone/Fax**	**Job Function**
Mr. John Q. Arnold Chief Financial Officer		Chief Financial Officer
Mr. James LaBelle Senior Vice President	314/425-1341	Bond Department Head Portfolio Mgr – Structured Notes

Mercantile – Safe Deposit & Trust Co. (Trust)

Bank/Trust

Sub of Mercantile Bankshares Corporation

Location: Two Hopkins Plaza
Third Floor
Baltimore, MD 21201

Fax: 410/237-5380 **Phone:** 410/237-5900

Profile: Total return investor

Investment Portfolio: $ 9.2 billion

Use: **Investment Purposes**
Provide incremental return

Currencies: US dollar

Regions: United States

DERIVATIVES ACTIVITIES: **CAC Class: 2**

Structured Notes Corporate MTNs

OTHER ALTERNATIVE INVESTMENTS:

CMOs/REMICs – Govt. CMOs/REMICs – Private

KEY MANAGERS & DERIVATIVES SPECIALISTS:	**Direct Phone/Fax**	**Job Function**
Mr. Kevin Dachille Senior Vice President	410/237-5599	Bond Department Head Portfolio Mgr – Structured Notes
Mr. James D. Hardesty Executive Vice President	410/237-5557	Chief Investment Officer

The Merchants Bank of New York

Bank/Portfolio

Location: 275 Madison Avenue
2nd Floor
New York, NY 10016

Fax: 212/966-4813 **Phone:** 212/973-6637

Profile: Total return investor

Investment Portfolio: $ 950.0 million

Use: **Investment Purposes**

Currencies: US dollar

Regions: United States

DERIVATIVES ACTIVITIES:

Structured Notes Corporate MTNs Govt. agency MTNs

OTHER ALTERNATIVE INVESTMENTS:

Strips

KEY MANAGERS & DERIVATIVES SPECIALISTS:	**Direct Phone/Fax**	**Job Function**
Mr. Eric W. Gould Assistant Treasurer	212/973-6372	Portfolio Mgr – Structured Notes
Mr. Spencer Witty Chairman	212/973-6666	Chief Investment Officer

Merck & Co., Inc.

Corporation

Location: One Merck Drive
Whitehouse Station, NJ 08889

Fax: 908/735-1275 **Phone:** 908/423-7958

Profile: Total return investor

Investment Portfolio: $ 1.0 - 3.0 billion

Use:

Balance Sheet/Risk Management
- Create synthetic fixed/floating rate
- Hedge balance sheet
- Hedge commercial paper
- Hedge currency risk
- Hedge interest rate risk
- Hedge overseas investments
- Reduce cost of capital
- Strategic liability management

Investment Purposes
- Adjust portfolio duration
- Capture extra yield

Currencies: US dollar, French franc, German mark, Japanese yen, Spanish peseta, Swiss franc, UK pound

Regions: United States, Europe, Pacific Rim

DERIVATIVES ACTIVITIES: **CAC Class: 4**

OTC Derivatives	**Currency, Interest rate**	
Plain Vanilla Derivatives	Swaps	
Structured Notes	Corporate MTNs Govt. agency MTNs CMT notes Floaters	Inverse floaters Periodic capped floaters Multi-step-up callable bonds
Counterparty Rating Requirement:	BBB	

OTHER ALTERNATIVE INVESTMENTS:

CMOs/REMICs – Govt.

CMOs/REMICs – Private

KEY MANAGERS & DERIVATIVES SPECIALISTS:	**Direct Phone/Fax**	**Job Function**
Mr. Douglas R. Rees Senior Director	908/423-7958	Chief Investment Officer Portfolio Mgr – Derivatives Portfolio Mgr – Structured Notes

Merganser Capital Management Corporation

Investment Manager

Location: One Cambridge Center
Suite 402
Cambridge, MA 02142-1611

Fax: 617/494-1899 **Phone:** 617/494-1000

Profile: Total return investor

Investment Portfolio: $ 2.4 billion

Use: **Investment Purposes**

Currencies: US dollar

Regions: United States

Merganser Capital Management Corporation – continued

DERIVATIVES ACTIVITIES:		**CAC Class: 1**
Structured Notes	Corporate MTNs Govt. agency MTNs	Floaters

OTHER ALTERNATIVE INVESTMENTS:		
	CMOs/REMICs – Govt. CMOs/REMICs – Private	Repos/reverse repos

KEY MANAGERS & DERIVATIVES SPECIALISTS:	**Direct Phone/Fax**	**Job Function**
Mr. Peter Kaplan		Portfolio Mgr – Structured Notes
Mr. Edward M. Safran President		President Chief Investment Officer

Meridian Bancorp, Inc.

Bank Holding Company

Location: 35 North Sixth Street
Reading, PA 19601

Fax: 610/655-2428 **Phone:** 610/655-2000

Use: **Balance Sheet/Risk Management**
Create synthetic fixed/floating rate
Strategic liability management

Currencies: US dollar **Regions:** United States

DERIVATIVES ACTIVITIES:		**CAC Class: 6**
Exchange-traded Options & Futures U.S. Treasury futures	Municipal options	
OTC Derivatives **Plain Vanilla Derivatives**	**Bond, Interest rate** Swaps Forwards	 Caps Floors

KEY MANAGERS & DERIVATIVES SPECIALISTS:	**Direct Phone/Fax**	**Job Function**
Mr. Samuel A. McCullough Chairman, President & C.E.O.		President
Mr. David E. Sparks Vice Chairman & C.F.O.		Chief Financial Officer Portfolio Mgr – Derivatives

Meridian Bank (Portfolio)

Bank/Portfolio

Sub of Meridian Bancorp, Inc.

Location: One Meridian Boulevard
Funds Management SR4B50
Wyomissing, PA 19610

Fax: 610/655-3916 **Phone:** 610/655-2788

Profile: Hold to maturity investor

Investment Portfolio: $ 3.2 billion

Use: **Balance Sheet/Risk Management**
Hedge balance sheet
Hedge interest rate risk
Incremental return
Strategic liability management

Currencies: US dollar

Regions: United States

DERIVATIVES ACTIVITIES: **CAC Class: 2**

Exchange-traded Options & Futures	**Interest rate**	
U.S. Treasury options		
OTC Derivatives	**Bond, Interest rate**	
Plain Vanilla Derivatives	Swaps	Caps
	Forwards	Floors
	Swaptions	
Exotic Derivatives	Index amortizing swaps	Periodic caps/floors
Structured Notes	Govt. agency MTNs	Periodic capped floaters
	Floaters	Multi-step-up callable bonds
Counterparty Rating Requirement:	AA	

OTHER ALTERNATIVE INVESTMENTS:

CMOs/REMICs – Govt.	Strips
CMOs/REMICs – Private	Repos/reverse repos

KEY MANAGERS & DERIVATIVES SPECIALISTS:	**Direct Phone/Fax**	**Job Function**
Mr. Jeffrey Faber	610/655-3661	Portfolio Mgr – Derivatives Portfolio Mgr – Options
Mr. Wayne Hardenbrook	610/655-2788	Chief Investment Officer Portfolio Mgr – Structured Notes

Meridian Investment Company

Bank/Management Division

Sub of Meridian Bancorp, Inc.

Location: 55 Valley Stream Parkway
Malvern, PA 19355-1462

Fax: 610/251-5985 **Phone:** 610/251-7991

Profile: Total return investor

Investment Portfolio: $ 4.0 - 10.0 billion

Use: **Investment Purposes**

Currencies: US dollar

Regions: United States

Meridian Investment Company – continued

DERIVATIVES ACTIVITIES:		**CAC Class: 2**
Structured Notes	Corporate MTNs	Multi-step-up callable bonds

OTHER ALTERNATIVE INVESTMENTS:		
	CMOs/REMICs – Govt.	Strips
	CMOs/REMICs – Private	Repos/reverse repos

KEY MANAGERS & DERIVATIVES SPECIALISTS:	**Direct Phone/Fax**	**Job Function**
Mr. Philip H. Brown II President	610/251-7966	President Chief Investment Officer
Ms. Eve Dintino Senior Investment Manager	610/251-7970	Fixed-Income Strategist
Mr. George W. Grosz President & C.E.O.	610/251-7984	President
Mr. Terrence J. Soffera Senior Portfolio Manager		Portfolio Mgr – Structured Notes

Merita Bank

Bank/Portfolio

Location: 437 Madison Avenue
21st Floor
New York, NY 10022

Fax: 212/421-4420 **Phone:** 212/318-9300

Profile: Total return investor

Investment Portfolio: $ 40.0 billion

Use:

Balance Sheet/Risk Management
Access global mkts
Create synthetic fixed/floating rate
Hedge balance sheet
Hedge currency risk
Hedge interest rate risk
Hedge overseas investments
Incremental return
Protect currency gains
Reduce cost of capital
Strategic liability management

Investment Purposes
Adjust portfolio duration
Asset allocation
Capture extra yield
Diversify portfolio
Enter new mkts/lower risk
Hedge bond portfolio risk
Hedge currency risk
Hedge interest rate risk
Protect currency gains
Provide incremental return
Reduce variability of returns

Currencies: US dollar
Australian dollar
Canadian dollar
French franc
German mark
Japanese yen
Swiss franc
UK pound

Regions: United States
Europe

Merita Bank – continued

DERIVATIVES ACTIVITIES:

Exchange-traded Options & Futures
U.S. Treasury futures

OTC Derivatives

Plain Vanilla Derivatives	Swaps Forwards Swaptions	Caps Floors Collars
Structured Notes	Govt. agency MTNs CMT notes Floaters	Inverse floaters Periodic capped floaters Multi-step-up callable bonds
Counterparty Rating Requirement:	A	

OTHER ALTERNATIVE INVESTMENTS:

	CMOs/REMICs – Govt. CMOs/REMICs – Private	Repos/reverse repos

KEY MANAGERS & DERIVATIVES SPECIALISTS:	Direct Phone/Fax	Job Function
Mr. Guy Caruso		Trader – Derivatives Trader – Futures Trader – Structured Investments
Mr. Lawrence Chan Deputy Treasurer	Ext. 395	Bond Department Head Portfolio Mgr – Derivatives
Mr. John L. Hickey Senior Vice President		Chief Investment Officer

Merrill Lynch Asset Management Inc.

Broker/Management Sub

Sub of Merrill Lynch & Co., Inc.

Location: 800 Scudders Mill Road
Plainsboro, NJ 08536-1606

Fax: 609/282-3055 **Phone:** 609/282-1212

Profile: Total return investor

Investment Portfolio: $ 159.0 billion

Use:

Balance Sheet/Risk Management
Hedge balance sheet
Hedge currency risk
Hedge interest rate risk

Investment Purposes
Alter portfolio weighting
Adjust portfolio duration
Asset allocation
Expand international investments
Hedge bond portfolio risk
Hedge currency risk
Hedge interest rate risk
Protect currency gains
Reduce variability of returns

Currencies: US dollar, Mexican peso

Regions: United States, Canada, Europe, Latin America, Pacific Rim, Emerging mkts

Merrill Lynch Asset Management Inc. – continued

DERIVATIVES ACTIVITIES: **CAC Class: 8**

Exchange-traded Options & Futures	**Bond, Currency, Interest rate**	
U.S. Treasury futures	U.S. Treasury options	
OTC Derivatives	**Bond, Currency, Interest rate**	
Plain Vanilla Derivatives	Swaps	Swaptions
	Forwards	
Structured Notes	Corporate MTNs	CMT notes
	Govt. agency MTNs	Floaters
Counterparty Rating Requirement:	A	

OTHER ALTERNATIVE INVESTMENTS:

	CMOs/REMICs – Govt.	MOPs/TOPs
	CMOs/REMICs – Private	

KEY MANAGERS & DERIVATIVES SPECIALISTS:	Direct Phone/Fax	Job Function
Mr. Vincent R. Giordano Senior Vice President	609/282-2101	Bond Department Head *Muni*
Mr. Jay Harbeck	609/282-2818	Portfolio Mgr – Derivatives
Mr. Joseph T. Monagle Senior Vice President	609/282-2070 609/282-3360	Portfolio Mgr – Derivatives Portfolio Mgr – Options Portfolio Mgr – Structured Notes
Mr. Arthur H. Zeikel Senior Vice President	609/282-2012	Chief Investment Officer

MERUS Capital Management

Bank/Management Division

Sub of The Mitsubishi Bank, Limited

Location: 475 Sansome Street
Suite 1400
San Francisco, CA 94111

Fax: 415/296-6472 **Phone:** 415/296-6401

Profile: Total return investor

Investment Portfolio: $ 6.3 billion

Use: **Investment Purposes**

Currencies: US dollar

Regions: United States

DERIVATIVES ACTIVITIES: **CAC Class: Inactive**

OTHER ALTERNATIVE INVESTMENTS:

	CMOs/REMICs – Govt.	Repos/reverse repos
	CMOs/REMICs – Private	

MERUS Capital Management – continued

KEY MANAGERS & DERIVATIVES SPECIALISTS:	Direct Phone/Fax	Job Function
Mr. Luke C. Mazur	415/291-7468	Chief Investment Officer
Mr. E. Jack Montgomery	415/296-6820 415/552-7880	Bond Department Head *Taxable*

Metropolitan Life Insurance Company

Insurance Co/Management

Location: One Madison Avenue
New York, NY 10010

Fax: 212/578-3910 **Phone:** 212/578-2211

Profile: Total return investor

Investment Portfolio: $ 118.2 billion

Use: **Balance Sheet/Risk Management**
Hedge commercial paper
Hedge currency risk
Hedge interest rate risk

Currencies: US dollar

Regions: United States

DERIVATIVES ACTIVITIES:

OTC Derivatives	**Currency, Interest rate**	
Plain Vanilla Derivatives	Swaps Forwards	Caps Floors
Exotic Derivatives	CMT options	
Counterparty Rating Requirement:	None	

OTHER ALTERNATIVE INVESTMENTS:

CMOs/REMICs – Govt.	Strips
CMOs/REMICs – Private	Repos/reverse repos
GICs	

KEY MANAGERS & DERIVATIVES SPECIALISTS:	Direct Phone/Fax	Job Function
Mr. Gerald Clark Chief Executive Officer	212/578-0337	Chief Investment Officer Bond Department Head Portfolio Mgr – Derivatives
Mr. Paul Delaney Assistant Vice President	212/578-9212	Portfolio Mgr – Derivatives

MGIC Investment Corporation

Insurance Co/Management

Location: 270 East Kilbourn Avenue
MGIC Plaza 3rd Floor
Milwaukee, WI 53202

Fax: 414/347-6382 **Phone:** 414/347-2569

Profile: Total return investor

Investment Portfolio: $ 1.5 billion

Use: **Balance Sheet/Risk Management**
Hedge balance sheet

Currencies: US dollar

Regions: United States

MGIC Investment Corporation – continued

DERIVATIVES ACTIVITIES:

OTC Derivatives	**Bond**	
Plain Vanilla Derivatives	Swaps	Collars
Structured Notes	Corporate MTNs	Floaters
Counterparty Rating Requirement:	AA	

OTHER ALTERNATIVE INVESTMENTS:

CMOs/REMICs – Govt.	Strips
CMOs/REMICs – Private	

KEY MANAGERS & DERIVATIVES SPECIALISTS:	Direct Phone/Fax	Job Function
Mr. James A. Karpowicz Vice President – Investments	414/347-6382	Chief Investment Officer Portfolio Mgr – Derivatives Portfolio Mgr – Options Portfolio Mgr – Structured Notes
Mr. William H. Lacy President & C.E.O.		President

M & I Investment Management Corp.

Bank/Management Division

Sub of Marshall & Ilsley Corporation

Location: 1000 North Water Street
13th Floor
Milwaukee, WI 53202-6629

Fax: 414/287-8730 **Phone:** 414/287-7300

Profile: Total return investor

Investment Portfolio: $ 6.8 billion

Use: **Investment Purposes**

Currencies: US dollar

Regions: United States

DERIVATIVES ACTIVITIES: **CAC Class: Inactive**

OTHER ALTERNATIVE INVESTMENTS:

CMOs/REMICs – Govt.	Strips
CMOs/REMICs – Private	Repos/reverse repos

KEY MANAGERS & DERIVATIVES SPECIALISTS:	Direct Phone/Fax	Job Function
Mr. Lawrence J. Pavelec V.P./Director-Fixed Income	414/287-8785	Bond Department Head
Mr. David W. Schulz President	414/287-8755	President Chief Investment Officer

Michigan Department of Treasury

Government Pension Fund

Location: 430 West Allegan Street
Bureau of Investments
Lansing, MI 48922

Fax: 517/335-2164 **Phone:** 517/373-3140

Profile: Hold to maturity investor

Investment Portfolio: $ 25.8 billion

Use: **Investment Purposes**

Currencies: US dollar

Regions: United States

DERIVATIVES ACTIVITIES: **CAC Class: Inactive**

OTHER ALTERNATIVE INVESTMENTS:

CMOs/REMICs – Govt.

KEY MANAGERS & DERIVATIVES SPECIALISTS:	**Direct Phone/Fax**	**Job Function**
Mr. Paul R. Nelson	517/373-9151	Bond Department Head *Corp, Govt, MBS*
Mr. Barry L. Stevens Director	517/373-3140	Chief Investment Officer

Michigan National Bank (Portfolio)

Bank/Portfolio

Sub of Michigan National Corporation

Location: 27777 Inkster Road
Farmington Hills, MI 48334

Fax: 810/473-3250 **Phone:** 810/473-3000

Profile: Hold to maturity investor

Investment Portfolio: $ 1.0 - 3.0 billion

Use: **Balance Sheet/Risk Management**
Hedge interest rate risk

Currencies: US dollar

Regions: United States

DERIVATIVES ACTIVITIES: **CAC Class: 6**

OTC Derivatives **Plain Vanilla Derivatives**	**Interest rate** Swaps
Counterparty Rating Requirement:	BBB

OTHER ALTERNATIVE INVESTMENTS:

CMOs/REMICs – Govt.
CMOs/REMICs – Private
Repos/reverse repos

KEY MANAGERS & DERIVATIVES SPECIALISTS:	**Direct Phone/Fax**	**Job Function**
Mr. James C. Buysse First V.P. – Portfolio Invts.	810/473-2606	Chief Investment Officer
Ms. Wendy Eisenshtadt Vice President	810/473-2610	Portfolio Mgr – Derivatives

Midland National Life Insurance Company

Insurance Co/Life

Location: One Midland Plaza
Sioux Falls, SD 57193

Fax: 605/335-3621 **Phone:** 605/335-5700

Profile: Total return investor

Investment Portfolio: $ 2.3 billion

Use: **Investment Purposes**
Capture extra yield

Currencies: US dollar, Canadian dollar **Regions:** United States

DERIVATIVES ACTIVITIES: **CAC Class: 2**

Structured Notes Govt. agency MTNs

OTHER ALTERNATIVE INVESTMENTS:

CMOs/REMICs – Govt.
CMOs/REMICs – Private
Repos/reverse repos

KEY MANAGERS & DERIVATIVES SPECIALISTS:	**Direct Phone/Fax**	**Job Function**
Mr. Jason Berrie	605/373-2392	Portfolio Mgr – Structured Notes
Mr. E. John Fromelt Head – Fixed-Income Department		Chief Investment Officer
Mr. John C. Watson Chairman, C.E.O. & President		President

Millipore Corporation

Corporation

Location: 80 Ashby Road
Bedford, MA 01730-9125

Fax: 617/275-5550 **Phone:** 617/275-9200

Use: **Balance Sheet/Risk Management**
Create synthetic fixed/floating rate
Hedge balance sheet
Hedge currency risk
Hedge interest rate risk
Strategic liability management

Currencies: US dollar, German mark, Japanese yen **Regions:** United States

DERIVATIVES ACTIVITIES:

OTC Derivatives
Plain Vanilla Derivatives Swaps

Counterparty Rating Requirement: None

KEY MANAGERS & DERIVATIVES SPECIALISTS:	**Direct Phone/Fax**	**Job Function**
Mr. George Heilliwell		Portfolio Mgr – Derivatives
Mr. William Zadel Chairman, President & C.E.O.		President

MIMLIC Asset Management Company

Insurance Co/Management

Sub of Minnesota Mutual Life Insurance Company

Location: 400 Robert Street North
St. Paul, MN 55101-2006

Fax: 612/223-5959 **Phone:** 612/298-3826

Profile: Current yield investor

Investment Portfolio: $ 7.1 billion

Use: **Balance Sheet/Risk Management**
Hedge interest rate risk

Currencies: US dollar

Regions: United States

DERIVATIVES ACTIVITIES: **CAC Class: 2**

Structured Notes	Corporate MTNs	Floaters

OTHER ALTERNATIVE INVESTMENTS:

	CMOs/REMICs – Govt. CMOs/REMICs – Private	GICs

KEY MANAGERS & DERIVATIVES SPECIALISTS:	**Direct Phone/Fax**	**Job Function**
Mr. Fritz Feuerherm Vice President	612/298-3837	Bond Department Head
Mr. Paul Gooding	612/298-3840	President Chief Investment Officer Treasurer
Mr. Thomas Gunderson	612/298-3845	Portfolio Mgr – Futures *Corp, Govt*
Ms. Lynne M. Mills Vice President	612/223-4434	Portfolio Mgr – Structured Notes

Minnesota State Board of Investment

Government Pension Fund

Location: 55 Sherburne Avenue
MEA Building Room 105
St. Paul, MN 55155

Fax: 612/296-9572 **Phone:** 612/296-3328

Profile: Total return investor

Investment Portfolio: $ 11.0 - 20.0 billion

Use: **Balance Sheet/Risk Management**
Hedge interest rate risk

Currencies: US dollar

Regions: United States

DERIVATIVES ACTIVITIES:

Exchange-traded Options & Futures	**Interest rate**	
OTC Derivatives **Plain Vanilla Derivatives**	**Interest rate** Swaps Forwards	Swaptions

Minnesota State Board of Investment – continued

OTHER ALTERNATIVE INVESTMENTS:

CMOs/REMICs – Govt. GICs

KEY MANAGERS & DERIVATIVES SPECIALISTS:	**Direct Phone/Fax**	**Job Function**
Mr. N. Robert Barman	612/296-5100	Research Analyst – Derivatives
Mr. James H. Lukens Manager – Fixed Income		Bond Department Head Portfolio Mgr – Derivatives
Mr. Thomas Stevens Senior Vice President		Chief Investment Officer

Minton Investment Management

Investment Manager

Location: 650 Sentry Parkway
Suite One
Blue Bell, PA 19422

Fax: 610/940-0696 **Phone:** 610/940-0695

Profile: Total return investor

Investment Portfolio: $ 600.0 million

Use: **Investment Purposes**

Currencies: US dollar

Regions: United States

DERIVATIVES ACTIVITIES: **CAC Class: Inactive**

OTHER ALTERNATIVE INVESTMENTS:

CMOs/REMICs – Govt.

KEY MANAGERS & DERIVATIVES SPECIALISTS:	**Direct Phone/Fax**	**Job Function**
Mr. Lee W. Minton, Jr. President		President Chief Investment Officer

Mitchell Hutchins Asset Management, Inc.

Mutual Fund Manager

Sub of PaineWebber Incorporated

Location: 1285 Avenue of the Americas
15th Floor
New York, NY 10019

Fax: 212/713-1459 **Phone:** 212/713-4000

Profile: Total return investor

Investment Portfolio: $ 43.6 billion

Use: **Investment Purposes**

Currencies: US dollar

Regions: United States

Mitchell Hutchins Asset Management, Inc. – continued

DERIVATIVES ACTIVITIES: **CAC Class: Inactive**

OTHER ALTERNATIVE INVESTMENTS:

CMOs/REMICs – Govt.	Strips
CMOs/REMICs – Private	

KEY MANAGERS & DERIVATIVES SPECIALISTS:	Direct Phone/Fax	Job Function
Ms. Margo Alexander President & C.E.O.	212/713-2402	President
Mr. Dennis McCauley	212/713-1842	Chief Investment Officer

Modern Woodmen of America

Insurance Co/Life

Location: 1701 First Avenue
Rock Island, IL 61201

Fax: 309/786-1701 **Phone:** 309/786-6481

Profile: Total return investor

Investment Portfolio: $ 1.0 - 3.0 billion

Use: **Investment Purposes**

Currencies: US dollar

Regions: United States

DERIVATIVES ACTIVITIES: **CAC Class: Inactive**

OTHER ALTERNATIVE INVESTMENTS:

CMOs/REMICs – Govt.	CMOs/REMICs – Private

KEY MANAGERS & DERIVATIVES SPECIALISTS:	Direct Phone/Fax	Job Function
Mr. Gary Stoefen	309/793-5560	Chief Investment Officer

Montag & Caldwell, Incorporated

Investment Manager

Location: 3343 Peachtree Road N.E.
Suite 1100
Atlanta, GA 30326-1450

Fax: 404/262-0105 **Phone:** 404/262-0100

Profile: Total return investor

Investment Portfolio: $ 4.3 billion

Use: **Investment Purposes**

Currencies: US dollar

Regions: United States

DERIVATIVES ACTIVITIES: **CAC Class: Inactive**

OTHER ALTERNATIVE INVESTMENTS:

CMOs/REMICs – Govt.	Strips
CMOs/REMICs – Private	Repos/reverse repos

Montag & Caldwell, Incorporated – continued

KEY MANAGERS & DERIVATIVES SPECIALISTS:	Direct Phone/Fax	Job Function
Mr. Ronald E. Canakaris President	404/262-0112	President Chief Investment Officer
Mr. David F. Seng Executive Vice President	404/262-0115	Fixed-Income Strategist

Montana Board of Investments

Government Pension Fund

Location: 555 Fuller Avenue
Helena, MT 59601-0126

Fax: 406/449-6579 **Phone:** 406/444-0001

Profile: Hold to maturity investor

Investment Portfolio: $ 5.6 billion

Use: **Investment Purposes**
Provide incremental return

Currencies: US dollar

Regions: United States

DERIVATIVES ACTIVITIES:

Structured Notes	Inverse floaters
Counterparty Rating Requirement:	None

OTHER ALTERNATIVE INVESTMENTS:

CMOs/REMICs – Govt.	Strips
CMOs/REMICs – Private	Repos/reverse repos

KEY MANAGERS & DERIVATIVES SPECIALISTS:	Direct Phone/Fax	Job Function
Mr. Robert T. Bugni Assistant Investment Officer		Portfolio Mgr – Structured Notes
Mr. James R. Penner Chief Investment Officer	406/444-0578	Chief Investment Officer Portfolio Mgr – Structured Notes

MONY Financial Services

Insurance Co/Management

Sub of The Mutual Life Insurance Co. of New York

Location: 1740 Broadway
11th Floor
New York, NY 10019-4315

Fax: 212/708-2491 **Phone:** 212/708-2000

Profile: Hold to maturity investor

Investment Portfolio: $ 11.0 billion

Use: **Balance Sheet/Risk Management**
Hedge balance sheet

Investment Purposes
Capture extra yield
Provide incremental return

Currencies: US dollar

Regions: United States

MONY Financial Services – continued

DERIVATIVES ACTIVITIES: **CAC Class: 5**

OTC Derivatives	**Bond**	
Plain Vanilla Derivatives	Swaps	Forwards
Structured Notes	Corporate MTNs	Floaters
Counterparty Rating Requirement:	A	

OTHER ALTERNATIVE INVESTMENTS:

	CMOs/REMICs – Govt.	Strips
	CMOs/REMICs – Private	Repos/reverse repos

KEY MANAGERS & DERIVATIVES SPECIALISTS:	Direct Phone/Fax	Job Function
Mr. Thomas M. Donohue President	212/708-2651	President Bond Department Head *Taxable*
Mr. William B. Goodwin Senior Managing Director	212/708-2666	Portfolio Mgr – Derivatives Portfolio Mgr – Structured Notes
Mr. Kenneth M. Levine Executive Vice President	212/708-2907	Chief Investment Officer
Mr. Gregory Staples Managing Director	212/708-2643	Portfolio Mgr – Futures *Corp*

J.P. Morgan & Company Inc.

Bank Holding Company

Location: 60 Wall Street, New York, NY 10260

Fax: 212/509-7628 **Phone:** 212/483-2323

Profile: Total return investor

Use:

Balance Sheet/Risk Management
- Create synthetic fixed/floating rate
- Hedge balance sheet
- Hedge currency risk
- Hedge interest rate risk
- Incremental return
- Protect currency gains
- Strategic liability management

Investment Purposes
- Capture extra yield
- Convexity objectives
- Discretionary situations
- Diversify portfolio
- Hedge bond portfolio risk
- Hedge currency risk
- Hedge equity portfolio risk
- Hedge interest rate risk
- Provide incremental return

Currencies: US dollar, Belgian franc, French franc, German mark, Italian lira, Japanese yen, Swiss franc, UK pound

Regions: United States

DERIVATIVES ACTIVITIES: **CAC Class: 8**

Exchange-traded Options & Futures	**Bond, Currency, Interest rate**	
OTC Derivatives	**Currency, Interest rate**	
Plain Vanilla Derivatives	Swaps Forwards	Swaptions
Exotic Derivatives		
Structured Notes		

J.P. Morgan & Company Inc. – continued

KEY MANAGERS & DERIVATIVES SPECIALISTS:	Direct Phone/Fax	Job Function
Mr. James T. Flynn Chief Financial Officer		Chief Financial Officer Treasurer
Mr. Douglas A. Warner III Chairman, President & C.E.O.		President

J.P. Morgan Investment Management, Inc. (U.S.A.)

Bank/Management Division

Sub of J.P. Morgan & Company Inc.

Location: 522 Fifth Avenue
New York, NY 10036

Fax: 212/575-0392 **Phone:** 212/837-2300

Investment Portfolio: $ 77.0 billion

Use: **Investment Purposes**

Currencies: US dollar

Regions: United States

DERIVATIVES ACTIVITIES:

Exchange-traded Options & Futures

OTC Derivatives
Plain Vanilla Derivatives

Structured Notes

OTHER ALTERNATIVE INVESTMENTS:

GICs
Strips
Repos/reverse repos

KEY MANAGERS & DERIVATIVES SPECIALISTS:	Direct Phone/Fax	Job Function
Mr. Robert W. Holland Vice President – Fixed Income	212/837-2096	Portfolio Mgr – Options Portfolio Mgr – Structured Notes
Mr. Charles T. Kimball	212/837-2115	Fixed-Income Strategist
Mr. Nicholas P. Sargen Managing Director		Fixed-Income Strategist *Govt*
Mr. Keith M. Schappert President & C.E.O.		President Chief Investment Officer

Morgan Grenfell Capital Management Inc.

Broker/Management Sub

Location: 1435 Walnut Street
Fourth Floor
Philadelphia, PA 19102

Fax: 215/963-0200 **Phone:** 215/246-0200

Profile: Total return investor

Investment Portfolio: $ 6.3 billion

Use: **Investment Purposes**

Currencies: US dollar

Regions: United States

Morgan Grenfell Capital Management Inc. – continued

DERIVATIVES ACTIVITIES:		**CAC Class: Inactive**

OTHER ALTERNATIVE INVESTMENTS:		
	CMOs/REMICs – Govt.	CMOs/REMICs – Private

KEY MANAGERS & DERIVATIVES SPECIALISTS:	**Direct Phone/Fax**	**Job Function**
Mr. David W. Baldt Executive Vice President	215/963-1190	Chief Investment Officer

Morgan Stanley Asset Management, Inc.

Broker/Management Sub

Location: 1221 Avenue of the Americas
21st Floor
New York, NY 10020

Fax: 212/296-7289 **Phone:** 212/296-7100

Profile: Total return investor

Investment Portfolio: $ 48.5 billion

Use: **Investment Purposes**
Adjust portfolio duration
Capture extra yield
Diversify portfolio
Hedge bond portfolio risk
Hedge currency risk
Hedge interest rate risk
Protect currency gains
Provide incremental return
Reduce variability of returns

Currencies: US dollar

Regions: United States, Canada, Europe, Latin America

DERIVATIVES ACTIVITIES:		**CAC Class: 4**
OTC Derivatives **Plain Vanilla Derivatives**	**Currency** Forwards	
Structured Notes	Corporate MTNs Govt. agency MTNs CMT notes	Periodic capped floaters Multi-step-up callable bonds
Counterparty Rating Requirement:	AA	

OTHER ALTERNATIVE INVESTMENTS:		
	CMOs/REMICs – Govt. CMOs/REMICs – Private	Strips Repos/reverse repos

KEY MANAGERS & DERIVATIVES SPECIALISTS:	**Direct Phone/Fax**	**Job Function**
Mr. Barton M. Biggs Chairman	212/296-7150	Chief Investment Officer
Mr. Charles B. Hintz Managing Director – Treasury	212/723-7178	Treasurer Portfolio Mgr – Derivatives Portfolio Mgr – Futures Portfolio Mgr – Options
Mr. Peter A. Nadosy President	212/296-7115	President Bond Department Head

Morgan Stanley Asset Management, Inc. – continued

KEY MANAGERS & DERIVATIVES SPECIALISTS:	Direct Phone/Fax	Job Function
Mr. Robert M. Smith Principal	212/296-7087	Portfolio Mgr – Derivatives Portfolio Mgr – Structured Notes

Munder Capital Management, Inc.

Investment Manager

Location: 480 Pierce Street, Suite 300, Birmingham, MI 48009

Fax: 810/647-5931 **Phone:** 810/647-9200

Profile: Total return investor

Investment Portfolio: $ 9.0 billion

Use: **Investment Purposes**

Currencies: US dollar

Regions: United States

DERIVATIVES ACTIVITIES:

CAC Class: Inactive

OTHER ALTERNATIVE INVESTMENTS:

CMOs/REMICs – Govt.
CMOs/REMICs – Private
GICs
Strips
Repos/reverse repos

KEY MANAGERS & DERIVATIVES SPECIALISTS:	Direct Phone/Fax	Job Function
Mr. James C. Robinson Director – Fixed Income		Bond Department Head
Mr. Gerald Seizert		Chief Investment Officer

Mutual of America Capital Management Corporation

Insurance Co/Life

Sub of Mutual of America Life Insurance Company

Location: 320 Park Avenue, 2nd – 9th Floors, New York, NY 10022

Fax: 212/224-2539 **Phone:** 212/224-1600

Profile: Hold to maturity investor

Investment Portfolio: $ 7.6 billion

Use: **Investment Purposes**

Currencies: US dollar

Regions: United States

DERIVATIVES ACTIVITIES:

CAC Class: Inactive

OTHER ALTERNATIVE INVESTMENTS:

CMOs/REMICs – Govt.
CMOs/REMICs – Private
Strips

KEY MANAGERS & DERIVATIVES SPECIALISTS:	Direct Phone/Fax	Job Function
Ms. Dolores J. Morrissey Executive Vice President	212/224-1939	Chief Investment Officer Bond Department Head

National Bank of Alaska

Bank/Portfolio

Sub of National Bancorp of Alaska Inc.

Location: 301 West Northern Lights Boulevard
Anchorage, AK 99503

Fax: 907/265-2139 **Phone:** 907/276-1132

Profile: Stable asset investor

Investment Portfolio: $ 1.0 - 3.0 billion

Use: **Balance Sheet/Risk Management**

Investment Purposes

Currencies: US dollar

Regions: United States

DERIVATIVES ACTIVITIES: **CAC Class: Inactive**

OTHER ALTERNATIVE INVESTMENTS:

CMOs/REMICs – Govt. CMOs/REMICs – Private

KEY MANAGERS & DERIVATIVES SPECIALISTS:	**Direct Phone/Fax**	**Job Function**
Ms. Mary Wladkowski Investment Manager	907/265-2975	Chief Investment Officer

National Bank of Commerce (Portfolio)

Bank/Portfolio

Sub of National Commerce Bancorporation

Location: One Commerce Square
Ninth Floor
Memphis, TN 38150

Fax: 901/523-3879 **Phone:** 901/523-3700

Profile: Total return investor

Investment Portfolio: $ 1.1 billion

Use: **Balance Sheet/Risk Management**
Hedge interest rate risk
Strategic liability management

Currencies: US dollar

Regions: United States

DERIVATIVES ACTIVITIES: **CAC Class: 3**

OTC Derivatives	**Interest rate**	
Plain Vanilla Derivatives	Swaps	Forwards
Exotic Derivatives	CMT options	

OTHER ALTERNATIVE INVESTMENTS:

CMOs/REMICs – Govt.

KEY MANAGERS & DERIVATIVES SPECIALISTS:	**Direct Phone/Fax**	**Job Function**
Mr. Wright Eddrington	901/523-3711	Trader – Derivatives *MBS*
Mr. Gary L. Lazarini Executive Vice President	901/523-3797 901/523-3910	Bond Department Head Portfolio Mgr – Derivatives
Mr. John Womble Senior Vice President	901/523-3271	Portfolio Mgr – Derivatives

National City Bank of Akron

Bank/Trust

Sub of National City Corporation

Location: One Cascade Plaza
Sixth Floor
Akron, OH 44308

Fax: 216/375-8434 **Phone:** 216/375-8433

Profile: Hold to maturity investor

Investment Portfolio: $ 1.4 billion

Use: **Investment Purposes**
Provide incremental return

Currencies: US dollar

Regions: United States

DERIVATIVES ACTIVITIES: **CAC Class: 1**

Structured Notes	Floaters

OTHER ALTERNATIVE INVESTMENTS:

CMOs/REMICs – Govt.
CMOs/REMICs – Private
Strips

KEY MANAGERS & DERIVATIVES SPECIALISTS:	**Direct Phone/Fax**	**Job Function**
Mr. Geoff Hauck Vice President		Chief Investment Officer
Mr. Barry Hollis Assistant Vice President		Portfolio Mgr – Structured Notes

National City Bank, Indiana

Bank/Trust

Sub of National City Corporation

Location: 101 West Washington Street
Indianapolis, IN 46255

Fax: 317/267-6112 **Phone:** 317/267-7000

Profile: Total return investor

Investment Portfolio: $ 1.0 billion

Use: **Investment Purposes**

Currencies: US dollar

Regions: United States

DERIVATIVES ACTIVITIES: **CAC Class: Inactive**

OTHER ALTERNATIVE INVESTMENTS:

CMOs/REMICs – Govt.
CMOs/REMICs – Private
GICs

KEY MANAGERS & DERIVATIVES SPECIALISTS:	**Direct Phone/Fax**	**Job Function**
Ms. Elizabeth Meitzler	317/267-6283	Bond Department Head

National Life Investment Management Co.

Insurance Co/Management

Sub of National Life of Vermont

Location: One National Life Drive
Montpelier, VT 05604

Fax: 802/223-9332 **Phone:** 802/223-9300

Profile: Total return investor

Investment Portfolio: $ 4.2 billion

Use: **Investment Purposes**

Currencies: US dollar

Regions: United States

DERIVATIVES ACTIVITIES: **CAC Class: Inactive**

OTHER ALTERNATIVE INVESTMENTS:

CMOs/REMICs – Govt. CMOs/REMICs – Private

KEY MANAGERS & DERIVATIVES SPECIALISTS:	Direct Phone/Fax	Job Function
Mr. Rodney A. Buck Chairman, President & C.E.O.	802/223-9350	President Bond Department Head

National Mutual Funds Management Inc.

Investment Manager

Location: 2029 Century Park East
Suite 2050
Los Angeles, CA 90067-3006

Fax: 310/286-2314 **Phone:** 310/557-1500

Profile: Total return investor

Investment Portfolio: $ 1.2 billion

Use: **Investment Purposes**
Asset allocation
Hedge bond portfolio risk
Hedge equity portfolio risk

Currencies: US dollar

Regions: United States

DERIVATIVES ACTIVITIES:

Exchange-traded Options & Futures
U.S. Treasury futures

Bond
U.S. Treasury options

OTHER ALTERNATIVE INVESTMENTS:

CMOs/REMICs – Govt.

KEY MANAGERS & DERIVATIVES SPECIALISTS:	Direct Phone/Fax	Job Function
Mr. Guy Elliffe Managing Director		Portfolio Mgr – Futures Portfolio Mgr – Options
Mr. Vache Mahseredjian Managing Director		Bond Department Head
Mr. Joel R. Swanson President		President Chief Investment Officer

National Western Asset Management, Inc.

Insurance Co/Management

Sub of National Western Life Insurance Company

Location: 850 East Anderson Lane
Austin, TX 78752-1602

Fax: 512/835-2729 **Phone:** 512/836-1010

Profile: Total return investor

Investment Portfolio: $ 1.0 - 3.0 billion

Use: **Investment Purposes**

Currencies: US dollar

Regions: United States

DERIVATIVES ACTIVITIES: **CAC Class: Inactive**

OTHER ALTERNATIVE INVESTMENTS:

CMOs/REMICs – Govt. CMOs/REMICs – Private

KEY MANAGERS & DERIVATIVES SPECIALISTS:	**Direct Phone/Fax**	**Job Function**
Ms. Patricia Scheuer		Chief Investment Officer

NationsBank (Charlotte) (Funds Management)

Bank/Portfolio

Sub of NationsBank Corporation

Location: 100 North Tryon Street
Charlotte, NC 28255

Fax: 704/339-6490 **Phone:** 704/386-5000

Profile: Total return investor

Investment Portfolio: $ 52.0 billion

Use: **Balance Sheet/Risk Management**
Create synthetic fixed/floating rate
Hedge balance sheet
Lower transaction costs
Reduce cost of capital
Strategic liability management

Currencies: US dollar

Regions: United States

DERIVATIVES ACTIVITIES: **CAC Class: 8**

Exchange-traded Options & Futures	**Bond, Currency, Interest rate**	
U.S. Treasury futures	U.S. Treasury options	
OTC Derivatives	**Bond, Currency, Interest rate**	
Plain Vanilla Derivatives	Swaps	Forwards
Exotic Derivatives	CMT swaps	Index amortizing swaps
	Govt. agency MTNs	Floaters
	Index amortizing notes	
Counterparty Rating Requirement:	AAA	

OTHER ALTERNATIVE INVESTMENTS:

CMOs/REMICs – Govt. Repos/reverse repos
CMOs/REMICs – Private

NationsBank (Charlotte) (Funds Management) – continued

KEY MANAGERS & DERIVATIVES SPECIALISTS:	Direct Phone/Fax	Job Function
Mr. Alvaro deMolina Senior Vice President	704/386-1500	Portfolio Mgr – Derivatives Portfolio Mgr – Futures
Mr. Thomas T. Houghton	704/388-2375	Portfolio Mgr – Derivatives Portfolio Mgr – Futures
Mr. Craig M. Wardlaw Executive Vice President	704/386-7696 704/388-0602	Chief Investment Officer Portfolio Mgr – Structured Notes

Nationwide Financial Services

Mutual Fund Manager

Location: One Nationwide Plaza
33rd Floor
Columbus, OH 43215

Fax: 614/249-4698 **Phone:** 614/249-7111

Profile: Hold to maturity investor

Investment Portfolio: $ 2.2 billion

Use: **Investment Purposes**

Currencies: US dollar

Regions: United States

DERIVATIVES ACTIVITIES:

Structured Notes	Corporate MTNs	Govt. agency MTNs
Counterparty Rating Requirement:	None	

OTHER ALTERNATIVE INVESTMENTS:

	CMOs/REMICs – Govt. CMOs/REMICs – Private	Repos/reverse repos

KEY MANAGERS & DERIVATIVES SPECIALISTS:	Direct Phone/Fax	Job Function
Mr. Charles Bath	614/249-7668	Portfolio Mgr – Structured Notes
Ms. Alpha L. Benson Senior Portfolio Manager	614/249-7851	Bond Department Head *Muni*
Mr. Wayne T. Frisbee Director – Investments	614/249-4125	Portfolio Mgr – Structured Notes
Mr. Robert Woodward		Chief Investment Officer

NatWest Bank, N.A. (Portfolio)

Bank/Portfolio

Sub of National Westminster Bancorp, Inc.

Location: Ten Exchange Place
22nd Floor
Jersey City, NJ 07302

Fax: 201/547-2979 **Phone:** 201/547-7000

Profile: Total return investor

Investment Portfolio: $ 5.4 billion

Use: **Balance Sheet/Risk Management**
Hedge interest rate risk

Investment Purposes
Capture extra yield
Discretionary situations
Hedge bond portfolio risk
Hedge currency risk

Currencies: US dollar, Canadian dollar, French franc, German mark, Italian lira, Swiss franc, UK pound

Regions: United States

DERIVATIVES ACTIVITIES: **CAC Class: 8**

Exchange-traded Options & Futures	**Bond, Currency, Interest rate**	
U.S. Treasury futures	Municipal futures	
U.S. Treasury options	Municipal options	
OTC Derivatives	**Bond, Currency, Interest rate**	
Plain Vanilla Derivatives	Swaps	Caps
	Forwards	Floors
Counterparty Rating Requirement:	A	

OTHER ALTERNATIVE INVESTMENTS:

CMOs/REMICs – Govt. CMOs/REMICs – Private

KEY MANAGERS & DERIVATIVES SPECIALISTS:	**Direct Phone/Fax**	**Job Function**
Mr. Klaus Dietrich Vice President & Manager	201/547-2871 201/547-2737	Chief Investment Officer
Mr. Howard Rosof		Portfolio Mgr – Derivatives Portfolio Mgr – Futures

Navy Federal Credit Union

Credit Union

Location: 820 Follin Lane
Vienna, VA 22180-4907

Fax: 703/255-7755 **Phone:** 703/255-8000

Profile: Hold to maturity investor

Investment Portfolio: $ 4.0 - 10.0 billion

Use: **Investment Purposes**
Capture extra yield

Currencies: US dollar

Regions: United States

Navy Federal Credit Union – continued

DERIVATIVES ACTIVITIES:		CAC Class: 2
Structured Notes	Multi-step-up callable bonds	

OTHER ALTERNATIVE INVESTMENTS:		
	CMOs/REMICs – Govt.	Strips

KEY MANAGERS & DERIVATIVES SPECIALISTS:	Direct Phone/Fax	Job Function
Mr. Donald Chapman		Chief Investment Officer Portfolio Mgr – Structured Notes

NBD Bank, N.A. (Trust)

Bank/Trust

Sub of First Chicago/NBD Corporation

Location: 611 Woodward Avenue
Detroit, MI 48226-7754

Fax: 313/225-1038 **Phone:** 313/225-1000

Profile: Total return investor

Investment Portfolio: $ 14.0 billion

Use: **Investment Purposes**

Currencies: US dollar

Regions: United States

DERIVATIVES ACTIVITIES:		CAC Class: Inactive

OTHER ALTERNATIVE INVESTMENTS:		
	CMOs/REMICs – Govt. CMOs/REMICs – Private	MOPs/TOPs

KEY MANAGERS & DERIVATIVES SPECIALISTS:	Direct Phone/Fax	Job Function
Mr. George F. Abel Senior Vice President	313/225-3049	Chief Investment Officer
Mr. Timothy B. Kerr First Vice President	313/225-1064	Bond Department Head

NCM Capital Management Group, Inc.

Investment Manager

Location: 103 West Main Street
Suite 400
Durham, NC 27701-3638

Fax: 919/682-0414 **Phone:** 919/688-0620

Profile: Total return investor

Investment Portfolio: $ 2.9 billion

Use: **Investment Purposes**
Capture extra yield
Provide incremental return

Currencies: US dollar

Regions: United States

NCM Capital Management Group, Inc. – continued

DERIVATIVES ACTIVITIES:		**CAC Class: 3**
Structured Notes	Corporate MTNs Floaters	Inverse floaters

OTHER ALTERNATIVE INVESTMENTS:		
	CMOs/REMICs – Govt.	Strips

KEY MANAGERS & DERIVATIVES SPECIALISTS:	**Direct Phone/Fax**	**Job Function**
Mr. David Carter Vice President		Portfolio Mgr – Structured Notes
Mr. Maceo K. Sloan Chairman, President & C.E.O.	919/688-5333	President Chief Investment Officer
Mr. Paul Van Kampen S.V.P. & Dir. – Fixed Income		Portfolio Mgr – Structured Notes

Nebraska State Investment Council

Government Pension Fund

Location: 941 O Street
Suite 500
Lincoln, NE 68508

Fax: 402/471-2498 **Phone:** 402/471-2043

Profile: Total return investor

Investment Portfolio: $ 2.3 billion

Use: **Investment Purposes**
Capture extra yield

Currencies: US dollar

Regions: United States

DERIVATIVES ACTIVITIES:		**CAC Class: 3**
Structured Notes	Govt. agency MTNs	Floaters

OTHER ALTERNATIVE INVESTMENTS:		
	CMOs/REMICs – Govt. GICs	Repos/reverse repos

KEY MANAGERS & DERIVATIVES SPECIALISTS:	**Direct Phone/Fax**	**Job Function**
Mr. Michael Hansen		Portfolio Mgr – Structured Notes
Mr. Rex W. Holsapple State Investment Officer		Chief Investment Officer Portfolio Mgr – Structured Notes

Neuberger & Berman Management Inc.

Broker/Management Sub

Location: 605 Third Avenue
Second Floor
New York, NY 10158

Fax: 212/476-5535 **Phone:** 212/476-9000

Profile: Total return investor

Investment Portfolio: $ 34.3 billion

Use: **Balance Sheet/Risk Management**
Create synthetic fixed/floating rate
Hedge balance sheet
Hedge currency risk
Hedge interest rate risk
Hedge overseas investments
Protect currency gains

Currencies: US dollar, French franc, German mark, Italian lira, Japanese yen

Regions: United States, Canada, Europe, Pacific Rim

DERIVATIVES ACTIVITIES: **CAC Class: 6**

Exchange-traded Options & Futures	**Bond, Currency, Interest rate**	
U.S. Treasury futures	Municipal futures	
U.S. Treasury options		
OTC Derivatives	**Bond, Currency, Interest rate**	
Plain Vanilla Derivatives	Caps	Collars
	Floors	
Structured Notes	Corporate MTNs	CMT notes
	Govt. agency MTNs	Floaters
Counterparty Rating Requirement:	AA	

OTHER ALTERNATIVE INVESTMENTS:

	CMOs/REMICs – Govt.	Repos/reverse repos
	CMOs/REMICs – Private	

KEY MANAGERS & DERIVATIVES SPECIALISTS:	Direct Phone/Fax	Job Function
Mr. Richard A. Cantor President & Executive Partner		President Chief Investment Officer
Mr. Theodore P. Giuliano General Partner	212/476-5523	Portfolio Mgr – Derivatives Portfolio Mgr – Options Portfolio Mgr – Structured Notes
Ms. Theresa A. Havell Director		Bond Department Head

New Jersey Division of Investments

Government Pension Fund

Location: 50 West State Street
Ninth Floor
Trenton, NJ 08625

Fax: 609/396-1073 **Phone:** 609/292-5106

Profile: Hold to maturity investor

Investment Portfolio: $ 44.1 billion

Use: **Investment Purposes**
Capture extra yield
Hedge bond portfolio risk
Hedge currency risk
Provide incremental return

Currencies: US dollar, French franc, German mark, Japanese yen

Regions: United States

DERIVATIVES ACTIVITIES: **CAC Class: 4**

OTC Derivatives
Plain Vanilla Derivatives

Structured Notes	Corporate MTNs
Counterparty Rating Requirement:	A

OTHER ALTERNATIVE INVESTMENTS:

CMOs/REMICs – Govt.
CMOs/REMICs – Private
Repos/reverse repos

KEY MANAGERS & DERIVATIVES SPECIALISTS:	Direct Phone/Fax	Job Function
Mr. Roland Machold		Chief Investment Officer
Mr. Timothy Patton	609/292-5025	Portfolio Mgr – Derivatives Portfolio Mgr – Structured Notes

New Mexico Educational Retirement Board

Government Pension Fund

Location: 701 Caminos de Los Marquez
Santa Fe, NM 87501

Fax: 505/989-7738 **Phone:** 505/827-8030

Profile: Total return investor

Investment Portfolio: $ 3.9 billion

Use: **Investment Purposes**
Hedge bond portfolio risk
Hedge interest rate risk

Currencies: US dollar

Regions: United States

DERIVATIVES ACTIVITIES:

Structured Notes	Corporate MTNs Govt. agency MTNs	Multi-step-up callable bonds
Counterparty Rating Requirement:	None	

New Mexico Educational Retirement Board – continued

OTHER ALTERNATIVE INVESTMENTS:

	CMOs/REMICs – Govt.	Strips
	CMOs/REMICs – Private	Repos/reverse repos

KEY MANAGERS & DERIVATIVES SPECIALISTS:	**Direct Phone/Fax**	**Job Function**
Mr. Frank C. Foy		Chief Investment Officer Portfolio Mgr – Derivatives

New Mexico State Permanent Funds

Foundation/Endowment

Location: 2025 South Pacheco Street
Suite 203
Santa Fe, NM 87505

Fax: 505/827-6242 **Phone:** 505/827-6226

Profile: Hold to maturity investor

Investment Portfolio: $ 5.9 billion

Use: **Investment Purposes**

Currencies: US dollar

Regions: United States

DERIVATIVES ACTIVITIES: **CAC Class: Inactive**

OTHER ALTERNATIVE INVESTMENTS:

CMOs/REMICs – Govt.

KEY MANAGERS & DERIVATIVES SPECIALISTS:	**Direct Phone/Fax**	**Job Function**
Mr. Phillip J. Archibeck State Investment Officer		Chief Investment Officer

New York Life Insurance Company (U.S.A)

Insurance Co/Life

Location: 51 Madison Avenue
New York, NY 10010

Fax: 212/576-8163 **Phone:** 212/576-7000

Profile: Total return investor

Investment Portfolio: $ 31.5 billion

Use: **Balance Sheet/Risk Management**
Hedge currency risk
Hedge interest rate risk
Strategic liability management

Currencies: US dollar

Regions: United States, Europe, Pacific Rim

New York Life Insurance Company (U.S.A) – continued

DERIVATIVES ACTIVITIES:

Exchange-traded Options & Futures		
U.S. Treasury futures	U.S. Treasury options	
OTC Derivatives		
Plain Vanilla Derivatives	Swaps Forwards	Caps Floors
Exotic Derivatives	CMT swaps	Index amortizing swaps
Counterparty Rating Requirement:	AA	

OTHER ALTERNATIVE INVESTMENTS:

	CMOs/REMICs – Govt.	Strips

KEY MANAGERS & DERIVATIVES SPECIALISTS:	Direct Phone/Fax	Job Function
Mr. William Cheng Vice President	212/576-6525	Portfolio Mgr – Derivatives
Ms. Celia Holtzberg Vice President	212/576-4837 212/447-4166	Bond Department Head
Ms. Jean E. Hoysradt Senior Vice President	212/576-4965	Chief Investment Officer
Mr. Joseph Sindelar Vice President	212/576-4257	Portfolio Mgr – Derivatives
Mr. Seymour Sternberg President & C.O.O.		President

New York State & Local Retirement Systems

Government Pension Fund

Location: Governor Alfred E. Smith Building
Sixth Floor
Albany, NY 12236

Fax: 518/473-6755 **Phone:** 518/474-6035

Profile: Stable asset investor

Investment Portfolio: $ 60.2 billion

Use: **Investment Purposes**
Adjust portfolio duration
Asset allocation
Capture extra yield
Diversify portfolio

Currencies: US dollar

Regions: United States

DERIVATIVES ACTIVITIES: **CAC Class: 5**

OTC Derivatives	**Bond**	
Plain Vanilla Derivatives	Swaps	
Structured Notes	Corporate	MTNs

New York State & Local Retirement Systems – continued

OTHER ALTERNATIVE INVESTMENTS:

	CMOs/REMICs – Govt. Strips	Repos/reverse repos

KEY MANAGERS & DERIVATIVES SPECIALISTS:	**Direct Phone/Fax**	**Job Function**
Mr. William M. Barrett	518/473-6396	Chief Investment Officer
Mr. Robert J. Limage Senior Investment Officer	518/474-6035	Bond Department Head
Mr. Thomas J. Miller Investment Officer	518/473-4558	Portfolio Mgr – Derivatives Portfolio Mgr – Structured Notes

New York State Teachers' Retirement System

Government Pension Fund

Location: Ten Corporate Woods Drive
Albany, NY 12211-2395

Fax: 518/447-2630 **Phone:** 518/447-2666

Profile: Hold to maturity investor

Investment Portfolio: $ 40.0 billion

Use: **Investment Purposes**

Currencies: US dollar

Regions: United States

DERIVATIVES ACTIVITIES: **CAC Class: Inactive**

OTHER ALTERNATIVE INVESTMENTS:

	CMOs/REMICs – Govt. CMOs/REMICs – Private	Strips

KEY MANAGERS & DERIVATIVES SPECIALISTS:	**Direct Phone/Fax**	**Job Function**
Mr. George M. Philip Executive Director		Chief Investment Officer

Nicholas-Applegate Capital Management

Investment Manager

Location: 600 West Broadway
29th Floor
San Diego, CA 92101

Fax: 619/687-8040 **Phone:** 619/687-8000

Profile: Total return investor

Investment Portfolio: $ 27.0 billion

Use: **Investment Purposes**

Currencies: US dollar

Regions: United States

Nicholas-Applegate Capital Management – continued

DERIVATIVES ACTIVITIES: **CAC Class: Inactive**

OTHER ALTERNATIVE INVESTMENTS:

CMOs/REMICs – Govt.	Strips
CMOs/REMICs – Private	Repos/reverse repos

KEY MANAGERS & DERIVATIVES SPECIALISTS:	**Direct Phone/Fax**	**Job Function**
Mr. Arthur Nicholas Partner		Chief Investment Officer
Mr. Thomas Pindelski Chief Financial Officer		Chief Financial Officer

Nicholas-Applegate Capital Management (Houston)

Investment Manager

Location: 1990 Post Oak Boulevard
Suite 1100
Houston, TX 77056-3890

Fax: 713/963-5235 **Phone:** 713/963-5200

Profile: Total return investor

Investment Portfolio: $ 27.0 billion

Use: **Balance Sheet/Risk Management**
Hedge interest rate risk
Incremental return

Currencies: US dollar

Regions: United States

DERIVATIVES ACTIVITIES: **CAC Class: 3**

Exchange-traded Options & Futures
U.S. Treasury futures

Bond

OTHER ALTERNATIVE INVESTMENTS:

CMOs/REMICs – Private GICs

KEY MANAGERS & DERIVATIVES SPECIALISTS:	**Direct Phone/Fax**	**Job Function**
Mr. Terence S. Ellis Partner	713/963-2460	Chief Investment Officer Bond Department Head
Mr. James Kellerman	713/963-5250 713/963-5280	Portfolio Mgr – Futures
Mr. David Kroon	713/963-5243 713/963-5280	Portfolio Mgr – Futures

Nike Securities (UIT Management)

Unit Investment Trust

Location: 1001 Warrenville Road
Suite 300
Lisle, IL 60532

Fax: 708/241-8727 **Phone:** 708/241-4141

Profile: Stable asset investor

Investment Portfolio: $ 11.0 - 20.0 billion

Use: **Investment Purposes**

Currencies: US dollar

Regions: United States

DERIVATIVES ACTIVITIES:

Exchange-traded Options & Futures	**Currency**

OTHER ALTERNATIVE INVESTMENTS:

CMOs/REMICs – Govt.

KEY MANAGERS & DERIVATIVES SPECIALISTS:	Direct Phone/Fax	Job Function
Mr. Scott Hall		Bond Department Head
Mr. Frank Kuhlman	708/241-8637	Portfolio Mgr – Futures

Nikko Capital Management (U.S.A.)

Broker/Management Sub

Location: 489 Fifth Avenue
Sixth Floor
New York, NY 10017

Fax: 212/599-4640 **Phone:** 212/599-0300

Profile: Total return investor

Investment Portfolio: $ 2.0 billion

Use:

Balance Sheet/Risk Management
Hedge currency risk

Investment Purposes
Alter portfolio weighting
Adjust portfolio duration
Asset allocation
Hedge bond portfolio risk
Hedge currency risk
Hedge interest rate risk

Currencies: US dollar, Canadian dollar, French franc, German mark, Italian lira, Japanese yen, Mexican peso, UK pound

Regions: United States, Canada, Europe, Pacific Rim

DERIVATIVES ACTIVITIES: **CAC Class: 5**

Exchange-traded Options & Futures U.S. Treasury futures	**Bond, Currency**
OTC Derivatives **Plain Vanilla Derivatives**	**Bond, Currency** Forwards
Counterparty Rating Requirement:	A

OTHER ALTERNATIVE INVESTMENTS:

CMOs/REMICs – Govt. Repos/reverse repos

Nikko Capital Management (U.S.A.) – continued

KEY MANAGERS & DERIVATIVES SPECIALISTS:	Direct Phone/Fax	Job Function
Mr. Stanley Kirtman President	212/559-4631	President Chief Investment Officer
Mr. Clifford W. Stober V.P. & Senior Portfolio Mgr	212/559-4632	Portfolio Mgr – Derivatives Portfolio Mgr – Futures

Nomura Capital Management (U.S.A.)

Investment Manager

Sub of Nomura Investment Management Co. Ltd.

Location: 180 Maiden Lane
Suite 2903
New York, NY 10038

Fax: 212/509-8835 **Phone:** 212/509-9253

Profile: Total return investor

Investment Portfolio: $ 5.3 billion

Use: **Balance Sheet/Risk Management**
Hedge currency risk
Hedge overseas Investments

Currencies: US dollar, Australian dollar, Belgian franc, Canadian dollar, French franc, German mark, Italian lira, Japanese yen, Mexican peso, Spanish peseta, Swiss franc, Thai baht, UK pound

Regions: United States, Canada, Europe, Latin America, Pacific Rim, Emerging mkts

DERIVATIVES ACTIVITIES:

OTC Derivatives
Plain Vanilla Derivatives

Currency
Forwards

OTHER ALTERNATIVE INVESTMENTS:

CMOs/REMICs – Govt.

KEY MANAGERS & DERIVATIVES SPECIALISTS:	Direct Phone/Fax	Job Function
Mr. Benjamin DeNigris Assistant Vice President	212/509-6527	Trader – Derivatives
Mr. Milton J. Ezrati Senior Vice President	212/509-6527	Chief Investment Officer Portfolio Mgr – Derivatives
Mr. Iwao Komatsu President		President

North Carolina Department of State Treasurer

Government Pension Fund

Location: 325 North Salisbury Street
Investment & Banking Division
Raleigh, NC 27603-1385

Fax: 919/733-0075 **Phone:** 919/733-4191

Profile: Total return investor

Investment Portfolio: $ 21.0 - 49.0 billion

Use: **Investment Purposes**

Currencies: US dollar

Regions: United States

DERIVATIVES ACTIVITIES: **CAC Class: Inactive**

OTHER ALTERNATIVE INVESTMENTS:

CMOs/REMICs – Govt. Strips

KEY MANAGERS & DERIVATIVES SPECIALISTS:	**Direct Phone/Fax**	**Job Function**
Mr. C. Douglas Chappell Deputy Treasurer	919/733-7282	Bond Department Head *Taxable*

North Fork Bank (Portfolio)

Bank/Portfolio

Sub of North Fork Bancorporation, Inc.

Location: 9025 Main Road
Route 25
Mattituck, NY 11952

Fax: 516/298-5769 **Phone:** 516/298-5000

Profile: Total return investor

Investment Portfolio: $ 734.9 million

Use: **Balance Sheet/Risk Management**
Hedge interest rate risk

Currencies: US dollar

Regions: United States

DERIVATIVES ACTIVITIES:

OTC Derivatives **Plain Vanilla Derivatives**	**Interest rate** Swaps Caps	 Floors
Counterparty Rating Requirement:	AAA	

OTHER ALTERNATIVE INVESTMENTS:

CMOs/REMICs – Govt. CMOs/REMICs – Private

KEY MANAGERS & DERIVATIVES SPECIALISTS:	**Direct Phone/Fax**	**Job Function**
Mr. Kevin O'Connor Senior Vice President		Chief Investment Officer Portfolio Mgr – Derivatives

North Side Savings Bank

Savings Bank/Bldg Society

Location: 170 Tulip Avenue
Floral Park, NY 11001-2792

Fax: 516/488-6546 **Phone:** 516/488-6900

Profile: Total return investor

Investment Portfolio: $ 1.1 billion

Use: **Balance Sheet/Risk Management**
Hedge interest rate risk

Investment Purposes
Alter portfolio weighting
Asset allocation
Capture extra yield

Currencies: US dollar

Regions: United States

DERIVATIVES ACTIVITIES:

Structured Notes Multi-step-up callable bonds

OTHER ALTERNATIVE INVESTMENTS:

CMOs/REMICs – Govt.
CMOs/REMICs – Private
Repos/reverse repos

KEY MANAGERS & DERIVATIVES SPECIALISTS:	**Direct Phone/Fax**	**Job Function**
Mr. Donald C. Fleming Executive Vice President		Chief Financial Officer
Ms. Kathleen Mallon Treasurer		Chief Investment Officer Treasurer Portfolio Mgr – Structured Notes
Mr. Thomas M. O'Brien President & C.E.O.		President

The Northern Trust Company (Treasury)

Bank/Portfolio

Sub of Northern Trust Corporation

Location: 50 South LaSalle Street
B – 12
Chicago, IL 60675

Fax: 312/444-5666 **Phone:** 312/630-6000

Profile: Spread investor

Investment Portfolio: $ 19.0 billion

Use: **Balance Sheet/Risk Management**
Hedge balance sheet
Hedge currency risk
Hedge interest rate risk

Currencies: US dollar
Canadian dollar
UK pound

Regions: United States

The Northern Trust Company (Treasury) – continued

DERIVATIVES ACTIVITIES: **CAC Class: 6**

Exchange-traded Options & Futures	**Currency**	
OTC Derivatives	**Currency**	
Plain Vanilla Derivatives	Swaps	Caps
	Forwards	Floors
Structured Notes	Govt. agency MTNs	Multi-step-up callable bonds
	Floaters	

OTHER ALTERNATIVE INVESTMENTS:

	CMOs/REMICs – Govt.	Repos/reverse repos
	CMOs/REMICs – Private	

KEY MANAGERS & DERIVATIVES SPECIALISTS:	Direct Phone/Fax	Job Function
Mr. Robert Gann Vice President	312/630-6678	Portfolio Mgr – Derivatives Portfolio Mgr – Options
Mr. Donald L. Raiff Senior Vice President		Chief Investment Officer

Northern Trust Corporation

Bank Holding Company

Location: 50 South LaSalle Street
Chicago, IL 60675

Fax: 312/444-7843 **Phone:** 312/630-6000

Profile: Spread investor

Use:

Balance Sheet/Risk Management
Hedge balance sheet
Hedge currency risk
Hedge interest rate risk
Strategic liability management

Investment Purposes
Asset allocation
Capture extra yield

Currencies: US dollar

Regions: United States

DERIVATIVES ACTIVITIES: **CAC Class: 8**

Exchange-traded Options & Futures	**Interest rate**	
OTC Derivatives	**Currency, Interest rate**	
Plain Vanilla Derivatives	Swaps	Caps
	Forwards	Floors
Counterparty Rating Requirement:	AA	

OTHER ALTERNATIVE INVESTMENTS:

Repos/reverse repos

Northern Trust Corporation – continued

KEY MANAGERS & DERIVATIVES SPECIALISTS:	Direct Phone/Fax	Job Function
Mr. David L. Eddy S.V.P. & Treasurer		Treasurer Portfolio Mgr – Derivatives
Mr. William A. Osborn President & C.O.O.		President
Mr. Perry R. Pero Sr. Exec. V.P. & C.F.O.		Chief Financial Officer

Northrop Grumman Corporation

Corporation

Location: 1840 Century Park East
Los Angeles, CA 90067

Fax: 310/201-3023 **Phone:** 310/553-6262

Use: **Balance Sheet/Risk Management**
Bypass regulations
Create synthetic fixed/floating rate
Hedge balance sheet
Hedge interest rate risk
Hedge overseas Investments
Incremental return
Reduce cost of capital
Strategic liability management

Currencies: US dollar

Regions: United States

DERIVATIVES ACTIVITIES:

OTC Derivatives **Plain Vanilla Derivatives**	**Currency, Interest rate** Swaps
Structured Notes	

KEY MANAGERS & DERIVATIVES SPECIALISTS:	Direct Phone/Fax	Job Function
Mr. Kent Kresa Chairman, President & C.E.O.		President
Mr. Albert F. Myers Vice President & Treasurer		Treasurer Portfolio Mgr – Derivatives Portfolio Mgr – Structured Notes
Mr. Richard B. Waugh Vice President & C.F.O.		Chief Financial Officer

Northwestern Mutual Life Insurance Co.

Insurance Co/Life

Location: 720 East Wisconsin Avenue
17th Floor
Milwaukee, WI 53202

Fax: 414/299-7124 **Phone:** 414/271-1444

Profile: Total return investor

Investment Portfolio: $ 36.1 billion

Use:

Balance Sheet/Risk Management
Hedge balance sheet
Hedge currency risk
Hedge interest rate risk

Investment Purposes
Alter portfolio weighting
Asset allocation
Hedge bond portfolio risk
Hedge currency risk
Hedge equity portfolio risk
Hedge interest rate risk

Currencies: US dollar, Australian dollar, Belgian franc, Canadian dollar, French franc, German mark, Italian lira, Indonesian rupiah, Japanese yen, Mexican peso, Spanish peseta, Thai baht, UK pound

Regions: United States, Canada, Europe, Latin America, Pacific Rim, Emerging mkts

DERIVATIVES ACTIVITIES: **CAC Class: 5**

Exchange-traded Options & Futures U.S. Treasury futures	**Bond**	
OTC Derivatives **Plain Vanilla Derivatives**	**Currency, Interest rate** Swaps	Forwards
Counterparty Rating Requirement:	A	

OTHER ALTERNATIVE INVESTMENTS:

CMOs/REMICs – Govt.
CMOs/REMICs – Private
Strips

KEY MANAGERS & DERIVATIVES SPECIALISTS:	**Direct Phone/Fax**	**Job Function**
Mr. Jefferson DeAngelis	414/299-5291	Portfolio Mgr – Futures Portfolio Mgr – Options
Mr. Mark Doll Sr. Vice President & Treasurer	414/299-7336	Treasurer
Mr. James Jackson	414/299-3340	Portfolio Mgr – Futures Portfolio Mgr – Options
Mr. Edward J. Zore Senior Vice President	414/299-7339	Chief Investment Officer

Norwest Bank Indiana, N.A.

Bank/Trust

Sub of Lincoln Financial Corporation

Location: 116 East Berry Street
Fort Wayne, IN 46802

Fax: 219/461-6678 **Phone:** 219/461-6000

Profile: Total return investor

Investment Portfolio: $ 1.8 billion

Use: **Investment Purposes**
Provide incremental return

Currencies: US dollar

Regions: United States

DERIVATIVES ACTIVITIES: **CAC Class: 2**

Structured Notes	Govt. agency MTNs	Multi-step-up callable bonds

OTHER ALTERNATIVE INVESTMENTS:

CMOs/REMICs – Govt.

KEY MANAGERS & DERIVATIVES SPECIALISTS:	**Direct Phone/Fax**	**Job Function**
Mr. Jerry Harms	219/461-6473	Chief Investment Officer
Mr. Ned Lee Vice President		Portfolio Mgr – Structured Notes

Norwest Bank Iowa, N.A.

Bank/Trust

Location: 666 Walnut Street
Des Moines, IA 50309

Fax: 515/245-8117 **Phone:** 515/245-3131

Profile: Current yield investor

Investment Portfolio: $ 5.0 billion

Use: **Investment Purposes**
Capture extra yield

Currencies: US dollar

Regions: United States

DERIVATIVES ACTIVITIES:

Exchange-traded Options & Futures

Structured Notes	Corporate MTNs Govt. agency MTNs Floaters	Inverse floaters Multi-step-up callable bonds

OTHER ALTERNATIVE INVESTMENTS:

CMOs/REMICs – Govt.	Strips
CMOs/REMICs – Private	Repos/reverse repos

Norwest Bank Iowa, N.A. – continued

KEY MANAGERS & DERIVATIVES SPECIALISTS:	Direct Phone/Fax	Job Function
Mr. Mark J. McGrew Senior Investment Officer	515/245-3226	Portfolio Mgr – Structured Notes
Mr. Donald S. Mears Vice President	515/245-3233	Chief Investment Officer

Norwest Investment Management (Minnesota)

Bank/Trust

Sub of Norwest Corporation

Location: Sixth & Marquette
Norwest Center 9th Floor
Minneapolis, MN 55479-2059

Fax: 612/667-0127 **Phone:** 612/667-1234

Profile: Spread investor

Investment Portfolio: $ 17.3 billion

Use: **Investment Purposes**
Adjust portfolio duration
Asset allocation
Beat conventional rates
Capture extra yield
Diversify portfolio
Enter new mkts/lower risk
Expand international Investments
Hedge bond portfolio risk
Hedge interest rate risk
Provide incremental return
Reduce variability of returns

Currencies: US dollar

Regions: United States

DERIVATIVES ACTIVITIES: **CAC Class: 6**

Exchange-traded Options & Futures U.S. Treasury options	**Bond**	
OTC Derivatives **Plain Vanilla Derivatives**	**Bond** Swaps Caps	 Floors Collars
Structured Notes	Corporate MTNs Govt. agency MTNs Bond index notes CMT notes Floaters	Inverse floaters Periodic capped floaters Tender options bonds Multi-step-up callable bonds
Counterparty Rating Requirement:	A	

OTHER ALTERNATIVE INVESTMENTS:

CMOs/REMICs – Govt.	MOPs/TOPs
CMOs/REMICs – Private	Repos/reverse repos

Norwest Investment Management (Minnesota) – continued

KEY MANAGERS & DERIVATIVES SPECIALISTS:	Direct Phone/Fax	Job Function
Mr. Stephen Gianoli Senior Vice President	612/667-5856	Portfolio Mgr – Futures Portfolio Mgr – Options Portfolio Mgr – Structured Notes

Norwest Investments & Trust Services

Bank/Trust

Location: 1740 Broadway
Denver, CO 80274-8698

Fax: 303/863-4879 **Phone:** 303/863-6800

Profile: Total return investor

Investment Portfolio: $ 4.2 billion

Use: **Investment Purposes**

Currencies: US dollar

Regions: United States

DERIVATIVES ACTIVITIES: **CAC Class: Inactive**

OTHER ALTERNATIVE INVESTMENTS:

CMOs/REMICs – Govt.

KEY MANAGERS & DERIVATIVES SPECIALISTS:	Direct Phone/Fax	Job Function
Mr. Richard Havey Vice President	303/863-4760	Bond Department Head

NYNEX Corporation

Corporation

Location: 1111 Westchester Avenue
White Plains, NY 10604

Fax: 914/644-6287 **Phone:** 914/644-7300

Use: **Balance Sheet/Risk Management**
Create synthetic fixed/floating rate
Hedge commercial paper
Hedge currency risk
Hedge interest rate risk
Protect currency gains
Reduce cost of capital

Currencies: US dollar

Regions: United States

DERIVATIVES ACTIVITIES: **CAC Class: 6**

Exchange-traded Options & Futures	**Currency, Interest rate**	
OTC Derivatives **Plain Vanilla Derivatives**	**Currency, Interest rate** Swaps Forwards	 Swaptions Caps
Structured Notes		
Counterparty Rating Requirement:	AA	

KEY MANAGERS & DERIVATIVES SPECIALISTS:	Direct Phone/Fax	Job Function
Mr. Per Stahlkrantz Assistant Treasurer		Portfolio Mgr – Derivatives

Oak Hill Partners

Investment Manager

Location: 65 East 55th Street
New York, NY 10022

Fax: 212/593-3596 **Phone:** 212/326-1500

Profile: Total return investor

Investment Portfolio: $ 1.4 billion

Use:
Balance Sheet/Risk Management
Create synthetic fixed/floating rate
Hedge balance sheet
Hedge interest rate risk

Investment Purposes
Provide incremental return

Currencies: US dollar

Regions: United States

DERIVATIVES ACTIVITIES: **CAC Class: 3**

Exchange-traded Options & Futures	**Interest rate**	
U.S. Treasury futures	U.S. Treasury options	
OTC Derivatives	**Interest rate**	
Plain Vanilla Derivatives	Swaps	Caps
	Forwards	Floors
	Swaptions	Collars
Structured Notes		
Counterparty Rating Requirement:	BBB	

OTHER ALTERNATIVE INVESTMENTS:

Repos/reverse repos

KEY MANAGERS & DERIVATIVES SPECIALISTS:	**Direct Phone/Fax**	**Job Function**
Mr. Glenn R. August Managing Director		Bond Department Head *Corp*
Mr. Scott D. Krase Vice President		Portfolio Mgr – Derivatives Portfolio Mgr – Futures Portfolio Mgr – Options Portfolio Mgr – Structured Notes

OFFITBANK

Bank/Trust

Location: 520 Madison Avenue
27th Floor
New York, NY 10022

Fax: 212/486-6957 **Phone:** 212/758-9600

Profile: Total return investor

Investment Portfolio: $ 6.1 billion

Use:
Investment Purposes
Hedge bond portfolio risk
Hedge currency risk
Hedge equity portfolio risk
Provide incremental return

Currencies: US dollar

Regions: United States

OFFITBANK – continued

DERIVATIVES ACTIVITIES:

Exchange-traded Options & Futures	**Bond, Currency**	
U.S. Treasury futures	U.S. Treasury options	
OTC Derivatives	**Bond, Currency, Interest rate**	
Plain Vanilla Derivatives	Swaps	Forwards
Structured Notes	Corporate MTNs	Bond index notes
	Govt. agency MTNs	

OTHER ALTERNATIVE INVESTMENTS:

CMOs/REMICs – Govt. | CMOs/REMICs – Private

KEY MANAGERS & DERIVATIVES SPECIALISTS:	**Direct Phone/Fax**	**Job Function**
Mr. Steven Blitz	212/350-3712 212/319-6148	Portfolio Mgr – Derivatives Portfolio Mgr – Futures
Mr. Morris W. Offit Chairman, President & C.E.O.	212/350-3800	President Chief Investment Officer

The Ohio National Life Insurance Company

Insurance Co/Life

Sub of The Ohio National Companies

Location: 237 William Howard Taft Road
Cincinnati, OH 45219

Fax: 513/559-6589 **Phone:** 513/861-3600

Profile: Total return investor

Investment Portfolio: $ 4.0 billion

Use: **Balance Sheet/Risk Management**

Currencies: US dollar

Regions: United States

DERIVATIVES ACTIVITIES: **CAC Class: Inactive**

OTHER ALTERNATIVE INVESTMENTS:

CMOs/REMICs – Govt. | Repos/reverse repos
CMOs/REMICs – Private

KEY MANAGERS & DERIVATIVES SPECIALISTS:	**Direct Phone/Fax**	**Job Function**
Mr. Michael A. Boedeker Vice President	513/559-6317	Bond Department Head *ABS, Corp, MBS*
Mr. Joseph P. Brom Senior Vice President	513/559-6214	Chief Investment Officer
Mr. David B. O'Maley Chairman, President & C.E.O.		President

Ohio Police & Firemen's Disability & Pension Fund

Government Pension Fund

Location: 230 East Town Street
Columbus, OH 43215-4650

Fax: 614/228-0451 **Phone:** 614/228-4076

Profile: Total return investor

Investment Portfolio: $ 1.0 - 3.0 billion

Use: **Investment Purposes**

Currencies: US dollar

Regions: United States

DERIVATIVES ACTIVITIES: **CAC Class: 1**

Structured Notes

OTHER ALTERNATIVE INVESTMENTS:

CMOs/REMICs – Govt. CMOs/REMICs – Private

KEY MANAGERS & DERIVATIVES SPECIALISTS:	**Direct Phone/Fax**	**Job Function**
Mr. Michael P. Downs		Portfolio Mgr – Structured Notes
Mr. Theodore G. Hall Director – Investments		Chief Investment Officer

Ohio Public Employees' Retirement System

Government Pension Fund

Location: 277 East Town Street
Fourth Floor
Columbus, OH 43215

Fax: 614/469-8276 **Phone:** 614/466-5155

Profile: Total return investor

Investment Portfolio: $ 31.4 billion

Use: **Investment Purposes**
Adjust portfolio duration
Asset allocation
Beat conventional rates
Capture extra yield
Hedge bond portfolio risk
Hedge interest rate risk
Provide incremental return

Currencies: US dollar

Regions: United States

DERIVATIVES ACTIVITIES:

Structured Notes Corporate MTNs

OTHER ALTERNATIVE INVESTMENTS:

CMOs/REMICs – Govt. Repos/reverse repos
Strips

KEY MANAGERS & DERIVATIVES SPECIALISTS:	**Direct Phone/Fax**	**Job Function**
Mr. Joel S. Buck Investment Officer	614/466-7320	Chief Investment Officer Bond Department Head
Mr. Todd C. Thompson	614/466-7320	Portfolio Mgr – Structured Notes

Old Kent Bank & Trust Company (Portfolio)

Bank/Portfolio

Sub of Old Kent Financial Corporation

Location: One Vandenberg Center
Grand Rapids, MI 49503-1438

Fax: 616/771-4317 **Phone:** 616/771-5000

Profile: Total return investor

Investment Portfolio: $ 2.9 billion

Use: **Balance Sheet/Risk Management**
Hedge balance sheet
Hedge interest rate risk

Currencies: US dollar

Regions: United States

DERIVATIVES ACTIVITIES: **CAC Class: 5**

OTC Derivatives		
Plain Vanilla Derivatives	Swaps Caps	Floors
Structured Notes	Corporate MTNs Govt. agency MTNs	Floaters
Counterparty Rating Requirement:	AAA	

OTHER ALTERNATIVE INVESTMENTS:

	CMOs/REMICs – Govt. CMOs/REMICs – Private	Repos/reverse repos

KEY MANAGERS & DERIVATIVES SPECIALISTS:	**Direct Phone/Fax**	**Job Function**
Mr. Thomas Powell Senior Vice President	616/771-1957	Chief Investment Officer
Mr. B. P. Sherwood III Vice Chairman & Treasurer	616/771-5589	Treasurer
Mr. David J. Wagner President & C.E.O.	616/771-5899	President Chief Investment Officer
Ms. Cynthia Welton Vice President	616/771-5230	Portfolio Mgr – Derivatives Portfolio Mgr – Structured Notes
Mr. Richard W. Wroten Exec. Vice President & C.F.O.	616/771-5808	Chief Financial Officer

Old Kent Bank & Trust Company (Trust)

Bank/Trust

Sub of Old Kent Financial Corporation

Location: One Vandenberg Center
Grand Rapids, MI 49506

Fax: 616/771-4640 **Phone:** 616/771-5469

Profile: Total return investor

Investment Portfolio: $ 7.0 billion

Use: **Investment Purposes**

Currencies: US dollar

Regions: United States

DERIVATIVES ACTIVITIES: **CAC Class: Inactive**

OTHER ALTERNATIVE INVESTMENTS:

CMOs/REMICs – Govt.

KEY MANAGERS & DERIVATIVES SPECIALISTS:	Direct Phone/Fax	Job Function
Mr. Joseph T. Keating Senior Vice President	616/771-5875	Chief Investment Officer
Mr. Allan J. Meyers V.P. & Director – Fixed Income	616/771-5219	Bond Department Head Fixed-Income Strategist

Old National Bank in Evansville (Portfolio)

Bank/Portfolio

Sub of Old National Bancorp

Location: 420 Main Street
Evansville, IN 47708

Fax: 812/464-1567 **Phone:** 812/464-1200

Profile: Total return investor

Investment Portfolio: $ 3.6 billion

Use: **Balance Sheet/Risk Management**

Currencies: US dollar

Regions: United States

DERIVATIVES ACTIVITIES: **CAC Class: 3**

OTC Derivatives **Plain Vanilla Derivatives**	Caps	Floors
Structured Notes	Floaters	
Counterparty Rating Requirement:	AAA	

OTHER ALTERNATIVE INVESTMENTS:

CMOs/REMICs – Govt.
CMOs/REMICs – Private
Strips

Old National Bank in Evansville (Portfolio) – continued

KEY MANAGERS & DERIVATIVES SPECIALISTS:	Direct Phone/Fax	Job Function
Mr. John Claybon	812/464-1442	Portfolio Mgr – Derivatives Portfolio Mgr – Structured Notes
Mr. Jeffrey W. Foye Assistant Vice President	812/464-1315	Chief Investment Officer

Olympic Capital Management, Inc.

Investment Manager

Sub of United Asset Management Corporation

Location: 1301 Fifth Avenue
Suite 3320
Seattle, WA 98101

Fax: 206/624-3871 **Phone:** 206/447-9399

Profile: Total return investor

Investment Portfolio: $ 1.3 billion

Use: **Investment Purposes**

Currencies: US dollar

Regions: United States

DERIVATIVES ACTIVITIES:

Structured Notes	Corporate MTNs	Floaters

OTHER ALTERNATIVE INVESTMENTS:

	CMOs/REMICs – Govt.	CMOs/REMICs – Private

KEY MANAGERS & DERIVATIVES SPECIALISTS:	Direct Phone/Fax	Job Function
Mr. John S. Crowl Principal		Chief Investment Officer
Mr. John F. Dagres Principal	206/621-9177	Portfolio Mgr – Structured Notes
Mr. Craig F. Hintze Principal		Bond Department Head *Taxable* Portfolio Mgr – Structured Notes

OnBank, Inc. (Portfolio)

Bank/Portfolio

Sub of ONBANCorp

Location: 101 South Salina Street
Syracuse, NY 13221

Fax: 315/424-5992 **Phone:** 315/424-4400

Profile: Total return investor

Investment Portfolio: $ 4.0 - 10.0 billion

Use:

Balance Sheet/Risk Management
Create synthetic fixed/floating rate
Hedge interest rate risk
Incremental return
Reduce cost of capital
Strategic liability management

Investment Purposes
Adjust portfolio duration
Capture extra yield
Hedge bond portfolio risk
Hedge interest rate risk
Provide incremental return
Reduce variability of returns

Currencies: US dollar

Regions: United States

DERIVATIVES ACTIVITIES: **CAC Class: 4**

OTC Derivatives **Plain Vanilla Derivatives**	**Interest rate** Swaps	
Structured Notes	Govt. agency MTNs Bond index notes Index amortizing notes	CMT notes Floaters Multi-step-up callable bonds
Counterparty Rating Requirement:	A	

OTHER ALTERNATIVE INVESTMENTS:

CMOs/REMICs – Govt.
CMOs/REMICs – Private
Repos/reverse repos

KEY MANAGERS & DERIVATIVES SPECIALISTS:	**Direct Phone/Fax**	**Job Function**
Mr. Michael Frenz Assistant Vice President	315/424-4566	Portfolio Mgr – Derivatives Portfolio Mgr – Structured Notes
Mr. Randy J. Wiley Vice President	315/424-4559 315/424-4439	Chief Investment Officer

One Valley Bancorp of West Virginia

Bank/Portfolio

Location: Summers & Lee Streets
One Valley Square
Charleston, WV 25301

Fax: 304/348-7315 **Phone:** 304/348-7000

Profile: Total return investor

Investment Portfolio: $ 986.4 million

Use:

Balance Sheet/Risk Management
Hedge interest rate risk
Strategic liability management

Currencies: US dollar

Regions: United States

One Valley Bancorp of West Virginia – continued

DERIVATIVES ACTIVITIES: **CAC Class: Inactive**

OTHER ALTERNATIVE INVESTMENTS:

CMOs/REMICs – Govt.

KEY MANAGERS & DERIVATIVES SPECIALISTS:	**Direct Phone/Fax**	**Job Function**
Mr. Laurance G. Jones Exec. V.P., Treasurer & C.F.O.	304/348-7062	Chief Financial Officer Treasurer
Mr. John Randall Valentine President	304/348-7258	President Chief Investment Officer

Oppenheimer Management Corporation

Mutual Fund Manager

Sub of Massachusetts Mutual Life Insurance Co.

Location: Two World Trade Center
34th Floor
New York, NY 10048

Fax: 212/323-0558 **Phone:** 212/323-0200

Profile: Total return investor

Investment Portfolio: $ 17.0 billion

Use:

Balance Sheet/Risk Management
- Access global mkts
- Create synthetic fixed/floating rate
- Hedge balance sheet
- Hedge commercial paper
- Hedge currency risk
- Hedge interest rate risk
- Hedge overseas investments
- Incremental return
- Lower transaction costs
- Protect currency gains

Investment Purposes
- Alter portfolio weighting
- Adjust portfolio duration
- Asset allocation
- Capture extra yield
- Discretionary situations
- Expand international investments
- Hedge bond portfolio risk
- Hedge currency risk
- Hedge equity portfolio risk
- Hedge interest rate risk
- Protect currency gains
- Provide incremental return

Currencies: US dollar, German mark, Italian lira, Japanese yen, Swiss franc

Regions: United States, Canada, Europe, Latin America, Pacific Rim, Emerging mkts

DERIVATIVES ACTIVITIES: **CAC Class: 6**

Exchange-traded Options & Futures	**Bond, Currency, Interest rate**	
U.S. Treasury futures	Municipal futures	
U.S. Treasury options		
OTC Derivatives	**Bond, Currency, Interest rate**	
Plain Vanilla Derivatives	Forwards	Caps
	Swaptions	Floors
Exotic Derivatives	Detached calls	
Structured Notes	Bond index notes	Inverse floaters
Counterparty Rating Requirement:	None	

Oppenheimer Management Corporation – continued

OTHER ALTERNATIVE INVESTMENTS:

	CMOs/REMICs – Govt.	GICs
	CMOs/REMICs – Private	Strips

KEY MANAGERS & DERIVATIVES SPECIALISTS:	**Direct Phone/Fax**	**Job Function**
Mr. O. Leonard Darling E.V.P./Director – Fixed Income	212/323-0680 212/323-0640	Bond Department Head Portfolio Mgr – Derivatives *Muni* Portfolio Mgr – Structured Notes
Ms. Bridget Macaskill President & C.E.O. & C.O.O.		President Chief Investment Officer
Mr. Russell Reed Vice President	212/323-0588	Portfolio Mgr – Derivatives Research Analyst – Derivatives
Mr. David A. Rosenberg Vice President	212/323-0584	Portfolio Mgr – Futures *Govt* Portfolio Mgr – Options *Govt*

Oregon State Treasury Investment Division – Fixed Income

Government

Location: 350 Winter Street Northeast
100 Labor & Industries Building
Salem, OR 97310

Fax: 503/378-6772 **Phone:** 503/378-4111

Investment Portfolio: $ 6.8 billion

Use: **Investment Purposes**

Currencies: US dollar

Regions: United States

DERIVATIVES ACTIVITIES:

OTC Derivatives
Plain Vanilla Derivatives

OTHER ALTERNATIVE INVESTMENTS:

	CMOs/REMICs – Govt.	CMOs/REMICs – Private

KEY MANAGERS & DERIVATIVES SPECIALISTS:	**Direct Phone/Fax**	**Job Function**
Mr. William S. Unverzagt Senior Investment Officer	503/378-4113	Bond Department Head *Corp, Govt, MBS*

Oryx Energy Company

Corporation

Location: 13155 Noel Road, Dallas, TX 75240-5067 | **Fax:** 214/715-3311 | **Phone:** 214/715-4000

Use: **Balance Sheet/Risk Management**
- Create synthetic fixed/floating rate
- Hedge commercial paper
- Hedge currency risk
- Hedge interest rate risk
- Lower transaction costs
- Meet interest rate target
- Meet cash flow target
- Protect currency gains
- Reduce cost of capital
- Strategic liability management

Currencies: US dollar, UK pound | **Regions:** United States

DERIVATIVES ACTIVITIES:

OTC Derivatives		
Plain Vanilla Derivatives	Swaps Forwards Swaptions	Caps Floors Collars
Exotic Derivatives	Index amortizing swaps	
Structured Notes	Corporate MTNs	Floaters
Counterparty Rating Requirement:	A	

KEY MANAGERS & DERIVATIVES SPECIALISTS:	**Direct Phone/Fax**	**Job Function**
Mr. David Chavenson Treasurer	214/715-4293	Treasurer Portfolio Mgr – Derivatives
Mr. Robert L. Keiser President & C.O.O.		President
Mr. Edward W. Moneypenny S.V.P. – Finance & C.F.O.	214/715-8950	Chief Financial Officer

Owens-Corning Fiberglass Corporation

Corporation

Location: Fiberglas Tower, Toledo, OH 43659 | **Fax:** 419/248-6227 | **Phone:** 419/248-8000

Use: **Balance Sheet/Risk Management**
- Hedge currency risk
- Hedge interest rate risk
- Hedge overseas Investments
- Protect currency gains
- Reduce cost of capital

Currencies: US dollar, Belgian franc, French franc, German mark, UK pound | **Regions:** United States

Owens-Corning Fiberglass Corporation – continued

DERIVATIVES ACTIVITIES:		CAC Class: 5
OTC Derivatives	**Currency, Interest rate**	
Plain Vanilla Derivatives	Swaps	Forwards
Counterparty Rating Requirement:	AA	

KEY MANAGERS & DERIVATIVES SPECIALISTS:	Direct Phone/Fax	Job Function
Mr. David W. Devonshire Senior Vice President & C.F.O.		Chief Financial Officer
Mr. Michael I. Miller Vice President & Treasurer		Treasurer Portfolio Mgr – Derivatives

PACCAR Incorporated

Corporation

Location: Business Center Building
777 106th Avenue N.E.
Bellevue, WA 98004

Fax: 206/453-4900 **Phone:** 206/455-7400

Profile: Total return investor

Use:

Balance Sheet/Risk Management
Incremental return
Protect currency gains

Investment Purposes
Adjust portfolio duration
Capture extra yield
Discretionary situations
Hedge interest rate risk
Lower transactions costs
Reduce variability of returns

Currencies: US dollar

Regions: United States

DERIVATIVES ACTIVITIES:		
Exchange-traded Options & Futures	**Bond**	
U.S. Treasury futures	Municipal futures	
OTC Derivatives	**Bond**	
Plain Vanilla Derivatives	Swaps	Forwards
Structured Notes	Index amortizing notes	Inverse floaters
Counterparty Rating Requirement:	AAA	

PACCAR Incorporated – continued

KEY MANAGERS & DERIVATIVES SPECIALISTS:	Direct Phone/Fax	Job Function
Mr. William E. Boisvert Exec. Vice President & C.F.O.		Chief Financial Officer
Mr. David J. Hovind President		President
Ms. Judith M. Swain Manager – Treasury Operations		Portfolio Mgr – Derivatives
Mr. John J. Wagoneer Treasurer		Chief Investment Officer Treasurer Portfolio Mgr – Derivatives

Pacholder Associates, Inc.

Investment Manager

Location: 8044 Montgomery Road
Suite 382
Cincinnati, OH 45236

Fax: 513/985-3217 **Phone:** 513/985-3200

Profile: Total return investor

Investment Portfolio: $ 1.2 billion

Use: **Investment Purposes**
Provide incremental return

Currencies: US dollar

Regions: United States

DERIVATIVES ACTIVITIES: **CAC Class: 2**

Structured Notes Corporate MTNs

OTHER ALTERNATIVE INVESTMENTS:

CMOs/REMICs – Govt.

KEY MANAGERS & DERIVATIVES SPECIALISTS:	Direct Phone/Fax	Job Function
Mr. Anthony L. Longi, Jr. Executive Vice President		Portfolio Mgr – Structured Notes
Mr. William J. Morgan President		President Bond Department Head *Corp, Govt, MBS*
Dr. Asher Pacholder Chairman	713/784-2350	Bond Department Head

Pacific Income Advisers

Investment Manager

Location: 1299 Ocean Avenue
Suite 210
Santa Monica, CA 90401

Fax: 310/393-0714 **Phone:** 310/393-1039

Profile: Total return investor

Investment Portfolio: $ 1.7 billion

Use: **Investment Purposes**

Currencies: US dollar

Regions: United States

DERIVATIVES ACTIVITIES: **CAC Class: Inactive**

OTHER ALTERNATIVE INVESTMENTS:

CMOs/REMICs – Private
Strips

Repos/reverse repos

KEY MANAGERS & DERIVATIVES SPECIALISTS:	**Direct Phone/Fax**	**Job Function**
Mr. Lloyd McAdams Chairman		Chief Investment Officer

Pacific Investment Management Co. (PIMCO)

Insurance Co/Management

Sub of Pacific Mutual Life Insurance Company

Location: 840 Newport Center Drive
Suite 360
Newport Beach, CA 92660

Fax: 714/720-1376 **Phone:** 714/640-3031

Profile: Total return investor

Investment Portfolio: $ 65.0 billion

Use:

Balance Sheet/Risk Management
- Access global mkts
- Create synthetic fixed/floating rate
- Hedge balance sheet
- Hedge commercial paper
- Hedge currency risk
- Hedge interest rate risk
- Hedge overseas investments
- Incremental return
- Strategic liability management

Investment Purposes
- Alter portfolio weighting
- Capture extra yield
- Convexity objectives
- Expand international investments
- Hedge bond portfolio risk
- Hedge currency risk
- Hedge interest rate risk
- Protect currency gains

Currencies: US dollar

Regions: United States Europe

Pacific Investment Management Co. (PIMCO) – continued

DERIVATIVES ACTIVITIES:		**CAC Class: 8**
Exchange-traded Options & Futures	**Bond, Currency, Interest rate**	
U.S. Treasury futures		
OTC Derivatives	**Bond, Currency, Interest rate**	
Plain Vanilla Derivatives	Swaps	Caps
	Forwards	Floors
	Swaptions	Collars
Exotic Derivatives	Bond index swaps	Detached calls
	CMT swaps	Periodic caps/floors
	CMT options	
Structured Notes	Corporate MTNs	CMT notes
	Govt. agency MTNs	Tender options bonds

OTHER ALTERNATIVE INVESTMENTS:		
	CMOs/REMICs – Govt.	Strips
	CMOs/REMICs – Private	Repos/reverse repos
	GICs	

KEY MANAGERS & DERIVATIVES SPECIALISTS:	**Direct Phone/Fax**	**Job Function**
Mr. Steven Bailey Executive Vice President		Chief Financial Officer
Ms. Leslie Barbi		Portfolio Mgr – Futures
Mr. John B. Brynjolfsson Vice President	714/640-3420	Fixed-Income Strategist *Taxable* Research Analyst – Derivatives
Mr. David H. Edington Managing Director	714/640-3025 714/640-3419	Portfolio Mgr – Derivatives Portfolio Mgr – Futures *Govt*
Mr. William H. Gross Managing Director	714/640-3317 714/640-3419	Chief Investment Officer Portfolio Mgr – Futures *Corp, Govt*
Mr. Frank B. Rabinowitz Managing Director	714/640-3843 714/640-3419	Portfolio Mgr – Derivatives Portfolio Mgr – Futures Trader – Derivatives
Mr. Ivor Schucking	714/640-3507	Portfolio Mgr – Derivatives Portfolio Mgr – Options Portfolio Mgr – Structured Notes
Mr. Lee Thomas, III Sr. Portfolio Manager		Bond Department Head

Pacific Mutual Life Insurance Company

Insurance Co/Life

Location: 700 Newport Center Drive
Newport Beach, CA 92660

Fax: 714/640-3199 **Phone:** 714/640-3011

Use: **Investment Purposes**

Investment Portfolio: $ 14.7 billion

Currencies: US dollar

Regions: United States

DERIVATIVES ACTIVITIES:

OTC Derivatives	**Interest rate**
Plain Vanilla Derivatives	Swaps

OTHER ALTERNATIVE INVESTMENTS:

CMOs/REMICs – Govt. CMOs/REMICs – Private

KEY MANAGERS & DERIVATIVES SPECIALISTS:	**Direct Phone/Fax**	**Job Function**
Mr. Larry J. Card Executive Vice President		Chief Investment Officer Portfolio Mgr – Derivatives
Mr. Mark Holmlund Assistant Vice President		Portfolio Mgr – Derivatives
Mr. Raymond J. Lee Senior Vice President	714/640-3199	Portfolio Mgr – Derivatives

Pacificorp

Corporation

Location: 700 N.E. Multnomah Street
Suite 1600
Portland, OR 97232-2000

Fax: 503/731-2136 **Phone:** 503/731-2000

Use: **Balance Sheet/Risk Management**
Create synthetic fixed/floating rate
Hedge currency risk
Hedge interest rate risk
Protect currency gains
Strategic liability management

Currencies: US dollar Japanese yen

Regions: United States

DERIVATIVES ACTIVITIES: **CAC Class: 3**

OTC Derivatives	**Currency, Interest rate**
Plain Vanilla Derivatives	Swaps
Counterparty Rating Requirement:	AA

KEY MANAGERS & DERIVATIVES SPECIALISTS:	**Direct Phone/Fax**	**Job Function**
Mr. Frederick W. Buckman President & C.E.O.		President
Mr. William E. Peressini Treasurer		Treasurer Portfolio Mgr – Derivatives

PanAgora Asset Management, Inc. (U.S.A.)

Investment Manager

Location: 260 Franklin Street
22nd Floor
Boston, MA 02110

Fax: 617/439-6302 **Phone:** 617/439-6300

Profile: Total return investor

Investment Portfolio: $ 13.2 billion

Use: **Investment Purposes**
Alter portfolio weighting
Adjust portfolio duration
Asset allocation
Diversify portfolio
Enter new mkts/lower risk
Expand international investments
Hedge bond portfolio risk
Hedge currency risk
Hedge equity portfolio risk
Reduce variability of returns

Currencies: US dollar, Austrian dollar, Belgian franc, Canadian dollar, French franc, German mark, Italian lira, Japanese yen, Swiss franc, UK pound

Regions: United States, Canada, Europe, Latin America, Pacific Rim

DERIVATIVES ACTIVITIES:

Exchange-traded Options & Futures	**Bond, Currency, Interest rate**	
U.S. Treasury futures	U.S. Treasury options	
OTC Derivatives	**Currency**	
Plain Vanilla Derivatives	Forwards	
Structured Notes	Corporate MTNs	Floaters
	Govt. agency MTNs	Periodic capped floaters

OTHER ALTERNATIVE INVESTMENTS:

CMOs/REMICs – Govt.	Repos/reverse repos
Strips	

KEY MANAGERS & DERIVATIVES SPECIALISTS:	**Direct Phone/Fax**	**Job Function**
Mr. Bruce Clarke President		President
Ms. Kristine Lino Manager – Global Investments		Portfolio Mgr – Derivatives Portfolio Mgr – Options
Mr. Roland Lochoff Senior Mgr-U.S. Fixed Income		Portfolio Mgr – Futures Portfolio Mgr – Structured Notes
Mr. Edgar E. Peters Chief Investment Strategist		Fixed-Income Strategist Research Analyst – Derivatives
Mr. Paul R. Samuelson Chief Investment Officer		Chief Investment Officer

The Patterson Capital Corporation

Investment Manager

Location: 2029 Century Park East
Suite 2950
Los Angeles, CA 90067

Fax: 310/553-3605 **Phone:** 310/556-2496

Profile: **Total return investor**

Investment Portfolio: $ 2.5 billion

Use: **Investment Purposes**
Alter portfolio weighting
Adjust portfolio duration
Asset allocation
Capture extra yield
Diversify portfolio
Provide incremental return
Reduce variability of returns

Currencies: US dollar

Regions: United States

DERIVATIVES ACTIVITIES: **CAC Class: 4**

Structured Notes	Corporate MTNs

OTHER ALTERNATIVE INVESTMENTS:

	CMOs/REMICs – Govt.	Repos/reverse repos

KEY MANAGERS & DERIVATIVES SPECIALISTS:	**Direct Phone/Fax**	**Job Function**
Mr. Brian Allen		Portfolio Mgr – Structured Notes
Mr. Joseph B. Patterson President		President Chief Investment Officer
Mr. David Sacherman		Portfolio Mgr – Structured Notes

Paul Revere Investment Management Corp.

Corporate Pension Fund

Location: 18 Chestnut Street
Worcester, MA 01608

Fax: 508/751-7240 **Phone:** 508/799-4441

Profile: Total return investor

Investment Portfolio: $ 4.4 billion

Use: **Balance Sheet/Risk Management**
Hedge interest rate risk

Currencies: US dollar

Regions: United States

DERIVATIVES ACTIVITIES: **CAC Class: 2**

OTC Derivatives **Plain Vanilla Derivatives**	**Interest rate** Swaps	
Structured Notes	Corporate MTNs	Govt. agency MTNs
Counterparty Rating Requirement:	A	

OTHER ALTERNATIVE INVESTMENTS:

	CMOs/REMICs – Govt.	CMOs/REMICs – Private

Paul Revere Investment Management Corp. – continued

KEY MANAGERS & DERIVATIVES SPECIALISTS:	Direct Phone/Fax	Job Function
Mr. Lee Herdle Vice President – Investments	508/751-7224	Bond Department Head
Mr. John D. Lemery President	508/751-7220	President Chief Investment Officer

Payden & Rygel Investment Counsel

Investment Manager

Location: 333 South Grand Avenue
32nd Floor
Los Angeles, CA 90071

Fax: 213/628-8488 **Phone:** 213/625-1900

Profile: Total return investor

Investment Portfolio: $ 16.5 billion

Use: **Balance Sheet/Risk Management**
Hedge interest rate risk

Currencies: US dollar, Australian dollar, Canadian dollar, German mark, UK pound

Regions: United States

DERIVATIVES ACTIVITIES: **CAC Class: 6**

Exchange-traded Options & Futures	**Bond, Currency, Interest rate**
Structured Notes	

OTHER ALTERNATIVE INVESTMENTS:

CMOs/REMICs – Govt.	Strips
CMOs/REMICs – Private	Repos/reverse repos

KEY MANAGERS & DERIVATIVES SPECIALISTS:	Direct Phone/Fax	Job Function
Ms. Lynda L. Faber Senior Vice President		Portfolio Mgr – Futures Portfolio Mgr – Options Portfolio Mgr – Structured Notes
Mr. John P. Isaacson Executive Vice President		Portfolio Mgr – Derivatives
Mr. Scott A. King Executive Vice President		Fixed-Income Strategist Portfolio Mgr – Futures Portfolio Mgr – Options
Mr. Brian W. Matthews Vice President		Portfolio Mgr – Futures Portfolio Mgr – Options
Mr. Christopher Orndorff Vice President		Portfolio Mgr – Futures Portfolio Mgr – Options
Ms. Joan A. Payden President		President Chief Investment Officer

Pekin Insurance Company

Insurance Co/P & C

Location: 2505 Court Street
Pekin, IL 61558-0001

Fax: 309/346-8512 **Phone:** 309/346-1161

Profile: Stable asset investor

Investment Portfolio: $ 500.0 - 999.0 million

Use: **Investment Purposes**

Currencies: US dollar

Regions: United States

DERIVATIVES ACTIVITIES: **CAC Class: Inactive**

Counterparty Rating Requirement: A

OTHER ALTERNATIVE INVESTMENTS:

CMOs/REMICs – Govt. CMOs/REMICs – Private

KEY MANAGERS & DERIVATIVES SPECIALISTS:	**Direct Phone/Fax**	**Job Function**
Mr. William Tunis S.V.P.-Treasurer-Secretary		Chief Investment Officer Treasurer

Pennsylvania Public School Employees' Retirement System

Government Pension Fund

Location: 5 North Fifth Street
Harrisburg, PA 17101

Fax: 717/783-9424 **Phone:** 717/783-5613

Profile: Total return investor

Investment Portfolio:$ 7.0 billion

Use: **Investment Purposes**
Capture extra yield
Hedge currency risk

Currencies: US dollar

Regions: United States, Canada, Europe, Latin America, Pacific Rim

DERIVATIVES ACTIVITIES: **CAC Class: 5**

Exchange-traded Options & Futures — **Bond, Interest rate**
U.S. Treasury futures

Counterparty Rating Requirement: A

OTHER ALTERNATIVE INVESTMENTS:

CMOs/REMICs – Govt.

KEY MANAGERS & DERIVATIVES SPECIALISTS:	**Direct Phone/Fax**	**Job Function**
Mr. John Lane Chief Financial Officer		Chief Investment Officer Chief Financial Officer
Mr. Jerry Peters	717/720-4715	Portfolio Mgr – Futures Portfolio Mgr – Options

Pension Boards – United Church of Christ

Union Pension Fund

Location: 475 Riverside Drive
Room 1020
New York, NY 10115

Fax: 212/870-2877 **Phone:** 212/870-2777

Profile: Total return investor

Investment Portfolio: $ 1.3 billion

Use: **Investment Purposes**

Currencies: US dollar

Regions: United States

DERIVATIVES ACTIVITIES: **CAC Class: Inactive**

OTHER ALTERNATIVE INVESTMENTS:

CMOs/REMICs – Govt. CMOs/REMICs – Private

KEY MANAGERS & DERIVATIVES SPECIALISTS:	**Direct Phone/Fax**	**Job Function**
Mr. Raymond Healy Senior Investment Advisor		Chief Investment Officer

People's Bank

Bank Holding Company

Location: 850 Main Street
Bridgeport, CT 06604

Fax: 203/338-2502 **Phone:** 203/338-7171

Use: **Balance Sheet/Risk Management**
Create synthetic fixed/floating rate
Hedge interest rate risk
Incremental return
Meet interest rate target

Currencies: US dollar

Regions: United States

DERIVATIVES ACTIVITIES: **CAC Class: 6**

Exchange-traded Options & Futures	**Interest rate**	
OTC Derivatives	**Interest rate**	
Plain Vanilla Derivatives	Swaps	Forwards
Counterparty Rating Requirement:	AA	

OTHER ALTERNATIVE INVESTMENTS:

Repos/reverse repos

KEY MANAGERS & DERIVATIVES SPECIALISTS:	**Direct Phone/Fax**	**Job Function**
Ms. Dorothea E. Brennan First Vice President		Portfolio Mgr – Derivatives
Mr. David E. Carson President & C.E.O.		President

People's Bank – continued

KEY MANAGERS & DERIVATIVES SPECIALISTS:	Direct Phone/Fax	Job Function
Mr. Dennis J. Colwell First Vice President		Treasurer
Mr. George W. Morriss Exec. Vice President & C.F.O.		Chief Financial Officer

People's Bank (Investment)

Savings Bank/Bldg Society

Sub of People's Bank

Location: 850 Main Street
Bridgeport, CT 06604

Fax: 203/338-4927 **Phone:** 203/338-7210

Profile: Hold to maturity investor

Investment Portfolio: $ 6.2 billion

Use: **Balance Sheet/Risk Management**
Hedge balance sheet
Hedge interest rate risk

Currencies: US dollar

Regions: United States

DERIVATIVES ACTIVITIES: **CAC Class: 6**

Exchange-traded Options & Futures

OTC Derivatives	**Interest rate**	
Plain Vanilla Derivatives	Swaps Forwards Caps	Floors Collars
Exotic Derivatives	Index amortizing swaps	
Counterparty Rating Requirement:	A	

OTHER ALTERNATIVE INVESTMENTS:

	CMOs/REMICs – Govt. CMOs/REMICs – Private	Repos/reverse repos

KEY MANAGERS & DERIVATIVES SPECIALISTS:	Direct Phone/Fax	Job Function
Ms. Debbie Assetta V.P.-Interest Rate Risk Mgmt.	203/338-4937	Portfolio Mgr – Derivatives Portfolio Mgr – Futures Portfolio Mgr – Options
Mr. Raymond P. Granville Senior Vice President	203/338-7443	Chief Investment Officer

Peregrine Capital Management

Investment Manager

Sub of Norwest Corporation

Location: 800 LaSalle Avenue
Suite 1850
Minneapolis, MN 55402-2018

Fax: 612/343-7636 **Phone:** 612/343-7600

Profile: Total return investor

Investment Portfolio: $ 3.2 billion

Use: **Investment Purposes**

Currencies: US dollar

Regions: United States

DERIVATIVES ACTIVITIES: **CAC Class: 2**

OTC Derivatives
Plain Vanilla Derivatives

Structured Notes

OTHER ALTERNATIVE INVESTMENTS:

CMOs/REMICs – Govt. CMOs/REMICs – Private

KEY MANAGERS & DERIVATIVES SPECIALISTS:	**Direct Phone/Fax**	**Job Function**
Ms. Patricia Burns Senior Vice President	612/343-7606	Portfolio Mgr – Derivatives Portfolio Mgr – Structured Notes
Mr. William D. Giese Senior Vice President	612/343-7607	Bond Department Head
Mr. Robert B. Mersky President	612/343-7602	President Chief Investment Officer

Phoenix Duff & Phelps Investment Management Co. (Chicago)

Investment Manager

Sub of Phoenix Duff & Phelps Investment Management Co. (Hartford)

Location: 55 East Monroe Street
Suite 3800
Chicago, IL 60603

Fax: 312/368-5512 **Phone:** 312/368-5500

Profile: Total return investor

Investment Portfolio: $ 16.4 billion

Use: **Investment Purposes**

Currencies: US dollar

Regions: United States

DERIVATIVES ACTIVITIES: **CAC Class: Inactive**

OTHER ALTERNATIVE INVESTMENTS:

CMOs/REMICs – Govt.

Phoenix Duff & Phelps Investment Management Co. (Chicago) – continued

KEY MANAGERS & DERIVATIVES SPECIALISTS:	Direct Phone/Fax	Job Function
Mr. Robert J. Moore Senior Vice President		Bond Department Head
Mr. Wayne C. Stevens President	312/368-5540	President Chief Investment Officer Fixed-Income Strategist

Phoenix Duff & Phelps Investment Management Co. (Hartford)

Insurance Co/Life

Location: One American Row
Hartford, CT 06115

Fax: 203/275-5509 **Phone:** 203/275-5000

Profile: Total return investor

Investment Portfolio: $ 24.4 billion

Use: **Investment Purposes**

Currencies: US dollar

Regions: United States

DERIVATIVES ACTIVITIES: **CAC Class: Inactive**

OTHER ALTERNATIVE INVESTMENTS:

CMOs/REMICs – Govt.
CMOs/REMICs – Private
GICs

KEY MANAGERS & DERIVATIVES SPECIALISTS:	Direct Phone/Fax	Job Function
Mr. Robert W. Fiondella Chairman, President & C.E.O.		President
Mr. Michael Haylon Senior Vice President	203/275-5835	Bond Department Head
Mr. Philip R. McLoughlin Executive Vice President	203/275-5365 203/275-5543	Chief Investment Officer
Mr. William Newman Chief Investment Strategist	203/275-5969	Fixed-Income Strategist

Physicians Mutual Insurance Company

Insurance Co/Life

Location: 2600 Dodge Street
Omaha, NE 68131

Fax: 402/633-1096 **Phone:** 402/633-1000

Profile: Current yield investor

Investment Portfolio: $ 1.0 - 3.0 billion

Use: **Balance Sheet/Risk Management**
Hedge interest rate risk
Strategic liability management

Currencies: US dollar

Regions: United States

Physicians Mutual Insurance Company – continued

DERIVATIVES ACTIVITIES:		**CAC Class: 2**
OTC Derivatives	**Interest rate**	
Plain Vanilla Derivatives	Swaps	Caps
Counterparty Rating Requirement:	A	

OTHER ALTERNATIVE INVESTMENTS:

CMOs/REMICs – Govt.

KEY MANAGERS & DERIVATIVES SPECIALISTS:	**Direct Phone/Fax**	**Job Function**
Mr. Jerome J. Coon S.V.P. – Assistant Treasurer	402/633-1197	Chief Investment Officer Portfolio Mgr – Derivatives

Pillar Point Capital Management Inc.

Insurance Co/Management

Sub of California Casualty

Location: 2000 Alameda de las Pulgas
Suite 154
San Mateo, CA 94403

Fax: 415/573-0672 **Phone:** 415/377-3900

Profile: Total return investor

Investment Portfolio: $ 689.1 million

Use: **Investment Purposes**

Currencies: US dollar

Regions: United States

DERIVATIVES ACTIVITIES:		**CAC Class: Inactive**
Counterparty Rating Requirement:	None	

OTHER ALTERNATIVE INVESTMENTS:

CMOs/REMICs – Govt.

KEY MANAGERS & DERIVATIVES SPECIALISTS:	**Direct Phone/Fax**	**Job Function**
Mr. Stuart Waters President & C.E.O.		President Chief Investment Officer

Pioneer Financial Services, Inc.

Insurance Co/Management

Location: 1750 East Golf Road
Schaumburg, IL 60173

Fax: 708/413-7192 **Phone:** 708/995-0400

Profile: Total return investor

Investment Portfolio: $ 724.0 million

Use: **Balance Sheet/Risk Management**
Hedge currency risk
Strategic liability management

Currencies: US dollar

Regions: United States

DERIVATIVES ACTIVITIES:

Exchange-traded Options & Futures	Bond
U.S. Treasury futures	

OTHER ALTERNATIVE INVESTMENTS:

	CMOs/REMICs – Govt.	CMOs/REMICs – Private

KEY MANAGERS & DERIVATIVES SPECIALISTS:	Direct Phone/Fax	Job Function
Mr. Thomas J. Brophy President – Health Division		President
Mr. Philip J. Fiskow Senior Vice President & C.I.O.		Chief Investment Officer Portfolio Mgr – Options *Govt*
Mr. Charles R. Scheper President – Life Division		President
Mr. David I. Vickers V.P., Treasurer & C.F.O.		Chief Financial Officer Treasurer Portfolio Mgr – Options

Pioneering Management Corporation

Investment Manager

Sub of The Pioneer Group, Inc.

Location: 60 State Street
18th Floor
Boston, MA 02109-1820

Fax: 617/422-4281 **Phone:** 617/742-7825

Profile: Total return investor

Investment Portfolio: $ 11.0 billion

Use: **Investment Purposes**

Currencies: US dollar

Regions: United States

Pioneering Management Corporation – continued

DERIVATIVES ACTIVITIES:		CAC Class: 2
Structured Notes	Corporate MTNs Floaters	Multi-step-up callable bonds

OTHER ALTERNATIVE INVESTMENTS:		
	CMOs/REMICs – Private	Strips

KEY MANAGERS & DERIVATIVES SPECIALISTS:	Direct Phone/Fax	Job Function
Mr. Salvatore Pramas V.P. – Global Fixed Income	617/422-4812	Bond Department Head
Mr. Sherman B. Russ Vice President	617/422-4830	Portfolio Mgr – Structured Notes
Mr. Richard A. Schlanger Vice President	617/422-4835	Portfolio Mgr – Structured Notes
Mr. David D. Tripple President	617/742-8810	President Chief Investment Officer

Piper Capital Management Inc.

Mutual Fund Manager

Sub of Piper Jaffray Companies

Location: 222 South Ninth Street
20th Floor
Minneapolis, MN 55402

Fax: 612/342-6992 **Phone:** 612/342-5800

Profile: Total return investor

Investment Portfolio: $ 10.4 billion

Use: **Balance Sheet/Risk Management**
Hedge balance sheet
Hedge interest rate risk

Investment Purposes
Capture extra yield
Hedge interest rate risk
Provide incremental return

Currencies: US dollar

Regions: United States

DERIVATIVES ACTIVITIES:		CAC Class: 3
OTC Derivatives **Plain Vanilla Derivatives**	**Interest rate** Caps	
Structured Notes	Floaters	Inverse floaters
Counterparty Rating Requirement:	A	

OTHER ALTERNATIVE INVESTMENTS:		
	CMOs/REMICs – Govt. CMOs/REMICs – Private	Strips Repos/reverse repos

Piper Capital Management Inc. – continued

KEY MANAGERS & DERIVATIVES SPECIALISTS:	**Direct Phone/Fax**	**Job Function**
Mr. Paul Dow	612/342-6379	Chief Investment Officer
Mr. Bruce D. Salvog Director	612/342-1155	Bond Department Head Portfolio Mgr – Derivatives Portfolio Mgr – Structured Notes

Plaza Investment Managers, Inc.

Insurance Co/Management

Sub of GEICO Corporation

Location: One GEICO Plaza
Washington, DC 20076

Fax: 301/718-5362 **Phone:** 301/718-5358

Profile: Total return investor

Investment Portfolio: $ 4.7 billion

Use: **Investment Purposes**

Currencies: US dollar

Regions: United States

DERIVATIVES ACTIVITIES: **CAC Class: Inactive**

OTHER ALTERNATIVE INVESTMENTS:

CMOs/REMICs – Govt.
CMOs/REMICs – Private
Strips
Repos/reverse repos

KEY MANAGERS & DERIVATIVES SPECIALISTS:	**Direct Phone/Fax**	**Job Function**
Mr. Douglas E. Fedynak Managing Director & Treasurer		Treasurer Bond Department Head

PNC Bank – Asset Liability (Portfolio)

Bank/Portfolio

Sub of PNC Bank Corporation

Location: Fifth Avenue & Wood Street
One PNC Plaza
Pittsburgh, PA 15265

Fax: 412/762-4167 **Phone:** 412/762-2000

Profile: Current yield investor

Investment Portfolio: $ 43.7 billion

Use: **Balance Sheet/Risk Management**
Hedge balance sheet
Hedge interest rate risk

Investment Purposes
Provide incremental return

Currencies: US dollar

Regions: United States

PNC Bank – Asset Liability (Portfolio) – continued

DERIVATIVES ACTIVITIES:		**CAC Class: 8**
Exchange-traded Options & Futures U.S. Treasury futures	**Interest rate**	
OTC Derivatives **Plain Vanilla Derivatives**	**Interest rate** Swaps Caps	 Floors Collars
Exotic Derivatives	Index amortizing swaps	
Structured Notes	Govt. agency MTNs	Floaters

OTHER ALTERNATIVE INVESTMENTS:

	CMOs/REMICs – Govt. CMOs/REMICs – Private	Repos/reverse repos

KEY MANAGERS & DERIVATIVES SPECIALISTS:	**Direct Phone/Fax**	**Job Function**
Mr. Randall C. King S.V.P. & Treasurer	412/762-8235	Bond Department Head *Govt, MBS* Portfolio Mgr – Structured Notes
Mr. Mark R. Mershon Vice President	412/762-8402	Portfolio Mgr – Derivatives

PNC Bank Ohio (Trust)

Bank/Trust

Sub of PNC Bank Corporation

Location: 201 East Fifth Street
3rd Floor
Cincinnati, OH 45202

Fax: 513/651-7156 **Phone:** 513/651-8896

Profile: Total return investor

Investment Portfolio: $ 3.6 billion

Use: **Investment Purposes**
Provide incremental return

Currencies: US dollar

Regions: United States

DERIVATIVES ACTIVITIES:		**CAC Class: 2**
Exchange-traded Options & Futures		
Structured Notes	Floaters	

OTHER ALTERNATIVE INVESTMENTS:

	CMOs/REMICs – Govt. CMOs/REMICs – Private	Strips Repos/reverse repos

PNC Bank Ohio (Trust) – continued

KEY MANAGERS & DERIVATIVES SPECIALISTS:	Direct Phone/Fax	Job Function
Mr. Edward Arbaugh	513/651-8405	Chief Investment Officer
Ms. Karen Bowie V.P. & Sr. Investment Officer	513/651-7159	Portfolio Mgr – Options Portfolio Mgr – Structured Notes
Ms. Jacqueline R. Moore	513/651-8484	Trader – Futures Trader – Options Trader – Structured Investments

PNC Institutional Management Corp.

Mutual Fund Manager

Sub of PNC Bank Corporation

Location: 400 Bellevue Parkway
Wilmington, DE 19809

Fax: 302/791-2467 **Phone:** 302/791-1700

Profile: Total return investor

Investment Portfolio: $ 31.0 billion

Use: **Investment Purposes**
Alter portfolio weighting
Adjust portfolio duration
Asset allocation
Capture extra yield
Diversify portfolio
Provide incremental return

Currencies: US dollar

Regions: United States

DERIVATIVES ACTIVITIES: **CAC Class: 2**

Structured Notes	Corporate MTNs Govt. agency MTNs Index amortizing notes	CMT notes Floaters Multi-step-up callable bonds

OTHER ALTERNATIVE INVESTMENTS:

CMOs/REMICs – Govt. CMOs/REMICs – Private	GICs Repos/reverse repos

KEY MANAGERS & DERIVATIVES SPECIALISTS:	Direct Phone/Fax	Job Function
Mr. Patrick Ford Group Manager – Taxable F/I	302/791-1730 302/791-1898	Portfolio Mgr – Structured Notes
Mr. Richard Hoerner		Portfolio Mgr – Structured Notes
Mr. Thomas Nevin President	302/791-1728	President Chief Investment Officer

Ponder Investment Company

Investment Manager

Location: 1600 Airport Freeway
Suite 400
Bedford, TX 76022

Fax: 817/354-1437 **Phone:** 817/354-8282

Investment Portfolio: $ 1.0 billion

Use: **Investment Purposes**
Asset allocation
Provide incremental return

Currencies: US dollar

Regions: United States

DERIVATIVES ACTIVITIES: **CAC Class: Inactive**

OTHER ALTERNATIVE INVESTMENTS:

CMOs/REMICs – Govt.
CMOs/REMICs – Private
Repos/reverse repos

KEY MANAGERS & DERIVATIVES SPECIALISTS:	**Direct Phone/Fax**	**Job Function**
Mr. C. Lee Ponder President		President Chief Investment Officer

The Portfolio Group, Inc.

Bank/Management Division

Sub of Chemical Banking Corporation

Location: 600 Fifth Avenue
Fourth Floor
New York, NY 10020

Fax: 212/332-4296 **Phone:** 212/332-4200

Profile: Total return investor

Investment Portfolio: $ 11.0 billion

Use: **Investment Purposes**
Asset allocation
Capture extra yield

Currencies: US dollar

Regions: United States

DERIVATIVES ACTIVITIES: **CAC Class: Inactive**

OTHER ALTERNATIVE INVESTMENTS:

CMOs/REMICs – Govt.
CMOs/REMICs – Private
Repos/reverse repos

KEY MANAGERS & DERIVATIVES SPECIALISTS:	**Direct Phone/Fax**	**Job Function**
Mr. Henry E. Gooss		Chief Investment Officer

PPM America Inc.

Investment Manager

Sub of Prudential Corporation p.l.c.

Location: 225 West Wacker Drive
Suite 1200
Chicago, IL 60606-1228

Fax: 312/634-0050 **Phone:** 312/634-2500

Profile: Spread investor

Investment Portfolio: $ 21.0 billion

Use: **Balance Sheet/Risk Management**
Create synthetic fixed/floating rate
Hedge balance sheet
Hedge interest rate risk
Strategic liability management

Investment Purposes
Alter portfolio weighting
Asset allocation
Capture extra yield
Hedge interest rate risk

Currencies: US dollar

Regions: United States

DERIVATIVES ACTIVITIES:

Exchange-traded Options & Futures		
OTC Derivatives		
Plain Vanilla Derivatives	Swaps	Swaptions
Exotic Derivatives	Bond index swaps	CMT swaps
Structured Notes	Corporate MTNs Govt. agency MTNs Bond index notes	CMT notes Floaters
Counterparty Rating Requirement:	BBB	

OTHER ALTERNATIVE INVESTMENTS:

CMOs/REMICs – Govt.	Strips
CMOs/REMICs – Private	Repos/reverse repos

KEY MANAGERS & DERIVATIVES SPECIALISTS:	**Direct Phone/Fax**	**Job Function**
Mr. Mark Alter Vice President	312/201-0279	Portfolio Mgr – Derivatives
Mr. Russell Swansen President		President Chief Investment Officer

Premier Investment Advisors

Bank/Management Division

Location: 451 Florida Street
North Tower 20th Floor
Baton Rouge, LA 70801

Fax: 504/332-7350 **Phone:** 504/332-4011

Profile: Total return investor

Investment Portfolio: $ 1.5 billion

Use: **Investment Purposes**

Currencies: US dollar

Regions: United States

Premier Investment Advisors – continued

DERIVATIVES ACTIVITIES: **CAC Class: Inactive**

OTHER ALTERNATIVE INVESTMENTS:

CMOs/REMICs – Govt.
Repos/reverse repos

KEY MANAGERS & DERIVATIVES SPECIALISTS:	Direct Phone/Fax	Job Function
Mr. Donald E. Allred President & C.E.O.	504/332-4336	President Chief Investment Officer

Presidential Life Insurance Company

Insurance Co/Life

Location: 69 Lydecker Street
Nyack, NY 10960

Fax: 914/358-2818 **Phone:** 914/358-2300

Profile: Hold to maturity investor

Investment Portfolio: $ 2.1 billion

Use: **Investment Purposes**

Currencies: US dollar

Regions: United States

DERIVATIVES ACTIVITIES:

Structured Notes

Corporate MTNs
Govt. agency MTNs
Bond index notes
Floaters
Periodic capped floaters

OTHER ALTERNATIVE INVESTMENTS:

CMOs/REMICs – Govt.
CMOs/REMICs – Private
Repos/reverse repos

KEY MANAGERS & DERIVATIVES SPECIALISTS:	Direct Phone/Fax	Job Function
Ms. Shirley P. Jordan Executive Vice President	Ext. 220	Chief Investment Officer Portfolio Mgr – Structured Notes

T. Rowe Price Associates, Inc.

Mutual Fund Manager

Location: 100 East Pratt Street
Baltimore, MD 21202-1008

Fax: 410/659-0965 **Phone:** 410/547-2000

Profile: Total return investor

Investment Portfolio: $ 54.0 billion

Use: **Investment Purposes**
Adjust portfolio duration
Capture extra yield
Provide incremental return
Reduce variability of returns

Currencies: US dollar

Regions: United States

T. Rowe Price Associates, Inc. – continued

DERIVATIVES ACTIVITIES:

Exchange-traded Options & Futures		
U.S. Treasury futures	Municipal futures	
OTC Derivatives	**Currency**	
Plain Vanilla Derivatives	Swaps	Forwards
Exotic Derivatives		
Structured Notes	Corporate MTNs Govt. agency MTNs Bond index notes	CMT notes Inverse floaters
Counterparty Rating Requirement:	AA	

OTHER ALTERNATIVE INVESTMENTS:

CMOs/REMICs – Govt.	GICs
CMOs/REMICs – Private	Strips

KEY MANAGERS & DERIVATIVES SPECIALISTS:	Direct Phone/Fax	Job Function
Mr. George J. Collins President & C.E.O.	410/547-2118	President Chief Investment Officer Bond Department Head
Mr. William T. Reynolds Mng. Director-Municipal Bonds	410/547-5703	Bond Department Head *Muni* Portfolio Mgr – Derivatives Portfolio Mgr – Futures Portfolio Mgr – Structured Notes
Mr. Alvin M. Younger, Jr. Managing Director & Treasurer		Treasurer

PriMerit Bank, A Federal Savings Bank

Savings Bank/Bldg Society

Location: 3300 West Sahara Avenue
Las Vegas, NV 89102

Fax: 702/365-3477 **Phone:** 702/362-5555

Profile: Hold to maturity investor

Investment Portfolio: $ 1.8 billion

Use: **Balance Sheet/Risk Management**
Hedge balance sheet
Hedge interest rate risk
Strategic liability management

Currencies: US dollar

Regions: United States

PriMerit Bank, A Federal Savings Bank – continued

DERIVATIVES ACTIVITIES: **CAC Class: 2**

OTC Derivatives	**Interest rate**
Plain Vanilla Derivatives	Swaps
Counterparty Rating Requirement:	BBB

OTHER ALTERNATIVE INVESTMENTS:

CMOs/REMICs – Govt.	Repos/reverse repos
CMOs/REMICs – Private	

KEY MANAGERS & DERIVATIVES SPECIALISTS:	Direct Phone/Fax	Job Function
Mr. Dan Cheever President	702/365-3480	President
Mr. Michael T. Kabat Assistant Vice President	702/365-3458	Chief Investment Officer Portfolio Mgr – Derivatives

Princeton Insurance Companies

Insurance Co/P & C

Location: 746 Alexander Road
Princeton, NJ 08540-5322

Fax: 609/734-8461 **Phone:** 609/452-9404

Profile: Total return investor

Investment Portfolio: $ 770.0 million

Use: **Investment Purposes**

Currencies: US dollar

Regions: United States

DERIVATIVES ACTIVITIES: **CAC Class: Inactive**

OTHER ALTERNATIVE INVESTMENTS:

CMOs/REMICs – Govt. CMOs/REMICs – Private

KEY MANAGERS & DERIVATIVES SPECIALISTS:	Direct Phone/Fax	Job Function
Mr. Arthur Aaronson Vice President		Chief Investment Officer Bond Department Head

Principal Mutual Life Insurance Company

Insurance Co/Life

Sub of The Principal Financial Group

Location: 711 High Street
Des Moines, IA 50392-0001

Fax: 515/248-8486 **Phone:** 515/247-5111

Profile: Hold to maturity investor

Investment Portfolio: $ 45.0 billion

Use: **Balance Sheet/Risk Management**
Hedge balance sheet
Hedge currency risk
Hedge interest rate risk
Strategic liability management

Currencies: US dollar

Regions: United States

DERIVATIVES ACTIVITIES: **CAC Class: 6**

Exchange-traded Options & Futures U.S. Treasury futures	**Bond, Currency**	
OTC Derivatives **Plain Vanilla Derivatives**	Swaps Forwards Caps	Floors Collars
Structured Notes	Corporate MTNs	Govt. agency MTNs
Counterparty Rating Requirement:	None	

OTHER ALTERNATIVE INVESTMENTS:

	CMOs/REMICs – Govt. CMOs/REMICs – Private	GICs

KEY MANAGERS & DERIVATIVES SPECIALISTS:	**Direct Phone/Fax**	**Job Function**
Mr. Donald D. Brattebo Second Vice President	515/247-6042	Portfolio Mgr – Futures *Corp, Govt*
Mr. Ronald E. Keller	515/247-5192	Chief Investment Officer Portfolio Mgr – Derivatives Portfolio Mgr – Structured Notes
Mr. Jay Windsor	515/248-9621	Portfolio Mgr – Derivatives

The Private Bank of Bank of Boston

Bank/Management Division

Sub of Bank of Boston Corporation

Location: 100 Federal Street
10th Floor
Boston, MA 02110

Fax: 617/434-6311 **Phone:** 617/434-2920

Profile: Total return investor

Investment Portfolio: $ 13.0 billion

Use: **Investment Purposes**

Currencies: US dollar

Regions: United States

DERIVATIVES ACTIVITIES: **CAC Class: Inactive**

OTHER ALTERNATIVE INVESTMENTS:

CMOs/REMICs – Govt.
CMOs/REMICs – Private
Repos/reverse repos

KEY MANAGERS & DERIVATIVES SPECIALISTS:	Direct Phone/Fax	Job Function
Ms. Susan A. Sanderson Senior Fund Manager	617/434-6637	Fixed-Income Strategist
Mr. David H. Thompson Director – Fixed Income Funds	617/434-2559	Chief Investment Officer

Protective Life Corporation

Insurance Co/Life

Location: 2801 Highway 280 South
Birmingham, AL 35223-2488

Fax: 205/868-3609 **Phone:** 205/879-9230

Profile: Hold to maturity investor

Investment Portfolio: $ 4.4 billion

Use: **Balance Sheet/Risk Management**
Create synthetic fixed/floating rate
Hedge interest rate risk
Reduce cost of capital
Strategic liability management

Currencies: US dollar

Regions: United States

Protective Life Corporation – continued

DERIVATIVES ACTIVITIES:		CAC Class: 3
Exchange-traded Options & Futures	**Bond**	
U.S. Treasury futures	U.S. Treasury options	
OTC Derivatives	**Interest rate**	
Plain Vanilla Derivatives	Swaps	Caps
	Swaptions	Floors
Structured Notes	Corporate MTNs	Inverse floaters
	Govt. agency MTNs	Periodic capped floaters
	Floaters	
Counterparty Rating Requirement:	A	

OTHER ALTERNATIVE INVESTMENTS:		
	CMOs/REMICs – Govt.	Repos/reverse repos
	CMOs/REMICs – Private	

KEY MANAGERS & DERIVATIVES SPECIALISTS:	Direct Phone/Fax	Job Function
Mr. Carl S. Thigpen Second V.P. – Investments	205/868-3620	Portfolio Mgr – Derivatives Portfolio Mgr – Futures Portfolio Mgr – Structured Notes
Mr. A. Steve Williams III Sr. Vice President-Investments	205/868-3600	Chief Investment Officer

The Provident Bank (Portfolio)

Bank/Portfolio

Sub of Provident Bancorp, Inc.

Location: One East Fourth Street
Cincinnati, OH 45202

Fax: 513/579-2233 **Phone:** 513/579-2075

Profile: Spread investor

Investment Portfolio: $ 645.0 million

Use: **Balance Sheet/Risk Management**
Create synthetic fixed/floating rate
Hedge balance sheet
Hedge interest rate risk
Strategic liability management

Investment Purposes
Provide incremental return

Currencies: US dollar

Regions: United States

The Provident Bank (Portfolio) – continued

DERIVATIVES ACTIVITIES:		**CAC Class: 6**
Exchange-traded Options & Futures U.S. Treasury futures		
OTC Derivatives **Plain Vanilla Derivatives**	**Interest rate** Swaps Caps	 Floors Collars
Structured Notes	Floaters	
Counterparty Rating Requirement:	BBB	

OTHER ALTERNATIVE INVESTMENTS:		
	CMOs/REMICs – Govt. CMOs/REMICs – Private	Repos/reverse repos

KEY MANAGERS & DERIVATIVES SPECIALISTS:	**Direct Phone/Fax**	**Job Function**
Mr. Robert W. Neu, Jr. Vice President	513/579-2075	Chief Investment Officer Portfolio Mgr – Derivatives Portfolio Mgr – Futures Portfolio Mgr – Structured Notes

Provident Life & Accident Insurance Co.

Insurance Co/P & C

Location: One Fountain Square
Chattanooga, TN 37402-1330

Fax: 615/755-1671 **Phone:** 615/755-1011

Profile: Total return investor

Investment Portfolio: $ 15.0 billion

Use:

Balance Sheet/Risk Management
Create synthetic fixed/floating rate
Hedge balance sheet
Hedge interest rate risk
Incremental return

Investment Purposes
Adjust portfolio duration
Capture extra yield
Enter new mkts/lower risk
Hedge bond portfolio risk
Hedge interest rate risk
Provide incremental return
Reduce variability of returns

Currencies: US dollar

Regions: United States

DERIVATIVES ACTIVITIES:	
OTC Derivatives **Plain Vanilla Derivatives**	**Bond, Currency, Interest rate** Swaps
Exotic Derivatives	Index amortizing swaps
Structured Notes	Corporate MTNs

OTHER ALTERNATIVE INVESTMENTS:		
	CMOs/REMICs – Govt. CMOs/REMICs – Private	Strips Repos/reverse repos

Provident Life & Accident Insurance Co. – continued

KEY MANAGERS & DERIVATIVES SPECIALISTS:	Direct Phone/Fax	Job Function
Mr. J. Harold Chandler President & C.E.O.		President
Mr. David Fussell Vice President – Securities	615/755-1916	Bond Department Head *Corp, Govt*
Mr. Kevin Lund	615/755-8931	Portfolio Mgr – Derivatives
Mr. James Ramsay V.P. – M.B.S. & Derivatives	615/755-8341	Bond Department Head *MBS* Portfolio Mgr – Derivatives Portfolio Mgr – Structured Notes
Mr. Thomas Watjen Chief Financial Officer		Chief Investment Officer Chief Financial Officer

Provident Mutual Life Insurance Company

Insurance Co/Life

Location: 1600 Market Street
Philadelphia, PA 19103

Fax: 215/636-8322 **Phone:** 215/636-5000

Profile: Total return investor

Investment Portfolio: $ 5.0 billion

Use: **Balance Sheet/Risk Management**
Hedge interest rate risk

Investment Purposes
Hedge bond portfolio risk
Hedge interest rate risk

Currencies: US dollar

Regions: United States

DERIVATIVES ACTIVITIES:	**CAC Class: 2**
Exchange-traded Options & Futures U.S. Treasury futures	**Interest rate**
OTC Derivatives **Plain Vanilla Derivatives**	**Interest rate** Swaps Govt. agency MTNs
Counterparty Rating Requirement:	AA

OTHER ALTERNATIVE INVESTMENTS:

CMOs/REMICs – Govt. CMOs/REMICs – Private

KEY MANAGERS & DERIVATIVES SPECIALISTS:	Direct Phone/Fax	Job Function
Ms. Rosanne Gatta A.V.P. & Treasurer	215/636-5212	Treasurer
Mr. Timothy P. Henry Assistant Vice President	215/636-8147	Portfolio Mgr – Derivatives Portfolio Mgr – Futures
Mr. James Kestner V.P.-Securities Research	215/636-5291 215/636-5036	Portfolio Mgr – Derivatives Portfolio Mgr – Futures

Provident Mutual Life Insurance Company – continued

KEY MANAGERS & DERIVATIVES SPECIALISTS:	Direct Phone/Fax	Job Function
Ms. Sara C. Lange V.P. – Portfolio Management	215/636-5326	Portfolio Mgr – Derivatives Portfolio Mgr – Futures
Mr. Stanley R. Reber Executive Vice President	215/636-5215	Chief Investment Officer
Ms. Dina M. Welch Assistant Vice President	215/636-5597	Portfolio Mgr – Derivatives Portfolio Mgr – Futures

Providian Corporation

Insurance Co/P & C

Location: 400 West Market Street
Louisville, KY 40202-3302

Fax: 502/560-3080 **Phone:** 502/560-2000

Profile: Current yield investor

Investment Portfolio: $ 16.7 billion

Use: **Balance Sheet/Risk Management**
Hedge balance sheet
Hedge interest rate risk

Currencies: US dollar

Regions: United States

DERIVATIVES ACTIVITIES: **CAC Class: 6**

Exchange-traded Options & Futures U.S. Treasury futures	**Bond, Interest rate** Municipal futures	
OTC Derivatives **Plain Vanilla Derivatives**	**Bond, Interest rate** Swaps Swaptions	 Caps
Exotic Derivatives	Bond index swaps	CMT swaps
Counterparty Rating Requirement:	A	

OTHER ALTERNATIVE INVESTMENTS:

CMOs/REMICs – Govt. CMOs/REMICs – Private

KEY MANAGERS & DERIVATIVES SPECIALISTS:	Direct Phone/Fax	Job Function
Mr. William S. Cook Director	502/560-3015	Bond Department Head
Mr. Eric B. Goodman Director	502/560-2960	Portfolio Mgr – Derivatives Portfolio Mgr – Futures
Mr. Frederick C. Kessell Chief Investment Officer	502/560-2393	Chief Investment Officer
Mr. Mark Lamb Director	502/560-3202	Portfolio Mgr – Derivatives Portfolio Mgr – Futures

Prudential Capital Management

Mutual Fund Manager

Location: 100 Mulberry St.
Two Gateway Center 7th Floor
Newark, NJ 07102-5096

Fax: 201/802-8845 **Phone:** 201/802-8476

Profile: Total return investor

Investment Portfolio: $ 74.0 billion

Use:

Balance Sheet/Risk Management
Access global mkts
Create synthetic fixed/floating rate
Hedge balance sheet
Hedge commercial paper
Hedge currency risk
Hedge interest rate risk
Hedge overseas investments
Protect currency gains

Investment Purposes
Alter portfolio weighting
Adjust portfolio duration
Asset allocation
Hedge bond portfolio risk
Hedge currency risk
Hedge equity portfolio risk
Hedge interest rate risk
Protect currency gains
Reduce variability of returns

Currencies: US dollar, UK pound

Regions: United States, Canada, Europe, Pacific Rim, Emerging mkts

DERIVATIVES ACTIVITIES: **CAC Class: 6**

Exchange-traded Options & Futures	**Bond, Currency, Interest rate**	
U.S. Treasury futures	U.S. Treasury options	
OTC Derivatives	**Bond, Currency, Interest rate**	
Plain Vanilla Derivatives	Swaps	Caps
	Forwards	Floors
	Swaptions	Collars
Exotic Derivatives	Bond index swaps	Detached calls
Structured Notes	Corporate MTNs	CMT notes
	Govt. agency MTNs	Floaters
	Bond index notes	Inverse floaters
Counterparty Rating Requirement:	BBB	

OTHER ALTERNATIVE INVESTMENTS:

CMOs/REMICs – Govt.	Strips
CMOs/REMICs – Private	Repos/reverse repos
GICs	

KEY MANAGERS & DERIVATIVES SPECIALISTS:	**Direct Phone/Fax**	**Job Function**
Mr. Peter J. Allegrini Managing Director		Bond Department Head *Muni*
Mr. Dennis Bushe Managing Director	201/802-9116	Fixed-Income Strategist
Mr. Garnett Keith	201/802-8126	Chief Investment Officer Portfolio Mgr – Derivatives
Mr. Steven Kellner Vice President	201/802-4762 201/802-7021	Portfolio Mgr – Futures *Corp, Govt*
Mr. Gary F. Neubeck Managing Director	201/802-6279 201/802-9272	Portfolio Mgr – Derivatives

Prudential Capital Management – continued

KEY MANAGERS & DERIVATIVES SPECIALISTS:	Direct Phone/Fax	Job Function
Mr. Julian M. Rappa	201/802-6497 201/467-4806	Fixed-Income Strategist

Public Employees Retirement Association of Colorado

Government Pension Fund

Location: 1300 Logan Street
5th Floor
Denver, CO 80203

Fax: 303/863-3753 **Phone:** 303/832-9550

Profile: Total return investor

Investment Portfolio: $ 12.2 billion

Use: **Balance Sheet/Risk Management**

Currencies: US dollar

Regions: United States

DERIVATIVES ACTIVITIES: **CAC Class: 6**

Exchange-traded Options & Futures

Structured Notes Floaters

OTHER ALTERNATIVE INVESTMENTS:

CMOs/REMICs – Govt.

KEY MANAGERS & DERIVATIVES SPECIALISTS:	Direct Phone/Fax	Job Function
Mr. Norman G. Benedict Deputy Executive Director	Ext. 564	Chief Investment Officer
Mr. Brant DeMuth		Research Analyst – Derivatives
Mr. Kenneth Mokray Director	Ext. 572 303/831-8521	Bond Department Head *Corp, Govt, MBS, Muni*
Ms. Jennifer Paquette	Ext. 568	Research Analyst – Derivatives

Public Service Enterprise Group Incorporated

Corporation

Location: 80 Park Plaza
Newark, NJ 07101-1171

Fax: 201/430-5845 **Phone:** 201/430-7000

Use: **Balance Sheet/Risk Management**
Create synthetic fixed/floating rate
Hedge balance sheet
Hedge currency risk
Hedge interest rate risk
Incremental return
Protect currency gains
Strategic liability management

Currencies: US dollar, UK pound

Regions: United States, Europe

Public Service Enterprise Group Incorporated – continued

DERIVATIVES ACTIVITIES:		CAC Class: 3
Exchange-traded Options & Futures	**Currency**	
OTC Derivatives	**Interest rate**	
Plain Vanilla Derivatives	Swaps	Forwards

KEY MANAGERS & DERIVATIVES SPECIALISTS:	Direct Phone/Fax	Job Function
Mr. E. James Ferland Chairman, President & C.E.O.		President
Mr. Robert C. Murray Vice President & C.F.O.		Chief Financial Officer
Mr. Francis J. Riepl Treasurer		Treasurer Portfolio Mgr – Derivatives

The Putnam Management Company Inc.

Mutual Fund Manager

Sub of Marsh & McLennan Companies, Inc.

Location: One Post Office Square
9th Floor
Boston, MA 02109

Fax: 617/292-1713 **Phone:** 617/292-1000

Profile: Stable asset investor

Investment Portfolio: $ 65.0 billion

Use:

Balance Sheet/Risk Management
Hedge balance sheet
Hedge currency risk
Hedge interest rate risk
Protect currency gains

Investment Purposes
Capture extra yield
Hedge currency risk
Hedge interest rate risk

Currencies: US dollar, Canadian dollar, French franc, German mark, Italian lira, Japanese yen, Swiss franc, UK pound

Regions: United States, Canada, Europe, Pacific Rim

DERIVATIVES ACTIVITIES:		
Exchange-traded Options & Futures		
OTC Derivatives		
Plain Vanilla Derivatives	Swaps Forwards	Swaptions
Structured Notes	Corporate MTNs Govt. agency MTNs	Floaters Inverse floaters

OTHER ALTERNATIVE INVESTMENTS:		
	CMOs/REMICs – Govt. CMOs/REMICs – Private	Strips Repos/reverse repos

The Putnam Management Company Inc. – continued

KEY MANAGERS & DERIVATIVES SPECIALISTS:	Direct Phone/Fax	Job Function
Mr. Alan J. Bankart Managing Director	617/292-1497 617/423-9589	Chief Investment Officer
Mr. Gary N. Coburn Senior Managing Director	617/292-1789	Bond Department Head
Mr. Edward H. D'Alelio Managing Director	617/292-1339	Chief Investment Officer
Mr. James E. Erickson Managing Director	617/292-1338	Bond Department Head *Muni*
Mr. David J. Eurkus Senior Vice President	617/292-1345	Fixed-Income Strategist
Mr. Jonathan Francis		Fixed-Income Strategist
Mr. Timothy Moran Managing Director & Treasurer	617/292-1776	Treasurer Portfolio Mgr – Derivatives Portfolio Mgr – Futures Portfolio Mgr – Options
Mr. Michael A. Mullaney Managing Director	617/292-1266 617/423-9589	Fixed-Income Strategist
Mr. Steven Spiegel Senior Managing Director		Fixed-Income Strategist
Ms. Hilary Till	617/292-1633	Portfolio Mgr – Futures

The Quaker Oats Company

Corporation

Location: Quaker Tower
321 North Clark Street
Chicago, IL 60610-4714

Fax: 312/222-8323 **Phone:** 312/222-7111

Use: **Balance Sheet/Risk Management**
Hedge currency risk
Hedge overseas investments
Strategic liability management

Currencies: US dollar, Canadian dollar, French franc, Italian lira, UK pound

Regions: United States

DERIVATIVES ACTIVITIES: **CAC Class: 4**

Exchange-traded Options & Futures

OTC Derivatives **Plain Vanilla Derivatives**	**Currency** Swaps Forwards	 Caps Floors
Counterparty Rating Requirement:	AA	

The Quaker Oats Company – continued

KEY MANAGERS & DERIVATIVES SPECIALISTS:	Direct Phone/Fax	Job Function
Ms. Janet K. Cooper Vice President & Treasurer		Treasurer Portfolio Mgr – Derivatives
Mr. Robert Thomason Vice President & C.F.O.		Chief Financial Officer

Qualivest Capital Management, Inc.

Bank/Management Division

Sub of U.S. Bancorp

Location: 111 Southwest Fifth Avenue
Suite 1500
Portland, OR 97204-1818

Fax: 503/274-0405 **Phone:** 503/275-6806

Profile: Total return investor

Investment Portfolio: $ 6.5 billion

Use: **Investment Purposes**

Currencies: US dollar

Regions: United States

DERIVATIVES ACTIVITIES: **CAC Class: Inactive**

OTHER ALTERNATIVE INVESTMENTS:

CMOs/REMICs – Govt. CMOs/REMICs – Private

KEY MANAGERS & DERIVATIVES SPECIALISTS:	Direct Phone/Fax	Job Function
Mr. Timothy Leach		Chief Investment Officer

Quantilogic Asset Management

Investment Manager

Location: 44 Montgomery Street
Suite 1950
San Francisco, CA 94104-4610

Fax: 415/434-1139 **Phone:** 415/434-1130

Profile: Total return investor

Investment Portfolio: $ 1.6 billion

Use: **Balance Sheet/Risk Management**
Hedge interest rate risk

Investment Purposes
Asset allocation
Hedge bond portfolio risk
Provide incremental return

Currencies: US dollar

Regions: United States

Quantilogic Asset Management – continued

DERIVATIVES ACTIVITIES: **CAC Class: 5**

Exchange-traded Options & Futures	**Bond**
U.S. Treasury futures	U.S. Treasury options

OTHER ALTERNATIVE INVESTMENTS:

CMOs/REMICs – Govt.	GICs
CMOs/REMICs – Private	

KEY MANAGERS & DERIVATIVES SPECIALISTS:	**Direct Phone/Fax**	**Job Function**
Mr. A. Darrell Braswell Managing Director		Chief Investment Officer Portfolio Mgr – Futures *Govt*
Mr. Michael J. Januzik Vice President		Portfolio Mgr – Futures *Govt*
Ms. Helen Potter		Portfolio Mgr – Futures
Mr. Jeffrey L. Winter Managing Director		Portfolio Mgr – Futures *Govt*

Raytheon Company

Corporation

Location: 141 Spring Street
Lexington, MA 02173

Fax: 617/860-2172 **Phone:** 617/862-6600

Use: **Balance Sheet/Risk Management**
Hedge currency risk
Lower transaction costs

Currencies: US dollar, Canadian dollar, French franc, German mark, Japanese yen, Spanish peseta, Thai baht, UK pound

Regions: United States, Canada, Europe, Pacific Rim

DERIVATIVES ACTIVITIES:

Exchange-traded Options & Futures	**Currency, Interest rate**	
OTC Derivatives **Plain Vanilla Derivatives**	Swaps	Forwards
Counterparty Rating Requirement:	None	

KEY MANAGERS & DERIVATIVES SPECIALISTS:	**Direct Phone/Fax**	**Job Function**
Mr. Max E. Bleck President		President
Mr. Herbert Deitcher S.V.P. & Treasurer		Treasurer Portfolio Mgr – Derivatives
Mr. Sheldon Rutstein Senior Vice President & C.F.O.		Chief Financial Officer

RCM Capital Management

Investment Manager

Sub of Travelers Group

Location: Four Embarcadero Center
Suite 2900
San Francisco, CA 94111-4189

Fax: 415/954-8200 **Phone:** 415/954-5400

Profile: Total return investor

Investment Portfolio: $ 26.7 billion

Use: **Balance Sheet/Risk Management**
Hedge currency risk

Currencies: US dollar, French franc, German mark, Italian lira, Japanese yen, Spanish peseta, UK pound

Regions: United States

DERIVATIVES ACTIVITIES: **CAC Class: 2**

Exchange-traded Options & Futures	**Currency**	
OTC Derivatives	**Currency**	
Plain Vanilla Derivatives	Swaps	Forwards
Counterparty Rating Requirement:	AA	

OTHER ALTERNATIVE INVESTMENTS:

CMOs/REMICs – Govt. CMOs/REMICs – Private

KEY MANAGERS & DERIVATIVES SPECIALISTS:	**Direct Phone/Fax**	**Job Function**
Mr. Eamonn F. Dolan Principal	415/954-5389	Fixed-Income Strategist
Mr. Stephen Kim Principal		Fixed-Income Strategist
Mr. Mark E. Raaberg Senior Portfolio Strategist	415/954-5419	Portfolio Mgr – Derivatives Portfolio Mgr – Futures
Mr. Gary W. Schreyer Principal	415/954-5304	Chief Investment Officer

Reams Asset Management Company Inc.

Investment Manager

Location: 227 Washington Street
Columbus, IN 47202

Fax: 812/376-3137 **Phone:** 812/372-6606

Use: **Investment Purposes**
Beat conventional rates
Convexity objectives
Provide incremental return

Investment Portfolio: $ 2.0 billion

Currencies: US dollar

Regions: United States

Reams Asset Management Company Inc. – continued

DERIVATIVES ACTIVITIES: **CAC Class: 3**

Structured Notes	Corporate MTNs Govt. agency MTNs	Inverse floaters
Counterparty Rating Requirement:	None	

OTHER ALTERNATIVE INVESTMENTS:

	CMOs/REMICs – Govt.	CMOs/REMICs – Private

KEY MANAGERS & DERIVATIVES SPECIALISTS:	Direct Phone/Fax	Job Function
Mr. Robert A. Crider Senior Vice President		Bond Department Head *Taxable* Portfolio Mgr – Structured Notes
Mr. Frederick W. Reams President		President Chief Investment Officer

Regents of the University of California

Foundation/Endowment

Location: 300 Lakeside Drive
17th Floor
Oakland, CA 94612-3550

Fax: 510/987-9617 **Phone:** 510/987-9600

Profile: Total return investor

Investment Portfolio: $ 16.9 billion

Use: **Investment Purposes**
Hedge currency risk
Hedge interest rate risk
Provide incremental return

Currencies: US dollar

Regions: United States

DERIVATIVES ACTIVITIES:

Exchange-traded Options & Futures	**Currency, Interest rate**
OTC Derivatives **Plain Vanilla Derivatives**	**Currency, Interest rate**

OTHER ALTERNATIVE INVESTMENTS:

	CMOs/REMICs – Govt.	CMOs/REMICs – Private

KEY MANAGERS & DERIVATIVES SPECIALISTS:	Direct Phone/Fax	Job Function
Mr. Herbert M. Gordon Treasurer	510/987-9620	Chief Investment Officer Treasurer Portfolio Mgr – Derivatives Portfolio Mgr – Futures Portfolio Mgr – Options

Regions Financial Corporation (Investments)

Bank/Portfolio

Location: 417 North 20th Street
9th Floor
Birmingham, AL 35203

Fax: 205/326-7775 **Phone:** 205/326-7100

Profile: Total return investor

Investment Portfolio: $ 3.6 billion

Use: **Investment Purposes**

Currencies: US dollar

Regions: United States

DERIVATIVES ACTIVITIES: **CAC Class: Inactive**

OTHER ALTERNATIVE INVESTMENTS:

CMOs/REMICs – Govt.
Repos/reverse repos

KEY MANAGERS & DERIVATIVES SPECIALISTS:	Direct Phone/Fax	Job Function
Ms. Ruth Nail	205/326-7016	Bond Department Head

Reich & Tang L.P.

Mutual Fund Manager

Sub of New England Investment Companies, L.P.

Location: 600 Fifth Avenue
8th Floor
New York, NY 10020

Fax: 212/830-5350 **Phone:** 212/830-5200

Profile: Total return investor

Investment Portfolio: $ 9.2 billion

Use: **Investment Purposes**

Currencies: US dollar

Regions: United States

DERIVATIVES ACTIVITIES: **CAC Class: Inactive**

OTHER ALTERNATIVE INVESTMENTS:

CMOs/REMICs – Govt.
CMOs/REMICs – Private
Strips

KEY MANAGERS & DERIVATIVES SPECIALISTS:	Direct Phone/Fax	Job Function
Mr. Oscar Tang President		President Chief Investment Officer

Reliance Insurance Company

Insurance Co/P & C

Sub of Reliance Group Holdings, Inc.

Location: 55 East 52nd Street
29th Floor
New York, NY 10055

Fax: 212/909-1844 **Phone:** 212/909-1100

Profile: Total return investor

Investment Portfolio: $ 3.9 billion

Use: **Investment Purposes**

Currencies: US dollar, UK pound, Mexican peso

Regions: United States, Europe

DERIVATIVES ACTIVITIES: **CAC Class: Inactive**

OTHER ALTERNATIVE INVESTMENTS:

CMOs/REMICs – Govt.
CMOs/REMICs – Private
Strips
Repos/reverse repos

KEY MANAGERS & DERIVATIVES SPECIALISTS:	**Direct Phone/Fax**	**Job Function**
Mr. Jerome H. Carr Sr. Vice President & C.F.O.		Chief Financial Officer
Mr. John H. Pankratz Vice President & Director	212/909-1320	Bond Department Head *Muni*
Mr. James E. Yacobucci S.V.P. – Investments	212/909-1850 212/909-1864	Chief Investment Officer

Renaissance Investment Management Inc.

Investment Manager

Location: 1700 Young Street
Cincinnati, OH 45210

Fax: 513/723-4512 **Phone:** 513/723-4500

Profile: Total return investor

Investment Portfolio: $ 1.3 billion

Use: **Investment Purposes**
Alter portfolio weighting
Capture extra yield
Hedge bond portfolio risk
Hedge equity portfolio risk

Currencies: US dollar

Regions: United States

DERIVATIVES ACTIVITIES: **CAC Class: 2**

Exchange-traded Options & Futures **Bond**
U.S. Treasury futures

OTHER ALTERNATIVE INVESTMENTS:

CMOs/REMICs – Govt.
CMOs/REMICs – Private

Renaissance Investment Management Inc. – continued

KEY MANAGERS & DERIVATIVES SPECIALISTS:	Direct Phone/Fax	Job Function
Mr. Mark A. Anderson Vice President		Portfolio Mgr – Futures Portfolio Mgr – Options
Mr. Frank W. Terrizzi Managing Director		Chief Investment Officer

Republic National Bank of NY (Treasury)

Bank/Portfolio

Sub of Republic New York Corporation

Location: 452 Fifth Avenue
Treasury Department 10th Floor
New York, NY 10018-2778

Fax: 212/525-6200 **Phone:** 212/221-6000

Profile: Total return investor

Investment Portfolio: $ 11.0 - 20.0 billion

Use: **Balance Sheet/Risk Management**
Access global mkts
Hedge balance sheet
Hedge interest rate risk

Currencies: US dollar, Australian dollar, Belgian franc, Canadian dollar, ECU, French franc, German mark, Italian lira, Indonesian rupiah, Japanese yen, Mexican peso, Spanish peseta, Swiss franc, Thai baht, UK pound

Regions: United States, Canada, Europe, Latin America

DERIVATIVES ACTIVITIES: **CAC Class: 3**

Exchange-traded Options & Futures	**Bond, Currency**	
U.S. Treasury futures	Municipal futures	
U.S. Treasury options	Municipal options	
OTC Derivatives	**Bond, Currency**	
Plain Vanilla Derivatives	Swaps	Floors
	Forwards	

OTHER ALTERNATIVE INVESTMENTS:

	CMOs/REMICs – Govt.	Strips
	CMOs/REMICs – Private	Repos/reverse repos

KEY MANAGERS & DERIVATIVES SPECIALISTS:	Direct Phone/Fax	Job Function
Mr. Ralph Attie First Vice President	212/525-6151	Bond Department Head
Mr. Mark Cahill First Vice President	212/525-8000	Portfolio Mgr – Derivatives Portfolio Mgr – Futures Portfolio Mgr – Options

Richmond Capital Management, Inc.

Investment Manager

Location: 10800 Midlothian Turnpike
Suite 217
Richmond, VA 23235

Fax: 804/379-9362 **Phone:** 804/379-8280

Profile: Total return investor

Investment Portfolio: $ 1.7 billion

Use: **Investment Purposes**
Asset allocation
Provide incremental return

Currencies: US dollar

Regions: United States

DERIVATIVES ACTIVITIES: **CAC Class: Inactive**

OTHER ALTERNATIVE INVESTMENTS:

CMOs/REMICs – Govt.
CMOs/REMICs – Private
Strips

KEY MANAGERS & DERIVATIVES SPECIALISTS:	Direct Phone/Fax	Job Function
Mr. Charles E. Keller President	804/379-8285	President Chief Investment Officer

Riggs Investment Management Corporation

Bank/Management Division

Sub of The Riggs National Corporation

Location: 808 17th Street N.W.
Washington, DC 20006

Fax: 202/835-6806 **Phone:** 202/835-6000

Profile: Total return investor

Investment Portfolio: $ 1.0 - 3.0 billion

Use: **Investment Purposes**

Currencies: US dollar

Regions: United States

DERIVATIVES ACTIVITIES: **CAC Class: Inactive**

OTHER ALTERNATIVE INVESTMENTS:

CMOs/REMICs – Govt.
Repos/reverse repos

KEY MANAGERS & DERIVATIVES SPECIALISTS:	Direct Phone/Fax	Job Function
Mr. William Wivel V.P. & Trust Officer	202/835-6879	Chief Investment Officer

Rite Aid Corporation

Corporation

Location: 30 Hunter Lane
Camp Hill, PA 17011-2404

Fax: 717/975-5905 **Phone:** 717/761-2633

Use: **Balance Sheet/Risk Management**
Hedge interest rate risk

Currencies: US dollar

Regions: United States

DERIVATIVES ACTIVITIES: **CAC Class: Inactive**

OTC Derivatives	**Interest rate**
Plain Vanilla Derivatives	Swaps

KEY MANAGERS & DERIVATIVES SPECIALISTS:	**Direct Phone/Fax**	**Job Function**
Mr. Frank M. Bergonzi S.V.P. – Finance		Chief Financial Officer
Mr. Thomas R. Coogan Vice President & Treasurer		Treasurer
Mr. Martin L. Grass President & C.O.O.		President

Rittenhouse Financial Services Inc.

Investment Manager

Location: 100 Matsonford Road
Two Radnor Corporate Center Suite 400
Radnor, PA 19087-4514

Fax: 610/293-2444 **Phone:** 610/971-9300

Profile: Total return investor

Investment Portfolio: $ 4.3 billion

Use: **Investment Purposes**
Asset allocation

Currencies: US dollar

Regions: United States

DERIVATIVES ACTIVITIES: **CAC Class: Inactive**

OTHER ALTERNATIVE INVESTMENTS:

CMOs/REMICs – Govt.

KEY MANAGERS & DERIVATIVES SPECIALISTS:	**Direct Phone/Fax**	**Job Function**
Mr. George W. Connell President		President
Mr. Leonard H. McCandless Vice President		Chief Investment Officer

The Rochester Community Savings Bank

Savings Bank/Bldg Society

Location: 228 East Main Street
Suite 300
Rochester, NY 14609

Fax: 716/423-7365 **Phone:** 716/258-3000

Profile: Spread investor

Investment Portfolio: $ 4.0 billion

Use: **Balance Sheet/Risk Management**
Hedge interest rate risk

Currencies: US dollar

Regions: United States

DERIVATIVES ACTIVITIES: **CAC Class: 5**

Exchange-traded Options & Futures	**Interest rate**
U.S. Treasury futures	U.S. Treasury options
OTC Derivatives	**Interest rate**
Plain Vanilla Derivatives	Swaps
Counterparty Rating Requirement:	A

OTHER ALTERNATIVE INVESTMENTS:

CMOs/REMICs – Govt.
CMOs/REMICs – Private
Repos/reverse repos

KEY MANAGERS & DERIVATIVES SPECIALISTS:	**Direct Phone/Fax**	**Job Function**
Mr. Robert Mahany	716/238-8862	Chief Investment Officer
Treasurer	716/423-7210	Treasurer
		Portfolio Mgr – Derivatives
		Portfolio Mgr – Futures
		Portfolio Mgr – Options

Rodney Square Management Corporation

Bank/Management Division

Sub of Wilmington Trust Company (Fixed Income)

Location: 1100 North Market Street
10th Floor
Wilmington, DE 19890-0001

Fax: 302/651-1507 **Phone:** 302/651-8280

Profile: Total return investor

Investment Portfolio: $ 1.7 billion

Use: **Investment Purposes**
Asset allocation
Diversify portfolio

Currencies: US dollar

Regions: United States

DERIVATIVES ACTIVITIES: **CAC Class: Inactive**

OTHER ALTERNATIVE INVESTMENTS:

CMOs/REMICs – Govt.
CMOs/REMICs – Private
Repos/reverse repos

Rodney Square Management Corporation – continued

KEY MANAGERS & DERIVATIVES SPECIALISTS:	Direct Phone/Fax	Job Function
Mr. Martin L. Klopping President	302/651-1923	President Chief Investment Officer Fixed-Income Strategist

Roosevelt Bank, A Federal Savings Bank

Savings Bank/Bldg Society

Sub of Roosevelt Financial Group, Inc.

Location: 900 Roosevelt Parkway
Chesterfield, MO 63017-2064

Fax: 314/532-6358 **Phone:** 314/532-6200

Profile: Hold to maturity investor

Investment Portfolio: $ 5.0 billion

Use: **Balance Sheet/Risk Management**
Hedge interest rate risk

Currencies: US dollar

Regions: United States

DERIVATIVES ACTIVITIES:

Exchange-traded Options & Futures	**Interest rate**	
OTC Derivatives	**Interest rate**	
Plain Vanilla Derivatives	Swaps Caps	Floors
Counterparty Rating Requirement:	AAA	

OTHER ALTERNATIVE INVESTMENTS:

CMOs/REMICs – Govt.	Strips
CMOs/REMICs – Private	Repos/reverse repos

KEY MANAGERS & DERIVATIVES SPECIALISTS:	Direct Phone/Fax	Job Function
Mr. Matthew G. Herries Vice President		Portfolio Mgr – Derivatives Portfolio Mgr – Futures
Mr. John Mason		Chief Investment Officer

Royal Caribbean Cruises Ltd.

Corporation

Location: 1050 Caribbean Way
Miami, FL 33132

Fax: 305/539-0562 **Phone:** 305/539-6000

Use: **Balance Sheet/Risk Management**
Hedge interest rate risk

Currencies: US dollar

Regions: United States

Royal Caribbean Cruises Ltd. – continued

DERIVATIVES ACTIVITIES:		**CAC Class: 5**
OTC Derivatives	**Interest rate**	
Plain Vanilla Derivatives	Swaps	
Counterparty Rating Requirement:	AA	

KEY MANAGERS & DERIVATIVES SPECIALISTS:	Direct Phone/Fax	Job Function
Mr. Kenneth D. Dubbin Vice President & Treasurer		Treasurer Portfolio Mgr – Derivatives
Mr. Richard J. Glasier S.V.P. & C.F.O.		Chief Financial Officer
Mr. Edwin W. Stephan President		President

The Rushmore Funds, Inc.

Mutual Fund Manager

Location: 4922 Fairmont Avenue
Bethesda, MD 20814

Fax: 301/657-1511 **Phone:** 301/657-1500

Profile: Total return investor

Investment Portfolio: $ 1.0 - 3.0 billion

Use: **Investment Purposes**
Asset allocation
Diversify portfolio

Currencies: US dollar

Regions: United States

DERIVATIVES ACTIVITIES:	**CAC Class: Inactive**

OTHER ALTERNATIVE INVESTMENTS:		
	CMOs/REMICs – Govt.	CMOs/REMICs – Private

KEY MANAGERS & DERIVATIVES SPECIALISTS:	Direct Phone/Fax	Job Function
Mr. Richard J. Garvey Director		Chief Investment Officer Bond Department Head

Frank Russell Investment Management Co.

Investment Manager

Sub of Frank Russell Company

Location: 909 A Street
Tacoma, WA 98401

Fax: 206/596-3120 **Phone:** 206/627-7001

Profile: Total return investor

Investment Portfolio: $ 3.8 billion

Use: **Investment Purposes**
Alter portfolio weighting
Capture extra yield
Hedge interest rate risk

Currencies: US dollar

Regions: United States

DERIVATIVES ACTIVITIES:

Exchange-traded Options & Futures

Structured Notes

Corporate MTNs	Floaters
Govt. agency MTNs	Multi-step-up callable bonds

OTHER ALTERNATIVE INVESTMENTS:

CMOs/REMICs – Govt.	Strips
CMOs/REMICs – Private	Repos/reverse repos

KEY MANAGERS & DERIVATIVES SPECIALISTS:	**Direct Phone/Fax**	**Job Function**
Mr. Peter F. Apanovitch		Portfolio Mgr – Structured Notes *Corp, Govt*
Mr. Randall Lert		Chief Investment Officer

RXR Capital Management, Inc.

Investment Manager

Sub of RXR Group

Location: 695 East Main Street
Suite 102
Stamford, CT 06901

Fax: 203/325-5999 **Phone:** 203/323-5015

Profile: Stable asset investor

Investment Portfolio: $ 1.1 billion

Use:

Balance Sheet/Risk Management
Hedge balance sheet
Hedge currency risk
Hedge interest rate risk
Hedge overseas investments

Investment Purposes
Hedge bond portfolio risk
Hedge currency risk
Hedge equity portfolio risk
Hedge interest rate risk

Currencies: US dollar, Australian dollar, German mark, Japanese yen

Regions: United States, Europe, Pacific Rim

RXR Capital Management, Inc. – continued

DERIVATIVES ACTIVITIES: **CAC Class: 6**

Exchange-traded Options & Futures U.S. Treasury futures	**Bond, Currency, Interest rate** U.S. Treasury options
OTC Derivatives **Plain Vanilla Derivatives**	**Bond, Currency, Interest rate** Forwards
Counterparty Rating Requirement:	AAA

OTHER ALTERNATIVE INVESTMENTS:

CMOs/REMICs – Govt.	GICs
CMOs/REMICs – Private	Strips

KEY MANAGERS & DERIVATIVES SPECIALISTS:	Direct Phone/Fax	Job Function
Mr. Mark Rosenberg President		President Chief Investment Officer Portfolio Mgr – Derivatives
Mr. Thomas K. Sullivan		Trader – Futures *Govt*

Ryan Labs, Inc.

Investment Manager

Location: 45 Broadway
Atrium 21st Floor
New York, NY 10006

Fax: 212/635-2309 **Phone:** 212/635-2300

Profile: Total return investor

Investment Portfolio: $ 1.9 billion

Use: **Investment Purposes**
Asset allocation
Diversify portfolio

Currencies: US dollar

Regions: United States

DERIVATIVES ACTIVITIES: **CAC Class: Inactive**

OTHER ALTERNATIVE INVESTMENTS:

CMOs/REMICs – Govt. GICs

KEY MANAGERS & DERIVATIVES SPECIALISTS:	Direct Phone/Fax	Job Function
Mr. Ronald J. Ryan President		President
Mr. Thomas J. Winters, Sr.		Chief Investment Officer

SAFECO Insurance Companies

Insurance Co/Management

Sub of SAFECO Corporation

Location: 4333 Brooklyn Avenue N.E.
SAFECO Plaza Tower 13
Seattle, WA 98185-0001

Fax: 206/545-3446 **Phone:** 206/545-5000

Profile: Hold to maturity investor

Investment Portfolio: $ 12.5 billion

Use:

Balance Sheet/Risk Management
Create synthetic fixed/floating rate
Hedge interest rate risk
Strategic liability management

Investment Purposes
Alter portfolio weighting
Adjust portfolio duration
Hedge bond portfolio risk
Hedge equity portfolio risk
Hedge interest rate risk

Currencies: US dollar

Regions: United States

DERIVATIVES ACTIVITIES: **CAC Class: 3**

Exchange-traded Options & Futures	**Bond**
OTC Derivatives **Plain Vanilla Derivatives**	**Bond, Interest rate** Swaps
Counterparty Rating Requirement:	A

OTHER ALTERNATIVE INVESTMENTS:

CMOs/REMICs – Govt.
CMOs/REMICs – Private
Strips

KEY MANAGERS & DERIVATIVES SPECIALISTS:	**Direct Phone/Fax**	**Job Function**
Mr. Stephen C. Bauer Vice President	206/545-5742	Bond Department Head *Muni*
Mr. Michael C. Knebel Vice President	206/545-3129	Bond Department Head
Mr. Ronald L. Spaulding	206/545-5734	Chief Investment Officer Portfolio Mgr – Derivatives Portfolio Mgr – Options

The St. Paul Companies Inc.

Insurance Co/P & C

Location: 385 Washington Street
St. Paul, MN 55102-1396

Fax: 612/221-8439 **Phone:** 612/221-7911

Profile: Stable asset investor

Investment Portfolio: $ 10.0 billion

Use: **Investment Purposes**

Currencies: US dollar

Regions: United States

The St. Paul Companies Inc. – continued

DERIVATIVES ACTIVITIES:

Structured Notes	Corporate MTNs Govt. agency MTNs Floaters	Inverse floaters Tender options bonds Multi-step-up callable bonds

OTHER ALTERNATIVE INVESTMENTS:

	CMOs/REMICs – Govt.	CMOs/REMICs – Private

KEY MANAGERS & DERIVATIVES SPECIALISTS:	Direct Phone/Fax	Job Function
Mr. Edward G. Pendergast Vice President – Fixed Income	612/221-7903	Bond Department Head Portfolio Mgr – Structured Notes

St. Paul Federal Bank for Savings

Savings Bank/Bldg Society

Sub of St. Paul Bancorp Inc.

Location: 6700 West North Avenue
Chicago, IL 60635

Fax: 312/804-2285 **Phone:** 312/804-2110

Profile: Net asset value investor

Investment Portfolio: $ 4.0 billion

Use: **Balance Sheet/Risk Management**
Create synthetic fixed/floating rate
Hedge interest rate risk
Strategic liability management

Currencies: US dollar

Regions: United States

DERIVATIVES ACTIVITIES: **CAC Class: 3**

OTC Derivatives **Plain Vanilla Derivatives**	**Interest rate** Swaps
Structured Notes	Govt. agency MTNs

OTHER ALTERNATIVE INVESTMENTS:

	CMOs/REMICs – Govt. CMOs/REMICs – Private	Repos/reverse repos

KEY MANAGERS & DERIVATIVES SPECIALISTS:	Direct Phone/Fax	Job Function
Mr. William Wogstad Treasurer & C.I.O.	Ext. 2238	Chief Investment Officer Treasurer Portfolio Mgr – Derivatives Portfolio Mgr – Structured Notes

Sallie Mae

Corporation

Location: 1050 Thomas Jefferson Street N.W.
Washington, DC 20007

Fax: 202/965-7085 **Phone:** 202/333-8000

Profile: Spread investor

Investment Portfolio: $ 10.0 billion

Use: **Balance Sheet/Risk Management**
Hedge interest rate risk

Investment Purposes
Capture extra yield

Currencies: US dollar

Regions: United States

DERIVATIVES ACTIVITIES:

Exchange-traded Options & Futures
U.S. Treasury futures

Interest rate
U.S. Treasury options

OTHER ALTERNATIVE INVESTMENTS:

CMOs/REMICs – Govt.
Strips

Repos/reverse repos

KEY MANAGERS & DERIVATIVES SPECIALISTS:	**Direct Phone/Fax**	**Job Function**
Mr. Robert J. Lavin Vice President-Investments	202/298-2668	Portfolio Mgr – Futures Portfolio Mgr – Options Trader – Futures Trader – Options
Mr. Robert R. Levine Vice President & Treasurer	202/298-2632 202/298-2726	Chief Investment Officer Treasurer
Ms. Denise McGlone Chief Financial Officer		Chief Financial Officer
Mr. William Rachal, Jr.		OTC Deriv/Swaps – Head Structured Notes – Head

Salomon Brothers Asset Management Inc. (U.S.A.)

Broker/Management Sub

Location: Seven World Trade Center
38th Floor
New York, NY 10048

Fax: 212/783-4014 **Phone:** 212/783-7000

Profile: Total return investor

Investment Portfolio: $ 18.0 billion

Use: **Balance Sheet/Risk Management**
Hedge interest rate risk

Investment Purposes
Provide incremental return

Currencies: US dollar

Regions: United States Europe

Salomon Brothers Asset Management Inc. (U.S.A.) – continued

DERIVATIVES ACTIVITIES:

Exchange-traded Options & Futures

OTC Derivatives
Plain Vanilla Derivatives — Swaps

Counterparty Rating Requirement: A

OTHER ALTERNATIVE INVESTMENTS:

CMOs/REMICs – Govt. | CMOs/REMICs – Private

KEY MANAGERS & DERIVATIVES SPECIALISTS:	**Direct Phone/Fax**	**Job Function**
Mr. Thomas W. Brock Chairman & C.E.O.	212/783-7990	Chief Investment Officer
Mr. Steven Guterman Managing Director		Bond Department Head
Mr. Michael S. Hyland President	212/783-7416	President Bond Department Head
Ms. Nancy Noyes Director-Asset Management	212/783-6315	Portfolio Mgr – Derivatives Portfolio Mgr – Futures Portfolio Mgr – Options
Mr. Allan R. White III Managing Director	212/783-7413	Portfolio Mgr – Derivatives

Santander National Bank

Bank/Portfolio

Location: Highway 2 & Road 167
Bayamon, PR 00960-1435

Fax: 809/798-4480 **Phone:** 809/740-4444

Profile: Hold to maturity investor

Investment Portfolio: $ 1.2 billion

Use:

Balance Sheet/Risk Management
Create synthetic fixed/floating rate
Hedge interest rate risk
Strategic liability management

Investment Purposes
Beat conventional rates
Capture extra yield
Discretionary situations

Currencies: US dollar

Regions: United States

DERIVATIVES ACTIVITIES: **CAC Class: 2**

Exchange-traded Options & Futures
Municipal options

Structured Notes — Govt. agency MTNs; Index amortizing notes; Multi-step-up callable bonds

Counterparty Rating Requirement: AAA

Santander National Bank – continued

OTHER ALTERNATIVE INVESTMENTS:

	CMOs/REMICs – Govt. CMOs/REMICs – Private	Repos/reverse repos

KEY MANAGERS & DERIVATIVES SPECIALISTS:	Direct Phone/Fax	Job Function
Ms. Alicia Rojo		Chief Investment Officer Portfolio Mgr – Derivatives Portfolio Mgr – Structured Notes

M.D. Sass Investors Services, Inc.

Investment Manager

Location: 1185 Avenue of the Americas
New York, NY 10036

Fax: 212/764-0381 **Phone:** 212/730-2000

Profile: Hold to maturity investor

Investment Portfolio: $ 2.3 billion

Use: **Balance Sheet/Risk Management**
Hedge balance sheet
Hedge interest rate risk
Incremental return
Strategic liability management

Currencies: US dollar

Regions: United States

DERIVATIVES ACTIVITIES: **CAC Class: 4**

Exchange-traded Options & Futures U.S. Treasury futures	**Bond** Municipal futures	
Structured Notes	Floaters	Tender options bonds

OTHER ALTERNATIVE INVESTMENTS:

	CMOs/REMICs – Govt. Strips	Repos/reverse repos

KEY MANAGERS & DERIVATIVES SPECIALISTS:	Direct Phone/Fax	Job Function
Mr. James H. Evans Vice President	212/843-2419 212/843-5949	Portfolio Mgr – Futures Portfolio Mgr – Structured Notes
Mr. Hugh R. Lamle Executive Vice President	Ext. 2112	Fixed-Income Strategist Portfolio Mgr – Futures
Mr. Martin D. Sass President	Ext. 2115	President Chief Investment Officer

Schlumberger, Ltd.

Corporation

Location: 277 Park Avenue
New York, NY 10172

Fax: 212/350-9564 **Phone:** 212/350-9400

Use: **Balance Sheet/Risk Management**
Hedge currency risk
Hedge overseas investments

Currencies: US dollar, German mark, French franc, UK pound

Regions: United States, Europe

DERIVATIVES ACTIVITIES: **CAC Class: 3**

OTC Derivatives	**Currency, Interest rate**	
Plain Vanilla Derivatives	Swaps	Forwards
Counterparty Rating Requirement:	AA	

KEY MANAGERS & DERIVATIVES SPECIALISTS:	**Direct Phone/Fax**	**Job Function**
Mr. Arthur Lindenauer E.V.P. – Finance & C.F.O.		Chief Financial Officer
Mr. Michel Soublin Vice President & Treasurer		Treasurer Portfolio Mgr – Derivatives

Schroder Wertheim Investment Services

Broker/Management Sub

Sub of Schroder Wertheim & Company, Inc.

Location: 787 Seventh Avenue
34th Floor
New York, NY 10019-6016

Fax: 212/641-3985 **Phone:** 212/641-3900

Profile: Total return investor

Investment Portfolio: $ 3.6 billion

Use: **Investment Purposes**

Currencies: US dollar

Regions: United States

DERIVATIVES ACTIVITIES: **CAC Class: Inactive**

OTHER ALTERNATIVE INVESTMENTS:

CMOs/REMICs – Govt. CMOs/REMICs – Private

KEY MANAGERS & DERIVATIVES SPECIALISTS:	**Direct Phone/Fax**	**Job Function**
Mr. William Smethurst President & C.I.O.		President Chief Investment Officer

Charles Schwab Investment Management

Broker/Management Sub

Sub of The Charles Schwab Corporation

Location: 101 Market Street
Federal Reserve Bank Bldg. 8th Floor
San Francisco, CA 94105-1530

Fax: 415/974-7660 **Phone:** 415/974-7600

Profile: Total return investor

Investment Portfolio: $ 15.4 billion

Use: **Investment Purposes**
Asset allocation
Diversify portfolio

Currencies: US dollar

Regions: United States

DERIVATIVES ACTIVITIES: **CAC Class: Inactive**

OTHER ALTERNATIVE INVESTMENTS:

CMOs/REMICs – Govt.
MOPs/TOPs
Repos/reverse repos

KEY MANAGERS & DERIVATIVES SPECIALISTS:	**Direct Phone/Fax**	**Job Function**
Mr. Stephen Ward	415/974-7613	Chief Investment Officer

SCOR Reinsurance Company

Reinsurance Company

Sub of SCOR U.S. Corporation

Location: Two World Trade Center
New York, NY 10048

Fax: 212/488-8608 **Phone:** 212/390-5200

Profile: Spread investor

Investment Portfolio: $ 621.6 million

Use: **Balance Sheet/Risk Management**
Create synthetic fixed/floating rate
Hedge interest rate risk
Incremental return
Strategic liability management

Currencies: US dollar

Regions: United States

DERIVATIVES ACTIVITIES: **CAC Class: 2**

OTC Derivatives
Plain Vanilla Derivatives — **Interest rate**

OTHER ALTERNATIVE INVESTMENTS:

CMOs/REMICs – Govt.

KEY MANAGERS & DERIVATIVES SPECIALISTS:	**Direct Phone/Fax**	**Job Function**
Ms. Linda Grant Vice President & Treasurer		Chief Investment Officer Treasurer Portfolio Mgr – Derivatives

Scudder Stevens & Clark, Inc. (Boston)

Investment Manager

Sub of Scudder Stevens & Clark, Inc. (U.S.A.)

Location: Two International Place
Boston, MA 02110-4103

Fax: 617/295-1111 **Phone:** 617/295-1000

Profile: Total return investor

Investment Portfolio: $ 67.0 billion

Use: **Investment Purposes**
- Alter portfolio weighting
- Adjust portfolio duration
- Asset allocation
- Capture extra yield
- Diversify portfolio
- Enter new mkts/lower risk
- Expand international investments
- Hedge bond portfolio risk
- Hedge currency risk
- Hedge equity portfolio risk
- Hedge interest rate risk
- Protect currency gains
- Provide incremental return
- Reduce variability of returns

Currencies:
- US dollar
- Australian dollar
- Belgian franc
- Canadian dollar
- ECU
- French franc
- German mark
- Italian lira
- Indonesian rupiah
- Japanese yen
- Mexican peso
- Spanish peseta
- Swiss franc
- Thai baht
- UK pound

Regions:
- United States
- Canada
- Europe
- Pacific Rim

DERIVATIVES ACTIVITIES:

Exchange-traded Options & Futures
- U.S. Treasury futures
- U.S. Treasury options

Bond, Currency, interest rate
- Municipal futures
- Municipal options

OTC Derivatives

Plain Vanilla Derivatives
- Swaps
- Forwards

Structured Notes
- Corporate MTNs
- Govt. agency MTNs
- Bond index notes
- Index amortizing notes
- CMT notes
- Floaters
- Inverse floaters
- Periodic capped floaters
- Tender options bonds
- Multi-step-up callable bonds

Counterparty Rating Requirement: AAA

OTHER ALTERNATIVE INVESTMENTS:
- CMOs/REMICs – Govt.
- CMOs/REMICs – Private
- GICs
- Strips
- Repos/reverse repos

Scudder Stevens & Clark, Inc. (Boston) – continued

KEY MANAGERS & DERIVATIVES SPECIALISTS:	Direct Phone/Fax	Job Function
Ms. Margaret D. Hadzima Managing Director	617/728-9260	Research Analyst – Derivatives
Mr. Gary P. Johnson Managing Director	617/728-9319	Research Analyst – Derivatives
Mr. Robert E. Pruyne Managing Director	617/295-1000	Bond Department Head *Taxable*
Mr. Michael T. Sullivan	617/295-2522	Trader – Derivatives Trader – Futures Trader – Options Trader – Structured Investments

Scudder Stevens & Clark, Inc. (Chicago)

Investment Manager

Location: 180 North Stetson Avenue
Two Prudential Plaza Suite 5400
Chicago, IL 60601-6713

Fax: 312/861-1472 **Phone:** 312/861-2700

Profile: Total return investor

Investment Portfolio: $ 67.0 billion

Use: **Investment Purposes**
Asset allocation
Capture extra yield
Diversify portfolio
Provide incremental return

Currencies: US dollar

Regions: United States

DERIVATIVES ACTIVITIES:

Exchange-traded Options & Futures	**Bond, Currency, Interest rate**	
Structured Notes	Corporate MTNs Govt. agency MTNs	Floaters

OTHER ALTERNATIVE INVESTMENTS:

CMOs/REMICs – Govt.	Strips
CMOs/REMICs – Private	Repos/reverse repos

KEY MANAGERS & DERIVATIVES SPECIALISTS:	Direct Phone/Fax	Job Function
Mr. Kevin D. Holt Vice President	312/861-2743	Portfolio Mgr – Options Portfolio Mgr – Structured Notes Trader – Options Trader – Structured Investments
Mr. Richard A. Holt Managing Director	312/861-2718	Bond Department Head *Corp, Govt, MBS*

Scudder Stevens & Clark, Inc. (Cincinnati)

Investment Manager

Location: 600 Vine Street
Cincinnati Commerce Center Suite 2000
Cincinnati, OH 45202

Fax: 513/621-5081 **Phone:** 513/621-2733

Profile: Total return investor

Investment Portfolio: $ 67.0 billion

Use: **Investment Purposes**

Currencies: US dollar

Regions: United States

DERIVATIVES ACTIVITIES: **CAC Class: Inactive**

OTHER ALTERNATIVE INVESTMENTS:

CMOs/REMICs – Govt.
CMOs/REMICs – Private

KEY MANAGERS & DERIVATIVES SPECIALISTS:	**Direct Phone/Fax**	**Job Function**
Mr. Thomas Crain		Chief Investment Officer
Mr. Leon Loewenstine		Bond Department Head

Scudder Stevens & Clark, Inc. (Los Angeles)

Investment Manager

Sub of Scudder Stevens & Clark, Inc. (U.S.A.)

Location: 333 South Hope Street
37th Floor
Los Angeles, CA 90071-1470

Fax: 213/626-1005 **Phone:** 213/628-1144

Profile: Total return investor

Investment Portfolio: $ 67.0 billion

Use: **Balance Sheet/Risk Management**
Hedge currency risk
Hedge interest rate risk
Protect currency gains

Currencies: US dollar

Regions: United States
Canada
Europe
Pacific Rim

Scudder Stevens & Clark, Inc. (Los Angeles) – continued

DERIVATIVES ACTIVITIES: **CAC Class: 6**

Exchange-traded Options & Futures		
U.S. Treasury futures	Municipal futures	
U.S. Treasury options	Municipal options	
OTC Derivatives		
Plain Vanilla Derivatives	Swaps	Caps
	Forwards	Floors
	Swaptions	Collars
Structured Notes	Corporate MTNs	Inverse floaters
	Govt. agency MTNs	Periodic capped floaters
	Floaters	Tender options bonds
Counterparty Rating Requirement:	AAA	

OTHER ALTERNATIVE INVESTMENTS:

	CMOs/REMICs – Govt.	Strips
	CMOs/REMICs – Private	Repos/reverse repos

KEY MANAGERS & DERIVATIVES SPECIALISTS:	**Direct Phone/Fax**	**Job Function**
Mr. Edward Chisholm		Portfolio Mgr – Derivatives Portfolio Mgr – Futures Portfolio Mgr – Options Portfolio Mgr – Structured Notes
Ms. Debra Hanson Principal		Portfolio Mgr – Derivatives Portfolio Mgr – Options Portfolio Mgr – Structured Notes
Mr. Jack W. Smock, Jr. Principal	213/229-0260	Bond Department Head

Scudder Stevens & Clark, Inc. (San Francisco)

Investment Manager

Sub of Scudder Stevens & Clark, Inc. (U.S.A.)

Location: 101 California Street
Suite 4100
San Francisco, CA 94111-5886

Fax: 415/403-0784 **Phone:** 415/981-8191

Profile: Total return investor

Investment Portfolio: $ 67.0 billion

Use:

Balance Sheet/Risk Management
- Hedge currency risk
- Hedge interest rate risk
- Lower transaction costs

Investment Purposes
- Alter portfolio weighting
- Adjust portfolio duration
- Asset allocation
- Diversify portfolio
- Hedge bond portfolio risk
- Hedge currency risk
- Hedge equity portfolio risk
- Hedge interest rate risk
- Reduce variability of returns

Currencies: US dollar, Australian dollar, Canadian dollar, ECU, French franc, German mark, Italian lira, Mexican peso, Spanish peseta, Thai baht, UK pound

Regions: United States, Canada, Europe, Latin America, Pacific Rim, Emerging mkts

DERIVATIVES ACTIVITIES: **CAC Class: 7**

Exchange-traded Options & Futures	**Bond, Currency, Interest rate**	
U.S. Treasury futures	Municipal futures	
U.S. Treasury options	Municipal options	
OTC Derivatives	**Bond, Currency, Interest rate**	
Plain Vanilla Derivatives	Forwards	Collars
	Caps	
Structured Notes	Corporate MTNs	Floaters
	Govt. agency MTNs	Inverse floaters
	Bond index notes	
Counterparty Rating Requirement:	AA	

OTHER ALTERNATIVE INVESTMENTS:

	CMOs/REMICs – Govt.	Strips
	CMOs/REMICs – Private	

KEY MANAGERS & DERIVATIVES SPECIALISTS:	**Direct Phone/Fax**	**Job Function**
Mr. John T. Packard	415/403-0715	Chief Investment Officer
		Portfolio Mgr – Derivatives
		Portfolio Mgr – Options
		Portfolio Mgr – Structured Notes

Seaboard Investment Advisers Inc.

Investment Manager

Location: 345 West Freemason Street
Norfolk, VA 23510

Fax: 804/622-0918 **Phone:** 804/622-7300

Profile: Total return investor

Investment Portfolio: $ 500.0 - 999.0 million

Use: **Investment Purposes**
Provide incremental return

Currencies: US dollar

Regions: United States

DERIVATIVES ACTIVITIES:

Exchange-traded Options & Futures

Structured Notes	Govt. agency MTNs	Multi-step-up callable bonds

OTHER ALTERNATIVE INVESTMENTS:

CMOs/REMICs – Govt.

KEY MANAGERS & DERIVATIVES SPECIALISTS:	Direct Phone/Fax	Job Function
Mr. Bruce DiPietro Vice President		Fixed-Income Strategist
Mr. Eugene W. Hansen Chairman		Chief Investment Officer Fixed-Income Strategist Portfolio Mgr – Options Portfolio Mgr – Structured Notes
Ms. Lisa Harrison		Trader – Options Trader – Structured Investments

Sears Roebuck and Company

Corporation

Location: Sears Tower
Chicago, IL 60684

Fax: 312/875-8351 **Phone:** 312/875-2500

Profile: Total return investor

Use: **Balance Sheet/Risk Management**
Hedge balance sheet
Hedge interest rate risk
Strategic liability management

Investment Purposes
Hedge bond portfolio risk
Hedge interest rate risk

Currencies: US dollar

Regions: United States

Sears Roebuck and Company – continued

DERIVATIVES ACTIVITIES:		**CAC Class: 6**
Exchange-traded Options & Futures U.S. Treasury futures	**Bond** U.S. Treasury options	
OTC Derivatives **Plain Vanilla Derivatives**	**Bond, Interest rate** Swaps Forwards Swaptions	 Caps Floors Collars
Counterparty Rating Requirement:	AA	

KEY MANAGERS & DERIVATIVES SPECIALISTS:	Direct Phone/Fax	Job Function
Mr. Alan J. Lacy E.V.P. & C.F.O.		Chief Financial Officer
Ms. Alice M. Peterson Vice President & Treasurer		Treasurer Portfolio Mgr – Derivatives

Securities Management and Research Inc.

Insurance Co/Management

Sub of American National Insurance Company

Location: One Moody Plaza
17th Floor
Galveston, TX 77550

Fax: 409/766-6608 **Phone:** 409/763-0726

Profile: Total return investor

Investment Portfolio: $ 6.3 billion

Use: **Investment Purposes**
Asset allocation
Diversify portfolio

Currencies: US dollar

Regions: United States

DERIVATIVES ACTIVITIES: **CAC Class: Inactive**

OTHER ALTERNATIVE INVESTMENTS:

CMOs/REMICs – Govt.

KEY MANAGERS & DERIVATIVES SPECIALISTS:	Direct Phone/Fax	Job Function
Mr. Gordon D. Dixon Senior Vice President	Ext. 258	Chief Investment Officer

Security Benefit Life Insurance Co. of Kansas

Insurance Co/Life

Location: 700 S.W. Harrison Street
Topeka, KS 66636-0002

Fax: 913/295-3099 **Phone:** 913/295-3000

Profile: Spread investor

Investment Portfolio: $ 5.0 billion

Use: **Balance Sheet/Risk Management**
Hedge balance sheet
Hedge interest rate risk
Strategic liability management

Investment Purposes
Adjust portfolio duration
Capture extra yield
Hedge bond portfolio risk
Hedge interest rate risk
Immunize from volatility

Currencies: US dollar

Regions: United States

DERIVATIVES ACTIVITIES: **CAC Class: 7**

Exchange-traded Options & Futures U.S. Treasury futures	**Bond**
OTC Derivatives **Plain Vanilla Derivatives**	**Bond** Forwards
Counterparty Rating Requirement:	AAA

OTHER ALTERNATIVE INVESTMENTS:

CMOs/REMICs – Govt. CMOs/REMICs – Private

KEY MANAGERS & DERIVATIVES SPECIALISTS:	Direct Phone/Fax	Job Function
Mr. Jeffrey A. Pantages Senior Vice President	913/295-3184	Chief Investment Officer Bond Department Head Portfolio Mgr – Derivatives Portfolio Mgr – Futures Portfolio Mgr – Options
Mr. James Woods Sr. Vice President & Treasurer	913/295-3131	Treasurer

Security Life of Denver Insurance Co.

Insurance Co/Life

Sub of Internationale Nederlanden Group (ING) NV

Location: 1290 Broadway
Denver, CO 80203-5699

Fax: 303/860-2049 **Phone:** 303/860-1290

Profile: Spread investor

Investment Portfolio: $ 4.0 billion

Use: **Balance Sheet/Risk Management**
Create synthetic fixed/floating rate
Hedge balance sheet
Hedge interest rate risk
Incremental return
Strategic liability management

Currencies: US dollar

Regions: United States Canada

Security Life of Denver Insurance Co. – continued

DERIVATIVES ACTIVITIES:		**CAC Class: 6**
Exchange-traded Options & Futures		
U.S. Treasury futures	U.S. Treasury options	
OTC Derivatives	**Bond, Interest rate**	
Plain Vanilla Derivatives	Swaps	Floors
	Swaptions	Collars
	Caps	
Exotic Derivatives	CMT swaps	Index amortizing swaps
	CMT options	
Structured Notes	Corporate MTNs	Floaters
	Govt. agency MTNs	Inverse floaters
	Index amortizing notes	Periodic capped floaters
Counterparty Rating Requirement:	A	

OTHER ALTERNATIVE INVESTMENTS:		
	CMOs/REMICs – Govt.	Strips
	CMOs/REMICs – Private	Repos/reverse repos

KEY MANAGERS & DERIVATIVES SPECIALISTS:	**Direct Phone/Fax**	**Job Function**
Mr. Kevin Ahern	303/860-2051	Portfolio Mgr – Derivatives
Mr. John G. Grant Vice President	303/860-2618	Portfolio Mgr – Derivatives
Mr. Jeffrey Seel S.V.P. & Managing Director	303/860-2041	Chief Investment Officer

Selective Insurance of America

Insurance Co/P & C

Sub of Selective Insurance Group, Inc.

Location: 40 Wantage Avenue
Branchville, NJ 07890

Fax: 201/948-6709 **Phone:** 201/948-3000

Profile: Hold to maturity investor

Investment Portfolio: $ 1.4 billion

Use: **Investment Purposes**
Asset allocation
Capture extra yield

Currencies: US dollar

Regions: United States

DERIVATIVES ACTIVITIES: **CAC Class: Inactive**

OTHER ALTERNATIVE INVESTMENTS:

CMOs/REMICs – Govt.

Selective Insurance of America – continued

KEY MANAGERS & DERIVATIVES SPECIALISTS:	Direct Phone/Fax	Job Function
Mr. James W. Entringer Chairman, President & C.E.O.		President
Mr. Gregory E. Murphy Sr. Vice President – Finance	201/948-1292	Chief Financial Officer
Mr. Robert P. Rank Sr. Vice President & C.I.O.		Chief Investment Officer

J & W Seligman & Co., Incorporated

Mutual Fund Manager

Location: 100 Park Avenue
New York, NY 10017-5598

Fax: 212/922-5747 **Phone:** 212/850-1864

Profile: Total return investor

Investment Portfolio: $ 15.2 billion

Use: **Investment Purposes**
Alter portfolio weighting
Asset allocation
Provide incremental return

Currencies: US dollar

Regions: United States

DERIVATIVES ACTIVITIES: **CAC Class: Inactive**

OTHER ALTERNATIVE INVESTMENTS:

CMOs/REMICs – Govt.
CMOs/REMICs – Private
GICs

KEY MANAGERS & DERIVATIVES SPECIALISTS:	Direct Phone/Fax	Job Function
Mr. Thomas G. Moles Managing Director	212/850-1467	Bond Department Head *Corp, Govt, MBS, Muni*
Mr. Ronald T. Schroeder Managing Director	212/850-1351	Chief Investment Officer

Shay Assets Management Co.

Investment Manager

Location: 111 East Wacker Drive
Suite 2600
Chicago, IL 60601

Fax: 312/938-2548 **Phone:** 312/938-2586

Profile: Total return investor

Investment Portfolio: $ 1.0 - 3.0 billion

Use: **Investment Purposes**
Asset allocation
Discretionary situations

Currencies: US dollar

Regions: United States

DERIVATIVES ACTIVITIES:

OTC Derivatives
Plain Vanilla Derivatives

Structured Notes	Govt. agency MTNs	Floaters
Counterparty Rating Requirement:	None	

OTHER ALTERNATIVE INVESTMENTS:

	CMOs/REMICs – Govt. CMOs/REMICs – Private	Repos/reverse repos

KEY MANAGERS & DERIVATIVES SPECIALISTS:	**Direct Phone/Fax**	**Job Function**
Mr. J. Douglas Bennett Vice President	312/644-3100	Portfolio Mgr – Derivatives Portfolio Mgr – Structured Notes
Mr. Rodger D. Shay, Sr. President & C.E.O.		President Chief Investment Officer Portfolio Mgr – Derivatives Portfolio Mgr – Structured Notes

Shell Oil Company

Corporate Pension Fund

Location: 777 Walker Street
26th Floor
Houston, TX 77002-5311

Fax: 713/241-2341 **Phone:** 713/241-6161

Profile: Total return investor

Investment Portfolio: $ 5.9 billion

Use: **Investment Purposes**
Adjust portfolio duration
Asset allocation
Capture extra yield
Hedge bond portfolio risk

Currencies: US dollar, Canadian dollar, French franc, German mark, Japanese yen, UK pound

Regions: United States, Canada, Europe, Pacific Rim

Shell Oil Company – continued

DERIVATIVES ACTIVITIES:		CAC Class: 6
Exchange-traded Options & Futures U.S. Treasury futures	**Bond, Currency**	
OTC Derivatives **Plain Vanilla Derivatives**	**Currency** Swaps	Forwards
Structured Notes	Corporate MTNs Govt. agency MTNs	Floaters

OTHER ALTERNATIVE INVESTMENTS:		
	CMOs/REMICs – Govt. CMOs/REMICs – Private	Strips Repos/reverse repos

KEY MANAGERS & DERIVATIVES SPECIALISTS:	Direct Phone/Fax	Job Function
Mr. W. L. Schroeder	713/241-2847	Chief Investment Officer
Mr. Ronald J. Stapleton Manager – Fixed Income	713/241-0285	Bond Department Head *Taxable* Portfolio Mgr – Derivatives Portfolio Mgr – Options Portfolio Mgr – Structured Notes

Signet Banking Corporation

Bank Holding Company

Location: Seven North Eighth Street
Richmond, VA 23260-5970

Fax: 804/771-7599 **Phone:** 804/747-2000

Use:

Balance Sheet/Risk Management
Create synthetic fixed/floating rate
Hedge interest rate risk
Incremental return
Strategic liability management

Investment Purposes
Capture extra yield
Discretionary situations
Provide incremental return

Currencies: US dollar

Regions: United States

DERIVATIVES ACTIVITIES:		CAC Class: 6
Exchange-traded Options & Futures	**Interest rate**	
OTC Derivatives **Plain Vanilla Derivatives**	**Interest rate** Swaps Forwards	Caps Floors

KEY MANAGERS & DERIVATIVES SPECIALISTS:	Direct Phone/Fax	Job Function
Mr. David L. Brantley E.V.P. & Treasurer		Treasurer Portfolio Mgr – Derivatives
Mr. Malcolm S. McDonald President & C.O.O.		President
Mr. Wallace B. Millner III Sr. Vice President & C.F.O.		Chief Financial Officer

Sit Investment Fixed Income Advisors Inc.

Investment Manager

Sub of Sit Investment Associates

Location: 90 South Seventh Street
4600 Norwest Center
Minneapolis, MN 55402-4130

Fax: 612/342-2018 **Phone:** 612/332-3223

Profile: Total return investor

Investment Portfolio: $ 1.0 billion

Use: **Investment Purposes**
Asset allocation
Capture extra yield
Provide incremental return

Currencies: US dollar

Regions: United States

DERIVATIVES ACTIVITIES: **CAC Class: 2**

OTC Derivatives	**Bond**
Plain Vanilla Derivatives	Swaps
Counterparty Rating Requirement:	None

OTHER ALTERNATIVE INVESTMENTS:

CMOs/REMICs – Govt. CMOs/REMICs – Private

KEY MANAGERS & DERIVATIVES SPECIALISTS:	**Direct Phone/Fax**	**Job Function**
Mr. Michael C. Brilley Senior Vice President	612/359-2561	Chief Investment Officer Portfolio Mgr – Derivatives
Ms. Debra A. Sit Vice President		Portfolio Mgr – Derivatives

Skandia Investment Management Inc. (U.S.A.)

Insurance Co/Management

Sub of Skandia International

Location: 165 Broadway
One Liberty Plaza 34th Floor
New York, NY 10006

Fax: 212/385-2169 **Phone:** 212/978-2700

Profile: Total return investor

Investment Portfolio: $ 2.5 billion

Use: **Investment Purposes**
Asset allocation
Discretionary situations
Provide incremental return

Currencies: US dollar

Regions: United States

DERIVATIVES ACTIVITIES: **CAC Class: Inactive**

OTHER ALTERNATIVE INVESTMENTS:

CMOs/REMICs – Govt. Repos/reverse repos

Skandia Investment Management Inc. (U.S.A.) – continued

KEY MANAGERS & DERIVATIVES SPECIALISTS:	Direct Phone/Fax	Job Function
Mr. Frederick K. Ellis	212/978-2800	Chief Investment Officer
Mr. John J. Murphy Vice President	212/978-2806	Bond Department Head

Herbert R. Smith, Inc.

Investment Manager

Location: 1105 Holliday, Wichita Falls, TX 76301

Fax: 817/322-3887 **Phone:** 817/723-5565

Use: **Investment Purposes**
- Adjust portfolio duration
- Capture extra yield
- Diversify portfolio
- Hedge bond portfolio risk
- Hedge interest rate risk
- Provide incremental return
- Reduce variability of returns

Investment Portfolio: $ 2.6 billion

Currencies: US dollar

Regions: United States

DERIVATIVES ACTIVITIES: **CAC Class: 2**

Structured Notes	Govt. agency MTNs Bond index notes Index amortizing notes CMT notes	Floaters Inverse floaters Periodic capped floaters Multi-step-up callable bonds

OTHER ALTERNATIVE INVESTMENTS:

CMOs/REMICs – Govt. CMOs/REMICs – Private	Strips

KEY MANAGERS & DERIVATIVES SPECIALISTS:	Direct Phone/Fax	Job Function
Mr. John J. Ford Senior Vice President		Portfolio Mgr – Structured Notes
Mr. Herbert R. Smith Chairman & C.E.O.		Chief Investment Officer

William B. Smith & Company Inc.

Investment Manager

Location: 57 Wharf Street, Pickering Wharf, Salem, MA 01970

Fax: 617/289-9555 **Phone:** 508/741-4933

Profile: Total return investor

Investment Portfolio: $ 1.0 - 3.0 billion

Use: **Investment Purposes**
- Capture extra yield

Currencies: US dollar

Regions: United States

William B. Smith & Company Inc. – continued

DERIVATIVES ACTIVITIES:		CAC Class: 1
Structured Notes	Corporate MTNs	Govt. agency MTNs

OTHER ALTERNATIVE INVESTMENTS:		
	CMOs/REMICs – Govt.	CMOs/REMICs – Private

KEY MANAGERS & DERIVATIVES SPECIALISTS:	Direct Phone/Fax	Job Function
Mr. William B. Smith III President		President Chief Investment Officer Portfolio Mgr – Structured Notes

Smith Affiliated Capital Corporation

Investment Manager

Location: 880 Third Avenue
8th Floor
New York, NY 10022

Fax: 212/644-1979 **Phone:** 212/644-9440

Profile: Total return investor

Investment Portfolio: $ 1.1 billion

Use: **Balance Sheet/Risk Management**
Hedge currency risk

Currencies: US dollar, Canadian dollar, Australian dollar

Regions: Canada, Pacific Rim

DERIVATIVES ACTIVITIES:		CAC Class: 2
Exchange-traded Options & Futures	**Currency**	
OTC Derivatives **Plain Vanilla Derivatives**	Forwards	
Counterparty Rating Requirement:	None	

OTHER ALTERNATIVE INVESTMENTS:		
	CMOs/REMICs – Govt.	CMOs/REMICs – Private

KEY MANAGERS & DERIVATIVES SPECIALISTS:	Direct Phone/Fax	Job Function
Mr. John Jenney Head of Fixed Income		Bond Department Head *Corp, Govt*
Mr. Dennis P. Slattery Manager		Portfolio Mgr – Derivatives Portfolio Mgr – Futures
Mr. Robert G. Smith, Sr. President & C.E.O.		President Chief Investment Officer Fixed-Income Strategist Portfolio Mgr – Derivatives Portfolio Mgr – Futures Portfolio Mgr – Options

Smith Barney, Inc. (Capital Management)

Mutual Fund Manager

Sub of Smith Barney, Inc.

Location: 388 Greenwich Street
25th Floor
New York, NY 10013

Fax: 212/816-6167 **Phone:** 212/816-6700

Profile: Total return investor

Investment Portfolio: $ 9.0 billion

Use: **Investment Purposes**
Asset allocation
Discretionary situations
Provide incremental return

Currencies: US dollar

Regions: United States

DERIVATIVES ACTIVITIES: **CAC Class: Inactive**

OTHER ALTERNATIVE INVESTMENTS:

CMOs/REMICs – Govt.
CMOs/REMICs – Private
Repos/reverse repos

KEY MANAGERS & DERIVATIVES SPECIALISTS:	Direct Phone/Fax	Job Function
Mr. Bruce D. Sargent Chairman & C.E.O.	212/816-2233	Chief Investment Officer

Smith Barney Investment Advisors

Broker/Management Sub

Sub of Smith Barney, Inc.

Location: 388 Greenwich Street
24th Floor
New York, NY 10013

Fax: 212/816-6101 **Phone:** 212/816-6999

Profile: Total return investor

Investment Portfolio: $ 13.0 billion

Use: **Investment Purposes**

Currencies: US dollar

Regions: United States

DERIVATIVES ACTIVITIES: **CAC Class: Inactive**

OTHER ALTERNATIVE INVESTMENTS:

CMOs/REMICs – Govt.
Strips

Smith Barney Investment Advisors – continued

KEY MANAGERS & DERIVATIVES SPECIALISTS:	Direct Phone/Fax	Job Function
Mr. Hersh Cohen President	212/816-5673	President Chief Investment Officer

Smith, Breeden Associates

Investment Manager

Location: 7300 College Boulevard
Suite 430
Overland Park, KS 66210-1879

Fax: 913/451-6313 **Phone:** 913/451-1566

Profile: Total return investor

Investment Portfolio: $ 11.0 - 20.0 billion

Use: **Balance Sheet/Risk Management**
Hedge balance sheet
Hedge interest rate risk

Currencies: US dollar

Regions: United States

DERIVATIVES ACTIVITIES: **CAC Class: 7**

Exchange-traded Options & Futures	**Bond, Interest rate**	
U.S. Treasury futures	U.S. Treasury options	
OTC Derivatives	**Bond, Interest rate**	
Plain Vanilla Derivatives	Swaps	Caps
	Forwards	Floors
	Swaptions	
Counterparty Rating Requirement:	BBB	

OTHER ALTERNATIVE INVESTMENTS:

CMOs/REMICs – Govt.	Strips
CMOs/REMICs – Private	Repos/reverse repos

KEY MANAGERS & DERIVATIVES SPECIALISTS:	Direct Phone/Fax	Job Function
Mr. William F. Quinn Principal		Bond Department Head *MBS, Muni* Portfolio Mgr – Derivatives Portfolio Mgr – Futures Portfolio Mgr – Options

Smith, Breeden Associates (Boulder)

Investment Manager

Location: 1050 Walnut Street
Suite 210
Boulder, CO 80302

Fax: 303/440-5131 **Phone:** 303/440-5151

Profile: Total return investor

Investment Portfolio: $ 1.0 billion

Use: **Balance Sheet/Risk Management**
Hedge interest rate risk

Currencies: US dollar

Regions: United States

Smith, Breeden Associates (Boulder) – continued

DERIVATIVES ACTIVITIES:

Exchange-traded Options & Futures

OTC Derivatives		
Plain Vanilla Derivatives	Swaps	Floors
	Caps	Collars
Counterparty Rating Requirement:	AAA	

OTHER ALTERNATIVE INVESTMENTS:

CMOs/REMICs – Govt.	Strips
CMOs/REMICs – Private	Repos/reverse repos

KEY MANAGERS & DERIVATIVES SPECIALISTS:	Direct Phone/Fax	Job Function
Mr. Gerald Madigan Executive Vice President		Chief Investment Officer Portfolio Mgr – Derivatives

Smith, Breeden Associates (Chapel Hill)

Investment Manager

Sub of Smith, Breeden Associates

Location: 100 Europa Drive
Suite 200
Chapel Hill, NC 27514-2310

Fax: 919/933-3157 **Phone:** 919/967-7221

Profile: Total return investor

Investment Portfolio: $ 11.0 - 20.0 billion

Use: **Balance Sheet/Risk Management**
Create synthetic fixed/floating rate
Hedge balance sheet
Hedge interest rate risk

Currencies: US dollar

Regions: United States

DERIVATIVES ACTIVITIES: **CAC Class: 5**

Exchange-traded Options & Futures	**Bond, Interest rate**	
U.S. Treasury futures	U.S. Treasury options	
OTC Derivatives	**Bond, Interest rate**	
Plain Vanilla Derivatives	Swaps	Floors
	Caps	
Counterparty Rating Requirement:	AAA	

OTHER ALTERNATIVE INVESTMENTS:

CMOs/REMICs – Govt. CMOs/REMICs – Private

Smith, Breeden Associates (Chapel Hill) – continued

KEY MANAGERS & DERIVATIVES SPECIALISTS:	Direct Phone/Fax	Job Function
Mr. Douglas T. Breeden Chairman & President	919/933-3356	President Chief Investment Officer
Mr. Michael Giarla Principal		Bond Department Head *MBS* Portfolio Mgr – Derivatives Portfolio Mgr – Options

Smith, Breeden Associates (Dallas)

Investment Manager

Sub of Smith, Breeden Associates

Location: 500 North Akard Street
2575 Lincoln Plaza Suite 2575
Dallas, TX 75201-3302

Fax: 214/871-1329 **Phone:** 214/871-2575

Profile: Total return investor

Investment Portfolio: $ 3.5 billion

Use: **Balance Sheet/Risk Management**
Hedge balance sheet
Hedge interest rate risk
Strategic liability management

Currencies: US dollar

Regions: United States

DERIVATIVES ACTIVITIES: **CAC Class: 3**

Exchange-traded Options & Futures U.S. Treasury futures	**Interest rate** U.S. Treasury options	
OTC Derivatives **Plain Vanilla Derivatives**	**Interest rate** Swaps Caps	 Floors
Structured Notes	Govt. agency MTNs	
Counterparty Rating Requirement:	AA	

OTHER ALTERNATIVE INVESTMENTS:

	CMOs/REMICs – Govt. CMOs/REMICs – Private	Strips Repos/reverse repos

KEY MANAGERS & DERIVATIVES SPECIALISTS:	Direct Phone/Fax	Job Function
Mr. Stephen Nix		Portfolio Mgr – Derivatives Portfolio Mgr – Futures Portfolio Mgr – Options Portfolio Mgr – Structured Notes

Smith, Graham & Co. Asset Managers

Investment Manager

Location: 333 Clay Street
Three Allen Center Suite 4470
Houston, TX 77002

Fax: 713/227-0912 **Phone:** 713/227-1100

Use: **Investment Purposes**
Asset allocation
Hedge bond portfolio risk
Provide incremental return

Investment Portfolio: $ 1.6 billion

Currencies: US dollar

Regions: United States

DERIVATIVES ACTIVITIES: **CAC Class: 2**

OTC Derivatives
Plain Vanilla Derivatives

OTHER ALTERNATIVE INVESTMENTS:

CMOs/REMICs – Govt.

KEY MANAGERS & DERIVATIVES SPECIALISTS:	**Direct Phone/Fax**	**Job Function**
Mr. Ladell Graham President	713/739-8436	President Chief Investment Officer
Mr. Gerald Smith Chairman & C.E.O.		Portfolio Mgr – Derivatives

Smith's Food & Drug Centers Inc.

Corporation

Location: 1550 South Redwood Road
Salt Lake City, UT 84104

Fax: 801/974-1662 **Phone:** 801/974-1400

Use: **Balance Sheet/Risk Management**
Hedge balance sheet

Currencies: US dollar

Regions: United States

DERIVATIVES ACTIVITIES:

OTC Derivatives	**Interest rate**
Plain Vanilla Derivatives	Swaps
Exotic Derivatives	Bond index swaps
Counterparty Rating Requirement:	A

KEY MANAGERS & DERIVATIVES SPECIALISTS:	**Direct Phone/Fax**	**Job Function**
Mr. Paul Tezak Vice President & Treasurer		Treasurer Portfolio Mgr – Derivatives

Society Asset Management, Inc.

Bank/Management Division

Sub of KeyCorp

Location: 127 Public Square
20th Floor
Cleveland, OH 44114-1306

Fax: 216/689-7083 **Phone:** 216/689-3000

Profile: Total return investor

Investment Portfolio: $ 31.0 billion

Use: **Balance Sheet/Risk Management**
Hedge currency risk

Investment Purposes
Capture extra yield

Currencies: US dollar, German mark, Australian dollar, Japanese yen, French franc, UK pound

Regions: United States, Pacific Rim, Europe

DERIVATIVES ACTIVITIES: **CAC Class: 4**

Exchange-traded Options & Futures U.S. Treasury futures	**Bond**	
OTC Derivatives **Plain Vanilla Derivatives**	**Currency** Forwards	
Structured Notes	Govt. agency MTNs	Floaters

OTHER ALTERNATIVE INVESTMENTS:

	Strips	Repos/reverse repos

KEY MANAGERS & DERIVATIVES SPECIALISTS:	Direct Phone/Fax	Job Function
Mr. Frank J. Riccardi Senior Vice President	216/689-9838	Bond Department Head Portfolio Mgr – Derivatives Portfolio Mgr – Futures Portfolio Mgr – Structured Notes

Society National Bank (Portfolio)

Bank/Portfolio

Sub of KeyCorp

Location: 127 Public Square
4th Floor
Cleveland, OH 44114-1306

Fax: 216/689-3832 **Phone:** 216/689-3000

Profile: Spread investor

Investment Portfolio: $ 21.0 billion

Use:

Balance Sheet/Risk Management
- Bypass regulations
- Create synthetic fixed/floating rate
- Hedge balance sheet
- Hedge currency risk
- Hedge interest rate risk
- Hedge overseas investments
- Incremental return
- Lower transaction costs
- Meet interest rate target
- Meet cash flow target
- Reduce cost of capital
- Strategic liability management

Investment Purposes
- Beat conventional rates
- Capture extra yield
- Convexity objectives
- Discretionary situations
- Diversify portfolio
- Enter new mkts/lower risk
- Expand international investments
- Hedge bond portfolio risk
- Hedge currency risk
- Hedge interest rate risk
- Immunize from volatility
- Lower transactions costs
- Provide incremental return
- Reduce variability of returns

Currencies: US dollar, Canadian dollar, German mark, UK pound

Regions: United States, Canada, Europe, Pacific Rim

DERIVATIVES ACTIVITIES: **CAC Class: 7**

Exchange-traded Options & Futures	**Bond, Interest rate**	
U.S. Treasury futures		
OTC Derivatives	**Bond, Currency, Interest rate**	
Plain Vanilla Derivatives	Swaps	Caps
	Forwards	Floors
	Swaptions	
Exotic Derivatives	CMT swaps	Index amortizing swaps
Structured Notes	Periodic capped floaters	
Counterparty Rating Requirement:	None	

OTHER ALTERNATIVE INVESTMENTS:

CMOs/REMICs – Govt. Repos/reverse repos

KEY MANAGERS & DERIVATIVES SPECIALISTS:	**Direct Phone/Fax**	**Job Function**
Mr. Terrence Burns	216/689-5859	Portfolio Mgr – Derivatives Portfolio Mgr – Futures Portfolio Mgr – Structured Notes
Mr. Michael Dontje Senior Vice President	216/689-3631	Portfolio Mgr – Derivatives Portfolio Mgr – Futures Portfolio Mgr – Structured Notes
Mr. Trenton Fletcher	216/689-4012	Portfolio Mgr – Derivatives Portfolio Mgr – Futures Portfolio Mgr – Structured Notes

South Boston Savings Bank Savings

Bank/Bldg Society

Sub of The Boston Bancorp

Location: 460 West Broadway
Boston, MA 02127-2298

Fax: 617/269-5354 **Phone:** 617/268-2500

Profile: Spread investor

Investment Portfolio: $ 2.1 billion

Use: **Balance Sheet/Risk Management**
Hedge interest rate risk

Currencies: US dollar

Regions: United States

DERIVATIVES ACTIVITIES: **CAC Class: 3**

OTC Derivatives	**Interest rate**	
Plain Vanilla Derivatives	Swaps	Caps
Structured Notes	Govt. agency MTNs	
Counterparty Rating Requirement:	BBB	

OTHER ALTERNATIVE INVESTMENTS:

CMOs/REMICs – Govt.	Strips
CMOs/REMICs – Private	Repos/reverse repos

KEY MANAGERS & DERIVATIVES SPECIALISTS:	Direct Phone/Fax	Job Function
Mr. Robert E. Lee President		President Chief Investment Officer
Mr. Greg Shaw Senior Vice President		Portfolio Mgr – Derivatives Portfolio Mgr – Structured Notes

South Carolina Retirement System

Government Pension Fund

Location: Wade Hampton Building
1st Floor
Columbia, SC 29202

Fax: 803/734-2039 **Phone:** 803/737-6800

Profile: Hold to maturity investor

Investment Portfolio: $ 11.0 - 20.0 billion

Use: **Investment Purposes**
Asset allocation
Capture extra yield

Currencies: US dollar

Regions: United States

DERIVATIVES ACTIVITIES: **CAC Class: Inactive**

OTHER ALTERNATIVE INVESTMENTS:

CMOs/REMICs – Govt.	Strips
CMOs/REMICs – Private	Repos/reverse repos

South Carolina Retirement System – continued

KEY MANAGERS & DERIVATIVES SPECIALISTS:	Direct Phone/Fax	Job Function
Mr. Charles C. Sanders, Jr. Sr. Assistant State Treasurer	803/734-2114	Chief Investment Officer
Ms. Shakun Tahiliani Assistant State Treasurer	803/734-2641 803/737-6810	Bond Department Head *Taxable*

South Dakota Investment Council

Government Pension Fund

Location: 4009 West 49th Street
Suite 300
Sioux Falls, SD 57106-3784

Fax: 605/367-5863 **Phone:** 605/367-5850

Profile: Total return investor

Investment Portfolio: $ 2.2 billion

Use: **Investment Purposes**
Alter portfolio weighting
Adjust portfolio duration
Asset allocation
Hedge bond portfolio risk
Hedge currency risk
Hedge equity portfolio risk
Reduce variability of returns

Currencies: US dollar, German mark, French franc

Regions: United States, Pacific Rim, Europe

DERIVATIVES ACTIVITIES:		**CAC Class: 2**
Exchange-traded Options & Futures U.S. Treasury futures	**Bond, Currency**	
OTC Derivatives **Plain Vanilla Derivatives**	**Bond**	
Counterparty Rating Requirement:	AAA	

OTHER ALTERNATIVE INVESTMENTS:

CMOs/REMICs – Govt.
CMOs/REMICs – Private
GICs
Strips
Repos/reverse repos

KEY MANAGERS & DERIVATIVES SPECIALISTS:	Direct Phone/Fax	Job Function
Mr. Stephen R. Myers State Investment Officer		Chief Investment Officer
Mr. Christopher L. Nelson	605/335-5832	Portfolio Mgr – Derivatives Portfolio Mgr – Futures *Govt*
Ms. Tammy V. Otten		Portfolio Mgr – Derivatives Portfolio Mgr – Futures *Govt*

Southern Farm Bureau Casualty Insurance Co.

Insurance Co/P & C

Location: 1800 East County Line Road
Suite 400
Ridgeland, MS 39157

Fax: 601/957-4329 **Phone:** 601/957-7777

Profile: Hold to maturity investor

Investment Portfolio: $ 1.3 billion

Use: **Investment Purposes**
Asset allocation

Currencies: US dollar

Regions: United States

DERIVATIVES ACTIVITIES: **CAC Class: Inactive**

OTHER ALTERNATIVE INVESTMENTS:

CMOs/REMICs – Govt.

KEY MANAGERS & DERIVATIVES SPECIALISTS:	Direct Phone/Fax	Job Function
Mr. Harry Hyslop		Bond Department Head *ABS, Corp, Govt, Muni*
Mr. Roderick Moore Vice President		Chief Investment Officer

Southern Farm Bureau Life Insurance Co.

Insurance Co/Management

Location: 1401 Livingston Lane
Jackson, MS 39215-1985

Fax: 601/981-1670 **Phone:** 601/981-7422

Profile: Hold to maturity investor

Investment Portfolio: $ 2.6 billion

Use: **Investment Purposes**

Currencies: US dollar

Regions: United States

DERIVATIVES ACTIVITIES:

Structured Notes

Corporate MTNs
Govt. agency MTNs
Floaters
Inverse floaters
Multi-step-up callable bonds

OTHER ALTERNATIVE INVESTMENTS:

CMOs/REMICs – Govt.
CMOs/REMICs – Private
Repos/reverse repos

KEY MANAGERS & DERIVATIVES SPECIALISTS:	Direct Phone/Fax	Job Function
Mr. Lloyd Ellis		Portfolio Mgr – Structured Notes
Mr. Walter J. Olson III Vice President	601/981-3605	Chief Investment Officer Portfolio Mgr – Structured Notes

SouthTrust Bank of Alabama, N.A. (Portfolio)

Bank/Portfolio

Sub of SouthTrust Corporation

Location: 112 North 20th Street
Birmingham, AL 35203

Fax: 205/254-5839 **Phone:** 205/254-6856

Profile: Total return investor

Investment Portfolio: $ 3.9 billion

Use: **Balance Sheet/Risk Management**
Hedge interest rate risk

Currencies: US dollar

Regions: United States

DERIVATIVES ACTIVITIES: **CAC Class: 5**

OTC Derivatives
Plain Vanilla Derivatives

Interest rate
Swaps
Caps
Floors

OTHER ALTERNATIVE INVESTMENTS:

CMOs/REMICs – Govt.
CMOs/REMICs – Private

KEY MANAGERS & DERIVATIVES SPECIALISTS:	**Direct Phone/Fax**	**Job Function**
Mr. Aubrey D. Barnard Secty., Treasurer & Controller		Treasurer Portfolio Mgr – Derivatives

SouthTrust Bank of Alabama, N.A. (Trust)

Bank/Trust

Sub of SouthTrust Corporation

Location: 420 North 20th Street
Eighth Floor
Birmingham, AL 35203

Fax: 205/254-5989 **Phone:** 205/254-5000

Profile: Total return investor

Investment Portfolio: $ 1.4 billion

Use: **Investment Purposes**
Provide incremental return

Currencies: US dollar

Regions: United States

DERIVATIVES ACTIVITIES: **CAC Class: 1**

Structured Notes

Corporate MTNs
Govt. agency MTNs

OTHER ALTERNATIVE INVESTMENTS:

Strips

KEY MANAGERS & DERIVATIVES SPECIALISTS:	**Direct Phone/Fax**	**Job Function**
Mr. Jon F. Goebel	205/254-5477	Chief Investment Officer
Mr. David J. Howell	205/254-6780	Portfolio Mgr – Structured Notes
Mr. R. Ponder Parks Senior Vice President	205/254-5428 205/254-5839	Bond Department Head Portfolio Mgr – Structured Notes *Corp*

Southwest Corporate Federal Credit Union

Credit Union

Location: 7920 Belt Line Road
Dallas, TX 75240

Fax: 214/861-3322 **Phone:** 214/861-3000

Profile: Spread investor

Investment Portfolio: $ 3.0 billion

Use: **Balance Sheet/Risk Management**
Hedge interest rate risk
Strategic liability management

Currencies: US dollar

Regions: United States

DERIVATIVES ACTIVITIES: **CAC Class: 4**

Exchange-traded Options & Futures Municipal futures	**Interest rate**
OTC Derivatives **Plain Vanilla Derivatives**	**Interest rate** Swaps
Structured Notes	CMT notes

OTHER ALTERNATIVE INVESTMENTS:

CMOs/REMICs – Govt.
CMOs/REMICs – Private
Repos/reverse repos

KEY MANAGERS & DERIVATIVES SPECIALISTS:	**Direct Phone/Fax**	**Job Function**
Mr. Bruce Fox Vice President		Chief Investment Officer Portfolio Mgr – Derivatives Portfolio Mgr – Futures Portfolio Mgr – Structured Notes
Mr. Francis Lee President		President

Sovereign Bank, A Federal Savings Bank

Savings Bank/Bldg Society

Sub of Sovereign Bancorp Inc.

Location: 1130 Berkshire Boulevard
Wyomissing, PA 19610

Fax: 610/320-8448 **Phone:** 610/320-8400

Profile: Spread investor

Investment Portfolio: $ 1.7 billion

Use: **Balance Sheet/Risk Management**
Hedge interest rate risk
Strategic liability management

Currencies: US dollar

Regions: United States

DERIVATIVES ACTIVITIES: **CAC Class: 6**

OTC Derivatives **Plain Vanilla Derivatives**	**Interest rate** Swaps

OTHER ALTERNATIVE INVESTMENTS:

CMOs/REMICs – Govt.
CMOs/REMICs – Private

Sovereign Bank, A Federal Savings Bank Savings – continued

KEY MANAGERS & DERIVATIVES SPECIALISTS:	Direct Phone/Fax	Job Function
Ms. Jacquelyn Blue		Chief Investment Officer Portfolio Mgr – Derivatives
Mr. Thomas Brugger	610/320-8439	Portfolio Mgr – Derivatives
Mr. Karl D. Gerhart C.F.O. & Treasuer		Chief Financial Officer Treasurer Portfolio Mgr – Derivatives
Mr. Jay S. Sidhu President & C.E.O.		President

Sprint Corporation

Corporation

Location: 2330 Shawnee Mission Parkway
Westwood, KS 66205

Fax: 913/624-3281 **Phone:** 913/624-3000

Use: **Balance Sheet/Risk Management**
Hedge currency risk
Hedge interest rate risk

Currencies: US dollar, French franc, German mark, Japanese yen, UK pound

Regions: United States

DERIVATIVES ACTIVITIES: **CAC Class: 5**

Exchange-traded Options & Futures	**Currency**	
OTC Derivatives	**Currency, Interest rate**	
Plain Vanilla Derivatives	Swaps	Forwards
Counterparty Rating Requirement:	A	

KEY MANAGERS & DERIVATIVES SPECIALISTS:	Direct Phone/Fax	Job Function
Mr. Michael Cline Manager – Financial Risk Mgmt.		Portfolio Mgr – Derivatives
Mr. Arthur B. Krause Exec. Vice President & C.F.O.		Chief Financial Officer
Ms. M. Jeannine Standjord Sr. Vice President & Treasurer		Treasurer

Standard Federal Bank

Savings Bank/Bldg Society

Location: 2600 West Big Beaver Road
Troy, MI 48084-3306

Fax: 810/643-0329 **Phone:** 810/643-9600

Profile: Spread investor

Investment Portfolio: $ 3.0 billion

Use: **Balance Sheet/Risk Management**
Hedge interest rate risk

Currencies: US dollar

Regions: United States

DERIVATIVES ACTIVITIES: **CAC Class: 3**

Exchange-traded Options & Futures
U.S. Treasury futures
U.S. Treasury options

OTC Derivatives
Plain Vanilla Derivatives
Interest rate
Swaps

OTHER ALTERNATIVE INVESTMENTS:

CMOs/REMICs – Govt.
CMOs/REMICs – Private
Repos/reverse repos

KEY MANAGERS & DERIVATIVES SPECIALISTS:	**Direct Phone/Fax**	**Job Function**
Mr. Joseph E. Krul Senior Vice President & C.F.O.	810/637-2530	Chief Financial Officer
Mr. Thomas R. Ricketts Chairman, President & C.E.O.	810/643-2500	President
Mr. Clayton J. Trible, Jr. S.V.P. & Treasurer	810/643-2508	Treasurer Bond Department Head *Corp, Govt, MBS* Portfolio Mgr – Derivatives Portfolio Mgr – Futures Portfolio Mgr – Options

Standard Insurance Company

Insurance Co/P & C

Location: 1100 Southwest Sixth Avenue
8th Floor
Portland, OR 97204

Fax: 503/321-8431 **Phone:** 503/321-8844

Profile: Total return investor

Investment Portfolio: $ 1.0 - 3.0 billion

Use: **Balance Sheet/Risk Management**

Currencies: US dollar

Regions: United States

DERIVATIVES ACTIVITIES: **CAC Class: Inactive**

OTHER ALTERNATIVE INVESTMENTS:

CMOs/REMICs – Govt.
CMOs/REMICs – Private

Standard Insurance Company – continued

KEY MANAGERS & DERIVATIVES SPECIALISTS:	Direct Phone/Fax	Job Function
Mr. Eric E. Parsons Vice President – Investments	503/321-8616	Chief Investment Officer

Standish, Ayer & Wood Inc.

Investment Manager

Location: One Financial Center
26th Floor
Boston, MA 02111

Fax: 617/350-7520 **Phone:** 617/350-6100

Profile: Total return investor

Investment Portfolio: $ 26.3 billion

Use:

Balance Sheet/Risk Management
Access global mkts
Hedge balance sheet
Hedge commercial paper
Hedge currency risk
Hedge interest rate risk
Hedge overseas investments
Incremental return

Investment Purposes
Capture extra yield
Hedge bond portfolio risk
Hedge currency risk
Hedge equity portfolio risk
Hedge interest rate risk
Lower transactions costs

Currencies: US dollar, Australian dollar, Belgian franc, Canadian dollar, ECU, French franc, German mark, Italian lira, Indonesian rupiah, Japanese yen, Mexican peso, Spanish peseta, Swiss franc, Thai baht, UK pound

Regions: United States, Canada, Europe, Latin America, Pacific Rim, Emerging mkts

DERIVATIVES ACTIVITIES:

Exchange-traded Options & Futures
U.S. Treasury futures
U.S. Treasury options

Bond, Currency, Interest rate
Municipal futures
Municipal options

OTC Derivatives
Plain Vanilla Derivatives

Bond, Currency, Interest rate
Swaps
Forwards
Swaptions
Caps
Floors
Collars

Exotic Derivatives

Structured Notes

Counterparty Rating Requirement: AA

OTHER ALTERNATIVE INVESTMENTS:

CMOs/REMICs – Govt.
GICs
Strips
Repos/reverse repos

KEY MANAGERS & DERIVATIVES SPECIALISTS:	Direct Phone/Fax	Job Function
Mr. Mark Flaherty Director of Equities Trading	617/457-5072	Portfolio Mgr – Derivatives Trader – Derivatives
Mr. George W. Noyes President	617/457-7312	President Chief Investment Officer
Mr. Mark Seidner	617/457-5025	Portfolio Mgr – Options Trader – Options

Standish International Management Co., L.P.

Investment Manager

Location: One Financial Center
26th Floor
Boston, MA 02111

Fax: 617/350-7520 **Phone:** 617/350-6100

Profile: Total return investor

Investment Portfolio: $ 1.0 - 3.0 billion

Use:

Balance Sheet/Risk Management
Access global mkts
Hedge balance sheet
Hedge currency risk
Hedge interest rate risk
Hedge overseas investments
Incremental return

Investment Purposes
Capture extra yield
Hedge bond portfolio risk
Hedge currency risk
Hedge equity portfolio risk
Hedge interest rate risk
Lower transactions costs

Currencies: US dollar, Australian dollar, Belgian franc, Canadian dollar, ECU, French franc, German mark, Italian lira, Indonesian rupiah, Japanese yen, Mexican peso, Spanish peseta, Swiss franc, Thai baht, UK pound

Regions: United States, Canada, Europe, Latin America, Pacific Rim, Emerging mkts

DERIVATIVES ACTIVITIES:

Exchange-traded Options & Futures
U.S. Treasury futures
U.S. Treasury options

Bond, Currency, Interest rate
Municipal futures
Municipal options

OTC Derivatives
Plain Vanilla Derivatives

Bond, Currency, Interest rate
Swaps
Forwards
Swaptions
Caps
Floors
Collars

Exotic Derivatives

Structured Notes

Counterparty Rating Requirement: AA

OTHER ALTERNATIVE INVESTMENTS:

CMOs/REMICs – Govt.
CMOs/REMICs – Private
Strips
Repos/reverse repos

KEY MANAGERS & DERIVATIVES SPECIALISTS:

Name	Direct Phone/Fax	Job Function
Mr. Mark Flaherty Director of Equities Trading	617/457-5072	Portfolio Mgr – Derivatives Trader – Derivatives
Mr. Richard S. Wood Executive Vice President		Chief Investment Officer Bond Department Head

Stanford Management Company

Foundation/Endowment

Location: 2770 Sand Hill Road
Menlo Park, CA 94025

Fax: 415/854-9188 **Phone:** 415/926-0200

Profile: Total return investor

Investment Portfolio: $ 2.5 billion

Use:

Balance Sheet/Risk Management
Create synthetic fixed/floating rate
Hedge currency risk
Strategic liability management

Investment Purposes
Alter portfolio weighting
Adjust portfolio duration
Asset allocation
Beat conventional rates
Capture extra yield
Discretionary situations
Hedge bond portfolio risk
Hedge currency risk
Hedge equity portfolio risk
Hedge interest rate risk
Immunize from volatility
Lower transactions costs
Provide incremental return
Reduce variability of returns

Currencies: US dollar, Canadian dollar, ECU, French franc, German mark, Italian lira, Japanese yen, Mexican peso, Spanish peseta, Swiss franc, UK pound

Regions: United States, Canada, Europe, Latin America, Pacific Rim, Emerging mkts

DERIVATIVES ACTIVITIES: **CAC Class: 3**

Exchange-traded Options & Futures	**Bond, Currency, Interest rate**	
Municipal futures		
OTC Derivatives	**Bond, Currency, Interest rate**	
Plain Vanilla Derivatives	Swaps	Forwards
Exotic Derivatives	CMT options	
Structured Notes	Corporate MTNs Govt. agency MTNs Index amortizing notes CMT notes	Inverse floaters Periodic capped floaters Multi-step-up callable bonds
Counterparty Rating Requirement:	None	

OTHER ALTERNATIVE INVESTMENTS:

CMOs/REMICs – Govt. Strips	Repos/reverse repos

KEY MANAGERS & DERIVATIVES SPECIALISTS:	**Direct Phone/Fax**	**Job Function**
Mr. Charles Froland Managing Director	415/926-0232	Chief Investment Officer
Mr. Daniel J. Kingston Portfolio Manager	415/926-0228	Portfolio Mgr – Derivatives Portfolio Mgr – Options Portfolio Mgr – Structured Notes

Star Bank, N.A. (Cincinnati) (Portfolio)

Bank/Portfolio

Sub of Star Banc Corporation

Location: 425 Walnut Street
Cincinnati, OH 45201

Fax: 513/632-4653 **Phone:** 513/632-4000

Profile: Total return investor

Investment Portfolio: $ 1.8 billion

Use: **Balance Sheet/Risk Management**
Hedge interest rate risk

Currencies: US dollar

Regions: United States

DERIVATIVES ACTIVITIES: **CAC Class: 3**

OTC Derivatives	**Interest rate**	
Plain Vanilla Derivatives	Swaps	Caps
	Forwards	

OTHER ALTERNATIVE INVESTMENTS:

CMOs/REMICs – Govt.	Strips
CMOs/REMICs – Private	Repos/reverse repos

KEY MANAGERS & DERIVATIVES SPECIALISTS:	**Direct Phone/Fax**	**Job Function**
Mr. Bruce E. Barnes S.V.P. & Treasurer	513/632-4089	Bond Department Head Portfolio Mgr – Derivatives
Mr. David Moffett Chief Financial Officer	513/632-4534	Chief Financial Officer

State Compensation Insurance Fund

Insurance Co/P & C

Location: 1275 Market Street
San Francisco, CA 94103

Fax: 415/565-1783 **Phone:** 415/565-1234

Profile: Total return investor

Investment Portfolio: $ 6.0 billion

Use: **Balance Sheet/Risk Management**

Currencies: US dollar

Regions: United States

DERIVATIVES ACTIVITIES: **CAC Class: Inactive**

OTHER ALTERNATIVE INVESTMENTS:

CMOs/REMICs – Govt.	Strips

KEY MANAGERS & DERIVATIVES SPECIALISTS:	**Direct Phone/Fax**	**Job Function**
Ms. Leslie Dawe Investment Manager		Bond Department Head

State Street Bank & Trust (Trust)

Bank/Trust

Sub of State Street Boston Corporation

Location: 225 Franklin Street
3rd Floor
Boston, MA 02110

Fax: 617/654-4449 **Phone:** 617/786-3000

Profile: Hold to maturity investor

Investment Portfolio: $ 170.0 billion

Use: **Investment Purposes**

Currencies: US dollar

Regions: United States

DERIVATIVES ACTIVITIES: **CAC Class: Inactive**

OTHER ALTERNATIVE INVESTMENTS:

CMOs/REMICs – Govt. Strips

KEY MANAGERS & DERIVATIVES SPECIALISTS:	**Direct Phone/Fax**	**Job Function**
Mr. Brenton Dickson	617/654-3201	Fixed-Income Strategist
Mr. James A. Quale Senior Vice President	617/664-5301	Chief Investment Officer

State Street Boston Corporation

Bank Holding Company

Location: 225 Franklin Street
Boston, MA 02110

Fax: 617/664-5377 **Phone:** 617/786-3000

Profile: Total return investor

Use:

Balance Sheet/Risk Management
- Create synthetic fixed/floating rate
- Hedge currency risk
- Hedge interest rate risk
- Reduce cost of capital
- Strategic liability management

Investment Purposes
- Adjust portfolio duration
- Capture extra yield
- Discretionary situations
- Hedge bond portfolio risk
- Hedge interest rate risk

Currencies: US dollar, Australian dollar, Belgian franc, Canadian dollar, ECU, French franc, German mark, Italian lira, Japanese yen, Mexican peso, Spanish peseta, Swiss franc, UK pound

Regions: United States

DERIVATIVES ACTIVITIES: **CAC Class: 8**

Exchange-traded Options & Futures	**Currency, Interest rate**	
OTC Derivatives	**Currency, Interest rate**	
Plain Vanilla Derivatives	Swaps	Caps
	Forwards	Floors
Counterparty Rating Requirement:	A	

OTHER ALTERNATIVE INVESTMENTS:

Repos/reverse repos

State Street Boston Corporation – continued

KEY MANAGERS & DERIVATIVES SPECIALISTS:	Direct Phone/Fax	Job Function
Mr. David A. Spina Vice Chairman		Treasurer Portfolio Mgr – Derivatives

State Street Global Advisors

Bank/Management Division

Sub of State Street Boston Corporation

Location: Two International Place
Boston, MA 02110

Fax: 617/654-6176 **Phone:** 617/654-4738

Profile: Total return investor

Investment Portfolio: $ 96.5 billion

Use: **Balance Sheet/Risk Management**
Access global mkts
Hedge interest rate risk
Strategic liability management

Investment Purposes
Capture extra yield
Hedge equity portfolio risk
Hedge interest rate risk

Currencies: US dollar, Australian dollar, Belgian franc, Canadian dollar, ECU, French franc, German mark, Italian lira, Indonesian rupiah, Japanese yen, Mexican peso, Spanish peseta, Swiss franc, Thai baht, UK pound

Regions: United States, Canada, Europe, Latin America, Pacific Rim, Emerging mkts

DERIVATIVES ACTIVITIES:		
Exchange-traded Options & Futures	**Bond, Currency, Interest rate**	
OTC Derivatives	**Bond, Currency, Interest rate**	
Plain Vanilla Derivatives	Swaps	Forwards

OTHER ALTERNATIVE INVESTMENTS:		
	CMOs/REMICs – Govt.	CMOs/REMICs – Private

KEY MANAGERS & DERIVATIVES SPECIALISTS:	Direct Phone/Fax	Job Function
Mr. Robert V. Callahan Chief Financial Officer		Chief Financial Officer
Mr. Robert E. Furdak Managing Director	617/654-3379	Portfolio Mgr – Derivatives
Mr. Nicholas Lopardo Chairman & C.E.O.	617/654-3312	Chief Investment Officer
Mr. James Qualie Senior Vice President		Bond Department Head
Mr. J. Victor Thompson, Jr. Principal	617/654-3271 617/654-4338	Portfolio Mgr – Derivatives Portfolio Mgr – Futures

State Street Research & Management Co.

Mutual Fund Manager

Sub of Metropolitan Life Insurance Company

Location: One Financial Center
38th Floor
Boston, MA 02111-2690

Fax: 617/542-7753 **Phone:** 617/357-1200

Profile: Total return investor

Investment Portfolio: $ 24.3 billion

Use: **Balance Sheet/Risk Management**
Hedge balance sheet
Hedge currency risk
Incremental return
Protect currency gains

Investment Purposes
Hedge bond portfolio risk
Hedge currency risk
Reduce variability of returns

Currencies: US dollar

Regions: United States, Canada, Europe, Pacific Rim

DERIVATIVES ACTIVITIES: **CAC Class: 6**

Exchange-traded Options & Futures U.S. Treasury futures	**Bond** Municipal futures	
OTC Derivatives **Plain Vanilla Derivatives**	**Bond** Swaps	Forwards
Structured Notes	Corporate MTNs Govt. agency MTNs	Floaters
Counterparty Rating Requirement:	AAA	

OTHER ALTERNATIVE INVESTMENTS:

CMOs/REMICs – Govt.	GICs
CMOs/REMICs – Private	Strips

KEY MANAGERS & DERIVATIVES SPECIALISTS:	**Direct Phone/Fax**	**Job Function**
Mr. Peter C. Bennett Vice President		Chief Investment Officer
Mr. Edward Finch Vice President	617/357-1222	Portfolio Mgr – Derivatives *Corp, MBS* Research Analyst – Derivatives *Corp, MBS*
Mr. John H. Kallis Senior Vice President		Portfolio Mgr – Derivatives Portfolio Mgr – Futures *Govt* Portfolio Mgr – Structured Notes
Mr. Thomas A. Shively Senior Vice President	617/357-1256	Bond Department Head *Taxable*
Mr. Ralph Verni Chairman, President & C.E.O.		President
Mr. Jeff Ward	617/357-1270	Trader – Derivatives Trader – Futures Trader – Options

Staten Island Savings Bank

Savings Bank/Bldg Society

Location: 15 Beach Street
Staten Island, NY 10304-2713

Fax: 718/727-3794 **Phone:** 718/447-7900

Profile: Total return investor

Investment Portfolio: $ 900.0 million

Use: **Investment Purposes**
Asset allocation

Currencies: US dollar

Regions: United States

DERIVATIVES ACTIVITIES: **CAC Class: Inactive**

OTHER ALTERNATIVE INVESTMENTS:

CMOs/REMICs – Govt.
CMOs/REMICs – Private
Repos/reverse repos

KEY MANAGERS & DERIVATIVES SPECIALISTS:	Direct Phone/Fax	Job Function
Mr. Edward Klungele Chief Financial Officer		Chief Investment Officer Chief Financial Officer

Stein Roe & Farnham Incorporated

Investment Manager

Sub of Liberty Mutual Insurance Companies

Location: One South Wacker Drive
Chicago, IL 60606

Fax: 312/368-8103 **Phone:** 312/368-7700

Profile: Total return investor

Investment Portfolio: $ 23.0 billion

Use: **Balance Sheet/Risk Management**
Hedge balance sheet

Currencies: US dollar

Regions: United States

DERIVATIVES ACTIVITIES: **CAC Class: 5**

OTC Derivatives
Plain Vanilla Derivatives Forwards

Counterparty Rating Requirement: AAA

OTHER ALTERNATIVE INVESTMENTS:

CMOs/REMICs – Govt.
CMOs/REMICs – Private
Strips

KEY MANAGERS & DERIVATIVES SPECIALISTS:	Direct Phone/Fax	Job Function
Mr. William D. Andrews Director – Fixed-Income	312/368-7682 312/368-5776	Bond Department Head Portfolio Mgr – Derivatives
Mr. Steven P. Luetger Vice President & Principal	312/368-7645	Portfolio Mgr – Derivatives
Mr. Timothy A. Schlindlwein Chairman	312/368-7678	Chief Investment Officer

Stein Roe & Farnham Incorporated – continued

KEY MANAGERS & DERIVATIVES SPECIALISTS:	Direct Phone/Fax	Job Function
Mr. Hans P. Ziegler President & C.E.O.		President

STI Capital Management

Bank/Management Division

Sub of SunTrust Banks Inc.

Location: 200 South Orange Avenue
8th Floor
Orlando, FL 32801-3495

Fax: 407/237-4285 **Phone:** 407/237-4472

Profile: Total return investor

Investment Portfolio: $ 11.7 billion

Use: **Investment Purposes**
Asset allocation
Provide incremental return

Currencies: US dollar

Regions: United States

DERIVATIVES ACTIVITIES: **CAC Class: Inactive**

OTHER ALTERNATIVE INVESTMENTS:

CMOs/REMICs – Govt.

KEY MANAGERS & DERIVATIVES SPECIALISTS:	Direct Phone/Fax	Job Function
Mr. L. Earl Denney Senior Vice President	407/237-4910	Bond Department Head *Corp, Govt*
Mr. Anthony R. Gray Chairman	407/237-4369	Chief Investment Officer
Mr. Ronald H. Schwartz Senior Vice President	407/237-4176	Bond Department Head *Muni*
Mr. James R. Wood President & C.F.O.		President Chief Financial Officer

Strategic Fixed Income L.P.

Investment Manager

Location: 1001 19th Street North
Suite 1600
Arlington, VA 22201

Fax: 703/812-9554 **Phone:** 703/812-8300

Profile: Hold to maturity investor

Investment Portfolio: $ 4.8 billion

Use: **Balance Sheet/Risk Management**
Hedge balance sheet
Hedge currency risk
Hedge interest rate risk
Hedge overseas investments
Protect currency gains

Currencies: US dollar

Regions: United States

Strategic Fixed Income L.P. – continued

DERIVATIVES ACTIVITIES: **CAC Class: 6**

Exchange-traded Options & Futures	**Currency**	
OTC Derivatives	**Currency, Interest rate**	
Plain Vanilla Derivatives	Forwards	Swaptions

OTHER ALTERNATIVE INVESTMENTS:

	CMOs/REMICs – Govt. CMOs/REMICs – Private	Repos/reverse repos

KEY MANAGERS & DERIVATIVES SPECIALISTS:	**Direct Phone/Fax**	**Job Function**
Ms. Patricia Arcoleo Vice President		Portfolio Mgr – Derivatives
Mr. Kenneth Windheim President		President Chief Investment Officer

Strong Capital Management Inc.

Investment Manager

Location: 100 Heritage Reserve
Menomonee Falls, WI 53051

Fax: 414/359-3460 **Phone:** 414/359-3600

Profile: Total return investor

Investment Portfolio: $ 5.7 billion

Use: **Investment Purposes**
Adjust portfolio duration
Expand international investments
Hedge bond portfolio risk
Hedge currency risk
Hedge interest rate risk
Provide incremental return

Currencies: US dollar, Australian dollar, Belgian franc, Canadian dollar, French franc, German mark, Italian lira, Indonesian rupiah, Japanese yen, Spanish peseta, Swiss franc, Thai baht, UK pound

Regions: United States, Canada, Europe, Latin America, Pacific Rim

DERIVATIVES ACTIVITIES: **CAC Class: 5**

Exchange-traded Options & Futures U.S. Treasury futures U.S. Treasury options	**Bond, Currency, Interest rate** Municipal futures	
OTC Derivatives	**Bond, Currency, Interest rate**	
Plain Vanilla Derivatives	Swaps	Forwards
Structured Notes	Corporate MTNs Floaters	Inverse floaters
Counterparty Rating Requirement:	AAA	

OTHER ALTERNATIVE INVESTMENTS:

	CMOs/REMICs – Govt. CMOs/REMICs – Private GICs	Strips Repos/reverse repos

Strong Capital Management Inc. – continued

KEY MANAGERS & DERIVATIVES SPECIALISTS:	Direct Phone/Fax	Job Function
Mr. Lyle Fitterer		Trader – Derivatives Trader – Futures
Mr. Richard S. Strong		Chief Investment Officer Bond Department Head
Mr. Bradley C. Tank Principal	414/359-3861 414/359-3745	Portfolio Mgr – Derivatives Portfolio Mgr – Futures Portfolio Mgr – Options Portfolio Mgr – Structured Notes

Summit Bank (Portfolio)

Bank/Portfolio

Location: One Main Street
Chatham, NJ 07928

Fax: 201/701-2675 **Phone:** 201/701-6200

Profile: Stable asset investor

Investment Portfolio: $ 1.9 billion

Use: **Balance Sheet/Risk Management**
Hedge interest rate risk

Currencies: US dollar

Regions: United States

DERIVATIVES ACTIVITIES: **CAC Class: 3**

OTC Derivatives	**Interest rate**	
Plain Vanilla Derivatives	Swaps	Caps
Counterparty Rating Requirement:	AA	

KEY MANAGERS & DERIVATIVES SPECIALISTS:	Direct Phone/Fax	Job Function
Mr. Bradley Condit Vice President	201/701-2527	Portfolio Mgr – Derivatives
Mr. Barry S. Duerk S.V.P. & Sr. Investment Offcr.	201/701-2525	Chief Investment Officer Portfolio Mgr – Derivatives

SunFinancial Group

Insurance Co/Management

Location: One Sun Life Executive Park
Wellesley Hills, MA 02181

Fax: 617/431-7521 **Phone:** 617/237-6030

Profile: Total return investor

Investment Portfolio: $ 10.0 billion

Use:

Balance Sheet/Risk Management
Hedge interest rate risk
Incremental return
Strategic liability management

Investment Purposes
Asset allocation
Capture extra yield
Convexity objectives
Discretionary situations
Hedge bond portfolio risk
Hedge interest rate risk
Immunize from volatility
Lower transactions costs
Provide incremental return
Reduce variability of returns

Currencies: US dollar, Canadian dollar, UK pound

Regions: United States

DERIVATIVES ACTIVITIES: **CAC Class: 5**

Exchange-traded Options & Futures	**Bond, Interest rate**	
U.S. Treasury futures		
OTC Derivatives	**Bond**	
Plain Vanilla Derivatives	Swaps	Swaptions
Exotic Derivatives	Bond index swaps	
Structured Notes	Corporate MTNs	
Counterparty Rating Requirement:	AA	

OTHER ALTERNATIVE INVESTMENTS:

CMOs/REMICs – Govt.
GICs
Strips
Repos/reverse repos

KEY MANAGERS & DERIVATIVES SPECIALISTS:	**Direct Phone/Fax**	**Job Function**
Mr. Richard Gordon Assistant Vice President	Ext. 7171	Bond Department Head *Taxable*
Mr. C. James Prieur Vice President – Investments	Ext. 1139	Chief Investment Officer Portfolio Mgr – Derivatives Portfolio Mgr – Structured Notes

SunTrust Bank, Nashville, N.A. (Trust)

Bank/Trust

Sub of SunTrust Banks Inc.

Location: 424 Church Street
Nashville, TN 37219

Fax: 615/255-2804 **Phone:** 615/748-4736

Profile: Hold to maturity investor

Investment Portfolio: $ 5.1 billion

Use: **Investment Purposes**

Currencies: US dollar

Regions: United States

SunTrust Bank, Nashville, N.A. (Trust) – continued

DERIVATIVES ACTIVITIES: **CAC Class: Inactive**

OTHER ALTERNATIVE INVESTMENTS:

	CMOs/REMICs – Govt.	Repos/reverse repos
	Strips	

KEY MANAGERS & DERIVATIVES SPECIALISTS:	Direct Phone/Fax	Job Function
Mr. Parker W. Thomas, Jr.	615/748-5154	Chief Investment Officer Fixed-Income Strategist

SwissRe Advisers Inc.

Insurance Co/Management

Sub of Schweizerische Rückversicherungs Gesellschaft

Location: 200 Park Avenue
16th Floor
New York, NY 10166

Fax: 212/973-5035 **Phone:** 212/973-5000

Profile: Total return investor

Investment Portfolio: $ 5.0 billion

Use: **Investment Purposes**

Currencies: US dollar

Regions: United States

DERIVATIVES ACTIVITIES: **CAC Class: Inactive**

OTHER ALTERNATIVE INVESTMENTS:

	CMOs/REMICs – Govt.	Repos/reverse repos

KEY MANAGERS & DERIVATIVES SPECIALISTS:	Direct Phone/Fax	Job Function
Mr. Thomas N. Farmakis Executive Vice President	212/973-5041	Chief Investment Officer Bond Department Head

Synovus Financial Corporation

Bank/Portfolio

Location: 901 Front Avenue
Suite 301
Columbus, GA 31901

Fax: 706/649-2479 **Phone:** 706/649-2311

Profile: Current yield investor

Investment Portfolio: $ 1.5 billion

Use: **Balance Sheet/Risk Management**
Hedge interest rate risk

Currencies: US dollar

Regions: United States

DERIVATIVES ACTIVITIES: **CAC Class: 3**

OTC Derivatives	**Interest rate**	
Plain Vanilla Derivatives	Swaps	Forwards
Structured Notes	Govt. agency MTNs	
Counterparty Rating Requirement:	A	

Synovus Financial Corporation – continued

OTHER ALTERNATIVE INVESTMENTS:

	Strips	Repos/reverse repos

KEY MANAGERS & DERIVATIVES SPECIALISTS:	**Direct Phone/Fax**	**Job Function**
Mr. Joseph M. Lowery	706/649-4424	Chief Investment Officer Portfolio Mgr – Derivatives Portfolio Mgr – Structured Notes

TCF Bank Minnesota fsb

Savings Bank/Bldg Society

Sub of TCF Financial Corporation

Location: 801 Marquette Avenue
Suite 302
Minneapolis, MN 55402-3476

Fax: 612/376-9089 **Phone:** 612/661-6500

Profile: Total return investor

Investment Portfolio: $ 1.2 billion

Use: **Balance Sheet/Risk Management**
Hedge interest rate risk

Investment Purposes
Discretionary situations

Currencies: US dollar

Regions: United States

DERIVATIVES ACTIVITIES: **CAC Class: 1**

OTC Derivatives	**Interest rate**
Plain Vanilla Derivatives	Swaps
Counterparty Rating Requirement:	AAA

OTHER ALTERNATIVE INVESTMENTS:

	CMOs/REMICs – Govt. CMOs/REMICs – Private	Repos/reverse repos

KEY MANAGERS & DERIVATIVES SPECIALISTS:	**Direct Phone/Fax**	**Job Function**
Mr. Leon Eicten	612/661-8799	Portfolio Mgr – Derivatives
Mr. Kevin Fink Director – Investments	612/661-8798	Chief Investment Officer
Mr. Lynn A. Nagorske E.V.P., Treasurer & C.F.O.		Chief Financial Officer Treasurer Portfolio Mgr – Derivatives
Mr. James E. Tuite President & C.O.O.		President

Teachers Insurance & Annuity Association

Union Pension Fund

Location: 730 Third Avenue
New York, NY 10017-3206

Fax: 212/916-6690 **Phone:** 212/490-9000

Investment Portfolio: $ 50.0 - 100.0 billion

Use: **Balance Sheet/Risk Management**
Hedge balance sheet
Hedge commercial paper
Hedge currency risk
Hedge interest rate risk

Currencies: US dollar

Regions: United States

DERIVATIVES ACTIVITIES: **CAC Class: 6**

Exchange-traded Options & Futures	**Interest rate**	
OTC Derivatives	**Interest rate**	
Plain Vanilla Derivatives	Swaps	Forwards
Structured Notes		
Counterparty Rating Requirement:	AA	

OTHER ALTERNATIVE INVESTMENTS:

CMOs/REMICs – Govt.	Strips
CMOs/REMICs – Private	Repos/reverse repos
GICs	

KEY MANAGERS & DERIVATIVES SPECIALISTS:	**Direct Phone/Fax**	**Job Function**
Mr. David B. Bullett Senior Vice President	212/916-4303	Bond Department Head
Mr. J. Daniel Lee, Jr. Executive Vice President	212/916-4300	Chief Investment Officer
Mr. Martin Leibowitz Vice Chairman & C.I.O.	212/916-4010	Chief Investment Officer Portfolio Mgr – Derivatives Portfolio Mgr – Futures Portfolio Mgr – Structured Notes

Teachers' Retirement System of Texas

Government Pension Fund

Location: 1000 Red River Street
Austin, TX 78701

Fax: 512/370-0519 **Phone:** 512/397-6460

Profile: Total return investor

Investment Portfolio: $ 38.0 billion

Use: **Investment Purposes**
Asset allocation
Provide incremental return

Currencies: US dollar

Regions: United States

DERIVATIVES ACTIVITIES: **CAC Class: Inactive**

Teachers' Retirement System of Texas – continued

OTHER ALTERNATIVE INVESTMENTS:

	CMOs/REMICs – Govt.	Strips
	CMOs/REMICs – Private	Repos/reverse repos
	CMOs/REMICs – Private	Repos/reverse repos

KEY MANAGERS & DERIVATIVES SPECIALISTS:	**Direct Phone/Fax**	**Job Function**
Mr. R. Jack Cooper Director	512/397-6471 512/370-0568	Bond Department Head *Corp, Govt, MBS*
Mr. John E. Young		Chief Investment Officer

Teledyne Inc.

Corporation

Location: 2049 Century Park East
Suite 15
Los Angeles, CA 90067

Fax: 310/551-4365 **Phone:** 310/277-3311

Profile: Total return investor

Investment Portfolio: $ 3.2 - 3.9 billion

Use: **Balance Sheet/Risk Management**

Investment Purposes

Currencies: US dollar

Regions: United States

DERIVATIVES ACTIVITIES: **CAC Class: Inactive**

OTHER ALTERNATIVE INVESTMENTS:

	CMOs/REMICs – Govt.	CMOs/REMICs – Private

KEY MANAGERS & DERIVATIVES SPECIALISTS:	**Direct Phone/Fax**	**Job Function**
Mr. Paul H. Newmark Manager – Investments	310/551-4240 310/551-4225	Chief Investment Officer

Templeton Global Bond Managers, Inc.

Investment Manager

Sub of Franklin Resources, Inc.

Location: 500 East Broward Boulevard
Suite 2100
Fort Lauderdale, FL 33394

Fax: 954/462-2504 **Phone:** 954/764-7390

Profile: Total return investor

Investment Portfolio: $ 2.3 billion

Use: **Balance Sheet/Risk Management**
Access global mkts
Hedge balance sheet

Investment Purposes
Hedge bond portfolio risk

Currencies: US dollar, Canadian dollar, Japanese yen, UK pound

Regions: United States, Canada, Europe, Pacific Rim

DERIVATIVES ACTIVITIES: **CAC Class: 3**

OTC Derivatives **Plain Vanilla Derivatives**	**Bond** Swaps	 Forwards
Structured Notes	Corporate MTNs	
Counterparty Rating Requirement:	A	

Templeton Global Bond Managers, Inc. – continued

OTHER ALTERNATIVE INVESTMENTS:

	CMOs/REMICs – Govt. CMOs/REMICs – Private	GICs

KEY MANAGERS & DERIVATIVES SPECIALISTS:	**Direct Phone/Fax**	**Job Function**
Mr. Neil S. Devlin Vice President	954/527-7444	Chief Investment Officer
Mr. Samuel J. Forester, Jr. President	Ext. 449	President
Mr. Thomas Latta Vice President	954/527-7434	Portfolio Mgr – Derivatives Portfolio Mgr – Structured Notes
Mr. Thomas Wilkinson Vice President	954/527-7442	Portfolio Mgr – Derivatives

Tenneco Inc.

Corporation

Location: 1010 Milam
Houston, TX 77002

Fax: 713/757-4257 **Phone:** 713/757-2131

Use: **Balance Sheet/Risk Management**
Hedge currency risk
Hedge interest rate risk
Protect currency gains
Strategic liability management

Currencies: US dollar, Australian dollar, Belgian franc, Canadian dollar, French franc, German mark, Italian lira, Spanish peseta, UK pound

Regions: United States, Canada, Europe

DERIVATIVES ACTIVITIES: **CAC Class: 6**

OTC Derivatives	**Currency, Interest rate**	
Plain Vanilla Derivatives	Swaps	Forwards
Counterparty Rating Requirement:	AA	

KEY MANAGERS & DERIVATIVES SPECIALISTS:	**Direct Phone/Fax**	**Job Function**
Mr. Robert T. Blakely Senior Vice President & C.F.O.		Chief Financial Officer
Ms. Karen R. Osar Vice President & Treasurer		Treasurer Portfolio Mgr – Derivatives

Tennessee Consolidated Retirement System

Government Pension Fund

Location: 1160 Andrew Jackson Building, 11th Floor, Nashville, TN 37243-0245

Fax: 615/741-1061 **Phone:** 615/741-2643

Profile: Total return investor

Investment Portfolio: $ 13.7 billion

Use:

Balance Sheet/Risk Management
Asset allocation
Hedge currency risk

Investment Purposes

Currencies: US dollar, German mark, Japanese yen, UK pound

Regions: Europe, Pacific Rim

DERIVATIVES ACTIVITIES: **CAC Class: 6**

OTC Derivatives	**Currency**
Plain Vanilla Derivatives	Forwards
Counterparty Rating Requirement:	A

OTHER ALTERNATIVE INVESTMENTS:

CMOs/REMICs – Govt.
CMOs/REMICs – Private

KEY MANAGERS & DERIVATIVES SPECIALISTS:	**Direct Phone/Fax**	**Job Function**
Mr. Charles H. Webb Chief Investment Officer	615/532-1157	Chief Investment Officer Portfolio Mgr – Derivatives
Mr. Roy O. Wellington III	615/532-1151	Trader – Derivatives

Texaco Inc.

Corporation

Location: 2000 Westchester Avenue, White Plains, NY 10650

Fax: 914/253-7753 **Phone:** 914/253-4000

Use:

Balance Sheet/Risk Management
Access global mkts
Create synthetic fixed/floating rate
Hedge commercial paper
Hedge currency risk
Hedge interest rate risk
Hedge overseas investments
Incremental return
Lower transaction costs
Protect currency gains
Reduce cost of capital

Investment Purposes
Beat conventional rates
Capture extra yield
Discretionary situations
Hedge currency risk
Hedge interest rate risk
Lower transactions costs
Protect currency gains
Provide incremental return

Currencies: US dollar, Australian dollar

Regions: United States, Europe, Latin America, Pacific Rim

DERIVATIVES ACTIVITIES: **CAC Class: 6**

Exchange-traded Options & Futures		
OTC Derivatives	**Currency**	
Plain Vanilla Derivatives	Swaps Forwards	Caps
Counterparty Rating Requirement:	AA	

Texaco Inc. – continued

KEY MANAGERS & DERIVATIVES SPECIALISTS:	Direct Phone/Fax	Job Function
Mr. William C. Bousquette S.V.P. & C.F.O.		Chief Financial Officer
Mr. James F. Link Treasurer		Treasurer Portfolio Mgr – Derivatives

Texas Commerce Bank, N.A. (Houston) (Trust)

Bank/Trust

Location: 600 Travis Street
Houston, TX 77002

Fax: 713/216-5674 **Phone:** 713/236-4865

Profile: Total return investor

Investment Portfolio: $ 4.0 billion

Use: **Investment Purposes**
Asset allocation

Currencies: US dollar

Regions: United States

DERIVATIVES ACTIVITIES: **CAC Class: Inactive**

OTHER ALTERNATIVE INVESTMENTS:

CMOs/REMICs – Govt. CMOs/REMICs – Private

KEY MANAGERS & DERIVATIVES SPECIALISTS:	Direct Phone/Fax	Job Function
Mr. Thomas Franckowiak Vice President	713/216-7770	Chief Investment Officer

Texas County & District Retirement System

Government Pension Fund

Location: 400 West 14th Street
Austin, TX 78701-1688

Fax: 512/479-8114 **Phone:** 512/469-9668

Profile: Hold to maturity investor

Investment Portfolio: $ 4.0 - 10.0 billion

Use: **Investment Purposes**

Currencies: US dollar

Regions: United States

DERIVATIVES ACTIVITIES: **CAC Class: Inactive**

OTHER ALTERNATIVE INVESTMENTS:

CMOs/REMICs – Govt. CMOs/REMICs – Private

Texas County & District Retirement System – continued

KEY MANAGERS & DERIVATIVES SPECIALISTS:	Direct Phone/Fax	Job Function
Mr. Terrence Horton Director		Chief Investment Officer
Mr. Ronald Schultz Investment Manager	512/479-6021	Chief Investment Officer

Third Federal Savings & Loan Association of Cleveland

Savings Bank/Bldg Society

Location: 7007 Broadway Avenue
Cleveland, OH 44105

Fax: 216/441-0055 **Phone:** 216/441-6000

Profile: Hold to maturity investor

Investment Portfolio: $ 4.5 billion

Use: **Investment Purposes**
Alter portfolio weighting
Asset allocation

Currencies: US dollar

Regions: United States

DERIVATIVES ACTIVITIES: **CAC Class: Inactive**

OTHER ALTERNATIVE INVESTMENTS:

CMOs/REMICs – Govt. CMOs/REMICs – Private

KEY MANAGERS & DERIVATIVES SPECIALISTS:	Direct Phone/Fax	Job Function
Mr. Mark Allio Chief Financial Officer		Chief Financial Officer Bond Department Head

Thompson, Siegel & Walmsley, Inc.

Investment Manager

Sub of United Asset Management Corporation

Location: 5000 Monument Avenue
Richmond, VA 23230

Fax: 804/353-0925 **Phone:** 804/353-4500

Profile: Total return investor

Investment Portfolio: $ 3.7 billion

Use: **Investment Purposes**

Currencies: US dollar

Regions: United States

DERIVATIVES ACTIVITIES: **CAC Class: Inactive**

OTHER ALTERNATIVE INVESTMENTS:

CMOs/REMICs – Govt.

Thompson, Siegel & Walmsley, Inc. – continued

KEY MANAGERS & DERIVATIVES SPECIALISTS:	Direct Phone/Fax	Job Function
Mr. Charles A. Gomer Vice President	804/353-9914	Bond Department Head
Mr. John T. Siegel President & Treasurer		President Chief Investment Officer Treasurer
Mr. Matthew G. Thompson Managing Director		Chief Investment Officer

Thornburg Management Company, Inc.

Mutual Fund Manager

Location: 119 East Marcy Street
Suite 202
Santa Fe, NM 87501-2018

Fax: 505/984-0310 **Phone:** 505/984-0200

Profile: Total return investor

Investment Portfolio: $ 2.0 billion

Use: **Investment Purposes**
Capture extra yield

Currencies: US dollar
Canadian dollar

Regions: United States

DERIVATIVES ACTIVITIES: **CAC Class: 2**

Structured Notes Inverse floaters

OTHER ALTERNATIVE INVESTMENTS:

CMOs/REMICs – Govt. CMOs/REMICs – Private

KEY MANAGERS & DERIVATIVES SPECIALISTS:	Direct Phone/Fax	Job Function
Mr. Brian J. McMahon Managing Director		Chief Investment Officer Bond Department Head *MBS* Portfolio Mgr – Structured Notes Trader – Structured Investments

TIG Holdings Inc.

Insurance Co/Life

Location: 65 East 55th Street
28th Floor
New York, NY 10022

Fax: 212/371-8360 **Phone:** 212/446-2700

Profile: Total return investor

Investment Portfolio: $ 4.4 billion

Use: **Balance Sheet/Risk Management**
Hedge interest rate risk

Investment Purposes
Adjust portfolio duration
Hedge interest rate risk

Currencies: US dollar

Regions: United States

TIG Holdings Inc. – continued

DERIVATIVES ACTIVITIES: **CAC Class: 3**

Exchange-traded Options & Futures	**Bond**
U.S. Treasury futures	

OTHER ALTERNATIVE INVESTMENTS:

Repos/reverse repos

KEY MANAGERS & DERIVATIVES SPECIALISTS:	**Direct Phone/Fax**	**Job Function**
Mr. David M. Finkelstein Director Corporate Finance	212/446-2711	Portfolio Mgr – Futures
Mr. Louis Paglia S.V.P. & Treasurer	212/446-2708	Treasurer Bond Department Head
Mr. Orest Stelmach Chief Investment Officer	212/446-2717	Chief Investment Officer Portfolio Mgr – Futures

Todd Investment Advisors Inc.

Investment Manager

Sub of Stifel Financial Corporation

Location: 3160 National City Tower
Louisville, KY 40202

Fax: 502/585-4203 **Phone:** 502/585-3121

Profile: Total return investor

Investment Portfolio: $ 2.3 billion

Use: **Investment Purposes**
Alter portfolio weighting

Currencies: US dollar

Regions: United States

DERIVATIVES ACTIVITIES: **CAC Class: Inactive**

OTHER ALTERNATIVE INVESTMENTS:

CMOs/REMICs – Govt.	Strips
CMOs/REMICs – Private	

KEY MANAGERS & DERIVATIVES SPECIALISTS:	**Direct Phone/Fax**	**Job Function**
Mr. Robert Cregor President		President Fixed-Income Strategist
Mr. Bosworth M. Todd, Jr. Chairman		Chief Investment Officer

Torchmark Corporation

Insurance Co/Management

Location: 2001 Third Avenue South
Birmingham, AL 35233

Fax: 205/325-4157 **Phone:** 205/325-4200

Profile: Total return investor

Investment Portfolio: $ 5.4 billion

Use: **Investment Purposes**
Diversify portfolio

Currencies: US dollar

Regions: United States

DERIVATIVES ACTIVITIES: **CAC Class: Inactive**

OTHER ALTERNATIVE INVESTMENTS:

	CMOs/REMICs – Govt. Strips	Repos/reverse repos

KEY MANAGERS & DERIVATIVES SPECIALISTS:	**Direct Phone/Fax**	**Job Function**
Mr. Michael J. Klyce Vice President & Treasurer	205/325-2051	Chief Investment Officer Treasurer

The Transamerica Corporation

Corporation

Location: 600 Montgomery Street
San Francisco, CA 94111

Fax: 415/983-4888 **Phone:** 415/983-4000

Use: **Balance Sheet/Risk Management**
Create synthetic fixed/floating rate
Hedge balance sheet
Hedge interest rate risk
Incremental return
Strategic liability management

Currencies: US dollar

Regions: United States

DERIVATIVES ACTIVITIES: **CAC Class: 6**

Exchange-traded Options & Futures	**Interest rate**	
OTC Derivatives **Plain Vanilla Derivatives**	**Interest rate** Swaps Forwards Swaptions	 Caps Floors
Counterparty Rating Requirement:	AA	

KEY MANAGERS & DERIVATIVES SPECIALISTS:	**Direct Phone/Fax**	**Job Function**
Mr. Edgar H. Grubb Exec. Vice President & C.F.O.		Chief Financial Officer
Mr. Frank C. Herringer President & C.E.O.		President
Mr. Richard N. Latzer Sr. Vice President & C.I.O.		Chief Investment Officer
Mr. Robert R. Lindberg Vice President & Treasurer		Treasurer Portfolio Mgr – Derivatives

The Transamerica Corporation – continued

KEY MANAGERS & DERIVATIVES SPECIALISTS:	Direct Phone/Fax	Job Function
Ms. Judith M. Tornese V.P. – Risk Management		Portfolio Mgr – Derivatives

Transamerica Investment Services Inc.

Insurance Co/Management

Sub of The Transamerica Corporation

Location: 1150 South Olive Street
Suite T 2700
Los Angeles, CA 90015

Fax: 213/742-4150 **Phone:** 213/742-4141

Profile: Hold to maturity investor

Investment Portfolio: $ 26.0 billion

Use: **Balance Sheet/Risk Management**
Hedge balance sheet
Hedge interest rate risk

Currencies: US dollar

Regions: United States

DERIVATIVES ACTIVITIES: **CAC Class: 6**

Exchange-traded Options & Futures

OTC Derivatives	**Interest rate**	
Plain Vanilla Derivatives	Swaps Forwards Swaptions	Caps Floors Collars
Exotic Derivatives	CMT swaps Index amortizing swaps	Periodic caps/floors
Counterparty Rating Requirement:	AA	

OTHER ALTERNATIVE INVESTMENTS:

	CMOs/REMICs – Govt. CMOs/REMICs – Private	Strips Repos/reverse repos

KEY MANAGERS & DERIVATIVES SPECIALISTS:	Direct Phone/Fax	Job Function
Mr. William Griffin Vice President	213/742-4161	Portfolio Mgr – Derivatives Portfolio Mgr – Futures Portfolio Mgr – Options Trader – Derivatives
Mr. Perry D. Preusch Vice President	213/742-3556	Bond Department Head *Muni*
Mr. Gary U. Rolle Executive Vice President	213/742-3551	Chief Investment Officer
Ms. Susan A. Silbert Senior Vice President	213/742-3553	Fixed-Income Strategist

Travelers Group

Corporation

Location: 388 Greenwich Street
New York, NY 10013

Fax: 212/816-8912 **Phone:** 212/816-8000

Use: **Balance Sheet/Risk Management**
Create synthetic fixed/floating rate
Hedge currency risk
Hedge interest rate risk
Hedge overseas investments
Protect currency gains

Currencies: US dollar

Regions: United States

DERIVATIVES ACTIVITIES: **CAC Class: 6**

Exchange-traded Options & Futures U.S. Treasury futures	**Interest rate**	
OTC Derivatives **Plain Vanilla Derivatives**	**Currency, Interest rate** Swaps	Forwards
Counterparty Rating Requirement:	AA	

OTHER ALTERNATIVE INVESTMENTS:

Repos/reverse repos

KEY MANAGERS & DERIVATIVES SPECIALISTS:	**Direct Phone/Fax**	**Job Function**
Mr. James Dimon President & C.O.O.	212/816-8800 212/816-8999	President
Mr. Jerome T. Fadden Vice President & Treasurer		Treasurer Portfolio Mgr – Derivatives Portfolio Mgr – Futures
Ms. Heidi G. Miller Chief Financial Officer		Chief Financial Officer

The Travelers Insurance Company

Insurance Co/Life

Sub of Travelers Group

Location: One Tower Square
Nine Plaza Building
Hartford, CT 06183-2030

Fax: 203/277-3667 **Phone:** 203/277-0111

Profile: Current yield investor

Investment Portfolio: $ 53.6 billion

Use: **Balance Sheet/Risk Management**
Hedge interest rate risk

Currencies: US dollar

Regions: United States

The Travelers Insurance Company – continued

DERIVATIVES ACTIVITIES:		CAC Class: 4
Exchange-traded Options & Futures U.S. Treasury futures	**Interest rate**	
OTC Derivatives **Plain Vanilla Derivatives**	**Interest rate** Swaps	
Structured Notes	Corporate MTNs Govt. agency MTNs	Bond index notes
Counterparty Rating Requirement:	AAA	

OTHER ALTERNATIVE INVESTMENTS:

	CMOs/REMICs – Govt. CMOs/REMICs – Private	GICs Repos/reverse repos

KEY MANAGERS & DERIVATIVES SPECIALISTS:	Direct Phone/Fax	Job Function
Mr. Jay Fishman Chief Financial Officer	203/954-1155	Chief Financial Officer
Mr. Jordan Stitzer Vice President	203-277-3992	Portfolio Mgr – Derivatives Portfolio Mgr – Futures Portfolio Mgr – Structured Notes
Dr. David A. Tyson Vice President	203/954-2041 203/954-4278	Bond Department Head
Mr. Marc Weill Senior Vice President	203/954-8423	Chief Investment Officer

Trust Company Bank of Georgia (Trust)

Bank/Trust

Sub of SunTrust Banks Inc.

Location: One Park Place
2nd Floor
Atlanta, GA 30303

Fax: 404/581-1793 **Phone:** 404/588-7711

Profile: Total return investor

Investment Portfolio: $ 10.3 billion

Use: **Investment Purposes**
Diversify portfolio

Currencies: US dollar

Regions: United States

DERIVATIVES ACTIVITIES: **CAC Class: Inactive**

OTHER ALTERNATIVE INVESTMENTS:

	CMOs/REMICs – Govt. Strips	Repos/reverse repos

Trust Company Bank of Georgia (Trust) – continued

KEY MANAGERS & DERIVATIVES SPECIALISTS:	**Direct Phone/Fax**	**Job Function**
Mr. Gerald T. Adams Senior Vice President	404/588-8569	Chief Investment Officer
Mr. James R. Albach	404/588-8240	Bond Department Head

Trust Company of the West (TCW) (High Yield Dept.)

Investment Manager

Sub of Trust Company of the West (TCW)

Location: 11100 Santa Monica Boulevard, Los Angeles, CA 90025

Fax: 310/575-1997 **Phone:** 310/575-9700

Profile: Total return investor

Investment Portfolio: $ 1.8 billion

Use: **Investment Purposes**

Currencies: US dollar

Regions: United States

DERIVATIVES ACTIVITIES: **CAC Class: Inactive**

OTHER ALTERNATIVE INVESTMENTS:

CMOs/REMICs – Govt.

KEY MANAGERS & DERIVATIVES SPECIALISTS:	**Direct Phone/Fax**	**Job Function**
Ms. Melissa Weiler		Bond Department Head *Corp*

Trustmark National Bank (Portfolio)

Bank/Portfolio

Sub of Trustmark Corporation

Location: 248 East Capitol Street, Jackson, MS 39201

Fax: 601/949-2382 **Phone:** 601/354-5111

Profile: Total return investor

Investment Portfolio: $ 1.8 billion

Use: **Investment Purposes**

Currencies: US dollar

Regions: United States

DERIVATIVES ACTIVITIES: **CAC Class: 2**

Structured Notes Multi-step-up callable bonds

OTHER ALTERNATIVE INVESTMENTS:

CMOs/REMICs – Govt.
CMOs/REMICs – Private
Strips
Repos/reverse repos

Trustmark National Bank (Portfolio) – continued

KEY MANAGERS & DERIVATIVES SPECIALISTS:	Direct Phone/Fax	Job Function
Mr. Gerard Host Senior Vice President	601/949-6651	Chief Financial Officer
Mr. Jonathan Rogers Assistant Vice President	601/961-6561	Trader – Structured Investments
Mr. Zach Wasson Vice President & Treasury Mgr	601/949-6816	Treasurer Portfolio Mgr – Structured Notes

Twentieth Century Insurance Company

Insurance Co/P & C

Sub of Twentieth Century Companies

Location: 6301 Owensmouth Avenue
Suite 950
Woodland Hills, CA 91367

Fax: 818/716-1308 **Phone:** 818/704-3700

Profile: Hold to maturity investor

Investment Portfolio: $ 1.0 billion

Use: **Investment Purposes**
Diversify portfolio
Hedge bond portfolio risk

Currencies: US dollar

Regions: United States

DERIVATIVES ACTIVITIES: **CAC Class: 1**

Structured Notes Corporate MTNs

OTHER ALTERNATIVE INVESTMENTS:

CMOs/REMICs – Govt. CMOs/REMICs – Private

KEY MANAGERS & DERIVATIVES SPECIALISTS:	Direct Phone/Fax	Job Function
Mr. Charles W. Hanks Assistant Vice President	818/704-3166 818/704-2989	Chief Investment Officer Portfolio Mgr – Structured Notes

UBS Asset Management, Inc. (U.S.A.)

Bank/Management Division

Sub of Schweizerische Bankgesellschaft

Location: 1211 Avenue of the Americas
37th Floor
New York, NY 10036-8796

Fax: 212/789-7237 **Phone:** 212/789-7100

Profile: Total return investor

Investment Portfolio: $ 32.0 billion

Use: **Investment Purposes**
Capture extra yield
Hedge interest rate risk

Currencies: US dollar

Regions: United States

UBS Asset Management, Inc. (U.S.A.) – continued

DERIVATIVES ACTIVITIES:

OTC Derivatives	**Interest rate**
Plain Vanilla Derivatives	Swaps

OTHER ALTERNATIVE INVESTMENTS:

CMOs/REMICs – Govt.

KEY MANAGERS & DERIVATIVES SPECIALISTS:	Direct Phone/Fax	Job Function
Mr. Louis N. Cohen Vice President	212/789-7219 212/869-2169	Portfolio Mgr – Derivatives
Mr. Thomas E. Messmore President & C.E.O.		President
Mr. Bradley Nelson		Bond Department Head
Mr. Daniel C. Roberts Managing Director		Chief Investment Officer

Union Bank – Los Angeles

Bank/Portfolio

Sub of Union Bank

Location: 445 South Figueroa Street
38th Floor
Los Angeles, CA 90071

Fax: 213/236-7983 **Phone:** 213/236-5000

Profile: Stable asset investor

Investment Portfolio: $ 1.6 billion

Use: **Balance Sheet/Risk Management**
Hedge interest rate risk
Strategic liability management

Currencies: US dollar

Regions: United States

DERIVATIVES ACTIVITIES:

OTC Derivatives	**Interest rate**	
Plain Vanilla Derivatives	Swaps	Floors
	Caps	Collars

OTHER ALTERNATIVE INVESTMENTS:

CMOs/REMICs – Govt.

KEY MANAGERS & DERIVATIVES SPECIALISTS:	Direct Phone/Fax	Job Function
Mr. Michael W. Cunningham Vice President	213/236-6040	Bond Department Head Fixed-Income Strategist Research Analyst – Futures/Options *Corp*
Mr. K. Hamahashi Senior Vice President	213/236-5007	Chief Investment Officer Treasurer

Union Bank – Los Angeles – continued

KEY MANAGERS & DERIVATIVES SPECIALISTS:	Direct Phone/Fax	Job Function
Mr. J. Michael McGonagle Vice President	213/236-7484 213/236-7366	Research Analyst – Futures/Options *Govt*
Mr. Takahiro Moriguchi Vice Chairman & C.F.O.		Chief Financial Officer
Mr. Merrick L. Sterling E.V.P. – Portfolio Risk		Portfolio Mgr – Derivatives

Union Bank of Switzerland Private Banking

Bank/Trust

Location: 299 Park Avenue
40th Floor
New York, NY 10171-0026

Fax: 212/715-3498 **Phone:** 212/715-3000

Profile: Total return investor

Investment Portfolio: $ 1.0 - 3.0 billion

Use: **Balance Sheet/Risk Management**
Hedge currency risk

Currencies: US dollar, Australian dollar, Belgian franc, Canadian dollar, French franc, German mark, Japanese yen, Swiss franc, Thai baht, UK pound

Regions: United States, Canada, Europe, Pacific Rim

DERIVATIVES ACTIVITIES:

OTC Derivatives	**Currency**	
Plain Vanilla Derivatives	Swaps	Forwards
Counterparty Rating Requirement:	A	

OTHER ALTERNATIVE INVESTMENTS:

	CMOs/REMICs – Govt. CMOs/REMICs – Private	Repos/reverse repos

KEY MANAGERS & DERIVATIVES SPECIALISTS:	Direct Phone/Fax	Job Function
Mr. Peter Daytz Vice President	212/821-3779	Portfolio Mgr – Derivatives
Mr. J. Michael Gaffney Senior Vice President	212/821-3670 212/821-3932	Chief Investment Officer
Mr. Hans P. Lochmeier Senior Vice President	212/715-3730	Bond Department Head

Union Capital Advisors (San Diego)

Bank/Trust

Sub of Union Bank

Location: 530 B Street
San Diego, CA 92101

Fax: 619/230-4391 **Phone:** 619/230-4714

Profile: Total return investor

Investment Portfolio: $ 4.2 billion

Use: **Investment Purposes**
Adjust portfolio duration

Currencies: US dollar, Japanese yen, German mark, UK pound

Regions: United States, Pacific Rim, Europe

DERIVATIVES ACTIVITIES:

Exchange-traded Options & Futures	**Currency, Interest rate**	
Structured Notes	Corporate MTNs Govt. agency MTNs	CMT notes Floaters

OTHER ALTERNATIVE INVESTMENTS:

	Strips	Repos/reverse repos

KEY MANAGERS & DERIVATIVES SPECIALISTS:	**Direct Phone/Fax**	**Job Function**
Mr. James V. Atkinson Vice President	619/230-4584 619/230-3480	Bond Department Head *ABS, Corp, Govt* Portfolio Mgr – Futures Portfolio Mgr – Options Portfolio Mgr – Structured Notes
Mr. Carl J. Colombo	619/230-3156	Portfolio Mgr – Futures Portfolio Mgr – Options
Mr. Clark Gates President	619/230-4700	President Chief Investment Officer Portfolio Mgr – Futures Portfolio Mgr – Options Portfolio Mgr – Structured Notes
Mr. Martin D. Standish Vice President	619/230-3344 619/230-3480	Portfolio Mgr – Futures Portfolio Mgr – Options Portfolio Mgr – Structured Notes
Mr. David Urben	619/230-4712	Portfolio Mgr – Options

Union Carbide Corporation

Corporation

Location: 39 Old Ridgebury Road
Danbury, CT 06817-0001

Fax: 203/794-3334 **Phone:** 203/794-2000

Use:

Balance Sheet/Risk Management
Hedge currency risk
Hedge interest rate risk
Protect currency gains

Investment Purposes
Alter portfolio weighting
Adjust portfolio duration
Convexity objectives
Hedge bond portfolio risk
Hedge currency risk
Hedge equity portfolio risk
Protect currency gains
Reduce variability of returns

Currencies: US dollar, Belgian franc, Canadian dollar, French franc, German mark, Italian lira, Indonesian rupiah, Japanese yen, Spanish peseta, Swiss franc, Thai baht, UK pound

Regions: United States, Canada, Europe, Latin America, Pacific Rim

DERIVATIVES ACTIVITIES:

Exchange-traded Options & Futures
U.S. Treasury options

OTC Derivatives	**Currency, Interest rate**	
Plain Vanilla Derivatives	Swaps	Caps
	Forwards	Floors
	Swaptions	Collars
Structured Notes	Periodic capped floaters	
Counterparty Rating Requirement:	A	

OTHER ALTERNATIVE INVESTMENTS:

Repos/reverse repos

KEY MANAGERS & DERIVATIVES SPECIALISTS:	**Direct Phone/Fax**	**Job Function**
Mr. John Fitzpatrick Assistant Treasurer		Portfolio Mgr – Derivatives Portfolio Mgr – Structured Notes
Mr. William H. Joyce President & C.O.O.		President
Mr. John K. Wulff Vice President		Chief Financial Officer Treasurer

Union Labor Life Insurance Co. (ULLICO)

Insurance Co/Life

Location: 111 Massachusetts Avenue N.W.
Washington, DC 20001-1498

Fax: 202/682-7932 **Phone:** 202/682-0900

Profile: Total return investor

Investment Portfolio: $ 1.5 billion

Use: **Balance Sheet/Risk Management**

Currencies: US dollar

Regions: United States

Union Labor Life Insurance Co. (ULLICO) – continued

DERIVATIVES ACTIVITIES: **CAC Class: Inactive**

OTHER ALTERNATIVE INVESTMENTS:

	CMOs/REMICs – Govt.	CMOs/REMICs – Private

KEY MANAGERS & DERIVATIVES SPECIALISTS:	Direct Phone/Fax	Job Function
Mr. Herbert C. Canapary Vice President – Investments	202/682-6681	Portfolio Mgr – Derivatives
Mr. Michael Steed S.V.P. – Investments		Chief Investment Officer

Union Planters National Bank (Funds Management)

Bank/Portfolio

Sub of Union Planters Corporation

Location: 7130 Goodlett Farms Parkway
Cordova, TN 38018-0001

Fax: 901/383-6947 **Phone:** 901/383-6940

Profile: Spread investor

Investment Portfolio: $ 2.3 billion

Use: **Balance Sheet/Risk Management**
Create synthetic fixed/floating rate
Hedge balance sheet
Hedge interest rate risk
Reduce cost of capital

Currencies: US dollar

Regions: United States

DERIVATIVES ACTIVITIES: **CAC Class: 3**

OTC Derivatives	**Interest rate**	
Plain Vanilla Derivatives	Swaps	Caps
Exotic Derivatives	Index amortizing swaps	Periodic caps/floors
Structured Notes	Govt. agency MTNs Index amortizing notes	Multi-step-up callable bonds
Counterparty Rating Requirement:	A	

OTHER ALTERNATIVE INVESTMENTS:

	CMOs/REMICs – Govt.	CMOs/REMICs – Private

KEY MANAGERS & DERIVATIVES SPECIALISTS:	Direct Phone/Fax	Job Function
Mr. Richard Conway V.P. & Senior Portfolio Mgr	901/383-6261	Bond Department Head Portfolio Mgr – Derivatives Portfolio Mgr – Structured Notes

United Air Lines Employees Credit Union

Credit Union

Location: 125 East Algonquin Road
Arlington Heights, IL 60005-4600

Fax: 708/952-6593 **Phone:** 708/952-6600

Profile: Total return investor

Investment Portfolio: $ 1.2 billion

Use: **Balance Sheet/Risk Management**
Hedge interest rate risk

Investment Purposes
Capture extra yield

Currencies: US dollar

Regions: United States

DERIVATIVES ACTIVITIES: **CAC Class: 2**

Structured Notes
CMT notes
Floaters
Multi-step-up callable bonds

OTHER ALTERNATIVE INVESTMENTS:

CMOs/REMICs – Govt.
CMOs/REMICs – Private
Repos/reverse repos

KEY MANAGERS & DERIVATIVES SPECIALISTS:	**Direct Phone/Fax**	**Job Function**
Mr. Timothy Wartman Manager – Investments		Portfolio Mgr – Structured Notes

United Asset Management Corporation

Corporation

Location: One International Plaza
Boston, MA 02110

Fax: 617/330-1133 **Phone:** 617/330-8900

Use: **Balance Sheet/Risk Management**
Hedge interest rate risk

Currencies: US dollar

Regions: United States

DERIVATIVES ACTIVITIES: **CAC Class: 3**

OTC Derivatives
Plain Vanilla Derivatives
Interest rate

KEY MANAGERS & DERIVATIVES SPECIALISTS:	**Direct Phone/Fax**	**Job Function**
Ms. Juliana M. Coyle Treasurer		Treasurer Portfolio Mgr – Derivatives
Mr. William H. Park Exec. Vice President & C.F.O.		Chief Financial Officer
Mr. Norton H. Reamer President & C.E.O.		President

United Farm Bureau Life Insurance Co.

Insurance Co/Life

Location: 225 South East Street
Indianapolis, IN 46202

Fax: 317/692-7525 **Phone:** 317/692-7200

Profile: Total return investor

Investment Portfolio: $ 972.0 million

Use: **Investment Purposes**
Diversify portfolio

Currencies: US dollar

Regions: United States

DERIVATIVES ACTIVITIES: **CAC Class: Inactive**

OTHER ALTERNATIVE INVESTMENTS:

CMOs/REMICs – Govt. Strips

KEY MANAGERS & DERIVATIVES SPECIALISTS:	**Direct Phone/Fax**	**Job Function**
Mr. Joseph Martin Senior Vice President	317/692-7504	Chief Investment Officer

United Jersey Bank (Portfolio)

Bank/Portfolio

Sub of Summit Bancorp

Location: 214 Main Street
3rd Floor
Hackensack, NJ 07601-7317

Fax: 201/646-1849 **Phone:** 201/646-5000

Profile: Hold to maturity investor

Investment Portfolio: $ 4.2 billion

Use: **Balance Sheet/Risk Management**
Create synthetic fixed/floating rate
Hedge balance sheet
Hedge interest rate risk
Strategic liability management

Currencies: US dollar

Regions: United States

DERIVATIVES ACTIVITIES: **CAC Class: 5**

Exchange-traded Options & Futures	**Currency, Interest rate**	
OTC Derivatives **Plain Vanilla Derivatives**	**Currency, Interest rate** Swaps Caps	Floors
Exotic Derivatives	Index extendible swaps	
Structured Notes	Index amortizing notes	Floaters

OTHER ALTERNATIVE INVESTMENTS:

CMOs/REMICs – Private Repos/reverse repos

KEY MANAGERS & DERIVATIVES SPECIALISTS:	**Direct Phone/Fax**	**Job Function**
Mr. Dennis Porterfield Executive Vice President	201/646-5208 201/489-7909	Chief Investment Officer Portfolio Mgr – Derivatives Portfolio Mgr – Structured Notes Trader – Derivatives Trader – Structured Investments

United Jersey Bank (Princeton) (Trust)

Bank/Trust

Sub of Summit Bancorp

Location: 90 Nassau Street
Princeton, NJ 08542-4520

Fax: 609/921-2474 **Phone:** 609/987-3680

Profile: Total return investor

Investment Portfolio: $ 1.4 billion

Use: **Investment Purposes**
Provide incremental return

Currencies: US dollar

Regions: United States

DERIVATIVES ACTIVITIES:

Exchange-traded Options & Futures	**Interest Rate**
Structured Notes	Govt. agency MTNs

OTHER ALTERNATIVE INVESTMENTS:

CMOs/REMICs – Govt. CMOs/REMICs – Private

KEY MANAGERS & DERIVATIVES SPECIALISTS:	**Direct Phone/Fax**	**Job Function**
Mr. Robert B. Lowe, Jr. Vice President	609/987-3688	Bond Department Head *Corp, Govt, MBS, Muni* Portfolio Mgr – Structured Notes

United Missouri Bank, N.A. (Portfolio)

Bank/Portfolio

Sub of United Missouri Bancshares, Inc.

Location: 1010 Grand Avenue
Kansas City, MO 64106-2220

Fax: 816/860-4829 **Phone:** 816/860-7200

Profile: Stable asset investor

Investment Portfolio: $ 6.5 billion

Use: **Balance Sheet/Risk Management**
Hedge interest rate risk

Currencies: US dollar

Regions: United States

DERIVATIVES ACTIVITIES: **CAC Class: 2**

Exchange-traded Options & Futures U.S. Treasury futures	**Bond**
OTC Derivatives **Plain Vanilla Derivatives**	Forwards
Structured Notes	Govt. agency MTNs
Counterparty Rating Requirement:	None

OTHER ALTERNATIVE INVESTMENTS:

CMOs/REMICs – Govt. Repos/reverse repos

United Missouri Bank, N.A. (Portfolio) – continued

KEY MANAGERS & DERIVATIVES SPECIALISTS:	Direct Phone/Fax	Job Function
Mr. Donald LaPiana		Trader – Futures Trader – Options Trader – Structured Investments
Mr. James C. Thompson, Jr. Divisional E.V.P.	Ext. 7200	Bond Department Head Portfolio Mgr – Derivatives Portfolio Mgr – Structured Notes *Govt*

United Missouri Investment Counsel Service

Bank/Trust

Sub of United Missouri Bancshares, Inc.

Location: 1010 Grand Avenue
Third Floor
Kansas City, MO 64106

Fax: 816/860-4829 **Phone:** 816/860-7000

Profile: Total return investor

Investment Portfolio: $ 4.5 billion

Use: **Balance Sheet/Risk Management**
Strategic liability management

Currencies: US dollar

Regions: United States

DERIVATIVES ACTIVITIES:

Exchange-traded Options & Futures

OTHER ALTERNATIVE INVESTMENTS:

CMOs/REMICs – Govt.
Strips
Repos/reverse repos

KEY MANAGERS & DERIVATIVES SPECIALISTS:	Direct Phone/Fax	Job Function
Mr. David B. Anderson Executive Vice President	816/860-7351	Chief Investment Officer Portfolio Mgr – Futures Portfolio Mgr – Options

United of Omaha Life Insurance Company

Insurance Co/Life

Location: Mutual of Omaha Plaza
4th Floor
Omaha, NE 68175-0001

Fax: 402/351-2913 **Phone:** 402/342-7600

Profile: Total return investor

Investment Portfolio: $ 10.5 billion

Use: **Investment Purposes**
Hedge interest rate risk

Currencies: US dollar

Regions: United States

United of Omaha Life Insurance Company – continued

DERIVATIVES ACTIVITIES:

Exchange-traded Options & Futures

OTC Derivatives
Plain Vanilla Derivatives

OTHER ALTERNATIVE INVESTMENTS:

CMOs/REMICs – Govt. | CMOs/REMICs – Private

KEY MANAGERS & DERIVATIVES SPECIALISTS:	**Direct Phone/Fax**	**Job Function**
Mr. John L. Maginn	402/351-2530	Chief Investment Officer
Mr. Steve Miller VP-Investment Derivatives	402/351-3004	Portfolio Mgr – Derivatives
Mr. Richard A. Witt Sr. Vice President & Manager	402/351-2503	Bond Department Head

United Services Advisors Inc.

Mutual Fund Manager

Location: 7900 Callaghan Road
San Antonio, TX 78229

Fax: 210/308-1270 **Phone:** 210/308-1234

Profile: Stable asset investor

Investment Portfolio: $ 1.2 billion

Use: **Investment Purposes**
Alter portfolio weighting
Capture extra yield

Currencies: US dollar

Regions: United States

DERIVATIVES ACTIVITIES: **CAC Class: 5**

Structured Notes

Govt. agency MTNs
Bond index notes
CMT notes
Floaters

OTHER ALTERNATIVE INVESTMENTS:

CMOs/REMICs – Govt.
CMOs/REMICs – Private
GICs
Strips
Repos/reverse repos

KEY MANAGERS & DERIVATIVES SPECIALISTS:	**Direct Phone/Fax**	**Job Function**
Mr. Victor Flores Executive Vice President		Chief Investment Officer
Mr. Creston A. King III		Portfolio Mgr – Structured Notes *Govt*

U.S. National Bank of Oregon (Portfolio)

Bank/Portfolio

Sub of U.S. Bancorp

Location: 111 Southwest Fifth Avenue
Portland, OR 97204

Fax: 503/275-5032 **Phone:** 503/275-5006

Profile: Total return investor

Investment Portfolio: $ 4.1 billion

Use: **Balance Sheet/Risk Management**
Create synthetic fixed/floating rate
Hedge balance sheet
Hedge interest rate risk
Strategic liability management

Investment Purposes
Alter portfolio weighting
Asset allocation
Capture extra yield
Hedge interest rate risk

Currencies: US dollar

Regions: United States

DERIVATIVES ACTIVITIES: **CAC Class: 8**

Exchange-traded Options & Futures	**Interest rate**	
OTC Derivatives	**Interest rate**	
Plain Vanilla Derivatives	Swaps	Caps
	Swaptions	Collars
Counterparty Rating Requirement:	A	

OTHER ALTERNATIVE INVESTMENTS:

CMOs/REMICs – Govt.

KEY MANAGERS & DERIVATIVES SPECIALISTS:	Direct Phone/Fax	Job Function
Mr. William Ellsworth		Chief Investment Officer
Mr. Thomas McKernan VP-Hedging & Derivatives	503/275-3686	Portfolio Mgr – Derivatives Portfolio Mgr – Futures Portfolio Mgr – Options Trader – Derivatives Trader – Futures Trader – Options
Mr. Lawrence B. Prescott Vice President		Chief Investment Officer

U.S. Steel & Carnegie Pension Fund

Corporate Pension Fund

Location: 767 Fifth Avenue
9th Floor
New York, NY 10153

Fax: 212/826-8443 **Phone:** 212/593-5151

Profile: Total return investor

Investment Portfolio: $ 8.5 billion

Use: **Investment Purposes**
Diversify portfolio

Currencies: US dollar

Regions: United States

U.S. Steel & Carnegie Pension Fund – continued

DERIVATIVES ACTIVITIES: — **CAC Class: Inactive**

OTHER ALTERNATIVE INVESTMENTS:

CMOs/REMICs – Govt. | CMOs/REMICs – Private

KEY MANAGERS & DERIVATIVES SPECIALISTS:	Direct Phone/Fax	Job Function
Mr. Gary A. Glynn President	212/826-8420	President Chief Investment Officer

United States Trust Company of Boston

Bank/Trust

Sub of UST Corporation

Location: 40 Court Street
10th Floor
Boston, MA 02108-2203

Fax: 617/695-4775 **Phone:** 617/726-7000

Profile: Total return investor

Investment Portfolio: $ 3.1 billion

Use: **Balance Sheet/Risk Management**
Strategic liability management

Investment Purposes
Provide incremental return

Currencies: US dollar

Regions: United States

DERIVATIVES ACTIVITIES: — **CAC Class: 2**

Structured Notes — Govt. agency MTNs

OTHER ALTERNATIVE INVESTMENTS:

CMOs/REMICs – Govt. | Strips

KEY MANAGERS & DERIVATIVES SPECIALISTS:	Direct Phone/Fax	Job Function
Mr. William H. Apfel	617/726-7280	Portfolio Mgr – Structured Notes
Mr. Domenic Colasacco President	617/726-7252	President Chief Investment Officer

United States Trust Co. of California., N.A.

Bank/Trust

Sub of United States Trust Corporation of New York

Location: 555 South Flower Street
Suite 2700
Los Angeles, CA 90071-2429

Fax: 213/488-4029 **Phone:** 213/488-4000

Profile: Hold to maturity investor

Investment Portfolio: $ 3.6 billion

Use: **Investment Purposes**
Diversify portfolio

Currencies: US dollar

Regions: United States

United States Trust Co. of California., N.A. – continued

DERIVATIVES ACTIVITIES: **CAC Class: Inactive**

OTHER ALTERNATIVE INVESTMENTS:

CMOs/REMICs – Govt.
CMOs/REMICs – Private

KEY MANAGERS & DERIVATIVES SPECIALISTS:	Direct Phone/Fax	Job Function
Mr. Robert M. Raney Managing Director	213/488-4011	Chief Investment Officer

United States Trust Company of New York (Portfolio)

Bank/Portfolio

Sub of United States Trust Corporation of New York

Location: 114 West 47th Street
New York, NY 10036-1532

Fax: 212/635-3580 **Phone:** 212/852-1000

Profile: Hold to maturity investor

Investment Portfolio: $ 4.0 - 10.0 billion

Use: **Balance Sheet/Risk Management**
Create synthetic fixed/floating rate
Hedge balance sheet
Hedge interest rate risk
Strategic liability management

Currencies: US dollar

Regions: United States

DERIVATIVES ACTIVITIES: **CAC Class: 3**

OTC Derivatives	**Interest rate**
Plain Vanilla Derivatives	Swaps

OTHER ALTERNATIVE INVESTMENTS:

CMOs/REMICs – Govt.
CMOs/REMICs – Private
Repos/reverse repos

KEY MANAGERS & DERIVATIVES SPECIALISTS:	Direct Phone/Fax	Job Function
Mr. Kenneth J. McAlley E.V.P./Head-Fixed Inc. Invsts.	212/852-3374	Bond Department Head Portfolio Mgr – Derivatives
Mr. David Quinn Senior Vice President	212/852-3151	Portfolio Mgr – Derivatives

United States Trust Company of New York (Trust)

Bank/Trust

Sub of United States Trust Corporation of New York

Location: 114 West 47th Street
New York, NY 10036

Fax: 212/852-3370 **Phone:** 212/852-1000

Profile: Total return investor

Investment Portfolio: $ 21.0 billion

Use: **Investment Purposes**
Diversify portfolio

Currencies: US dollar

Regions: United States

DERIVATIVES ACTIVITIES: **CAC Class: 2**

OTC Derivatives
Plain Vanilla Derivatives

Structured Notes

OTHER ALTERNATIVE INVESTMENTS:

CMOs/REMICs – Govt.
CMOs/REMICs – Private
GICs
Repos/reverse repos

KEY MANAGERS & DERIVATIVES SPECIALISTS:	**Direct Phone/Fax**	**Job Function**
Mr. David Fann Division Mgr-Alternative Inv.	212/852-3773	Portfolio Mgr – Derivatives Portfolio Mgr – Structured Notes
Mr. Frederick B. Taylor Vice Chairman	212/852-3756	Chief Investment Officer
Mr. Leigh Weiss Vice President	212/852-3578	Portfolio Mgr – Structured Notes

U.S. West, Inc.

Corporate Pension Fund

Location: 9785 Maroon Circle
Suite 360
Englewood, CO 80112-5918

Fax: 303/649-4520 **Phone:** 303/649-4500

Profile: Spread investor

Investment Portfolio: $ 3.8 billion

Use: **Balance Sheet/Risk Management**
Create synthetic fixed/floating rate
Hedge currency risk

Investment Purposes
Alter portfolio weighting
Asset allocation
Hedge bond portfolio risk
Hedge currency risk
Hedge equity portfolio risk
Hedge interest rate risk

Currencies: US dollar
German mark
Italian lira
Japanese yen
UK pound

Regions: United States
Europe
Pacific Rim

U.S. West, Inc. – continued

DERIVATIVES ACTIVITIES:		**CAC Class: 2**
Exchange-traded Options & Futures U.S. Treasury futures	**Bond**	
OTC Derivatives **Plain Vanilla Derivatives**	Swaps	Forwards
Counterparty Rating Requirement:	AA	

OTHER ALTERNATIVE INVESTMENTS:

	CMOs/REMICs – Govt. CMOs/REMICs – Private	Strips Repos/reverse repos

KEY MANAGERS & DERIVATIVES SPECIALISTS:	**Direct Phone/Fax**	**Job Function**
Mr. James R. Belquist Head Director – Trust Invt. Mgmt.	303/649-4503	Bond Department Portfolio Mgr – Derivatives Portfolio Mgr – Futures
Mr. James J. Biundo Exec. Dir. – Trust Invt. Mgmt.	303/649-4501	Chief Investment Officer
Mr. Michael Jensen	303/649-4509	Portfolio Mgr – Derivatives Portfolio Mgr – Futures Portfolio Mgr – Options
Mr. Stanley Willie Director – Trust Invt. Mgmt.	303/649-4514	Portfolio Mgr – Derivatives Portfolio Mgr – Futures

University of Texas System – Office of Investments

Foundation/Endowment

Location: 210 West Sixth Street
2nd Floor
Austin, TX 78701-2980

Fax: 512/499-4429 **Phone:** 512/499-4317

Profile: Total return investor

Investment Portfolio: $ 5.4 billion

Use: **Investment Purposes**
Asset allocation
Diversify portfolio

Currencies: US dollar

Regions: United States

DERIVATIVES ACTIVITIES: **CAC Class: Inactive**

OTHER ALTERNATIVE INVESTMENTS:

	CMOs/REMICs – Govt.	CMOs/REMICs – Private

KEY MANAGERS & DERIVATIVES SPECIALISTS:	**Direct Phone/Fax**	**Job Function**
Mr. Robert W. Holland Executive Director		Bond Department Head *Corp, Govt, MBS*

UNUM Life Insurance Company

Insurance Co/Life

Sub of UNUM Corporation

Location: 2211 Congress Street
Portland, ME 04122-1941

Fax: 207/770-4152 **Phone:** 207/770-2211

Profile: Total return investor

Investment Portfolio: $ 10.4 billion

Use: **Investment Purposes**
Asset allocation
Diversify portfolio

Currencies: US dollar

Regions: United States

DERIVATIVES ACTIVITIES:

Structured Notes	Corporate MTNs

OTHER ALTERNATIVE INVESTMENTS:

CMOs/REMICs – Govt.	Repos/reverse repos
CMOs/REMICs – Private	

KEY MANAGERS & DERIVATIVES SPECIALISTS:	**Direct Phone/Fax**	**Job Function**
Mr. John F. Burns	207/770-4115	Portfolio Mgr – Structured Notes
Mr. Robert L. Crispin, Jr. Executive Vice President	207/770-4322	Chief Investment Officer
Mr. Daniel Redmond Vice President	207/770-4108	Bond Department Head

USBANCORP, Inc.

Bank/Portfolio

Location: Main & Franklin Streets
Johnstown, PA 15901

Fax: 814/533-5430 **Phone:** 814/533-5300

Profile: Total return investor

Investment Portfolio: $ 760.9 million

Use: **Balance Sheet/Risk Management**
Create synthetic fixed/floating rate
Hedge balance sheet
Hedge interest rate risk

Currencies: US dollar

Regions: United States

DERIVATIVES ACTIVITIES: **CAC Class: 3**

OTC Derivatives **Plain Vanilla Derivatives**	**Interest rate** Swaps
Counterparty Rating Requirement:	AA

OTHER ALTERNATIVE INVESTMENTS:

CMOs/REMICs – Govt.	Repos/reverse repos
CMOs/REMICs – Private	

USBANCORP, Inc. – continued

KEY MANAGERS & DERIVATIVES SPECIALISTS:	Direct Phone/Fax	Job Function
Mr. Raymond M. Fisher Vice President & C.I.O.	814/533-5355 814/533-5427	Chief Investment Officer Portfolio Mgr – Derivatives
Mr. Orlando B. Hanselman President		President

USLIFE Advisers Inc.

Insurance Co/Management

Sub of USLIFE Corporation

Location: 125 Maiden Lane
New York, NY 10038-4992

Fax: 212/709-6064 **Phone:** 212/709-6000

Profile: Hold to maturity investor

Investment Portfolio: $ 6.1 billion

Use: **Investment Purposes**
Asset allocation
Diversify portfolio

Currencies: US dollar

Regions: United States

DERIVATIVES ACTIVITIES: **CAC Class: Inactive**

OTHER ALTERNATIVE INVESTMENTS:

CMOs/REMICs – Govt.

KEY MANAGERS & DERIVATIVES SPECIALISTS:	Direct Phone/Fax	Job Function
Mr. Richard J. Chouinard President	212/709-6077	President Chief Investment Officer

Valley National Bank (New Jersey) (Portfolio)

Bank/Portfolio

Location: 1455 Valley Road
Wayne, NJ 07470

Fax: 201/305-8415 **Phone:** 201/305-4058

Profile: Total return investor

Investment Portfolio: $ 1.4 billion

Use: **Balance Sheet/Risk Management**

Currencies: US dollar

Regions: United States

DERIVATIVES ACTIVITIES: **CAC Class: Inactive**

OTHER ALTERNATIVE INVESTMENTS:

CMOs/REMICs – Govt. CMOs/REMICs – Private

KEY MANAGERS & DERIVATIVES SPECIALISTS:	Direct Phone/Fax	Job Function
Mr. Jack Blackin		Chief Investment Officer

The Vanguard Group, Inc.

Mutual Fund Manager

Location: 100 Vanguard Boulevard
Malvern, PA 19355

Fax: 610/640-6894 **Phone:** 610/669-1000

Profile: Total return investor

Investment Portfolio: $ 95.0 billion

Use: **Investment Purposes**

Currencies: US dollar

Regions: United States

DERIVATIVES ACTIVITIES:		**CAC Class: 7**
Exchange-traded Options & Futures	**Bond**	
U.S. Treasury futures	Municipal futures	
OTC Derivatives		
Plain Vanilla Derivatives	Forwards	
Structured Notes	Floaters	Inverse floaters

OTHER ALTERNATIVE INVESTMENTS:		
	CMOs/REMICs – Govt.	Strips
	GICs	Repos/reverse repos

KEY MANAGERS & DERIVATIVES SPECIALISTS:	**Direct Phone/Fax**	**Job Function**
Mr. Robert F. Auwaerter Vice President	610/669-6341	Portfolio Mgr – Derivatives Portfolio Mgr – Options Portfolio Mgr – Structured Notes
Mr. John J. Brennan President & C.E.O.		President Chief Investment Officer
Mr. Richard F. Hyland Treasurer		Treasurer
Mr. Ian A. MacKinnon Senior Vice President	610/669-6340	Bond Department Head
Mr. Ralph K. Packard Chief Financial Officer		Chief Financial Officer

Van Kampen American Capital Investment Advisory Corp.

Mutual Fund Manager

Sub of Clayton Dublier & Rice

Location: One Parkview Plaza, Oakbrook Terrace, IL 60181-4400
Fax: 708/684-6270 **Phone:** 708/684-6000

Profile: Total return investor
Investment Portfolio: $ 17.4 billion

Use:

Balance Sheet/Risk Management
Create synthetic fixed/floating rate
Hedge currency risk
Hedge interest rate risk
Incremental return
Protect currency gains
Reduce cost of capital
Strategic liability management

Investment Purposes
Adjust portfolio duration
Diversify portfolio
Enter new mkts/lower risk
Hedge bond portfolio risk
Hedge currency risk
Hedge interest rate risk
Protect currency gains
Reduce variability of returns

Currencies: US dollar, Australian dollar, Belgian franc, Canadian dollar, French franc, German mark, Italian lira, Japanese yen, Spanish peseta, Swiss franc, UK pound

Regions: United States, Canada, Europe

DERIVATIVES ACTIVITIES: **CAC Class: 5**

Exchange-traded Options & Futures	**Bond, Currency, Interest rate**
U.S. Treasury futures	Municipal futures
U.S. Treasury options	Municipal options
OTC Derivatives	**Bond, Currency, Interest rate**
Plain Vanilla Derivatives	
Exotic Derivatives	
Structured Notes	Inverse floaters

OTHER ALTERNATIVE INVESTMENTS:

CMOs/REMICs – Govt.
CMOs/REMICs – Private
GICs
Strips
Repos/reverse repos

KEY MANAGERS & DERIVATIVES SPECIALISTS:	**Direct Phone/Fax**	**Job Function**
Mr. Peter W. Hegel Executive Vice President	708/684-6290	Bond Department Head
Mr. Robert J. Hickey Vice President	708/684-6296	Portfolio Mgr – Derivatives Portfolio Mgr – Futures Portfolio Mgr – Options Portfolio Mgr – Structured Notes
Mr. Dennis J. McDonnell President	708/684-6330	President Chief Investment Officer
Mr. Thomas J. Slefinger First Vice President	708/684-6295	Portfolio Mgr – Derivatives Portfolio Mgr – Futures Portfolio Mgr – Options
Mr. Edward A. Treichel Senior Vice President	708/684-6346 708/684-5966	Fixed-Income Strategist

Van Kampen American Capital Management & Research

Mutual Fund Manager

Location: 2800 Post Oak Boulevard
45th Floor
Houston, TX 77056-6198

Fax: 713/966-7411 **Phone:** 713/993-0500

Profile: Total return investor

Investment Portfolio: $ 13.7 billion

Use: **Investment Purposes**

Currencies: US dollar

Regions: United States

DERIVATIVES ACTIVITIES:

OTC Derivatives	**Bond**	
Plain Vanilla Derivatives	Forwards	

OTHER ALTERNATIVE INVESTMENTS:

	CMOs/REMICs – Govt.	CMOs/REMICs – Private

KEY MANAGERS & DERIVATIVES SPECIALISTS:	Direct Phone/Fax	Job Function
Mr. Robert C. Peck, Jr. Senior Vice President	713/993-4167	Chief Investment Officer Bond Department Head *Corp, Govt, MBS* Portfolio Mgr – Derivatives

Vaughan, Nelson, Scarborough & McConnell Inc.

Investment Manager

Location: 6300 Texas Commerce Tower
Houston, TX 77002-3071

Fax: 713/247-9534 **Phone:** 713/224-2545

Profile: Total return investor

Investment Portfolio: $ 1.0 billion

Use: **Investment Purposes**
Capture extra yield
Diversify portfolio

Currencies: US dollar

Regions: United States

DERIVATIVES ACTIVITIES:

Structured Notes	Corporate MTNs	Govt. agency MTNs

OTHER ALTERNATIVE INVESTMENTS:

	CMOs/REMICs – Govt.	CMOs/REMICs – Private

KEY MANAGERS & DERIVATIVES SPECIALISTS:	Direct Phone/Fax	Job Function
Mr. Eugene H. Vaughan President & C.E.O.		President Chief Investment Officer Portfolio Mgr – Structured Notes
Mr. Allan J. Waldron Principal		Bond Department Head

Victoria Bank & Trust Company (Trust)

Bank/Trust

Sub of Victoria Bankshares, Inc.

Location: One O'Connor Plaza
Sixth Floor
Victoria, TX 77901

Fax: 512/574-5669 **Phone:** 512/574-5869

Profile: Total return investor

Investment Portfolio: $ 1.2 billion

Use: **Investment Purposes**
Diversify portfolio

Currencies: US dollar

Regions: United States

DERIVATIVES ACTIVITIES: **CAC Class: Inactive**

OTHER ALTERNATIVE INVESTMENTS:

CMOs/REMICs – Govt.

KEY MANAGERS & DERIVATIVES SPECIALISTS:	Direct Phone/Fax	Job Function
Mr. Friench S. Tarkington S.V.P./Trust Invt. Officer		Chief Investment Officer

Virtus Capital Management

Bank/Management Division

Sub of Signet Banking Corporation

Location: 707 East Main Street
13th Floor
Richmond, VA 23219

Fax: 804/771-7908 **Phone:** 804/771-7164

Profile: Total return investor

Investment Portfolio: $ 2.2 billion

Use: **Investment Purposes**
Discretionary situations
Diversify portfolio

Currencies: US dollar

Regions: United States

DERIVATIVES ACTIVITIES: **CAC Class: Inactive**

OTHER ALTERNATIVE INVESTMENTS:

CMOs/REMICs – Govt.

KEY MANAGERS & DERIVATIVES SPECIALISTS:	Direct Phone/Fax	Job Function
Mr. Garry M. Allen President		President Chief Investment Officer
Mr. E. Christian Goetz Senior Vice President	804/771-7987 804/775-3948	Bond Department Head Fixed-Income Strategist

Voyageur Asset Management

Investment Manager

Sub of Dougherty Dawkins Strand & Bigelow Inc.

Location: 717 17th Street
Suite 2720
Denver, CO 80202

Fax: 303/292-5376 **Phone:** 303/293-0782

Profile: Total return investor

Investment Portfolio: $ 1.4 billion

Use: **Balance Sheet/Risk Management**

Currencies: US dollar

Regions: United States

DERIVATIVES ACTIVITIES: **CAC Class: Inactive**

OTHER ALTERNATIVE INVESTMENTS:

CMOs/REMICs – Govt. CMOs/REMICs – Private

Voyageur Fund Managers

Mutual Fund Manager

Sub of Dougherty Dawkins Strand & Bigelow Inc.

Location: 90 South Seventh Street
Suite 4400
Minneapolis, MN 55402-4115

Fax: 612/341-2818 **Phone:** 612/376-7000

Profile: Total return investor

Investment Portfolio: $ 8.1 billion

Use: **Investment Purposes**
Asset allocation
Diversify portfolio

Currencies: US dollar

Regions: United States

DERIVATIVES ACTIVITIES: **CAC Class: Inactive**

OTHER ALTERNATIVE INVESTMENTS:

CMOs/REMICs – Govt. CMOs/REMICs – Private

KEY MANAGERS & DERIVATIVES SPECIALISTS:	**Direct Phone/Fax**	**Job Function**
Mr. John G. Taft President	612/376-7040	President
Ms. Jane M. Wyatt Chief Investment Officer	612/376-7063	Chief Investment Officer Bond Department Head *Taxable*

Wachovia Corporation

Bank Holding Company

Location: 301 North Main Street
Winston-Salem, NC 27102

Fax: 910/770-6667 **Phone:** 910/770-5000

Profile: Total return investor

Use: **Balance Sheet/Risk Management**
Strategic liability management

Investment Purposes
Hedge currency risk
Hedge interest rate risk

Currencies: US dollar

Regions: United States

DERIVATIVES ACTIVITIES: **CAC Class: 6**

Exchange-traded Options & Futures	**Interest rate**	
OTC Derivatives	**Currency, Interest rate**	
Plain Vanilla Derivatives	Swaps	Forwards

KEY MANAGERS & DERIVATIVES SPECIALISTS:	**Direct Phone/Fax**	**Job Function**
Mr. L. M. Baker, Jr. President & C.E.O	910/770-5581	President
Mr. Robert S. McCoy, Jr. Exec. Vice President & C.F.O.	910/770-5926 910/770-5959	Chief Financial Officer
Mr. Richard B. Roberts E.V.P. & Treasurer	910/732-4554	Treasurer

Wachovia Bank Capital Management

Bank/Management Division

Sub of Wachovia Corporation

Location: 301 North Main Street
Winston-Salem, NC 27150

Fax: 910/770-6630 **Phone:** 910/732-4385

Profile: Total return investor

Investment Portfolio: $ 17.0 billion

Use: **Investment Purposes**
Provide incremental return

Currencies: US dollar

Regions: United States

DERIVATIVES ACTIVITIES:

Exchange-traded Options & Futures

OTHER ALTERNATIVE INVESTMENTS:

CMOs/REMICs – Govt.

KEY MANAGERS & DERIVATIVES SPECIALISTS:	**Direct Phone/Fax**	**Job Function**
Mr. Dennis Monroe Senior Vice President	910/732-6317	Chief Investment Officer Bond Department Head
Mr. Mark I. Thompson Vice President	910/732-5915	Portfolio Mgr – Options

Wachovia Bank Capital Management (Atlanta)

Bank/Management Division

Sub of Wachovia Corporation

Location: 191 Peachtree Street N.E.
Atlanta, GA 30303-1757

Fax: 404/332-4163 **Phone:** 404/332-4162

Profile: Total return investor

Investment Portfolio: $ 17.0 billion

Use: **Investment Purposes**
Diversify portfolio

Currencies: US dollar

Regions: United States

DERIVATIVES ACTIVITIES: **CAC Class: Inactive**

OTHER ALTERNATIVE INVESTMENTS:

CMOs/REMICs – Govt. Strips

KEY MANAGERS & DERIVATIVES SPECIALISTS:	**Direct Phone/Fax**	**Job Function**
Mr. Barry Berlin Senior Vice President	404/332-4160	Bond Department Head

Waddell & Reed Investment Management Co.

Mutual Fund Manager

Sub of Torchmark Corporation

Location: 6300 Lamar Avenue
Shawnee Mission, KS 66202-4247

Fax: 913/236-1885 **Phone:** 913/236-2000

Profile: Spread investor

Investment Portfolio: $ 17.0 billion

Use:

Balance Sheet/Risk Management
Hedge balance sheet
Hedge currency risk
Hedge interest rate risk

Investment Purposes
Asset allocation
Capture extra yield
Discretionary situations
Diversify portfolio
Enter new mkts/lower risk
Hedge bond portfolio risk
Hedge currency risk
Hedge equity portfolio risk
Hedge interest rate risk
Lower transactions costs
Protect currency gains
Provide incremental return

Currencies: US dollar
Canadian dollar
French franc
German mark
Italian lira
Japanese yen
Mexican peso
Swiss franc
UK pound

Regions: United States

Waddell & Reed Investment Management Co. – continued

DERIVATIVES ACTIVITIES:

Exchange-traded Options & Futures	**Bond, Currency, Interest rate**	
U.S. Treasury futures	Municipal futures	
U.S. Treasury options	Municipal options	
OTC Derivatives	**Bond, Currency, Interest rate**	
Plain Vanilla Derivatives	Swaps	Floors
	Forwards	Collars
	Caps	
Exotic Derivatives	Bond index swaps	
Structured Notes	Corporate MTNs	Inverse floaters
	Floaters	

OTHER ALTERNATIVE INVESTMENTS:

CMOs/REMICs – Govt.	Strips
CMOs/REMICs – Private	

KEY MANAGERS & DERIVATIVES SPECIALISTS:	Direct Phone/Fax	Job Function
Ms. Diane Dercher	913/236-1874	Fixed-Income Strategist
Mr. Henry J. Herrmann Executive Vice President	913/236-1750	Chief Investment Officer
Mr. Daniel Vrabac Vice President	913/236-1834	Bond Department Head Portfolio Mgr – Derivatives

Warburg, Pincus Counsellors, Inc.

Investment Manager

Sub of E.M. Warburg, Pincus & Co., Inc.

Location: 466 Lexington Avenue
10th Floor
New York, NY 10017-3147

Fax: 212/878-9351 **Phone:** 212/878-0600

Profile: Total return investor

Investment Portfolio: $ 11.0 billion

Use:

Balance Sheet/Risk Management
- Access global mkts
- Hedge balance sheet
- Hedge currency risk
- Hedge interest rate risk
- Hedge overseas investments
- Protect currency gains

Investment Purposes
- Alter portfolio weighting
- Asset allocation
- Capture extra yield
- Hedge equity portfolio risk
- Hedge interest rate risk

Currencies: US dollar, Australian dollar, Belgian franc, Canadian dollar, ECU, French franc, German mark, Italian lira, Indonesian rupiah, Japanese yen, Mexican peso, Spanish peseta, Swiss franc, Thai baht, UK pound

Regions: United States, Canada, Europe, Latin America, Pacific Rim, Emerging mkts

Warburg, Pincus Counsellors, Inc. – continued

DERIVATIVES ACTIVITIES:		CAC Class: 6
Exchange-traded Options & Futures		
OTC Derivatives **Plain Vanilla Derivatives**	**Currency** Swaps	 Forwards
Structured Notes	Corporate MTNs Govt. agency MTNs Floaters	Inverse floaters Periodic capped floaters
Counterparty Rating Requirement:	AA	

OTHER ALTERNATIVE INVESTMENTS:		
	CMOs/REMICs – Govt. Strips	Repos/reverse repos

KEY MANAGERS & DERIVATIVES SPECIALISTS:	Direct Phone/Fax	Job Function
Mr. Dale C. Christensen Managing Director	212/878-9368	Bond Department Head *Corp* Portfolio Mgr – Derivatives
Mr. Andrew H. Massie, Jr.		Chief Investment Officer
Mr. Latchmi Vandari Vice President	212/878-9366	Portfolio Mgr – Derivatives Portfolio Mgr – Structured Notes

Washington Federal Savings & Loan Association

Savings Bank/Bldg Society

Sub of Washington Federal, Inc.

Location: 425 Pike Street
Seattle, WA 98101-2334

Fax: 206/467-0524 **Phone:** 206/624-7930

Profile: Hold to maturity investor

Investment Portfolio: $ 1.4 billion

Use: **Investment Purposes**
Asset allocation
Diversify portfolio

Currencies: US dollar

Regions: United States

DERIVATIVES ACTIVITIES:		CAC Class: Inactive

OTHER ALTERNATIVE INVESTMENTS:		
	CMOs/REMICs – Govt.	Repos/reverse repos

KEY MANAGERS & DERIVATIVES SPECIALISTS:	Direct Phone/Fax	Job Function
Mr. Ronald L. Saper Exec. Vice President & C.F.O.		Chief Investment Officer Chief Financial Officer

Washington Square Advisers Inc.

Insurance Co/Management

Sub of ReliaStar Financial Corporation

Location: 100 Washington Square
Suite 800
Minneapolis, MN 55401-2147

Fax: 612/342-7541 **Phone:** 612/342-3736

Profile: Spread investor

Investment Portfolio: $ 11.3 billion

Use: **Balance Sheet/Risk Management**
Hedge interest rate risk

Currencies: US dollar

Regions: United States

DERIVATIVES ACTIVITIES:

Exchange-traded Options & Futures	**Currency, Interest rate**	
OTC Derivatives	**Currency, Interest rate**	
Plain Vanilla Derivatives	Swaps Caps	Floors
Structured Notes	Corporate MTNs Govt. agency MTNs	Floaters Periodic capped floaters
Counterparty Rating Requirement:	A	

OTHER ALTERNATIVE INVESTMENTS:

	CMOs/REMICs – Govt. CMOs/REMICs – Private	Repos/reverse repos

KEY MANAGERS & DERIVATIVES SPECIALISTS:	**Direct Phone/Fax**	**Job Function**
Ms. Nancy Esch Vice President	612/372-1123 612/342-3575	Portfolio Mgr – Derivatives Portfolio Mgr – Futures Portfolio Mgr – Structured Notes
Mr. Douglas P. Hedberg Senior Vice President	612/372-5220	Chief Investment Officer
Mr. Richard S. Nelson Vice President	612/372-5539	Fixed-Income Strategist
Ms. Susan Ripley Vice President	612/372-5595	Portfolio Mgr – Derivatives Portfolio Mgr – Futures
Mr. Steven W. Wishart President	612/372-5262	President

Washington State Investment Board

Government Pension Fund

Location: 2424 Heritage Court Southwest
Olympia, WA 98502

Fax: 360/664-8912 **Phone:** 360/664-8900

Profile: Total return investor

Investment Portfolio: $ 26.0 billion

Use: **Investment Purposes**
Diversify portfolio

Currencies: US dollar

Regions: United States

Washington State Investment Board – continued

DERIVATIVES ACTIVITIES:		**CAC Class: Inactive**

OTHER ALTERNATIVE INVESTMENTS:		
	CMOs/REMICs – Govt.	CMOs/REMICs – Private

KEY MANAGERS & DERIVATIVES SPECIALISTS:	**Direct Phone/Fax**	**Job Function**
Mr. Philip Halpern		Chief Investment Officer

Webster Bank

Savings Bank/Bldg Society

Sub of Webster Financial Corporation

Location: Webster Plaza
Waterbury, CT 06702-2211

Fax: 203/573-8301 **Phone:** 203/755-1422

Profile: Current yield investor

Investment Portfolio: $ 858.3 million

Use: **Investment Purposes**
Immunize from volatility

Currencies: US dollar

Regions: United States

DERIVATIVES ACTIVITIES:		**CAC Class: 2**
Exchange-traded Options & Futures U.S. Treasury futures	**Bond**	

OTHER ALTERNATIVE INVESTMENTS:		
	CMOs/REMICs – Govt.	CMOs/REMICs – Private

KEY MANAGERS & DERIVATIVES SPECIALISTS:	**Direct Phone/Fax**	**Job Function**
Mr. John V. Brennan E.V.P., C.F.O. & Treasurer		Chief Financial Officer Treasurer
Mr. Bernard Schumacher Senior Vice President	203/578-2446	Chief Investment Officer Portfolio Mgr – Futures
Mr. James C. Smith President & C.E.O.		President

Wellington Management Company

Investment Manager

Location:	75 State Street 19th Floor Boston, MA 02109-1809	**Fax:** 617/951-5250	**Phone:** 617/951-5000
Profile:	Total return investor	**Investment Portfolio:**	$ 95.0 billion
Use:	**Balance Sheet/Risk Management** Hedge interest rate risk	**Investment Purposes** Alter portfolio weighting Asset allocation Capture extra yield	

Currencies:	US dollar Australian dollar Canadian dollar French franc	German mark Japanese yen Swiss franc UK pound	**Regions:**	United States Canada	Europe Pacific Rim

DERIVATIVES ACTIVITIES:

Exchange-traded Options & Futures U.S. Treasury futures	**Bond, Currency, Interest rate**	
OTC Derivatives **Plain Vanilla Derivatives**	**Bond, Interest rate** Swaps Forwards Swaptions	 Caps Floors Collars

OTHER ALTERNATIVE INVESTMENTS:

	CMOs/REMICs – Govt. CMOs/REMICs – Private GICs	Strips Repos/reverse repos

KEY MANAGERS & DERIVATIVES SPECIALISTS:	**Direct Phone/Fax**	**Job Function**
Mr. Robert W. Doran Chairman	617/951-5446	Chief Investment Officer
Mr. Paul D. Kaplan Senior Vice President	617/951-5038 617/951-5130	Fixed-Income Strategist
Mr. Thomas L. Pappas Vice President	617/951-5037	Portfolio Mgr – Derivatives Portfolio Mgr – Futures

Wells Fargo Bank, N.A. (Treasury)

Bank/Portfolio

Location:	444 Market Street San Francisco, CA 94111	**Fax:** 415/399-1614	**Phone:** 415/477-1000
		Investment Portfolio:	$ 10.9 billion
Use:	**Balance Sheet/Risk Management** Hedge interest rate risk	**Investment Purposes** Capture extra yield	
Currencies:	US dollar	**Regions:**	United States

Wells Fargo Bank, N.A. (Treasury) – continued

DERIVATIVES ACTIVITIES: **CAC Class: Inactive**

OTHER ALTERNATIVE INVESTMENTS:

CMOs/REMICs – Govt.
CMOs/REMICs – Private
Repos/reverse repos

KEY MANAGERS & DERIVATIVES SPECIALISTS:	Direct Phone/Fax	Job Function
Mr. Alan Pabst Treasurer	415/396-6264 415/989-3851	Chief Investment Officer Treasurer

Wentworth, Hauser & Violich, Inc.

Investment Manager

Location: 333 Sacramento Street
San Francisco, CA 94111-3697

Fax: 415/788-7281 **Phone:** 415/981-6911

Profile: Total return investor

Investment Portfolio: $ 1.4 billion

Use: **Investment Purposes**
Asset allocation
Diversify portfolio

Currencies: US dollar

Regions: United States

DERIVATIVES ACTIVITIES: **CAC Class: Inactive**

OTHER ALTERNATIVE INVESTMENTS:

CMOs/REMICs – Govt.

KEY MANAGERS & DERIVATIVES SPECIALISTS:	Direct Phone/Fax	Job Function
Mr. W. Kurt Hauser President		President Chief Investment Officer
Mr. Allan P. Wentworth Treasurer		Treasurer

WESTAMERICA Bank

Bank/Portfolio

Sub of WESTAMERICA Bancorporation

Location: 1108 Fifth Avenue
2nd Floor
San Rafael, CA 94901

Fax: 415/257-8127 **Phone:** 415/456-8000

Profile: Hold to maturity investor

Investment Portfolio: $ 600.0 million

Use: **Balance Sheet/Risk Management**
Create synthetic fixed/floating rate
Hedge balance sheet
Hedge interest rate risk
Strategic liability management

Investment Purposes
Asset allocation
Hedge bond portfolio risk
Hedge interest rate risk

Currencies: US dollar

Regions: United States

WESTAMERICA Bank – continued

DERIVATIVES ACTIVITIES: **CAC Class: 2**

Exchange-traded Options & Futures	**Bond, Interest rate**	
OTC Derivatives		
Plain Vanilla Derivatives	Swaps	Forwards
Structured Notes	Corporate MTNs Floaters	Periodic capped floaters
Counterparty Rating Requirement:	None	

OTHER ALTERNATIVE INVESTMENTS:

	CMOs/REMICs – Govt.	Repos/reverse repos

KEY MANAGERS & DERIVATIVES SPECIALISTS:	**Direct Phone/Fax**	**Job Function**
Mr. E. Joseph Bowler S.V.P. & Treasurer	415/257-8040	Chief Investment Officer Treasurer Portfolio Mgr – Derivatives Portfolio Mgr – Structured Notes
Mr. Douglas S. Young Vice President	415/257-8047	Portfolio Mgr – Derivatives Portfolio Mgr – Structured Notes

Western Asset Management Company

Investment Manager

Sub of Legg Mason, Inc.

Location: 117 East Colorado Boulevard
6th Floor
Pasadena, CA 91105-1986

Fax: 818/584-4390 **Phone:** 818/584-4300

Profile: Total return investor

Investment Portfolio: $ 19.1 billion

Use: **Investment Purposes**

Currencies: US dollar, Canadian dollar, French franc, German mark, Italian lira, Japanese yen

Regions: United States, Canada, Europe

DERIVATIVES ACTIVITIES:

Exchange-traded Options & Futures

OTHER ALTERNATIVE INVESTMENTS:

	CMOs/REMICs – Govt.	CMOs/REMICs – Private

KEY MANAGERS & DERIVATIVES SPECIALISTS:	**Direct Phone/Fax**	**Job Function**
Mr. Kent S. Engel Chief Investment Officer	Ext. 364 818/683-2270	Chief Investment Officer
Mr. S. Kenneth Leech Director-Portfolio Management	Ext. 368	Portfolio Mgr – Futures *Corp, Govt*

Western Financial Savings Bank, Fsb

Savings Bank/Bldg Society

Sub of Westcorp

Location: 23 Pasteur Road
Irvine, CA 92718-3804

Fax: 714/727-2306 **Phone:** 714/727-1000

Profile: Total return investor

Investment Portfolio: $ 835.0 million

Use: **Balance Sheet/Risk Management**
Hedge balance sheet
Hedge interest rate risk

Investment Purposes
Convexity objectives
Hedge interest rate risk

Currencies: US dollar

Regions: United States, Europe

DERIVATIVES ACTIVITIES: **CAC Class: 5**

Exchange-traded Options & Futures

OTC Derivatives	**Interest rate**	
Plain Vanilla Derivatives	Swaps	Caps
	Forwards	
Counterparty Rating Requirement:	AA	

OTHER ALTERNATIVE INVESTMENTS:

CMOs/REMICs – Govt.	Repos/reverse repos
CMOs/REMICs – Private	

KEY MANAGERS & DERIVATIVES SPECIALISTS:	Direct Phone/Fax	Job Function
Mr. Don Kasle President & C.E.O.		President
Ms. Joy Schaefer Vice President & C.O.O.		Chief Financial Officer Bond Department Head Portfolio Mgr – Derivatives Portfolio Mgr – Options
Mr. Lee A. Whatcott Asst. Vice President & C.F.O.		Chief Financial Officer Treasurer

Westfield Companies

Insurance Co/P & C

Location: One Park Circle
Westfield Center, OH 44251

Fax: 330/887-0840 **Phone:** 330/887-0101

Profile: Total return investor

Investment Portfolio: $ 1.4 billion

Use: **Investment Purposes**

Currencies: US dollar

Regions: United States

DERIVATIVES ACTIVITIES: **CAC Class: 1**

Structured Notes	Govt. agency MTNs	Inverse floaters

Westfield Companies – continued

OTHER ALTERNATIVE INVESTMENTS:

	CMOs/REMICs – Govt.	Repos/reverse repos
	Strips	
	Repos/reverse repos	

KEY MANAGERS & DERIVATIVES SPECIALISTS:	**Direct Phone/Fax**	**Job Function**
Mr. Otto Bosshard Sr. Vice President & Treasurer	330/887-0400	Chief Investment Officer Treasurer
Mr. Ronald C. Stephonic Assistant Treasurer	330/887-0411	Portfolio Mgr – Structured Notes

Whitney National Bank (Portfolio)

Bank/Portfolio

Sub of Whitney Holding Corporation

Location: 228 St. Charles Avenue
New Orleans, LA 70130-2615

Fax: 504/586-7383 **Phone:** 504/586-7272

Profile: Total return investor

Investment Portfolio: $ 1.5 billion

Use: **Balance Sheet/Risk Management**
Hedge interest rate risk

Investment Purposes
Asset allocation
Diversify portfolio

Currencies: US dollar

Regions: United States

DERIVATIVES ACTIVITIES: **CAC Class: Inactive**

OTHER ALTERNATIVE INVESTMENTS:

	CMOs/REMICs – Govt.	Repos/reverse repos
	CMOs/REMICs – Private	

KEY MANAGERS & DERIVATIVES SPECIALISTS:	**Direct Phone/Fax**	**Job Function**
Mr. Edward B. Grimball Exec. Vice President & C.F.O.		Chief Investment Officer Chief Financial Officer

Williams, Jones & Associates Inc.

Investment Manager

Location: 717 Fifth Avenue
Suite 2400
New York, NY 10022

Fax: 212/753-3072 **Phone:** 212/935-8750

Profile: Total return investor

Investment Portfolio: $ 800.0 million

Use: **Investment Purposes**
Diversify portfolio
Provide incremental return

Currencies: US dollar

Regions: United States

Williams, Jones & Associates Inc. – continued

DERIVATIVES ACTIVITIES: **CAC Class: Inactive**

OTHER ALTERNATIVE INVESTMENTS:

CMOs/REMICs – Govt.

KEY MANAGERS & DERIVATIVES SPECIALISTS:	**Direct Phone/Fax**	**Job Function**
Mr. Frederic Williams Chairman		Chief Investment Officer

Wilmington Trust Company (Fixed Income)

Bank/Trust

Location: 1100 North Market Street
Rodney Square North
Wilmington, DE 19890-0001

Fax: 302/651-1758 **Phone:** 302/651-1000

Profile: Total return investor

Investment Portfolio: $ 23.3 billion

Use: **Investment Purposes**
Capture extra yield

Currencies: US dollar

Regions: United States

DERIVATIVES ACTIVITIES: **CAC Class: 2**

Structured Notes

Corporate MTNs
Govt. agency MTNs
CMT notes
Multi-step-up callable bonds

OTHER ALTERNATIVE INVESTMENTS:

CMOs/REMICs – Govt.
CMOs/REMICs – Private
Repos/reverse repos

KEY MANAGERS & DERIVATIVES SPECIALISTS:	**Direct Phone/Fax**	**Job Function**
Mr. Clayton M. Albright III Vice President	302/651-1858 302/651-1979	Portfolio Mgr – Structured Notes
Mr. Robert F. Collins Assistant Vice President	302/651-8193	Bond Department Head
Mr. Andrew Hopkins Assistant Vice President	302/651-8698	Portfolio Mgr – Structured Notes
Mr. Peter Succoso Vice President	302/651-8784	Chief Investment Officer

Wilmington Trust Company (Portfolio)

Bank/Portfolio

Location: 1100 North Market Street
Rodney Square North
Wilmington, DE 19890-0001

Fax: 302/651-1187 **Phone:** 302/651-1000

Profile: Hold to maturity investor

Investment Portfolio: $ 1.0 - 3.0 billion

Use: **Balance Sheet/Risk Management**
Hedge interest rate risk

Currencies: US dollar

Regions: United States

DERIVATIVES ACTIVITIES: **CAC Class: 5**

OTC Derivatives	**Interest rate**	
Plain Vanilla Derivatives	Swaps	Floors
Structured Notes	Govt. agency MTNs	
Counterparty Rating Requirement:	A	

OTHER ALTERNATIVE INVESTMENTS:

	CMOs/REMICs – Govt.	Repos/reverse repos
	CMOs/REMICs – Private	

KEY MANAGERS & DERIVATIVES SPECIALISTS:	**Direct Phone/Fax**	**Job Function**
Mr. John A. Sitek Vice President	302/651-1862	Chief Investment Officer Portfolio Mgr – Derivatives Portfolio Mgr – Structured Notes

Winterthur Swiss Group

Insurance Co/P & C

Sub of Winterthur Versicherungen

Location: 225 Liberty Street
42nd Floor
New York, NY 10281-1008

Fax: 212/524-6839 **Phone:** 212/416-5700

Profile: Total return investor

Investment Portfolio: $ 1.0 - 3.0 billion

Use: **Investment Purposes**
Asset allocation
Diversify portfolio
Provide incremental return

Currencies: US dollar

Regions: United States Europe

DERIVATIVES ACTIVITIES: **CAC Class: Inactive**

OTHER ALTERNATIVE INVESTMENTS:

	CMOs/REMICs – Govt.	CMOs/REMICs – Private

KEY MANAGERS & DERIVATIVES SPECIALISTS:	**Direct Phone/Fax**	**Job Function**
Mr. Reto Koller Vice President	212/416-5855	Chief Investment Officer

State of Wisconsin Investment Board

Government Pension Fund

Location: 121 East Wilson Street
Madison, WI 53702

Fax: 608/266-2436 **Phone:** 608/266-2381

Profile: Total return investor

Investment Portfolio: $ 26.0 billion

Use: **Balance Sheet/Risk Management**
Hedge interest rate risk

Currencies: US dollar, Italian lira, Mexican peso

Regions: United States

DERIVATIVES ACTIVITIES: **CAC Class: 4**

Exchange-traded Options & Futures

OTC Derivatives	**Bond, Currency, Interest rate**	
Plain Vanilla Derivatives	Swaps	Caps
	Forwards	Floors
Structured Notes	Bond index notes	Floaters
Counterparty Rating Requirement:	AA	

OTHER ALTERNATIVE INVESTMENTS:

CMOs/REMICs – Govt.	Repos/reverse repos
Strips	

KEY MANAGERS & DERIVATIVES SPECIALISTS:	**Direct Phone/Fax**	**Job Function**
Ms. Patricia Lipton Executive Director	608/266-9451	Chief Investment Officer
Mr. John Zwadzich Investment Director	608/266-2047	Bond Department Head *Taxable* Portfolio Mgr – Derivatives Portfolio Mgr – Futures Portfolio Mgr – Structured Notes

WMX Technologies, Inc.

Corporation

Location: 3003 Butterfield Road
Oak Brook, IL 60521

Fax: 708/572-3094 **Phone:** 708/572-8800

Use: **Balance Sheet/Risk Management**
Create synthetic fixed/floating rate
Hedge balance sheet
Hedge currency risk
Hedge interest rate risk
Protect currency gains
Strategic liability management

Currencies: US dollar, Australian dollar, French franc, German mark, Italian lira, UK pound

Regions: United States

WMX Technologies, Inc. – continued

DERIVATIVES ACTIVITIES:		CAC Class: 6
Exchange-traded Options & Futures	**Currency**	
OTC Derivatives	**Currency, Interest rate**	
Plain Vanilla Derivatives	Swaps Forwards Swaptions	Caps Collars
Counterparty Rating Requirement:	AAA	

KEY MANAGERS & DERIVATIVES SPECIALISTS:	Direct Phone/Fax	Job Function
Mr. James E. Koenig S.V.P., Treasurer & C.F.O.		Chief Financial Officer Treasurer Portfolio Mgr – Derivatives
Ms. Susan C. Nustra Vice President – Treasury		Treasurer Portfolio Mgr – Derivatives
Mr. Phillip B. Rooney President & C.O.O.		President

Wolf, Webb, Burk & Campbell Inc.

Investment Manager

Location: 1525 Locust Street
11th Floor
Philadelphia, PA 19102

Fax: 215/735-7892 **Phone:** 215/735-5910

Profile: Total return investor

Investment Portfolio: $ 1.0 billion

Use: **Investment Purposes**
Diversify portfolio

Currencies: US dollar

Regions: United States

DERIVATIVES ACTIVITIES: **CAC Class: Inactive**

OTHER ALTERNATIVE INVESTMENTS:

CMOs/REMICs – Govt.

KEY MANAGERS & DERIVATIVES SPECIALISTS:	Direct Phone/Fax	Job Function
Mr. H. Jerry Wolf President & Principal		President Chief Investment Officer

Woodmen of the World Life Insurance Society

Insurance Co/Life

Location: 1700 Farnam Street
Omaha, NE 68102

Fax: 402/342-5136 **Phone:** 402/342-1890

Profile: Total return investor

Investment Portfolio: $ 3.9 billion

Use: **Balance Sheet/Risk Management** **Investment Purposes**

Currencies: US dollar

Regions: United States

Woodmen of the World Life Insurance Society – continued

DERIVATIVES ACTIVITIES:		**CAC Class: Inactive**

OTHER ALTERNATIVE INVESTMENTS:

	CMOs/REMICs – Govt.	CMOs/REMICs – Private

KEY MANAGERS & DERIVATIVES SPECIALISTS:	**Direct Phone/Fax**	**Job Function**
Mr. Don L. Miller		Chief Investment Officer

The World Bank

Government

Location: 1818 H Street N.W.
Washington, DC 20433

Fax: 202/477-8589 **Phone:** 202/477-1234

Profile: Stable asset investor

Investment Portfolio: $ 20.4 billion

Use:

Balance Sheet/Risk Management
Hedge currency risk
Hedge interest rate risk
Lower transaction costs
Reduce cost of capital

Investment Purposes
Adjust portfolio duration
Capture extra yield
Provide incremental return

Currencies: US dollar, German mark, Japanese yen, Spanish peseta, Swiss franc, UK pound

Regions: United States, Canada, Europe

DERIVATIVES ACTIVITIES:		**CAC Class: 7**
Exchange-traded Options & Futures	**Bond, Interest rate**	
U.S. Treasury futures	U.S. Treasury options	
OTC Derivatives	**Currency, Interest rate**	
Plain Vanilla Derivatives	Swaps	Caps
	Forwards	Floors
	Swaptions	Collars
Structured Notes	Govt. agency MTNs	Floaters
Counterparty Rating Requirement:	AAA	

OTHER ALTERNATIVE INVESTMENTS:

	CMOs/REMICs – Govt.	Repos/reverse repos
	Strips	

KEY MANAGERS & DERIVATIVES SPECIALISTS:	**Direct Phone/Fax**	**Job Function**
Ms. Veronique Lavorel Director	202/458-0040	Chief Investment Officer Portfolio Mgr – Derivatives Portfolio Mgr – Options Portfolio Mgr – Structured Notes
Mr. James D. Wolfensohn President	202/458-5120	President

World Savings & Loan Association, A Fed. Svgs. & Loan Assn.

Savings Bank/Bldg Society

Sub of Golden West Financial Corp.

Location: 1901 Harrison Street
Oakland, CA 94612

Fax: 510/446-4672 **Phone:** 510/446-6000

Profile: Total return investor

Investment Portfolio: $ 3.4 billion

Use: **Balance Sheet/Risk Management**
Hedge interest rate risk

Currencies: US dollar

Regions: United States

DERIVATIVES ACTIVITIES: **CAC Class: 7**

OTC Derivatives	**Interest rate**	
Plain Vanilla Derivatives	Swaps	Caps
	Forwards	

OTHER ALTERNATIVE INVESTMENTS:

CMOs/REMICs – Govt.

KEY MANAGERS & DERIVATIVES SPECIALISTS:	Direct Phone/Fax	Job Function
Mr. Peter Beall	510/446-3536	Chief Investment Officer
Ms. Berta Conger	510/446-3218	Portfolio Mgr – Derivatives

YMCA Retirement Fund

Corporate Pension Fund

Location: 225 Broadway
8th Floor
New York, NY 10007-3083

Fax: 212/227-6941 **Phone:** 212/766-4150

Profile: Total return investor

Investment Portfolio: $ 2.3 billion

Use: **Investment Purposes**
Alter portfolio weighting
Adjust portfolio duration
Asset allocation
Beat conventional rates
Capture extra yield
Diversify portfolio
Hedge bond portfolio risk
Hedge currency risk
Hedge equity portfolio risk
Immunize from volatility
Provide incremental return

Currencies: US dollar, Canadian dollar, French franc, German mark, Japanese yen, Swiss franc, UK pound

Regions: United States, Canada, Europe

YMCA Retirement Fund – continued

DERIVATIVES ACTIVITIES: **CAC Class: 3**

Exchange-traded Options & Futures	**Bond, Currency, Interest rate**	
U.S. Treasury futures	U.S. Treasury options	
OTC Derivatives	**Bond, Currency, Interest rate**	
Plain Vanilla Derivatives	Swaps	Floors
	Caps	Collars
Structured Notes		
Counterparty Rating Requirement:	None	

OTHER ALTERNATIVE INVESTMENTS:

	CMOs/REMICs – Govt.	Repos/reverse repos

KEY MANAGERS & DERIVATIVES SPECIALISTS:	**Direct Phone/Fax**	**Job Function**
Mr. Jack Cosgrove Vice President	212/766-2113	Portfolio Mgr – Futures Portfolio Mgr – Options Portfolio Mgr – Structured Notes
Mr. Harold C. Smith President	212/766-4173 212/766-4178	President Chief Investment Officer Portfolio Mgr – Derivatives Portfolio Mgr – Structured Notes

The Zenith Insurance Company

Insurance Co/P & C

Location: 21255 Califa Street
Woodland Hills, CA 91367-5005

Fax: 818/713-0177 **Phone:** 818/713-1000

Profile: Current yield investor

Investment Portfolio: $ 1.5 billion

Use: **Investment Purposes**

Currencies: US dollar

Regions: United States

DERIVATIVES ACTIVITIES:

Structured Notes	Corporate MTNs

OTHER ALTERNATIVE INVESTMENTS:

	CMOs/REMICs – Govt.

KEY MANAGERS & DERIVATIVES SPECIALISTS:	**Direct Phone/Fax**	**Job Function**
Mr. Daniel Petrula Vice President	818/594-5266	Portfolio Mgr – Structured Notes *Corp*
Mr. Keith Trotman Senior Vice President	818/594-5590	Chief Investment Officer Portfolio Mgr – Derivatives

Zions First National Bank (Portfolio)

Bank/Portfolio

Sub of Zions Bancorporation

Location: One South Main Street
13th Floor
Salt Lake City, UT 84111-1923

Fax: 801/524-2129 **Phone:** 801/524-4711

Profile: Spread investor

Investment Portfolio: $ 500.0 - 999.0 million

Use: **Balance Sheet/Risk Management**
Strategic liability management

Currencies: US dollar

Regions: United States

DERIVATIVES ACTIVITIES: **CAC Class: 4**

OTC Derivatives	**Interest rate**	
Plain Vanilla Derivatives	Swaps	Floors
	Caps	

OTHER ALTERNATIVE INVESTMENTS:

CMOs/REMICs – Govt.	Strips
CMOs/REMICs – Private	Repos/reverse repos

KEY MANAGERS & DERIVATIVES SPECIALISTS:	**Direct Phone/Fax**	**Job Function**
Mr. Jonathan E. Bacon Assistant Vice President	801/524-2304	Trader – Derivatives
Mr. W. David Hemingway Executive Vice President	801/524-4640 801/524-4664	Chief Investment Officer Portfolio Mgr – Derivatives

Zirkin Cutler Investments

Investment Manager

Location: 805 15th Street N.W.
Suite 240
Washington, DC 20005

Fax: 202/842-5107 **Phone:** 202/371-9000

Profile: Total return investor

Investment Portfolio: $ 1.0 - 3.0 billion

Use: **Investment Purposes**
Diversify portfolio
Provide incremental return

Currencies: US dollar

Regions: United States

DERIVATIVES ACTIVITIES: **CAC Class: Inactive**

OTHER ALTERNATIVE INVESTMENTS:

CMOs/REMICs – Govt.	CMOs/REMICs – Private

KEY MANAGERS & DERIVATIVES SPECIALISTS:	**Direct Phone/Fax**	**Job Function**
Mr. Marshall Cutler		Chief Investment Officer

Zurich-Kemper Investments, Inc.

Insurance Co/Management

Sub of Zurich Versicherungs-Gesellschaft

Location: 120 South LaSalle Street
Chicago, IL 60603-9932

Fax: 312/499-1001 **Phone:** 312/781-1121

Profile: Total return investor

Investment Portfolio: $ 62.4 billion

Use: **Balance Sheet/Risk Management**
Hedge currency risk
Hedge interest rate risk
Protect currency gains

Currencies: US dollar, Belgian franc, Canadian dollar, Japanese yen, UK pound

Regions: United States, Canada, Europe, Pacific Rim

DERIVATIVES ACTIVITIES: **CAC Class: 6**

Exchange-traded Options & Futures	**Bond**	
U.S. Treasury futures	U.S. Treasury options	
OTC Derivatives	**Currency**	
Plain Vanilla Derivatives	Swaps	Forwards
Structured Notes	Corporate MTNs CMT notes	Tender options bonds
Counterparty Rating Requirement:	A	

OTHER ALTERNATIVE INVESTMENTS:

CMOs/REMICs – Govt.	Strips
CMOs/REMICs – Private	Repos/reverse repos

KEY MANAGERS & DERIVATIVES SPECIALISTS:	Direct Phone/Fax	Job Function
Mr. J. Patrick Beimford, Jr. Director – Fixed-Income	312/499-1976	Chief Investment Officer Bond Department Head Portfolio Mgr – Derivatives Portfolio Mgr – Options
Mr. Frank E. Collecchia Senior Vice President	312/499-1552	Fixed-Income Strategist *Corp, Govt, MBS, Muni*
Mr. John E. Neal President & C.O.O.		President
Mr. Robert H. Schumacher Senior Vice President	312/499-1046 312/499-5601	Fixed-Income Strategist *Corp, Govt, MBS, Muni*
Mr. Stephen B. Timbers Chairman & C.E.O.	312/499-1984	Chief Investment Officer

Sellside Derivatives

ABN AMRO Securities (USA) Inc.

Bank/Dealer

Sub of ABN AMRO Holdings

Location: 181 West Madison Street
Suite 3201
Chicago, IL 60602

Fax: 312/781-8167

Phone: 312/781-8600

KEY MANAGERS & DERIVATIVES SPECIALISTS	Direct Phone/Fax	Job Function
Mr. Timothy Aburano Trader	312/904-5590	Trader – Currency Options
Mr. Thomas Dolan Senior Vice President	312/904-8647 312/904-8495	Bond Department Head
Mr. Rudy Frank Vice President	312/904-6181	Sales – Derivatives
Mr. Thomas J. Johnston Group Senior Vice President	312/904-7001	Bond Department Head *ABS, Govt, Agency, MBS, Muni, Money Mkt*
Mr. Thomas Plodzeen Vice President	312/904-6405	Marketing – Derivatives
Mr. Robert VanParidon Treasurer	312/904-5510	Trader – Currency Futures Trader – Currency Options

J. Aron & Company

Broker/Dealer – Regional

Sub of Goldman, Sachs & Company

Location: 85 Broad Street
New York, NY 10004

Fax: 212/346-2687

Phone: 212/902-5326

KEY MANAGERS & DERIVATIVES SPECIALISTS	Direct Phone/Fax	Job Function
Ms. Tracey McCabe Vice President	212/902-7850	Sales – Currency
Ms. Maria Nordone Vice President	212/902-7850	Sales – Currency
Mr. Marc Spilker Vice President	212/902-7746	Trader – Currency Options
Mr. Christopher Webb Vice President	212/902-7747	Trader – Currency Options

BA Futures Inc.

Bank/Dealer

Sub of BankAmerica Corporation

Location: BA Building
200 West Adams Street, Suite 2700
Chicago, IL 60606

Fax: 312/987-0644 **Phone:** 312/828-2345

KEY MANAGERS & DERIVATIVES SPECIALISTS	Direct Phone/Fax	Job Function
Mr. Thomas Baran Vice President	312/269-4558	Trader – Currency Futures
Mr. Richard Durso Vice President	312/269-4582	Trader – Interest Rate Futures
Mr. Michael Farrell Vice President	312/269-4558	Trader – Currency Futures
Mr. Taylor Hurst Managing Director	312/269-4552	Sales – Currency
Mr. Daniel Knytych Account Executive	312/269-4510	Sales – Derivatives

Banco Santander of New York (Dealer)

Bank/Dealer

Sub of Banco Santander (Spain)

Location: 45 East 53rd Street
New York, NY 10022

Fax: 212/350-3535 **Phone:** 212/350-3500

KEY MANAGERS & DERIVATIVES SPECIALISTS	Direct Phone/Fax	Job Function
Mr. Melchor Armenta Vice President	212/756-9222	Trader – FRA's
Mr. Leo Borenstein Senior Dealer	212/756-9222	Sales – Currency Trader – Currency Futures Trader – Currency Options
Mr. Eduardo Fernandez Senior Dealer	212/756-9222	Trader – Currency Futures Trader – Currency Options
Mr. Juan Carlos Garrido Senior Dealer	212/756-9222	Trader – Options
Mr. Kenneth Kolber Vice President	212/756-9200	Trader – Derivatives
Mr. Jaime Suarez Vice President	212/756-9222 212/350-3579	Trader – Currency Options Head Trader – Derivatives Head

Bank of America NT & SA – Capital Markets

Bank/Dealer

Sub of BankAmerica Corporation

Location: 555 California Street, San Francisco, CA 94104 **Fax:** 415/622-5901 **Phone:** 415/622-4386

KEY MANAGERS & DERIVATIVES SPECIALISTS	Direct Phone/Fax	Job Function
Mr. Joseph P. Bauman Senior Vice President	415/953-1234 415/953-3198	Derivatives Products Head Research Analyst – Derivatives Trader – Derivatives
Mr. James H. Gill, Jr. Manager – Structured Securities	415/953-5306	Derivatives Specialist
Mr. Robert J. Oxenburgh Manager – Risk Management	415/953-5310	Derivatives Specialist
Mr. Scott Rosebrook V.P. & Manager	415/622-9182	Derivatives Specialist
Ms. Elizabeth Stanners Manager – Emerging Markets	415/622-8965	Derivatives Specialist
Mr. Richard S. Turney Vice President	415/622-3007	Trading – Derivatives Head

Bank of America Illinois (Dealer)

Bank/Dealer

Sub of BankAmerica Corporation

Location: 231 South LaSalle Street, Chicago, IL 60697-0001 **Fax:** 312/828-3820 **Phone:** 312/828-2345

KEY MANAGERS & DERIVATIVES SPECIALISTS	Direct Phone/Fax	Job Function
Mr. James J. Baldino Managing Director	312/828-2281	Bond Department Head Sales – Derivatives Trader – Derivatives
Mr. Steven Saratore Managing Director	312/828-8933	Marketing – Derivatives

Bank of America NT & SA – Capital Markets (New York)

Bank/Dealer

Sub of BankAmerica Corporation

Location: 40 East 52nd Street, Unit #7664, New York, NY 10022 **Fax:** 212/836-5390 **Phone:** 212/503-7000

Bank of America NT & SA – Capital Markets (New York) – continued

KEY MANAGERS & DERIVATIVES SPECIALISTS	Direct Phone/Fax	Job Function
Mr. Eugene Chang Vice President	212/836-5508	Trader – Options
Ms. Christine Mandell Senior Vice President	212/836-5500	Trader – Derivatives Head
Mr. V. K. Ranganadhan Manager	212/836-5585	Trader – Currency Swaps Trader – Interest Rate Swaps
Mr. John Richards Vice President	212/836-5572	Trader – Currency Futures Head Trader – Currency Options Head

Bank Julius Baer & Co., Ltd.

Broker/Dealer – National

Sub of Bär Holdings A.G.

Location: 330 Madison Avenue
New York, NY 10017

Fax: 212/297-1935

Phone: 212/297-3600

KEY MANAGERS & DERIVATIVES SPECIALISTS	Direct Phone/Fax	Job Function
Ms. Donna Calandrillo Vice President	212/818-9130	Trader – Futures Trader – Options
Ms. Jeanette Kulka Assistant Vice President	212/297-1911	Trader – Options
Mr. Peter Mayers Assistant Vice President	212/297-1979	Trader – Interest Rate Futures Trader – Interest Rate Options
Ms. Donna Seferian Vice President	212/297-1981	Bond Department Head *Muni, Money Mkt* Derivatives Products Head
Mr. Walter Simon Vice President	212/808-9392	Trader – Options
Mr. Bernard Spilko Managing Director	212/297-3939	Bond Department Head *Govt, MBS*
Mr. Peter Wild Senior Vice President	212/297-1950	Derivatives Products Head

Bank of Boston Corporation

Bank/Dealer

Location: 100 Federal Street, Boston, MA 02110-1898 **Fax:** 617/434-8330 **Phone:** 617/434-2200

KEY MANAGERS & DERIVATIVES SPECIALISTS	**Direct Phone/Fax**	**Job Function**
Mr. Mark Burgess Vice President	617/434-8074	Structured Notes – Head *Corp*
Mr. Darrell J. Hendrix Director	617/434-8074	Trader – Derivatives Head
Mr. T. J. Hughes Managing Director	617/434-4884	Derivatives Specialist
Mr. William LePard Director	617/434-7129	Derivatives Products Head Sales – Derivatives
Mr. James Mather Vice President	212/415-9743	Trader – Currency Swaps Trader – Interest Rate Swaps

Bank of Montreal (Chicago)

Bank/Dealer

Sub of Bank of Montréal (Canada)

Location: 115 South LaSalle Street, 19 West, Chicago, IL 60603 **Fax:** 312/845-4198 **Phone:** 312/845-4100

KEY MANAGERS & DERIVATIVES SPECIALISTS	**Direct Phone/Fax**	**Job Function**
Mr. Eric Bergstrom Associate – Risk Management	312/845-4360	Trader – Options
Mr. Donald Lloyd Chief Trader	312/845-4060	Trader – Currency Futures Head Trader – Currency Options Head
Ms. Donna Morlack Vice President	312/845-5020	Trader – Derivatives
Ms. Susan Spinner Director	312/845-5020	Trader – FRA's
Ms. Jamie K. Thorsen Managing Director	312/845-4107	Marketing – Currency
Mr. David Wales Director	312/845-5020	Trader – Structured Investments
Mr. Roland Wikstrom Assistant Vice President	312/845-5021	Trader – Options
Mr. Trevor Woodland Vice President	312/845-4080 312/461-7385	Sales – Currency

Bank of Montreal (New York)

Bank/Dealer

Sub of Bank of Montréal (Canada)

Location: 430 Park Avenue
8th Floor
New York, NY 10022

Fax: 212/702-1193

Phone: 212/758-6300

KEY MANAGERS & DERIVATIVES SPECIALISTS	Direct Phone/Fax	Job Function
Mr. Thomas Benfer Vice President	212/702-1284	Sales – Currency
Ms. Christine Cromarty Vice President	212/702-1284	Derivatives Specialist
Mr. Harold Guardiola Vice President	212/702-1284	Trader – Currency Futures Head Trader – Currency Options Head Sales – Currency

The Bank of New York (Dealer)

Bank/Dealer

Sub of The Bank of New York Company, Inc.

Location: 48 Wall Street
13th Floor
New York, NY 10005-2901

Fax: 212/495-1014

Phone: 212/495-1784

KEY MANAGERS & DERIVATIVES SPECIALISTS	Direct Phone/Fax	Job Function
Ms. Marlene Alonzo Vice President	212/804-2137	Sales – Derivatives Trader – Currency Swaps
Mr. James Amato Assistant Vice President	212/804-2108	Trader – Derivatives
Mr. John Cipriani Vice President	212/804-2100	Trader – Currency Futures Trader – Currency Options
Mr. John R. Gaines Vice President	212/804-2035	Trader – Currency Options Head
Mr. James C. Gerber Vice President & Manager	212/804-2222 212/495-1017	Bond Department Head *Muni*
Mr. Thomas P. Gibbons Senior Vice President	212/804-2006	Bond Department Head *Funding, Money Mkt* Trader– Derivatives
Mr. William Hardis Vice President	212/804-2108	Trader – Currency Futures
Mr. Thomas G. Kane Vice President	212/804-2179 212/495-1019	Bond Department Head *Treas, Agency*
Mr. James McAuliffe Vice President	212/804-2137	OTC Deriv/Swaps – Head Trader – Currency Swaps

The Bank of New York (Dealer) – continued

KEY MANAGERS & DERIVATIVES SPECIALISTS	Direct Phone/Fax	Job Function
Ms. Tazmeen Rajwani Vice President	212/804-2142	Derivatives Products Head *Funding, Money Mkt* Sales – Derivatives Trader – Interest Rate Futures Trader – Interest Rate Options Trader – Interest Rate Swaps
Mr. Robert C. Ryan Vice President	212/804-2165	Trader – Currency Futures Trader – Currency Options
Mr. Michael Wootton Assistant Vice President	212/804-2109	Trader – Options

Banque Nationale de Paris (New York)

Bank/Dealer

Sub of Banque Nationale de Paris S.A. (BNP) (Compte de Tiers)

Location: 499 Park Avenue
New York, NY 10024

Fax: 212/415-9798

Phone: 212/750-1400

KEY MANAGERS & DERIVATIVES SPECIALISTS	Direct Phone/Fax	Job Function
Mr. Lawrence Bassallo Vice President	212/415-9743	Sales – Derivatives
Ms. Rhonda Black Vice President	212/415-9743	Sales – Derivatives
Mr. Daniel Brooks Vice President	212/415-9755	Trader – Currency Futures Trader – Currency Options
Mr. Barry Calder Vice President	212/415-9755	Trader – Currency Futures Head Trader – Currency Options Head
Mr. Thomas Corper Vice President	212/415-9743	Marketing – Derivatives Sales – Derivatives
Ms. Yuko Deudon Vice President	212/415-9743	Trader – Currency Swaps Trader – Interest Rate Futures Trader – Interest Rate Options Trader – Interest Rate Swaps
Ms. Eleanor Diabala-Smith Vice President	212/415-1636	Trader – Futures Trader – Options
Mr. Christophe Gouelo Vice President	212/415-9751	Trader – Options
Mr. Timothy McWalters Vice President	212/415-9755	Trader – Derivatives

Banque Paribas Ltd. Corporation

Bank/Dealer

Sub of Compagnie Financière de Paribas

Location: The Equitable Tower
787 Seventh Avenue
New York, NY 10019

Fax: 212/841-2146

Phone: 212/841-2000

KEY MANAGERS & DERIVATIVES SPECIALISTS	Direct Phone/Fax	Job Function
Mr. Francois Boisson	212/841-3717	Derivatives Specialist
Mr. John Goldfield	212/841-2400	Trader – Derivatives
Mr. John Light	212/841-2425	Trader – Currency Futures Trader – FRA's
Ms. Ellen Nose	212/841-3442	Marketing – Structured Notes Trader – Currency Swaps
Mr. Kent Oz	212/841-3740	Derivatives Specialist
Mr. Christian Picot	212/841-3670	Derivatives Specialist
Mr. Shahriar Shahida	212/841-3900	Derivatives Products Head
Mr. Jonathan Simmons	212/841-2400	Trader – Currency Futures Head Trader – Currency Options Head Trader – Derivatives Head
Mr. Theodore Tsao	212/841-3716	Derivatives Specialist
Mr. Srinivasa Varathan	212/841-3750	Derivatives Products Head Structured Notes – Head Sales – Structured Notes Trader – Currency Swaps Trader – Interest Rate Swaps Trader – Structured Investments
Mr. George Vere-Laurie	212/841-3433	Trader – Currency Swaps Trader – Interest Rate Swaps

Banque Worms Capital Corporation

Bank/Dealer

Sub of Banque Worms

Location: 450 Park Avenue
New York, NY 10022

Fax: 212/593-4854

Phone: 212/758-9205

KEY MANAGERS & DERIVATIVES SPECIALISTS	Direct Phone/Fax	Job Function
Mr. Andre Chatelain Vice President	212/826-5462	Trader – Derivatives Head
Mr. Lawrence Fafalak Vice President	212/826-5465	Trader – FRA's

Banque Worms Capital Corporation – continued

KEY MANAGERS & DERIVATIVES SPECIALISTS	Direct Phone/Fax	Job Function
Mr. Terrence Sullivan Vice President	212/826-5463	Trader – Currency Futures Head
Mr. Timothy Walz Vice President	212/826-5464	Sales – Derivatives Trader – Derivatives

BayBank Boston, N.A. (Dealer)

Bank/Dealer

Sub of BayBanks, Inc.

Location: 155 Federal Street
7th Floor
Boston, MA 02110-1735

Fax: 617/556-6650 **Phone:** 617/482-1040

KEY MANAGERS & DERIVATIVES SPECIALISTS	Direct Phone/Fax	Job Function
Mr. Jonathan Cottrell Senior Vice President	617/556-6822 617/556-6604	Trader – Currency Futures Trader – Currency Options
Mr. John Croft Vice President	617/556-6248	OTC Deriv/Swaps – Head Sales – Derivatives
Ms. Karen M. Epstein Vice President	617/556-6722 617/556-6650	Bond Department Head *Funding, Money Mkt*
Ms. Lois Scheirer Senior Vice President	617/556-6996	Trader – Currency Futures Head Trader – Currency Options Head
Mr. Brian D. Stewart Vice President	617/556-6717 617/556-6650	Bond Department Head *Treas, Agency, MBS*
Ms. Elizabeth W. Whitehead Director – Public Finance	617/556-6990 617/556-6650	Bond Department Head *Muni*

Bayerische Vereinsbank AG (New York)

Bank/Dealer

Sub of Bayerische Vereinsbank AG

Location: 335 Madison Avenue
New York, NY 10017

Fax: 212/210-0330 **Phone:** 212/210-0300

KEY MANAGERS & DERIVATIVES SPECIALISTS	Direct Phone/Fax	Job Function
Mr. Robert B. Butler Vice President	212/210-0303	Sales – Derivatives

Bayerische Vereinsbank AG (New York) – continued

KEY MANAGERS & DERIVATIVES SPECIALISTS	Direct Phone/Fax	Job Function
Mr. Thomas J. Glynn Vice President	212/210-0302	Derivatives Products Head OTC Deriv/Swaps – Head Structured Notes – Head Trader – Currency Futures Head Trader – Currency Options Head Trader – Derivatives Head
Ms. Nancy Henderson Vice President	212/210-0303	Trader – Interest Rate Futures Trader – Interest Rate Options Trader – Interest Rate Swaps

Bear, Stearns & Company Inc.

Broker/Dealer – National

Location: 245 Park Avenue
New York, NY 10167

Fax: 212/272-6291

Phone: 212/272-2000

KEY MANAGERS & DERIVATIVES SPECIALISTS	Direct Phone/Fax	Job Function
Mr. Michael G. Barnes Managing Director	212/272-8015	Sales – Structured Notes
Mr. William Byers Managing Director	212/272-2716	Sales – Futures
Mr. Peter Cherasia Senior Managing Director	212/272-6366	Fixed-Income Strategist
Mr. Peter S. Croncota Managing Director	212/272-7744	Marketing – Derivatives
Mr. Nestor Cybrwisky Head – Emerging Markets	212/272-9429	Bond Department Head
Ms. Wendy deMonchaux Senior Managing Director	212/272-3452 212/272-6550	Derivatives Products Head
Mr. Michael Ehrlich Senior Managing Director	212/272-9272	Trader – Currency Futures Trader – Currency Options
Ms. Phyllis Esposito Senior Managing Director	212/272-4936 212/272-5948	Derivatives Products Head *Muni* Trader – Derivatives *Muni*
Mr. Michael S. Fedak Head – Fixed Income Risk Management	212/272-9633	Derivatives Product Head
Mr. Kevin J. Finnerty Senior Managing Director	212/272-6014 212/272-5593	Bond Department Head *MBS*
Mr. Bjorn Flesaker Managing Director	212/272-3690	Research Analyst – Derivatives

Bear, Stearns & Company Inc. – continued

KEY MANAGERS & DERIVATIVES SPECIALISTS	Direct Phone/Fax	Job Function
Mr. David Goldman Managing Director	212/272-2876	Fixed-Income Strategist
Mr. James Held Senior Managing Director	212/272-5136	Trader – Derivatives Head
Mr. Ronald M. Hersch Managing Director	212/272-9866	Trader – Currency Futures Head Trader – Futures
Ms. Marjorie E. Hogan Senior Managing Director	212/272-3666	Trader – Currency Swaps *MBS*
Mr. Evan Kalimtgis	212/272-2597	Fixed-Income Strategist
Mr. Daniel L. Keating Senior Managing Director	212/272-4911 212/272-6291	Bond Department Head *Muni*
Mr. Michael L. Kolodner Managing Director	212/272-4936	Research Analyst – Derivatives
Mr. Andrew D. Langerman Managing Director	212/272-6459	Sales – Structured Notes
Mr. Gary McLoughlin Senior Managing Director	212/272-5514 212/272-6247	Bond Department Head *Govt*
Mr. Timothy Murray Managing Director	212/272-5138	Derivatives Specialist
Mr. Emmanuel Rousseau Trader – Hybrid Derivatives	212/272-5135	Trader – Derivatives Head
Mr. David Schoenthal Head – Foreign Exchange	212/272-4518	Trader – Currency Futures Head Trader – Currency Options Head
Mr. Nathaniel R. Singer Senior Managing Director	212/272-5630	Trader – Futures *Muni*
Mr. Warren J. Spector Senior Managing Director	212/272-5719	Bond Department Head *MBS* Derivatives Products Head
Ms. Lisa Y. Whitley Vice President	212/272-5631	Research Analyst – Futures/Options *Muni*
Mr. Elliot K. Wolk Senior Managing Director	212/272-4806	Derivatives Specialist
Mr. Martin Woodhams Managing Director	212/272-4518	Trader – Currency Futures Trader – Currency Options

Bear, Stearns Securities Corp.

Broker/Dealer – National

Sub of Bear, Stearns & Company Inc.

Location: 30 South Wacker Drive
Suite 2000
Chicago, IL 60606

Fax: 312/474-4615

Phone: 312/474-4600

KEY MANAGERS & DERIVATIVES SPECIALISTS	**Direct Phone/Fax**	**Job Function**
Mr. John R. Finnegen Managing Director	312/474-4720 312/474-4736	Sales – Currency Sales – Futures
Mr. Steven Trimble Trader	312/474-4726 312/474-4690	Sales – Currency Sales – Futures Trader – Futures

Bloom Staloff Brokerage Services Inc.

Brokers' Broker

Location: 2000 Market Street
18th Floor
Philadelphia, PA 19103

Fax: 215/569-3377

Phone: 215/567-0200

KEY MANAGERS & DERIVATIVES SPECIALISTS	**Direct Phone/Fax**	**Job Function**
Mr. Richard T. Alba Trader	215/568-9311	Trader – Currency Futures Head Trader – Currency Options Head Sales – Currency
Mr. George Morgan President	215/568-9311	Sales – Derivatives

BR Associates

Broker/Dealer – Regional

Location: 867 River Road
Chatham, NJ 07928

Fax: 908/771-7452

Phone: 908/771-7452

KEY MANAGERS & DERIVATIVES SPECIALISTS	**Direct Phone/Fax**	**Job Function**
Mr. Luke Diehl Managing Director		Derivatives Products Head Trader – Currency Futures Head Trader – Derivatives Head
Ms. Katherine A. Everett Manager		Structured Notes – Head Sales – Derivatives Sales – Structured Notes
Mr. Wendell J. Hanna Vice President		Trader – Futures
Ms. E. T. Mitchell Vice President		Bond Department Head

BR Associates – continued

KEY MANAGERS & DERIVATIVES SPECIALISTS	Direct Phone/Fax	Job Function
Ms. Kimberly Wales Trader		Trader – Currency Options *Corp, Govt, Muni* Trader – Interest Rate Options *Corp, Govt, Muni* Trader – Options *Corp, Govt, Muni*

BT Securities Corporation

Bank/Dealer

Sub of Bankers Trust – New York Corporation

Location: 130 Liberty Street
One Bankers Trust Plaza 33rd Floor
New York, NY 10006

Fax: 212/250-7071 **Phone:** 212/250-2500

KEY MANAGERS & DERIVATIVES SPECIALISTS	Direct Phone/Fax	Job Function
Mr. Lee Barba Managing Director	212/250-7600	Derivatives Specialist
Mr. Ari Bergmann Managing Director	212/250-9596	Derivatives Specialist
Mr. Philip Borg Managing Director	212/775-3336	Trader – Derivatives *Corp*
Mr. Yves deBalmann Managing Director	212/775-2625	Derivatives Products Head
Ms. Donna E. Garban Vice President	212/775-3991	Trader – Derivatives *Muni*
Mr. David Gittings Managing Director	212/775-2043	OTC Deriv/Swaps – Head Structured Notes – Head Sales – Derivatives
Mr. William Hirschberg Managing Director	212/775-5611	Trader – Currency Options Head Trader – Derivatives Head Trader – Currency Swaps Trader – Interest Rate Futures Trader – Interest Rate Options Trader – Interest Rate Swaps
Ms. Lisa Polsky Managing Director	212/775-3418	Derivatives Specialist
Mr. Simon Ross Associate	212/775-4937	Derivatives Specialist
Ms. Kimberley Turner Vice President	212/250-7616	Trader – Derivatives *Muni*
Mr. Michael Wohl Managing Director	212/250-7602	Derivatives Products Head *Muni*

BZW/Barclays Bank

Bank/Dealer

Sub of Barclays de Zoete Wedd Securities

Location: 222 Broadway
8th Floor
New York, NY 10038

Fax: 212/412-1768

Phone: 212/412-4000

KEY MANAGERS & DERIVATIVES SPECIALISTS	Direct Phone/Fax	Job Function
Mr. Bruce Burns Senior Dealer	212/693-4070	Trader – Currency Futures Trader – Currency Options
Mr. Joseph J. Cammarata Chief Dealer	212/412-2001	Trader – Currency Options Head Trader – Derivatives Head
Mr. Kevin Collins Director	212/412-2159	Trader – Futures
Mr. Nigel Denison Managing Director	212/412-6900	Trader – Derivatives
Mr. Fernando Fernandez Senior Dealer	212/412-2001	Trader – FRA's
Mr. David Greenberg Associate Director	212/412-6859	Sales – Derivatives
Mr. Richard Krause Senior Dealer	212/693-4070	Trader – Derivatives
Mr. Kevin McGivern Manager	212/412-6850	OTC Deriv/Swaps – Head Trader – Currency Swaps Trader – Interest Rate Swaps
Mr. Eric Miller Director	212/412-1768	Sales – Futures Trader – Futures
Mr. John Nasti Director	212/693-4070	Trader – Currency Futures Trader – Currency Options
Mr. Mark Schaefer Dealer	212/693-4070	Trader – Derivatives
Mr. Oka Usi Managing Director	212/492-6900	Derivatives Products Head Trader – Derivatives Head
Mr. Brian Warner Associate	212/412-6850	Sales – Futures Sales – Options

Canadian Imperial Bank of Commerce (U.S.A.)

Bank/Dealer

Sub of Canadian Imperial Bank of Commerce (Canada)

Location: 425 Lexington Avenue
5th Floor
New York, NY 10017

Fax: 212/856-6699

Phone: 212/856-4000

KEY MANAGERS & DERIVATIVES SPECIALISTS	Direct Phone/Fax	Job Function
Mr. Charbel Abourached Managing Director	212/856-6036	Trader – Interest Rate Futures Trader – Interest Rate Options
Mr. Bruce Berger Managing Director	212/856-6052	Trader – Derivatives
Mr. George Courtadone Managing Director	212/856-6598	Derivatives Products Head
Mr. Anthony Franz Vice President	212/856-6601	Trader – Currency Options
Ms. Mary Galvin Trader	212/856-6648	Trader – Currency Options
Mr. Robert J. Giordano Managing Director	212/856-4600	Bond Department Head *Govt* Trader – Derivatives *Govt* Trader – Futures *Govt*
Ms. Cynthia Johnson Vice President	212/856-6601	Trader – Currency Futures Head Trader – Currency Options Head
Mr. James Phoenix Vice President	212/856-6647	Trader – Currency Futures
Mr. Shaiy Pilpel Managing Director	212/856-4233	Trader – Derivatives *MBS*
Mr. Shaun N. Rai Vice President	212/648-6502 212/856-6099	Derivatives Products Head *Muni*
Mr. David Ricketts Manager	212/856-6602	Trader – Currency Options
Mr. Michael Rulle Executive Managing Director	212/856-6050	Derivatives Products Head Trader -- Derivatives Head Research Analyst – Derivatives
Mr. David E. Wagner Director	212/856-6513	Derivatives Products Head *Muni*

Chase Securities Inc.

Bank/Dealer

Sub of The Chase Manhattan Corporation

Location: One Chase Manhattan Plaza
35th Floor
New York, NY 10081

Fax: 212/425-1404

Phone: 212/552-2222

KEY MANAGERS & DERIVATIVES SPECIALISTS	Direct Phone/Fax	Job Function
Mr. James Borden Senior Vice President	212/552-7543	Trader – Currency Futures Trader – Currency Options
Mr. Frederick J. Chapey, Jr. Managing Director	212/552-4222	Derivatives Products Head Marketing – Swaps
Mr. Dexter H. Charles Managing Director	212/552-2749	Trader – Interest Rate Futures Trader – Interest Rate Options Trader – Interest Rate Swaps
Mr. Robert S. Cohen Managing Director	212/552-4912 212/552-5054	Bond Department Head
Mr. Andrew Feldman Managing Director	212/552-2744	Marketing – Derivatives
Mr. Anthony Hamer Vice President	212/552-2752	OTC Deriv/Swaps – Head
Ms. Marian Hayden Vice President	212/552-0754	Trader – Currency Futures Trader – Currency Options
Mr. Jorge Jasson Senior Vice President	212/552-1475 212/552-6163	Bond Department Head *MBS*
Ms. Barbara Luttich Managing Director	212/834-4440	Marketing – Derivatives Sales – Derivatives
Ms. Patricia Lynott-Bonan Managing Director	212/552-1401 212/552-0630	Bond Department Head *Corp*
Mr. James MeVay Managing Director	212/552-1780	Marketing – Derivatives
Mr. Douglas Muller Vice President	212/552-5183	OTC Deriv/Swaps – Head Sales – Derivatives
Mr. Atsuo Ogaki Second Vice President	212/552-5222	Trader – Options
Mr. Demitri Papacostas Vice President	212/552-5222	Trader – Currency Options Head
Mr. Bruce Rigione Managing Director	212/552-2716 212/552-4907	Bond Department Head *ABS*

Chase Securities Inc. – continued

KEY MANAGERS & DERIVATIVES SPECIALISTS	Direct Phone/Fax	Job Function
Mr. Randolph W. Sides Managing Director	212/552-3081 212/552-7955	Bond Department Head *Govt*
Ms. Kathleen Smith Vice President	212/552-6318	Derivatives Specialist

Chemical Futures & Options Inc.

Bank/Dealer

Sub of Chemical Banking Corporation

Location: One Penn Center
Suite 610
Philadelphia, PA 19103

Fax: 215/561-3027

Phone: 215/561-3030

KEY MANAGERS & DERIVATIVES SPECIALISTS	Direct Phone/Fax	Job Function
Mr. David S. Bateman Trader	215/561-0880	Trader – Currency Options
Mr. Glenn S. Dydak Trader	215/561-0880	Trader – Derivatives
Ms. Kathryn A. Newell Trader	215/561-0880	Trader – Derivatives

Chemical Securities Incorporated

Bank/Dealer

Sub of Chemical Banking Corporation

Location: 270 Park Avenue
6th Floor
New York, NY 10017

Fax: 212/834-6527

Phone: 212/270-6000

KEY MANAGERS & DERIVATIVES SPECIALISTS	Direct Phone/Fax	Job Function
Mr. William Arnold Vice President	212/834-4600	Trader – Currency Options
Mr. Hartley Connett Vice President	212/834-3636	Marketing – Derivatives
Mr. Samuel Derosa-Farag Managing Director	212/270-1309	Fixed-Income Strategist *Taxable*
Mr. Simon Lack Managing Director	212/834-4445	Derivatives Products Head *Corp*
Mr. Jeffrey R. Larsen Managing Director	212/834-5240	Derivatives Products Head Trader – Derivatives
Ms. Regina Morellino Vice President	212/834-5062	Trader – Currency Futures Trader – Currency Options
Mr. William H. Pike Managing Director	212/834-4500 212/834-6024	Bond Department Head *Govt*

Chemical Securities Incorporated – continued

KEY MANAGERS & DERIVATIVES SPECIALISTS	Direct Phone/Fax	Job Function
Mr. Paul Plesser Vice President	212/834-4610	Trader – Currency Futures Trader – Currency Options
Mr. Theodor K. Plomgren Managing Director	212/834-4567 212/834-6521	Bond Department Head *Money Mkt*
Mr. David Puth Managing Director	212/834-5060	Trader – Interest Rate Futures Trader – Interest Rate Options Trader – Interest Rate Swaps
Mr. Robert R. Rupp Managing Director	212/834-5305 212/834-6539	Bond Department Head
Mr. Per Sekse Vice President	212/834-4486	Marketing – Derivatives
Mr. David Sheppe Vice President	212/834-3895	Marketing – Derivatives
Mr. Scott B. Verch Vice President	212/834-5207	Marketing – Options *Muni* Marketing – Swaps *Muni*

Christiana Bank, New York Branch

Bank/Dealer

Sub of Christiana Bank (Norway)

Location: 11 West 42nd Street
7th Floor
New York, NY 10036

Fax: 212/827-4888

Phone: 212/827-4800

KEY MANAGERS & DERIVATIVES SPECIALISTS	Direct Phone/Fax	Job Function
Mr. Harold Haugli Treasurer	212/827-4850	Derivatives Products Head
Mr. David Nahor Vice President	212/827-4852	Trader – Derivatives

Citicorp Global Derivatives

Bank/Dealer

Sub of Citicorp

Location: 200 South Wacker Drive
29th Floor
Chicago, IL 60606

Fax: 312/993-6830

Phone: 312/993-3000

KEY MANAGERS & DERIVATIVES SPECIALISTS	Direct Phone/Fax	Job Function
Mr. David Alfano Vice President	312/993-3105	Sales – Derivatives
Mr. John Bruce Vice President	312/993-3044	Sales – Derivatives

Citicorp Global Derivatives – continued

KEY MANAGERS & DERIVATIVES SPECIALISTS	Direct Phone/Fax	Job Function
Mr. William Gust Vice President	312/993-3797	Derivatives Products Head
Ms. Marie N. Hollein Vice President	312/993-3733	Sales – Currency
Mr. John Murphy Vice President	312/993-3868	Trader – Derivatives Head
Ms. Maryann O'Brien Vice President	312/993-3165	Trader – Currency Futures Trader – Currency Options
Mr. Joel Schweitzer Vice President	312/993-3796	OTC Deriv/Swaps – Head Structured Notes – Head

Citicorp Securities, Inc.

Bank/Dealer

Sub of Citicorp

Location: 399 Park Avenue
7th Floor
New York, NY 10043

Fax: 212/425-3857

Phone: 212/559-1000

KEY MANAGERS & DERIVATIVES SPECIALISTS	Direct Phone/Fax	Job Function
Mr. Vincent Amaru Vice President	212/291-7492	Trader – Currency Futures Trader – Currency Options
Mr. David Buchen Vice President	212/291-7353	Trader – Currency Options Head Trader – Currency Futures Trader – FRA's
Mr. David A. Croft Vice President	212/559-5333	Bond Department Head *Muni*
Mr. John Dorans Managing Director	212/559-0148	Bond Department Head *MBS*
Mr. Jeffrey Feig Vice President	212/291-7464	Trader – FRA's
Mr. David Hickey Vice President	212/559-5236	Trader – Derivatives *Muni*
Ms. Nancy Humphreys Managing Director	212/291-7120	Derivatives Specialist
Mr. Robert Khanna Vice President	212/291-2155	Derivatives Products Head

Citicorp Securities, Inc. – continued

KEY MANAGERS & DERIVATIVES SPECIALISTS	Direct Phone/Fax	Job Function
Mr. Mark Koenigsberg Vice President	212/559-5902	Research Analyst – Derivatives Research Analyst – Futures/Options *Govt*
Mr. David Madden Vice President	212/291-7452	Trader – Currency Futures Trader – Currency Options
Mr. Michael E. Morandi Vice President	212/291-2954	Research Analyst – Derivatives Trader – Derivatives
Mr. Anil Prasad Vice President	212/291-7120	Trader – Options
Mr. Narayan Prasad Managing Director	212/559-4971	Derivatives Products Head *Muni*
Mr. Dipak K. Rastogi Managing Director	212/291-6121 212/291-3158	Derivatives Products Head *ABS, Treas, Agency, MBS, Money Mkt*
Mr. Michael Ricciardi Managing Director	212/291-6407 212/291-3454	Bond Department Head
Mr. Michael Sbabo Vice President	212/291-2782	OTC Deriv/Swaps – Head Sales – Currency
Mr. Steven Thatcher Vice President	212/559-5292	Research Analyst – Derivatives *Muni*
Mr. Douglas Warren Vice President	212/291-4783	Trader – Derivatives *Muni*

Commander Corporation

Broker/Dealer – Regional

Location: 738 Chestnut Street, Meadville, PA 16335 **Fax:** No fax **Phone:** 814/724-5078

KEY MANAGERS & DERIVATIVES SPECIALISTS	Direct Phone/Fax	Job Function
Mr. Homer M. Douglass Associate Vice President		Research Analyst – Derivatives Trader – Currency Options Trader – Interest Rate Options Trader – Options
Ms. Martha J. Ingraham Vice President		Derivatives Products Head Trader – Currency Futures Head Trader – Derivatives Head
Mr. E. T. Moss Vice President		Bond Department Head Fixed-Income Strategist

Commander Corporation – continued

KEY MANAGERS & DERIVATIVES SPECIALISTS	Direct Phone/Fax	Job Function
Mr. Paul E. Passman Manager		Trader – Currency Futures Trader – Futures Trader – Interest Rate Futures

Commerz Financial Products

Bank/Dealer

Sub of Commerzbank AG

Location: Two World Financial Center
New York, NY 10281-1050

Fax: 212/266-7567

Phone: 212/266-7700

KEY MANAGERS & DERIVATIVES SPECIALISTS	Direct Phone/Fax	Job Function
Mr. Patrice Cohen Vice President	212/266-7515	Trader – Currency Options Head Trader – Derivatives Head
Mr. Butch Fischer Vice President	212/266-7562	Trader – Currency Options
Mr. Harold Fisher Vice President	212/266-7515	Sales – Derivatives Trader – Derivatives
Mr. Michael Levy Vice President	212/266-7515	Sales – Derivatives Trader – Currency Options

Commerzbank Capital Markets

Bank/Dealer

Sub of Commerzbank AG

Location: Two World Financial Center
New York, NY 10281-1050

Fax: 212/266-7797

Phone: 212/266-7700

KEY MANAGERS & DERIVATIVES SPECIALISTS	Direct Phone/Fax	Job Function
Mr. Robert Donohue Vice President	212/266-7336	Sales – Derivatives
Mr. Michael Lundquist Vice President	212/266-7559	Trader – FRA's
Mr. Andreas Mann Chief Dealer	212/266-7414	Trader – Currency Futures Head
Mr. Anthony Ortiaga Assistant Treasurer	212/266-7414	Trader – FRA's
Mr. Michael Purdy Assistant Vice President	212/266-7417	Trader – FRA's Trader – Interest Rate Options Trader – Interest Rate Swaps

Commerzbank Capital Markets – continued

KEY MANAGERS & DERIVATIVES SPECIALISTS	Direct Phone/Fax	Job Function
Mr. Beat Reinhart Assistant Vice President	212/266-7575	Trader – Options
Mr. Cyrus Whitney Vice President	212/266-7412	Trader – Currency Futures Trader – Currency Options

Credit Lyonnais Bank

Bank/Dealer

Sub of Crédit Lyonnais

Location: 1301 Avenue of the Americas
117th Floor
New York, NY 10019-6022

Fax: 212/459-3170

Phone: 212/261-7000

KEY MANAGERS & DERIVATIVES SPECIALISTS	Direct Phone/Fax	Job Function
Mr. Omar Abukhadra Managing Director	212/459-3086	Derivatives Products Head
Mr. Lukasz Cianciara Vice President	212/261-7940	Sales – Derivatives
Mr. Kevin Cronin Manager – Fixed Income	212/261-3510	Bond Department Head
Mr. David S. French Director	212/459-3060 212/459-3193	Bond Department Head *Treas*
Mr. Robert Friedberg Vice President	212/459-3033	Trader – Currency Options Head
Mr. John D. Hendrickson Assistant Vice President	212/261-7953 212/261-7969	Bond Department Head *MBS* Structured Notes – Head
Mr. Ivan Sands First Vice President	212/261-7979	OTC Deriv/Swaps – Head
Mr. Mark A. Thompson Director	212/261-7932 212/261-3641	Derivatives Products Head *Funding, Money Mkt* Trader – Derivatives Head Trader – Currency Swaps Trader – Interest Rate Futures Trader – Interest Rate Options Trader – Interest Rate Swaps
Mr. Jack Veffer First Vice President	212/261-7981 212/459-3152	Bond Department Head *Funding, Money Mkt* Trader – Derivatives
Mr. Mario Yrun Director	212/459-3065	Marketing – Derivatives Sales – Derivatives

Credit Suisse Financial Products

Broker/Dealer – National

Sub of CS Holding Group

Location: 55 East 52nd Street
Park Avenue Plaza
New York, NY 10055

Fax: 212/238-5332

Phone: 212/322-5900

KEY MANAGERS & DERIVATIVES SPECIALISTS	Direct Phone/Fax	Job Function
Mr. Wilson Ervin Director	212/322-5960	Trader – Derivatives Head *Corp*
Mr. Steven Lazarus Director	212/322-5960	Trader – Derivatives
Mr. Yves Leyson Director	212/322-5900	Derivatives Products Head Marketing – Derivatives Sales – Derivatives
Mr. Bruce T. Miller Managing Director	212/322-5960	Bond Department Head *ABS, MBS*
Mr. David Pierce-Jones Director	212/322-5960	Trader – Derivatives Head
Mr. Benjamin Weston Managing Director	212/322-5998 212/318-0730	Derivatives Products Head *ABS, Treas, Agency, Funding, MBS, Money Mkt*

CS First Boston Corporation

Broker/Dealer – National

Sub of CS Holding Group

Location: 55 East 52nd Street
Park Avenue Plaza
New York, NY 10055

Fax: 212/308-1187

Phone: 212/909-2000

KEY MANAGERS & DERIVATIVES SPECIALISTS	Direct Phone/Fax	Job Function
Mr. Matthew Alexy Director	212/909-2670 212/318-0752	Fixed-Income Strategist *Govt*
Mr. Andrew Brenner Director	212/909-3915	Trader – Derivatives
Mr. Philippe Buhannic Director	212/909-2318	Trader – Derivatives Head
Mr. John Chrystal Director – Structuring	212/322-5903 212/308-2357	Derivatives Products Head Structured Notes – Head
Mr. Benjamin Cohen Managing Director	212/909-3009	Derivatives Products Head
Mr. John P. Costas Managing Director	212/909-3610 212/318-0783	Bond Department Head

CS First Boston Corporation – continued

KEY MANAGERS & DERIVATIVES SPECIALISTS	Direct Phone/Fax	Job Function
Mr. Kenneth Ford Director		Sales – Currency Sales – Futures Sales – Options Sales – Structured Notes
Mr. Irvin J. Goldman Managing Director	212/909-2854 212/479-0145	Bond Department Head *Funding*
Mr. Robert E. Griffith Director	212/909-3525 212/318-1226	Bond Department Head *Agency*
Ms. Terry Ludwig Director	212/909-3700	Sales – Currency
Mr. John Mahoney Director	212/909-2730	Sales – Derivatives
Mr. B. Scott Minerd Managing Director	212/909-3728 212/318-1354	Bond Department Head *Money Mkt*
Mr. John Moubayed Vice President	212/909-3180	Trader – Currency Futures Trader – Currency Options
Mr. Joseph Mullally Vice President	212/909-3265 212/318-1354	Fixed-Income Strategist
Mr. C. Lee Quaintance Managing Director	212/909-4166 212/318-1226	Bond Department Head *Treas*
Mr. Andrew Stone Managing Director	212/909-2131	Bond Department Head *MBS*
Mr. Jay S. Tucker Manager	212/909-3180	Trader – Currency Futures Trader – Currency Options
Mr. Philip Vasan Director	212/909-4222	Trader – Currency Options Head

Dai-Ichi Kangyo Bank Ltd. (New York)

Bank/Dealer

Sub of Dai-Ichi Kangyo Bank Ltd.

Location: One World Trade Center
Suite 4811
New York, NY 10048

Fax: 212/912-0915

Phone: 212/466-5200

Dai-Ichi Kangyo Bank Ltd. (New York) – continued

KEY MANAGERS & DERIVATIVES SPECIALISTS	Direct Phone/Fax	Job Function
Mr. Hideaki Ikeuchi Vice President	212/466-5271	Trader – Derivatives
Mr. Masami Inoue Senior Vice President	212/466-5270	Trader – Derivatives Head *Corp*
Mr. Masao Okada Vice President	212/466-6656	Trader – Currency Options Head
Mr. Yoshiaka Yamaka Senior Vice President	212/432-6670	Trader – Currency Futures Head

Daiwa Securities America, Inc.

Bank/Dealer

Sub of Daiwa Securities Co., Ltd.

Location: Financial Square
32 Old Slip
New York, NY 10005

Fax: 212/612-7100

Phone: 212/612-7000

KEY MANAGERS & DERIVATIVES SPECIALISTS	Direct Phone/Fax	Job Function
Mr. Gaku Aizawa Executive Vice President	212/612-6612 212/341-0710	Marketing – Futures Sales – Futures Trader – Futures
Mr. John Dunlop Manager – Foreign Exchange	212/612-7200 212/612-7125	Trader – Currency Futures Head Trader – Currency Options Head
Mr. Marc Edwards Executive Vice President	212/612-6602	Derivatives Products Head
Mr. Anthony Gibbons Senior Vice President	212/612-6594	Trader – Interest Rate Futures Trader – Interest Rate Options Trader – Interest Rate Swaps
Mr. Frank L. McDermott Senior Vice President	212/612-6540	Bond Department Head *Funding, Money Mkt*
Mr. John McVey Vice President – Sales	212/612-6500	Sales – Derivatives
Mr. Nobuaki Ohmura President & C.O.O.	212/612-6660	Bond Department Head Sales – Futures Trader – Futures
Mr. W. Terrence Pigott Senior Vice President	212/612-6566	Bond Department Head *Treas, Agency*
Mr. Steven J. Turi Vice President	212/612-6607	Derivatives Specialist

Dean Witter Reynolds Inc.

Broker/Dealer – National

Sub of Dean Witter, Discover & Co.

Location: Two World Trade Center
59th Floor
New York, NY 10048

Fax: 212/392-0188 **Phone:** 212/392-2222

KEY MANAGERS & DERIVATIVES SPECIALISTS	**Direct Phone/Fax**	**Job Function**
Mr. Brian D. Barry Senior Vice President	212/392-5155 212/392-8811	Bond Department Head *ABS, MBS* Derivatives Products Head *ABS, MBS*
Mr. Ian N. Bernstein Senior Vice President	212/392-3884 212/392-7686	Bond Department Head *Treas, Agency, Funding, Money Mkt*
Mr. Barry Fetner Senior Vice President	212/392-2600 212/392-1355	Trader – Currency Futures Head Trader – Currency Options Head
Mr. Jeffrey Hammer Vice President	212/392-8302	OTC Deriv/Swaps – Head
Mr. James P. Kelly First Vice President	212/392-3770	Trader – Options
Mr. Tony Miliote	212/392-4472	Trader – Options
Ms. Marilyn Needleman Director	212/392-2950	Derivatives Products Head
Mr. Robert Santora Executive Vice President	212/392-1922 212/392-2887	Bond Department Head

Dean Witter Reynolds Institutional Futures

Broker/Dealer – Regional

Sub of Dean Witter, Discover & Co.

Location: 150 South Wacker Drive
Suite 1500
Chicago, IL 60606

Fax: 312/641-0463 **Phone:** 312/984-4345

KEY MANAGERS & DERIVATIVES SPECIALISTS	**Direct Phone/Fax**	**Job Function**
Mr. Irwin Bernstein Senior Vice President	312/984-4760	Sales – Futures
Mr. Lawrence Mollner Executive Vice President	312/984-4205	Trader – Futures

Dean Witter Reynolds Inc. (Philadelphia)

Broker/Dealer – National

Sub of Dean Witter, Discover & Co.

Location: 1900 Market Street
Trading Floor
Philadelphia, PA 19103

Fax: 215/665-1486

Phone: 215/665-1485

KEY MANAGERS & DERIVATIVES SPECIALISTS	**Direct Phone/Fax**	**Job Function**
Mr. Ralph A. Elia Vice President	215/665-1481	Trader – Currency Options Head Trader – Currency Futures Trader – Currency Options
Mr. Jose Ortiz Assistant Vice President	215/665-1481	Trader – Currency Options

Deutsche Morgan Grenfell

Broker/Dealer – Regional

Sub of Deutsche Bank North America

Location: 31 West 52nd Street
New York, NY 10019

Fax: 212/474-8212

Phone: 212/474-8000

KEY MANAGERS & DERIVATIVES SPECIALISTS	**Direct Phone/Fax**	**Job Function**
Mr. Daniel V. Almeida Managing Director	212/474-8370	Trader – Currency Futures Head Trader – Currency Options Head
Mr. Thomas Brush Director	212/469-7714	Sales – Currency Sales – Futures Sales – Options Sales – Structured Notes
Mr. David Duebendorfer Managing Director	212/469-5880 212/469-6025	Derivatives Products Head
Mr. Howard B. Hill Managing Director	212/469-6706	Bond Department Head *ABS, MBS*
Mr. Paul F. Jacobson Managing Director	212/469-6708	Bond Department Head
Mr. Jorge Nagel Director	212/469-8046	Trader – Currency Futures Trader – Currency Options
Mr. Andrew O'Flaherty Managing Director	212/469-6715	Bond Department Head *Agency*
Mr. Mario J. Pierro Managing Director	212/469-7194	Bond Department Head *Funding, Money Mkt*
Mr. Gopal Verdahan Director	212/469-7401	Trader – Derivatives Head
Mr. Puru Voruganti Director	212/469-7231	Research Analyst – Derivatives

DKB Financial Products, Inc.

Bank/Dealer

Sub of Dai-Ichi Kangyo Bank Ltd.

Location: One World Trade Center
50th Floor
New York, NY 10048

Fax: 212/432-8464

Phone: 212/488-8460

KEY MANAGERS & DERIVATIVES SPECIALISTS	Direct Phone/Fax	Job Function
Mr. Koichi Ino Vice President	212/313-0530	Derivatives Specialist
Mr. Richard Robb Chief Trader	212/313-0530	Derivatives Products Head Structured Notes – Head Trader – Interest Rate Futures Trader – Interest Rate Options Trader – Interest Rate Swaps
Mr. Kirk Schubert Senior Vice President	212/313-0480	Marketing – Derivatives Sales – Derivatives

Dresdner Securities (USA) Inc.

Bank/Dealer

Sub of Dresdner Bank AG

Location: 75 Wall Street
New York, NY 10005-2889

Fax: 212/429-4496

Phone: 212/429-2100

KEY MANAGERS & DERIVATIVES SPECIALISTS	Direct Phone/Fax	Job Function
Mr. Matthew Balestiero Assistant Vice President	212/429-4120	Derivatives Specialist
Mr. Michael Boland Vice President	212/429-4135 212/429-4171	Trader – FRA's Trader – Interest Rate Swaps
Mr. Brian Cronin Vice President	212/429-4144	Derivatives Specialist
Mr. Thomas Devine Vice President	212/429-4148	Trader – Currency Options Head
Mr. Matthew DiPallo Vice President	212/429-4410	Derivatives Specialist
Mr. James Fantozzi Assistant Vice President	212/429-4147	Trader – FRA's Trader – Interest Rate Swaps
Mr. Donald S. Galante Senior Vice President	212/429-4401	Bond Department Head
Mr. Patrick Griffin Vice President	212/429-4100	Sales – Currency
Mr. John Ignaszak Assistant Vice President	212/429-4100	Trader – Derivatives

Dresdner Securities (USA) Inc. – continued

KEY MANAGERS & DERIVATIVES SPECIALISTS	Direct Phone/Fax	Job Function
Mr. Christopher King Assistant Vice President	212/429-4120	Trader – Derivatives
Mr. Paul Loffredo First Vice President	212/429-4140	Derivatives Products Head
Mr. Timothy McKessy Assistant Vice President	212/429-4120	Trader – Derivatives
Mr. Vinayek Singh Vice President	212/429-0437	Trader – Derivatives
Ms. Hey Ran Toh Vice President	212/429-4120 212/429-4171	Trader – Currency Futures Head Trader – Currency Options Head Trader – Derivatives Head Trader – FRA's
Mr. Kenneth Weisman Vice President	212/429-4120	Trader – Currency Futures Trader – Currency Options

Essex Radez Company

Broker/Dealer – Regional

Location: 327 South LaSalle Street
Suite 1137
Chicago, IL 60605

Fax: No fax

Phone: 312/362-2916

KEY MANAGERS & DERIVATIVES SPECIALISTS	Direct Phone/Fax	Job Function
Mr. Stephen A. Radez President		Derivatives Products Head Trader – Derivatives Head Sales – Derivatives

Euro Brokers Maxcor, Inc.

Brokers' Broker

Sub of Euro Brokers Inc.

Location: Two World Trade Center
Suite 8400
New York, NY 10048

Fax: 212/748-7050

Phone: 212/748-7000

KEY MANAGERS & DERIVATIVES SPECIALISTS	Direct Phone/Fax	Job Function
Mr. Jeremy Blum Senior Vice President	212/748-7060	Trader – FRA's
Mr. Walter E. Dulski Senior Vice President	212/748-7018 212/748-7329	Bond Department Head *Agency, MBS*
Mr. Craig Flynn Senior Vice President	212/748-7100	Derivatives Specialist

Euro Brokers Maxcor, Inc. – continued

KEY MANAGERS & DERIVATIVES SPECIALISTS	Direct Phone/Fax	Job Function
Mr. Colton Heppe Vice President	212/748-7100	Trader – Interest Rate Swaps
Mr. Ronald Jampel Vice President	212/748-7080	Derivatives Specialist *Muni*
Mr. Alistair Johnstone Executive Vice President	212/748-7012 212/748-7329	Bond Department Head *Money Mkt*
Mr. John D. Keenan Vice President	212/748-7080 212/748-7088	Bond Department Head *Muni* Derivatives Products Head *Muni* Trader – Interest Rate Options *Muni* Trader – Interest Rate Swaps *Muni*
Mr. Thomas Kinnally Manager – Repos	212/748-7180 212/748-7343	Bond Department Head *Funding*
Mr. David Lessing Senior Vice President	212/748-7100	Derivatives Products Head
Mr. T. J. Masonius Vice President	212/748-7160	Trader – FRA's
Mr. Peter Shapiro Senior Vice President	212/748-7416	Structured Notes – Head Trader – Structured Investments
Mr. Kevin York Vice President	212/748-7220	Trader – Interest Rate Options

Exco Noonan Inc.

Broker/Dealer – Regional

Sub of Exco International (London)

Location: 10 Exchange Place
Jersey City, NJ 07302

Fax: 201/200-5069

Phone: 201/200-4500

KEY MANAGERS & DERIVATIVES SPECIALISTS	Direct Phone/Fax	Job Function
Mr. Joshua Jacobs Manager	201/200-4960	OTC Deriv/Swaps – Head Trader – FRA's Trader – Interest Rate Swaps
Mr. James Kenny Manager	201/200-4950	Trader – Interest Rate Swaps
Mr. Peter F. Rotondo Executive Vice President	201/200-4610	Trader – Currency Futures Head Trader – Currency Options Head

FIMAT Futures U.S.A., Inc.

Broker/Dealer – National

Sub of Société Générale AG

Location: 12 East 49th Street
Suite 2203
New York, NY 10017

Fax: 212/759-2898

Phone: 212/527-8100

KEY MANAGERS & DERIVATIVES SPECIALISTS	**Direct Phone/Fax**	**Job Function**
Mr. Stanley Jonas Manager	212/759-2626	OTC Deriv/Swaps – Head Structured Notes – Head Trader – Currency Futures Head Trader – Currency Options Head Sales – Derivatives
Mr. Brian Kaye Chairman	212/527-8101	Sales – Derivatives Sales – Futures
Ms. Suzanne Schonman Vice President	212/527-8115	Marketing – Derivatives Sales – Derivatives
Mr. Pierre Wolf Managing Director	212/759-2626	Derivatives Products Head Sales – Derivatives Trader – Interest Rate Futures Trader – Interest Rate Options Trader – Interest Rate Swaps
Ms. Cynthia Zeltwanger General Manager	212/527-8125	Sales – Derivatives

FIMAT Futures U.S.A. Inc. (Chicago)

Broker/Dealer – National

Sub of Société Générale AG

Location: 181 West Madison Street
Suite 3450
Chicago, IL 60602

Fax: 312/578-5277

Phone: 312/578-5200

KEY MANAGERS & DERIVATIVES SPECIALISTS	**Direct Phone/Fax**	**Job Function**
Mr. James Cannon Desk Manager	312/578-5250	Sales – Derivatives Trader – Derivatives
Mr. Alexander Lamb General Manager	312/578-5201	Derivatives Products Head Sales – Derivatives
Mr. Azza Meleik Co-Manager	312/578-5212	Marketing – Derivatives Sales – Derivatives
Mr. James Olney Senior Vice President	312/578-5201	Trader – Currency Futures Head Trader – Currency Options Head Trader – Derivatives Head
Mr. Edouard Ziecina Desk Manager	312/578-5250	Sales – Derivatives Trader – Derivatives

First Chicago Capital Markets, Inc.

Broker/Dealer – Regional

Sub of First Chicago/NBD Corporation

Location: One First National Plaza
7th Floor
Chicago, IL 60670

Fax: 312/732-8733

Phone: 312/732-4000

KEY MANAGERS & DERIVATIVES SPECIALISTS	Direct Phone/Fax	Job Function
Ms. Catherine L. Althoff Managing Director	312/732-4889 312/732-1033	Marketing – Derivatives *Muni*
Ms. Nancy Amicangelo Managing Director	312/732-8338 312/732-4670	Bond Department Head *Funding*
Mr. Thomas J. Campbell Senior Managing Director	312/732-1318 312/732-4239	Bond Department Head *Muni*
Mr. Claudio Cerulli Vice President	312/732-6298	Trader – Options *Treas*
Mr. David Donovan Senior Vice President	312/732-6312	Bond Department Head *ABS*
Mr. Russell Lau Vice President	312/732-8378	OTC Deriv/Swaps – Head *Muni*
Mr. Richard Morton Managing Director	312/732-4440 312/732-5442	Trader – Derivatives Head
Mr. Alfred G. Roth Senior Managing Director	312/732-4401 312/732-4239	Bond Department Head *Govt*

First Chicago Futures

Brokers' Broker

Sub of First Chicago/NBD Corporation

Location: One First National Plaza
Chicago, IL 60670

Fax: 312/732-3348

Phone: 312/408-8300

KEY MANAGERS & DERIVATIVES SPECIALISTS	Direct Phone/Fax	Job Function
Mr. W. Robert Felker Senior Vice President	312/732-4174	Derivatives Products Head
Mr. Frank Mullins Vice President	312/732-5595	Marketing – Futures

First National Bank of Chicago (Dealer)

Bank/Dealer

Sub of First Chicago/NBD Corporation

Location: One First National Plaza
Chicago, IL 60670

Fax: 312/732-4840

Phone: 312/732-4000

First National Bank of Chicago (Dealer) – continued

KEY MANAGERS & DERIVATIVES SPECIALISTS	Direct Phone/Fax	Job Function
Mr. Paul Abbenhaus Vice President	312/732-3183	Trader – Currency Options
Mr. Craig Bouchard Senior Vice President	312/732-2155	Derivatives Products Head
Mr. Timothy M. Clark Vice President	312/732-7338	Trader – Currency Options Head
Mr. Steven Matsuo Vice President	312/732-9090	Trader – Currency Futures Head
Ms. Kathryn Shafer Vice President	312/732-1347	Marketing – Currency
Mr. L. Britt Swofford Senior Vice President	312/732-7029	Derivatives Products Head
Ms. Phyllis Thomas Vice President	312/732-7768	Marketing – Derivatives

Fuji Bank Ltd.

Bank/Dealer

Sub of The Fuji Bank

Location: Two World Trade Center
89th Floor
New York, NY 10048

Fax: 212/321-9408

Phone: 212/898-2000

KEY MANAGERS & DERIVATIVES SPECIALISTS	Direct Phone/Fax	Job Function
Mr. Bruce Campbell Associate Director	212/898-2900	Marketing – Derivatives
Mr. Barry Drucker Vice President & Manager	212/898-2330	Trader – Currency Futures Head Trader – Currency Options Head
Mr. Thomas Dwyer Vice President	212/898-2800	Trader – Currency Swaps Trader – Interest Rate Swaps Trader – Options
Mr. David Harbison Vice President	212/898-2330	Trader – FRA's
Mr. Sham Ito Manager	212/898-2324	Trader – Interest Rate Futures Trader – Interest Rate Options Trader – Interest Rate Swaps

Fuji Bank Ltd. – continued

KEY MANAGERS & DERIVATIVES SPECIALISTS	Direct Phone/Fax	Job Function
Mr. Brendon Lavelle Vice President	212/898-2805	Trader – Derivatives
Mr. Steven Mullaney Vice President	212/898-2810	Trader – Derivatives
Mr. Sherif Sweillam Associate Director	212/898-2827	Trader – Derivatives Head

Fuji Securities, Inc.

Bank/Dealer

Sub of The Fuji Bank

Location: 140 South Dearborn Street
Chicago, IL 60603

Fax: 312/899-4701

Phone: 312/899-4700

KEY MANAGERS & DERIVATIVES SPECIALISTS	Direct Phone/Fax	Job Function
Mr. Robert Dickey Vice President	312/899-4574 312/899-4606	Derivatives Products Head

Garvin GuyButler Corporation

Broker/Dealer – Regional

Location: 120 Broadway
New York, NY 10271

Fax: 212/815-6587

Phone: 212/732-6900

KEY MANAGERS & DERIVATIVES SPECIALISTS	Direct Phone/Fax	Job Function
Mr. Nick Farr Senior Vice President		Trader – FRA's
Mr. Peter J. McGuire Senior Vice President		Trader – Currency Swaps Trader – Interest Rate Swaps
Mr. Daniel J. McMorrow Senior Vice President		Trader – Currency Swaps Trader – Interest Rate Swaps
Mr. Philip Moody Senior Vice President		Trader – Currency Swaps
Mr. Will Nichols Senior Vice President		Trader – Structured Investments
Mr. J. Douglas Rhoten Managing Director		OTC Deriv/Swaps – Head
Ms. Karen Towler Senior Vice President		Trader – Interest Rate Options

General Re Securities Corporation

Broker/Dealer – Regional

Sub of General Re Corporation

Location: 630 Fifth Avenue
Suite 450
New York, NY 10111

Fax: 212/307-2320

Phone: 212/307-2300

KEY MANAGERS & DERIVATIVES SPECIALISTS	Direct Phone/Fax	Job Function
Mr. Jeffrey Dodgson Vice President	212/307-2342	Marketing – Derivatives
Mr. T. Timothy Foxe Vice President	212/307-2327	Trader – Structured Investments
Mr. James D. Haas Vice President	212/307-2360	Marketing – Derivatives
Mr. Daniel Ho Vice President	212/307-2327	Trader – Structured Investments
Mr. Ralph Hodgson President & C.E.O.	212/307-2321	Derivatives Products Head
Ms. Susan Ip Managing Director	212/307-2299	Sales – Derivatives
Mr. Tong Lee Vice President	212/307-2341	Trader – Currency Futures Head Trader – Currency Options Head Trader – Currency Swaps
Mr. Matthew J. Nelson Vice President	212/307-2327	Trader – Interest Rate Options
Mr. Timothy Prister Vice President	212/307-2327	Trader – Interest Rate Futures Trader – Interest Rate Options Trader – Interest Rate Swaps
Mr. David W. Rose Vice President	212/307-2327	Bond Department Head Structured Notes – Head
Mr. Charles L. Stafford Vice President	212/307-2327	Trader – Derivatives *Muni*
Mr. Shelly Sussman Vice President	212/307-2327	Trader – Derivatives *Muni*

Goldman Sachs & Company

Broker/Dealer – National

Sub of Goldman Sachs

Location: 85 Broad Street
New York, NY 10004

Fax: 212/902-1512

Phone: 212/902-1000

Goldman Sachs & Company – continued

KEY MANAGERS & DERIVATIVES SPECIALISTS	Direct Phone/Fax	Job Function
Mr. Howard Altarescu Vice President	212/902-3277	Bond Department Head *ABS, MBS*
Mr. Calvin Carver Vice President	212/902-8257	Trader – Interest Rate Swaps
Mr. David Covin Associate	212/902-4650	Trader – Interest Rate Swaps
Ms. Lynn Edens Vice President	212/902-1720	Fixed-Income Strategist
Mr. Stephen Einhorn Partner	212/902-6732	Fixed-Income Strategist
Mr. Frederic B. Garonzik Vice President	212/902-8717	Bond Department Head
Mr. Jacob D. Goldfield Partner	212/902-0388	Derivatives Products Head
Mr. Aaron S. Gurwitz Vice President & Manager	212/902-6705	Fixed-Income Strategist
Mr. Kevin Ingram Vice President	212/902-8362	Bond Department Head *Govt*
Mr. Scott McDermott Vice President	212/902-5052	Research Analyst – Derivatives
Mr. Thomas K. Montag Partner	212/902-8285	Derivatives Products Head
Mr. Brian Mooney Vice President	212/902-8366	Trader – Options
Mr. Bruce Petersen Vice President	212/902-8228	Trader – Interest Rate Swaps
Mr. Vijay Popat Vice President	212/902-4402	Sales – Derivatives
Mr. Derrick Smith Vice President	212/902-8366	Trader – Options
Mr. John Tormondsen Senior Vice President	212/902-8340	Bond Department Head *Govt*
Mr. Mark Zurack Partner	212/902-8654	Research Analyst – Futures/Options *Corp*

Goldman Sachs & Company (Chicago)

Broker/Dealer – National

Sub of Goldman Sachs

Location: 233 South Wacker Drive
4900 Sears Tower
Chicago, IL 60606

Fax: 312/655-4555 **Phone:** 312/655-4600

KEY MANAGERS & DERIVATIVES SPECIALISTS	Direct Phone/Fax	Job Function
Mr. Robert Bierman Vice President	312/655-4728	Sales – Futures Trader – Futures
Mr. John R. Gilmore Partner	312/655-4720 312/655-4552	Bond Department Head

Greenwich Capital Markets, Inc.

Broker/Dealer – Regional

Sub of Long Term Credit Bank of Japan

Location: 600 Steamboat Road
Greenwich, CT 06830

Fax: 203/629-4426 **Phone:** 203/625-2700

KEY MANAGERS & DERIVATIVES SPECIALISTS	Direct Phone/Fax	Job Function
Mr. Derick B. Burgher Senior Vice President	203/625-7660	Derivatives Products Head Trader – Currency Futures Head Trader – Currency Options Head
Mr. Blake S. Drexler Senior Vice President	203/625-7818	OTC Deriv/Swaps – Head Trader – Options
Mr. Raymond Humiston Executive Vice President	203/625-2818 203/629-8743	Bond Department Head *Govt, Agency* Trader – Derivatives *Govt*
Mr. Anthony R. Mauro Vice President	203/625-2828 203/629-2513	Bond Department Head *Funding*
Mr. Stephen M. Peet Executive Vice President	203/625-2712 203/629-1686	Bond Department Head *ABS, MBS*

HSBC Markets

Bank/Dealer

Sub of Midland Global Markets

Location: 140 Broadway
New York, NY 10005

Fax: 212/658-1905 **Phone:** 212/658-2700

KEY MANAGERS & DERIVATIVES SPECIALISTS	Direct Phone/Fax	Job Function
Mr. Dev Bhagat Senior Vice President	212/658-2217	Structured Notes – Head Trader – Derivatives Head
Mr. Stephen Blyth Vice President	212/658-1282	Trader – Structured Investments

HSBC Markets – continued

KEY MANAGERS & DERIVATIVES SPECIALISTS	Direct Phone/Fax	Job Function
Mr. Charles Crookshank Vice President	212/658-6710	Trader – Interest Rate Options
Mr. Andrew Ead Vice President	212/658-2217	Trader – FRA's
Mr. Remy Grandury Vice President	212/658-1282	Trader – Interest Rate Swaps
Mr. A. J. Karanikolas Vice President	212/658-5690	Trader – Currency Options Head
Mr. Craig Knebel Vice President	212/658-2217	Trader – FRA's
Mr. Azam Mistry Vice President	212/658-1047	Sales – Derivatives
Mr. Robert Powers Vice President	212/658-6710	Sales – Derivatives

ING Barings

Bank/Dealer

Sub of Internationale Nederlanden Group (ING) NV

Location: 135 East 57th Street
New York, NY 10022-2101

Fax: 212/644-0428

Phone: 212/446-1500

KEY MANAGERS & DERIVATIVES SPECIALISTS	Direct Phone/Fax	Job Function
Mr. Michael Babcock Vice President	212/446-1550	Trader – Derivatives
Mr. Phillip Berniman Vice President	212/319-3930 212/758-4905	Bond Department Head *MBS*
Mr. Kenneth Bradt Managing Director	212/446-1946 212/593-3362	Bond Department Head *ABS*
Mr. Carlos Cerritti Assistant Vice President	212/758-2929	Trader – Currency Options Trader – Interest Rate Options
Mr. Peter Fitzpatrick Treasurer	212/446-1550 212/935-3811	Bond Department Head *Govt, Agency, Money Mkt*
Mr. Scott Gordon President – Capital Markets	212/446-0399	Bond Department Head
Mr. Mark Katzelnick Vice President	212/446-0905 212/688-0582	Bond Department Head *Funding*

ING Barings – continued

KEY MANAGERS & DERIVATIVES SPECIALISTS	Direct Phone/Fax	Job Function
Mr. John McCarthy Vice President	212/446-1553	Trader – Currency Futures Head Trader – Currency Options Head Trader – Derivatives Head
Mr. Richard Prager Managing Director	212/446-1961 212/935-3811	Derivatives Products Head
Mr. George Schott Co-Head – Global Derivatives	212/446-0403	Sales – Derivatives
Mr. Steven Whiting Vice President	212/446-1555 212/935-3811	Bond Department Head *Muni*

Intercapital Securities Inc.

Brokers' Broker

Location: 153 East 53rd Street
38th Floor
New York, NY 10022

Fax: 212/319-4001 **Phone:** 212/888-8756

KEY MANAGERS & DERIVATIVES SPECIALISTS	Direct Phone/Fax	Job Function
Mr. Richard Fuchs Vice President	212/688-0900	Derivatives Products Head
Mr. Richard Walsh Director	212/888-5242	Trader – Options

Lehman Brothers, Inc.

Broker/Dealer – National

Location: Three World Financial Center
New York, NY 10285

Fax: 212/526-3738 **Phone:** 212/526-7000

KEY MANAGERS & DERIVATIVES SPECIALISTS	Direct Phone/Fax	Job Function
Mr. Philippe Burke Senior Vice President	212/526-8886 212/528-6187	Fixed-Income Strategist Derivatives Specialist
Mr. John Coghlan Managing Director	212/526-8258 212/528-8061	Bond Department Head *Money Mkt*
Mr. William J. Curtin Senior Vice President	212/526-7617	Fixed-Income Strategist
Mr. Douglas Dachille Managing Director	212/526-6600 212/528-7920	Trader – Currency Futures Head Trader – Currency Options Head Trader – Derivatives *MBS*

Lehman Brothers, Inc. – continued

KEY MANAGERS & DERIVATIVES SPECIALISTS	**Direct Phone/Fax**	**Job Function**
Mr. Paul Edwards Managing Director	212/526-8257 212/528-6187	Derivatives Products Head
Mr. Patrick M. Fay Managing Director	212/526-8033 212/528-6885	Bond Department Head *Funding*
Mr. Joseph M. Gregory Managing Director	212/526-8625 212/528-6786	Bond Department Head
Mr. D. Lee Hayes Managing Director	212/528-1313 212/528-0821	Bond Department Head *Muni*
Mr. Matthew Jacobs Managing Director	212/526-6610 212/528-7920	Trader – Derivatives Head
Mr. Theodore Janulis Managing Director	212/526-7406 212/528-8955	Bond Department Head *ABS*
Mr. Timothy W. Jay Managing Director	212/526-6420 212/528-6786	Bond Department Head *Treas, Agency*
Mr. Gary Killian Managing Director	212/528-6027 212/528-7891	Derivatives Products Head *Muni*
Ms. Joan LoCascio Vice President	212/528-0656	Trader – Futures *Muni*
Mr. John V. Malvey Managing Director	212/526-6686	Fixed-Income Strategist
Mr. Ravi Mattu Senior Vice President	212/526-0206 212/528-6384	Fixed-Income Strategist
Mr. Bart McDade Managing Director	212/526-7067	Bond Department Head *Corp*
Mr. Kenneth D. Phillips Vice President	212/528-0656	Trader – Futures *Muni*
Mr. James Roper Managing Director	212/526-0392 212/528-6885	Fixed-Income Strategist
Mr. Craig Schiffer Managing Director	212/526-4445	Research Analyst – Derivatives Trader – Derivatives
Mr. Kenneth Umezaki Senior Vice President	212/526-6570 212/528-7920	Trader – Structured Investments

Lehman Brothers, Inc. – continued

KEY MANAGERS & DERIVATIVES SPECIALISTS	Direct Phone/Fax	Job Function
Mr. Jeffrey A. Vanderbeek Managing Director	212/526-0770 212/528-6187	Derivatives Products Head *Treas, Funding, Money Mkt*
Mr. Brian R. Zipp Managing Director	212/526-8817 212/528-8955	Bond Department Head *MBS*

Lehman Brothers, Inc. (Chicago)

Broker/Dealer – National

Location: 190 South LaSalle Street
Suite 2600
Chicago, IL 60603

Fax: 312/609-8562

Phone: 312/609-8000

KEY MANAGERS & DERIVATIVES SPECIALISTS	Direct Phone/Fax	Job Function
Mr. Leonard Teifeld Senior Vice President	312/609-4007	Derivatives Products Head Trader – Currency Futures Head Sales – Futures

E.D. & F. Man International Securities Corp.

Broker/Dealer – National

Location: Two World Financial Center
27th Floor
New York, NY 10821

Fax: 212/566-9456

Phone: 212/566-9000

KEY MANAGERS & DERIVATIVES SPECIALISTS	Direct Phone/Fax	Job Function
Ms. Kathleen Eagye Senior Vice President	212/566-9452	Derivatives Products Head Sales – Futures Sales – Options
Mr. E. Murray Hood Vice President	212/902-6170	Sales – Derivatives Trader – Derivatives
Mr. Ira Polk Executive Vice President	212/566-9008	Trader – Currency Options Head Trader – Futures
Mr. Howard J. Stover Vice President	212/902-6170	Sales – Derivatives Trader – Derivatives

E.D. & F. Man International Inc. (Chicago)

Broker/Dealer – National

Sub of E.D. & F. Man International Securities Corp.

Location: 440 South LaSalle Street
20th Floor
Chicago, IL 60605

Fax: 312/663-7710

Phone: 312/663-7500

E.D. & F. Man International Inc. (Chicago) – continued

KEY MANAGERS & DERIVATIVES SPECIALISTS	Direct Phone/Fax	Job Function
Mr. David Vincent Vice President	312/663-7503	Derivatives Products Head OTC Deriv/Swaps – Head Trader – Currency Options Head Trader – Derivatives Head Sales – Derivatives Trader – Currency Swaps Trader – Futures

Merrill Lynch Capital Markets

Broker/Dealer – National

Sub of Merrill Lynch & Co., Inc.

Location: 250 Vesey Street World Financial Center
North Tower
New York, NY 10281

Fax: 212/449-2805 **Phone:** 212/449-1000

KEY MANAGERS & DERIVATIVES SPECIALISTS	Direct Phone/Fax	Job Function
Mr. Joseph Argilagos Managing Director	212/449-8026 212/449-6629	Derivatives Products Head *ABS, Treas, Agency, Funding, MBS, Money Mkt* Sales – Currency Trader – Derivatives
Mr. Keith Bailey Managing Director	212/449-6177	Trader – Currency Swaps Trader – Interest Rate Swaps
Mr. Vincent Balducci Vice President		Marketing – Swaps
Mr. Robert C. Barber Managing Director	212/449-2734	Trader – Derivatives *Muni*
Mr. Harley Bassman Managing Director	212/449-6828 212/449-5868	Trader – Derivatives *Govt, MBS* Trader – Futures *Govt*
Mr. Charles Clough, Jr. Chief Economist	212/449-0904 212/449-5871	Fixed-Income Strategist
Mr. Geoffrey S. Domm Director	212/449-7358	Trader – Derivatives *Muni*
Mr. Philip J. Fischer First Vice President	212/449-0218	Research Analyst – Derivatives *Muni*
Mr. Edward Fluss Assistant Vice President	212/449-5578	Trader – Currency Futures Trader – Currency Options
Mr. Martin S. Fridson Managing Director	212/449-1102 212/449-8150	Fixed-Income Strategist

Merrill Lynch Capital Markets – continued

KEY MANAGERS & DERIVATIVES SPECIALISTS	Direct Phone/Fax	Job Function
Mr. Seth Garrett Director	212/449-5578	Trader – Currency Options Head
Mr. William Kenny Vice President	212/449-5911	Trader – Futures Trader – Options
Mr. Jeffrey W. Kronthal Managing Director	212/449-1635 212/449-6639	Bond Department Head *MBS* Derivatives Specialist
Mr. Boon Chai Lee Director	212/449-6177	Derivatives Specialist
Mr. Thomas R. Lynett, Jr. Managing Director & C.O.O.	212/449-5843 212/449-6673	Bond Department Head *Govt*
Mr. James McCarthy, Jr. Director	212/449-5578	Trader – Currency Futures Trader – Currency Options
Mr. Joseph H. Moglia Managing Director	212/449-5730 212/449-3774	Bond Department Head *Muni*
Mr. David T. Napoli Senior Vice President	212/449-5841	Trader – Derivatives Head
Mr. Michael Normile Managing Director	212/449-5835 212/449-9015	Bond Department Head *ABS*
Mr. Mark J. Paris Director	212/449-0679	Trader – Derivatives *Muni*
Mr. William Perfit Manager	212/449-5578	Trader – Currency Futures Trader – Currency Options
Mr. Guy Piserchia Vice President	212/449-5578	Trader – Currency Options
Mr. Thomas R. Robinson Manager	212/449-0916	Fixed-Income Strategist
Mr. Ronald Rosenberg Managing Director	212/449-5390	Marketing – Derivatives Sales – Derivatives
Mr. Robert Q. Scott Director	212/449-6177	Trader – Derivatives *Muni*
Mr. Robert M. Simonson Managing Director	212/449-5693 212/449-8896	Bond Department Head *Money Mkt*
Mr. Winthrop A. Smith Executive Vice President	212/449-6349	Bond Department Head

Merrill Lynch Capital Markets – continued

KEY MANAGERS & DERIVATIVES SPECIALISTS	Direct Phone/Fax	Job Function
Mr. Edward Somekh Managing Director	212/449-7860	Trader – Derivatives
Mr. Thomas J. Sowanick Chief Fixed Income Strategist	212/449-0230 212/449-3111	Fixed-Income Strategist
Mr. Wesley Sparks Managing Director	212/449-5003 212/449-6339	Derivatives Products Head *MBS*
Mr. Glenn Stevens Chief Director	212/449-5578	Trader – Currency Futures Head Trader – Currency Options Head
Mr. Anthony Wegener Vice President	212/449-5578	Trader – Currency Futures

Mitsubishi Capital Markets Services

Bank/Dealer

Sub of The Mitsubishi Bank, Limited

Location: Two World Financial Centre
225 Liberty Street
New York, NY 10281

Fax: 212/667-3560

Phone: 212/667-2500

KEY MANAGERS & DERIVATIVES SPECIALISTS	Direct Phone/Fax	Job Function
Mr. Yoshiyuki Adachi Vice President	212/667-3300	Trader – Currency Options Head
Mr. James Arsenault Senior Trader	212/667-3343	Trader – Derivatives Head
Mr. Eric Burns Vice President	212/667-3441	Trader – Interest Rate Futures Trader – Interest Rate Options Trader – Interest Rate Swaps
Mr. Ichiro Chitani Vice President	212/667-3410	Trader – Currency Futures Trader – Currency Options
Mr. Jeffrey K. Davis Vice President	212/667-3298	Sales – Derivatives
Mr. Truaki Fujimoto Vice President	212/667-3300	Trader – FRA's
Mr. Akio Fujiwara Vice President	212/667-3410	Trader – Currency Futures Head
Mr. Susumu Hanada President & C.E.O.	212/667-3358	Derivatives Products Head

Mitsubishi Financial Futures Inc.

Bank/Dealer

Sub of The Mitsubishi Bank, Limited

Location: 10 South Wacker Drive
Suite 1030
Chicago, IL 60606

Fax: 312/930-2320

Phone: 312/930-2300

KEY MANAGERS & DERIVATIVES SPECIALISTS	Direct Phone/Fax	Job Function
Mr. M. Scott Gordon Executive Vice President	312/930-2301	Derivatives Products Head
Mr. John Nyhoff Vice President	312/930-2310	Trader – Derivatives Head Trader – Futures

Mitsui T & B Futures Inc.

Bank/Dealer

Sub of Mitsui Marine Insurance Ltd

Location: 30 South Wacker Drive
Suite 1520
Chicago, IL 60606

Fax: 312/362-4568

Phone: 312/362-2244

KEY MANAGERS & DERIVATIVES SPECIALISTS	Direct Phone/Fax	Job Function
Mr. Thomas Piersanti Vice President		Derivatives Products Head Trader – Currency Options Head Trader – Derivatives Head Trader – Futures

J.P. Morgan Futures Inc. (Chicago)

Broker/Dealer – National

Sub of J.P. Morgan & Company Inc.

Location: 227 West Monroe Street
Suite 2800
Chicago, IL 60606

Fax: 312/541-3381

Phone: 312/541-3300

KEY MANAGERS & DERIVATIVES SPECIALISTS	Direct Phone/Fax	Job Function
Mr. Richard McVey Managing Director	312/541-3344	Derivatives Products Head Marketing – Futures Sales – Futures Trader – Futures

J.P. Morgan Securities Inc.

Broker/Dealer – National

Sub of J.P. Morgan & Company Inc.

Location: 60 Wall Street
New York, NY 10260-0060

Fax: 212/648-5253

Phone: 212/483-2323

J.P. Morgan Securities Inc. – continued

KEY MANAGERS & DERIVATIVES SPECIALISTS	Direct Phone/Fax	Job Function
Mr. Peter W. Atwater Managing Director	212/648-4498 212/648-5251	Bond Department Head *ABS*
Mr. Albert C. Bashawaty Managing Director	212/648-0189 212/648-5604	Derivatives Products Head Trader – Derivatives
Mr. Rhahime A. Bell Managing Director	212/648-4420	Derivatives Specialist Trader – Currency Swaps *Muni* Trader – Interest Rate Swaps *Muni*
Mr. Mark C. Brickell Managing Director	212/648-6605 212/648-5376	Research Analyst – Derivatives
Mr. John Caccavale Vice President	212/648-2000	Trader – Currency Futures Head Trader – Currency Options Head
Mr. John Corrie Managing Director	212/648-2410	OTC Deriv/Swaps – Head
Mr. William S. Demchak Managing Director	212/648-0772	Marketing – Swaps
Mr. Christopher M. Dillon Vice President	212/648-0949	Fixed-Income Strategist
Mr. Paul Frean Vice President	212/648-0213	Fixed-Income Strategist *MBS*
Mr. Brian C. Gendreau Vice President	212/648-3069	Fixed-Income Strategist
Ms. Stephany Hanbury-Brown Managing Director	212/826-1465	Sales – Derivatives
Mr. Peter Hancock Managing Director	212/648-2200 212/648-5925	Bond Department Head Derivatives Products Head
Mr. Christopher Harvey Managing Director	212/648-2121	Trader – Currency Options
Ms. Maureen A. Hendricks Managing Director	212/648-2500	Bond Department Head *Corp*
Mr. Thomas L. Kalaris Managing Director	212/648-0925 212/648-5181	Bond Department Head
Mr. Norman Klath Managing Director	212/648-3080	Fixed-Income Strategist

J.P. Morgan Securities Inc. – continued

KEY MANAGERS & DERIVATIVES SPECIALISTS	Direct Phone/Fax	Job Function
Mr. John Mullen Managing Director	212/648-0743 212/648-5953	Bond Department Head *ABS, MBS*
Mr. David Pryde Managing Director	212/648-9307	Derivatives Products Head
Mr. Andrew Readinger Vice President	212/648-2429	Derivatives Products Head *Muni*
Mr. Steven Sinacore Managing Director	212/648-2333	Derivatives Specialist
Mr. Damon P. Smith III Managing Director	212/648-0916 212/648-5916	Bond Department Head *Muni*

Morgan Stanley & Co., Incorporated (NYC Branch)

Broker/Dealer – National

Location: 1221 Avenue of the Americas
New York, NY 10020

Fax: 212/764-7490 **Phone:** 212/703-4000

KEY MANAGERS & DERIVATIVES SPECIALISTS	Direct Phone/Fax	Job Function
Ms. Zoe Cruz Managing Director	212/761-2855	Sales – Currency Trader – Currency Futures Trader – Currency Options
Mr. Steven D'Antonio MBS Product Manager	212/761-2080	Derivatives Products Head *MBS*
Mr. Ignacio Fanlo Managing Director	212/761-2080 212/921-5861	Trader – Derivatives *MBS*
Mr. Marc W. Gordon Principal	212/296-5098	Bond Department Head
Mr. Peter F. Karches Managing Director	212/296-6502 212/296-5256	Bond Department Head
Mr. Gary Latainer	212/296-4140	Fixed-Income Strategist
Ms. Elaine Lloyd Managing Director	212/761-2700	Derivatives Specialist
Mr. Gary Meyerson Vice President	212/761-2433	Trader – Currency Options Head Trader – Currency Swaps Trader – Interest Rate Swaps
Mr. Paul S. Miller Principal	212/761-2328	Derivatives Specialist

Morgan Stanley & Co., Incorporated (NYC Branch) – continued

KEY MANAGERS & DERIVATIVES SPECIALISTS	Direct Phone/Fax	Job Function
Mr. Philip Nucomb Director	212/761-2840	Trader – Currency Options Head Marketing – Options
Mr. William B. O'Keefe Managing Director	212/296-7654 212/719-3141	Bond Department Head *Muni* Trader – Derivatives *Muni* Trader – Futures *Muni*
Mr. Craig S. Phillips Managing Director	212/296-4311 212/921-5861	Bond Department Head *MBS*
Ms. Elaine Pochtar Vice President	212/761-2324 212/719-3141	Trader – Futures *Muni*
Mr. Guy Randolph Principal	212/761-2700	Sales – Currency
Mr. Kevin J. Straine Dealer	212/761-1786	Sales – Futures Sales – Options
Mr. Alan J. Tulp Principal	212/761-7640 212/719-3141	Trader – Futures
Mr. Eric M. Vandercar	212/296-5855	Fixed-Income Strategist
Mr. Benjamin Wolkowitz Managing Director	212/761-1700	Derivatives Products Head Trader – Derivatives Head

NationsBanc – CRT

Bank/Dealer

Sub of NationsBank Corporation

Location: 233 South Wacker Drive
Suite 2800
Chicago, IL 60606

Fax: 312/234-3089

Phone: 312/234-5000

KEY MANAGERS & DERIVATIVES SPECIALISTS	Direct Phone/Fax	Job Function
Mr. Stuart Adams Trader	312/234-3545	Trader – Interest Rate Options
Ms. Dorie Boyce Trader	312/234-2613	Trader – Currency Options
Ms. Denise DeMeure Trader	312/234-2613	Trader – Currency Options
Mr. Patrick Donahue Global Manager	312/234-2613	Trader – Currency Futures Head Trader – Currency Options Head Trader – Derivatives Head

NationsBanc – CRT – continued

KEY MANAGERS & DERIVATIVES SPECIALISTS	Direct Phone/Fax	Job Function
Mr. Sean Doyle Trader	312/234-2585	Trader – Interest Rate Swaps
Mr. William Fall Manager	312/234-5737	Sales – Futures Sales – Options Sales – Structured Notes
Mr. John Gannon Trader	312/234-2613	Trader – Currency Options
Mr. Duncan Goldie-Morrison Global Manager	312/234-2540	Trader – Interest Rate Futures Trader – Interest Rate Options Trader – Interest Rate Swaps
Mr. Mark Henrici Trader	312/234-2613	Trader – Currency Options
Mr. John Hughes Trader	312/234-5437	OTC Deriv/Swaps – Head
Mr. John Kuhn Trader	312/234-2585	Trader – Interest Rate Swaps
Mr. Michael Kukanza Trader	312/234-2349	Trader – Currency Options
Ms. Denise Lilien Trader	312/234-3545	Trader – Interest Rate Options Trader – Options
Mr. James O'Donnell Trader	312/234-2585	Trader – Interest Rate Swaps
Mr. Howard Stolar Trader	312/234-5437	Trader – Interest Rate Options Trader – Structured Investments
Mr. Brett Tidland Trader	312/234-5437	OTC Deriv/Swaps – Head
Mr. Lawrence Weithers Trader	312/234-3110	Trader – Interest Rate Options

NatWest Securities Corporation

Bank/Dealer

Sub of National Westminster Bancorp, Inc.

Location: 175 Water Street
New York, NY 10038

Fax: 212/602-4939

Phone: 212/602-4800

NatWest Securities Corporation – continued

KEY MANAGERS & DERIVATIVES SPECIALISTS	Direct Phone/Fax	Job Function
Mr. Joseph P. Adams Executive Vice President	212/602-5606 212/495-5790	Bond Department Head *ABS*
Mr. Joseph Cambria Senior Vice President	212/602-4060	Trader – Currency Options Head
Mr. Christopher Carman Vice President	212/602-5561	Trader – Derivatives
Mr. Robert E. Kline Vice President & Manager	212/602-1880	Bond Department Head *Money Mkt*
Mr. Chad Loweth Senior Vice President	212/602-4880 212/495-5803	Derivatives Products Head
Mr. Christopher Mackenzie Senior Vice President	212/602-4357	Structured Notes – Head Sales – Currency
Mr. Tuulikki Matthews Vice President	212/602-4050	Trader – Derivatives
Mr. Kelvin Norman Vice President	212/602-4060	Trader – Derivatives
Mr. Peter Rading Manager	212/602-4265	Trader – Derivatives
Mr. Richard Simon Assistant Vice President	212/602-4050	Trader – Derivatives
Mr. Matthew Spelker Vice President	212/602-4060	Trader – Currency Futures Trader – Currency Options
Mr. Vincent Tomasi Senior Vice President	212/602-4377 212/602-4547	Derivatives Products Head *ABS* Trader – Derivatives Head
Mr. David Wald Co-Director	212/602-5651	Derivatives Specialist
Mr. Christopher Wilkinson Assistant Vice President	212/602-4060	Trader – Currency Futures

Nomura Securities International, Inc.

Broker/Dealer – Regional

Sub of Nomura Securities Ltd.

Location: Two World Financial Center
Building B
New York, NY 10281-1198

Fax: 212/667-1058

Phone: 212/667-9300

Nomura Securities International, Inc. – continued

KEY MANAGERS & DERIVATIVES SPECIALISTS	Direct Phone/Fax	Job Function
Mr. Gary Aronstein Director	212/667-2118 212/667-1044	Bond Department Head *Money Mkt*
Mr. Thomas I. Blinten Managing Director	212/667-2332	Marketing – Derivatives Sales – Derivatives
Mr. Jeffrey E. Davis Vice President	212/667-1490	Sales – Derivatives
Mr. Daniel Frommer Vice President	212/667-1483	Marketing – Derivatives Sales – Derivatives
Mr. Sean C. Gallop Director	212/667-2050 212/667-1041	Sales – Derivatives *MBS*
Mr. Sean Kelleher Director	212/667-2240 212/667-1006	Trader – Derivatives
Mr. Sanjeev Khullar Director	212/667-2334	OTC Deriv/Swaps – Head Trader – Derivatives Head
Mr. William Mansfield Vice President	212/667-1480 212/667-9000	Trader – Derivatives
Mr. Edward Neminski Vice President	212/667-2174	Trader – Currency Futures Head Trader – Currency Options Head
Mr. Christopher Phelan Vice President	212/667-1489	Sales – Derivatives
Mr. Joseph Schmuckler Executive Managing Director	212/667-2099	Trader – Interest Rate Futures Trader – Interest Rate Options Trader – Interest Rate Swaps
Mr. Dean Trotzuk Vice President	212/667-2331	Sales – Derivatives
Mr. William Wraith Executive Managing Director	212/667-1355	Bond Department Head *MBS*
Mr. Hajime Yoshida Executive Managing Director	212/667-2335 212/667-9000	Derivatives Products Head

Oppenheimer & Co., Inc.

Broker/Dealer – National

Sub of Oppenheimer Group

Location: 200 Liberty Street
One World Financial Center
New York, NY 10281

Fax: 212/667-5302

Phone: 212/667-7000

Oppenheimer & Co., Inc. – continued

KEY MANAGERS & DERIVATIVES SPECIALISTS	Direct Phone/Fax	Job Function
Mr. William H. Frazier Managing Director	212/667-5251	Bond Department Head *Muni*
Mr. Thomas Gallagher Vice Chairman	212/667-7387	Bond Department Head
Mr. Thomas V. Herlihy Vice President	212/667-5263 212/667-2302	Derivatives Products Head *Muni* Trader – Derivatives *Muni*
Mr. Keith Kursner Senior Vice President	212/667-5328	Trader – Options
Mr. Alan Leiderman Senior Vice President	212/667-5430	Derivatives Products Head Trader – Derivatives Head
Mr. William Malone Vice President	212/667-5430 212/667-5488	Bond Department Head *MBS* Derivatives Products Head *MBS*
Mr. E. Michael Metz Chief Investment Strategist	212/667-7073 212/667-5580	Fixed-Income Strategist
Mr. Seth Novatt Managing Director	212/667-7365 212/667-5514	Sales – Derivatives
Mr. Kyle A. Permut Managing Director	212/667-5634 212/667-5995	Bond Department Head *Treas, Agency, Funding*
Mr. Michael Schwartz Senior Vice President	212/667-7130	Trader – Options

PaineWebber Incorporated

Broker/Dealer – National

Sub of PaineWebber Group, Inc.

Location: 1285 Avenue of the Americas
New York, NY 10019

Fax: 212/713-1303 **Phone:** 212/713-2000

KEY MANAGERS & DERIVATIVES SPECIALISTS	Direct Phone/Fax	Job Function
Mr. Terrence L. Atkinson Managing Director & Co-Head	212/713-2814 212/713-2998	Bond Department Head *Muni*
Mr. Daniel J. Callahan, Jr. Managing Director	212/713-1449	Bond Department Head *Govt*
Mr. Steven Ciccarello Vice President	212/713-1101	Sales – Options

PaineWebber Incorporated – continued

KEY MANAGERS & DERIVATIVES SPECIALISTS	**Direct Phone/Fax**	**Job Function**
Mr. Timothy E. Cronin E.V.P. & Co-Head	212/713-3553 212/586-7994	Bond Department Head
Mr. Stephen DeVoe Managing Director	212/713-1457	Derivatives Specialist
Ms. Laurie S. Goodman Senior Vice President	212/713-4141	Fixed-Income Strategist
Ms. Johanna Griffin Vice President	212/713-6135	Derivatives Specialist
Mr. Thomas P. Hart Vice President	212/713-3582	Derivatives Products Head
Mr. Patrick Hughes Director	212/713-2412	Marketing – Derivatives
Mr. Robert B. Jacobs Managing Director & Co-Head	212/713-2740 212/713-6051	Bond Department Head *Muni*
Mr. Gregory Kiernan Managing Director	212/713-2344	Bond Department Head *Corp*
Ms. Linda Lowell First Vice President	212/713-6257	Fixed-Income Strategist
Mr. Edward Lynn Trader	212/713-4498	Trader – Interest Rate Options Trader – Options
Mr. Michael P. Ryan	212/713-4671	Fixed-Income Strategist
Mr. Steven Schwimmer Senior Vice President	212/713-8700	Derivatives Products Head
Ms. Mary Lynn Soulas Trader	212/713-1101	Trader – Currency Options
Mr. Bert F. Verdicchio Vice President	212/713-2548	Trader – Derivatives *Muni*

Peregrine Derivatives Ltd.

Broker/Dealer – Regional

Location: 780 Third Avenue
New York, NY 10017

Fax: 212/593-5932

Phone: 212/593-5920

Peregrine Derivatives Ltd. – continued

KEY MANAGERS & DERIVATIVES SPECIALISTS	Direct Phone/Fax	Job Function
Mr. Steven Coller Vice President		Derivatives Products Head Trader – Currency Options Head Trader – Interest Rate Options Trader – Options
Mr. John Sullivan Assistant Vice President		Sales – Options

Prebon Yamane (U.S.A.)

Brokers' Broker

Location: 101 Hudson Street
24th Floor
Jersey City, NJ 07302

Fax: 201/557-5895

Phone: 201/557-5000

KEY MANAGERS & DERIVATIVES SPECIALISTS	Direct Phone/Fax	Job Function
Mr. Carmine Capobianco First Vice President	201/557-5105	Trader – Currency Futures Head Trader – Currency Options Head
Mr. Andrew Freeman Vice President	201/557-5440	Derivatives Products Head Trader – Derivatives Head
Mr. Harry A. Fry President	201/557-5135 201/557-5996	Bond Department Head *Money Mkt*
Mr. John S. Hottinger Senior Vice President	201/557-5270 201/557-5941	Bond Department Head *ABS, MBS*
Mr. George J. Quinn Executive Vice President	201/557-5210 201/557-5920	Bond Department Head *Funding*

Prudential Securities Inc.

Broker/Dealer – National

Sub of The Prudential Insurance Company of America (U.S.A.)

Location: One Seaport Plaza
New York, NY 10292-2014

Fax: 212/776-3463

Phone: 212/214-1000

KEY MANAGERS & DERIVATIVES SPECIALISTS	Direct Phone/Fax	Job Function
Mr. Jack Annizuato Vice President	212/778-3960	Sales – Currency
Mr. Richard J. Barry Managing Director	212/778-3406 212/778-1648	Derivatives Products Head *MBS*
Mr. Anand K. Bhattacharya Managing Director	212/778-4930 212/778-3716	Bond Department Head *Taxable*
Mr. Marc Chodera Assistant Vice President	212/778-3985	Trader – Currency Options

Prudential Securities Inc. – continued

KEY MANAGERS & DERIVATIVES SPECIALISTS	Direct Phone/Fax	Job Function
Mr. Gerard Cudzil President & Director	212/778-3999	Trader – Currency Futures Head Trader – Currency Options Head
Mr. Kenneth F. Entler S.V.P. & Manager	212/778-3373 212/778-3165	Bond Department Head *Funding*
Mr. Robert T. Johnson Senior Vice President	212/778-6165 212/778-6154	Bond Department Head *MBS* Sales – Derivatives
Mr. James M. Kelso Director	212/778-7860	Trader – Futures
Ms. Gail Kreitman Vice President	212/778-2166	Trader – Derivatives *MBS*
Mr. Raymond Lemanski Managing Director	212/778-5500 212/778-5297	Bond Department Head *Corp*
Mr. Gerald P. McBride E.V.P. & National Manager	212/778-3688 212/778-7137	Bond Department Head *Muni*
Mr. A. Laurence Norton Director	212/778-6355	Marketing – Futures
Mr. Michael Pillari		Trader – Derivatives *MBS*
Mr. Mark Razzano Vice President	212/778-3988	Trader – Currency Futures Trader – Currency Options
Ms. Donna Redel Director	212/778-7926	Marketing – Futures
Mr. Gregory P. Richter Managing Director	212/778-2741 212/778-1905	Bond Department Head *ABS*
Mr. Gregory Smith Vice President	212/778-1416	Fixed-Income Strategist
Mr. Michael J. Sullivan Vice President	212/778-3399 212/778-2279	Bond Department Head *Money Mkt*
Ms. Carol Sze Director – F/I Strategies	212/778-1741	Fixed-Income Strategist
Mr. Jeffrey J. Theodorou Managing Director	212/778-7444 212/778-4516	Bond Department Head *MBS*

Rabobank Nederland North America

Bank/Dealer

Sub of Rabobank Nederland

Location: 245 Park Avenue
36th Floor
New York, NY 10167

Fax: 212/818-0233

Phone: 212/916-7800

KEY MANAGERS & DERIVATIVES SPECIALISTS	Direct Phone/Fax	Job Function
Mr. Keith L. Bigwood V.P. & Investment Manager	212/808-7900	Bond Department Head *Govt, MBS*
Mr. Charles R. Gates Vice President	212/808-2531 212/808-2578	Marketing – Derivatives Trader – Derivatives
Mr. Randy Himelfarb Vice President	212/808-2520 212/808-2574	Trader – Derivatives Head
Mr. Steven H. Lim Vice President	212/808-2531 212/808-2578	Derivatives Products Head Trader – Derivatives
Ms. Aimee McCormack Vice President	212/808-7900	Bond Department Head *Funding, Money Mkt* Derivatives Specialist

Republic New York Securities Corporation

Bank/Dealer

Sub of Republic National Bank of New York

Location: 452 Fifth Avenue
Tower 12
New York, NY 10018

Fax: 212/525-6958

Phone: 212/525-6600

KEY MANAGERS & DERIVATIVES SPECIALISTS	Direct Phone/Fax	Job Function
Mr. Boaz Ben-Moshe Senior Vice President	212/525-5725	Trader – Derivatives Head
Ms. Joyce Covello Vice President	212/525-6531	Marketing – Options Trader – Options
Mr. James F. Curley Chairman & C.E.O.	212/525-6737	Sales – Futures Trader – Futures
Mr. Victor Fattal Managing Director	212/221-3556	Trader – Currency Futures Head Trader – Currency Options Head
Mr. Brendan Lynch Vice President	212/525-8611	Trader – Options
Mr. Jerry Marer Senior Vice President	212/525-6736	Sales – Futures Trader – Futures
Mr. Joseph Randazzo Senior Vice President	212/525-6734	Sales – Futures Trader – Futures
Mr. Robert Schwartz President	212/525-6837	Derivatives Products Head
Mr. James E. Sweeney President – Futures Division	212/525-6117	Sales – Futures Trader – Futures

The Sakura Bank Ltd. (New York)

Bank/Dealer

Sub of The Sakura Bank Ltd. (Japan)

Location: 277 Park Avenue
New York, NY 10172-0121

Fax: 212/644-9565

Phone: 212/756-6700

KEY MANAGERS & DERIVATIVES SPECIALISTS	Direct Phone/Fax	Job Function
Mr. Paul Chludzinski Vice President	212/756-6867	Trader – Derivatives Head
Mr. Francois Chu-Fong Vice President	212/756-6931	Trader – Currency Futures Head Trader – Currency Options Head
Mr. Koichi Masuda Senior Vice President	212/756-6900	Derivatives Products Head Trader – Interest Rate Futures Trader – Interest Rate Options Trader – Interest Rate Swaps
Mr. Hiroshi Nakazawa Assistant Vice President	212/756-6931	Trader – Currency Futures Trader – Currency Options
Mr. Thomas Sharpe Manager	212/756-6931	Trader – Currency Futures Trader – Currency Options Trader – FRA's

Sakura Global Capital, Inc.

Bank/Dealer

Sub of The Sakura Bank Ltd. (Japan)

Location: Park Avenue Tower
65 East 55th Street 20th Floor
New York, NY 10022

Fax: 212/355-4271

Phone: 212/486-8282

KEY MANAGERS & DERIVATIVES SPECIALISTS	Direct Phone/Fax	Job Function
Ms. Joanne Coulson Assistant Vice President	212/486-8454	OTC Deriv/Swaps – Head
Mr. Marko Issever Managing Director	212/486-8269	Marketing – Derivatives Sales – Currency Sales – Futures Sales – Options
Ms. Kathy Schmidt Director	212/486-8716	Derivatives Specialist
Mr. Elwyn Wong Managing Director	212/486-5193	Trader – Currency Futures Head Trader – Currency Options Head Trader – Interest Rate Futures Trader – Interest Rate Options Trader – Interest Rate Swaps Trader – Structured Investments

Salomon Brothers Inc.

Broker/Dealer – National

Sub of Salomon Inc.

Location: Seven World Trade Center
New York, NY 10048

Fax: 212/783-2284

Phone: 212/783-7000

KEY MANAGERS & DERIVATIVES SPECIALISTS	Direct Phone/Fax	Job Function
Mr. Ravit Efraty Vice President	212/783-4733	Research Analyst – Derivatives
Mr. Paul Fjeldsted Vice President	212/783-2917	Trader – Derivatives
Mr. John L. Haseltine Head – Fixed Income	212/783-3216	Bond Department Head
Mr. Max Holmes High-Yield Bond Strategist	212/783-3155	Fixed-Income Strategist
Mr. Michael T. Hutchins Managing Director	212/783-2849 212/783-2318	Bond Department Head *ABS, MBS*
Mr. Paul E. Jablansky Director	212/783-3335 212/783-4004	Fixed-Income Strategist
Mr. Anthony C. Lemke Director	212/783-6623	Fixed-Income Strategist
Mr. Sumit Roy Vice President	212/783-2917	Trader – Derivatives
Mr. Jonathan Sandelman Managing Director	212/783-3180	Derivatives Specialist
Mr. Alan Shaffran Vice President	212/783-2693	OTC Deriv/Swaps – Head
Ms. Janet Showers Managing Director	212/783-6612	Fixed-Income Strategist Research Analyst – Futures/Options *Corp*
Mr. Richard Stuckey Managing Director	212/783-2693	Derivatives Products Head Trader – Derivatives Head
Mr. Gordon Tanner Vice President	212/783-2917	Trader – Derivatives

Santander Financial Products

Bank/Dealer

Sub of Banco Santander (Spain)

Location: 45 East 53rd Street
New York, NY 10022

Fax: 212/350-3535

Phone: 212/350-3500

Santander Financial Products – continued

KEY MANAGERS & DERIVATIVES SPECIALISTS	Direct Phone/Fax	Job Function
Mr. Joaquin Avila Managing Director	212/407-7808	Trader – Interest Rate Futures Trader – Interest Rate Options
Mr. Thomas Buttke Vice President	212/407-7822	Trader – Structured Investments
Mr. Michael Driscoll Senior Vice President	212/407-7824	Trader – Structured Investments
Mr. Anthony Pesco Managing Director	212/407-2975	Derivatives Products Head Trader – Interest Rate Futures Trader – Interest Rate Options Trader – Interest Rate Swaps
Mr. Gregory Young Senior Vice President	212/407-7821	Trader – Structured Investments

Sanwa Bank

Bank/Dealer

Sub of Sanwa Bank Ltd.

Location: Park Avenue Plaza
55 East 52nd Street
New York, NY 10055

Fax: 212/750-3284

Phone: 212/339-6500

KEY MANAGERS & DERIVATIVES SPECIALISTS	Direct Phone/Fax	Job Function
Mr. Steven Engel Assistant Vice President	212/339-6294	Structured Notes – Head Trader – Structured Investments
Mr. Yohisuke Inoue Assistant Vice President	212/339-6531	Trader – Interest Rate Futures Trader – Interest Rate Options Trader – Interest Rate Swaps
Mr. Koudou Kamimura Assistant Vice President	212/339-6516	Trader – Currency Futures Trader – Currency Options
Mr. Mitsuo Kamimura Assistant Vice President	212/339-6533	Trader – Interest Rate Futures Trader – Interest Rate Options Trader – Interest Rate Swaps
Mr. Hideshu Yoshimura Vice President	212/339-6512	Trader – Currency Futures Head Trader – Currency Options Head

Sanwa Securities (USA) Co., L.P.

Bank/Dealer

Sub of Sanwa Bank Ltd.

Location: 599 Lexington Avenue
19th Floor
New York, NY 10022-6063

Fax: 212/935-1024

Phone: 212/527-2600

Sanwa Securities (USA) Co., L.P. – continued

KEY MANAGERS & DERIVATIVES SPECIALISTS	Direct Phone/Fax	Job Function
Mr. Jeffrey Cohen Vice President	212/527-2883	Trader – Currency Options Head Trader – Derivatives Head Trader – Futures
Mr. James P. Coughlin Executive Vice President	212/527-2501 212/486-1279	Bond Department Head *Treas, Agency*
Mr. Salvatore DeMarco Executive Vice President	212/527-2533 212/527-2596	Bond Department Head *Funding*
Mr. Glenn Doran Senior Vice President	212/527-2450 212/486-1279	Derivatives Products Head Trader – Futures *Govt* Trader – Options
Mr. William Feezer, Jr. Executive Vice President	212/527-2501 212/754-0587	Bond Department Head *Treas*
Mr. Dennis Flynn Senior Vice President	212/527-2565 212/754-0587	Bond Department Head *Money Mkt*
Mr. George Kegler Senior Vice President	212/527-2450 212/486-1279	Bond Department Head *Treas, Agency*

Smith Barney, Inc. (Chicago)

Broker/Dealer – National

Sub of Travelers Group

Location: 70 West Madison Street
Three First National Plaza Suite 5000
Chicago, IL 60602

Fax: 312/419-3490 **Phone:** 312/419-3600

KEY MANAGERS & DERIVATIVES SPECIALISTS	Direct Phone/Fax	Job Function
Mr. Thomas Dugan Vice President	312/419-3631	Sales – Currency Sales – Options

Smith Barney, Inc. (Greenwich Street)

Broker/Dealer – National

Sub of Travelers Group

Location: 390 Greenwich Street
New York, NY 10013

Fax: 212/723-8792 **Phone:** 212/816-6000

KEY MANAGERS & DERIVATIVES SPECIALISTS	Direct Phone/Fax	Job Function
Ms. Deborah J. Elliot Managing Director	212/723-7448	Bond Department Head *Funding*
Mr. Bruce E. Fox Director	212/723-7585	Derivatives Products Head OTC Deriv/Swaps – Head Structured Notes – Head Sales – Derivatives

Smith Barney, Inc. (Greenwich Street) – continued

KEY MANAGERS & DERIVATIVES SPECIALISTS	Direct Phone/Fax	Job Function
Mr. George D. Friedlander Managing Director	212/698-3262	Fixed-Income Strategist
Mr. Ralph Hallenborg Managing Director	212/723-5815 212/723-8764	Bond Department Head *Treas, Agency*
Mr. Curt Lin Vice President	212/723-7585	Structured Notes – Head Trader – Derivatives Head
Mr. Alan D. Marks Executive Vice President	212/723-5671	Research Analyst – Derivatives Trader – Derivatives
Mr. Howard D. Marsh Managing Director	212/723-7097 212/723-8951	Bond Department Head *Muni*
Mr. Martin Marx Executive Vice President	212/723-7250	Trader – Derivatives
Mr. James Mulvey Senior Vice President	212/723-7001	Trader – Currency Futures Head Trader – FRA's
Ms. Christine Olivier Vice President	212/723-3262	Fixed-Income Strategist
Mr. Bruce J. Richards Managing Director	212/723-5287 212/723-8764	Bond Department Head *MBS*
Mr. Phillip M. Waterman Sr. Executive Vice President	212/723-5888	Sales – Futures
Mr. Matthew Weinberg Managing Director	212/723-7414 212/723-8846	Derivatives Products Head *MBS*

Societe Generale Securities Corporation

Broker/Dealer – National

Sub of Société Générale AG

Location: 1221 Avenue of the Americas
New York, NY 10020

Fax: 212/278-7195

Phone: 212/278-6000

KEY MANAGERS & DERIVATIVES SPECIALISTS	Direct Phone/Fax	Job Function
Mr. Michael Casper Vice President	212/278-7105	Trader – Interest Rate Futures Trader – Interest Rate Options Trader – Interest Rate Swaps
Mr. Stephen Dougherty Vice President	212/278-7100	Marketing – Derivatives

Societe Generale Securities Corporation – continued

KEY MANAGERS & DERIVATIVES SPECIALISTS	Direct Phone/Fax	Job Function
Mr. Dominque Errichetti First Vice President	212/278-6900	Trader – Currency Futures Head Trader – Currency Options Head
Mr. Jeremy Henderson First V.P. & Director	212/278-7100	Marketing – Futures Marketing – Options Marketing – Swaps Sales – Derivatives
Mr. Jean Pierre Lardy First Vice President	212/278-7100	Derivatives Products Head
Mr. Martin Levion First V.P. & Manager	212/278-7100	Derivatives Products Head Trader – Interest Rate Futures Trader – Interest Rate Options Trader – Interest Rate Swaps
Mr. Hector Negroni Vice President	212/278-7106	Trader – Interest Rate Futures Trader – Interest Rate Options Trader – Interest Rate Swaps
Mr. John O'Connor First Vice President	212/278-6739	Structured Notes – Head Trader – Structured Investments
Mr. Daniel Sauerhaft Vice President & Manager	212/278-7100	Marketing – Derivatives *Muni*
Mr. Phillip Schemel Vice President & Director	212/278-7105	Trader – Derivatives Head Trader – Interest Rate Futures Trader – Interest Rate Options Trader – Interest Rate Swaps
Mr. Michael Straine First Vice President	212/278-5316	Bond Department Head *Funding*
Mr. Jonathan Wilcox Vice President	212/278-7105	Trader – Derivatives *Muni* Trader – Options Trader – Structured Investments
Mr. William Zachary Vice President	212/278-7100	Marketing – Derivatives

Swiss Bank Corporation (SBC Warburg)

Bank/Dealer

Sub of Schweizerischer Bankverein (Basel)

Location: 222 Broadway
New York, NY 10038

Fax: 212/335-1389

Phone: 212/335-1000

KEY MANAGERS & DERIVATIVES SPECIALISTS	Direct Phone/Fax	Job Function
Ms. Linda Bammann Managing Director	212/574-6919	Sales – Derivatives

Swiss Bank Corporation (SBC Warburg) – continued

KEY MANAGERS & DERIVATIVES SPECIALISTS	Direct Phone/Fax	Job Function
Mr. Yves Bergin Managing Director	212/574-5186	Trader – Currency Swaps
Mr. Simon Bunce Managing Director	212/335-1384	Derivatives Products Head Marketing – Options Sales – Futures Sales – Options Sales – Structured Notes
Mr. Thomas Estes Director	212/574-6820	Bond Department Head *Govt*
Mr. E. Brian Finkelstein Executive Director	212/335-1007	Trader – Derivatives
Mr. Patrick MacDonald Executive Director	212/335-1331	Derivatives Products Head *Govt*
Mr. J. R. Tracy Executive Director	212/574-6088	OTC Deriv/Swaps – Head Trader – Derivatives Head Trader – Interest Rate Options Trader – Interest Rate Swaps
Mr. Eric Weinstein Executive Director	212/574-6042	Sales – Derivatives

The Tokai Bank Ltd.

Bank/Dealer

Sub of The Tokai Bank Ltd.

Location: 55 East 52nd Street
Park Avenue Plaza
New York, NY 10055

Fax: 212/754-2174

Phone: 212/339-1200

KEY MANAGERS & DERIVATIVES SPECIALISTS	Direct Phone/Fax	Job Function
Mr. Katsumasa Arai Assistant Vice President	212/339-1284	Trader – Currency Swaps Trader – Interest Rate Swaps
Mr. Takayuki Ishikawa Assistant Vice President	212/339-1267	Trader – Currency Options
Mr. Christopher Johansen Vice President	212/339-1268	Trader – Currency Futures
Mr. Yoshimi Kato Assistant Treasurer	212/339-1286	Sales – Derivatives
Mr. Gary Lakritz Vice President	212/339-1288	Trader – Interest Rate Options

The Tokai Bank Ltd. – continued

KEY MANAGERS & DERIVATIVES SPECIALISTS	Direct Phone/Fax	Job Function
Mr. Hitoshi Shimamura V.P. & Manager – Capital Mkts.	212/339-1282	Derivatives Products Head Trader – Derivatives Head
Mr. Donald Shiner Vice President	212/339-1276	Trader – Currency Swaps Trader – FRA's

The Toronto-Dominion Bank (New York – Dealer)

Bank/Dealer

Sub of The Toronto-Dominion Bank

Location: 31 West 52nd Street
New York, NY 10019

Fax: 212/262-1949

Phone: 212/468-0300

KEY MANAGERS & DERIVATIVES SPECIALISTS	Direct Phone/Fax	Job Function
Mr. Robert P. Baizer Manager	212/468-0375	Trader – Interest Rate Futures Trader – Interest Rate Options
Mr. P. Joseph Hegener Managing Director	212/468-0375	Derivatives Products Head
Mr. Timothy J. Jennings Director	212/468-0377	Derivatives Products Head OTC Deriv/Swaps – Head Structured Notes – Head
Mr. Kevin T. Lyons Director	212/468-0375	Trader – Interest Rate Futures Trader – Interest Rate Options Trader – Interest Rate Swaps
Mr. Steve McDougall Director	212/468-0375	Trader – Currency Options Head Trader – Derivatives Head Trader – Currency Swaps Trader – Futures
Mr. Srikane Sharma Manager	212/468-0375	Sales – Derivatives Sales – Structured Notes

UBS Securities, Inc.

Bank/Dealer

Sub of Union Bank of Switzerland (UBS)

Location: 299 Park Avenue
New York, NY 10171

Fax: 212/821-5805

Phone: 212/821-4000

KEY MANAGERS & DERIVATIVES SPECIALISTS	Direct Phone/Fax	Job Function
Mr. Andrew Beal Vice President	212/821-3039	Trader – Derivatives *MBS*
Mr. Alan G. Bozian Senior Managing Director	212/821-4048 212/821-5846	Bond Department Head *Govt, Agency*

UBS Securities, Inc. – continued

KEY MANAGERS & DERIVATIVES SPECIALISTS	Direct Phone/Fax	Job Function
Mr. Paul G. Cucchissi Manager	212/821-4098 212/821-5871	Marketing – Derivatives
Mr. Michael Damas Managing Director	212/821-6313 212/821-4873	Bond Department Head *ABS*
Mr. George Handjinicolaou Managing Director	212/821-5069 212/821-5062	Derivatives Products Head
Mr. Charles McLendon Vice President	212/821-4948 212/821-5871	Marketing – Derivatives
Mr. Simeon Schwartz Vice President	212/821-4131 212/821-5871	Trader – Derivatives Head
Mr. Michael Snow Senior Managing Director	212/821-3100 212/821-5846	Bond Department Head
Mr. Gary Taratunio Vice President	212/821-3580	Sales – Currency
Mr. Konrad Testwuide Managing Director	212/821-4592 212/821-4816	Marketing – Derivatives *Corp*
Ms. Virginia H. Tranchik Managing Director	212/821-3500 212/821-4815	Bond Department Head *Money Mkt*

Westdeutsche Landesbank Girozentrale – New York Branch

Bank/Dealer

Sub of West Merchant Bank Limited

Location: 1211 Avenue of the Americas
24th Floor
New York, NY 10036-8701

Fax: 212/852-6300

Phone: 212/852-6000

KEY MANAGERS & DERIVATIVES SPECIALISTS	Direct Phone/Fax	Job Function
Mr. Timothy Ball Senior Vice President	212/597-8541 212/597-8591	Derivatives Products Head OTC Deriv/Swaps – Head
Mr. Oliver A. Bergmann Vice President	212/597-8550	Trader – Interest Rate Options
Mr. James P. Bolton Vice President	212/597-8500	Trader – Derivatives
Mr. James E. Galowski Managing Director	212/852-6034 212/852-6140	Bond Department Head *Money Mkt*

Westdeutsche Landesbank Girozentrale – New York Branch – continued

KEY MANAGERS & DERIVATIVES SPECIALISTS	Direct Phone/Fax	Job Function
Mr. Ian Hawkins Vice President	212/597-8571	Structured Notes – Head Marketing – Derivatives
Ms. Kimberly Kassin Vice President	212/597-8500	Marketing – Derivatives Sales – Derivatives
Mr. Wolfgang Ketzer Assistant Vice President	212/852-6026	Bond Department Head *Govt*
Mr. David N. Lawrence Managing Director	212/852-6362 212/852-6140	Bond Department Head *ABS, Agency, Money Mkt*
Ms. Su Lum Vice President	212/597-8500	Trader – Derivatives
Mr. Thomas D. McCaffery Managing Director	212/852-6036 212/852-6140	Bond Department Head *Muni*
Mr. Michael Nesseler Vice President	212/597-8500	Trader – Derivatives
Mr. Jiro J. Okochi Vice President	212/597-8500	Sales – Derivatives
Mr. James Purnell Vice President	212/597-8500	Marketing – Derivatives Sales – Derivatives
Mr. Anthony Scamardolla Vice President	212/852-6052	Trader – Currency Futures Head Trader – Currency Options Head
Ms. Ellen Spiro Assistant Vice President	212/597-8500	Trader – Interest Rate Swaps
Mr. Patrick Trozzo Senior Vice President	212/597-8545	OTC Deriv/Swaps – Head
Mr. Peter F. Willard Vice President	212/597-8550	Trader – Interest Rate Swaps

Westpac Banking Corporation

Bank/Dealer

Sub of Westpac Banking Ltd. (Australia)

Location: 335 Madison Avenue
New York, NY 10023

Fax: 212/818-1499

Phone: 212/551-2700

KEY MANAGERS & DERIVATIVES SPECIALISTS	Direct Phone/Fax	Job Function
Mr. Robert Bosse Vice President	212/818-1578	Sales – Derivatives Trader – Currency Swaps Trader – Derivatives

Westpac Banking Corporation – continued

KEY MANAGERS & DERIVATIVES SPECIALISTS	Direct Phone/Fax	Job Function
Mr. Robert Goldwasser Vice President	212/818-1578	Sales – Derivatives
Mr. Wayne Howe Vice President	212/850-7821	Sales – Derivatives
Mr. Anthony Matthews Assistant Vice President	212/818-1578	Marketing – Derivatives Sales – Derivatives
Mr. Jack Richards Vice President	212/818-1578	Trader – Currency Futures Head Trader – Currency Options Head
Mr. Ian Stewart Vice President	212/850-7821	Marketing – Derivatives Sales – Derivatives

Yamaichi International (America), Inc.

Bank/Dealer

Sub of Yamaichi International Capital Management Co. Ltd.

Location: Two World Trade Center
Suite 9650
New York, NY 10048

Fax: 212/912-0172

Phone: 212/912-6400

KEY MANAGERS & DERIVATIVES SPECIALISTS	Direct Phone/Fax	Job Function
Mr. Kiyo Izutsu Vice President	212/524-8282	Sales – Futures Sales – Options
Mr. Patrick Q. Lynch Executive Vice President	212/524-6585	Bond Department Head *Govt, Agency, Money Mkt*
Mr. Mark O. Schultz Vice President	212/524-1160 212/524-1159	Bond Department Head *MBS*
Mr. Michael Welcome Executive Vice President	212/524-8260 212/390-8815	Trader – Derivatives Head

Derivatives Use: Investment Purposes

A Brief Illustration
Of Our Strength
In Risk Management
(Or, Why Choosing
The Right Bank Can Make
A World Of Difference)
Fact is, very few banks can equal our global strength and resources in risk management. As a major player in the world's capital markets, we are able to provide a broad range of derivative products tailored to your financial needs. In short, providing unparalleled risk management solutions is a feat we are superbly qualified to perform.
Bank of America
©1996 BankAmerica Corporation

The Acacia Group
Adams, Viner & Mosler
Advisers Capital Management Inc.
AEGON U.S.A. Investment Management (Cedar Rapids)
Aetna Life & Casualty (Portfolio Management Group)
Aid Association for Lutherans (AAL)
AIM Advisors, Inc.
Alaska Permanent Capital Management Company
Alaska Retirement Systems
Alfa Group
Allendale Mutual Insurance Company
Alliance Capital Management L.P.
Alliance Capital Management (Minneapolis)
Allied-Signal Inc.
Allstate Insurance Company
Amalgamated Bank of New York (Investment Management Group)
AMCORE Bank, N.A. Rockford
American Agricultural Insurance Company
American Family Insurance Group
American Money Management Corporation
American Mutual Life Insurance Company
American National Corporation
American National Bank & Trust (Chicago) (Trust)
American Savings Bank, F.A.
Ameritas Investment Advisors Inc.
Amoco Corporation
AMR Investment Services, Inc.
AmSouth Bank N.A. (Trust)
ANB Investment Management & Trust Co. of Chicago
Anhalt/O'Connell, Inc.
Ark Asset Management Company, Inc.
ASB Capital Management, Inc.
Asset Allocation & Management Company
Associated Bank Green Bay, N.A.
Atlantic Asset Management Partners Inc.
Auto Club Insurance Association
Auto-Owners Insurance Company
Avatar Investors Associates
Back Bay Advisors, L.P.
Banco Popular of Puerto Rico (Portfolio)
BancOklahoma Trust Company
Bank of America Illinois (Institutional Trust)
Bank of America NT & SA (Portfolio)
The Bank of California, N.A.
The Bank of New York Company, Inc.
Bank One, Dayton, N.A.
The Bank of Tokyo Trust Company (Pension & Investments)
Bankers Trust Global Investment Management
Bankers Trust — New York Corporation (Portfolio)
Baring Asset Management Company
Barnett Banks, Inc.
Barrow, Hanley, Mewhinney & Strauss, Inc.
Bartlett & Co.
BEA Associates
Bear, Stearns Asset Management Inc.
Bear, Stearns & Co. Inc. (Unit Trust)
Beneficial Life Insurance Company
Benefit Capital Management Corporation
Benham Capital Management Group
Berkeley Capital Management
Berkley Dean & Co.
Berkshire Life Insurance Co.
Sanford C. Bernstein & Co., Inc.
Bessemer Trust Company, N.A.
BlackRock Financial Management L.P.
The Boatmen's National Bank of St. Louis (Portfolio)
Boatmen's Trust (St. Louis) (Fixed Income)
Boatmen's Trust Company of Texas
Boeing Employee Credit Union
BofA Capital Management Inc. (Los Angeles)
The Boston Company Asset Management
Boston Safe Deposit and Trust Company

BPS Associates, Inc.
BR Investment Associates
Bradford & Marzec, Inc.
Branch Banking & Trust Company (Trust)
Stacey Braun Associates Incorporated
Bridgewater Associates Inc.
Brinson Partners, Inc.
Alex. Brown Investment Management
Brown Brothers Harriman & Co. (Investments)
Brown Brothers Harriman & Co. (Investments) (Chicago)
Brundage, Story and Rose
BZW Barclays Global Investors
Calamos Asset Management, Inc.
California Federal Bank, A Federal Savings Bank
California Public Employees' Retirement System
Calvert Asset Management Company, Inc.
Capital Guardian Trust Company
Capital Research & Management Company
Capital Research & Management Company (New York)
Capitol Federal Savings & Loan Association
Capitoline Investment Services, Inc. (Richmond)
Capitoline Investment Services, Inc. (Washington, DC)
Cardinal Management Corporation
Carillon Advisers, Inc.
Cashman, Farrell and Associates
Central Carolina Bank & Trust Co. (Portfolio)
Central Fidelity National Bank (Richmond) (Portfolio)
The Central Trust Bank
Century Investment Management Co. (CIMCO)
Charter One Bank, F.S.B.
Chase Manhattan Private Bank Investment Management
Chemical Bank (Portfolio)
Chevy Chase Federal Savings Bank
The Chicago Corporation — Asset Management Group
The Chubb Corporation
CIGNA Investment Management (U.S.A.)
CIGNA Investments, Inc.
Citibank, N.A. (Portfolio)
Citibank Private Banking Investment Division
Citicorp
Citizens Trust Company & Savings Bank (Trust)
Coastal Banc ssb
Collective Bank
Colonial Management Associates
Columbia Management Company
Columbus Circle Investors
Comerica Bank (Funds Management)
Commander Investment Corporation
Commerce Bancshares Inc.
Commerce Bank Investment Management Group
Commercial Federal Corporation
Commercial Union Investment Management
Commonwealth Investment Counsel
Compass Bank (Portfolio)
Compass Bank (Trust)
Conseco Capital Management
Consistent Asset Management Company
Continental Asset Management
CoreStates Investment Advisers, Inc.
The Crabbe-Huson Group, Inc.
CTT Investment Management Group
Dana Investment Advisors, Inc.
Dauphin Deposit Bank & Trust Company (Portfolio)
Dauphin Deposit Bank & Trust Company (Trust)
Davis Selected Advisers, L.P.
C.H. Dean Investment Associates
Dean Witter, Discover & Co.
Dean Witter InterCapital Inc.
Delaware Management Company Inc.
Delphi Capital Management, Inc.
Denver Investment Advisors Inc.
Deposit Guaranty Corp.

Deposit Guaranty National Bank (Portfolio)
Deposit Guaranty National Bank (Trust)
Dewey Square Investors Corporation
Dodge & Cox Inc.
The Dreyfus Corporation
Dreyfus Management
Eagle Asset Management, Inc.
Eastbridge Capital, Inc.
Eaton Corporation
Eaton Vance Management, Inc.
Employers Reinsurance Corporation
The Equitable Companies Incorporated
Equitable Investment Services, Inc.
Erie Insurance Group
Evangelical Lutheran Church-Board of Pensions
Evergreen Asset Management Corp. (New York)
Evergreen Asset Management, Inc. (Washington)
Exxon Corporation
Falcon Asset Management, Inc.
Federal Home Loan Bank of Chicago
Federal Home Loan Bank of Topeka
Federated Group
Federated Investors
Ferguson, Wellman, Rudd, Purdy & Van Winkle, Inc.
Fidelity Management & Research Company
Fidelity Management Trust Company
Fiduciary Asset Management
Fiduciary Trust Company International
Fiduciary Trust Company of Massachusetts
Fielding Management Company, Inc.
Fifth Third Bank
The Fifth Third Bank of Northwestern Ohio
Financial Counselors, Inc.
Financial Holding Corporation
First of America Investment Corporation
First American Corporation
First Asset Management
First Bank, N.A. (Omaha) (Trust)
First Bank Puerto Rico
First Chicago/NBD Corporation
First Citizens Bank & Trust Co.
First Commercial Corporation
First Commercial Capital Management
First Interstate Bank of California (Trust)
First Interstate Bank of Denver (Trust)
First Interstate Bank of Nevada
First Interstate Bank of Oregon (Trust)
First Interstate Bank of Texas (Portfolio)
First Manhattan Capital Management
First National Bank of Commerce (Investment)
First National Bank Gainesville (Portfolio)
First National Bank of Maryland (Portfolio)
First National Bank of Ohio
The First National Bank of Omaha (Trust)
First NH Bank
First NH Investment Services
First Tennessee Bank
First Union Corporation
First Union National Bank of Florida
First Union National Bank (New Jersey)
First Union National Bank (Pennsylvania) (Instl. Trust)
Fischer, Francis, Trees and Watts, Inc.
Fleet Bank of Maine (Portland)
Fleet Financial Group
Fleet Investment Advisors (Boston)
Florida State Board of Administration
The Ford Foundation
Fort Washington Investment Advisors Inc.
Fort Washington Investment Advisors Inc. (Cincinnati)
Fort Wayne National Bank (Trust)
Fortis Advisers, Inc.
Fortis Asset Management

Franklin Federal Bancorp, A Federal Savings Bank
Franklin Resources, Inc.
Fremont Investment Advisors Inc.
Fulton Bank (Trust)
Gabelli-O'Connor Fixed Income Management Co.
GEM Capital Management, Inc.
General Electric Investment Corporation
General Motors Investment Management Corp.
General Re Asset Management, Inc.
Gibraltar Advisors
The Glenmede Trust Company
Glickenhaus & Company (Investments)
GMG/Seneca Capital Management
GNA Capital Management Inc.
Golden Eagle Insurance Company
W.R. Grace & Company
Gradison-McDonald Asset Management
Grantham, Mayo, Van Otterloo & Company
Greenwich Street Advisors
Greenwich Street Advisors Municipal Management
Guardian Life Insurance Co. of America
Guardian Savings & Loan Association
Harbor Capital Management Company, Inc.
Harleysville Mutual Insurance Company
Harris Associates, L.P.
Harris Trust & Savings (Personal Trust)
Harvard Management Company
Hawaiian Electric Industries, Inc.
Hawaiian Trust Co., Ltd.
Heber Fuger Wendin Incorporated
Heine Securities Corporation
Heritage House Asset Management
Hibernia Corporation
Hibernia National Bank (Trust)
Hoisington Investment Management Co.
Hotchkis and Wiley
Howard Hughes Medical Institute
HSBC Asset Management Americas Inc.
Huntington Bancshares, Incorporated
The Huntington Trust Company, N.A.
Hyperion Capital Management, Inc.
IDS Fixed Income Advisors
Illinois State Board of Investment
Integra Financial Corporation
Intel Corporation
Inter-American Development Bank
Interstate/Johnson Lane, Inc.
INTRUST Bank (Trust)
INVESCO Management and Research, Inc.
INVESCO MIM Inc.
Investek Capital Management
Investment Advisers, Inc.
Investment Counselors of Maryland, Inc.
Investors Management Group, Ltd. (IMG)
Investors Savings Bank
Israel Discount Bank of New York
ITT Hartford Life Insurance Company
Jamaica Savings Bank, Fsb
John Alden Asset Management
John Hancock Advisers, Inc.
John Hancock Mutual Life Insurance Company
Johnson Investment Counsel Incorporated
Kansas City Life Insurance Company
Henry Kaufman & Company, Inc.
Kennedy Associates Inc.
Kentucky National Insurance Co.
Key Trust Company (Albany)
Key Trust Company (Syracuse)
KeyCorp
Keystone Custodian Funds, Inc.
Keystone Investment Services
Kiewit Investment Management

Luther King Capital Management
Laidlaw Capital Management, Inc.
The Laredo National Bank
Lazard Freres Asset Management
Leader Federal Bank for Savings
Lehman Brothers Global Asset Management, Inc. (New York)
Lexington Management Corporation
LGT Asset Management
Liberty Bank and Trust Co. (Oklahoma City) (Trust)
Liberty Capital Advisors, Inc.
Life Insurance Company of the Southwest
Life Partners Group
Lincoln National Corporation
Lipper & Company, L.P.
Loomis, Sayles & Company L.P.
Loomis, Sayles & Company L.P. (Bloomfield Hills)
Loomis, Sayles & Company L.P. (Milwaukee)
Loomis, Sayles & Company L.P. (Pasadena)
Loomis, Sayles & Company Inc. (San Francisco)
Loomis, Sayles & Company Inc. (Washington, D.C.)
Lord Abbett & Company
Lotsoff Capital Management
Lutheran Brotherhood
Madison Investment Advisors, Inc.
Madison Scottsdale
Manning & Napier Advisors Inc.
Manufacturers & Traders Trust Company (Portfolio)
Marine Midland Bank, N.A. (Trust)
Martin Marietta Corporation
Maryland State Retirement & Pension System
Masco Corporation
Massachusetts Financial Services Company
MBIA Securities Corporation
C.S. McKee & Company, Inc.
The Medical Protective Company
Mellon Bank, N.A. (Trust)
Mellon Private Asset Management Group
Mercantile — Safe Deposit & Trust Co. (Trust)
The Merchants Bank of New York
Merck & Co., Inc.
Merganser Capital Management Corporation
Meridian Investment Company
Merita Bank
Merrill Lynch Asset Management Inc.
MERUS Capital Management
M & I Investment Management Corp.
Michigan Department of Treasury
Midland National Life Insurance Company
Minton Investment Management
Mitchell Hutchins Asset Management, Inc.
Modern Woodmen of America
Montag & Caldwell, Incorporated
Montana Board of Investments
MONY Financial Services
J.P. Morgan & Company Inc.
J.P. Morgan Investment Management, Inc. (U.S.A.)
Morgan Grenfell Capital Management Inc.
Morgan Stanley Asset Management, Inc.
Munder Capital Management, Inc.
Mutual of America Capital Management Corporation
National Bank of Alaska
National City Bank of Akron
National City Bank, Indiana
National Life Investment Management Co.
National Mutual Funds Management Inc.
National Western Asset Management, Inc.
Nationwide Financial Services
NatWest Bank, N.A. (Portfolio)
Navy Federal Credit Union
NBD Bank, N.A. (Trust)
NCM Capital Management Group, Inc.
Nebraska State Investment Council

New Jersey Division of Investments
New Mexico Educational Retirement Board
New Mexico State Permanent Funds
New York State & Local Retirement Systems
New York State Teachers' Retirement System
Nicholas-Applegate Capital Management
Nike Securities (UIT Management)
Nikko Capital Management (U.S.A.)
North Carolina Department of State Treasurer
North Side Savings Bank
Northern Trust Corporation
Northwestern Mutual Life Insurance Co.
Norwest Bank Indiana, N.A.
Norwest Bank Iowa, N.A.
Norwest Investment Management (Minnesota)
Norwest Investments & Trust Services
Oak Hill Partners
OFFITBANK
Ohio Police & Firemen's Disability & Pension Fund
Ohio Public Employees' Retirement System
Old Kent Bank & Trust Company (Trust)
Olympic Capital Management, Inc.
OnBank, Inc. (Portfolio)
Oppenheimer Management Corporation
Oregon State Treasury Investment Division — Fixed Income
PACCAR Incorporated
Pacholder Associates, Inc.
Pacific Income Advisers
Pacific Investment Management Co. (PIMCO)
Pacific Mutual Life Insurance Company
PanAgora Asset Management, Inc. (U.S.A.)
The Patterson Capital Corporation
Pekin Insurance Company
Pennsylvania Public School Employees' Retirement System
Pension Boards — United Church of Christ
Peregrine Capital Management
Phoenix Duff & Phelps Investment Management Co. (Chicago)
Phoenix Duff & Phelps Investment Management Co. (Hartford)
Pillar Point Capital Management Inc.
Pioneering Management Corporation
Piper Capital Management Inc.
Plaza Investment Managers, Inc.
PNC Bank — Asset Liability (Portfolio)
PNC Bank Ohio (Trust)
PNC Institutional Management Corp.
Ponder Investment Company
The Portfolio Group, Inc.
PPM America Inc.
Premier Investment Advisors
Presidential Life Insurance Company
T. Rowe Price Associates, Inc.
Princeton Insurance Companies
The Private Bank of Bank of Boston
The Provident Bank (Portfolio)
Provident Life & Accident Insurance Co.
Provident Mutual Life Insurance Company
Prudential Capital Management
The Putnam Management Company Inc.
Qualivest Capital Management, Inc.
Quantilogic Asset Management
Reams Asset Management Company Inc.
Regents of the University of California
Regions Financial Corporation (Investments)
Reich & Tang L.P.
Reliance Insurance Company
Renaissance Investment Management Inc.
Richmond Capital Management, Inc.
Riggs Investment Management Corporation
Rittenhouse Financial Services Inc.
Rodney Square Management Corporation
The Rushmore Funds, Inc.
Frank Russell Investment Management Co.

RXR Capital Management, Inc.
Ryan Labs, Inc.
SAFECO Insurance Companies
The St. Paul Companies Inc.
Sallie Mae
Salomon Brothers Asset Management Inc. (U.S.A.)
Santander National Bank
Schroder Wertheim Investment Services
Charles Schwab Investment Management
Scudder Stevens & Clark, Inc. (Boston)
Scudder Stevens & Clark, Inc. (Chicago)
Scudder Stevens & Clark, Inc. (Cincinnati)
Scudder Stevens & Clark, Inc. (San Francisco)
Seaboard Investment Advisers Inc.
Sears Roebuck and Company
Securities Management and Research Inc.
Security Benefit Life Insurance Co. of Kansas
Selective Insurance of America
J & W Seligman & Co., Incorporated
Shay Assets Management Co.
Shell Oil Company
Signet Banking Corporation
Sit Investment Fixed Income Advisors Inc.
Skandia Investment Management Inc. (U.S.A.)
Herbert R. Smith, Inc.
William B. Smith & Company Inc.
Smith Barney, Inc. (Capital Management)
Smith Barney Investment Advisors
Smith, Graham & Co. Asset Managers
Society Asset Management, Inc.
Society National Bank (Portfolio)
South Carolina Retirement System
South Dakota Investment Council
Southern Farm Bureau Casualty Insurance Co.
Southern Farm Bureau Life Insurance Co.
SouthTrust Bank of Alabama, N.A. (Trust)
Standish, Ayer & Wood Inc.
Standish International Management Co., L.P.
Stanford Management Company
State Street Bank & Trust (Trust)
State Street Boston Corporation
State Street Global Advisors
State Street Research & Management Co.
Staten Island Savings Bank
STI Capital Management
Strong Capital Management Inc.
SunFinancial Group
SunTrust Bank, Nashville, N.A. (Trust)
SwissRe Advisers Inc.
TCF Bank Minnesota fsb
Teachers' Retirement System of Texas
Teledyne Inc.
Templeton Global Bond Managers, Inc.
Tennessee Consolidated Retirement System
Texaco Inc.
Texas Commerce Bank, N.A. (Houston) (Trust)
Texas County & District Retirement System
Third Federal Savings & Loan Association of Cleveland
Thompson, Siegel & Walmsley, Inc.
Thornburg Management Company, Inc.
TIG Holdings Inc.
Todd Investment Advisors Inc.
Torchmark Corporation
Trust Company Bank of Georgia (Trust)
Trust Company of the West (TCW) (High Yield Dept.)
Trustmark National Bank (Portfolio)
Twentieth Century Insurance Company
UBS Asset Management, Inc. (U.S.A.)
Union Capital Advisors (San Diego)
Union Carbide Corporation
United Air Lines Employees Credit Union
United Farm Bureau Life Insurance Co.

United Jersey Bank (Princeton) (Trust)
United of Omaha Life Insurance Company
United Services Advisors Inc.
U.S. National Bank of Oregon (Portfolio)
U.S. Steel & Carnegie Pension Fund
United States Trust Company of Boston
United States Trust Co. of California., N.A.
United States Trust Company of New York (Trust)
U.S. West, Inc.
University of Texas System — Office of Investments
UNUM Life Insurance Company
USLIFE Advisers Inc.
The Vanguard Group, Inc.
Van Kampen American Capital Investment Advisory Corp.
Van Kampen American Capital Management & Research
Vaughan, Nelson, Scarborough & McConnell Inc.
Victoria Bank & Trust Company (Trust)
Virtus Capital Management
Voyageur Fund Managers
Wachovia Corporation
Wachovia Bank Capital Management
Wachovia Bank Capital Management (Atlanta)
Waddell & Reed Investment Management Co.
Warburg, Pincus Counsellors, Inc.
Washington Federal Savings & Loan Association
Washington State Investment Board
Webster Bank
Wellington Management Company
Wells Fargo Bank, N.A. (Treasury)
Wentworth, Hauser & Violich, Inc.
WESTAMERICA Bank
Western Asset Management Company
Western Financial Savings Bank, Fsb
Westfield Companies
Whitney National Bank (Portfolio)
Williams, Jones & Associates Inc.
Wilmington Trust Company (Fixed Income)
Winterthur Swiss Group
Wolf, Webb, Burk & Campbell Inc.
Woodmen of the World Life Insurance Society
The World Bank
YMCA Retirement Fund
The Zenith Insurance Company
Zirkin Cutler Investments

Derivatives Use: Balance Sheet/ Risk Management

Acorn Derivatives Management Corp.
Advanced Micro Devices, Inc.
AEGON U.S.A. Investment Management (Cedar Rapids)
Aetna Life & Casualty (Portfolio Management Group)
AgriBank, FCB
H.F. Ahmanson & Company
Alcoa
Alfa Corporation
Alliance Capital Management L.P.
Allianz Investment Corporation
Allmerica Asset Management, Inc.
Allstate Insurance Company
AMBAC Inc.
AMBAC Financial Services, L.P.
AMCORE Bank, N.A. Rockford
AMCORE Financial, Inc.
American Express Company
American Express Bank Ltd.
American Express Financial Advisors
American Family Insurance Group
American Family Life Assurance Company (AFLAC)
American General Corporation
American Mutual Life Insurance Company
American National Corporation
American President Companies, Ltd.
American Savings Bank, F.A.
American United Life Insurance Company
Amoco Corporation
AMR Investment Services, Inc.
AmSouth Bank N.A. (Portfolio)
AON Advisors Incorporated
Arvin Industries, Inc.
Associates Corporation of North America
AT&T
Back Bay Advisors, L.P.
BANC ONE Corporation
Banco Popular of Puerto Rico (Portfolio)
Bank of America NT & SA (Portfolio)
Bank of America Texas, N.A.
Bank of Boston (Treasury)
The Bank of California, N.A.
Bank of Hawaii (Investments)
The Bank of New York Company, Inc.
The Bank of North Dakota
Bank of Oklahoma, N.A. (Portfolio)
The Bank of Tokyo Trust Company (Securities & Investments)
Bank United of Texas, FSB
Bank of the West (Portfolio)
Barnett Banks, Inc.
Bausch & Lomb Incorporated
Baxter International Inc.
Bay View Federal Bank, A Federal Savings Bank
BayBank Boston, N.A. (Portfolio)
BellSouth Corporation
Beneficial Insurance Group, Inc.
Bessemer Trust Company, N.A.
BlackRock Financial Management L.P.
Bluebonnet Savings Bank Fsb
The Boatmen's National Bank of St. Louis (Portfolio)
The Boeing Company
Branch Banking & Trust Company (BB&T-NC) (Portfolio)
BZW Barclays Global Investors
California Federal Bank, A Federal Savings Bank
California State Teachers' Retirement System
Calvert Asset Management Company, Inc.
Campbell Soup Company
Capital One Financial Corporation
Caremark International Inc.

Carillon Advisers, Inc.
CDC Investment Management Corp. (CIMCO)
Central Carolina Bank & Trust Co. (Portfolio)
Central Fidelity National Bank (Richmond) (Portfolio)
Century Investment Management Co. (CIMCO)
Charter One Bank, F.S.B.
Charter One Bank, F.S.B. (Michigan)
Chemical Bank (Portfolio)
CIGNA Investments, Inc.
Circus Circus Enterprises, Inc.
Citibank, N.A. (Portfolio)
Citicorp
Citizens Federal Bank, F.S.B.
Citizens National Bank of Evansville (Portfolio)
Coast Federal Bank, Federal Savings Bank (Administration)
Coastal Banc ssb
Colonial Management Associates
Comerica Bank (Funds Management)
Commercial Union Investment Management
Commonwealth Investment Counsel
Compass Bank (Portfolio)
Corning Incorporated
Crestar Bank (Portfolio)
Dean Witter, Discover & Co.
Deposit Guaranty Corp.
Deposit Guaranty National Bank (Portfolio)
The Dime Savings Bank of New York, FSB
Dimensional Fund Advisors, Inc.
Dominion Resources, Inc.
Dow Jones & Company, Inc.
The Dreyfus Corporation
Duke Power Company
Eaton Corporation
Ecolab Inc.
Employers Reinsurance Corporation
Enhance Financial Services Group Inc.
Equifax, Inc.
The Equitable Companies Incorporated
Evangelical Lutheran Church-Board of Pensions
Exxon Corporation
Farmers Insurance Group of Companies
Federal Home Loan Bank of Atlanta
Federal Home Loan Bank of Boston
Federal Home Loan Bank of Chicago
Federal Home Loan Bank of San Francisco
Federal Home Loan Bank of Seattle
Federal Home Loan Bank of Topeka
Federal National Mortgage Association
The FINOVA Group Inc.
First of America Bank Corporation
First American Corporation
First Bank Puerto Rico
First Bank System (Portfolio)
First Chicago/NBD Corporation
First Federal Savings and Loan Association of Rochester
First Interstate Bank of Texas (Portfolio)
First Investors Management Co., Inc.
First National Bank of Commerce (Investment)
First National Bank Evergreen Park (Portfolio)
First National Bank of Maryland (Portfolio)
First Nationwide Bank, A Federal Savings Bank
First NH Bank
First NH Investment Services
First Tennessee Bank
First Union Corporation
First Union National Bank of North Carolina — Funds Mgmt.
Flaherty & Crumrine, Inc.
Fleet Financial Group

Fleet Investment Advisors (Boston)
Fleming Companies, Inc.
Ford Motor Company
Freeport-McMoRan Inc.
Fremont General Corporation
The Frost National Bank (Portfolio)
General Accident Group
General American Investment Management Company (GAIMCO)
General Electric Company
General Electric Capital Corporation
General Motors Acceptance Corporation
General Re Asset Management, Inc.
GMG/Seneca Capital Management
GNA Capital Management Inc.
Goldman Sachs Asset Management (U.S.A.)
W.R. Grace & Company
Gradison-McDonald Asset Management
Great Western Bank, a Federal Savings Bank (Treasury)
The Greater New York Savings Bank
Guaranty Federal Bank, F.S.B.
Guardian Life Insurance Co. of America
M.A. Hanna Company
Harris Corporation
Harris Investment Management, Inc.
Harsco Corporation
Harvard Management Company
Heber Fuger Wendin Incorporated
Hercules Incorporated
Heritage Asset Management, Inc.
Hibernia Corporation
Honeywell, Inc.
Hotchkis and Wiley
Household International, Inc.
Humana Inc.
Huntington Bancshares, Incorporated
I.B.J.-Schroder Bank & Trust Co. (Trust)
Independence One Capital Management Corp.
Independent Bank Corp.
ING Investment Management Inc. — Americas Region
Integra Financial Corporation
Intel Corporation
Inter-Regional Financial Group, Inc.
Interstate/Johnson Lane, Inc.
ITT Corporation
ITT Hartford Life Insurance Company
John Hancock Mutual Life Insurance Company
Johnson Controls, Inc.
KeyCorp
Keystone Investment Services
Knights of Columbus
LaSalle National Bank (Portfolio)
Leader Federal Bank for Savings
Leucadia National Corporation
LGT Asset Management
Libby, Inc.
Liberty Bank and Trust Co. (Oklahoma City) (Portfolio)
Lincoln National Corporation
Lincoln National Investment Management Co.
Litton Industries, Inc.
The Long Island Savings Bank, F.S.B.
Los Angeles County Treasurer
Magna Group, Inc.
Manufacturers & Traders Trust Company (Portfolio)
Manufacturers & Traders Trust Company (Treasury)
Mark Twain Bank (Portfolio)
Marshall & Ilsley Corporation
Massachusetts Financial Services Company
Massachusetts Mutual Life Insurance Co.

MBNA Corporation
McDonald's Corporation
McDonnell Douglas Corporation
MCI Communications Corporation
McKesson Corporation
MCN Corporation
The Mead Corporation
Mellon Bank, N.A. (Portfolio)
Mercantile Banks of St. Louis, N.A.
Merck & Co., Inc.
Meridian Bancorp, Inc.
Meridian Bank (Portfolio)
Merita Bank
Merrill Lynch Asset Management Inc.
Metropolitan Life Insurance Company
MGIC Investment Corporation
Michigan National Bank (Portfolio)
Millipore Corporation
MIMLIC Asset Management Company
Minnesota State Board of Investment
MONY Financial Services
J.P. Morgan & Company Inc.
National Bank of Alaska
National Bank of Commerce (Portfolio)
NationsBank (Charlotte) (Funds Management)
NatWest Bank, N.A. (Portfolio)
Neuberger & Berman Management Inc.
New York Life Insurance Company (U.S.A)
Nicholas-Applegate Capital Management (Houston)
Nikko Capital Management (U.S.A.)
Nomura Capital Management (U.S.A.)
North Fork Bank (Portfolio)
North Side Savings Bank
The Northern Trust Company (Treasury)
Northern Trust Corporation
Northrop Grumman Corporation
Northwestern Mutual Life Insurance Co.
NYNEX Corporation
Oak Hill Partners
The Ohio National Life Insurance Company
Old Kent Bank & Trust Company (Portfolio)
Old National Bank in Evansville (Portfolio)
OnBank, Inc. (Portfolio)
One Valley Bancorp of West Virginia
Oppenheimer Management Corporation
Oryx Energy Company
Owens-Corning Fiberglass Corporation
PACCAR Incorporated
Pacific Investment Management Co. (PIMCO)
Pacificorp
Paul Revere Investment Management Corp.
Payden & Rygel Investment Counsel
People's Bank
People's Bank (Investment)
Physicians Mutual Insurance Company
Pioneer Financial Services, Inc.
Piper Capital Management Inc.
PNC Bank — Asset Liability (Portfolio)
PPM America Inc.
PriMerit Bank, A Federal Savings Bank
Principal Mutual Life Insurance Company
Protective Life Corporation
The Provident Bank (Portfolio)
Provident Life & Accident Insurance Co.
Provident Mutual Life Insurance Company
Providian Corporation
Prudential Capital Management
Public Employees Retirement Association of Colorado

Public Service Enterprise Group Incorporated
The Putnam Management Company Inc.
The Quaker Oats Company
Quantilogic Asset Management
Raytheon Company
RCM Capital Management
Republic National Bank of NY (Treasury)
Rite Aid Corporation
The Rochester Community Savings Bank
Roosevelt Bank, A Federal Savings Bank
Royal Caribbean Cruises Ltd.
RXR Capital Management, Inc.
SAFECO Insurance Companies
St. Paul Federal Bank for Savings
Sallie Mae
Salomon Brothers Asset Management Inc. (U.S.A.)
Santander National Bank
M.D. Sass Investors Services, Inc.
Schlumberger, Ltd.
SCOR Reinsurance Company
Scudder Stevens & Clark, Inc. (Los Angeles)
Scudder Stevens & Clark, Inc. (San Francisco)
Sears Roebuck and Company
Security Benefit Life Insurance Co. of Kansas
Security Life of Denver Insurance Co.
Signet Banking Corporation
Smith Affiliated Capital Corporation
Smith, Breeden Associates
Smith, Breeden Associates (Boulder)
Smith, Breeden Associates (Chapel Hill)
Smith, Breeden Associates (Dallas)
Smith's Food & Drug Centers Inc.
Society Asset Management, Inc.
Society National Bank (Portfolio)
South Boston Savings Bank
SouthTrust Bank of Alabama, N.A. (Portfolio)
Southwest Corporate Federal Credit Union
Sovereign Bank, A Federal Savings Bank
Sprint Corporation
Standard Federal Bank
Standard Insurance Company
Standish, Ayer & Wood Inc.
Standish International Management Co., L.P.
Stanford Management Company
Star Bank, N.A. (Cincinnati) (Portfolio)
State Compensation Insurance Fund
State Street Boston Corporation
State Street Global Advisors
State Street Research & Management Co.
Stein Roe & Farnham Incorporated
Strategic Fixed Income L.P.
Summit Bank (Portfolio)
SunFinancial Group
Synovus Financial Corporation
TCF Bank Minnesota fsb
Teachers Insurance & Annuity Association
Teledyne Inc.
Templeton Global Bond Managers, Inc.
Tenneco Inc.
Tennessee Consolidated Retirement System
Texaco Inc.
TIG Holdings Inc.
The Transamerica Corporation
Transamerica Investment Services Inc.
Travelers Group
The Travelers Insurance Company
Union Bank — Los Angeles
Union Bank of Switzerland Private Banking

Union Carbide Corporation
Union Labor Life Insurance Co. (ULLICO)
Union Planters National Bank (Funds Management)
United Air Lines Employees Credit Union
United Asset Management Corporation
United Jersey Bank (Portfolio)
United Missouri Bank, N.A. (Portfolio)
United Missouri Investment Counsel Service
U.S. National Bank of Oregon (Portfolio)
United States Trust Company of Boston
United States Trust Company of New York (Portfolio)
U.S. West, Inc.
USBANCORP, Inc.
Valley National Bank (New Jersey) (Portfolio)
Van Kampen American Capital Investment Advisory Corp.
Voyageur Asset Management
Wachovia Corporation
Waddell & Reed Investment Management Co.
Warburg, Pincus Counsellors, Inc.
Washington Square Advisers Inc.
Wellington Management Company
Wells Fargo Bank, N.A. (Treasury)
WESTAMERICA Bank
Western Financial Savings Bank, Fsb
Whitney National Bank (Portfolio)
Wilmington Trust Company (Portfolio)
State of Wisconsin Investment Board
WMX Technologies, Inc.
Woodmen of the World Life Insurance Society
The World Bank
World Savings & Loan Association, A Fed. Svgs. & Loan Assn.
Zions First National Bank (Portfolio)
Zurich-Kemper Investments, Inc.

Exchange-traded Options & Futures

Derivatives Week

A PUBLICATION OF INSTITUTIONAL INVESTOR, INC.

NOVEMBER 27, 1995
VOL. IV, NO. 47

II ACQUIRES FUND WORLD

Institutional Investor, Inc. has acquired **Fund World, Inc.**, publisher of the leading newsletters covering the mutual fund industry. The three newsletters, *Fund Action*, *Fund Decoder* and *Fund Directions*, bring the number of II newsletters to 20. For subscription call (212) 224-3233. For advertising, call (212) 224-3578.

IN THE NEWS

HSBC FIRES UP STRUCTURED PRODUCT BIZ 2
EXECUTIVES SCHUFFLE AT DEUTSCHE MORGAN 2
FRANKFURT BROKERAGE LOSES OPTIONS HEAD 4
SPANISH COMPANY LOOKS INTO RISKMETRICS 4
RANGE BINARY AND REVERSE BARRIER OPTIONS EYED 4
U.K. FORUM FOR END USERS READY TO LAUNCH 6
BASLE COMMITTEE TO SET RISK MODEL RULES 6
MANAGERS WARY OF J.P. MORGAN'S COVERED CALL PITCH 6

USER STRATEGIES

IRISH MANAGER BUYS PUTS AND CALLS AGAINST U.S. $ 8
G-BAR SELLS WESTINGHOUSE VOLATILITY 8
CHRISTIANA BANK LOCKS IN RATES 8

DEPARTMENTS

USER PROFILE: MORRIS GROSSFELD OF THE THOMAS COOK GROUP 9
LEARNING CURVE: BARRIER VARIETY 10
MARKETS 12

TRANSPORTATION EQUIPMENT GIANT CONSIDERS OPTIONS USE.

Bombardier Capital, the financing arm of **Bombardier**, is looking into increasing its use of over-the-counter options to manage the company's interest rate and currency risks, according to **Andrew Baranowsky**, treasurer. The company, with annual sales in excess of US$4 billion, wants to take a more proactive stance in managing its interest rate and currency exposures by using options in a greater quantity, he said.

The designer, developer, manufacturer and marketer of transportation, equipment,

(continued on page 15)

JAPANESE INVESTORS SAID TO DRIVE NOVEL TRIPLE CURRENCY BOND MARKET.

Japanese investors on a quest for yield have been driving a novel market for long-term triple currency bonds, according to market officials close to the transactions. The yen-denominated bonds make coupon payments in any of three designated currencies, determined by the issuer, and maintain yen principal payments.

The bonds have typically been issued in yen with an embedded strip of forex options that commit the issuer to make coupon payments in one of three currencies such as Australian dollars, Deutsche marks and U.S. dollars. Triple currency bonds pay an annualized

(continued on page 15)

WILL GOLDMAN SUSPEND INTEREST RATE DERIVATIVES MARKETING IN NON-JAPAN ASIA?

Goldman Sachs may be looking to halt interest rate derivatives marketing in non-Japan Asia—the major growth area of Asia—at least temporarily, according to a source familiar with the situation. The investment bank is reviewing its business plans for 1996 and has asked **Winston Chan**, currently executive director and head of interest rate derivatives marketing in Hong Kong, to transfer to debt capital markets to reignite that department, he added.

One source close to the situation confirmed that Goldman is reviewing its 1996

(continued on page 14)

PARIBAS TO CREATE DERIVATIVE HEDGE FUNDS THROUGH NEW FUND-OF-FUND OPERATION.

Paribas Asset Management is preparing an alternative investment operation in London that will develop and market fund-of-fund products, including derivative hedge funds, according to *Global Private Banking*, a new publication launched last week by *Institutional Investor*. Paribas runs a derivatives hedge fund internally called the Paribas Global Derivatives Fund, but it is intended for investors that can tolerate high risk, according to **Alexandre Leibeskind**, a private banking official at Paribas in Geneva. The derivative hedge funds created by the new desk will carry reduced risk because they will be

(continued on page 14)

Acorn Derivatives Management Corp.
Adams, Viner & Mosler
Advanced Micro Devices, Inc.
Advisers Capital Management Inc.
AEGON U.S.A. Investment Management (Cedar Rapids)
Aetna Life & Casualty (Portfolio Management Group)
AIM Advisors, Inc.
Alcoa
Alfa Corporation
Alliance Capital Management L.P.
Allied-Signal Inc.
Allmerica Asset Management, Inc.
Allstate Insurance Company
AMBAC Inc.
AMCORE Bank, N.A. Rockford
AMCORE Financial, Inc.
American Express Company
American Express Bank Ltd.
American Express Financial Advisors
American Mutual Life Insurance Company
Amoco Corporation
AMR Investment Services, Inc.
AmSouth Bank N.A. (Portfolio)
ANB Investment Management & Trust Co. of Chicago
Anhalt/O'Connell, Inc.
AON Advisors Incorporated
Ark Asset Management Company, Inc.
Arvin Industries, Inc.
Atlantic Asset Management Partners Inc.
AT&T
Back Bay Advisors, L.P.
Banco Popular of Puerto Rico (Portfolio)
Bank of America NT & SA (Portfolio)
Bank of Boston (Treasury)
The Bank of California, N.A.
The Bank of New York Company, Inc.
The Bank of Tokyo Trust Company (Pension & Investments)
Bank United of Texas, FSB
Bank of the West (Portfolio)
Bankers Trust Global Investment Management
Bankers Trust — New York Corporation (Portfolio)
Barnett Banks, Inc.
Baxter International Inc.
BEA Associates
Benham Capital Management Group
Berkeley Capital Management
Sanford C. Bernstein & Co., Inc.
BlackRock Financial Management L.P.
Bluebonnet Savings Bank Fsb
The Boatmen's National Bank of St. Louis (Portfolio)
The Boston Company Asset Management
BR Investment Associates
Branch Banking & Trust Company (BB&T-NC) (Portfolio)
Bridgewater Associates Inc.
Brinson Partners, Inc.
Brown Brothers Harriman & Co. (Investments)
BZW Barclays Global Investors
Calamos Asset Management, Inc.
California Federal Bank, A Federal Savings Bank
California Public Employees' Retirement System
California State Teachers' Retirement System
Calvert Asset Management Company, Inc.
Campbell Soup Company
Capital Guardian Trust Company
Capital Research & Management Company (New York)
Cardinal Management Corporation
Carillon Advisers, Inc.
CDC Investment Management Corp. (CIMCO)

Central Carolina Bank & Trust Co. (Portfolio)
Chase Manhattan Private Bank Investment Management
Chemical Bank (Portfolio)
The Chubb Corporation
CIGNA Investment Management (U.S.A.)
CIGNA Investments, Inc.
Circus Circus Enterprises, Inc.
Citibank, N.A. (Portfolio)
Citibank Private Banking Investment Division
Citicorp
Colonial Management Associates
Columbus Circle Investors
Comerica Bank (Funds Management)
Commander Investment Corporation
Commerce Bancshares Inc.
Commerce Bank Investment Management Group
Commonwealth Investment Counsel
Compass Bank (Portfolio)
Conseco Capital Management
Continental Asset Management
Corning Incorporated
Dean Witter, Discover & Co.
Dean Witter InterCapital Inc.
Delphi Capital Management, Inc.
Deposit Guaranty National Bank (Portfolio)
The Dime Savings Bank of New York, FSB
The Dreyfus Corporation
Eastbridge Capital, Inc.
Eaton Corporation
Eaton Vance Management, Inc.
Farmers Insurance Group of Companies
Federal Home Loan Bank of Boston
Federal Home Loan Bank of San Francisco
Federal Home Loan Bank of Seattle
Federal Home Loan Bank of Topeka
Federated Investors
Fidelity Management & Research Company
Fidelity Management Trust Company
Fiduciary Asset Management
Fiduciary Trust Company International
Fielding Management Company, Inc.
First Bank Puerto Rico
First Chicago/NBD Corporation
First Citizens Bank & Trust Co.
First Federal Savings and Loan Association of Rochester
First National Bank of Maryland (Portfolio)
First Union Corporation
First Union National Bank of North Carolina — Funds Mgmt.
Flaherty & Crumrine, Inc.
Fleet Financial Group
Fleet Investment Advisors (Boston)
Florida State Board of Administration
Ford Motor Company
Fortis Advisers, Inc.
General Motors Acceptance Corporation
General Re Asset Management, Inc.
GMG/Seneca Capital Management
GNA Capital Management Inc.
Goldman Sachs Asset Management (U.S.A.)
Gradison-McDonald Asset Management
Grantham, Mayo, Van Otterloo & Company
Greenwich Street Advisors
Guaranty Federal Bank, F.S.B.
M.A. Hanna Company
Harris Investment Management, Inc.
Harvard Management Company
Hawaiian Electric Industries, Inc.
Hercules Incorporated

Heritage Asset Management, Inc.
Hibernia Corporation
Humana Inc.
I.B.J.-Schroder Bank & Trust Co. (Trust)
IDS Fixed Income Advisors
Intel Corporation
Inter-American Development Bank
Inter-Regional Financial Group, Inc.
Interstate/Johnson Lane, Inc.
Investment Advisers, Inc.
Investment Counselors of Maryland, Inc.
ITT Hartford Life Insurance Company
John Hancock Advisers, Inc.
John Hancock Mutual Life Insurance Company
Kentucky National Insurance Co.
KeyCorp
Kiewit Investment Management
LaSalle National Bank (Portfolio)
Lazard Freres Asset Management
Leucadia National Corporation
LGT Asset Management
Lincoln National Corporation
Lincoln National Investment Management Co.
Litton Industries, Inc.
Los Angeles County Treasurer
Lotsoff Capital Management
Lutheran Brotherhood
Manufacturers & Traders Trust Company (Portfolio)
Masco Corporation
Massachusetts Financial Services Company
Massachusetts Mutual Life Insurance Co.
Mellon Bank, N.A. (Portfolio)
Mellon Bank, N.A. (Trust)
Meridian Bancorp, Inc.
Meridian Bank (Portfolio)
Merita Bank
Merrill Lynch Asset Management Inc.
Minnesota State Board of Investment
J.P. Morgan & Company Inc.
J.P. Morgan Investment Management, Inc. (U.S.A.)
National Mutual Funds Management Inc.
NationsBank (Charlotte) (Funds Management)
NatWest Bank, N.A. (Portfolio)
Neuberger & Berman Management Inc.
New York Life Insurance Company (U.S.A)
Nicholas-Applegate Capital Management (Houston)
Nike Securities (UIT Management)
Nikko Capital Management (U.S.A.)
The Northern Trust Company (Treasury)
Northern Trust Corporation
Northwestern Mutual Life Insurance Co.
Norwest Bank Iowa, N.A.
Norwest Investment Management (Minnesota)
NYNEX Corporation
Oak Hill Partners
OFFITBANK
Oppenheimer Management Corporation
PACCAR Incorporated
Pacific Investment Management Co. (PIMCO)
PanAgora Asset Management, Inc. (U.S.A.)
Payden & Rygel Investment Counsel
Pennsylvania Public School Employees' Retirement System
People's Bank
People's Bank (Investment)
Pioneer Financial Services, Inc.
PNC Bank — Asset Liability (Portfolio)
PNC Bank Ohio (Trust)
PPM America Inc.

GRADUATE AND PROFESSIONAL EDUCATION IN FINANCIAL DERIVATIVES/RISK MANAGEMENT

Center for the Study of Futures and Options Markets
Department of Finance
Pamplin College of Business
Virginia Tech

The Pamplin College of Business at Virginia Tech offers two programs in Financial Derivatives/Risk Management. A degree program leading to a track in Financial Risk Management within an MBA degree is offered at the Blacksburg campus (full-time) and the Falls Church graduate center (part-time/evening). A continuing education program leading to a certificate in Financial Risk Management is offered at the Falls Church graduate center with classes held on Fridays.

The programs are supported by Virginia Tech's Center for the Study of Futures and Options Markets (CSFOM), a leading source of research and education on economic and public policy issues in financial derivatives and risk management. The Center sponsors monthly luncheon meetings of the Financial Innovation Study Committee/Weird Instruments Study Committee.

For more information about the programs or the CSFOM or to interview students, contact Professor Don Chance, Ph.D., CFA, (dmc @ vt.edu) at 540-231-5061 or Professor Robert Mackay, Ph.D., at 703-698-6036.

T. Rowe Price Associates, Inc.
Principal Mutual Life Insurance Company
Protective Life Corporation
The Provident Bank (Portfolio)
Provident Mutual Life Insurance Company
Providian Corporation
Prudential Capital Management
Public Employees Retirement Association of Colorado
Public Service Enterprise Group Incorporated
The Putnam Management Company Inc.
The Quaker Oats Company
Quantilogic Asset Management
Raytheon Company
RCM Capital Management
Regents of the University of California
Renaissance Investment Management Inc.
Republic National Bank of NY (Treasury)
The Rochester Community Savings Bank
Roosevelt Bank, A Federal Savings Bank
Frank Russell Investment Management Co.
RXR Capital Management, Inc.
SAFECO Insurance Companies
Sallie Mae
Salomon Brothers Asset Management Inc. (U.S.A.)
Santander National Bank
M.D. Sass Investors Services, Inc.
Scudder Stevens & Clark, Inc. (Boston)
Scudder Stevens & Clark, Inc. (Chicago)
Scudder Stevens & Clark, Inc. (Los Angeles)
Scudder Stevens & Clark, Inc. (San Francisco)
Seaboard Investment Advisers Inc.
Sears Roebuck and Company
Security Benefit Life Insurance Co. of Kansas
Security Life of Denver Insurance Co.
Shell Oil Company
Signet Banking Corporation
Smith Affiliated Capital Corporation
Smith, Breeden Associates
Smith, Breeden Associates (Boulder)
Smith, Breeden Associates (Chapel Hill)
Smith, Breeden Associates (Dallas)
Society Asset Management, Inc.
Society National Bank (Portfolio)
South Dakota Investment Council
Southwest Corporate Federal Credit Union
Sprint Corporation
Standard Federal Bank
Standish, Ayer & Wood Inc.
Standish International Management Co., L.P.
Stanford Management Company
State Street Boston Corporation
State Street Global Advisors
State Street Research & Management Co.
Strategic Fixed Income L.P.
Strong Capital Management Inc.
SunFinancial Group
Teachers Insurance & Annuity Association
Texaco Inc.
TIG Holdings Inc.
The Transamerica Corporation
Transamerica Investment Services Inc.
Travelers Group
The Travelers Insurance Company
Union Capital Advisors (San Diego)
Union Carbide Corporation
United Jersey Bank (Portfolio)
United Missouri Bank, N.A. (Portfolio)
United Missouri Investment Counsel Service

United of Omaha Life Insurance Company
U.S. National Bank of Oregon (Portfolio)
U.S. West, Inc.
The Vanguard Group, Inc.
Van Kampen American Capital Investment Advisory Corp.
Wachovia Corporation
Wachovia Bank Capital Management
Waddell & Reed Investment Management Co.
Warburg, Pincus Counsellors, Inc.
Washington Square Advisers Inc.
Webster Bank
Wellington Management Company
WESTAMERICA Bank
Western Asset Management Company
Western Financial Savings Bank, Fsb
State of Wisconsin Investment Board
WMX Technologies, Inc.
The World Bank
YMCA Retirement Fund
Zurich-Kemper Investments, Inc.

OTC Derivatives

Acorn Derivatives Management Corp.
Adams, Viner & Mosler
Advanced Micro Devices, Inc.
AEGON U.S.A. Investment Management (Cedar Rapids)
Aetna Life & Casualty (Portfolio Management Group)
AgriBank, FCB
H.F. Ahmanson & Company
AIM Advisors, Inc.
Alcoa
Alfa Corporation
Alliance Capital Management L.P.
Alliance Capital Management (Minneapolis)
Allmerica Asset Management, Inc.
Allstate Insurance Company
AMBAC Inc.
AMBAC Financial Services, L.P.
AMCORE Bank, N.A. Rockford
AMCORE Financial, Inc.
American Express Company
American Express Bank Ltd.
American Express Financial Advisors
American Family Life Assurance Company (AFLAC)
American General Corporation
American Mutual Life Insurance Company
American National Corporation
American President Companies, Ltd.
American Savings Bank, F.A.
Amoco Corporation
AmSouth Bank N.A. (Portfolio)
AON Advisors Incorporated
Arvin Industries, Inc.
AT&T
Back Bay Advisors, L.P.
BANC ONE Corporation
Banco Popular of Puerto Rico (Portfolio)
Bank of America NT & SA (Portfolio)
Bank of America Texas, N.A.
Bank of Boston (Treasury)
The Bank of California, N.A.
Bank of Hawaii (Investments)
The Bank of New York Company, Inc.
The Bank of North Dakota
Bank of Oklahoma, N.A. (Portfolio)
The Bank of Tokyo Trust Company (Securities & Investments)
Bank United of Texas, FSB
Bank of the West (Portfolio)
Bankers Trust Global Investment Management
Baring Asset Management Company
Barnett Banks, Inc.
Bausch & Lomb Incorporated
Baxter International Inc.
Bay View Federal Bank, A Federal Savings Bank
BayBank Boston, N.A. (Portfolio)
BEA Associates
BellSouth Corporation
Sanford C. Bernstein & Co., Inc.
Bessemer Trust Company, N.A.
BlackRock Financial Management L.P.
Bluebonnet Savings Bank Fsb
The Boatmen's National Bank of St. Louis (Portfolio)
The Boeing Company
BR Investment Associates
Branch Banking & Trust Company (BB&T-NC) (Portfolio)
Bridgewater Associates Inc.
Brinson Partners, Inc.
Brown Brothers Harriman & Co. (Investments)
BZW Barclays Global Investors
Calamos Asset Management, Inc.

California Federal Bank, A Federal Savings Bank
California Public Employees' Retirement System
Campbell Soup Company
Capital Guardian Trust Company
Capital One Financial Corporation
Caremark International Inc.
Carillon Advisers, Inc.
CDC Investment Management Corp. (CIMCO)
Central Carolina Bank & Trust Co. (Portfolio)
Central Fidelity National Bank (Richmond) (Portfolio)
Century Investment Management Co. (CIMCO)
Charter One Bank, F.S.B.
Charter One Bank, F.S.B. (Michigan)
Chase Manhattan Private Bank Investment Management
Chemical Bank (Portfolio)
The Chubb Corporation
CIGNA Investment Management (U.S.A.)
CIGNA Investments, Inc.
Circus Circus Enterprises, Inc.
Citibank, N.A. (Portfolio)
Citicorp
Citizens Federal Bank, F.S.B.
Citizens National Bank of Evansville (Portfolio)
Coast Federal Bank, Federal Savings Bank (Administration)
Coastal Banc ssb
Colonial Management Associates
Comerica Bank (Funds Management)
Commerce Bancshares Inc.
Commonwealth Investment Counsel
Compass Bank (Portfolio)
Conseco Capital Management
Continental Asset Management
Corning Incorporated
Crestar Bank (Portfolio)
Dean Witter, Discover & Co.
Delaware Management Company Inc.
Delphi Capital Management, Inc.
Deposit Guaranty Corp.
Deposit Guaranty National Bank (Portfolio)
The Dime Savings Bank of New York, FSB
Dimensional Fund Advisors, Inc.
Dominion Resources, Inc.
Dow Jones & Company, Inc.
The Dreyfus Corporation
Duke Power Company
Eaton Corporation
Ecolab Inc.
Enhance Financial Services Group Inc.
Equifax, Inc.
The Equitable Companies Incorporated
Evangelical Lutheran Church-Board of Pensions
Exxon Corporation
Farmers Insurance Group of Companies
Federal Home Loan Bank of Atlanta
Federal Home Loan Bank of Boston
Federal Home Loan Bank of Chicago
Federal Home Loan Bank of San Francisco
Federal Home Loan Bank of Seattle
Federal Home Loan Bank of Topeka
Federal National Mortgage Association
Federated Investors
Fidelity Management & Research Company
The FINOVA Group Inc.
First of America Bank Corporation
First of America Investment Corporation
First American Corporation
First Bank Puerto Rico
First Bank System (Portfolio)

First Chicago/NBD Corporation
First Commercial Corporation
First Federal Savings and Loan Association of Rochester
First National Bank of Commerce (Investment)
First National Bank of Maryland (Portfolio)
First Nationwide Bank, A Federal Savings Bank
First NH Bank
First Tennessee Bank
First Union Corporation
First Union National Bank of Florida
First Union National Bank of North Carolina — Funds Mgmt.
Fleet Financial Group
Fleet Investment Advisors (Boston)
Fleming Companies, Inc.
Florida State Board of Administration
The Ford Foundation
Ford Motor Company
Freeport-McMoRan Inc.
Fremont General Corporation
The Frost National Bank (Portfolio)
General Electric Company
General Electric Capital Corporation
General Motors Acceptance Corporation
General Re Asset Management, Inc.
GMG/Seneca Capital Management
GNA Capital Management Inc.
Goldman Sachs Asset Management (U.S.A.)
W.R. Grace & Company
Great Western Bank, a Federal Savings Bank (Treasury)
The Greater New York Savings Bank
Greenwich Street Advisors
Guaranty Federal Bank, F.S.B.
M.A. Hanna Company
Harris Corporation
Harsco Corporation
Harvard Management Company
Heber Fuger Wendin Incorporated
Hercules Incorporated
Hibernia Corporation
Honeywell, Inc.
Household International, Inc.
Huntington Bancshares, Incorporated
IDS Fixed Income Advisors
Independent Bank Corp.
ING Investment Management Inc. — Americas Region
Integra Financial Corporation
Intel Corporation
Inter-American Development Bank
Interstate/Johnson Lane, Inc.
Investment Counselors of Maryland, Inc.
ITT Corporation
ITT Hartford Life Insurance Company
John Hancock Advisers, Inc.
John Hancock Mutual Life Insurance Company
Johnson Controls, Inc.
KeyCorp
Keystone Investment Services
LaSalle National Bank (Portfolio)
Lazard Freres Asset Management
Leader Federal Bank for Savings
Leucadia National Corporation
LGT Asset Management
Libby, Inc.
Liberty Bank and Trust Co. (Oklahoma City) (Portfolio)
Life Partners Group
Lincoln National Corporation
Lincoln National Investment Management Co.
Lipper & Company, L.P.

Litton Industries, Inc.
The Long Island Savings Bank, F.S.B.
Loomis, Sayles & Company Inc. (Washington, D.C.)
Los Angeles County Treasurer
Lotsoff Capital Management
Magna Group, Inc.
Manufacturers & Traders Trust Company (Treasury)
Mark Twain Bank (Portfolio)
Marshall & Ilsley Corporation
Masco Corporation
Massachusetts Financial Services Company
Massachusetts Mutual Life Insurance Co.
MBNA Corporation
McDonald's Corporation
McDonnell Douglas Corporation
MCI Communications Corporation
McKesson Corporation
MCN Corporation
The Mead Corporation
Mellon Bank, N.A. (Portfolio)
Mellon Bank, N.A. (Trust)
Merck & Co., Inc.
Meridian Bancorp, Inc.
Meridian Bank (Portfolio)
Merita Bank
Merrill Lynch Asset Management Inc.
Metropolitan Life Insurance Company
MGIC Investment Corporation
Michigan National Bank (Portfolio)
Millipore Corporation
Minnesota State Board of Investment
MONY Financial Services
J.P. Morgan & Company Inc.
J.P. Morgan Investment Management, Inc. (U.S.A.)
Morgan Stanley Asset Management, Inc.
National Bank of Commerce (Portfolio)
NationsBank (Charlotte) (Funds Management)
NatWest Bank, N.A. (Portfolio)
Neuberger & Berman Management Inc.
New Jersey Division of Investments
New York Life Insurance Company (U.S.A)
New York State & Local Retirement Systems
Nikko Capital Management (U.S.A.)
Nomura Capital Management (U.S.A.)
North Fork Bank (Portfolio)
The Northern Trust Company (Treasury)
Northern Trust Corporation
Northrop Grumman Corporation
Northwestern Mutual Life Insurance Co.
Norwest Investment Management (Minnesota)
NYNEX Corporation
Oak Hill Partners
OFFITBANK
Old Kent Bank & Trust Company (Portfolio)
Old National Bank in Evansville (Portfolio)
OnBank, Inc. (Portfolio)
Oppenheimer Management Corporation
Oregon State Treasury Investment Division — Fixed Income
Oryx Energy Company
Owens-Corning Fiberglass Corporation
PACCAR Incorporated
Pacific Investment Management Co. (PIMCO)
Pacific Mutual Life Insurance Company
Pacificorp
PanAgora Asset Management, Inc. (U.S.A.)
Paul Revere Investment Management Corp.
People's Bank
People's Bank (Investment)

Peregrine Capital Management
Physicians Mutual Insurance Company
Piper Capital Management Inc.
PNC Bank — Asset Liability (Portfolio)
PPM America Inc.
T. Rowe Price Associates, Inc.
PriMerit Bank, A Federal Savings Bank
Principal Mutual Life Insurance Company
Protective Life Corporation
The Provident Bank (Portfolio)
Provident Life & Accident Insurance Co.
Provident Mutual Life Insurance Company
Providian Corporation
Prudential Capital Management
Public Service Enterprise Group Incorporated
The Putnam Management Company Inc.
The Quaker Oats Company
Raytheon Company
RCM Capital Management
Regents of the University of California
Republic National Bank of NY (Treasury)
Rite Aid Corporation
The Rochester Community Savings Bank
Roosevelt Bank, A Federal Savings Bank
Royal Caribbean Cruises Ltd.
RXR Capital Management, Inc.
SAFECO Insurance Companies
St. Paul Federal Bank for Savings
Salomon Brothers Asset Management Inc. (U.S.A.)
Schlumberger, Ltd.
SCOR Reinsurance Company
Scudder Stevens & Clark, Inc. (Boston)
Scudder Stevens & Clark, Inc. (Los Angeles)
Scudder Stevens & Clark, Inc. (San Francisco)
Sears Roebuck and Company
Security Benefit Life Insurance Co. of Kansas
Security Life of Denver Insurance Co.
Shay Assets Management Co.
Shell Oil Company
Signet Banking Corporation
Sit Investment Fixed Income Advisors Inc.
Smith Affiliated Capital Corporation
Smith, Breeden Associates
Smith, Breeden Associates (Boulder)
Smith, Breeden Associates (Chapel Hill)
Smith, Breeden Associates (Dallas)
Smith, Graham & Co. Asset Managers
Smith's Food & Drug Centers Inc.
Society Asset Management, Inc.
Society National Bank (Portfolio)
South Boston Savings Bank
South Dakota Investment Council
SouthTrust Bank of Alabama, N.A. (Portfolio)
Southwest Corporate Federal Credit Union
Sovereign Bank, A Federal Savings Bank
Sprint Corporation
Standard Federal Bank
Standish, Ayer & Wood Inc.
Standish International Management Co., L.P.
Stanford Management Company
Star Bank, N.A. (Cincinnati) (Portfolio)
State Street Boston Corporation
State Street Global Advisors
State Street Research & Management Co.
Stein Roe & Farnham Incorporated
Strategic Fixed Income L.P.
Strong Capital Management Inc.
Summit Bank (Portfolio)

SunFinancial Group
Synovus Financial Corporation
TCF Bank Minnesota fsb
Teachers Insurance & Annuity Association
Templeton Global Bond Managers, Inc.
Tenneco Inc.
Tennessee Consolidated Retirement System
Texaco Inc.
The Transamerica Corporation
Transamerica Investment Services Inc.
Travelers Group
The Travelers Insurance Company
UBS Asset Management, Inc. (U.S.A.)
Union Bank — Los Angeles
Union Bank of Switzerland Private Banking
Union Carbide Corporation
Union Planters National Bank (Funds Management)
United Asset Management Corporation
United Jersey Bank (Portfolio)
United Missouri Bank, N.A. (Portfolio)
United of Omaha Life Insurance Company
U.S. National Bank of Oregon (Portfolio)
United States Trust Company of New York (Portfolio)
United States Trust Company of New York (Trust)
U.S. West, Inc.
USBANCORP, Inc.
The Vanguard Group, Inc.
Van Kampen American Capital Investment Advisory Corp.
Van Kampen American Capital Management & Research
Wachovia Corporation
Waddell & Reed Investment Management Co.
Warburg, Pincus Counsellors, Inc.
Washington Square Advisers Inc.
Wellington Management Company
WESTAMERICA Bank
Western Financial Savings Bank, Fsb
Wilmington Trust Company (Portfolio)
State of Wisconsin Investment Board
WMX Technologies, Inc.
The World Bank
World Savings & Loan Association, A Fed. Svgs. & Loan Assn.
YMCA Retirement Fund
Zions First National Bank (Portfolio)
Zurich-Kemper Investments, Inc.

Currency Swaps & Options

Advanced Micro Devices, Inc.
AIM Advisors, Inc.
Alcoa
Alfa Corporation
Alliance Capital Management L.P.
Alliance Capital Management (Minneapolis)
American Express Bank Ltd.
American Express Financial Advisors
American Family Life Assurance Company (AFLAC)
American National Corporation
American President Companies, Ltd.
Amoco Corporation
AON Advisors Incorporated
AT&T
Back Bay Advisors, L.P.
Bank of America NT & SA (Portfolio)
The Bank of New York Company, Inc.
The Bank of Tokyo Trust Company (Securities & Investments)
Bank of the West (Portfolio)
Bankers Trust Global Investment Management
Baring Asset Management Company
Bausch & Lomb Incorporated
Baxter International Inc.
BayBank Boston, N.A. (Portfolio)
BEA Associates
Bessemer Trust Company, N.A.
Bridgewater Associates Inc.
Brinson Partners, Inc.
Brown Brothers Harriman & Co. (Investments)
BZW Barclays Global Investors
Calamos Asset Management, Inc.
Caremark International Inc.
CDC Investment Management Corp. (CIMCO)
CIGNA Investment Management (U.S.A.)
CIGNA Investments, Inc.
Citibank, N.A. (Portfolio)
Citicorp
Colonial Management Associates
Continental Asset Management
Corning Incorporated
Dimensional Fund Advisors, Inc.
Dow Jones & Company, Inc.
The Dreyfus Corporation
Eaton Corporation
Ecolab Inc.
Equifax, Inc.
Exxon Corporation
Farmers Insurance Group of Companies
First Chicago/NBD Corporation
First National Bank of Maryland (Portfolio)
First NH Bank
First Union Corporation
First Union National Bank of North Carolina — Funds Mgmt.
Fleet Financial Group
Florida State Board of Administration
The Ford Foundation
Ford Motor Company
Freeport-McMoRan Inc.
General Electric Company
General Electric Capital Corporation
General Motors Acceptance Corporation
General Re Asset Management, Inc.
GNA Capital Management Inc.
Harris Corporation
Harsco Corporation
Heber Fuger Wendin Incorporated
Hercules Incorporated
Honeywell, Inc.

The way you first see them.
The way they will see you.
Junior Achievement

Household International, Inc.
Intel Corporation
ITT Corporation
ITT Hartford Life Insurance Company
John Hancock Advisers, Inc.
John Hancock Mutual Life Insurance Company
Johnson Controls, Inc.
KeyCorp
Lazard Freres Asset Management
LGT Asset Management
Lincoln National Corporation
Lincoln National Investment Management Co.
Loomis, Sayles & Company Inc. (Washington, D.C.)
Masco Corporation
Massachusetts Financial Services Company
Massachusetts Mutual Life Insurance Co.
MBNA Corporation
McDonald's Corporation
McDonnell Douglas Corporation
MCI Communications Corporation
McKesson Corporation
The Mead Corporation
Mellon Bank, N.A. (Trust)
Merck & Co., Inc.
Merrill Lynch Asset Management Inc.
Metropolitan Life Insurance Company
J.P. Morgan & Company Inc.
Morgan Stanley Asset Management, Inc.
NationsBank (Charlotte) (Funds Management)
NatWest Bank, N.A. (Portfolio)
Neuberger & Berman Management Inc.
Nikko Capital Management (U.S.A.)
Nomura Capital Management (U.S.A.)
The Northern Trust Company (Treasury)
Northern Trust Corporation
Northrop Grumman Corporation
Northwestern Mutual Life Insurance Co.
NYNEX Corporation
OFFITBANK
Oppenheimer Management Corporation
Owens-Corning Fiberglass Corporation
Pacific Investment Management Co. (PIMCO)
Pacificorp
PanAgora Asset Management, Inc. (U.S.A.)
T. Rowe Price Associates, Inc.
Provident Life & Accident Insurance Co.
Prudential Capital Management
The Quaker Oats Company
RCM Capital Management
Regents of the University of California
Republic National Bank of NY (Treasury)
RXR Capital Management, Inc.
Schlumberger, Ltd.
Scudder Stevens & Clark, Inc. (San Francisco)
Shell Oil Company
Society Asset Management, Inc.
Society National Bank (Portfolio)
Sprint Corporation
Standish, Ayer & Wood Inc.
Standish International Management Co., L.P.
Stanford Management Company
State Street Boston Corporation
State Street Global Advisors
Strategic Fixed Income L.P.
Strong Capital Management Inc.
Tenneco Inc.
Tennessee Consolidated Retirement System
Texaco Inc.

Travelers Group
Union Bank of Switzerland Private Banking
Union Carbide Corporation
United Jersey Bank (Portfolio)
Van Kampen American Capital Investment Advisory Corp.
Wachovia Corporation
Waddell & Reed Investment Management Co.
Warburg, Pincus Counsellors, Inc.
Washington Square Advisers Inc.
State of Wisconsin Investment Board
WMX Technologies, Inc.
The World Bank
YMCA Retirement Fund
Zurich-Kemper Investments, Inc.

Interest Rate Swaps & Options

Adams, Viner & Mosler
Advanced Micro Devices, Inc.
AEGON U.S.A. Investment Management (Cedar Rapids)
AgriBank, FCB
H.F. Ahmanson & Company
Alcoa
Alfa Corporation
Alliance Capital Management (Minneapolis)
Allmerica Asset Management, Inc.
Allstate Insurance Company
AMBAC Inc.
AMBAC Financial Services, L.P.
AMCORE Bank, N.A. Rockford
AMCORE Financial, Inc.
American Express Company
American Express Bank Ltd.
American Express Financial Advisors
American Family Life Assurance Company (AFLAC)
American General Corporation
American National Corporation
American Savings Bank, F.A.
Amoco Corporation
AmSouth Bank N.A. (Portfolio)
AON Advisors Incorporated
Arvin Industries, Inc.
AT&T
BANC ONE Corporation
Banco Popular of Puerto Rico (Portfolio)
Bank of America NT & SA (Portfolio)
Bank of America Texas, N.A.
The Bank of California, N.A.
Bank of Hawaii (Investments)
The Bank of New York Company, Inc.
The Bank of North Dakota
Bank of Oklahoma, N.A. (Portfolio)
The Bank of Tokyo Trust Company (Securities & Investments)
Bank United of Texas, FSB
Bank of the West (Portfolio)
Barnett Banks, Inc.
Bausch & Lomb Incorporated
Baxter International Inc.
Bay View Federal Bank, A Federal Savings Bank
BayBank Boston, N.A. (Portfolio)
BEA Associates
Bessemer Trust Company, N.A.
BlackRock Financial Management L.P.
Bluebonnet Savings Bank Fsb
The Boatmen's National Bank of St. Louis (Portfolio)
BR Investment Associates
Branch Banking & Trust Company (BB&T-NC) (Portfolio)
Bridgewater Associates Inc.
Brinson Partners, Inc.
BZW Barclays Global Investors
California Federal Bank, A Federal Savings Bank
Capital One Financial Corporation
Carillon Advisers, Inc.
CDC Investment Management Corp. (CIMCO)
Central Carolina Bank & Trust Co. (Portfolio)
Central Fidelity National Bank (Richmond) (Portfolio)
Charter One Bank, F.S.B.
Charter One Bank, F.S.B. (Michigan)
Chemical Bank (Portfolio)
The Chubb Corporation
CIGNA Investment Management (U.S.A.)
CIGNA Investments, Inc.
Circus Circus Enterprises, Inc.
Citibank, N.A. (Portfolio)
Citicorp

Citizens Federal Bank, F.S.B.
Citizens National Bank of Evansville (Portfolio)
Coast Federal Bank, Federal Savings Bank (Administration)
Coastal Banc ssb
Comerica Bank (Funds Management)
Commerce Bancshares Inc.
Commonwealth Investment Counsel
Compass Bank (Portfolio)
Continental Asset Management
Crestar Bank (Portfolio)
Dean Witter, Discover & Co.
Delphi Capital Management, Inc.
Deposit Guaranty Corp.
The Dime Savings Bank of New York, FSB
Dominion Resources, Inc.
The Dreyfus Corporation
Duke Power Company
Eaton Corporation
Enhance Financial Services Group Inc.
Equifax, Inc.
The Equitable Companies Incorporated
Exxon Corporation
Federal Home Loan Bank of Atlanta
Federal Home Loan Bank of Boston
Federal Home Loan Bank of Chicago
Federal Home Loan Bank of San Francisco
Federal Home Loan Bank of Seattle
Federal Home Loan Bank of Topeka
Federal National Mortgage Association
Federated Investors
Fidelity Management & Research Company
The FINOVA Group Inc.
First of America Bank Corporation
First of America Investment Corporation
First American Corporation
First Bank Puerto Rico
First Bank System (Portfolio)
First Chicago/NBD Corporation
First Commercial Corporation
First Federal Savings and Loan Association of Rochester
First National Bank of Commerce (Investment)
First National Bank of Maryland (Portfolio)
First Nationwide Bank, A Federal Savings Bank
First Tennessee Bank
First Union Corporation
First Union National Bank of North Carolina — Funds Mgmt.
Fleet Financial Group
Fleming Companies, Inc.
Ford Motor Company
Freeport-McMoRan Inc.
Fremont General Corporation
The Frost National Bank (Portfolio)
General Electric Company
General Electric Capital Corporation
General Motors Acceptance Corporation
General Re Asset Management, Inc.
GNA Capital Management Inc.
Great Western Bank, a Federal Savings Bank (Treasury)
Guaranty Federal Bank, F.S.B.
Heber Fuger Wendin Incorporated
Hercules Incorporated
Hibernia Corporation
Honeywell, Inc.
Household International, Inc.
Huntington Bancshares, Incorporated
Independent Bank Corp.
ING Investment Management Inc. — Americas Region
Integra Financial Corporation

Intel Corporation
Interstate/Johnson Lane, Inc.
ITT Corporation
ITT Hartford Life Insurance Company
John Hancock Mutual Life Insurance Company
KeyCorp
Keystone Investment Services
LaSalle National Bank (Portfolio)
Lazard Freres Asset Management
Leader Federal Bank for Savings
Leucadia National Corporation
Libby, Inc.
Liberty Bank and Trust Co. (Oklahoma City) (Portfolio)
Life Partners Group
Lincoln National Corporation
Lincoln National Investment Management Co.
Loomis, Sayles & Company Inc. (Washington, D.C.)
Los Angeles County Treasurer
Lotsoff Capital Management
Magna Group, Inc.
Manufacturers & Traders Trust Company (Treasury)
Masco Corporation
Massachusetts Financial Services Company
Massachusetts Mutual Life Insurance Co.
MBNA Corporation
McDonald's Corporation
MCI Communications Corporation
McKesson Corporation
MCN Corporation
The Mead Corporation
Mellon Bank, N.A. (Portfolio)
Merck & Co., Inc.
Meridian Bancorp, Inc.
Meridian Bank (Portfolio)
Merrill Lynch Asset Management Inc.
Metropolitan Life Insurance Company
Michigan National Bank (Portfolio)
Minnesota State Board of Investment
J.P. Morgan & Company Inc.
National Bank of Commerce (Portfolio)
NationsBank (Charlotte) (Funds Management)
NatWest Bank, N.A. (Portfolio)
Neuberger & Berman Management Inc.
North Fork Bank (Portfolio)
Northern Trust Corporation
Northrop Grumman Corporation
Northwestern Mutual Life Insurance Co.
NYNEX Corporation
Oak Hill Partners
OFFITBANK
OnBank, Inc. (Portfolio)
Oppenheimer Management Corporation
Owens-Corning Fiberglass Corporation
Pacific Investment Management Co. (PIMCO)
Pacific Mutual Life Insurance Company
Pacificorp
Paul Revere Investment Management Corp.
People's Bank
People's Bank (Investment)
Physicians Mutual Insurance Company
Piper Capital Management Inc.
PNC Bank — Asset Liability (Portfolio)
PriMerit Bank, A Federal Savings Bank
Protective Life Corporation
The Provident Bank (Portfolio)
Provident Life & Accident Insurance Co.
Provident Mutual Life Insurance Company
Providian Corporation

Prudential Capital Management
Public Service Enterprise Group Incorporated
Regents of the University of California
Rite Aid Corporation
The Rochester Community Savings Bank
Roosevelt Bank, A Federal Savings Bank
Royal Caribbean Cruises Ltd.
RXR Capital Management, Inc.
SAFECO Insurance Companies
St. Paul Federal Bank for Savings
Schlumberger, Ltd.
SCOR Reinsurance Company
Scudder Stevens & Clark, Inc. (San Francisco)
Sears Roebuck and Company
Security Life of Denver Insurance Co.
Signet Banking Corporation
Smith, Breeden Associates
Smith, Breeden Associates (Chapel Hill)
Smith, Breeden Associates (Dallas)
Smith's Food & Drug Centers Inc.
Society National Bank (Portfolio)
South Boston Savings Bank
SouthTrust Bank of Alabama, N.A. (Portfolio)
Southwest Corporate Federal Credit Union
Sovereign Bank, A Federal Savings Bank
Sprint Corporation
Standard Federal Bank
Standish, Ayer & Wood Inc.
Standish International Management Co., L.P.
Stanford Management Company
Star Bank, N.A. (Cincinnati) (Portfolio)
State Street Boston Corporation
State Street Global Advisors
Strategic Fixed Income L.P.
Strong Capital Management Inc.
Summit Bank (Portfolio)
Synovus Financial Corporation
TCF Bank Minnesota fsb
Teachers Insurance & Annuity Association
Tenneco Inc.
The Transamerica Corporation
Transamerica Investment Services Inc.
Travelers Group
The Travelers Insurance Company
UBS Asset Management, Inc. (U.S.A.)
Union Bank — Los Angeles
Union Carbide Corporation
Union Planters National Bank (Funds Management)
United Asset Management Corporation
United Jersey Bank (Portfolio)
U.S. National Bank of Oregon (Portfolio)
United States Trust Company of New York (Portfolio)
USBANCORP, Inc.
Van Kampen American Capital Investment Advisory Corp.
Wachovia Corporation
Waddell & Reed Investment Management Co.
Washington Square Advisers Inc.
Wellington Management Company
Western Financial Savings Bank, Fsb
Wilmington Trust Company (Portfolio)
State of Wisconsin Investment Board
WMX Technologies, Inc.
The World Bank
World Savings & Loan Association, A Fed. Svgs. & Loan Assn.
YMCA Retirement Fund
Zions First National Bank (Portfolio)

Structured Notes

The Acacia Group
Adams, Viner & Mosler
AEGON U.S.A. Investment Management (Cedar Rapids)
Aetna Life & Casualty (Portfolio Management Group)
AgriBank, FCB
AIM Advisors, Inc.
Alaska Permanent Capital Management Company
Alaska Retirement Systems
Alliance Capital Management L.P.
Allied-Signal Inc.
Allmerica Asset Management, Inc.
Allstate Insurance Company
AMCORE Bank, N.A. Rockford
American Express Financial Advisors
American Money Management Corporation
American Mutual Life Insurance Company
American Savings Bank, F.A.
AMR Investment Services, Inc.
AmSouth Bank N.A. (Portfolio)
AON Advisors Incorporated
Ark Asset Management Company, Inc.
Associated Bank Green Bay, N.A.
Atlantic Asset Management Partners Inc.
Auto-Owners Insurance Company
Back Bay Advisors, L.P.
Banco Popular of Puerto Rico (Portfolio)
Bank of America Illinois (Institutional Trust)
Bank of Boston (Treasury)
Bank of Hawaii (Investments)
The Bank of North Dakota
Bankers Trust Global Investment Management
Baring Asset Management Company
Bartlett & Co.
BEA Associates
Bear, Stearns Asset Management Inc.
BellSouth Corporation
Benham Capital Management Group
BlackRock Financial Management L.P.
Bluebonnet Savings Bank Fsb
The Boatmen's National Bank of St. Louis (Portfolio)
Boatmen's Trust (St. Louis) (Fixed Income)
Boatmen's Trust Company of Texas
The Boston Company Asset Management
BR Investment Associates
Branch Banking & Trust Company (BB&T-NC) (Portfolio)
Brinson Partners, Inc.
Brown Brothers Harriman & Co. (Investments) (Chicago)
BZW Barclays Global Investors
California Federal Bank, A Federal Savings Bank
California Public Employees' Retirement System
Calvert Asset Management Company, Inc.
Campbell Soup Company
Capital Guardian Trust Company
Capitol Federal Savings & Loan Association
Capitoline Investment Services, Inc. (Richmond)
Capitoline Investment Services, Inc. (Washington, DC)
Carillon Advisers, Inc.
CDC Investment Management Corp. (CIMCO)
Central Carolina Bank & Trust Co. (Portfolio)
Chase Manhattan Private Bank Investment Management
Chemical Bank (Portfolio)
The Chubb Corporation
CIGNA Investment Management (U.S.A.)
CIGNA Investments, Inc.
Citibank Private Banking Investment Division
Coast Federal Bank, Federal Savings Bank (Administration)
Collective Bank
Colonial Management Associates

Commander Investment Corporation
Compass Bank (Portfolio)
Conseco Capital Management
Continental Asset Management
CTT Investment Management Group
Dauphin Deposit Bank & Trust Company (Portfolio)
Dauphin Deposit Bank & Trust Company (Trust)
Davis Selected Advisers, L.P.
C.H. Dean Investment Associates
Dean Witter InterCapital Inc.
Delaware Management Company Inc.
Delphi Capital Management, Inc.
Denver Investment Advisors Inc.
Deposit Guaranty National Bank (Portfolio)
Dimensional Fund Advisors, Inc.
The Dreyfus Corporation
Eaton Vance Management, Inc.
Employers Reinsurance Corporation
Erie Insurance Group
Evangelical Lutheran Church-Board of Pensions
Falcon Asset Management, Inc.
Farmers Insurance Group of Companies
Federal Home Loan Bank of Atlanta
Federal Home Loan Bank of Boston
Federal Home Loan Bank of Chicago
Federal Home Loan Bank of San Francisco
Federal Home Loan Bank of Seattle
Federal Home Loan Bank of Topeka
Federal National Mortgage Association
Federated Group
Federated Investors
Ferguson, Wellman, Rudd, Purdy & Van Winkle, Inc.
Fidelity Management & Research Company
Fielding Management Company, Inc.
The Fifth Third Bank of Northwestern Ohio
Financial Counselors, Inc.
First of America Investment Corporation
First Asset Management
First Bank, N.A. (Omaha) (Trust)
First Bank Puerto Rico
First Chicago/NBD Corporation
First Citizens Bank & Trust Co.
First Commercial Corporation
First Commercial Capital Management
First Investors Management Co., Inc.
First National Bank Gainesville (Portfolio)
First National Bank of Maryland (Portfolio)
First Nationwide Bank, A Federal Savings Bank
First NH Bank
First NH Investment Services
First Union National Bank of Florida
First Union National Bank (New Jersey)
First Union National Bank (Pennsylvania) (Instl. Trust)
Flaherty & Crumrine, Inc.
Fleet Investment Advisors (Boston)
Florida State Board of Administration
General Motors Investment Management Corp.
GMG/Seneca Capital Management
GNA Capital Management Inc.
Goldman Sachs Asset Management (U.S.A.)
Gradison-McDonald Asset Management
Great Western Bank, a Federal Savings Bank (Treasury)
The Greater New York Savings Bank
Guardian Life Insurance Co. of America
Harleysville Mutual Insurance Company
Harris Investment Management, Inc.
Harris Trust & Savings (Personal Trust)
Harvard Management Company

Hawaiian Electric Industries, Inc.
Heber Fuger Wendin Incorporated
Hotchkis and Wiley
HSBC Asset Management Americas Inc.
IDS Fixed Income Advisors
Integra Financial Corporation
INVESCO Management and Research, Inc.
Investment Counselors of Maryland, Inc.
Israel Discount Bank of New York
ITT Hartford Life Insurance Company
John Hancock Advisers, Inc.
John Hancock Mutual Life Insurance Company
Kentucky National Insurance Co.
Keystone Custodian Funds, Inc.
Keystone Investment Services
The Laredo National Bank
Lazard Freres Asset Management
Leader Federal Bank for Savings
LGT Asset Management
Liberty Bank and Trust Co. (Oklahoma City) (Trust)
Life Insurance Company of the Southwest
Life Partners Group
Lincoln National Investment Management Co.
Litton Industries, Inc.
The Long Island Savings Bank, F.S.B.
Loomis, Sayles & Company Inc. (Washington, D.C.)
Los Angeles County Treasurer
Lutheran Brotherhood
Maryland State Retirement & Pension System
Massachusetts Financial Services Company
Massachusetts Mutual Life Insurance Co.
The Medical Protective Company
Mellon Bank, N.A. (Trust)
Mercantile Banks of St. Louis, N.A.
Mercantile — Safe Deposit & Trust Co. (Trust)
The Merchants Bank of New York
Merck & Co., Inc.
Merganser Capital Management Corporation
Meridian Bank (Portfolio)
Meridian Investment Company
Merita Bank
Merrill Lynch Asset Management Inc.
MGIC Investment Corporation
Midland National Life Insurance Company
MIMLIC Asset Management Company
Montana Board of Investments
MONY Financial Services
J.P. Morgan & Company Inc.
J.P. Morgan Investment Management, Inc. (U.S.A.)
Morgan Stanley Asset Management, Inc.
National City Bank of Akron
Nationwide Financial Services
Navy Federal Credit Union
NCM Capital Management Group, Inc.
Nebraska State Investment Council
Neuberger & Berman Management Inc.
New Jersey Division of Investments
New Mexico Educational Retirement Board
New York State & Local Retirement Systems
North Side Savings Bank
The Northern Trust Company (Treasury)
Northrop Grumman Corporation
Norwest Bank Indiana, N.A.
Norwest Bank Iowa, N.A.
Norwest Investment Management (Minnesota)
NYNEX Corporation
Oak Hill Partners
OFFITBANK

Ohio Police & Firemen's Disability & Pension Fund
Ohio Public Employees' Retirement System
Old Kent Bank & Trust Company (Portfolio)
Old National Bank in Evansville (Portfolio)
Olympic Capital Management, Inc.
OnBank, Inc. (Portfolio)
Oppenheimer Management Corporation
Oryx Energy Company
PACCAR Incorporated
Pacholder Associates, Inc.
Pacific Investment Management Co. (PIMCO)
PanAgora Asset Management, Inc. (U.S.A.)
The Patterson Capital Corporation
Paul Revere Investment Management Corp.
Payden & Rygel Investment Counsel
Peregrine Capital Management
Pioneering Management Corporation
Piper Capital Management Inc.
PNC Bank — Asset Liability (Portfolio)
PNC Bank Ohio (Trust)
PNC Institutional Management Corp.
PPM America Inc.
Presidential Life Insurance Company
T. Rowe Price Associates, Inc.
Principal Mutual Life Insurance Company
Protective Life Corporation
The Provident Bank (Portfolio)
Provident Life & Accident Insurance Co.
Prudential Capital Management
Public Employees Retirement Association of Colorado
The Putnam Management Company Inc.
Reams Asset Management Company Inc.
Frank Russell Investment Management Co.
The St. Paul Companies Inc.
St. Paul Federal Bank for Savings
Santander National Bank
M.D. Sass Investors Services, Inc.
Scudder Stevens & Clark, Inc. (Boston)
Scudder Stevens & Clark, Inc. (Chicago)
Scudder Stevens & Clark, Inc. (Los Angeles)
Scudder Stevens & Clark, Inc. (San Francisco)
Seaboard Investment Advisers Inc.
Security Life of Denver Insurance Co.
Shay Assets Management Co.
Shell Oil Company
Herbert R. Smith, Inc.
William B. Smith & Company Inc.
Smith, Breeden Associates (Dallas)
Society Asset Management, Inc.
Society National Bank (Portfolio)
South Boston Savings Bank
Southern Farm Bureau Life Insurance Co.
SouthTrust Bank of Alabama, N.A. (Trust)
Southwest Corporate Federal Credit Union
Standish, Ayer & Wood Inc.
Standish International Management Co., L.P.
Stanford Management Company
State Street Research & Management Co.
Strong Capital Management Inc.
SunFinancial Group
Synovus Financial Corporation
Teachers Insurance & Annuity Association
Templeton Global Bond Managers, Inc.
Thornburg Management Company, Inc.
The Travelers Insurance Company
Trustmark National Bank (Portfolio)
Twentieth Century Insurance Company
Union Capital Advisors (San Diego)

Union Carbide Corporation
Union Planters National Bank (Funds Management)
United Air Lines Employees Credit Union
United Jersey Bank (Portfolio)
United Jersey Bank (Princeton) (Trust)
United Missouri Bank, N.A. (Portfolio)
United Services Advisors Inc.
United States Trust Company of Boston
United States Trust Company of New York (Trust)
UNUM Life Insurance Company
The Vanguard Group, Inc.
Van Kampen American Capital Investment Advisory Corp.
Vaughan, Nelson, Scarborough & McConnell Inc.
Waddell & Reed Investment Management Co.
Warburg, Pincus Counsellors, Inc.
Washington Square Advisers Inc.
WESTAMERICA Bank
Westfield Companies
Wilmington Trust Company (Fixed Income)
Wilmington Trust Company (Portfolio)
State of Wisconsin Investment Board
The World Bank
YMCA Retirement Fund
The Zenith Insurance Company
Zurich-Kemper Investments, Inc.

Non-dollar Transactions

Advanced Micro Devices, Inc.
AIM Advisors, Inc.
Alcoa
Alliance Capital Management L.P.
Amoco Corporation
AON Advisors Incorporated
Bank of America NT & SA (Portfolio)
The Bank of New York Company, Inc.
Bank of the West (Portfolio)
Bankers Trust Global Investment Management
Baxter International Inc.
Sanford C. Bernstein & Co., Inc.
Bessemer Trust Company, N.A.
BlackRock Financial Management L.P.
The Boston Company Asset Management
Bridgewater Associates Inc.
Brinson Partners, Inc.
Calamos Asset Management, Inc.
California State Teachers' Retirement System
Campbell Soup Company
Capital Guardian Trust Company
Charter One Bank, F.S.B.
Chase Manhattan Private Bank Investment Management
Chemical Bank (Portfolio)
The Chubb Corporation
Citibank, N.A. (Portfolio)
Citicorp
Continental Asset Management
Corning Incorporated
C.H. Dean Investment Associates
Dean Witter, Discover & Co.
Dean Witter InterCapital Inc.
Dominion Resources, Inc.
Dow Jones & Company, Inc.
The Dreyfus Corporation
Eaton Corporation
Eaton Vance Management, Inc.
Ecolab Inc.
Exxon Corporation
Farmers Insurance Group of Companies
Federal National Mortgage Association
Fidelity Management & Research Company
Fiduciary Asset Management
Fielding Management Company, Inc.
The FINOVA Group Inc.
First Bank System (Portfolio)
First Chicago/NBD Corporation
First Union National Bank of North Carolina — Funds Mgmt.
Fortis Advisers, Inc.
Freeport-McMoRan Inc.
General Electric Company
General Electric Capital Corporation
Goldman Sachs Asset Management (U.S.A.)
Grantham, Mayo, Van Otterloo & Company
Hawaiian Electric Industries, Inc.
Honeywell, Inc.
Household International, Inc.
IDS Fixed Income Advisors
Investment Advisers, Inc.
ITT Corporation
John Hancock Advisers, Inc.
Johnson Controls, Inc.
KeyCorp
Keystone Custodian Funds, Inc.
LGT Asset Management
Lincoln National Corporation
Litton Industries, Inc.
Loomis, Sayles & Company Inc. (Washington, D.C.)

Manufacturers & Traders Trust Company (Portfolio)
Masco Corporation
Massachusetts Financial Services Company
MBNA Corporation
McDonald's Corporation
McDonnell Douglas Corporation
Merck & Co., Inc.
Merrill Lynch Asset Management Inc.
Millipore Corporation
J.P. Morgan & Company Inc.
J.P. Morgan Investment Management, Inc. (U.S.A.)
Neuberger & Berman Management Inc.
New Jersey Division of Investments
New York Life Insurance Company (U.S.A)
Nomura Capital Management (U.S.A.)
Northwestern Mutual Life Insurance Co.
OFFITBANK
Oppenheimer Management Corporation
Oryx Energy Company
Pacific Investment Management Co. (PIMCO)
PanAgora Asset Management, Inc. (U.S.A.)
T. Rowe Price Associates, Inc.
Provident Life & Accident Insurance Co.
Prudential Capital Management
Public Service Enterprise Group Incorporated
Regents of the University of California
RXR Capital Management, Inc.
Schlumberger, Ltd.
Scudder Stevens & Clark, Inc. (Boston)
Scudder Stevens & Clark, Inc. (Los Angeles)
Scudder Stevens & Clark, Inc. (San Francisco)
Shell Oil Company
Society Asset Management, Inc.
Standish, Ayer & Wood Inc.
Standish International Management Co., L.P.
State Street Boston Corporation
State Street Global Advisors
Strategic Fixed Income L.P.
Tenneco Inc.
Tennessee Consolidated Retirement System
Texaco Inc.
Thornburg Management Company, Inc.
UBS Asset Management, Inc. (U.S.A.)
Union Bank of Switzerland Private Banking
United of Omaha Life Insurance Company
U.S. West, Inc.
UNUM Life Insurance Company
Van Kampen American Capital Investment Advisory Corp.
Waddell & Reed Investment Management Co.
Wellington Management Company
Western Asset Management Company
State of Wisconsin Investment Board
The World Bank
World Savings & Loan Association, A Fed. Svgs. & Loan Assn.
Zurich-Kemper Investments, Inc.

Geographical Cross-reference

ALABAMA

Birmingham

AmSouth Bank N.A. (Portfolio)
AmSouth Bank N.A. (Trust)
Compass Bank (Portfolio)
Compass Bank (Trust)
Protective Life Corporation
Regions Financial Corporation (Investments)
SouthTrust Bank of Alabama, N.A. (Portfolio)
SouthTrust Bank of Alabama, N.A. (Trust)
Torchmark Corporation

Montgomery

Alfa Corporation
Alfa Group

ALASKA

Anchorage

Alaska Permanent Capital Management Company
National Bank of Alaska

Juneau

Alaska Retirement Systems

ARIZONA

Phoenix

The FINOVA Group Inc.

Scottsdale

Madison Scottsdale

ARKANSAS

Little Rock

First Commercial Corporation
First Commercial Capital Management

CALIFORNIA

Beverly Hills

Litton Industries, Inc.

Chatsworth

Great Western Bank, a Federal Savings Bank (Treasury)

Irvine

American Savings Bank, F.A.
Western Financial Savings Bank, Fsb

CALIFORNIA – continued

Irwindale

H.F. Ahmanson & Company

Los Angeles

Anhalt/O'Connell, Inc.
BofA Capital Management Inc. (Los Angeles)
Bradford & Marzec, Inc.
California Federal Bank, A Federal Savings Bank
Capital Guardian Trust Company
Capital Research & Management Company
Farmers Insurance Group of Companies
First Interstate Bank of California (Trust)
Hotchkis and Wiley
Los Angeles County Treasurer
National Mutual Funds Management Inc.
Northrop Grumman Corporation
The Patterson Capital Corporation
Payden & Rygel Investment Counsel
Scudder Stevens & Clark, Inc. (Los Angeles)
Teledyne Inc.
Transamerica Investment Services Inc.
Trust Company of the West (TCW) (High Yield Dept.)
Union Bank — Los Angeles
United States Trust Co. of California., N.A.

Menlo Park

Stanford Management Company

Mountain View

Benham Capital Management Group

Newport Beach

Pacific Investment Management Co. (PIMCO)
Pacific Mutual Life Insurance Company

Oakland

American President Companies, Ltd.
Regents of the University of California
World Savings & Loan Association, A Fed. Svgs. & Loan Assn.

Pasadena

Flaherty & Crumrine, Inc.
Loomis, Sayles & Company L.P. (Pasadena)
Western Asset Management Company

Sacramento

California Public Employees' Retirement System
California State Teachers' Retirement System

San Diego

Golden Eagle Insurance Company
Nicholas-Applegate Capital Management
Union Capital Advisors (San Diego)

San Francisco

Bank of America NT & SA — Capital Markets
The Bank of California, N.A.
Berkeley Capital Management

CALIFORNIA – continued

San Francisco – continued

BZW Barclays Global Investors
Dodge & Cox Inc.
Federal Home Loan Bank of San Francisco
First Nationwide Bank, A Federal Savings Bank
Fremont Investment Advisors Inc.
GMG/Seneca Capital Management
LGT Asset Management
Loomis, Sayles & Company Inc. (San Francisco)
McKesson Corporation
MERUS Capital Management
Quantilogic Asset Management
RCM Capital Management
Charles Schwab Investment Management
Scudder Stevens & Clark, Inc. (San Francisco)
State Compensation Insurance Fund
The Transamerica Corporation
Wells Fargo Bank, N.A. (Treasury)
Wentworth, Hauser & Violich, Inc.

San Mateo

Bay View Federal Bank, A Federal Savings Bank
Pillar Point Capital Management Inc.

San Rafael

WESTAMERICA Bank

Santa Clara

Intel Corporation

Santa Monica

Dimensional Fund Advisors, Inc.
Fremont General Corporation
Pacific Income Advisers

Sunnyvale

Advanced Micro Devices, Inc.

Walnut Creek

Bank of the West (Portfolio)

West Hills

Coast Federal Bank, Federal Savings Bank (Administration)

Woodland Hills

Twentieth Century Insurance Company
The Zenith Insurance Company

COLORADO

Boulder

Smith, Breeden Associates (Boulder)

Denver

Denver Investment Advisors Inc.
First Interstate Bank of Denver (Trust)
Norwest Investments & Trust Services

COLORADO – continued

Denver – continued

Public Employees Retirement Association of Colorado
Security Life of Denver Insurance Co.
Voyageur Asset Management

Englewood

Life Partners Group
U.S. West, Inc.

CONNECTICUT

Bridgeport

People's Bank
People's Bank (Investment)

Danbury

Benefit Capital Management Corporation
Union Carbide Corporation

Darien

Gabelli-O'Connor Fixed Income Management Co.

Fairfield

General Electric Company

Greenwich

Berkley Dean & Co.
Greenwich Capital Markets, Inc.

Hartford

Aetna Life & Casualty (Portfolio Management Group)
CIGNA Investment Management (U.S.A.)
CIGNA Investments, Inc.
Phoenix Duff & Phelps Investment Management Co. (Hartford)
The Travelers Insurance Company

New Haven

Knights of Columbus

Norwalk

Franklin Resources, Inc.

Simsbury

ITT Hartford Life Insurance Company

Stamford

Atlantic Asset Management Partners Inc.
Columbus Circle Investors
General Electric Capital Corporation
General Electric Investment Corporation
General Re Asset Management, Inc.
RXR Capital Management, Inc.

CONNECTICUT – continued

Waterbury

Webster Bank

Westport

Allianz Investment Corporation
AMBAC Financial Services, L.P.

Wilton

Bridgewater Associates Inc.

DELAWARE

Newark

MBNA Corporation

Wilmington

Hercules Incorporated
PNC Institutional Management Corp.
Rodney Square Management Corporation
Wilmington Trust Company (Fixed Income)
Wilmington Trust Company (Portfolio)

DISTRICT OF COLUMBIA

Washington

The Acacia Group
ASB Capital Management, Inc.
Capitoline Investment Services, Inc. (Washington, DC)
Federal National Mortgage Association
Inter-American Development Bank
Loomis, Sayles & Company Inc. (Washington, DC)
MCI Communications Corporation
Plaza Investment Managers, Inc.
Riggs Investment Management Corporation
Sallie Mae
Union Labor Life Insurance Co. (ULLICO)
The World Bank
Zirkin Cutler Investments

FLORIDA

Boca Raton

W.R. Grace & Company

Coral Gables

First Union National Bank of Florida

Fort Lauderdale

Templeton Global Bond Managers, Inc.

Jacksonville

Barnett Banks, Inc.

Melbourne

Harris Corporation

FLORIDA – continued

Miami

John Alden Asset Management
Royal Caribbean Cruises Ltd.

Orlando

STI Capital Management

St. Petersburg

Eagle Asset Management, Inc.
Heritage Asset Management, Inc.

Tallahassee

Florida State Board of Administration

West Palm Beach

Adams, Viner & Mosler

GEORGIA

Atlanta

BellSouth Corporation
Equifax, Inc.
Federal Home Loan Bank of Atlanta
ING Investment Management Inc. — Americas Region
INVESCO MIM Inc.
Montag & Caldwell, Incorporated
Trust Company Bank of Georgia (Trust)
Wachovia Bank Capital Management (Atlanta)

Columbus

American Family Life Assurance Company (AFLAC)
Synovus Financial Corporation

Gainesville

First National Bank Gainesville (Portfolio)

HAWAII

Honolulu

Bank of Hawaii (Investments)
Hawaiian Electric Industries, Inc.
Hawaiian Trust Co., Ltd.

ILLINOIS

Arlington Heights

United Air Lines Employees Credit Union

Chicago

ABN AMRO Securities (USA) Inc.
American National Corporation
American National Bank & Trust (Chicago) (Trust)
Amoco Corporation
ANB Investment Management & Trust Co. of Chicago
AON Advisors Incorporated

ILLINOIS – continued

Chicago – continued

Asset Allocation & Management Company
BA Futures Inc.
Bank of America Illinois (Dealer)
Bank of America Illinois (Institutional Trust)
Bank of Montreal (Chicago)
Bear, Stearns Securities Corp.
Brinson Partners, Inc.
Brown Brothers Harriman & Co. (Investments) (Chicago)
The Chicago Corporation — Asset Management Group
Citicorp Global Derivatives
CTT Investment Management Group
Dean Witter Reynolds Institutional Futures
Essex Radez Company
Federal Home Loan Bank of Chicago
FIMAT Futures U.S.A. Inc. (Chicago)
First Chicago Capital Markets, Inc.
First Chicago Futures
First Chicago/NBD Corporation
First National Bank of Chicago (Dealer)
Fuji Securities, Inc.
Goldman, Sachs & Company (Chicago)
Harris Associates, L.P.
Harris Investment Management, Inc.
Harris Trust & Savings (Personal Trust)
Illinois State Board of Investment
LaSalle National Bank (Portfolio)
Lehman Brothers, Inc. (Chicago)
Lotsoff Capital Management
E.D. & F. Man International Inc. (Chicago)
Mitsubishi Financial Futures Inc.
Mitsui T & B Futures Inc.
J.P. Morgan Futures Inc. (Chicago)
NationsBanc — CRT
The Northern Trust Company (Treasury)
Northern Trust Corporation
Phoenix Duff & Phelps Investment Management Co. (Chicago)
PPM America Inc.
The Quaker Oats Company
St. Paul Federal Bank for Savings
Scudder Stevens & Clark, Inc. (Chicago)
Sears Roebuck and Company
Shay Assets Management Co.
Smith Barney, Inc. (Chicago)
Stein Roe & Farnham Incorporated
Zurich-Kemper Investments, Inc.

Deerfield

Baxter International Inc.

Evergreen Park

First National Bank Evergreen Park (Portfolio)

Lisle

Nike Securities (UIT Management)

Naperville

Calamos Asset Management, Inc.

Northbrook

Allstate Insurance Company
Caremark International Inc.

ILLINOIS – continued

Oak Brook

McDonald's Corporation
WMX Technologies, Inc.

Oakbrook Terrace

Van Kampen American Capital Investment Advisory Corp.

Park Ridge

American Agricultural Insurance Company

Pekin

Pekin Insurance Company

Prospect Heights

Household International, Inc.

Rock Island

Modern Woodmen of America

Rockford

AMCORE Bank, N.A. Rockford
AMCORE Financial, Inc.

Schaumburg

Pioneer Financial Services, Inc.

INDIANA

Carmel

Conseco Capital Management

Columbus

Arvin Industries, Inc.
Reams Asset Management Company Inc.

Evansville

Citizens National Bank of Evansville (Portfolio)
Old National Bank in Evansville (Portfolio)

Fort Wayne

Fort Wayne National Bank (Trust)
Lincoln National Corporation
Lincoln National Investment Management Co.
The Medical Protective Company
Norwest Bank Indiana, N.A.

Indianapolis

American United Life Insurance Company
National City Bank, Indiana
United Farm Bureau Life Insurance Co.

IOWA

Cedar Rapids

AEGON U.S.A. Investment Management (Cedar Rapids)

IOWA – continued

Des Moines

American Mutual Life Insurance Company
Equitable Investment Services, Inc.
Investors Management Group, Ltd. (IMG)
Norwest Bank Iowa, N.A.
Principal Mutual Life Insurance Company

KANSAS

Overland Park

Employers Reinsurance Corporation
Smith, Breeden Associates

Shawnee Mission

Waddell & Reed Investment Management Co.

Topeka

Capitol Federal Savings & Loan Association
Federal Home Loan Bank of Topeka
Security Benefit Life Insurance Co. of Kansas

Westwood

Sprint Corporation

Wichita

INTRUST Bank (Trust)

KENTUCKY

Lexington

Kentucky National Insurance Co.

Louisville

Humana Inc.
Providian Corporation
Todd Investment Advisors Inc.

LOUISIANA

Baton Rouge

Premier Investment Advisors

New Orleans

First National Bank of Commerce (Investment)
Freeport-McMoRan Inc.
Hibernia Corporation
Hibernia National Bank (Trust)
Whitney National Bank (Portfolio)

MAINE

Portland

Fleet Bank of Maine (Portland)
UNUM Life Insurance Company

MARYLAND

Baltimore

Alex. Brown Investment Management
Falcon Asset Management, Inc.
First National Bank of Maryland (Portfolio)
Investment Counselors of Maryland, Inc.
Maryland State Retirement & Pension System
Mercantile — Safe Deposit & Trust Co. (Trust)
T. Rowe Price Associates, Inc.

Bethesda

Calvert Asset Management Company, Inc.
Martin Marietta Corporation
The Rushmore Funds, Inc.

Chevy Chase

Chevy Chase Federal Savings Bank
Howard Hughes Medical Institute

MASSACHUSETTS

Bedford

Millipore Corporation

Boston

Back Bay Advisors, L.P.
Bank of Boston Corporation
Bank of Boston (Treasury)
Baring Asset Management Company
BayBank Boston, N.A. (Dealer)
BayBank Boston, N.A. (Portfolio)
The Boston Company Asset Management
Boston Safe Deposit and Trust Company
Colonial Management Associates
Commercial Union Investment Management
Dewey Square Investors Corporation
Eaton Vance Management, Inc.
Federal Home Loan Bank of Boston
Fidelity Management & Research Company
Fidelity Management Trust Company
Fiduciary Trust Company of Massachusetts
Fleet Financial Group
Fleet Investment Advisors (Boston)
Grantham, Mayo, Van Otterloo & Company
Harbor Capital Management Company, Inc.
Harvard Management Company
Heritage House Asset Management
INVESCO Management and Research, Inc.
John Hancock Advisers, Inc.
John Hancock Mutual Life Insurance Company
Keystone Custodian Funds, Inc.
Loomis, Sayles & Company L.P.
Massachusetts Financial Services Company
Mellon Private Asset Management Group
PanAgora Asset Management, Inc. (U.S.A.)
Pioneering Management Corporation
The Private Bank of Bank of Boston

MASSACHUSETTS – continued

Boston – continued

The Putnam Management Company Inc.
Scudder Stevens & Clark, Inc. (Boston)
South Boston Savings Bank
Standish, Ayer & Wood Inc.
Standish International Management Co., L.P.
State Street Bank & Trust (Trust)
State Street Boston Corporation
State Street Global Advisors
State Street Research & Management Co.
United Asset Management Corporation
United States Trust Company of Boston
Wellington Management Company

Cambridge

Merganser Capital Management Corporation

Lexington

Raytheon Company

Pittsfield

Berkshire Life Insurance Co.

Rockland

Independent Bank Corp.

Salem

William B. Smith & Company Inc.

Springfield

Massachusetts Mutual Life Insurance Co.

Wellesley Hills

SunFinancial Group

Worcester

Allmerica Asset Management, Inc.
Paul Revere Investment Management Corp.

MICHIGAN

Birmingham

Heber Fuger Wendin Incorporated
Munder Capital Management, Inc.

Bloomfield Hills

Loomis, Sayles & Company L.P. (Bloomfield Hills)

Dearborn

Ford Motor Company

MICHIGAN – continued

Detroit

Charter One Bank, F.S.B. (Michigan)
Comerica Bank (Funds Management)
General Motors Acceptance Corporation
MCN Corporation
NBD Bank, N.A. (Trust)

Farmington Hills

Independence One Capital Management Corp.
Michigan National Bank (Portfolio)

Grand Rapids

Old Kent Bank & Trust Company (Portfolio)
Old Kent Bank & Trust Company (Trust)

Kalamazoo

First of America Bank Corporation
First of America Investment Corporation

Lansing

Auto-Owners Insurance Company
Michigan Department of Treasury

Livonia

Auto Club Insurance Association

Taylor

Masco Corporation

Troy

Standard Federal Bank

MINNESOTA

Bloomington

BPS Associates, Inc.

Golden Valley

Fortis Advisers, Inc.

Minneapolis

Alliance Capital Management (Minneapolis)
American Express Financial Advisors
Evangelical Lutheran Church-Board of Pensions
First Asset Management
First Bank System (Portfolio)
Honeywell, Inc.
IDS Fixed Income Advisors
Inter-Regional Financial Group, Inc.
Investment Advisers, Inc.
Lutheran Brotherhood
Norwest Investment Management (Minnesota)
Peregrine Capital Management
Piper Capital Management Inc.
Sit Investment Fixed Income Advisors Inc.
TCF Bank Minnesota fsb
Voyageur Fund Managers
Washington Square Advisers Inc.

MINNESOTA – continued

Owatonna

Federated Group

St. Paul

AgriBank, FCB
Ecolab Inc.
MIMLIC Asset Management Company
Minnesota State Board of Investment
The St. Paul Companies Inc.

MISSISSIPPI

Jackson

Deposit Guaranty Corp.
Deposit Guaranty National Bank (Portfolio)
Deposit Guaranty National Bank (Trust)
Investek Capital Management
Southern Farm Bureau Life Insurance Co.
Trustmark National Bank (Portfolio)

Ridgeland

Southern Farm Bureau Casualty Insurance Co.

MISSOURI

Chesterfield

Roosevelt Bank, A Federal Savings Bank

Clayton

Commerce Bancshares Inc.
Fiduciary Asset Management

Jefferson City

The Central Trust Bank

Kansas City

Commerce Bank Investment Management Group
Financial Counselors, Inc.
Financial Holding Corporation
Kansas City Life Insurance Company
United Missouri Bank, N.A. (Portfolio)
United Missouri Investment Counsel Service

St. Louis

The Boatmen's National Bank of St. Louis (Portfolio)
Boatmen's Trust (St. Louis) (Fixed Income)
General American Investment Management Company (GAIMCO)
Magna Group, Inc.
Mark Twain Bank (Portfolio)
McDonnell Douglas Corporation
Mercantile Banks of St. Louis, N.A.

MONTANA

Helena

Montana Board of Investments

NEBRASKA

Lincoln

Ameritas Investment Advisors Inc.
Nebraska State Investment Council

Omaha

Commercial Federal Corporation
First Bank, N.A. (Omaha) (Trust)
The First National Bank of Omaha (Trust)
Kiewit Investment Management
Physicians Mutual Insurance Company
United of Omaha Life Insurance Company
Woodmen of the World Life Insurance Society

NEVADA

Las Vegas

Circus Circus Enterprises, Inc.
First Interstate Bank of Nevada
PriMerit Bank, A Federal Savings Bank

Reno

Bank of America NT & SA (Portfolio)

NEW HAMPSHIRE

Manchester

First NH Bank
First NH Investment Services

NEW JERSEY

Branchville

Selective Insurance of America

Camden

Campbell Soup Company

Chatham

BR Associates
BR Investment Associates
Summit Bank (Portfolio)

Egg Harbor City

Collective Bank

Hackensack

United Jersey Bank (Portfolio)

Jersey City

Exco Noonan Inc.
NatWest Bank, N.A. (Portfolio)
Prebon Yamane (U.S.A.)

Millburn

Investors Savings Bank

NEW JERSEY – continued

Morristown

Allied-Signal Inc.

Newark

First Union National Bank (New Jersey)
Prudential Capital Management
Public Service Enterprise Group Incorporated

Peapack

Beneficial Insurance Group, Inc.

Plainsboro

Merrill Lynch Asset Management Inc.

Princeton

Princeton Insurance Companies
United Jersey Bank (Princeton) (Trust)

Saddle Brook

Lexington Management Corporation

Short Hills

Heine Securities Corporation

Trenton

New Jersey Division of Investments

Warren

The Chubb Corporation

Wayne

Valley National Bank (New Jersey) (Portfolio)

Whitehouse Station

Merck & Co., Inc.

NEW MEXICO

Santa Fe

Davis Selected Advisers, L.P.
New Mexico Educational Retirement Board
New Mexico State Permanent Funds
Thornburg Management Company, Inc.

NEW YORK

Albany

Key Trust Company (Albany)
New York State & Local Retirement Systems
New York State Teachers' Retirement System

Armonk

MBIA Securities Corporation

NEW YORK – continued

Buffalo

Manufacturers & Traders Trust Company (Treasury)
Marine Midland Bank, N.A. (Trust)

Corning

Corning Incorporated

Floral Park

North Side Savings Bank

Lynbrook

Jamaica Savings Bank, Fsb

Mattituck

North Fork Bank (Portfolio)

Melville

The Long Island Savings Bank, F.S.B.

New York

Advisers Capital Management Inc.
Alliance Capital Management L.P.
Amalgamated Bank of New York (Investment Management Group)
AMBAC Inc.
American Express Company
American Express Bank Ltd.
Ark Asset Management Company, Inc.
J. Aron & Company
AT&T
Avatar Investors Associates
Banco Santander of New York (Dealer)
Bank of America NT & SA — Capital Markets (New York)
Bank Julius Baer & Co., Ltd.
Bank of Montreal (New York)
The Bank of New York Company, Inc.
The Bank of New York (Dealer)
The Bank of Tokyo Trust Company (Pension & Investments)
The Bank of Tokyo Trust Company (Securities & Investments)
Bankers Trust Global Investment Management
Bankers Trust — New York Corporation (Portfolio)
Banque Nationale de Paris (New York)
Banque Paribas Ltd. Corporation
Banque Worms Capital Corporation
Bayerische Vereinsbank AG (New York)
BEA Associates
Bear, Stearns & Company Inc.
Bear, Stearns Asset Management Inc.
Bear, Stearns & Co. Inc. (Unit Trust)
Sanford C. Bernstein & Co., Inc.
Bessemer Trust Company, N.A.
BlackRock Financial Management L.P.
Stacey Braun Associates Incorporated
Brown Brothers Harriman & Co. (Investments)
Brundage, Story and Rose
BT Securities Corporation
BZW/Barclays Bank
Canadian Imperial Bank of Commerce (U.S.A.)
Capital Research & Management Company (New York)
CDC Investment Management Corp. (CIMCO)
Chase Manhattan Private Bank Investment Management
Chase Securities Inc.
Chemical Bank (Portfolio)

NEW YORK – continued

New York – continued

Chemical Securities Incorporated
Christiana Bank, New York Branch
Citibank, N.A. (Portfolio)
Citibank Private Banking Investment Division
Citicorp
Citicorp Securities, Inc.
Commerz Financial Products
Commerzbank Capital Markets
Continental Asset Management
Credit Lyonnais Bank
Credit Suisse Financial Products
CS First Boston Corporation
Dai-Ichi Kangyo Bank Ltd. (New York)
Daiwa Securities America, Inc.
Dean Witter, Discover & Co.
Dean Witter InterCapital Inc.
Dean Witter Reynolds Inc.
Delphi Capital Management, Inc.
Deutsche Morgan Grenfell
The Dime Savings Bank of New York, FSB
DKB Financial Products, Inc.
Dow Jones & Company, Inc.
Dresdner Securities (USA) Inc.
The Dreyfus Corporation
Dreyfus Management
Eastbridge Capital, Inc.
Enhance Financial Services Group Inc.
The Equitable Companies Incorporated
Euro Brokers Maxcor, Inc.
Fiduciary Trust Company International
FIMAT Futures U.S.A., Inc.
First Investors Management Co., Inc.
First Manhattan Capital Management
Fischer, Francis, Trees and Watts, Inc.
The Ford Foundation
Fortis Asset Management
Fuji Bank Ltd.
Garvin GuyButler Corporation
GEM Capital Management, Inc.
General Motors Investment Management Corp.
General Re Securities Corporation
Gibraltar Advisors
Glickenhaus & Company (Investments)
Goldman Sachs & Company
Goldman Sachs Asset Management (U.S.A.)
The Greater New York Savings Bank
Greenwich Street Advisors
Greenwich Street Advisors Municipal Management
Guardian Life Insurance Co. of America
HSBC Asset Management Americas Inc.
HSBC Markets
Hyperion Capital Management, Inc.
I.B.J.-Schroder Bank & Trust Co. (Trust)
ING Barings
Intercapital Securities Inc.
Israel Discount Bank of New York
ITT Corporation
Henry Kaufman & Company, Inc.
Laidlaw Capital Management, Inc.
Lazard Freres Asset Management
Lehman Brothers, Inc.
Lehman Brothers Global Asset Management, Inc. (New York)
Leucadia National Corporation

NEW YORK – continued

New York – continued

Lipper & Company, L.P.
Lord Abbett & Company
E.D. & F. Man International Securities Corp.
Manufacturers & Traders Trust Company (Portfolio)
The Merchants Bank of New York
Merita Bank
Merrill Lynch Capital Markets
Metropolitan Life Insurance Company
Mitchell Hutchins Asset Management, Inc.
Mitsubishi Capital Markets Services
MONY Financial Services
J.P. Morgan & Company Inc.
J.P. Morgan Investment Management, Inc. (U.S.A.)
J.P. Morgan Securities Inc.
Morgan Stanley & Co., Incorporated (NYC Branch)
Morgan Stanley Asset Management, Inc.
Mutual of America Capital Management Corporation
NatWest Securities Corporation
Neuberger & Berman Management Inc.
New York Life Insurance Company (U.S.A)
Nikko Capital Management (U.S.A.)
Nomura Capital Management (U.S.A.)
Nomura Securities International, Inc.
Oak Hill Partners
OFFITBANK
Oppenheimer & Co., Inc.
Oppenheimer Management Corporation
PaineWebber Incorporated
Pension Boards — United Church of Christ
Peregrine Derivatives Ltd.
The Portfolio Group, Inc.
Prudential Securities Inc.
Rabobank Nederland North America
Reich & Tang L.P.
Reliance Insurance Company
Republic National Bank of NY (Treasury)
Republic New York Securities Corporation
Ryan Labs, Inc.
The Sakura Bank Ltd. (New York)
Sakura Global Capital, Inc.
Salomon Brothers Inc.
Salomon Brothers Asset Management Inc. (U.S.A.)
Santander Financial Products
Sanwa Bank
Sanwa Securities (USA) Co., L.P.
M.D. Sass Investors Services, Inc.
Schlumberger, Ltd.
Schroder Wertheim Investment Services
SCOR Reinsurance Company
J & W Seligman & Co., Incorporated
Skandia Investment Management Inc. (U.S.A.)
Smith Affiliated Capital Corporation
Smith Barney, Inc. (Capital Management)
Smith Barney, Inc. (Greenwich Street)
Smith Barney Investment Advisors
Societe Generale Securities Corporation
Swiss Bank Corporation (SBC Warburg)
SwissRe Advisers Inc.
Teachers Insurance & Annuity Association
TIG Holdings Inc.
The Tokai Bank Ltd.
The Toronto-Dominion Bank (New York — Dealer)
Travelers Group

NEW YORK – continued

New York – continued

UBS Asset Management, Inc. (U.S.A.)
UBS Securities, Inc.
Union Bank of Switzerland Private Banking
U.S. Steel & Carnegie Pension Fund
United States Trust Company of New York (Portfolio)
United States Trust Company of New York (Trust)
USLIFE Advisers Inc.
Warburg, Pincus Counsellors, Inc.
Westdeutsche Landesbank Girozentrale — New York Branch
Westpac Banking Corporation
Williams, Jones & Associates Inc.
Winterthur Swiss Group
Yamaichi International (America), Inc.
YMCA Retirement Fund

Nyack

Presidential Life Insurance Company

Purchase

Evergreen Asset Management Corp. (New York)

Rochester

Bausch & Lomb Incorporated
Fielding Management Company, Inc.
First Federal Savings and Loan Association of Rochester
Manning & Napier Advisors Inc.
The Rochester Community Savings Bank

Staten Island

Staten Island Savings Bank

Syracuse

Key Trust Company (Syracuse)
OnBank, Inc. (Portfolio)

White Plains

Acorn Derivatives Management Corp.
NYNEX Corporation
Texaco Inc.

NORTH CAROLINA

Chapel Hill

Smith, Breeden Associates (Chapel Hill)

Charlotte

Duke Power Company
First Union Corporation
First Union National Bank of North Carolina — Funds Mgmt.
Interstate/Johnson Lane, Inc.
NationsBank (Charlotte) (Funds Management)

Durham

Central Carolina Bank & Trust Co. (Portfolio)
NCM Capital Management Group, Inc.

NORTH CAROLINA – continued

Raleigh

Branch Banking & Trust Company (Trust)
First Citizens Bank & Trust Co.
North Carolina Department of State Treasurer

Winston-Salem

Branch Banking & Trust Company (BB&T-NC) (Portfolio)
Wachovia Corporation
Wachovia Bank Capital Management

NORTH DAKOTA

Bismarck

The Bank of North Dakota

OHIO

Akron

First National Bank of Ohio
National City Bank of Akron

Cincinnati

American Money Management Corporation
Bartlett & Co.
Carillon Advisers, Inc.
Fifth Third Bank
Fort Washington Investment Advisors Inc.
Fort Washington Investment Advisors Inc. (Cincinnati)
Gradison-McDonald Asset Management
Johnson Investment Counsel Incorporated
The Ohio National Life Insurance Company
Pacholder Associates, Inc.
PNC Bank Ohio (Trust)
The Provident Bank (Portfolio)
Renaissance Investment Management Inc.
Scudder Stevens & Clark, Inc. (Cincinnati)
Star Bank, N.A. (Cincinnati) (Portfolio)

Cleveland

Charter One Bank, F.S.B.
Eaton Corporation
M.A. Hanna Company
KeyCorp
Society Asset Management, Inc.
Society National Bank (Portfolio)
Third Federal Savings & Loan Association of Cleveland

Columbus

BANC ONE Corporation
Cardinal Management Corporation
Huntington Bancshares, Incorporated
The Huntington Trust Company, N.A.
Nationwide Financial Services
Ohio Police & Firemen's Disability & Pension Fund
Ohio Public Employees' Retirement System

OHIO – continued

Dayton

Bank One, Dayton, N.A.
Citizens Federal Bank, F.S.B.
C.H. Dean Investment Associates
The Mead Corporation

Toledo

The Fifth Third Bank of Northwestern Ohio
Libby, Inc.
Owens-Corning Fiberglass Corporation

Westfield Center

Westfield Companies

OKLAHOMA

Oklahoma City

Fleming Companies, Inc.
Liberty Bank and Trust Co. (Oklahoma City) (Portfolio)
Liberty Bank and Trust Co. (Oklahoma City) (Trust)

Tulsa

BancOklahoma Trust Company
Bank of Oklahoma, N.A. (Portfolio)

OREGON

Portland

Columbia Management Company
The Crabbe-Huson Group, Inc.
Ferguson, Wellman, Rudd, Purdy & Van Winkle, Inc.
First Interstate Bank of Oregon (Trust)
Pacificorp
Qualivest Capital Management, Inc.
Standard Insurance Company
U.S. National Bank of Oregon (Portfolio)

Salem

Oregon State Treasury Investment Division — Fixed Income

PENNSYLVANIA

Berwyn

Cashman, Farrell and Associates

Blue Bell

Minton Investment Management

Camp Hill

Rite Aid Corporation

Chadds Ford

Consistent Asset Management Company

PENNSYLVANIA – continued

Erie
Erie Insurance Group

Harleysville
Harleysville Mutual Insurance Company

Harrisburg
Dauphin Deposit Bank & Trust Company (Portfolio)
Dauphin Deposit Bank & Trust Company (Trust)
Keystone Investment Services
Pennsylvania Public School Employees' Retirement System

Johnstown
USBANCORP, Inc.

Lancaster
Fulton Bank (Trust)

Malvern
Meridian Investment Company
The Vanguard Group, Inc.

Meadville
Commander Corporation
Commander Investment Corporation

Philadelphia
Bloom Staloff Brokerage Services Inc.
Chemical Futures & Options Inc.
CoreStates Investment Advisers, Inc.
Dean Witter Reynolds Inc. (Philadelphia)
Delaware Management Company Inc.
First Union National Bank (Pennsylvania) (Instl. Trust)
General Accident Group
The Glenmede Trust Company
Morgan Grenfell Capital Management Inc.
Provident Mutual Life Insurance Company
Wolf, Webb, Burk & Campbell Inc.

Pittsburgh
Alcoa
Federated Investors
Integra Financial Corporation
C.S. McKee & Company, Inc.
Mellon Bank, N.A. (Portfolio)
Mellon Bank, N.A. (Trust)
PNC Bank — Asset Liability (Portfolio)

Radnor
Rittenhouse Financial Services Inc.

Reading
Meridian Bancorp, Inc.

Wormleysburg
Harsco Corporation

PENNSYLVANIA – continued

Wyomissing

Meridian Bank (Portfolio)
Sovereign Bank, A Federal Savings Bank

PUERTO RICO

Bayamon

Santander National Bank

Hato Rey

Banco Popular of Puerto Rico (Portfolio)

Santurce

First Bank Puerto Rico

RHODE ISLAND

Johnston

Allendale Mutual Insurance Company

Providence

Citizens Trust Company & Savings Bank (Trust)

SOUTH CAROLINA

Columbia

South Carolina Retirement System

Greenville

Liberty Capital Advisors, Inc.

SOUTH DAKOTA

Sioux Falls

Midland National Life Insurance Company
South Dakota Investment Council

TENNESSEE

Chattanooga

Provident Life & Accident Insurance Co.

Cordova

Union Planters National Bank (Funds Management)

Memphis

First Tennessee Bank
Leader Federal Bank for Savings
National Bank of Commerce (Portfolio)

TENNESSEE – continued

Nashville

First American Corporation
SunTrust Bank, Nashville, N.A. (Trust)
Tennessee Consolidated Retirement System

TEXAS

Austin

Franklin Federal Bancorp, A Federal Savings Bank
Hoisington Investment Management Co.
National Western Asset Management, Inc.
Teachers' Retirement System of Texas
Texas County & District Retirement System
University of Texas System — Office of Investments

Bedford

Ponder Investment Company

Dallas

Barrow, Hanley, Mewhinney & Strauss, Inc.
Bluebonnet Savings Bank Fsb
Guaranty Federal Bank, F.S.B.
Life Insurance Company of the Southwest
Oryx Energy Company
Smith, Breeden Associates (Dallas)
Southwest Corporate Federal Credit Union

Fort Worth

AMR Investment Services, Inc.
Luther King Capital Management

Galveston

Securities Management and Research Inc.

Houston

AIM Advisors, Inc.
American General Corporation
Bank United of Texas, FSB
Boatmen's Trust Company of Texas
Coastal Banc ssb
First Interstate Bank of Texas (Portfolio)
Guardian Savings & Loan Association
Nicholas-Applegate Capital Management (Houston)
Shell Oil Company
Smith, Graham & Co. Asset Managers
Tenneco Inc.
Texas Commerce Bank, N.A. (Houston) (Trust)
Van Kampen American Capital Management & Research
Vaughan, Nelson, Scarborough & McConnell Inc.

Irving

Associates Corporation of North America
Bank of America Texas, N.A.
Exxon Corporation

Laredo

The Laredo National Bank

TEXAS – continued

San Antonio

The Frost National Bank (Portfolio)
United Services Advisors Inc.

Victoria

Victoria Bank & Trust Company (Trust)

Wichita Falls

Herbert R. Smith, Inc.

UTAH

Salt Lake City

Beneficial Life Insurance Company
Smith's Food & Drug Centers Inc.
Zions First National Bank (Portfolio)

VERMONT

Montpelier

National Life Investment Management Co.

VIRGINIA

Arlington

Strategic Fixed Income L.P.

Falls Church

Capital One Financial Corporation

Norfolk

Seaboard Investment Advisers Inc.

Richmond

Capitoline Investment Services, Inc. (Richmond)
Central Fidelity National Bank (Richmond) (Portfolio)
Commonwealth Investment Counsel
Crestar Bank (Portfolio)
Dominion Resources, Inc.
Richmond Capital Management, Inc.
Signet Banking Corporation
Thompson, Siegel & Walmsley, Inc.
Virtus Capital Management

Vienna

Navy Federal Credit Union

WASHINGTON

Bellevue

PACCAR Incorporated

WASHINGTON – continued

Olympia

Washington State Investment Board

Seattle

The Boeing Company
Evergreen Asset Management, Inc. (Washington)
Federal Home Loan Bank of Seattle
GNA Capital Management Inc.
Kennedy Associates Inc.
Olympic Capital Management, Inc.
SAFECO Insurance Companies
Washington Federal Savings & Loan Association

Tacoma

Frank Russell Investment Management Co.

Tukwila

Boeing Employee Credit Union

WEST VIRGINIA

Charleston

One Valley Bancorp of West Virginia

WISCONSIN

Appleton

Aid Association for Lutherans (AAL)

Brookfield

Dana Investment Advisors, Inc.

Green Bay

Associated Bank Green Bay, N.A.

Madison

American Family Insurance Group
Century Investment Management Co. (CIMCO)
Madison Investment Advisors, Inc.
State of Wisconsin Investment Board

Menomonee Falls

Strong Capital Management Inc.

Milwaukee

Johnson Controls, Inc.
Loomis, Sayles & Company L.P. (Milwaukee)
Marshall & Ilsley Corporation
MGIC Investment Corporation
M & I Investment Management Corp.
Northwestern Mutual Life Insurance Co.

Rapid Reference – Firms

WHILE YOU'RE PUTTING YOUR NOSE TO THE GRINDSTONE, WHERE'S THE GUY IN THE NEXT OFFICE PUTTING HIS?

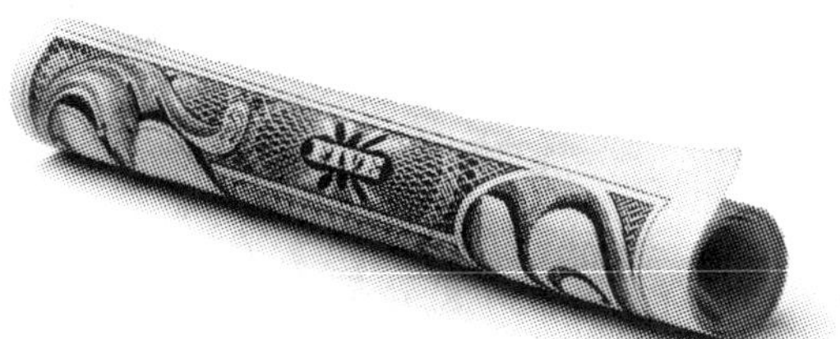

Nearly seven million employed Americans used an illicit drug at least once last month. Over 14 million used one in the past year. And while many users believe they are getting away with something, the consequences are everywhere.

Drug users are more likely to be absent, to file workers' comp claims, and to require disciplinary actions than non-drug-using employees. So the question isn't only what the guy in the next office is doing, it's whether he's even shown up for work.

It's enough to make you, the non-user, furious about having to carry the load. But, after you're finished being mad, do something. Get involved. Because more than anything, what a drug user in the workplace needs to know is he's not going to get away with it. Call **1-800-883-DRUG** and find out what you can do.

You'll be helping yourself, your company, and most of all, the guy in the next office.

PARTNERSHIP FOR A DRUG-FREE AMERICA®

Firm/Location	Buyside/Sellside	Telephone	Fax
ABN AMRO Securities (USA) Inc. Chicago, IL	S	312/781-8600	312/781-8167
The Acacia Group Washington, DC	B	202/628-4506	202/638-0345
Acorn Derivatives Management Corp. White Plains, NY	B	914/949-3516	914/949-3521
Adams, Viner & Mosler West Palm Beach, FL	B	407/655-4900	407/655-3059
Advanced Micro Devices, Inc. Sunnyvale, CA	B	408/732-2400	408/982-6161
Advisers Capital Management Inc. New York, NY	B	212/514-5110	212/514-5780
AEGON U.S.A. Investment Management (Cedar Rapids) Cedar Rapids, IA	B	319/363-5400	319/369-2009
Aetna Life & Casualty (Portfolio Management Group) Hartford, CT	B	203/273-0123	203/275-4846
AgriBank, FCB St. Paul, MN	B	612/282-8800	612/282-8666
H.F. Ahmanson & Company Irwindale, CA	B	818/960-6311	818/962-9679
Aid Association for Lutherans (AAL) Appleton, WI	B	414/734-5721	414/730-3752
AIM Advisors, Inc. Houston, TX	B	713/626-1919	713/626-0642
Alaska Permanent Capital Management Company Anchorage, AK	B	907/272-7575	907/272-7574
Alaska Retirement Systems Juneau, AK	B	907/465-4399	907/465-4397
Alcoa Pittsburgh, PA	B	412/553-4545	412/553-4498
Alfa Corporation Montgomery, AL	B	334/288-3900	334/288-0905
Alfa Group Montgomery, AL	B	334/288-3900	334/288-0905
Allendale Mutual Insurance Company Johnston, RI	B	401/275-3000	401/275-3022
Alliance Capital Management L.P. New York, NY	B	212/969-1000	212/969-2284
Alliance Capital Management (Minneapolis) Minneapolis, MN	B	612/332-1544	612/342-2149

Firm/Location	Buyside/Sellside	Telephone	Fax
Allianz Investment Corporation Westport, CT	B	203/221-8500	203/221-8529
Allied-Signal Inc. Morristown, NJ	B	201/455-2000	201/455-4807
Allmerica Asset Management, Inc. Worcester, MA	B	508/855-1000	508/852-6935
Allstate Insurance Company Northbrook, IL	B	708/402-5000	708/402-4347
Amalgamated Bank of New York (Investment Management Group) New York, NY	B	212/255-6200	212/675-6926
AMBAC Inc. New York, NY	B	212/668-0340	212/509-9190
AMBAC Financial Services, L.P. Westport, CT	B	203/222-9691	203/341-2351
AMCORE Bank, N.A. Rockford Rockford, IL	B	815/968-2241	815/961-7746
AMCORE Financial, Inc. Rockford, IL	B	815/968-2241	815/961-7749
American Agricultural Insurance Company Park Ridge, IL	B	312/399-5700	312/399-5896
American Express Company New York, NY	B	212/640-2000	212/611-9802
American Express Bank Ltd. New York, NY	B	212/306-9000	212/619-9872
American Express Financial Advisors Minneapolis, MN	B	612/671-3131	612/671-2733
American Family Insurance Group Madison, WI	B	608/242-4100	608/243-4923
American Family Life Assurance Company (AFLAC) Columbus, GA	B	706/323-3431	706/323-1838
American General Corporation Houston, TX	B	713/522-1111	713/831-6218
American Money Management Corporation Cincinnati, OH	B	513/579-2192	513/579-2580
American Mutual Life Insurance Company Des Moines, IA	B	515/283-2371	515/242-4670
American National Corporation Chicago, IL	B	312/661-5000	312/661-6417
American National Bank & Trust (Chicago) (Trust) Chicago, IL	B	312/661-5000	312/661-5341

Firm/Location	Buyside/Sellside	Telephone	Fax
American President Companies, Ltd. Oakland, CA	B	510/272-7000	510/272-7941
American Savings Bank, F.A. Irvine, CA	B	714/252-4300	714/252-6884
American United Life Insurance Company Indianapolis, IN	B	317/263-1877	317/263-1225
Ameritas Investment Advisors Inc. Lincoln, NE	B	402/467-6980	402/467-6970
Amoco Corporation Chicago, IL	B	312/856-6111	312/856-2454
AMR Investment Services, Inc. Fort Worth, TX	B	817/967-3509	817/967-9721
AmSouth Bank N.A. (Portfolio) Birmingham, AL	B	205/326-5120	205/326-5572
AmSouth Bank N.A. (Trust) Birmingham, AL	B	205/326-5120	205/581-7433
ANB Investment Management & Trust Co. of Chicago Chicago, IL	B	312/661-5866	312/661-5054
Anhalt/O'Connell, Inc. Los Angeles, CA	B	213/622-0066	213/613-0805
AON Advisors Incorporated Chicago, IL	B	312/701-3000	312/701-3900
Ark Asset Management Company, Inc. New York, NY	B	212/668-4800	212/668-6198
J. Aron & Company New York, NY	S	212/902-5326	212/346-2687
Arvin Industries, Inc. Columbus, IN	B	812/379-3000	812/379-3688
ASB Capital Management, Inc. Washington, DC	B	202/383-6300	202/347-8389
Asset Allocation & Management Company Chicago, IL	B	312/263-2900	312/263-1193
Associated Bank Green Bay, N.A. Green Bay, WI	B	414/433-3200	414/433-4381
Associates Corporation of North America Irving, TX	B	214/541-4000	214/541-4032
Atlantic Asset Management Partners Inc. Stamford, CT	B	203/363-5100	203/363-5110
AT&T New York, NY	B	212/387-5400	212/226-4935

Firm/Location	Buyside/Sellside	Telephone	Fax
Auto Club Insurance Association Livonia, MI	B	313/336-1234	313/462-8061
Auto-Owners Insurance Company Lansing, MI	B	517/323-1200	517/323-8796
Avatar Investors Associates New York, NY	B	212/753-7710	212/644-0332
BA Futures Inc. Chicago, IL	S	312/828-2345	312/987-0644
Back Bay Advisors, L.P. Boston, MA	B	617/578-1500	617/424-8665
BANC ONE Corporation Columbus, OH	B	614/248-5944	614/248-9344
Banco Popular of Puerto Rico (Portfolio) Hato Rey, PR	B	809/765-9800	809/754-9290
Banco Santander of New York (Dealer) New York, NY	S	212/350-3500	212/350-3535
BancOklahoma Trust Company Tulsa, OK	B	918/588-6000	918/588-6939
Bank of America NT & SA — Capital Markets San Francisco, CA	S	415/622-4386	415/622-5901
Bank of America Illinois (Dealer) Chicago, IL	S	312/828-2345	312/828-3820
Bank of America Illinois (Institutional Trust) Chicago, IL	B	312/828-7574	312/987-0500
Bank of America NT & SA — Capital Markets (New York) New York, NY	S	212/503-7000	212/836-5390
Bank of America NT & SA (Portfolio) Reno, NV	B	702/688-8600	702/688-8787
Bank of America Texas, N.A. Irving, TX	B	214/444-5555	214/444-5460
Bank Julius Baer & Co., Ltd. New York, NY	S	212/297-3600	212/297-1935
Bank of Boston Corporation Boston, MA	S	617/434-2200	617/434-8330
Bank of Boston (Treasury) Boston, MA	B	617/434-2200	617/434-6795
The Bank of California, N.A. San Francisco, CA	B	415/765-0400	415/765-2788
Bank of Hawaii (Investments) Honolulu, HI	B	808/847-8888	808/538-4471

Firm/Location	Buyside/Sellside	Telephone	Fax
Bank of Montreal (Chicago) Chicago, IL	S	312/845-4100	312/845-4198
Bank of Montreal (New York) New York, NY	S	212/758-6300	212/702-1193
The Bank of New York Company, Inc. New York, NY	B	212/495-1784	212/815-4023
The Bank of New York (Dealer) New York, NY	S	212/495-1784	212/495-1014
The Bank of North Dakota Bismarck, ND	B	701/328-5600	701/328-5632
Bank of Oklahoma, N.A. (Portfolio) Tulsa, OK	B	918/588-6000	918/588-6510
Bank One, Dayton, N.A. Dayton, OH	B	513/449-8600	513/449-7199
The Bank of Tokyo Trust Company (Pension & Investments) New York, NY	B	212/782-4000	212/571-5150
The Bank of Tokyo Trust Company (Securities & Investments) New York, NY	B	212/782-6705	212/782-6426
Bank United of Texas, FSB Houston, TX	B	713/543-6500	713/543-7927
Bank of the West (Portfolio) Walnut Creek, CA	B	510/942-8400	510/256-7202
Bankers Trust Global Investment Management New York, NY	B	212/250-2500	212/250-9857
Bankers Trust — New York Corporation (Portfolio) New York, NY	B	212/250-2500	212/775-2487
Banque Nationale de Paris (New York) New York, NY	S	212/750-1400	212/415-9798
Banque Paribas Ltd. Corporation New York, NY	S	212/841-2000	212/841-2146
Banque Worms Capital Corporation New York, NY	S	212/758-9205	212/593-4854
Baring Asset Management Company Boston, MA	B	617/951-0052	617/951-1432
Barnett Banks, Inc. Jacksonville, FL	B	904/791-7500	904/791-7185
Barrow, Hanley, Mewhinney & Strauss, Inc. Dallas, TX	B	214/665-1900	214/665-1965
Bartlett & Co. Cincinnati, OH	B	513/621-4612	513/621-6462

Firm/Location	Buyside/Sellside	Telephone	Fax
Bausch & Lomb Incorporated Rochester, NY	B	716/338-6000	716/338-6007
Baxter International Inc. Deerfield, IL	B	847/948-2000	847/948-3948
Bay View Federal Bank, A Federal Savings Bank San Mateo, CA	B	415/312-7268	415/573-1028
BayBank Boston, N.A. (Dealer) Boston, MA	S	617/482-1040	617/556-6650
BayBank Boston, N.A. (Portfolio) Boston, MA	B	617/556-6717	617/556-6650
Bayerische Vereinsbank AG (New York) New York, NY	S	212/210-0300	212/210-0330
BEA Associates New York, NY	B	212/832-2626	212/355-1545
Bear, Stearns & Company Inc. New York, NY	S	212/272-2000	212/272-6291
Bear, Stearns Asset Management Inc. New York, NY	B	212/272-2814	212/272-3107
Bear, Stearns Securities Corp. Chicago, IL	S	312/474-4600	312/474-4615
Bear, Stearns & Co. Inc. (Unit Trust) New York, NY	B	212/272-2500	212/272-3104
BellSouth Corporation Atlanta, GA	B	404/249-2000	404/249-5597
Beneficial Insurance Group, Inc. Peapack, NJ	B	908/781-4246	908/781-4479
Beneficial Life Insurance Company Salt Lake City, UT	B	801/531-7979	801/531-3315
Benefit Capital Management Corporation Danbury, CT	B	203/794-4762	203/794-2693
Benham Capital Management Group Mountain View, CA	B	415/965-8300	415/965-4902
Berkeley Capital Management San Francisco, CA	B	415/393-0300	415/393-0392
Berkley Dean & Co. Greenwich, CT	B	203/629-2880	203/629-4359
Berkshire Life Insurance Co. Pittsfield, MA	B	413/499-4321	413/443-9397
Sanford C. Bernstein & Co., Inc. New York, NY	B	212/486-5800	212/756-4550

Firm/Location	Buyside/Sellside	Telephone	Fax
Bessemer Trust Company, N.A. New York, NY	B	212/708-9100	212/265-5826
BlackRock Financial Management L.P. New York, NY	B	212/754-5560	212/754-8790
Bloom Staloff Brokerage Services Inc. Philadelphia, PA	S	215/567-0200	215/569-3377
Bluebonnet Savings Bank Fsb Dallas, TX	B	214/443-9000	214/443-4376
The Boatmen's National Bank of St. Louis (Portfolio) St. Louis, MO	B	314/466-6000	314/466-8480
Boatmen's Trust (St. Louis) (Fixed Income) St. Louis, MO	B	314/466-4086	314/466-4098
Boatmen's Trust Company of Texas Houston, TX	B	713/952-9100	713/952-9141
The Boeing Company Seattle, WA	B	206/655-2121	206/655-1177
Boeing Employee Credit Union Tukwila, WA	B	206/439-5700	206/439-5806
BofA Capital Management Inc. (Los Angeles) Los Angeles, CA	B	213/229-1400	213/626-2162
The Boston Company Asset Management Boston, MA	B	617/722-7000	617/722-7250
Boston Safe Deposit and Trust Company Boston, MA	B	617/722-7000	617/722-7807
BPS Associates, Inc. Bloomington, MN	B	612/893-0177	612/893-0909
BR Associates Chatham, NJ	S	908/771-7452	908/771-7452
BR Investment Associates Chatham, NJ	B	908/771-7452	908/771-7452
Bradford & Marzec, Inc. Los Angeles, CA	B	213/687-9170	213/687-9189
Branch Banking & Trust Company (BB&T-NC) (Portfolio) Winston-Salem, NC	B	910/733-2000	910/733-2238
Branch Banking & Trust Company (Trust) Raleigh, NC	B	919/831-3990	919/831-4397
Stacey Braun Associates Incorporated New York, NY	B	212/226-7707	212/941-0759
Bridgewater Associates Inc. Wilton, CT	B	203/762-8511	203/762-2615

Firm/Location	Buyside/Sellside	Telephone	Fax
Brinson Partners, Inc. Chicago, IL	B	312/220-7100	312/220-7199
Alex. Brown Investment Management Baltimore, MD	B	410/727-1700	410/837-8338
Brown Brothers Harriman & Co. (Investments) New York, NY	B	212/483-1818	212/493-8526
Brown Brothers Harriman & Co. (Investments) (Chicago) Chicago, IL	B	312/781-7111	312/368-1287
Brundage, Story and Rose New York, NY	B	212/269-3050	212/425-4286
BT Securities Corporation New York, NY	S	212/250-2500	212/250-7071
BZW Barclays Global Investors San Francisco, CA	B	415/597-2000	415/597-2011
BZW/Barclays Bank New York, NY	S	212/412-4000	212/412-1768
Calamos Asset Management, Inc. Naperville, IL	B	708/245-7200	708/245-7531
California Federal Bank, A Federal Savings Bank Los Angeles, CA	B	213/932-4321	213/930-6272
California Public Employees' Retirement System Sacramento, CA	B	916/326-3400	916/326-3363
California State Teachers' Retirement System Sacramento, CA	B	916/229-3870	916/387-9585
Calvert Asset Management Company, Inc. Bethesda, MD	B	301/951-4800	301/657-1982
Campbell Soup Company Camden, NJ	B	609/342-4800	609/342-3878
Canadian Imperial Bank of Commerce (U.S.A.) New York, NY	S	212/856-4000	212/856-6699
Capital Guardian Trust Company Los Angeles, CA	B	310/996-6000	310/996-6200
Capital One Financial Corporation Falls Church, VA	B	703/205-1000	703/205-1755
Capital Research & Management Company Los Angeles, CA	B	310/996-6000	310/996-6200
Capital Research & Management Company (New York) New York, NY	B	212/581-5000	212/582-7878
Capitol Federal Savings & Loan Association Topeka, KS	B	913/235-1341	913/231-6361

Firm/Location	Buyside/Sellside	Telephone	Fax
Capitoline Investment Services, Inc. (Richmond) Richmond, VA	B	804/782-7242	804/782-5839
Capitoline Investment Services, Inc. (Washington, DC) Washington, DC	B	202/879-6277	202/879-6333
Cardinal Management Corporation Columbus, OH	B	614/464-6811	614/464-8713
Caremark International Inc. Northbrook, IL	B	708/559-4700	708/559-4648
Carillon Advisers, Inc. Cincinnati, OH	B	513/595-2900	513/595-2843
Cashman, Farrell and Associates Berwyn, PA	B	610/889-1500	610/889-1665
CDC Investment Management Corp. (CIMCO) New York, NY	B	212/891-6100	212/891-6294
Central Carolina Bank & Trust Co. (Portfolio) Durham, NC	B	919/683-7777	919/682-3870
Central Fidelity National Bank (Richmond) (Portfolio) Richmond, VA	B	804/782-4000	804/783-8335
The Central Trust Bank Jefferson City, MO	B	314/634-1234	314/634-7813
Century Investment Management Co. (CIMCO) Madison, WI	B	608/232-6111	608/238-2316
Charter One Bank, F.S.B. Cleveland, OH	B	216/566-5300	216/566-5308
Charter One Bank, F.S.B. (Michigan) Detroit, MI	B	313/965-1400	313/965-5936
Chase Manhattan Private Bank Investment Management New York, NY	B	212/789-4000	212/398-1872
Chase Securities Inc. New York, NY	S	212/552-2222	212/425-1404
Chemical Bank (Portfolio) New York, NY	B	212/834-5000	212/834-6550
Chemical Futures & Options Inc. Philadelphia, PA	S	215/561-3030	215/561-3027
Chemical Securities Incorporated New York, NY	S	212/270-6000	212/834-6527
Chevy Chase Federal Savings Bank Chevy Chase, MD	B	301/986-7000	301/986-7002
The Chicago Corporation — Asset Management Group Chicago, IL	B	312/855-7600	312/855-4066

Firm/Location	Buyside/Sellside	Telephone	Fax
Christiana Bank, New York Branch New York, NY	S	212/827-4800	212/827-4888
The Chubb Corporation Warren, NJ	B	908/903-2000	908/580-3775
CIGNA Investment Management (U.S.A.) Hartford, CT	B	203/726-6000	203/726-8530
CIGNA Investments, Inc. Hartford, CT	B	203/726-6000	203/726-8137
Circus Circus Enterprises, Inc. Las Vegas, NV	B	702/734-0410	702/794-3831
Citibank, N.A. (Portfolio) New York, NY	B	212/559-1000	212/527-2737
Citibank Private Banking Investment Division New York, NY	B	212/559-2838	212/527-2099
Citicorp New York, NY	B	212/291-2542	212/291-4007
Citicorp Global Derivatives Chicago, IL	S	312/993-3000	312/993-6830
Citicorp Securities, Inc. New York, NY	S	212/559-1000	212/425-3857
Citizens Federal Bank, F.S.B. Dayton, OH	B	513/223-4234	513/228-5510
Citizens National Bank of Evansville (Portfolio) Evansville, IN	B	812/464-3400	812/464-3496
Citizens Trust Company & Savings Bank (Trust) Providence, RI	B	401/456-7000	401/455-5310
Coast Federal Bank, Federal Savings Bank (Administration) West Hills, CA	B	818/316-8000	818/316-3228
Coastal Banc ssb Houston, TX	B	713/623-2600	713/960-9864
Collective Bank Egg Harbor City, NJ	B	609/965-1235	609/625-9149
Colonial Management Associates Boston, MA	B	617/426-3750	617/737-0358
Columbia Management Company Portland, OR	B	503/222-3600	503/243-2928
Columbus Circle Investors Stamford, CT	B	203/353-6000	203/353-6041
Comerica Bank (Funds Management) Detroit, MI	B	313/222-4000	313/222-9825

Firm/Location	Buyside/Sellside	Telephone	Fax
Commander Corporation Meadville, PA	S	814/724-5078	No fax
Commander Investment Corporation Meadville, PA	B	814/724-5078	No fax
Commerce Bancshares Inc. Clayton, MO	B	314/726-2255	314/746-7432
Commerce Bank Investment Management Group Kansas City, MO	B	816/234-2000	816/234-2545
Commercial Federal Corporation Omaha, NE	B	402/554-9200	402/390-5143
Commercial Union Investment Management Boston, MA	B	617/725-6000	617/725-6702
Commerz Financial Products New York, NY	S	212/266-7700	212/266-7567
Commerzbank Capital Markets New York, NY	S	212/266-7700	212/266-7797
Commonwealth Investment Counsel Richmond, VA	B	804/782-3207	804/782-3629
Compass Bank (Portfolio) Birmingham, AL	B	205/933-3000	205/715-7997
Compass Bank (Trust) Birmingham, AL	B	205/558-6785	205/558-6754
Conseco Capital Management Carmel, IN	B	317/817-6100	317/817-2763
Consistent Asset Management Company Chadds Ford, PA	B	610/558-3000	610/558-3002
Continental Asset Management New York, NY	B	212/440-7526	212/440-7518
CoreStates Investment Advisers, Inc. Philadelphia, PA	B	215/973-3350	215/973-3460
Corning Incorporated Corning, NY	B	607/974-9000	607/974-8150
The Crabbe-Huson Group, Inc. Portland, OR	B	503/295-0111	503/295-2939
Credit Lyonnais Bank New York, NY	S	212/261-7000	212/459-3170
Credit Suisse Financial Products New York, NY	S	212/322-5900	212/238-5332
Crestar Bank (Portfolio) Richmond, VA	B	804/782-5000	804/782-5100

Firm/Location	Buyside/Sellside	Telephone	Fax
CS First Boston Corporation New York, NY	S	212/909-2000	212/308-1187
CTT Investment Management Group Chicago, IL	B	312/223-2000	312/223-5170
Dai-Ichi Kangyo Bank Ltd. (New York) New York, NY	S	212/466-5200	212/912-0915
Daiwa Securities America, Inc. New York, NY	S	212/612-7000	212/612-7100
Dana Investment Advisors, Inc. Brookfield, WI	B	414/782-3631	414/782-0581
Dauphin Deposit Bank & Trust Company (Portfolio) Harrisburg, PA	B	717/255-2121	717/255-2073
Dauphin Deposit Bank & Trust Company (Trust) Harrisburg, PA	B	717/255-2121	717/255-2073
Davis Selected Advisers, L.P. Santa Fe, NM	B	505/820-1000	505/820-1222
C.H. Dean Investment Associates Dayton, OH	B	513/222-9531	513/227-9313
Dean Witter, Discover & Co. New York, NY	B	212/392-2222	212/392-8405
Dean Witter InterCapital Inc. New York, NY	B	212/392-1600	212/392-4282
Dean Witter Reynolds Inc. New York, NY	S	212/392-2222	212/392-0188
Dean Witter Reynolds Institutional Futures Chicago, IL	S	312/984-4345	312/641-0463
Dean Witter Reynolds Inc. (Philadelphia) Philadelphia, PA	S	215/665-1485	215/665-1486
Delaware Management Company Inc. Philadelphia, PA	B	215/988-1200	215/988-1005
Delphi Capital Management, Inc. New York, NY	B	212/838-7000	212/838-7598
Denver Investment Advisors Inc. Denver, CO	B	303/312-5000	303/312-4900
Deposit Guaranty Corp. Jackson, MS	B	601/354-8211	601/354-8329
Deposit Guaranty National Bank (Portfolio) Jackson, MS	B	601/354-8486	601/354-8361
Deposit Guaranty National Bank (Trust) Jackson, MS	B	601/354-8128	601/354-8143

Firm/Location	Buyside/Sellside	Telephone	Fax
Deutsche Morgan Grenfell New York, NY	S	212/474-8000	212/474-8212
Dewey Square Investors Corporation Boston, MA	B	617/526-1300	617/526-1337
The Dime Savings Bank of New York, FSB New York, NY	B	212/326-6912	212/326-6907
Dimensional Fund Advisors, Inc. Santa Monica, CA	B	310/395-8005	310/395-6140
DKB Financial Products, Inc. New York, NY	S	212/488-8460	212/432-8464
Dodge & Cox Inc. San Francisco, CA	B	415/981-1710	415/986-5471
Dominion Resources, Inc. Richmond, VA	B	804/775-5700	804/775-5819
Dow Jones & Company, Inc. New York, NY	B	212/416-2000	212/416-2655
Dresdner Securities (USA) Inc. New York, NY	S	212/429-2100	212/429-4496
The Dreyfus Corporation New York, NY	B	212/922-6000	212/922-6076
Dreyfus Management New York, NY	B	212/922-6000	212/715-6014
Duke Power Company Charlotte, NC	B	704/594-9400	704/382-7363
Eagle Asset Management, Inc. St. Petersburg, FL	B	813/573-2453	813/573-8325
Eastbridge Capital, Inc. New York, NY	B	212/756-7200	212/756-7270
Eaton Corporation Cleveland, OH	B	216/523-5000	216/523-4787
Eaton Vance Management, Inc. Boston, MA	B	617/482-8260	617/451-0642
Ecolab Inc. St. Paul, MN	B	612/293-2233	612/293-2471
Employers Reinsurance Corporation Overland Park, KS	B	913/676-5200	913/676-5221
Enhance Financial Services Group Inc. New York, NY	B	212/983-3100	212/682-5377
Equifax, Inc. Atlanta, GA	B	404/885-8000	404/885-5452

Firm/Location	Buyside/Sellside	Telephone	Fax
The Equitable Companies Incorporated New York, NY	B	212/554-1234	212/554-2320
Equitable Investment Services, Inc. Des Moines, IA	B	515/282-0323	515/282-9538
Erie Insurance Group Erie, PA	B	814/870-2000	814/870-3126
Essex Radez Company Chicago, IL	S	312/362-2916	No fax
Euro Brokers Maxcor, Inc. New York, NY	S	212/748-7000	212/748-7050
Evangelical Lutheran Church-Board of Pensions Minneapolis, MN	B	612/333-7651	612/334-5307
Evergreen Asset Management Corp. (New York) Purchase, NY	B	914/694-2020	914/641-2279
Evergreen Asset Management, Inc. (Washington) Seattle, WA	B	206/224-9914	206/382-0950
Exco Noonan Inc. Jersey City, NJ	S	201/200-4500	201/200-5069
Exxon Corporation Irving, TX	B	214/444-1000	214/444-1348
Falcon Asset Management, Inc. Baltimore, MD	B	410/547-3660	410/547-3582
Farmers Insurance Group of Companies Los Angeles, CA	B	213/932-3200	213/930-3101
Federal Home Loan Bank of Atlanta Atlanta, GA	B	404/888-8000	404/897-1846
Federal Home Loan Bank of Boston Boston, MA	B	617/542-0150	617/292-9645
Federal Home Loan Bank of Chicago Chicago, IL	B	312/565-5700	312/565-5823
Federal Home Loan Bank of San Francisco San Francisco, CA	B	415/616-1000	415/616-2626
Federal Home Loan Bank of Seattle Seattle, WA	B	206/340-2300	206/340-2485
Federal Home Loan Bank of Topeka Topeka, KS	B	913/233-0507	913/234-1796
Federal National Mortgage Association Washington, DC	B	202/752-7000	202/752-4447
Federated Group Owatonna, MN	B	507/455-5200	507/455-5199

Firm/Location	Buyside/Sellside	Telephone	Fax
Federated Investors Pittsburgh, PA	B	412/288-1900	412/288-1982
Ferguson, Wellman, Rudd, Purdy & Van Winkle, Inc. Portland, OR	B	503/226-1444	503/226-3647
Fidelity Management & Research Company Boston, MA	B	617/563-2500	617/723-9637
Fidelity Management Trust Company Boston, MA	B	617/563-8700	617/476-9858
Fiduciary Asset Management Clayton, MO	B	314/726-5533	314/863-4360
Fiduciary Trust Company International New York, NY	B	212/466-4100	212/839-6403
Fiduciary Trust Company of Massachusetts Boston, MA	B	617/482-5270	617/482-3774
Fielding Management Company, Inc. Rochester, NY	B	716/383-1300	716/383-0914
Fifth Third Bank Cincinnati, OH	B	513/579-5300	513/579-4312
The Fifth Third Bank of Northwestern Ohio Toledo, OH	B	419/259-7890	419/259-7869
FIMAT Futures U.S.A., Inc. New York, NY	S	212/527-8100	212/759-2898
FIMAT Futures U.S.A. Inc. (Chicago) Chicago, IL	S	312/578-5200	312/578-5277
Financial Counselors, Inc. Kansas City, MO	B	816/751-5258	816/751-5265
Financial Holding Corporation Kansas City, MO	B	816/391-2000	816/391-2165
The FINOVA Group Inc. Phoenix, AZ	B	602/207-4900	602/207-5543
First of America Bank Corporation Kalamazoo, MI	B	616/376-7460	616/376-7484
First of America Investment Corporation Kalamazoo, MI	B	616/385-0200	616/385-0227
First American Corporation Nashville, TN	B	615/748-2000	615/541-6372
First Asset Management Minneapolis, MN	B	612/973-0999	612/973-0200
First Bank, N.A. (Omaha) (Trust) Omaha, NE	B	402/348-6000	402/348-7819

Firm/Location	Buyside/Sellside	Telephone	Fax
First Bank Puerto Rico Santurce, PR	B	809/729-8200	809/724-5965
First Bank System (Portfolio) Minneapolis, MN	B	612/973-1111	612/973-0965
First Chicago Capital Markets, Inc. Chicago, IL	S	312/732-4000	312/732-8733
First Chicago Futures Chicago, IL	S	312/408-8300	312/732-3348
First Chicago/NBD Corporation Chicago, IL	B	312/732-4000	312/732-3366
First Citizens Bank & Trust Co. Raleigh, NC	B	919/755-7285	919/755-7545
First Commercial Corporation Little Rock, AR	B	501/371-7000	501/371-7413
First Commercial Capital Management Little Rock, AR	B	501/371-6756	501/371-7487
First Federal Savings and Loan Association of Rochester Rochester, NY	B	716/238-2119	716/238-2056
First Interstate Bank of California (Trust) Los Angeles, CA	B	213/614-4111	213/614-2468
First Interstate Bank of Denver (Trust) Denver, CO	B	303/293-2211	303/293-5163
First Interstate Bank of Nevada Las Vegas, NV	B	702/791-6150	702/791-6131
First Interstate Bank of Oregon (Trust) Portland, OR	B	503/225-2376	503/225-4066
First Interstate Bank of Texas (Portfolio) Houston, TX	B	713/224-6611	713/226-1958
First Investors Management Co., Inc. New York, NY	B	212/858-8000	212/858-8078
First Manhattan Capital Management New York, NY	B	212/756-3300	212/223-4175
First National Bank of Chicago (Dealer) Chicago, IL	S	312/732-4000	312/732-4840
First National Bank of Commerce (Investment) New Orleans, LA	B	504/561-1380	504/561-1923
First National Bank Evergreen Park (Portfolio) Evergreen Park, IL	B	708/422-6700	708/422-6827
First National Bank Gainesville (Portfolio) Gainesville, GA	B	770/503-2000	770/503-2706

Firm/Location	Buyside/Sellside	Telephone	Fax
First National Bank of Maryland (Portfolio) Baltimore, MD	B	410/244-4000	410/244-4477
First National Bank of Ohio Akron, OH	B	216/384-8000	216/253-1849
The First National Bank of Omaha (Trust) Omaha, NE	B	402/633-3434	402/341-6556
First Nationwide Bank, A Federal Savings Bank San Francisco, CA	B	415/904-1100	415/904-1325
First NH Bank Manchester, NH	B	603/634-7145	603/634-7189
First NH Investment Services Manchester, NH	B	603/634-6165	603/224-9405
First Tennessee Bank Memphis, TN	B	901/523-4444	901/523-4266
First Union Corporation Charlotte, NC	B	704/374-6161	704/374-4609
First Union National Bank of Florida Coral Gables, FL	B	305/569-1904	305/569-1938
First Union National Bank (New Jersey) Newark, NJ	B	201/565-3200	201/430-4821
First Union National Bank of North Carolina — Funds Mgmt. Charlotte, NC	B	704/374-6161	704/374-6902
First Union National Bank (Pennsylvania) (Instl. Trust) Philadelphia, PA	B	215/985-6423	215/985-6441
Fischer, Francis, Trees and Watts, Inc. New York, NY	B	212/681-3000	212/681-3250
Flaherty & Crumrine, Inc. Pasadena, CA	B	818/795-7300	818/795-0269
Fleet Bank of Maine (Portland) Portland, ME	B	207/874-5000	207/874-5230
Fleet Financial Group Boston, MA	B	617/346-2000	617/346-0130
Fleet Investment Advisors (Boston) Boston, MA	B	617/346-5686	617/292-2061
Fleming Companies, Inc. Oklahoma City, OK	B	405/840-7200	405/841-8149
Florida State Board of Administration Tallahassee, FL	B	904/488-4406	904/921-2131
The Ford Foundation New York, NY	B	212/573-5000	212/599-4584

Firm/Location	Buyside/Sellside	Telephone	Fax
Ford Motor Company Dearborn, MI	B	313/322-3000	313/390-2106
Fort Washington Investment Advisors Inc. Cincinnati, OH	B	513/421-1800	513/629-1047
Fort Washington Investment Advisors Inc. (Cincinnati) Cincinnati, OH	B	513/361-7600	513/361-7699
Fort Wayne National Bank (Trust) Fort Wayne, IN	B	219/426-0555	219/461-6214
Fortis Advisers, Inc. Golden Valley, MN	B	612/544-1531	612/544-6363
Fortis Asset Management New York, NY	B	212/859-7000	212/859-7202
Franklin Federal Bancorp, A Federal Savings Bank Austin, TX	B	512/477-5000	512/479-3498
Franklin Resources, Inc. Norwalk, CT	B	203/866-8575	203/866-9961
Freeport-McMoRan Inc. New Orleans, LA	B	504/582-4000	504/582-4936
Fremont General Corporation Santa Monica, CA	B	310/315-5500	310/315-5599
Fremont Investment Advisors Inc. San Francisco, CA	B	415/768-4258	415/284-8122
The Frost National Bank (Portfolio) San Antonio, TX	B	210/220-4011	210/220-4614
Fuji Bank Ltd. New York, NY	S	212/898-2000	212/321-9408
Fuji Securities, Inc. Chicago, IL	S	312/899-4700	312/899-4701
Fulton Bank (Trust) Lancaster, PA	B	717/291-2411	717/291-2695
Gabelli-O'Connor Fixed Income Management Co. Darien, CT	B	203/655-1999	203/655-7719
Garvin GuyButler Corporation New York, NY	S	212/732-6900	212/815-6587
GEM Capital Management, Inc. New York, NY	B	212/753-0700	212/753-0735
General Accident Group Philadelphia, PA	B	215/625-1000	215/625-2103
General American Investment Management Company (GAIMCO) St. Louis, MO	B	314/231-1700	314/444-0486

Firm/Location	Buyside/Sellside	Telephone	Fax
General Electric Company Fairfield, CT	B	203/373-2211	203/373-3131
General Electric Capital Corporation Stamford, CT	B	203/357-4000	203/357-6791
General Electric Investment Corporation Stamford, CT	B	203/326-2300	203/326-4215
General Motors Acceptance Corporation Detroit, MI	B	313/974-1222	313/974-1244
General Motors Investment Management Corp. New York, NY	B	212/418-6100	212/418-3665
General Re Asset Management, Inc. Stamford, CT	B	203/328-5000	203/328-6504
General Re Securities Corporation New York, NY	S	212/307-2300	212/307-2320
Gibraltar Advisors New York, NY	B	212/415-5800	212/415-5885
The Glenmede Trust Company Philadelphia, PA	B	215/419-6000	215/419-6197
Glickenhaus & Company (Investments) New York, NY	B	212/953-7800	212/599-2537
GMG/Seneca Capital Management San Francisco, CA	B	415/677-1550	415/677-1692
GNA Capital Management Inc. Seattle, WA	B	206/625-1755	206/583-5606
Golden Eagle Insurance Company San Diego, CA	B	619/463-5800	619/460-3820
Goldman Sachs & Company New York, NY	S	212/902-1000	212/902-1512
Goldman Sachs Asset Management (U.S.A.) New York, NY	B	212/902-0800	212/902-9100
Goldman Sachs & Company (Chicago) Chicago, IL	S	312/655-4600	312/655-4555
W.R. Grace & Company Boca Raton, FL	B	407/362-2000	407/362-2193
Gradison-McDonald Asset Management Cincinnati, OH	B	513/579-5000	513/579-5080
Grantham, Mayo, Van Otterloo & Company Boston, MA	B	617/346-7610	617/439-0457
Great Western Bank, a Federal Savings Bank (Treasury) Chatsworth, CA	B	818/775-2800	818/775-2811

Firm/Location	Buyside/Sellside	Telephone	Fax
The Greater New York Savings Bank New York, NY	B	212/613-4000	212/613-4117
Greenwich Capital Markets, Inc. Greenwich, CT	S	203/625-2700	203/629-4426
Greenwich Street Advisors New York, NY	B	212/816-5700	212/816-6006
Greenwich Street Advisors Municipal Management New York, NY	B	212/816-5711	212/816-5117
Guaranty Federal Bank, F.S.B. Dallas, TX	B	214/360-3360	214/360-8983
Guardian Life Insurance Co. of America New York, NY	B	212/598-8000	212/777-6715
Guardian Savings & Loan Association Houston, TX	B	713/787-3100	713/787-3192
M.A. Hanna Company Cleveland, OH	B	216/589-4000	216/589-4200
Harbor Capital Management Company, Inc. Boston, MA	B	617/478-7200	617/439-9789
Harleysville Mutual Insurance Company Harleysville, PA	B	215/256-5000	215/256-5601
Harris Corporation Melbourne, FL	B	407/727-9100	407/727-9344
Harris Associates, L.P. Chicago, IL	B	312/621-0600	312/621-0372
Harris Investment Management, Inc. Chicago, IL	B	312/461-7699	312/765-8160
Harris Trust & Savings (Personal Trust) Chicago, IL	B	312/461-2121	312/461-7142
Harsco Corporation Wormleysburg, PA	B	717/763-7064	717/763-6424
Harvard Management Company Boston, MA	B	617/523-4400	617/523-1283
Hawaiian Electric Industries, Inc. Honolulu, HI	B	808/543-5662	808/543-7966
Hawaiian Trust Co., Ltd. Honolulu, HI	B	808/538-4444	808/538-1788
Heber Fuger Wendin Incorporated Birmingham, MI	B	810/258-6866	810/258-9295
Heine Securities Corporation Short Hills, NJ	B	201/912-2000	201/912-0147

Firm/Location	Buyside/Sellside	Telephone	Fax
Hercules Incorporated Wilmington, DE	B	302/594-5000	302/594-5405
Heritage Asset Management, Inc. St. Petersburg, FL	B	813/573-8320	813/573-8334
Heritage House Asset Management Boston, MA	B	617/482-8877	617/451-0800
Hibernia Corporation New Orleans, LA	B	504/586-5552	504/586-5841
Hibernia National Bank (Trust) New Orleans, LA	B	504/533-5531	504/533-0153
Hoisington Investment Management Co. Austin, TX	B	512/327-7200	512/327-8646
Honeywell, Inc. Minneapolis, MN	B	612/951-1000	612/951-3070
Hotchkis and Wiley Los Angeles, CA	B	213/362-8888	213/623-7880
Household International, Inc. Prospect Heights, IL	B	708/564-5000	708/564-6110
Howard Hughes Medical Institute Chevy Chase, MD	B	301/215-8687	301/215-8691
HSBC Asset Management Americas Inc. New York, NY	B	212/503-6815	212/503-6808
HSBC Markets New York, NY	S	212/658-2700	212/658-1905
Humana Inc. Louisville, KY	B	502/580-1000	502/580-4089
Huntington Bancshares, Incorporated Columbus, OH	B	614/480-8300	614/480-3761
The Huntington Trust Company, N.A. Columbus, OH	B	614/463-5345	614/480-5223
Hyperion Capital Management, Inc. New York, NY	B	212/980-8400	212/753-5869
I.B.J.-Schroder Bank & Trust Co. (Trust) New York, NY	B	212/858-2000	212/514-9279
IDS Fixed Income Advisors Minneapolis, MN	B	612/671-3335	612/671-2733
Illinois State Board of Investment Chicago, IL	B	312/793-5712	312/793-2266
Independence One Capital Management Corp. Farmington Hills, MI	B	810/473-3300	810/473-3094

Firm/Location	Buyside/Sellside	Telephone	Fax
Independent Bank Corp. Rockland, MA	B	617/878-6100	617/982-6591
ING Barings New York, NY	S	212/446-1500	212/644-0428
ING Investment Management Inc. — Americas Region Atlanta, GA	B	770/850-4800	770/850-4801
Integra Financial Corporation Pittsburgh, PA	B	412/644-7669	412/261-7279
Intel Corporation Santa Clara, CA	B	408/765-8080	408/765-1821
Inter-American Development Bank Washington, DC	B	202/623-1000	202/623-3096
Intercapital Securities Inc. New York, NY	S	212/888-8756	212/319-4001
Inter-Regional Financial Group, Inc. Minneapolis, MN	B	612/371-7750	612/371-7755
Interstate/Johnson Lane, Inc. Charlotte, NC	B	704/379-9000	704/379-9281
INTRUST Bank (Trust) Wichita, KS	B	316/383-1111	316/383-1140
INVESCO Management and Research, Inc. Boston, MA	B	617/345-8200	617/261-4560
INVESCO MIM Inc. Atlanta, GA	B	404/892-0896	404/892-3204
Investek Capital Management Jackson, MS	B	601/949-3105	601/949-3177
Investment Advisers, Inc. Minneapolis, MN	B	612/376-2600	612/376-2616
Investment Counselors of Maryland, Inc. Baltimore, MD	B	410/539-3838	410/783-7321
Investors Management Group, Ltd. (IMG) Des Moines, IA	B	515/244-5426	515/244-2353
Investors Savings Bank Millburn, NJ	B	201/376-5100	201/376-5243
Israel Discount Bank of New York New York, NY	B	212/551-8500	212/370-9623
ITT Corporation New York, NY	B	212/258-1000	212/258-1027
ITT Hartford Life Insurance Company Simsbury, CT	B	203/547-5000	203/843-6457

Firm/Location	Buyside/Sellside	Telephone	Fax
Jamaica Savings Bank, Fsb Lynbrook, NY	B	516/887-7000	516/596-1205
John Alden Asset Management Miami, FL	B	305/715-2000	305/715-3914
John Hancock Advisers, Inc. Boston, MA	B	617/375-1500	617/375-1831
John Hancock Mutual Life Insurance Company Boston, MA	B	617/572-6000	617/572-1605
Johnson Controls, Inc. Milwaukee, WI	B	414/228-1200	414/228-2302
Johnson Investment Counsel Incorporated Cincinnati, OH	B	513/385-4001	513/385-8947
Kansas City Life Insurance Company Kansas City, MO	B	816/753-7299	816/753-1354
Henry Kaufman & Company, Inc. New York, NY	B	212/755-3040	212/755-4090
Kennedy Associates Inc. Seattle, WA	B	206/624-9640	206/624-8515
Kentucky National Insurance Co. Lexington, KY	B	606/253-5200	606/253-5203
Key Trust Company (Albany) Albany, NY	B	518/488-5800	518/488-5846
Key Trust Company (Syracuse) Syracuse, NY	B	315/470-5209	315/470-5283
KeyCorp Cleveland, OH	B	216/689-0234	216/689-5115
Keystone Custodian Funds, Inc. Boston, MA	B	617/338-3200	617/338-3351
Keystone Investment Services Harrisburg, PA	B	717/231-5724	717/231-5758
Kiewit Investment Management Omaha, NE	B	402/342-2052	402/271-2918
Luther King Capital Management Fort Worth, TX	B	817/332-3235	817/332-4630
Knights of Columbus New Haven, CT	B	203/865-1710	203/772-0037
Laidlaw Capital Management, Inc. New York, NY	B	212/949-5400	212/233-7784
The Laredo National Bank Laredo, TX	B	210/723-1151	210/723-0260

Firm/Location	Buyside/Sellside	Telephone	Fax
LaSalle National Bank (Portfolio) Chicago, IL	B	312/781-8000	312/750-6244
Lazard Freres Asset Management New York, NY	B	212/632-6000	212/632-6060
Leader Federal Bank for Savings Memphis, TN	B	901/578-2000	901/524-5715
Lehman Brothers, Inc. New York, NY	S	212/526-7000	212/526-3738
Lehman Brothers, Inc. (Chicago) Chicago, IL	S	312/609-8000	312/609-8562
Lehman Brothers Global Asset Management, Inc. (New York) New York, NY	B	212/526-0600	212/528-6300
Leucadia National Corporation New York, NY	B	212/460-1900	212/598-4869
Lexington Management Corporation Saddle Brook, NJ	B	201/845-7300	201/845-5121
LGT Asset Management San Francisco, CA	B	415/392-6181	415/956-5617
Libby, Inc. Toledo, OH	B	419/727-2100	419/727-2585
Liberty Bank and Trust Co. (Oklahoma City) (Portfolio) Oklahoma City, OK	B	405/231-6000	405/231-6758
Liberty Bank and Trust Co. (Oklahoma City) (Trust) Oklahoma City, OK	B	405/231-6453	405/231-6725
Liberty Capital Advisors, Inc. Greenville, SC	B	803/268-8303	803/292-4097
Life Insurance Company of the Southwest Dallas, TX	B	214/638-7100	214/638-9393
Life Partners Group Englewood, CO	B	303/779-1111	303/796-7576
Lincoln National Corporation Fort Wayne, IN	B	219/455-2000	219/455-2301
Lincoln National Investment Management Co. Fort Wayne, IN	B	219/455-2000	219/455-1475
Lipper & Company, L.P. New York, NY	B	212/883-6333	212/883-8701
Litton Industries, Inc. Beverly Hills, CA	B	310/859-5000	310/859-5940
The Long Island Savings Bank, F.S.B. Melville, NY	B	516/547-2265	516/547-3029

Firm/Location	Buyside/Sellside	Telephone	Fax
Loomis, Sayles & Company L.P. Boston, MA	B	617/482-2450	617/482-1985
Loomis, Sayles & Company L.P. (Bloomfield Hills) Bloomfield Hills, MI	B	810/646-2100	810/645-8608
Loomis, Sayles & Company L.P. (Milwaukee) Milwaukee, WI	B	414/272-4844	414/272-1531
Loomis, Sayles & Company L.P. (Pasadena) Pasadena, CA	B	818/793-8989	818/584-1197
Loomis, Sayles & Company Inc. (San Francisco) San Francisco, CA	B	415/956-2424	415/956-1052
Loomis, Sayles & Company Inc. (Washington, D.C.) Washington, DC	B	202/463-6200	202/293-8264
Lord Abbett & Company New York, NY	B	212/848-1800	212/888-4405
Los Angeles County Treasurer Los Angeles, CA	B	213/974-2191	213/625-2249
Lotsoff Capital Management Chicago, IL	B	312/368-1442	312/750-1131
Lutheran Brotherhood Minneapolis, MN	B	612/340-7000	612/340-8328
Madison Investment Advisors, Inc. Madison, WI	B	608/274-0300	608/274-7905
Madison Scottsdale Scottsdale, AZ	B	602/596-3338	602/596-3303
Magna Group, Inc. St. Louis, MO	B	314/963-2500	314/963-2691
E.D. & F. Man International Securities Corp. New York, NY	S	212/566-9000	212/566-9456
E.D. & F. Man International Inc. (Chicago) Chicago, IL	S	312/663-7500	312/663-7710
Manning & Napier Advisors Inc. Rochester, NY	B	716/325-6880	716/325-1992
Manufacturers & Traders Trust Company (Portfolio) New York, NY	B	212/350-2000	212/350-2166
Manufacturers & Traders Trust Company (Treasury) Buffalo, NY	B	716/842-4200	716/842-5823
Marine Midland Bank, N.A. (Trust) Buffalo, NY	B	716/841-2424	716/841-4244
Mark Twain Bank (Portfolio) St. Louis, MO	B	314/727-1000	314/746-2609

Firm/Location	Buyside/Sellside	Telephone	Fax
Marshall & Ilsley Corporation Milwaukee, WI	B	414/765-7700	414/765-7645
Martin Marietta Corporation Bethesda, MD	B	301/897-6000	301/897-6929
Maryland State Retirement & Pension System Baltimore, MD	B	410/225-1020	410/523-8133
Masco Corporation Taylor, MI	B	313/274-7400	313/374-6666
Massachusetts Financial Services Company Boston, MA	B	617/954-5000	617/954-6603
Massachusetts Mutual Life Insurance Co. Springfield, MA	B	413/788-8411	413/744-6127
MBIA Securities Corporation Armonk, NY	B	914/273-4545	914/765-3375
MBNA Corporation Newark, DE	B	302/456-8588	302/456-8541
McDonald's Corporation Oak Brook, IL	B	708/575-3000	708/575-6941
McDonnell Douglas Corporation St. Louis, MO	B	314/232-0232	314/234-3826
MCI Communications Corporation Washington, DC	B	202/872-1600	202/887-2443
C.S. McKee & Company, Inc. Pittsburgh, PA	B	412/566-1234	412/566-1548
McKesson Corporation San Francisco, CA	B	415/983-8300	415/983-7160
MCN Corporation Detroit, MI	B	313/256-5500	313/256-5232
The Mead Corporation Dayton, OH	B	513/495-6323	513/461-2424
The Medical Protective Company Fort Wayne, IN	B	219/485-9622	219/486-0415
Mellon Bank, N.A. (Portfolio) Pittsburgh, PA	B	412/234-4100	412/234-8913
Mellon Bank, N.A. (Trust) Pittsburgh, PA	B	412/234-4100	412/236-0648
Mellon Private Asset Management Group Boston, MA	B	617/722-7000	617/722-7250
Mercantile Banks of St. Louis, N.A. St. Louis, MO	B	314/425-2525	314/425-2727

Firm/Location	Buyside/Sellside	Telephone	Fax
Mercantile — Safe Deposit & Trust Co. (Trust) Baltimore, MD	B	410/237-5900	410/237-5380
The Merchants Bank of New York New York, NY	B	212/973-6637	212/966-4813
Merck & Co., Inc. Whitehouse Station, NJ	B	908/423-7958	908/735-1275
Merganser Capital Management Corporation Cambridge, MA	B	617/494-1000	617/494-1899
Meridian Bancorp, Inc. Reading, PA	B	610/655-2000	610/655-2428
Meridian Bank (Portfolio) Wyomissing, PA	B	610/655-2788	610/655-3916
Meridian Investment Company Malvern, PA	B	610/251-7991	610/251-5985
Merita Bank New York, NY	B	212/318-9300	212/421-4420
Merrill Lynch Asset Management Inc. Plainsboro, NJ	B	609/282-1212	609/282-3055
Merrill Lynch Capital Markets New York, NY	S	212/449-1000	212/449-2805
MERUS Capital Management San Francisco, CA	B	415/296-6401	415/296-6472
Metropolitan Life Insurance Company New York, NY	B	212/578-2211	212/578-3910
MGIC Investment Corporation Milwaukee, WI	B	414/347-2569	414/347-6382
M & I Investment Management Corp. Milwaukee, WI	B	414/287-7300	414/287-8730
Michigan Department of Treasury Lansing, MI	B	517/373-3140	517/335-2164
Michigan National Bank (Portfolio) Farmington Hills, MI	B	810/473-3000	810/473-3250
Midland National Life Insurance Company Sioux Falls, SD	B	605/335-5700	605/335-3621
Millipore Corporation Bedford, MA	B	617/275-9200	617/275-5550
MIMLIC Asset Management Company St. Paul, MN	B	612/298-3826	612/223-5959
Minnesota State Board of Investment St. Paul, MN	B	612/296-3328	612/296-9572

Firm/Location	Buyside/Sellside	Telephone	Fax
Minton Investment Management Blue Bell, PA	B	610/940-0695	610/940-0696
Mitchell Hutchins Asset Management, Inc. New York, NY	B	212/713-4000	212/713-1459
Mitsubishi Capital Markets Services New York, NY	S	212/667-2500	212/667-3560
Mitsubishi Financial Futures Inc. Chicago, IL	S	312/930-2300	312/930-2320
Mitsui T & B Futures Inc. Chicago, IL	S	312/362-2244	312/362-4568
Modern Woodmen of America Rock Island, IL	B	309/786-6481	309/786-1701
Montag & Caldwell, Incorporated Atlanta, GA	B	404/262-0100	404/262-0105
Montana Board of Investments Helena, MT	B	406/444-0001	406/449-6579
MONY Financial Services New York, NY	B	212/708-2000	212/708-2491
J.P. Morgan & Company Inc. New York, NY	B	212/483-2323	212/509-7628
J.P. Morgan Futures Inc. (Chicago) Chicago, IL	S	312/541-3300	312/541-3381
J.P. Morgan Investment Management, Inc. (U.S.A.) New York, NY	B	212/837-2300	212/575-0392
J.P. Morgan Securities Inc. New York, NY	S	212/483-2323	212/648-5253
Morgan Grenfell Capital Management Inc. Philadelphia, PA	B	215/246-0200	215/963-0200
Morgan Stanley & Co., Incorporated (NYC Branch) New York, NY	S	212/703-4000	212/764-7490
Morgan Stanley Asset Management, Inc. New York, NY	B	212/296-7100	212/296-7289
Munder Capital Management, Inc. Birmingham, MI	B	810/647-9200	810/647-5931
Mutual of America Capital Management Corporation New York, NY	B	212/224-1600	212/224-2539
National Bank of Alaska Anchorage, AK	B	907/276-1132	907/265-2139
National Bank of Commerce (Portfolio) Memphis, TN	B	901/523-3700	901/523-3879

Firm/Location	Buyside/Sellside	Telephone	Fax
National City Bank of Akron Akron, OH	B	216/375-8433	216/375-8434
National City Bank, Indiana Indianapolis, IN	B	317/267-7000	317/267-6112
National Life Investment Management Co. Montpelier, VT	B	802/223-9300	802/223-9332
National Mutual Funds Management Inc. Los Angeles, CA	B	310/557-1500	310/286-2314
National Western Asset Management, Inc. Austin, TX	B	512/836-1010	512/835-2729
NationsBanc — CRT Chicago, IL	S	312/234-5000	312/234-3089
NationsBank (Charlotte) (Funds Management) Charlotte, NC	B	704/386-5000	704/339-6490
Nationwide Financial Services Columbus, OH	B	614/249-7111	614/249-4698
NatWest Bank, N.A. (Portfolio) Jersey City, NJ	B	201/547-7000	201/547-2979
NatWest Securities Corporation New York, NY	S	212/602-4800	212/602-4939
Navy Federal Credit Union Vienna, VA	B	703/255-8000	703/255-7755
NBD Bank, N.A. (Trust) Detroit, MI	B	313/225-1000	313/225-1038
NCM Capital Management Group, Inc. Durham, NC	B	919/688-0620	919/682-0414
Nebraska State Investment Council Lincoln, NE	B	402/471-2043	402/471-2498
Neuberger & Berman Management Inc. New York, NY	B	212/476-9000	212/476-5535
New Jersey Division of Investments Trenton, NJ	B	609/292-5106	609/396-1073
New Mexico Educational Retirement Board Santa Fe, NM	B	505/827-8030	505/989-7738
New Mexico State Permanent Funds Santa Fe, NM	B	505/827-6226	505/827-6242
New York Life Insurance Company (U.S.A) New York, NY	B	212/576-7000	212/576-8163
New York State & Local Retirement Systems Albany, NY	B	518/474-6035	518/473-6755

Firm/Location	Buyside/Sellside	Telephone	Fax
New York State Teachers' Retirement System Albany, NY	B	518/447-2666	518/447-2630
Nicholas-Applegate Capital Management San Diego, CA	B	619/687-8000	619/687-8040
Nicholas-Applegate Capital Management (Houston) Houston, TX	B	713/963-5200	713/963-5235
Nike Securities (UIT Management) Lisle, IL	B	708/241-4141	708/241-8727
Nikko Capital Management (U.S.A.) New York, NY	B	212/599-0300	212/599-4640
Nomura Capital Management (U.S.A.) New York, NY	B	212/509-9253	212/509-8835
Nomura Securities International, Inc. New York, NY	S	212/667-9300	212/667-1058
North Carolina Department of State Treasurer Raleigh, NC	B	919/733-4191	919/733-0075
North Fork Bank (Portfolio) Mattituck, NY	B	516/298-5000	516/298-5769
North Side Savings Bank Floral Park, NY	B	516/488-6900	516/488-6546
The Northern Trust Company (Treasury) Chicago, IL	B	312/630-6000	312/444-5666
Northern Trust Corporation Chicago, IL	B	312/630-6000	312/444-7843
Northrop Grumman Corporation Los Angeles, CA	B	310/553-6262	310/201-3023
Northwestern Mutual Life Insurance Co. Milwaukee, WI	B	414/271-1444	414/299-7124
Norwest Bank Indiana, N.A. Fort Wayne, IN	B	219/461-6000	219/461-6678
Norwest Bank Iowa, N.A. Des Moines, IA	B	515/245-3131	515/245-8117
Norwest Investment Management (Minnesota) Minneapolis, MN	B	612/667-1234	612/667-0127
Norwest Investments & Trust Services Denver, CO	B	303/863-6800	303/863-4879
NYNEX Corporation White Plains, NY	B	914/644-7300	914/644-6287
Oak Hill Partners New York, NY	B	212/326-1500	212/593-3596

Firm/Location	Buyside/Sellside	Telephone	Fax
OFFITBANK New York, NY	B	212/758-9600	212/486-6957
The Ohio National Life Insurance Company Cincinnati, OH	B	513/861-3600	513/559-6589
Ohio Police & Firemen's Disability & Pension Fund Columbus, OH	B	614/228-4076	614/228-0451
Ohio Public Employees' Retirement System Columbus, OH	B	614/466-5155	614/469-8276
Old Kent Bank & Trust Company (Portfolio) Grand Rapids, MI	B	616/771-5000	616/771-4317
Old Kent Bank & Trust Company (Trust) Grand Rapids, MI	B	616/771-5469	616/771-4640
Old National Bank in Evansville (Portfolio) Evansville, IN	B	812/464-1200	812/464-1567
Olympic Capital Management, Inc. Seattle, WA	B	206/447-9399	206/624-3871
OnBank, Inc. (Portfolio) Syracuse, NY	B	315/424-4400	315/424-5992
One Valley Bancorp of West Virginia Charleston, WV	B	304/348-7000	304/348-7315
Oppenheimer & Co., Inc. New York, NY	S	212/667-7000	212/667-5302
Oppenheimer Management Corporation New York, NY	B	212/323-0200	212/323-0558
Oregon State Treasury Investment Division — Fixed Income Salem, OR	B	503/378-4111	503/378-6772
Oryx Energy Company Dallas, TX	B	214/715-4000	214/715-3311
Owens-Corning Fiberglass Corporation Toledo, OH	B	419/248-8000	419/248-6227
PACCAR Incorporated Bellevue, WA	B	206/455-7400	206/453-4900
Pacholder Associates, Inc. Cincinnati, OH	B	513/985-3200	513/985-3217
Pacific Income Advisers Santa Monica, CA	B	310/393-1039	310/393-0714
Pacific Investment Management Co. (PIMCO) Newport Beach, CA	B	714/640-3031	714/720-1376
Pacific Mutual Life Insurance Company Newport Beach, CA	B	714/640-3011	714/640-3199

Firm/Location	Buyside/Sellside	Telephone	Fax
Pacificorp Portland, OR	B	503/731-2000	503/731-2136
PaineWebber Incorporated New York, NY	S	212/713-2000	212/713-1303
PanAgora Asset Management, Inc. (U.S.A.) Boston, MA	B	617/439-6300	617/439-6302
The Patterson Capital Corporation Los Angeles, CA	B	310/556-2496	310/553-3605
Paul Revere Investment Management Corp. Worcester, MA	B	508/799-4441	508/751-7240
Payden & Rygel Investment Counsel Los Angeles, CA	B	213/625-1900	213/628-8488
Pekin Insurance Company Pekin, IL	B	309/346-1161	309/346-8512
Pennsylvania Public School Employees' Retirement System Harrisburg, PA	B	717/783-5613	717/783-9424
Pension Boards — United Church of Christ New York, NY	B	212/870-2777	212/870-2877
People's Bank Bridgeport, CT	B	203/338-7171	203/338-2502
People's Bank (Investment) Bridgeport, CT	B	203/338-7210	203/338-4927
Peregrine Capital Management Minneapolis, MN	B	612/343-7600	612/343-7636
Peregrine Derivatives Ltd. New York, NY	S	212/593-5920	212/593-5932
Phoenix Duff & Phelps Investment Management Co. (Chicago) Chicago, IL	B	312/368-5500	312/368-5512
Phoenix Duff & Phelps Investment Management Co. (Hartford) Hartford, CT	B	203/275-5000	203/275-5509
Physicians Mutual Insurance Company Omaha, NE	B	402/633-1000	402/633-1096
Pillar Point Capital Management Inc. San Mateo, CA	B	415/377-3900	415/573-0672
Pioneer Financial Services, Inc. Schaumburg, IL	B	708/995-0400	708/413-7192
Pioneering Management Corporation Boston, MA	B	617/742-7825	617/422-4281
Piper Capital Management Inc. Minneapolis, MN	B	612/342-5800	612/342-6992

Firm/Location	Buyside/Sellside	Telephone	Fax
Plaza Investment Managers, Inc. Washington, DC	B	301/718-5358	301/718-5362
PNC Bank — Asset Liability (Portfolio) Pittsburgh, PA	B	412/762-2000	412/762-4167
PNC Bank Ohio (Trust) Cincinnati, OH	B	513/651-8896	513/651-7156
PNC Institutional Management Corp. Wilmington, DE	B	302/791-1700	302/791-2467
Ponder Investment Company Bedford, TX	B	817/354-8282	817/354-1437
The Portfolio Group, Inc. New York, NY	B	212/332-4200	212/332-4296
PPM America Inc. Chicago, IL	B	312/634-2500	312/634-0050
Prebon Yamane (U.S.A.) Jersey City, NJ	S	201/557-5000	201/557-5895
Premier Investment Advisors Baton Rouge, LA	B	504/332-4011	504/332-7350
Presidential Life Insurance Company Nyack, NY	B	914/358-2300	914/358-2818
T. Rowe Price Associates, Inc. Baltimore, MD	B	410/547-2000	410/659-0965
PriMerit Bank, A Federal Savings Bank Las Vegas, NV	B	702/362-5555	702/365-3477
Princeton Insurance Companies Princeton, NJ	B	609/452-9404	609/734-8461
Principal Mutual Life Insurance Company Des Moines, IA	B	515/247-5111	515/248-8486
The Private Bank of Bank of Boston Boston, MA	B	617/434-2920	617/434-6311
Protective Life Corporation Birmingham, AL	B	205/879-9230	205/868-3609
The Provident Bank (Portfolio) Cincinnati, OH	B	513/579-2075	513/579-2233
Provident Life & Accident Insurance Co. Chattanooga, TN	B	615/755-1011	615/755-1671
Provident Mutual Life Insurance Company Philadelphia, PA	B	215/636-5000	215/636-8322
Providian Corporation Louisville, KY	B	502/560-2000	502/560-3080

Firm/Location	Buyside/Sellside	Telephone	Fax
Prudential Capital Management Newark, NJ	B	201/802-8476	201/802-8845
Prudential Securities Inc. New York, NY	S	212/214-1000	212/776-3463
Public Employees Retirement Association of Colorado Denver, CO	B	303/832-9550	303/863-3753
Public Service Enterprise Group Incorporated Newark, NJ	B	201/430-7000	201/430-5845
The Putnam Management Company Inc. Boston, MA	B	617/292-1000	617/292-1713
The Quaker Oats Company Chicago, IL	B	312/222-7111	312/222-8323
Qualivest Capital Management, Inc. Portland, OR	B	503/275-6806	503/274-0405
Quantilogic Asset Management San Francisco, CA	B	415/434-1130	415/434-1139
Rabobank Nederland North America New York, NY	S	212/916-7800	212/818-0233
Raytheon Company Lexington, MA	B	617/862-6600	617/860-2172
RCM Capital Management San Francisco, CA	B	415/954-5400	415/954-8200
Reams Asset Management Company Inc. Columbus, IN	B	812/372-6606	812/376-3137
Regents of the University of California Oakland, CA	B	510/987-9600	510/987-9617
Regions Financial Corporation (Investments) Birmingham, AL	B	205/326-7100	205/326-7775
Reich & Tang L.P. New York, NY	B	212/830-5200	212/830-5350
Reliance Insurance Company New York, NY	B	212/909-1100	212/909-1844
Renaissance Investment Management Inc. Cincinnati, OH	B	513/723-4500	513/723-4512
Republic National Bank of NY (Treasury) New York, NY	B	212/221-6000	212/525-6200
Republic New York Securities Corporation New York, NY	S	212/525-6600	212/525-6958
Richmond Capital Management, Inc. Richmond, VA	B	804/379-8280	804/379-9362

Firm/Location	Buyside/Sellside	Telephone	Fax
Riggs Investment Management Corporation Washington, DC	B	202/835-6000	202/835-6806
Rite Aid Corporation Camp Hill, PA	B	717/761-2633	717/975-5905
Rittenhouse Financial Services Inc. Radnor, PA	B	610/971-9300	610/293-2444
The Rochester Community Savings Bank Rochester, NY	B	716/258-3000	716/423-7365
Rodney Square Management Corporation Wilmington, DE	B	302/651-8280	302/651-1507
Roosevelt Bank, A Federal Savings Bank Chesterfield, MO	B	314/532-6200	314/532-6358
Royal Caribbean Cruises Ltd. Miami, FL	B	305/539-6000	305/539-0562
The Rushmore Funds, Inc. Bethesda, MD	B	301/657-1500	301/657-1511
Frank Russell Investment Management Co. Tacoma, WA	B	206/627-7001	206/596-3120
RXR Capital Management, Inc. Stamford, CT	B	203/323-5015	203/325-5999
Ryan Labs, Inc. New York, NY	B	212/635-2300	212/635-2309
SAFECO Insurance Companies Seattle, WA	B	206/545-5000	206/545-3446
The St. Paul Companies Inc. St. Paul, MN	B	612/221-7911	612/221-8439
St. Paul Federal Bank for Savings Chicago, IL	B	312/804-2110	312/804-2285
The Sakura Bank Ltd. (New York) New York, NY	S	212/756-6700	212/644-9565
Sakura Global Capital, Inc. New York, NY	S	212/486-8282	212/355-4271
Sallie Mae Washington, DC	B	202/333-8000	202/965-7085
Salomon Brothers Inc. New York, NY	S	212/783-7000	212/783-2284
Salomon Brothers Asset Management Inc. (U.S.A.) New York, NY	B	212/783-7000	212/783-4014
Santander Financial Products New York, NY	S	212/350-3500	212/350-3535

Firm/Location	Buyside/Sellside	Telephone	Fax
Santander National Bank Bayamon, PR	B	809/740-4444	809/798-4480
Sanwa Bank New York, NY	S	212/339-6500	212/750-3284
Sanwa Securities (USA) Co., L.P. New York, NY	S	212/527-2600	212/935-1024
M.D. Sass Investors Services, Inc. New York, NY	B	212/730-2000	212/764-0381
Schlumberger, Ltd. New York, NY	B	212/350-9400	212/350-9564
Schroder Wertheim Investment Services New York, NY	B	212/641-3900	212/641-3985
Charles Schwab Investment Management San Francisco, CA	B	415/974-7600	415/974-7660
SCOR Reinsurance Company New York, NY	B	212/390-5200	212/488-8608
Scudder Stevens & Clark, Inc. (Boston) Boston, MA	B	617/295-1000	617/295-1111
Scudder Stevens & Clark, Inc. (Chicago) Chicago, IL	B	312/861-2700	312/861-1472
Scudder Stevens & Clark, Inc. (Cincinnati) Cincinnati, OH	B	513/621-2733	513/621-5081
Scudder Stevens & Clark, Inc. (Los Angeles) Los Angeles, CA	B	213/628-1144	213/626-1005
Scudder Stevens & Clark, Inc. (San Francisco) San Francisco, CA	B	415/981-8191	415/403-0784
Seaboard Investment Advisers Inc. Norfolk, VA	B	804/622-7300	804/622-0918
Sears Roebuck and Company Chicago, IL	B	312/875-2500	312/875-8351
Securities Management and Research Inc. Galveston, TX	B	409/763-0726	409/766-6608
Security Benefit Life Insurance Co. of Kansas Topeka, KS	B	913/295-3000	913/295-3099
Security Life of Denver Insurance Co. Denver, CO	B	303/860-1290	303/860-2049
Selective Insurance of America Branchville, NJ	B	201/948-3000	201/948-6709
J & W Seligman & Co., Incorporated New York, NY	B	212/850-1864	212/922-5747

Firm/Location	Buyside/Sellside	Telephone	Fax
Shay Assets Management Co. Chicago, IL	B	312/938-2586	312/938-2548
Shell Oil Company Houston, TX	B	713/241-6161	713/241-2341
Signet Banking Corporation Richmond, VA	B	804/747-2000	804/771-7599
Sit Investment Fixed Income Advisors Inc. Minneapolis, MN	B	612/332-3223	612/342-2018
Skandia Investment Management Inc. (U.S.A.) New York, NY	B	212/978-2700	212/385-2169
Herbert R. Smith, Inc. Wichita Falls, TX	B	817/723-5565	817/322-3887
William B. Smith & Company Inc. Salem, MA	B	508/741-4933	617/289-9555
Smith Affiliated Capital Corporation New York, NY	B	212/644-9440	212/644-1979
Smith Barney, Inc. (Capital Management) New York, NY	B	212/816-6700	212/816-6167
Smith Barney, Inc. (Chicago) Chicago, IL	S	312/419-3600	312/419-3490
Smith Barney, Inc. (Greenwich Street) New York, NY	S	212/816-6000	212/723-8792
Smith Barney Investment Advisors New York, NY	B	212/816-6999	212/816-6101
Smith, Breeden Associates Overland Park, KS	B	913/451-1566	913/451-6313
Smith, Breeden Associates (Boulder) Boulder, CO	B	303/440-5151	303/440-5131
Smith, Breeden Associates (Chapel Hill) Chapel Hill, NC	B	919/967-7221	919/933-3157
Smith, Breeden Associates (Dallas) Dallas, TX	B	214/871-2575	214/871-1329
Smith, Graham & Co. Asset Managers Houston, TX	B	713/227-1100	713/227-0912
Smith's Food & Drug Centers Inc. Salt Lake City, UT	B	801/974-1400	801/974-1662
Societe Generale Securities Corporation New York, NY	S	212/278-6000	212/278-7195
Society Asset Management, Inc. Cleveland, OH	B	216/689-3000	216/689-7083

Firm/Location	Buyside/Sellside	Telephone	Fax
Society National Bank (Portfolio) Cleveland, OH	B	216/689-3000	216/689-3832
South Boston Savings Bank Boston, MA	B	617/268-2500	617/269-5354
South Carolina Retirement System Columbia, SC	B	803/737-6800	803/734-2039
South Dakota Investment Council Sioux Falls, SD	B	605/367-5850	605/367-5863
Southern Farm Bureau Casualty Insurance Co. Ridgeland, MS	B	601/957-7777	601/957-4329
Southern Farm Bureau Life Insurance Co. Jackson, MS	B	601/981-7422	601/981-1670
SouthTrust Bank of Alabama, N.A. (Portfolio) Birmingham, AL	B	205/254-6856	205/254-5839
SouthTrust Bank of Alabama, N.A. (Trust) Birmingham, AL	B	205/254-5000	205/254-5989
Southwest Corporate Federal Credit Union Dallas, TX	B	214/861-3000	214/861-3322
Sovereign Bank, A Federal Savings Bank Wyomissing, PA	B	610/320-8400	610/320-8448
Sprint Corporation Westwood, KS	B	913/624-3000	913/624-3281
Standard Federal Bank Troy, MI	B	810/643-9600	810/643-0329
Standard Insurance Company Portland, OR	B	503/321-8844	503/321-8431
Standish, Ayer & Wood Inc. Boston, MA	B	617/350-6100	617/350-7520
Standish International Management Co., L.P. Boston, MA	B	617/350-6100	617/350-7520
Stanford Management Company Menlo Park, CA	B	415/926-0200	415/854-9188
Star Bank, N.A. (Cincinnati) (Portfolio) Cincinnati, OH	B	513/632-4000	513/632-4653
State Compensation Insurance Fund San Francisco, CA	B	415/565-1234	415/565-1783
State Street Bank & Trust (Trust) Boston, MA	B	617/786-3000	617/654-4449
State Street Boston Corporation Boston, MA	B	617/786-3000	617/664-5377

Firm/Location	Buyside/Sellside	Telephone	Fax
State Street Global Advisors Boston, MA	B	617/654-4738	617/654-6176
State Street Research & Management Co. Boston, MA	B	617/357-1200	617/542-7753
Staten Island Savings Bank Staten Island, NY	B	718/447-7900	718/727-3794
Stein Roe & Farnham Incorporated Chicago, IL	B	312/368-7700	312/368-8103
STI Capital Management Orlando, FL	B	407/237-4472	407/237-4285
Strategic Fixed Income L.P. Arlington, VA	B	703/812-8300	703/812-9554
Strong Capital Management Inc. Menomonee Falls, WI	B	414/359-3600	414/359-3460
Summit Bank (Portfolio) Chatham, NJ	B	201/701-6200	201/701-2675
SunFinancial Group Wellesley Hills, MA	B	617/237-6030	617/431-7521
SunTrust Bank, Nashville, N.A. (Trust) Nashville, TN	B	615/748-4736	615/255-2804
Swiss Bank Corporation (SBC Warburg) New York, NY	S	212/335-1000	212/335-1389
SwissRe Advisers Inc. New York, NY	B	212/973-5000	212/973-5035
Synovus Financial Corporation Columbus, GA	B	706/649-2311	706/649-2479
TCF Bank Minnesota fsb Minneapolis, MN	B	612/661-6500	612/376-9089
Teachers Insurance & Annuity Association New York, NY	B	212/490-9000	212/916-6690
Teachers' Retirement System of Texas Austin, TX	B	512/397-6460	512/370-0519
Teledyne Inc. Los Angeles, CA	B	310/277-3311	310/551-4365
Templeton Global Bond Managers, Inc. Fort Lauderdale, FL	B	954/764-7390	954/462-2504
Tenneco Inc. Houston, TX	B	713/757-2131	713/757-4257
Tennessee Consolidated Retirement System Nashville, TN	B	615/741-2643	615/741-1061

Firm/Location	Buyside/Sellside	Telephone	Fax
Texaco Inc. White Plains, NY	B	914/253-4000	914/253-7753
Texas Commerce Bank, N.A. (Houston) (Trust) Houston, TX	B	713/236-4865	713/216-5674
Texas County & District Retirement System Austin, TX	B	512/469-9668	512/479-8114
Third Federal Savings & Loan Association of Cleveland Cleveland, OH	B	216/441-6000	216/441-0055
Thompson, Siegel & Walmsley, Inc. Richmond, VA	B	804/353-4500	804/353-0925
Thornburg Management Company, Inc. Santa Fe, NM	B	505/984-0200	505/984-0310
TIG Holdings Inc. New York, NY	B	212/446-2700	212/371-8360
Todd Investment Advisors Inc. Louisville, KY	B	502/585-3121	502/585-4203
The Tokai Bank Ltd. New York, NY	S	212/339-1200	212/754-2174
Torchmark Corporation Birmingham, AL	B	205/325-4200	205/325-4157
The Toronto-Dominion Bank (New York — Dealer) New York, NY	S	212/468-0300	212/262-1949
The Transamerica Corporation San Francisco, CA	B	415/983-4000	415/983-4888
Transamerica Investment Services Inc. Los Angeles, CA	B	213/742-4141	213/742-4150
Travelers Group New York, NY	B	212/816-8000	212/816-8912
The Travelers Insurance Company Hartford, CT	B	203/277-0111	203/277-3667
Trust Company Bank of Georgia (Trust) Atlanta, GA	B	404/588-7711	404/581-1793
Trust Company of the West (TCW) (High Yield Dept.) Los Angeles, CA	B	310/575-9700	310/575-1997
Trustmark National Bank (Portfolio) Jackson, MS	B	601/354-5111	601/949-2382
Twentieth Century Insurance Company Woodland Hills, CA	B	818/704-3700	818/716-1308
UBS Asset Management, Inc. (U.S.A.) New York, NY	B	212/789-7100	212/789-7237

Firm/Location	Buyside/Sellside	Telephone	Fax
UBS Securities, Inc. New York, NY	S	212/821-4000	212/821-5805
Union Bank — Los Angeles Los Angeles, CA	B	213/236-5000	213/236-7983
Union Bank of Switzerland Private Banking New York, NY	B	212/715-3000	212/715-3498
Union Capital Advisors (San Diego) San Diego, CA	B	619/230-4714	619/230-4391
Union Carbide Corporation Danbury, CT	B	203/794-2000	203/794-3334
Union Labor Life Insurance Co. (ULLICO) Washington, DC	B	202/682-0900	202/682-7932
Union Planters National Bank (Funds Management) Cordova, TN	B	901/383-6940	901/383-6947
United Air Lines Employees Credit Union Arlington Heights, IL	B	708/952-6600	708/952-6593
United Asset Management Corporation Boston, MA	B	617/330-8900	617/330-1133
United Farm Bureau Life Insurance Co. Indianapolis, IN	B	317/692-7200	317/692-7525
United Jersey Bank (Portfolio) Hackensack, NJ	B	201/646-5000	201/646-1849
United Jersey Bank (Princeton) (Trust) Princeton, NJ	B	609/987-3680	609/921-2474
United Missouri Bank, N.A. (Portfolio) Kansas City, MO	B	816/860-7200	816/860-4829
United Missouri Investment Counsel Service Kansas City, MO	B	816/860-7000	816/860-4829
United of Omaha Life Insurance Company Omaha, NE	B	402/342-7600	402/351-2913
United Services Advisors Inc. San Antonio, TX	B	210/308-1234	210/308-1270
U.S. National Bank of Oregon (Portfolio) Portland, OR	B	503/275-5006	503/275-5032
U.S. Steel & Carnegie Pension Fund New York, NY	B	212/593-5151	212/826-8443
United States Trust Company of Boston Boston, MA	B	617/726-7000	617/695-4775
United States Trust Co. of California., N.A. Los Angeles, CA	B	213/488-4000	213/488-4029

Firm/Location	Buyside/Sellside	Telephone	Fax
United States Trust Company of New York (Portfolio) New York, NY	B	212/852-1000	212/635-3580
United States Trust Company of New York (Trust) New York, NY	B	212/852-1000	212/852-3370
U.S. West, Inc. Englewood, CO	B	303/649-4500	303/649-4520
University of Texas System — Office of Investments Austin, TX	B	512/499-4317	512/499-4429
UNUM Life Insurance Company Portland, ME	B	207/770-2211	207/770-4152
USBANCORP, Inc. Johnstown, PA	B	814/533-5300	814/533-5430
USLIFE Advisers Inc. New York, NY	B	212/709-6000	212/709-6064
Valley National Bank (New Jersey) (Portfolio) Wayne, NJ	B	201/305-4058	201/305-8415
The Vanguard Group, Inc. Malvern, PA	B	610/669-1000	610/640-6894
Van Kampen American Capital Investment Advisory Corp. Oakbrook Terrace, IL	B	708/684-6000	708/684-6270
Van Kampen American Capital Management & Research Houston, TX	B	713/993-0500	713/966-7411
Vaughan, Nelson, Scarborough & McConnell Inc. Houston, TX	B	713/224-2545	713/247-9534
Victoria Bank & Trust Company (Trust) Victoria, TX	B	512/574-5869	512/574-5669
Virtus Capital Management Richmond, VA	B	804/771-7164	804/771-7908
Voyageur Asset Management Denver, CO	B	303/293-0782	303/292-5376
Voyageur Fund Managers Minneapolis, MN	B	612/376-7000	612/341-2818
Wachovia Corporation Winston-Salem, NC	B	910/770-5000	910/770-6667
Wachovia Bank Capital Management Winston-Salem, NC	B	910/732-4385	910/770-6630
Wachovia Bank Capital Management (Atlanta) Atlanta, GA	B	404/332-4162	404/332-4163
Waddell & Reed Investment Management Co. Shawnee Mission, KS	B	913/236-2000	913/236-1885

Firm/Location	Buyside/Sellside	Telephone	Fax
Warburg, Pincus Counsellors, Inc. New York, NY	B	212/878-0600	212/878-9351
Washington Federal Savings & Loan Association Seattle, WA	B	206/624-7930	206/467-0524
Washington Square Advisers Inc. Minneapolis, MN	B	612/342-3736	612/342-7541
Washington State Investment Board Olympia, WA	B	360/664-8900	360/664-8912
Webster Bank Waterbury, CT	B	203/755-1422	203/573-8301
Wellington Management Company Boston, MA	B	617/951-5000	617/951-5250
Wells Fargo Bank, N.A. (Treasury) San Francisco, CA	B	415/477-1000	415/399-1614
Wentworth, Hauser & Violich, Inc. San Francisco, CA	B	415/981-6911	415/788-7281
WESTAMERICA Bank San Rafael, CA	B	415/456-8000	415/257-8127
Westdeutsche Landesbank Girozentrale — New York Branch New York, NY	S	212/852-6000	212/852-6300
Western Asset Management Company Pasadena, CA	B	818/584-4300	818/584-4390
Western Financial Savings Bank, Fsb Irvine, CA	B	714/727-1000	714/727-2306
Westfield Companies Westfield Center, OH	B	330/887-0101	330/887-0840
Westpac Banking Corporation New York, NY	S	212/551-2700	212/818-1499
Whitney National Bank (Portfolio) New Orleans, LA	B	504/586-7272	504/586-7383
Williams, Jones & Associates Inc. New York, NY	B	212/935-8750	212/753-3072
Wilmington Trust Company (Fixed Income) Wilmington, DE	B	302/651-1000	302/651-1758
Wilmington Trust Company (Portfolio) Wilmington, DE	B	302/651-1000	302/651-1187
Winterthur Swiss Group New York, NY	B	212/416-5700	212/524-6839
State of Wisconsin Investment Board Madison, WI	B	608/266-2381	608/266-2436

Firm/Location	Buyside/Sellside	Telephone	Fax
WMX Technologies, Inc. Oak Brook, IL	B	708/572-8800	708/572-3094
Wolf, Webb, Burk & Campbell Inc. Philadelphia, PA	B	215/735-5910	215/735-7892
Woodmen of the World Life Insurance Society Omaha, NE	B	402/342-1890	402/342-5136
The World Bank Washington, DC	B	202/477-1234	202/477-8589
World Savings & Loan Association, A Fed. Svgs. & Loan Assn. Oakland, CA	B	510/446-6000	510/446-4672
Yamaichi International (America), Inc. New York, NY	S	212/912-6400	212/912-0172
YMCA Retirement Fund New York, NY	B	212/766-4150	212/227-6941
The Zenith Insurance Company Woodland Hills, CA	B	818/713-1000	818/713-0177
Zions First National Bank (Portfolio) Salt Lake City, UT	B	801/524-4711	801/524-2129
Zirkin Cutler Investments Washington, DC	B	202/371-9000	202/842-5107
Zurich-Kemper Investments, Inc. Chicago, IL	B	312/781-1121	312/499-1001

Rapid Reference – Key Managers & Derivatives Professionals

Contact/Firm	Buyside/Sellside	Telephone	Fax
Mr. Arthur Aaronson Vice President Princeton Insurance Companies	B	609/452-9404	609/734-8461
Mr. Paul Abbenhaus Vice President First National Bank of Chicago (Dealer)	S	312/732-3183	312/732-4840
Mr. George F. Abel Senior Vice President NBD Bank, N.A. (Trust)	B	313/225-3049	313/225-1038
Mr. James Abitz Vice President — Securities Aid Association for Lutherans (AAL)	B	414/730-3788	414/730-3752
Mr. Foster L. Aborn Vice Chairman John Hancock Mutual Life Insurance Company	B	617/572-6625	617/572-1605
Mr. Charbel Abourached Managing Director Canadian Imperial Bank of Commerce (U.S.A.)	S	212/856-6036	212/856-6699
Mr. Omar Abukhadra Managing Director Credit Lyonnais Bank	S	212/459-3086	212/459-3170
Mr. Timothy Aburano Trader ABN AMRO Securities (USA) Inc.	S	312/904-5590	312/781-8167
Mr. Yoshiyuki Adachi Vice President Mitsubishi Capital Markets Services	S	212/667-3300	212/667-3560
Mr. Gerald T. Adams Senior Vice President Trust Company Bank of Georgia (Trust)	B	404/588-8569	404/581-1793
Mr. Joseph P. Adams Executive Vice President NatWest Securities Corporation	S	212/602-5606	212/495-5790
Mr. Stuart Adams Trader NationsBanc — CRT	S	312/234-3545	312/234-3089
Mr. Thomas Adams Senior Vice President First Tennessee Bank	B	901/523-4444	901/523-4266
Mr. Richard C. Adkerson Senior Vice President & C.F.O. Freeport-McMoRan Inc.	B	504/582-4000	504/582-4936
Mr. Kevin Ahern Security Life of Denver Insurance Co.	B	303/860-2051	303/860-2049
Mr. Gaku Aizawa Executive Vice President Daiwa Securities America, Inc.	S	212/612-6612	212/341-0710
Mr. Richard T. Alba Trader Bloom Staloff Brokerage Services Inc.	S	215/568-9311	215/569-3377
Mr. James R. Albach Trust Company Bank of Georgia (Trust)	B	404/588-8240	404/581-1793

Contact/Firm	Buyside/Sellside	Telephone	Fax
Mr. Clayton M. Albright III Vice President Wilmington Trust Company (Fixed Income)	B	302/651-1858	302/651-1979
Mr. David Alfano Vice President Citicorp Global Derivatives	S	312/993-3105	312/993-6830
Mr. Peter J. Allegrini Managing Director Prudential Capital Management	B	201/802-8476	201/802-8845
Mr. Brian Allen The Patterson Capital Corporation	B	310/556-2496	310/553-3605
Mr. Garry M. Allen President Virtus Capital Management	B	804/771-7164	804/771-7908
Mr. Lee C. Allen Vice President Bank of Oklahoma, N.A. (Portfolio)	B	918/588-6856	918/588-6510
Mr. Thomas W. Allen Trust Officer The First National Bank of Omaha (Trust)	B	402/633-3414	402/341-6556
Mr. Robert G. Alley Senior Vice President AIM Advisors, Inc.	B	713/626-1919	713/622-7350
Mr. Mark Allio Chief Financial Officer Third Federal Savings & Loan Association of Cleveland	B	216/441-6000	216/441-0055
Mr. Donald E. Allred President & C.E.O. Premier Investment Advisors	B	504/332-4336	504/332-7350
Mr. Daniel V. Almeida Managing Director Deutsche Morgan Grenfell	S	212/474-8370	212/474-8212
Ms. Marlene Alonzo Vice President The Bank of New York (Dealer)	S	212/804-2137	212/495-1014
Mr. Howard Altarescu Vice President Goldman Sachs & Company	S	212/902-3277	212/902-1512
Mr. Mark Alter Vice President PPM America Inc.	B	312/634-2500	312/201-0279
Mr. Vincent Amaru Vice President Citicorp Securities, Inc.	S	212/291-7492	212/425-3857
Mr. James Amato Assistant Vice President The Bank of New York (Dealer)	S	212/804-2108	212/495-1014
Mr. Joseph Amato V.P. — Portfolio Strategy Federal National Mortgage Association	B	202/752-5013	202/752-4447

Contact/Firm	Buyside/Sellside	Telephone	Fax
Mr. Scott M. Amero Vice President & Partner BlackRock Financial Management L.P.	B	212/754-5330	212/754-8790
Ms. Nancy Amicangelo Managing Director First Chicago Capital Markets, Inc.	S	312/732-8338	312/732-4670
Ms. Anne-Drue M. Anderson E.V.P. & Treasurer H.F. Ahmanson & Company	B	818/960-6311	818/962-9679
Mr. Charles Anderson President Denver Investment Advisors Inc.	B	303/312-5050	303/312-4900
Mr. David B. Anderson Executive Vice President United Missouri Investment Counsel Service	B	816/860-7351	816/860-4829
Mr. Mark A. Anderson Vice President Renaissance Investment Management Inc.	B	513/723-4500	513/723-4512
Mr. William D. Andrews Director — Fixed-Income Stein Roe & Farnham Incorporated	B	312/368-7682	312/368-5776
Mr. Wiley D. Angell Senior Vice President Fiduciary Asset Management	B	314/863-4488	314/863-4360
Mr. Dale Annis Vice President First Interstate Bank of Oregon (Trust)	B	503/225-2472	503/225-4066
Mr. Jack Annizuato Vice President Prudential Securities Inc.	S	212/778-3960	212/776-3463
Mr. Bruce Antenberg Treasurer Great Western Bank, a Federal Savings Bank (Treasury)	B	818/775-2800	818/775-2811
Mr. Yosuke Aoyagi Vice President & Manager The Bank of Tokyo Trust Company (Securities & Investments)	B	212/782-6706	212/782-6426
Mr. Peter F. Apanovitch Frank Russell Investment Management Co.	B	206/627-7001	206/596-3120
Mr. Ed Apelian Assistant Vice President First Union National Bank (New Jersey)	B	201/430-4412	201/430-4821
Mr. William H. Apfel United States Trust Company of Boston	B	617/726-7280	617/695-4775
Mr. Michael D. Aquilino Senior Vice President Heritage House Asset Management	B	617/482-8877	617/451-0800
Mr. Katsumasa Arai Assistant Vice President The Tokai Bank Ltd.	S	212/339-1284	212/754-2174
Mr. Andrew M. Aran Senior Vice President Alliance Capital Management L.P.	B	212/969-1237	212/969-1356

Contact/Firm	Buyside/Sellside	Telephone	Fax
Mr. Edward Arbaugh PNC Bank Ohio (Trust)	B	513/651-8405	513/651-7156
Mr. Phillip J. Archibeck State Investment Officer New Mexico State Permanent Funds	B	505/827-6226	505/827-6242
Ms. Patricia Arcoleo Vice President Strategic Fixed Income L.P.	B	703/812-8300	703/812-9554
Mr. Canfield Ardington BR Investment Associates	B	908/771-7452	908/771-7452
Mr. Joseph Argilagos Managing Director Merrill Lynch Capital Markets	S	212/449-8026	212/449-6629
Mr. Melchor Armenta Vice President Banco Santander of New York (Dealer)	S	212/756-9222	212/350-3535
Mr. John Q. Arnold Chief Financial Officer Mercantile Banks of St. Louis, N.A.	B	314/425-2525	314/425-2727
Mr. William Arnold Vice President Chemical Securities Incorporated	S	212/834-4600	212/834-6527
Mr. William L. Arnold Director — Risk Management Freeport-McMoRan Inc.	B	504/582-4000	504/582-4936
Mr. Gary Aronstein Director Nomura Securities International, Inc.	S	212/667-2118	212/667-1044
Mr. James Arsenault Senior Trader Mitsubishi Capital Markets Services	S	212/667-3343	212/667-3560
Ms. Debbie Assetta V.P.-Interest Rate Risk Mgmt. People's Bank (Investment)	B	203/338-4937	203/338-4927
Mr. Marvin Assofsky John Alden Asset Management	B	305/715-3190	305/715-3914
Ms. Annie Astor de Carbonell Exec. Vice President & C.F.O. First Bank Puerto Rico	B	809/729-8110	809/724-5965
Mr. Frank J. Aten Senior Vice President Boatmen's Trust (St. Louis) (Fixed Income)	B	314/466-4087	314/466-4098
Mr. James V. Atkinson Vice President Union Capital Advisors (San Diego)	B	619/230-4584	619/230-3480
Mr. Terrence L. Atkinson Managing Director & Co-Head PaineWebber Incorporated	S	212/713-2814	212/713-2998
Mr. Thomas H. Atteberry V.P. & Senior Trust Officer Fifth Third Bank	B	513/579-6100	513/579-4312

Contact/Firm	Buyside/Sellside	Telephone	Fax
Mr. Ralph Attie First Vice President Republic National Bank of NY (Treasury)	B	212/525-6151	212/525-6200
Mr. Peter W. Atwater Managing Director J.P. Morgan Securities Inc.	S	212/648-4498	212/648-5251
Mr. Robert T. Atwood Exec. Vice President & C.F.O. First Union Corporation	B	704/374-6161	704/374-4609
Mr. Richard W. Aubrey Bank of the West (Portfolio)	B	510/942-8475	510/256-7202
Mr. Glenn R. August Managing Director Oak Hill Partners	B	212/326-1500	212/593-3596
Mr. Jonathan E. Austad Vice President Allmerica Asset Management, Inc.	B	508/855-2427	508/852-6935
Mr. Robert F. Auwaerter Vice President The Vanguard Group, Inc.	B	610/669-6341	610/640-6894
Mr. Joaquin Avila Managing Director Santander Financial Products	S	212/407-7808	212/350-3535
Mr. Edward S. Babbitt, Jr. President Avatar Investors Associates	B	212/753-7710	212/644-0332
Mr. Michael Babcock Vice President ING Barings	S	212/446-1550	212/644-0428
Mr. Jonathan E. Bacon Assistant Vice President Zions First National Bank (Portfolio)	B	801/524-2304	801/524-2129
Mr. Fred Baechle American Agricultural Insurance Company	B	312/399-5718	312/399-5896
Mr. Keith Bailey Managing Director Merrill Lynch Capital Markets	S	212/449-6177	212/449-2805
Mr. Steven Bailey Executive Vice President Pacific Investment Management Co. (PIMCO)	B	714/640-3031	714/720-1376
Mr. Wayne Bailey Fremont General Corporation	B	310/315-5500	310/315-5599
Mr. John C. Baity First NH Bank	B	603/634-7145	603/634-7189
Mr. Robert P. Baizer Manager The Toronto-Dominion Bank (New York — Dealer)	S	212/468-0375	212/262-1949
Ms. Josephine A. Baker Harleysville Mutual Insurance Company	B	215/256-5027	215/256-5601

Contact/Firm	Buyside/Sellside	Telephone	Fax
Mr. Norman D. Baker, Jr. Senior Vice President Allendale Mutual Insurance Company	B	401/275-3000 Ext. 1570	401/275-3022
Mr. Thomas Balachowski President ING Investment Management Inc. — Americas Region	B	770/850-4800	770/850-4801
Mr. James J. Baldino Managing Director Bank of America Illinois (Dealer)	S	312/828-2281	312/828-3820
Mr. David W. Baldt Executive Vice President Morgan Grenfell Capital Management Inc.	B	215/246-0200	215/963-1190
Mr. Matthew Balestiero Assistant Vice President Dresdner Securities (USA) Inc.	S	212/429-4120	212/429-4496
Mr. Timothy Ball Senior Vice President Westdeutsche Landesbank Girozentrale — New York Branch	S	212/597-8541	212/597-8591
Mr. Chris Ballinger Vice President Bank of America NT & SA (Portfolio)	B	702/688-8820	702/688-8787
Ms. Linda Bammann Managing Director Swiss Bank Corporation (SBC Warburg)	S	212/574-6919	212/335-1389
Mr. Alan J. Bankart Managing Director The Putnam Management Company Inc.	B	617/292-1497	617/423-9589
Mr. Thomas Baran Vice President BA Futures Inc.	S	312/269-4558	312/987-0644
Mr. Lee Barba Managing Director BT Securities Corporation	S	212/250-7600	212/250-7071
Mr. Vernon R. Barback Managing Director Bankers Trust Global Investment Management	B	212/250-9205	212/250-9857
Mr. Doug Barber First Commercial Corporation	B	501/371-3387	501/371-7413
Mr. Freeman Barber First Vice President Interstate/Johnson Lane, Inc.	B	704/379-9135	704/379-9281
Mr. Robert C. Barber Managing Director Merrill Lynch Capital Markets	S	212/449-2734	212/449-2805
Ms. Leslie Barbi Pacific Investment Management Co. (PIMCO)	B	714/640-3031	714/720-1376
Mr. N. Robert Barman Minnesota State Board of Investment	B	612/296-5100	612/296-9572
Mr. Aubrey D. Barnard Secty., Treasurer & Controller SouthTrust Bank of Alabama, N.A. (Portfolio)	B	205/254-6856	205/254-5839

Contact/Firm	Buyside/Sellside	Telephone	Fax
Mr. Bruce E. Barnes S.V.P. & Treasurer Star Bank, N.A. (Cincinnati) (Portfolio)	B	513/632-4089	513/632-4653
Mr. Bryant P. Barnes President & C.F.O. Financial Counselors, Inc.	B	816/751-5268	816/751-5265
Mr. Michael G. Barnes Managing Director Bear, Stearns & Company, Inc.	S	212/272-8015	212/272-6291
Mr. Todd J. Barre Vice President Harris Trust & Savings (Personal Trust)	B	312/461-2773	312/394-8730
Mr. William M. Barrett New York State & Local Retirement Systems	B	518/473-6396	518/473-6755
Mr. Brian D. Barry Senior Vice President Dean Witter Reynolds Inc.	S	212/392-5155	212/392-8811
Mr. Richard J. Barry Managing Director Prudential Securities Inc.	S	212/778-3406	212/778-1648
Mr. William J. Barton Senior Vice President Hawaiian Trust Co., Ltd.	B	808/538-4622	808/538-1788
Mr. Albert C. Bashawaty Managing Director J.P. Morgan Securities Inc.	S	212/648-0189	212/648-5604
Mr. Anthony J. Basile Partner & Director Cashman, Farrell and Associates	B	610/889-1500	610/889-1665
Mr. Lawrence Bassallo Vice President Banque Nationale de Paris (New York)	S	212/415-9743	212/415-9798
Mr. Harley Bassman Managing Director Merrill Lynch Capital Markets	S	212/449-6828	212/449-5868
Mr. Ben C. M. Bastianen Treasurer Johnson Controls, Inc.	B	414/228-1200	414/228-2302
Mr. David S. Bateman Trader Chemical Futures & Options Inc.	S	215/561-0880	215/561-3027
Mr. Charles Bath Nationwide Financial Services	B	614/249-7668	614/249-4698
Mr. Fernando L. Batlle Senior Vice President First Bank Puerto Rico	B	809/729-8110	809/724-5965
Mr. Stephen C. Bauer Vice President SAFECO Insurance Companies	B	206/545-5742	206/545-3446
Mr. Joseph P. Bauman Senior Vice President Bank of America NT & SA — Capital Markets	S	415/622-5639	415/622-3198

Contact/Firm	Buyside/Sellside	Telephone	Fax
Mr. James E. Bayne Manager-Benefits, Fin. & Invt. Exxon Corporation	B	214/444-1574	214/444-1348
Mr. Andrew Beal Vice President UBS Securities, Inc.	S	212/821-3039	212/821-5805
Mr. Peter Beall World Savings & Loan Association, A Fed. Svgs. & Loan Assn.	B	510/446-3536	510/446-4672
Ms. Sue A. Becht Treasurer Duke Power Company	B	704/382-8695	704/382-7363
Mr. Clive Beck Commander Investment Corporation	B	814/724-5078	No fax
Ms. Meri Anne Beck Senior Partner Loomis, Sayles & Company L.P. (Pasadena)	B	818/793-8989	818/584-9831
Mr. Timothy P. Beck Senior Vice President & C.F.O. The Medical Protective Company	B	219/485-9622	219/486-0415
Mr. Robert Beckwitt Fidelity Management & Research Company	B	617/563-2537	617/723-9637
Mr. J. Patrick Beimford, Jr. Director — Fixed-Income Zurich-Kemper Investments, Inc.	B	312/499-1976	312/499-1001
Mr. Rhahime A. Bell Managing Director J.P. Morgan Securities Inc.	S	212/648-4420	212/648-5253
Mr. James R. Belquist Director — Trust Invt. Mgmt. U.S. West, Inc.	B	303/649-4503	303/649-4520
Mr. Norman G. Benedict Deputy Executive Director Public Employees Retirement Association of Colorado	B	303/832-9550 Ext. 564	303/863-3753
Mr. Thomas Benfer Vice President Bank of Montreal (New York)	S	212/702-1284	212/702-1193
Mr. Boaz Ben-Moshe Senior Vice President Republic New York Securities Corporation	S	212/525-5725	212/525-6958
Mr. H. Dean Benner Managing Director Brundage, Story and Rose	B	212/269-3050	212/425-4286
Mr. J. Douglas Bennett Vice President Shay Assets Management Co.	B	312/644-3100	312/938-2548
Mr. John F. Bennett S.V.P. — Investments Jamaica Savings Bank, Fsb	B	516/887-7000 Ext. 304	516/596-1205
Mr. Peter C. Bennett Vice President State Street Research & Management Co.	B	617/357-1200	617/542-7753
Ms. Alpha L. Benson Senior Portfolio Manager Nationwide Financial Services	B	614/249-7851	614/249-4698

Contact/Firm	Buyside/Sellside	Telephone	Fax
Mr. Stephen Bepler Senior Vice President Capital Research & Management Company (New York)	B	212/581-5000	212/582-7878
Mr. Bruce Berger Managing Director Canadian Imperial Bank of Commerce (U.S.A.)	S	212/856-6052	212/856-6699
Mr. James D. Berghausen Fifth Third Bank	B	513/744-7545	513/579-4312
Mr. Yves Bergin Managing Director Swiss Bank Corporation (SBC Warburg)	S	212/574-5186	212/335-1389
Mr. Ari Bergmann Managing Director BT Securities Corporation	S	212/250-9596	212/250-7071
Mr. Oliver A. Bergmann Vice President Westdeutsche Landesbank Girozentrale — New York Branch	S	212/597-8550	212/852-6300
Mr. Frank M. Bergonzi S.V.P. — Finance Rite Aid Corporation	B	717/761-2633	717/975-5905
Mr. Eric Bergstrom Associate — Risk Management Bank of Montreal (Chicago)	S	312/845-4360	312/845-4198
Mr. Barry Berlin Senior Vice President Wachovia Bank Capital Management (Atlanta)	B	404/332-4160	404/332-4163
Mr. Phillip Berniman Vice President ING Barings	S	212/319-3930	212/758-4905
Mr. Daniel Bernstein Bridgewater Associates Inc.	B	203/762-8511	203/762-2615
Mr. Ian N. Bernstein Senior Vice President Dean Witter Reynolds Inc.	S	212/392-3884	212/392-7686
Mr. Irwin Bernstein Senior Vice President Dean Witter Reynolds Institutional Futures	S	312/984-4760	312/641-0463
Mr. Jason Berrie Midland National Life Insurance Company	B	605/373-2392	605/335-3621
Mr. Bruce J. Besecker Vice President First Union National Bank (Pennsylvania) (Instl. Trust)	B	215/985-6423	215/985-6441
Ms. Lauren Best Vice President Advisers Capital Management Inc.	B	212/514-5110	212/514-5780
Mr. Dev Bhagat Senior Vice President HSBC Markets	S	212/658-2217	212/658-1905
Mr. Anand K. Bhattacharya Managing Director Prudential Securities Inc.	S	212/778-4930	212/778-3716

Contact/Firm	Buyside/Sellside	Telephone	Fax
Mr. Robert Bierman Vice President Goldman Sachs & Company (Chicago)	S	312/655-4728	312/655-4555
Mr. Barton M. Biggs Chairman Morgan Stanley Asset Management, Inc.	B	212/296-7150	212/296-7289
Mr. Jeremy H. Biggs Vice Chairman Fiduciary Trust Company International	B	212/466-4100 Ext. 2693	212/839-6403
Mr. Keith L. Bigwood V.P. & Investment Manager Rabobank Nederland North America	S	212/808-7900	212/818-0233
Mr. Peter Birkey AEGON U.S.A. Investment Management (Cedar Rapids)	B	319/369-2399	319/369-2009
Mr. James J. Biundo Exec. Dir. — Trust Invt. Mgmt. U.S. West, Inc.	B	303/649-4501	303/649-4520
Mr. Frank J. Bivona Senior Vice President & C.F.O. AMBAC Inc.	B	212/208-3236	212/509-9190
Mr. Rolf F. Bjelland Executive Vice President Lutheran Brotherhood	B	612/340-7274	612/340-8328
Ms. Betsy A. Blacher Vice President Keystone Custodian Funds, Inc.	B	617/338-3458	617/338-3351
Ms. Rhonda Black Vice President Banque Nationale de Paris (New York)	S	212/415-9743	212/415-9798
Mr. Jack Blackin Valley National Bank (New Jersey) (Portfolio)	B	201/305-4058	201/305-8415
Mr. Steve Blackwood A.V.P.-Derivatives Deposit Guaranty National Bank (Portfolio)	B	601/354-8016	601/354-8361
Mr. Robert T. Blakely Senior Vice President & C.F.O. Tenneco Inc.	B	713/757-2131	713/757-4257
Mr. Walter J. Blasberg President Continental Asset Management	B	212/440-7525	212/440-7518
Mr. Thomas I. Blinten Managing Director Nomura Securities International, Inc.	S	212/667-2332	212/667-1058
Mr. Steven Blitz OFFITBANK	B	212/350-3712	212/319-6148
Mr. Stephen W. Blocklin Vice President The Bank of Tokyo Trust Company (Pension & Investments)	B	212/782-4000	212/571-5150
Ms. Jacquelyn Blue Sovereign Bank, A Federal Savings Bank	B	610/320-8400	610/320-8448

Contact/Firm	Buyside/Sellside	Telephone	Fax
Mr. Jeremy Blum Senior Vice President Euro Brokers Maxcor, Inc.	S	212/748-7060	212/748-7050
Mr. Stephen Blyth Vice President HSBC Markets	S	212/658-1282	212/658-1905
Mr. Gregory D. Boal First Citizens Bank & Trust Co.	B	919/755-7265	919/755-7545
Mr. Ras Boateng Assistant Vice President Allmerica Asset Management, Inc.	B	508/855-3476	508/852-6935
Mr. Matthew Boatwright Assistant Vice President Federal Home Loan Bank of Topeka	B	913/233-0507 Ext. 557	913/234-1796
Mr. Michael A. Boedeker Vice President The Ohio National Life Insurance Company	B	513/559-6317	513/559-6589
Mr. Kenneth F. Boehl General Auditor — Risk Mgmt. MBNA Corporation	B	302/456-8588	302/456-8541
Mr. Phillip Boehmke Vice President First NH Investment Services	B	603/634-6156	603/224-9405
Mr. Francois Boisson Banque Paribas Ltd. Corporation	S	212/841-3717	212/841-2146
Mr. William E. Boisvert Exec. Vice President & C.F.O. PACCAR Incorporated	B	206/455-7400	206/453-4900
Mr. Michael Boland Vice President Dresdner Securities (USA) Inc.	S	212/429-4135	212/429-4171
Ms. Christina L. Boles Senior Vice President Compass Bank (Portfolio)	B	205/933-3881	205/715-7997
Mr. James P. Bolton Vice President Westdeutsche Landesbank Girozentrale — New York Branch	S	212/597-8500	212/852-6300
Ms. Kelli L. Bono Vice President & Treasurer Federal Home Loan Bank of Seattle	B	206/340-2300	206/340-2485
Mr. Joseph F. Bonomo, Jr. Senior Vice President C.S. McKee & Company, Inc.	B	412/566-1234	412/566-1548
Mr. James Borden Senior Vice President Chase Securities Inc.	S	212/552-7543	212/425-1404
Mr. Leo Borenstein Senior Dealer Banco Santander of New York (Dealer)	S	212/756-9222	212/350-3535
Mr. Philip Borg Managing Director BT Securities Corporation	S	212/775-3336	212/250-7071

Contact/Firm	Buyside/Sellside	Telephone	Fax
Mr. John Borland Brown Brothers Harriman & Co. (Investments) (Chicago)	B	312/781-7111	312/368-1287
Mr. Mark Borowy Erie Insurance Group	B	814/870-3197	814/870-3126
Mr. Robert Bosse Vice President Westpac Banking Corporation	S	212/818-1578	212/818-1499
Mr. Otto Bosshard Sr. Vice President & Treasurer Westfield Companies	B	330/887-0400	330/887-0840
Mr. Stephen K. Bossu Lotsoff Capital Management	B	312/368-1442	312/750-1131
Mr. Craig Bouchard Senior Vice President First National Bank of Chicago (Dealer)	S	312/732-2155	312/732-4840
Mr. William C. Bousquette S.V.P. & C.F.O. Texaco Inc.	B	914/253-4000	914/253-7753
Ms. Karen Bowie V.P. & Sr. Investment Officer PNC Bank Ohio (Trust)	B	513/651-7159	513/651-7156
Mr. E. Joseph Bowler S.V.P. & Treasurer WESTAMERICA Bank	B	415/257-8040	415/257-8127
Mr. Robert A. Bowman Exec. Vice President & C.F.O. ITT Corporation	B	212/258-1000	212/258-1027
Mr. Stephen R. Bowman Citizens National Bank of Evansville (Portfolio)	B	812/464-3446	812/464-3496
Ms. Dorie Boyce Trader NationsBanc — CRT	S	312/234-2613	312/234-3089
Mr. Alan G. Bozian Senior Managing Director UBS Securities, Inc.	S	212/821-4048	212/821-5846
Mr. Edward T. Bradford Managing Director & C.E.O. Bradford & Marzec, Inc.	B	213/687-9170	213/687-9189
Mr. Kenneth Bradt Managing Director ING Barings	S	212/446-1946	212/593-3362
Mr. Coleman Brandt Co-Chairman/Managing Director Ark Asset Management Company, Inc.	B	212/668-4870	212/668-6198
Mr. David L. Brantley E.V.P. & Treasurer Signet Banking Corporation	B	804/747-2000	804/771-7599
Mr. A. Darrell Braswell Managing Director Quantilogic Asset Management	B	415/434-1130	415/434-1139

Contact/Firm	Buyside/Sellside	Telephone	Fax
Mr. Donald D. Brattebo Second Vice President Principal Mutual Life Insurance Company	B	515/247-6042	515/248-8486
Mr. George H. Braun Vice President John Hancock Mutual Life Insurance Company	B	617/572-9615	617/572-1605
Mr. John Bredemus American Express Financial Advisors	B	612/671-1853	612/671-2733
Mr. Douglas T. Breeden Chairman & President Smith, Breeden Associates (Chapel Hill)	B	919/933-3356	919/933-3157
Ms. Dorothea E. Brennan First Vice President People's Bank	B	203/338-7171	203/338-2502
Mr. John J. Brennan President & C.E.O. The Vanguard Group, Inc.	B	610/669-1000	610/640-6894
Mr. John V. Brennan E.V.P., C.F.O. & Treasurer Webster Bank	B	203/755-1422	203/573-8301
Mr. Andrew Brenner Director CS First Boston Corporation	S	212/909-3915	212/308-1187
Mr. Mark C. Brickell Managing Director J.P. Morgan Securities Inc.	S	212/648-6605	212/648-5376
Mr. James Bridges Assistant Vice President AmSouth Bank N.A. (Portfolio)	B	205/581-7749	205/326-5572
Mr. Samuel L. Bright Vice President The Frost National Bank (Portfolio)	B	210/220-4859	210/220-4614
Mr. Christopher J. Brightman Partner Brinson Partners, Inc.	B	312/220-7100	312/220-7266
Mr. Michael C. Brilley Senior Vice President Sit Investment Fixed Income Advisors Inc.	B	612/359-2561	612/342-2018
Mr. Gary P. Brinson President Brinson Partners, Inc.	B	312/220-7100	312/220-7199
Mr. Thomas W. Brock Chairman & C.E.O. Salomon Brothers Asset Management Inc. (U.S.A.)	B	212/783-7990	212/783-4014
Mr. Joseph P. Brom Senior Vice President The Ohio National Life Insurance Company	B	513/559-6214	513/559-6589
Mr. Daniel Brooks Vice President Banque Nationale de Paris (New York)	S	212/415-9755	212/415-9798

Contact/Firm	Buyside/Sellside	Telephone	Fax
Mr. Gary Brown Managing Director Allianz Investment Corporation	B	203/221-8553	203/221-8529
Mr. H. Richard Brown Vice President First National Bank Evergreen Park (Portfolio)	B	708/422-6700	708/422-6827
Mr. J. Dorsey Brown III Managing Director & C.E.O. Alex. Brown Investment Management	B	410/727-1700	410/837-8338
Mr. Kenneth R. Brown Senior Vice President Liberty Bank and Trust Co. (Oklahoma City) (Portfolio)	B	405/231-6454	405/231-6758
Mr. Kirby Brown Vice President ING Investment Management Inc. — Americas Region	B	770/850-4807	770/850-4801
Mr. Philip H. Brown II President Meridian Investment Company	B	610/251-7966	610/251-5985
Mr. Mitchell Brownstein Continental Asset Management	B	212/440-3613	212/440-7518
Mr. John Bruce Vice President Citicorp Global Derivatives	S	312/993-3044	312/993-6830
Mr. Thomas Brugger Sovereign Bank, A Federal Savings Bank	B	610/320-8439	610/320-8448
Mr. Gary W. Brummett E.V.P., Controller & Co-C.F.O California Federal Bank, A Federal Savings Bank	B	213/932-4321	213/930-6272
Mr. Thomas Brush Director Deutsche Morgan Grenfell	S	212/469-7714	212/474-8212
Mr. Andrew D. Bryant Vice President & C.F.O. Intel Corporation	B	408/765-8080	408/765-1821
Mr. John B. Brynjolfsson Vice President Pacific Investment Management Co. (PIMCO)	B	714/640-3420	714/720-1376
Mr. Maxwell E. Bublitz Senior Vice President Conseco Capital Management	B	317/817-6100	317/817-6161
Mr. David Buchen Vice President Citicorp Securities, Inc.	S	212/291-7353	212/425-3857
Mr. Joel S. Buck Investment Officer Ohio Public Employees' Retirement System	B	614/466-7320	614/469-8276
Mr. Rodney A. Buck Chairman, President & C.E.O. National Life Investment Management Co.	B	802/223-9350	802/223-9332
Mr. Ronald Buerges Magna Group, Inc.	B	314/963-3030	314/963-2691

Contact/Firm	Buyside/Sellside	Telephone	Fax
Mr. Robert T. Bugni Assistant Investment Officer Montana Board of Investments	B	406/444-0001	406/449-6579
Mr. Philippe Buhannic Director CS First Boston Corporation	S	212/909-2318	212/308-1187
Mr. David Bulin American Mutual Life Insurance Company	B	515/283-3442	515/242-4670
Mr. David B. Bullett Senior Vice President Teachers Insurance & Annuity Association	B	212/916-4303	212/916-6690
Mr. Simon Bunce Managing Director Swiss Bank Corporation (SBC Warburg)	S	212/335-1384	212/335-1389
Mr. James R. Bunt Vice President & Treasurer General Electric Company	B	203/373-2211	203/373-3131
Ms. Catherine L. Bunting Senior Vice President Back Bay Advisors, L.P.	B	617/578-1743	617/424-8665
Mr. Jay W. Burden Senior Portfolio Manager Allied-Signal Inc.	B	201/455-4861	201/455-6761
Mr. Howard W. Burdett Vice President & Treasurer Alcoa	B	412/553-4545	412/553-4498
Mr. Frank E. Burgess President Madison Investment Advisors, Inc.	B	608/274-0300	608/274-7905
Mr. Mark Burgess Vice President Bank of Boston Corporation	S	617/434-8074	617/434-8330
Mr. Derick B. Burgher Senior Vice President Greenwich Capital Markets, Inc.	S	203/625-7660	203/629-4426
Mr. Philippe Burke Senior Vice President Lehman Brothers, Inc.	S	212/526-8886	212/528-6187
Mr. Marvin Burkett S.V.P., C.F.O. & Treasurer Advanced Micro Devices, Inc.	B	408/732-2400	408/982-6161
Mr. Bruce Burns Senior Dealer BZW/Barclays Bank	S	212/693-4070	212/412-1768
Mr. Eric Burns Vice President Mitsubishi Capital Markets Services	S	212/667-3441	212/667-3560
Mr. John F. Burns UNUM Life Insurance Company	B	207/770-4115	207/770-4152
Ms. Patricia Burns Senior Vice President Peregrine Capital Management	B	612/343-7606	612/343-7636

Contact/Firm	Buyside/Sellside	Telephone	Fax
Mr. Terrence Burns Society National Bank (Portfolio)	B	216/689-5859	216/689-3832
Mr. Thomas P. Burrows Vice President Mellon Bank, N.A. (Trust)	B	412/234-4697	412/236-0648
Mr. James Buskirk The Huntington Trust Company, N.A.	B	614/480-5566	614/480-5223
Mr. Robert B. Butler Vice President Bayerische Vereinsbank AG (New York)	S	212/210-0303	212/210-0330
Mr. Thomas Buttke Vice President Santander Financial Products	S	212/407-7822	212/350-3535
Mr. James C. Buysse First V.P. — Portfolio Invts. Michigan National Bank (Portfolio)	B	810/473-2606	810/473-3250
Mr. Joseph Bybee Boatmen's Trust Company of Texas	B	713/952-9100	713/952-9141
Mr. William Byers Managing Director Bear, Stearns & Company Inc.	S	212/272-2716	212/272-6291
Mr. John Caccavale Vice President J.P. Morgan Securities Inc.	S	212/648-2000	212/648-5253
Mr. Mark Cahill First Vice President Republic National Bank of NY (Treasury)	B	212/525-8000	212/525-6200
Mr. John P. Calamos President Calamos Asset Management, Inc.	B	708/245-7200	708/245-7531
Mr. Nicholas P. Calamos Senior Vice President Calamos Asset Management, Inc.	B	708/245-7200	708/245-7531
Ms. Donna Calandrillo Vice President Bank Julius Baer & Co., Ltd.	S	212/818-9130	212/297-1935
Mr. Barry Calder Vice President Banque Nationale de Paris (New York)	S	212/415-9755	212/415-9798
Mr. Daniel J. Callahan, Jr. Managing Director PaineWebber Incorporated	S	212/713-1449	212/713-1303
Mr. Robert V. Callahan Chief Financial Officer State Street Global Advisors	B	617/654-4738	617/654-6176
Mr. Bruce W. Calvert Vice Chairman & C.I.O. Alliance Capital Management L.P.	B	212/969-1070	212/969-2284
Mr. Joseph Cambria Senior Vice President NatWest Securities Corporation	S	212/602-4060	212/602-4939

Contact/Firm	Buyside/Sellside	Telephone	Fax
Mr. Joseph J. Cammarata Chief Dealer BZW/Barclays Bank	S	212/412-2001	212/412-1768
Mr. Randall Campanale Capital Management Manager First Interstate Bank of Nevada	B	702/791-6151	702/791-6131
Mr. Leonard A. Campanaro Senior Vice President & C.F.O. Harsco Corporation	B	717/763-7064	717/763-6424
Mr. Gary D. Campbell Senior Vice President Commerce Bancshares Inc.	B	314/746-7254	314/746-7432
Mr. Thomas J. Campbell Senior Managing Director First Chicago Capital Markets, Inc.	S	312/732-1318	312/732-4239
Mr. Van C. Campbell Vice Chairman & C.F.O. Corning Incorporated	B	607/974-9000	607/974-8150
Mr. Ronald E. Canakaris President Montag & Caldwell, Incorporated	B	404/262-0112	404/262-0105
Mr. Herbert C. Canapary Vice President — Investments Union Labor Life Insurance Co. (ULLICO)	B	202/682-6681	202/682-7932
Mr. James Cannon Desk Manager FIMAT Futures U.S.A. Inc. (Chicago)	S	312/578-5250	312/578-5277
Mr. Stephen E. Canter Chairman The Dreyfus Corporation	B	212/922-6360	212/922-6076
Mr. Richard A. Cantor President & Executive Partner Neuberger & Berman Management Inc.	B	212/476-9000	212/476-5535
Mr. Carmine Capobianco First Vice President Prebon Yamane (U.S.A.)	S	201/557-5105	201/557-5895
Mr. Larry J. Card Executive Vice President Pacific Mutual Life Insurance Company	B	714/640-3011	714/640-3199
Mr. John L. Carl Exec. Vice President & C.F.O. Amoco Corporation	B	312/856-6111	312/856-2454
Mr. John R. Carle Vice President Cardinal Management Corporation	B	614/464-8797	614/464-8713
Mr. Christopher Carman Vice President NatWest Securities Corporation	S	212/602-5561	212/602-4939
Mr. John M. Carmont Vice President & Treasurer Eaton Corporation	B	216/523-5000	216/523-4787

Contact/Firm	Buyside/Sellside	Telephone	Fax
Mr. J.J. Landers Carnal Senior Vice President Boatmen's Trust (St. Louis) (Fixed Income)	B	314/466-4088	314/466-4098
Mr. Jerome H. Carr Sr. Vice President & C.F.O. Reliance Insurance Company	B	212/909-1100	212/909-1844
Mr. David Carter Vice President NCM Capital Management Group, Inc.	B	919/688-0620	919/682-0414
Mr. Guy Caruso Merita Bank	B	212/318-9300	212/421-4420
Mr. Calvin Carver Vice President Goldman Sachs & Company	S	212/902-8257	212/902-1512
Mr. Joseph Carwile Assistant Vice President Falcon Asset Management, Inc.	B	410/547-3542	410/547-3582
Ms. Carol Casey Maryland State Retirement & Pension System	B	410/225-1021	410/523-8133
Ms. Mary Lou Casey Senior Managing Director CIGNA Investments, Inc.	B	203/726-3444	203/726-8137
Mr. Daniel V. Cashman Senior Partner Cashman, Farrell and Associates	B	610/889-1500	610/889-1665
Mr. Michael Casper Vice President Societe Generale Securities Corporation	S	212/278-7105	212/278-7195
Mr. Thomas Caton First Investors Management Co., Inc.	B	212/858-8062	212/858-8078
Mr. Carlos Cerritti Assistant Vice President ING Barings	S	212/758-2929	212/644-0428
Mr. Claudio Cerulli Vice President First Chicago Capital Markets, Inc.	S	312/732-6298	312/732-8733
Mr. George Chain First Union National Bank of Florida	B	305/569-1963	305/569-1938
Mr. Steven Champagne Bank United of Texas, FSB	B	713/543-6996	713/543-7927
Mr. Lawrence Chan Deputy Treasurer Merita Bank	B	212/318-9300 Ext. 395	212/421-4420
Mr. Enrique Chang Director-Quantitative Strategy General Re Asset Management, Inc.	B	203/328-5000	203/328-6504
Mr. Eugene Chang Vice President Bank of America NT & SA — Capital Markets (New York)	S	212/836-5508	212/836-5390

Contact/Firm	Buyside/Sellside	Telephone	Fax
Mr. Frederick J. Chapey, Jr. Managing Director Chase Securities Inc.	S	212/552-4222	212/425-1404
Mr. Donald Chapman Navy Federal Credit Union	B	703/255-8000	703/255-7755
Mr. C. Douglas Chappell Deputy Treasurer North Carolina Department of State Treasurer	B	919/733-7282	919/733-0075
Mr. Dexter H. Charles Managing Director Chase Securities Inc.	S	212/552-2749	212/425-1404
Mr. Andre Chatelain Vice President Banque Worms Capital Corporation	S	212/826-5462	212/593-4854
Mr. David Chavenson Treasurer Oryx Energy Company	B	214/715-4293	214/715-3311
Mr. William Cheng Vice President New York Life Insurance Company (U.S.A)	B	212/576-6525	212/576-8163
Mr. L. Robert Cheshire First Union National Bank (New Jersey)	B	201/430-4392	201/430-4821
Mr. Michael S. Cheung State Investment Officer Alaska Retirement Systems	B	907/465-3702	907/463-3565
Mr. Mario Chiodetti Bank United of Texas, FSB	B	713/543-6500	713/543-7927
Mr. Edward Chisholm Scudder Stevens & Clark, Inc. (Los Angeles)	B	213/628-1144	213/626-1005
Mr. Ichiro Chitani Vice President Mitsubishi Capital Markets Services	S	212/667-3410	212/667-3560
Mr. Paul Chludzinski Vice President The Sakura Bank Ltd. (New York)	S	212/756-6867	212/644-9565
Mr. Marc Chodera Assistant Vice President Prudential Securities Inc.	S	212/778-3985	212/776-3463
Mr. Richard J. Chouinard President USLIFE Advisers Inc.	B	212/709-6077	212/709-6064
Mr. Andrew S. Chow Second Vice President Conseco Capital Management	B	317/817-2602	317/817-6419
Mr. Dale C. Christensen Managing Director Warburg, Pincus Counsellors, Inc.	B	212/878-9368	212/878-9351
Mr. John Chrystal Director — Structuring CS First Boston Corporation	S	212/322-5903	212/308-2357

Contact/Firm	Buyside/Sellside	Telephone	Fax
Mr. Francois Chu-Fong Vice President The Sakura Bank Ltd. (New York)	S	212/756-6931	212/644-9565
Mr. John W. Church, Jr. Senior Vice President The Glenmede Trust Company	B	215/419-6030	215/419-6197
Mr. Lukasz Cianciara Vice President Credit Lyonnais Bank	S	212/261-7940	212/459-3170
Mr. Steven Ciccarello Vice President PaineWebber Incorporated	S	212/713-1101	212/713-1303
Mr. Joaquin G. Cigarroa III Executive Vice President The Laredo National Bank	B	210/723-1151	210/723-0260
Mr. Philip A. Cimino The Greater New York Savings Bank	B	212/613-4000	212/613-4117
Mr. John Cipriani Vice President The Bank of New York (Dealer)	S	212/804-2100	212/495-1014
Mr. Edward Clanuch Senior Vice President First Interstate Bank of Denver (Trust)	B	303/293-5527	303/293-5163
Mr. A. Bayard Clark Chief Financial Officer Commerce Bancshares Inc.	B	314/726-2255	314/746-7432
Mr. Gerald Clark Chief Executive Officer Metropolitan Life Insurance Company	B	212/578-0337	212/578-3910
Mr. Timothy M. Clark Vice President First National Bank of Chicago (Dealer)	S	312/732-7338	312/732-4840
Mr. Malcolm D. Clarke, Jr. Brundage, Story and Rose	B	212/269-3050	212/425-4286
Mr. Thomas D. Clarkson Partner Brinson Partners, Inc.	B	312/220-7263	312/220-7266
Mr. Dennis Clary Vice President First of America Investment Corporation	B	616/385-0203	616/385-0227
Mr. Michael Clawson First Vice President Great Western Bank, a Federal Savings Bank (Treasury)	B	818/775-3450	818/775-2811
Mr. John Claybon Old National Bank in Evansville (Portfolio)	B	812/464-1442	812/464-1567
Mr. Michael Cline Manager — Financial Risk Mgmt. Sprint Corporation	B	913/624-3000	913/624-3281
Mr. Kriss Cloninger III Exec. Vice President & C.F.O. American Family Life Assurance Company (AFLAC)	B	706/323-3431	706/323-1838

Contact/Firm	Buyside/Sellside	Telephone	Fax
Mr. Eric Clothier BZW Barclays Global Investors	B	415/597-2000	415/597-2011
Mr. George L. Clucas President & C.E.O. Carillon Advisers, Inc.	B	513/595-2476	513/595-2843
Mr. John A. Cobb American General Corporation	B	713/831-6209	713/831-6218
Mr. Gary N. Coburn Senior Managing Director The Putnam Management Company Inc.	B	617/292-1789	617/292-1713
Mr. Stuart Coco Vice President AIM Advisors, Inc.	B	713/214-1302	713/626-0642
Mr. Lewis Coffey President BPS Associates, Inc.	B	612/893-0177	612/893-0909
Mr. John Coghlan Managing Director Lehman Brothers, Inc.	S	212/526-8258	212/528-8061
Mr. Benjamin Cohen Managing Director CS First Boston Corporation	S	212/909-3009	212/308-1187
Mr. Dale E. Cohen E.V.P., Treasurer & Co-C.F.O. California Federal Bank, A Federal Savings Bank	B	213/932-4321	213/930-6272
Mr. Hersh Cohen President Smith Barney Investment Advisors	B	212/816-5673	212/816-6101
Mr. Jeffrey Cohen Vice President Sanwa Securities (USA) Co., L.P.	S	212/527-2883	212/935-1024
Mr. Louis N. Cohen Vice President UBS Asset Management, Inc. (U.S.A.)	B	212/789-7219	212/869-2169
Mr. Patrice Cohen Vice President Commerz Financial Products	S	212/266-7515	212/266-7567
Mr. Richard Cohen Senior Vice President Amalgamated Bank of New York (Investment Management Group)	B	212/620-8679	212/675-6926
Mr. Robert S. Cohen Managing Director Chase Securities Inc.	S	212/552-4912	212/552-5054
Mr. Domenic Colasacco President United States Trust Company of Boston	B	617/726-7252	617/695-4775
Mr. Scott Colbert Vice President Commerce Bancshares Inc.	B	314/746-8557	314/746-7432

Contact/Firm	Buyside/Sellside	Telephone	Fax
Ms. Lisa M. Coleman Vice President Allmerica Asset Management, Inc.	B	508/855-2393	508/855-6508
Mr. Michael B. Colgan Vice President INTRUST Bank (Trust)	B	316/383-1331	316/383-1140
Mr. James A. Colica S.V.P. — Risk Management General Electric Capital Corporation	B	203/357-4244	203/357-6791
Mr. Steven Coller Vice President Peregrine Derivatives Ltd.	S	212/593-5920	212/593-5932
Mr. George J. Collins President & C.E.O. T. Rowe Price Associates, Inc.	B	410/547-2118	410/659-0965
Mr. George H. Collins Vice President & Treasurer First Federal Savings and Loan Association of Rochester	B	716/238-2574	716/238-2056
Mr. Kevin Collins Director BZW/Barclays Bank	S	212/412-2159	212/412-1768
Mr. Robert F. Collins Assistant Vice President Wilmington Trust Company (Fixed Income)	B	302/651-8193	302/651-1758
Mr. Carl J. Colombo Union Capital Advisors (San Diego)	B	619/230-3156	619/230-4391
Mr. Steven Colton Benham Capital Management Group	B	415/967-9790	415/965-4902
Mr. Dennis J. Colwell First Vice President People's Bank	B	203/338-7171	203/338-2502
Mr. Allen Compton Second Vice President Massachusetts Mutual Life Insurance Co.	B	413/744-8491	413/744-6127
Mr. Bradley Condit Vice President Summit Bank (Portfolio)	B	201/701-2527	201/701-2675
Ms. Berta Conger World Savings & Loan Association, A Fed. Svgs. & Loan Assn.	B	510/446-3218	510/446-4672
Mr. Matthew Connolly First Vice President The Greater New York Savings Bank	B	212/613-4000	212/613-4117
Mr. James E. Conroy Managing Director Greenwich Street Advisors	B	212/816-4117	212/816-6006
Mr. Richard Conway V.P. & Senior Portfolio Mgr. Union Planters National Bank (Funds Management)	B	901/383-6261	901/383-6947
Mr. Thomas R. Coogan Vice President & Treasurer Rite Aid Corporation	B	717/761-2633	717/975-5905
Mr. Jeff Cook Branch Banking & Trust Company (BB&T-NC) (Portfolio)	B	910/733-2174	910/733-2238

Contact/Firm	Buyside/Sellside	Telephone	Fax
Mr. William S. Cook Director Providian Corporation	B	502/560-3015	502/560-3080
Mr. Jerome J. Coon S.V.P. — Assistant Treasurer Physicians Mutual Insurance Company	B	402/633-1197	402/633-1096
Ms. Janet K. Cooper Vice President & Treasurer The Quaker Oats Company	B	312/222-7111	312/222-8323
Mr. R. Jack Cooper Director Teachers' Retirement System of Texas	B	512/397-6471	512/370-0568
Mr. Daniel N. Copp E.V.P., C.F.O. & Treasurer Circus Circus Enterprises, Inc.	B	702/734-0410	702/794-3831
Mr. Kenneth Corba Eagle Asset Management, Inc.	B	813/573-2453	813/573-8325
Ms. Kathleen Corbet Senior Vice President Alliance Capital Management L.P.	B	212/969-2468	212/969-2284
Mr. M. Timothy Corbett Senior Portfolio Manager Aetna Life & Casualty (Portfolio Management Group)	B	203/275-3407	203/275-4496
Mr. John R. Cormey Vice President Denver Investment Advisors Inc.	B	303/312-5060	303/312-4900
Mr. Greg Cornell Treasurer Auto-Owners Insurance Company	B	517/323-1200	517/323-8796
Mr. Thomas Corper Vice President Banque Nationale de Paris (New York)	S	212/415-9743	212/415-9798
Mr. John Corrie Managing Director J.P. Morgan Securities Inc.	S	212/648-2410	212/648-5253
Mr. Jack Cosgrove Vice President YMCA Retirement Fund	B	212/766-2113	212/227-6941
Mr. John P. Costas Managing Director CS First Boston Corporation	S	212/909-3610	212/318-0783
Mr. Jonathan Cottrell Senior Vice President BayBank Boston, N.A. (Dealer)	S	617/556-6822	617/556-6604
Mr. Stephen B. Couch Vice President The Acacia Group	B	202/628-4506 Ext. 362	202/638-0345
Mr. James P. Coughlin Executive Vice President Sanwa Securities (USA) Co., L.P.	S	212/527-2501	212/486-1279

Contact/Firm	Buyside/Sellside	Telephone	Fax
Ms. Joanne Coulson Assistant Vice President Sakura Global Capital, Inc.	S	212/486-8454	212/355-4271
Mr. George Councill Executive Vice President Life Partners Group	B	303/779-1111	303/796-7576
Mr. George Courtadone Managing Director Canadian Imperial Bank of Commerce (U.S.A.)	S	212/856-6598	212/856-6699
Ms. Joyce Covello Vice President Republic New York Securities Corporation	S	212/525-6531	212/525-6958
Mr. David Covin Associate Goldman Sachs & Company	S	212/902-4650	212/902-1512
Mr. William F. Cox Senior Vice President Berkeley Capital Management	B	415/393-0346	415/393-0392
Ms. Juliana M. Coyle Treasurer United Asset Management Corporation	B	617/330-8900	617/330-1133
Mr. Thomas Crain Scudder Stevens & Clark, Inc. (Cincinnati)	B	513/621-2733	513/621-5081
Mr. Robert A. Crider Senior Vice President Reams Asset Management Company Inc.	B	812/372-6606	812/376-3137
Mr. David Crimmins Vice President First Union National Bank (New Jersey)	B	201/430-4407	201/430-4821
Mr. Robert L. Crispin, Jr. Executive Vice President UNUM Life Insurance Company	B	207/770-4322	207/770-4152
Mr. David A. Croft Vice President Citicorp Securities, Inc.	S	212/559-5333	212/425-3857
Mr. John Croft Vice President BayBank Boston, N.A. (Dealer)	S	617/556-6248	617/556-6650
Ms. Christine Cromarty Vice President Bank of Montreal (New York)	S	212/702-1284	212/702-1193
Mr. Peter S. Croncota Managing Director Bear, Stearns & Company Inc.	S	212/272-7744	212/272-6291
Mr. Brian Cronin Vice President Dresdner Securities (USA) Inc.	S	212/429-4144	212/429-4496
Mr. Kevin Cronin Manager — Fixed Income Credit Lyonnais Bank	S	212/261-3510	212/459-3170

Contact/Firm	Buyside/Sellside	Telephone	Fax
Mr. Timothy E. Cronin E.V.P. & Co-Head PaineWebber Incorporated	S	212/713-3553	212/586-7994
Mr. Charles Crookshank Vice President HSBC Markets	S	212/658-6710	212/658-1905
Mr. George E. Crosby Vice President Boatmen's Trust Company of Texas	B	713/952-9100	713/952-9141
Mr. Robert Crowell Senior Vice President Bank of Hawaii (Investments)	B	808/537-8313	808/538-4471
Mr. John S. Crowl Principal Olympic Capital Management, Inc.	B	206/447-9399	206/624-3871
Mr. Gary T. Crum President AIM Advisors, Inc.	B	713/214-1125	713/626-0642
Mr. Donald F. Crumrine Vice President Flaherty & Crumrine, Inc.	B	818/795-7300	818/795-0269
Ms. Zoe Cruz Managing Director Morgan Stanley & Co., Incorporated (NYC Branch)	S	212/761-2855	212/764-7490
Ms. Jane Cuddy Senior Vice President Alaska Permanent Capital Management Company	B	907/272-7575	907/272-7574
Mr. Gerard Cudzil President & Director Prudential Securities Inc.	S	212/778-3999	212/776-3463
Mr. Mark R. Cummins S.V.P., C.I.O. & Treasurer Harleysville Mutual Insurance Company	B	215/256-5036	215/256-5601
Mr. Bruce H. Cundick Beneficial Life Insurance Company	B	801/531-7979	801/531-3315
Mr. Bradley Cunningham Vice President The Boatmen's National Bank of St. Louis (Portfolio)	B	314/466-8321	314/466-8480
Ms. Deborah A. Cunningham V.P. & Senior Portfolio Mgr. Federated Investors	B	412/288-8481	412/288-8690
Ms. Michelle Cunningham Investment Officer California State Teachers' Retirement System	B	916/229-3743	916/387-9585
Mr. Michael W. Cunningham Vice President Union Bank — Los Angeles	B	213/236-6040	213/236-7983
Mr. James F. Curley Chairman & C.E.O. Republic New York Securities Corporation	S	212/525-6737	212/525-6958

Contact/Firm	Buyside/Sellside	Telephone	Fax
Mr. James Curtin First Vice President LaSalle National Bank (Portfolio)	B	312/904-8648	312/750-6244
Mr. Marshall Cutler Zirkin Cutler Investments	B	202/371-9000	202/842-5107
Mr. Nestor Cybrwisky Head — Emerging Markets Bear, Stearns & Company Inc.	S	212/272-9429	212/272-6291
Mr. Robert Cyr Vice President Fleet Bank of Maine (Portland)	B	207/874-5016	207/874-5230
Mr. Douglas Dachille Managing Director Lehman Brothers, Inc.	S	212/526-6600	212/528-7920
Mr. Kevin Dachille Senior Vice President Mercantile — Safe Deposit & Trust Co. (Trust)	B	410/237-5599	410/237-5380
Mr. John F. Dagres Principal Olympic Capital Management, Inc.	B	206/447-9399	206/621-9177
Mr. Edward H. D'Alelio Managing Director The Putnam Management Company Inc.	B	617/292-1339	617/292-1713
Mr. Jon W. d'Alessio Treasurer McKesson Corporation	B	415/983-8300	415/983-7160
Mr. Raymond Dalio President Bridgewater Associates Inc.	B	203/762-8511	203/762-2615
Mr. Michael Damas Managing Director UBS Securities, Inc.	S	212/821-6313	212/821-4873
Mr. Dennis D. Dammerman Senior Vice President-Finance General Electric Company	B	203/373-2211	203/373-3131
Mr. Lawrence D. Damon Treasurer Baxter International Inc.	B	847/948-2000	847/948-3948
Mr. David Daniel Commander Investment Corporation	B	814/724-5078	No fax
Mr. Richard Daniel Chief Financial Officer Bankers Trust — New York Corporation (Portfolio)	B	212/250-2500	212/775-2487
Mr. Steven D'Antonio MBS Product Manager Morgan Stanley & Co., Incorporated (NYC Branch)	S	212/761-2080	212/764-7490
Mr. James Daras Treasurer The Dime Savings Bank of New York, FSB	B	212/326-6912	212/326-6907
Mr. O. Leonard Darling E.V.P./Director — Fixed Income Oppenheimer Management Corporation	B	212/323-0680	212/323-0640

Contact/Firm	Buyside/Sellside	Telephone	Fax
Mr. Lawrence G. Darlington Manager — Fixed Income Illinois State Board of Investment	B	312/793-5712	312/793-2266
Mr. Michael S. Daubs Century Investment Management Co. (CIMCO)	B	608/231-7500	608/238-2316
Mr. John Davenport President Commonwealth Investment Counsel	B	804/782-3207	804/782-3629
Mr. Richard R. Davidson Vice President Loomis, Sayles & Company L.P. (Milwaukee)	B	414/272-4844	414/272-1531
Mr. Robert Guy Davidson III Director — Municipal Bonds Sanford C. Bernstein & Co., Inc.	B	212/756-4150	212/756-4550
Mr. Andrew A. Davis President Davis Selected Advisers, L.P.	B	505/982-7116	505/820-1222
Mr. Jeffrey E. Davis Vice President Nomura Securities International, Inc.	S	212/667-1490	212/667-1058
Mr. Jeffrey K. Davis Vice President Mitsubishi Capital Markets Services	S	212/667-3298	212/667-3560
Mr. Richard Davis Los Angeles County Treasurer	B	213/974-2191	213/625-2249
Mr. Robert C. Davis Life Insurance Company of the Southwest	B	214/638-9247	214/638-9393
Ms. Leslie Dawe Investment Manager State Compensation Insurance Fund	B	415/565-1234	415/565-1783
Ms. Pamela Dawson First Interstate Bank of Texas (Portfolio)	B	713/224-6611	713/226-1958
Mr. William D. Dawson Senior Vice President Federated Investors	B	412/288-1990	412/288-1982
Mr. James Day Executive Vice President Guardian Savings & Loan Association	B	713/787-3100	713/787-3192
Mr. Peter Daytz Vice President Union Bank of Switzerland Private Banking	B	212/821-3779	212/715-3498
Mr. Dennis D. Dean President C.H. Dean Investment Associates	B	513/222-9531	513/227-9313
Mr. Joseph P. Deane S.V.P. & Managing Director Greenwich Street Advisors	B	212/816-4275	212/816-6006
Mr. Jefferson DeAngelis Northwestern Mutual Life Insurance Co.	B	414/299-5291	414/299-7124

Contact/Firm	Buyside/Sellside	Telephone	Fax
Mr. Yves deBalmann Managing Director BT Securities Corporation	S	212/775-2625	212/250-7071
Mr. Spyro Degleris Manufacturers & Traders Trust Company (Portfolio)	B	212/350-2000	212/350-2166
Mr. Herbert Deitcher S.V.P. & Treasurer Raytheon Company	B	617/862-6600	617/860-2172
Mr. George Delaney Vice President First of America Investment Corporation	B	616/385-0203	616/385-0227
Mr. Paul Delaney Assistant Vice President Metropolitan Life Insurance Company	B	212/578-9212	212/578-3910
Mr. Peter J. DeMarco Managing Director Bear, Stearns & Co. Inc. (Unit Trust)	B	212/272-5500	212/272-3104
Mr. Salvatore DeMarco Executive Vice President Sanwa Securities (USA) Co., L.P.	S	212/527-2533	212/527-2596
Mr. Stephen G. DeMay Financial Analyst Duke Power Company	B	704/382-2620	704/382-7363
Ms. Denise DeMeure Trader NationsBanc — CRT	S	312/234-2613	312/234-3089
Mr. Robert M. DeMichele Chairman Lexington Management Corporation	B	201/845-7300	201/845-5121
Mr. Peter Demirale Assistant Vice President Greenwich Street Advisors	B	212/816-5700	212/816-6006
Mr. Alvaro deMolina Senior Vice President NationsBank (Charlotte) (Funds Management)	B	704/386-1500	704/339-6490
Ms. Wendy deMonchaux Senior Managing Director Bear, Stearns & Company Inc.	S	212/272-3452	212/272-6550
Mr. Nicholas Demonico CDC Investment Management Corp. (CIMCO)	B	212/891-6136	212/891-6116
Mr. Brant DeMuth Public Employees Retirement Association of Colorado	B	303/832-9550	303/863-3753
Mr. Benjamin DeNigris Assistant Vice President Nomura Capital Management (U.S.A.)	B	212/509-6527	212/509-8835
Mr. Nigel Denison Managing Director BZW/Barclays Bank	S	212/412-6900	212/412-1768
Mr. L. Earl Denney Senior Vice President STI Capital Management	B	407/237-4910	407/237-4285

Contact/Firm	Buyside/Sellside	Telephone	Fax
Mr. Edward DeNoble Harvard Management Company	B	617/523-4400	617/523-5308
Mr. Paul R. DeRosa Managing Director Eastbridge Capital, Inc.	B	212/756-7200	212/756-7270
Mr. Jerry M. de St. Paer Exec. Vice President & C.F.O. The Equitable Companies Incorporated	B	212/554-1234	212/554-2320
Mr. Ronald E. Desautels Massachusetts Mutual Life Insurance Co.	B	413/788-8411	413/744-6127
Ms. Yuko Deudon Vice President Banque Nationale de Paris (New York)	S	212/415-9743	212/415-9798
Mr. R. Randolph Devening Vice Chairman & C.F.O. Fleming Companies, Inc.	B	405/840-7200	405/841-8149
Mr. John M. Devine V.P. & Chief Financial Officer Ford Motor Company	B	313/322-3000	313/390-2106
Mr. Thomas Devine Vice President Dresdner Securities (USA) Inc.	S	212/429-4148	212/429-4496
Mr. Neil S. Devlin Vice President Templeton Global Bond Managers, Inc.	B	954/527-7444	954/462-2504
Mr. Stephen DeVoe Managing Director PaineWebber Incorporated	S	212/713-1457	212/713-1303
Mr. David W. Devonshire Senior Vice President & C.F.O. Owens-Corning Fiberglass Corporation	B	419/248-8000	419/248-6227
Ms. Eleanor Diabala-Smith Vice President Banque Nationale de Paris (New York)	S	212/415-1636	212/415-9798
Mr. Robert Dickey Vice President Fuji Securities, Inc.	S	312/899-4574	312/899-4606
Mr. Luke Diehl Managing Director BR Associates	S	908/771-7452	908/771-7452
Mr. Klaus Dietrich Vice President & Manager NatWest Bank, N.A. (Portfolio)	B	201/547-2871	201/547-2737
Mr. Stephen C. Dilbone Vice President Gradison-McDonald Asset Management	B	513/579-5966	513/579-5080
Mr. Ross Dillon Integra Financial Corporation	B	412/644-8528	412/261-7279
Mr. Matthew DiPallo Vice President Dresdner Securities (USA) Inc.	S	212/429-4410	212/429-4496

Contact/Firm	Buyside/Sellside	Telephone	Fax
Mr. Gordon D. Dixon Senior Vice President Securities Management and Research Inc.	B	409/763-0726 Ext. 258	409/766-6608
Mr. Steven J. Dixon Senior Vice President Bank of America NT & SA (Portfolio)	B	702/688-8888	702/688-8787
Mr. Leonard E. Doherty Treasurer & Asst. Secretary Dow Jones & Company, Inc.	B	212/416-2000	212/416-2655
Mr. Thomas Dolan Senior Vice President ABN AMRO Securities (USA) Inc.	S	312/904-8647	312/904-8495
Mr. Mark Doll Sr. Vice President & Treasurer Northwestern Mutual Life Insurance Co.	B	414/299-7336	414/299-7124
Mr. Geoffrey S. Domm Director Merrill Lynch Capital Markets	S	212/449-7358	212/449-2805
Mr. Patrick Donahue Global Manager NationsBanc — CRT	S	312/234-2613	312/234-3089
Mr. George Donner Vice President Fort Wayne National Bank (Trust)	B	219/426-0555	219/461-6214
Mr. John C. Donohue Assistant Vice President Allmerica Asset Management, Inc.	B	508/855-2159	508/852-6935
Mr. Robert Donohue Vice President Commerzbank Capital Markets	S	212/266-7336	212/266-7797
Mr. Thomas M. Donohue President MONY Financial Services	B	212/708-2651	212/708-2491
Mr. David Donovan Senior Vice President First Chicago Capital Markets, Inc.	S	312/732-6312	312/732-8733
Mr. Michael Dontje Senior Vice President Society National Bank (Portfolio)	B	216/689-3631	216/689-3832
Mr. Glenn Doran Senior Vice President Sanwa Securities (USA) Co., L.P.	S	212/527-2450	212/486-1279
Mr. Robert W. Doran Chairman Wellington Management Company	B	617/951-5446	617/951-5250
Mr. John Dorans Managing Director Citicorp Securities, Inc.	S	212/559-0148	212/425-3857
Mr. James W. Doucette Vice President Humana Inc.	B	502/580-1002	502/580-4089

Contact/Firm	Buyside/Sellside	Telephone	Fax
Mr. Homer M. Douglass Associate Vice President Commander Corporation	S	814/724-5078	No fax
Mr. Paul Dow Piper Capital Management Inc.	B	612/342-6379	612/342-6992
Mr. Robert S. Dow Executive Vice President Lord Abbett & Company	B	212/848-1873	212/888-4405
Ms. Paula Downey A.V.P. & Treasurer Auto Club Insurance Association	B	313/462-7008	313/462-8061
Mr. Thomas L. Downing Vice President Keystone Investment Services	B	717/231-5724	717/231-5758
Mr. Michael P. Downs Ohio Police & Firemen's Disability & Pension Fund	B	614/228-4076	614/228-0451
Mr. Sean Doyle Trader NationsBanc — CRT	S	312/234-2585	312/234-3089
Ms. Anne S. Drennan Vice President & Treasurer Alliance Capital Management L.P.	B	212/969-6443	212/969-2284
Ms. Ina Drew Senior Managing Director Chemical Bank (Portfolio)	B	212/834-5000	212/834-6550
Mr. Blake S. Drexler Senior Vice President Greenwich Capital Markets, Inc.	S	203/625-7818	203/629-4426
Mr. Michael Driscoll Senior Vice President Santander Financial Products	S	212/407-7824	212/350-3535
Mr. Joel Drube Second Vice President Federated Group	B	507/455-5200 Ext. 5301	507/455-5199
Mr. Barry Drucker Vice President & Manager Fuji Bank Ltd.	S	212/898-2330	212/321-9408
Mr. Kenneth D. Dubbin Vice President & Treasurer Royal Caribbean Cruises Ltd.	B	305/539-6000	305/539-0562
Mr. William H. Dudley Executive Vice President American Express Financial Advisors	B	612/671-3243	612/671-2733
Mr. David Duebendorfer Managing Director Deutsche Morgan Grenfell	S	212/469-5880	212/469-6025
Mr. Barry S. Duerk S.V.P. & Sr. Investment Offcr. Summit Bank (Portfolio)	B	201/701-2525	201/701-2675
Mr. Michael S. Duffey Treasurer M.A. Hanna Company	B	216/589-4000	216/589-4200

Contact/Firm	Buyside/Sellside	Telephone	Fax
Mr. Thomas Dugan Vice President Smith Barney, Inc. (Chicago)	S	312/419-3631	312/419-3490
Mr. Walter E. Dulski Senior Vice President Euro Brokers Maxcor, Inc.	S	212/748-7018	212/748-7329
Mr. R. Foster Duncan Treasurer Freeport-McMoRan Inc.	B	504/582-4000	504/582-4936
Mr. Mark Dunetz Assistant Vice President Guardian Life Insurance Co. of America	B	212/598-1961	212/777-6715
Ms. Jane R. Dunlap Vice President & Treasurer Delphi Capital Management, Inc.	B	215/787-3942	212/838-7598
Mr. John Dunlop Manager — Foreign Exchange Daiwa Securities America, Inc.	S	212/612-7200	212/612-7125
Mr. Robert Dunn AON Advisors Incorporated	B	312/701-3000	312/701-3900
Mr. Thomas F. Dunn Vice President Lazard Freres Asset Management	B	212/632-8267	212/632-6060
Ms. Karen Dunn-Kelly Senior Vice President AIM Advisors, Inc.	B	713/214-1188	713/626-0642
Mr. A. James Durica Senior Vice President Keystone Investment Services	B	717/231-5724	717/231-5758
Mr. Richard Durso Vice President BA Futures Inc.	S	312/269-4582	312/987-0644
Mr. Thomas Dwyer Vice President Fuji Bank Ltd.	S	212/898-2800	212/321-9408
Mr. William F. Dwyer Citizens Trust Company & Savings Bank (Trust)	B	401/456-7000	401/455-5310
Mr. Glenn S. Dydak Trader Chemical Futures & Options Inc.	S	215/561-0880	215/561-3027
Mr. Steve Dymant Managing Director AMBAC Financial Services, L.P.	B	203/222-9691	203/341-2351
Mr. Andrew Ead Vice President HSBC Markets	S	212/658-2217	212/658-1905
Ms. Kathleen Eagye Senior Vice President E.D. & F. Man International Securities Corp.	S	212/566-9452	212/566-9456
Mr. Warren East Leader Federal Bank for Savings	B	901/578-2419	901/524-5715

Contact/Firm	Buyside/Sellside	Telephone	Fax
Mr. Robert W. Eccles Vice President CIGNA Investments, Inc.	B	203/726-6000	203/726-8137
Mr. Wright Eddrington National Bank of Commerce (Portfolio)	B	901/523-3711	901/523-3879
Mr. David L. Eddy S.V.P. & Treasurer Northern Trust Corporation	B	312/630-6000	312/444-7843
Ms. Brenda E. Edgerton Vice President & Treasurer Campbell Soup Company	B	609/342-4800	609/342-3878
Mr. David H. Edington Managing Director Pacific Investment Management Co. (PIMCO)	B	714/640-3025	714/640-3419
Mr. David R. Edstam S.V.P. & Treasurer First Bank System (Portfolio)	B	612/973-2278	612/973-0965
Mr. Marc Edwards Executive Vice President Daiwa Securities America, Inc.	S	212/612-6602	212/612-7100
Mr. Paul Edwards Managing Director Lehman Brothers, Inc.	S	212/526-8257	212/528-6187
Mr. William A. Effler Vice President American Money Management Corporation	B	513/579-2515	513/579-0323
Mr. Ravit Efraty Vice President Salomon Brothers Inc.	S	212/783-4733	212/783-2284
Mr. Kenneth Egan Managing Director Greenwich Street Advisors	B	212/816-4732	212/816-6006
Mr. Raymond Egan Integra Financial Corporation	B	412/644-8557	412/261-7279
Mr. David W. Ehlers Exec. Vice President & C.F.O. The Bank of California, N.A.	B	415/765-0400	415/765-2788
Mr. Michael Ehrlich Senior Managing Director Bear, Stearns & Company Inc.	S	212/272-9272	212/272-6291
Mr. Leon Eicten TCF Bank Minnesota fsb	B	612/661-8799	612/376-9089
Mr. Neil Eigen Bear, Stearns Asset Management Inc.	B	212/272-2814	212/272-3107
Mr. Timothy Eisel First of America Investment Corporation	B	616/385-0224	616/385-0227
Ms. Wendy Eisenshtadt Vice President Michigan National Bank (Portfolio)	B	810/473-2610	810/473-3250

Contact/Firm	Buyside/Sellside	Telephone	Fax
Mr. Ralph A. Elia Vice President Dean Witter Reynolds Inc. (Philadelphia)	S	215/665-1481	215/665-1486
Mr. Donald Ellenberger Mellon Bank, N.A. (Portfolio)	B	412/234-8604	412/234-8913
Mr. Guy Elliffe Managing Director National Mutual Funds Management Inc.	B	310/557-1500	310/286-2314
Ms. Deborah J. Elliot Managing Director Smith Barney, Inc. (Greenwich Street)	S	212/723-7448	212/723-8792
Mr. Harold C. Elliot The Bank of Tokyo Trust Company (Pension & Investments)	B	212/766-8494	212/571-5150
Mr. Scott M. Elliot Integra Financial Corporation	B	412/644-8534	412/261-7279
Mr. Frank Elliott Bank United of Texas, FSB	B	713/543-6500	713/543-7927
Mr. R. Keith Elliott Senior Vice President & C.F.O. Hercules Incorporated	B	302/594-5250	302/594-5405
Mr. C. Lee Ellis III Executive Vice President Alfa Group	B	334/613-4326	334/288-0905
Mr. Frederick K. Ellis Skandia Investment Management Inc. (U.S.A.)	B	212/978-2800	212/385-2169
Mr. Lloyd Ellis Southern Farm Bureau Life Insurance Co.	B	601/981-7422	601/981-1670
Mr. Terence S. Ellis Partner Nicholas-Applegate Capital Management (Houston)	B	713/963-2460	713/963-5235
Mr. William Ellsworth U.S. National Bank of Oregon (Portfolio)	B	503/275-5006	503/275-5032
Mr. Jonathan T. Ender Senior Vice President The Chicago Corporation — Asset Management Group	B	312/855-7738	312/855-4066
Mr. Kent S. Engel Chief Investment Officer Western Asset Management Company	B	818/584-4300 Ext. 364	818/683-2270
Mr. Steven Engel Assistant Vice President Sanwa Bank	S	212/339-6294	212/750-3284
Mr. Frederick W. Engimann CTT Investment Management Group	B	312/223-3403	312/223-5170
Mr. Kenneth F. Entler S.V.P. & Manager Prudential Securities Inc.	S	212/778-3373	212/778-3165
Ms. Karen M. Epstein Vice President BayBank Boston, N.A. (Dealer)	S	617/556-6722	617/556-6650

Contact/Firm	Buyside/Sellside	Telephone	Fax
Mr. James E. Erickson Managing Director The Putnam Management Company Inc.	B	617/292-1338	617/292-1713
Mr. Carl C. Ericson Vice President Colonial Management Associates	B	617/772-3735	617/737-0358
Mr. Dominque Errichetti First Vice President Societe Generale Securities Corporation	S	212/278-6900	212/278-7195
Mr. Wilson Ervin Director Credit Suisse Financial Products	S	212/322-5960	212/238-5332
Ms. Nancy Esch Vice President Washington Square Advisers Inc.	B	612/372-1123	612/342-3575
Ms. Phyllis Esposito Senior Managing Director Bear, Stearns & Company Inc.	S	212/272-4936	212/272-5948
Mr. Thomas Estes Director Swiss Bank Corporation (SBC Warburg)	S	212/574-6820	212/335-1389
Mr. Robert Ettinger Vice President Flaherty & Crumrine, Inc.	B	818/795-7300	818/795-0269
Mr. Barry H. Evans Senior Vice President John Hancock Advisers, Inc.	B	617/375-1979	617/375-1831
Mr. James H. Evans Vice President M.D. Sass Investors Services, Inc.	B	212/843-2419	212/843-5949
Mr. Jay H. Evans AMCORE Bank, N.A. Rockford	B	815/961-7120	815/961-7746
Ms. Katherine A. Everett Manager BR Associates	S	908/771-7452	908/771-7452
Mr. Milton J. Ezrati Senior Vice President Nomura Capital Management (U.S.A.)	B	212/509-6527	212/509-8835
Mr. Jeffrey Faber Meridian Bank (Portfolio)	B	610/655-3661	610/655-3916
Ms. Lynda L. Faber Senior Vice President Payden & Rygel Investment Counsel	B	213/625-1900	213/628-8488
Mr. Jerome T. Fadden Vice President & Treasurer Travelers Group	B	212/816-8000	212/816-8912
Mr. Lawrence Fafalak Vice President Banque Worms Capital Corporation	S	212/826-5465	212/593-4854
Ms. Virginia Fagan Continental Asset Management	B	212/440-7511	212/440-7518

Contact/Firm	Buyside/Sellside	Telephone	Fax
Mr. William Fain Vice President Allmerica Asset Management, Inc.	B	508/855-4104	508/852-6935
Mr. Jack Falconi Director of Investments Guaranty Federal Bank, F.S.B.	B	214/360-3360 Ext. 4865	214/360-8983
Mr. Patrick Falconio Executive Vice President AEGON U.S.A. Investment Management (Cedar Rapids)	B	319/398-8660	319/369-2009
Mr. William Fall Manager NationsBanc — CRT	S	312/234-5737	312/234-3089
Mr. Mark Fallon Financial Holding Corporation	B	816/391-2000	816/391-2037
Mr. Ignacio Fanlo Managing Director Morgan Stanley & Co., Incorporated (NYC Branch)	S	212/761-2080	212/921-5861
Mr. David Fann Division Mgr.-Alternative Inv. United States Trust Company of New York (Trust)	B	212/852-3773	212/852-3370
Mr. James Fantozzi Assistant Vice President Dresdner Securities (USA) Inc.	S	212/429-4147	212/429-4496
Mr. Thomas N. Farmakis Executive Vice President SwissRe Advisers Inc.	B	212/973-5041	212/973-5035
Mr. Nick Farr Senior Vice President Garvin GuyButler Corporation	S	212/732-6900	212/815-6587
Mr. James H. Farrell, Jr. Senior Partner Cashman, Farrell and Associates	B	610/889-1500	610/889-1665
Mr. Michael Farrell Vice President BA Futures Inc.	S	312/269-4558	312/987-0644
Mr. Victor Fattal Managing Director Republic New York Securities Corporation	S	212/221-3556	212/525-6958
Mr. Patrick M. Fay Managing Director Lehman Brothers, Inc.	S	212/526-8033	212/528-6885
Ms. Marilyn G. Fedak Sanford C. Bernstein & Co., Inc.	B	212/756-4489	212/756-4550
Mr. Michael S. Fedak Head — Fixed Income Risk Mgmt. Bear, Stearns & Company, Inc.	S	212/272-9633	212/272-6291
Mr. Harry Feder Chief Investment Officer Israel Discount Bank of New York	B	212/551-8145	212/370-9623
Mr. Douglas E. Fedynak Managing Director & Treasurer Plaza Investment Managers, Inc.	B	301/718-5358	301/718-5362

Contact/Firm	Buyside/Sellside	Telephone	Fax
Mr. William Feeney Fremont Investment Advisors Inc.	B	415/768-0521	415/284-8122
Mr. William Feezer, Jr. Executive Vice President Sanwa Securities (USA) Co., L.P.	S	212/527-2501	212/754-0587
Mr. Jeffrey Feig Vice President Citicorp Securities, Inc.	S	212/291-7464	212/425-3857
Mr. Francis X. Felcon John Hancock Mutual Life Insurance Company	B	617/572-9617	617/572-1605
Mr. W. Robert Felker Senior Vice President First Chicago Futures	S	312/732-4174	312/732-3348
Ms. Darlene A. Fernald Vice President Charter One Bank, F.S.B.	B	216/566-5300	216/566-5308
Mr. Eduardo Fernandez Senior Dealer Banco Santander of New York (Dealer)	S	212/756-9222	212/350-3535
Mr. Fernando Fernandez Senior Dealer BZW/Barclays Bank	S	212/412-2001	212/412-1768
Mr. Barry Fetner Senior Vice President Dean Witter Reynolds Inc.	S	212/392-2600	212/392-1355
Mr. Fritz Feuerherm Vice President MIMLIC Asset Management Company	B	612/298-3837	612/223-5959
Mr. Ronald H. Fielding President Fielding Management Company, Inc.	B	716/383-1300	716/383-0914
Mr. Michael W. Fields Vice President AMR Investment Services, Inc.	B	817/967-1537	817/931-3797
Mr. Edward Finch Vice President State Street Research & Management Co.	B	617/357-1222	617/542-7753
Mr. Kevin Fink Director — Investments TCF Bank Minnesota fsb	B	612/661-8798	612/376-9089
Mr. Laurence D. Fink Chairman & C.E.O. BlackRock Financial Management L.P.	B	212/754-5546	212/754-8790
Mr. David M. Finkelstein Director Corporate Finance TIG Holdings Inc.	B	212/446-2711	212/371-8360
Mr. E. Brian Finkelstein Executive Director Swiss Bank Corporation (SBC Warburg)	S	212/335-1007	212/335-1389
Mr. Richard Finn Senior Vice President-Finance Kansas City Life Insurance Company	B	816/753-7299 Ext. 8216	816/753-1354

Contact/Firm	Buyside/Sellside	Telephone	Fax
Mr. John D. Finnegan Exec. Vice President & C.F.O. General Motors Acceptance Corporation	B	313/974-1222	313/974-1244
Mr. John R. Finnegen Managing Director Bear, Stearns Securities Corp.	S	312/474-4720	312/474-4736
Mr. Kevin J. Finnerty Senior Managing Director Bear, Stearns & Company Inc.	S	212/272-6014	212/272-5593
Mr. Butch Fischer Vice President Commerz Financial Products	S	212/266-7562	212/266-7567
Mr. Philip J. Fischer First Vice President Merrill Lynch Capital Markets	S	212/449-0218	212/449-2805
Mr. David S. Fisher Director First of America Bank Corporation	B	616/376-7464	616/376-7484
Mr. Harold Fisher Vice President Commerz Financial Products	S	212/266-7515	212/266-7567
Mr. Raymond M. Fisher Vice President & C.I.O. USBANCORP, Inc.	B	814/533-5355	814/533-5427
Mr. Jay Fishman Chief Financial Officer The Travelers Insurance Company	B	203/954-1155	203/277-3667
Mr. Philip J. Fiskow Senior Vice President & C.I.O. Pioneer Financial Services, Inc.	B	708/995-0400	708/413-7192
Mr. Lyle Fitterer Strong Capital Management Inc.	B	414/359-3600	414/359-3460
Mr. John Fitzpatrick Assistant Treasurer Union Carbide Corporation	B	203/794-2000	203/794-3334
Mr. Peter Fitzpatrick Treasurer ING Barings	S	212/446-1550	212/935-3811
Mr. Robert J. Fitzsimmons S.V.P. — Treasurer The FINOVA Group Inc.	B	602/207-4900	602/207-5543
Mr. Paul Fjeldsted Vice President Salomon Brothers Inc.	S	212/783-2917	212/783-2284
Mr. Mark Flaherty Director of Equities Trading Standish, Ayer & Wood Inc.	B	617/457-5072	617/350-7520
Mr. Michael J. Flaherty Vice President Marshall & Ilsley Corporation	B	414/765-7700	414/765-7645
Mr. Robert Flaherty President Flaherty & Crumrine, Inc.	B	818/795-7300	818/795-0269

Contact/Firm	Buyside/Sellside	Telephone	Fax
Mr. Thomas E. Flanigan California State Teachers' Retirement System	B	916/229-3736	916/387-9585
Mr. Donald C. Fleming Executive Vice President North Side Savings Bank	B	516/488-6900	516/488-6546
Mr. Bjorn Flesaker Managing Director Bear, Stearns & Company Inc.	S	212/272-3690	212/272-6291
Mr. Trenton Fletcher Society National Bank (Portfolio)	B	216/689-4012	216/689-3832
Mr. Victor Flores Executive Vice President United Services Advisors Inc.	B	210/308-1234	210/308-1270
Mr. Brian Fluck Assistant Treasurer AT&T	B	212/387-5400	212/226-4935
Mr. Stephen F. Fluegel President General Re Asset Management, Inc.	B	203/328-6522	203/328-6423
Mr. Edward Fluss Assistant Vice President Merrill Lynch Capital Markets	S	212/449-5578	212/449-2805
Mr. Craig Flynn Senior Vice President Euro Brokers Maxcor, Inc.	S	212/748-7100	212/748-7050
Mr. Dennis Flynn Senior Vice President Sanwa Securities (USA) Co., L.P.	S	212/527-2565	212/754-0587
Mr. James T. Flynn Chief Financial Officer J.P. Morgan & Company Inc.	B	212/483-2323	212/509-7628
Mr. John J. Ford Senior Vice President Herbert R. Smith, Inc.	B	817/723-5565	817/322-3887
Mr. Kenneth Ford Director CS First Boston Corporation	S	212/909-2000	212/308-1187
Mr. Patrick Ford Group Manager — Taxable F/I PNC Institutional Management Corp.	B	302/791-1730	302/791-1898
Mr. Richard H. Forde President CIGNA Investment Management (U.S.A.)	B	203/726-6686	203/726-8530
Mr. Louis C. Fornetti E.V.P., C.F.O. & Treasurer Inter-Regional Financial Group, Inc.	B	612/371-7750	612/371-7755
Ms. Kimberly P. Forsyth Senior Vice President Back Bay Advisors, L.P.	B	617/578-1751	617/424-8665
Mr. Michael C. Fosbury Humana Inc.	B	502/580-1004	502/580-4089

Contact/Firm	Buyside/Sellside	Telephone	Fax
Mr. Arthur Foster E.V.P.- Finance Collective Bank	B	609/965-1235	609/625-9149
Mr. D. Haddon Foster II V.P. & Mgr.-Invest. Portfolio Federal Home Loan Bank of Atlanta	B	404/888-8183	404/897-1846
Mr. Marc Fovinci Ferguson, Wellman, Rudd, Purdy & Van Winkle, Inc.	B	503/226-1444	503/226-3647
Mr. Bryce Fowler Bluebonnet Savings Bank Fsb	B	214/443-9000 Ext. 3320	214/443-4376
Mr. Bruce Fox Vice President Southwest Corporate Federal Credit Union	B	214/861-3000	214/861-3322
Mr. Bruce E. Fox Director Smith Barney, Inc. (Greenwich Street)	S	212/723-7585	212/723-8792
Mr. David Fox Managing Director HSBC Asset Management Americas Inc.	B	212/503-6848	212/503-6756
Mr. T. Timothy Foxe Vice President General Re Securities Corporation	S	212/307-2327	212/307-2320
Mr. Frank C. Foy New Mexico Educational Retirement Board	B	505/827-8030	505/989-7738
Mr. Jeffrey W. Foye Assistant Vice President Old National Bank in Evansville (Portfolio)	B	812/464-1315	812/464-1567
Mr. Thomas Franckowiak Vice President Texas Commerce Bank, N.A. (Houston) (Trust)	B	713/216-7770	713/216-5674
Mr. Rudy Frank Vice President ABN AMRO Securities (USA) Inc.	S	312/904-6181	312/781-8167
Mr. Anthony Franz Vice President Canadian Imperial Bank of Commerce (U.S.A.)	S	212/856-6601	212/856-6699
Mr. William H. Frazier Managing Director Oppenheimer & Co., Inc.	S	212/667-5251	212/667-5302
Ms. Nancy Freedman Lipper & Company, L.P.	B	212/883-2215	212/883-8701
Mr. Robert G. Freedman President John Hancock Advisers, Inc.	B	617/375-1968	617/375-1831
Mr. Andrew Freeman Vice President Prebon Yamane (U.S.A.)	S	201/557-5440	201/557-5895
Mr. David S. French Director Credit Lyonnais Bank	S	212/459-3060	212/459-3193
Mr. Michael Frenz Assistant Vice President OnBank, Inc. (Portfolio)	B	315/424-4566	315/424-5992

Contact/Firm	Buyside/Sellside	Telephone	Fax
Mr. Dale F. Frey Chairman & President General Electric Investment Corporation	B	203/326-2310	203/326-4215
Mr. Robert Friedberg Vice President Credit Lyonnais Bank	S	212/459-3033	212/459-3170
Mr. Wayne T. Frisbee Director — Investments Nationwide Financial Services	B	614/249-4125	614/249-4698
Mr. Steven L. Fritze Vice President & Treasurer Ecolab Inc.	B	612/293-2233	612/293-2471
Mr. Ernest C. Frohboese Sr. Vice President & C.E.O. General Re Asset Management, Inc.	B	203/328-6506	203/328-6504
Mr. Charles Froland Managing Director Stanford Management Company	B	415/926-0232	415/854-9188
Mr. E. John Fromelt Head — Fixed-Income Department Midland National Life Insurance Company	B	605/335-5700	605/335-3621
Mr. Daniel Frommer Vice President Nomura Securities International, Inc.	S	212/667-1483	212/667-1058
Mr. Harry A. Fry President Prebon Yamane (U.S.A.)	S	201/557-5135	201/557-5996
Mr. Richard Fuchs Vice President Intercapital Securities Inc.	S	212/688-0900	212/319-4001
Mr. Truaki Fujimoto Vice President Mitsubishi Capital Markets Services	S	212/667-3300	212/667-3560
Mr. Akio Fujiwara Vice President Mitsubishi Capital Markets Services	S	212/667-3410	212/667-3560
Mr. Robert E. Furdak Managing Director State Street Global Advisors	B	617/654-3379	617/654-6176
Mr. Daniel J. Fuss Executive Vice President Loomis, Sayles & Company L.P.	B	617/482-2450	617/951-2747
Mr. David Fussell Vice President — Securities Provident Life & Accident Insurance Co.	B	615/755-1916	615/755-1671
Mr. Nicholas Gabriel Treasurer The Ford Foundation	B	212/573-4613	212/599-4584
Mr. Frederick W. Gaertner Vice President The Chubb Corporation	B	908/580-3752	908/580-3775

Contact/Firm	Buyside/Sellside	Telephone	Fax
Mr. J. Michael Gaffney Senior Vice President Union Bank of Switzerland Private Banking	B	212/821-3670	212/821-3932
Mr. John R. Gaines Vice President The Bank of New York (Dealer)	S	212/804-2035	212/495-1014
Mr. Donald S. Galante Senior Vice President Dresdner Securities (USA) Inc.	S	212/429-4401	212/429-4496
Mr. Thomas Gallagher Vice Chairman Oppenheimer & Co., Inc.	S	212/667-7387	212/667-5302
Dr. Henry J. Galliot Federated Investors	B	412/288-1931	412/288-1982
Mr. Sean C. Gallop Director Nomura Securities International, Inc.	S	212/667-2050	212/667-1041
Mr. James E. Galowski Managing Director Westdeutsche Landesbank Girozentrale — New York Branch	S	212/852-6034	212/852-6140
Ms. Mary Galvin Trader Canadian Imperial Bank of Commerce (U.S.A.)	S	212/856-6648	212/856-6699
Ms. Susan Gammill First Commercial Capital Management	B	501/371-6755	501/371-7487
Mr. Arthur E. Gandolfi Eastbridge Capital, Inc.	B	212/756-7200	212/756-7270
Mr. Robert Gann Vice President The Northern Trust Company (Treasury)	B	312/630-6678	312/444-5666
Mr. John Gannon Trader NationsBanc — CRT	S	312/234-2613	312/234-3089
Ms. Donna E. Garban Vice President BT Securities Corporation	S	212/775-3991	212/250-7071
Mr. Joseph H. Gareau Executive Vice President ITT Hartford Life Insurance Company	B	203/843-3295	203/843-6457
Mr. Frederic B. Garonzik Vice President Goldman Sachs & Company	S	212/902-8717	212/902-1512
Mr. Seth Garrett Director Merrill Lynch Capital Markets	S	212/449-5578	212/449-2805
Mr. Juan Carlos Garrido Senior Dealer Banco Santander of New York (Dealer)	S	212/756-9222	212/350-3535
Mr. Richard J. Garvey Director The Rushmore Funds, Inc.	B	301/657-1500	301/657-1511

Contact/Firm	Buyside/Sellside	Telephone	Fax
Mr. Charles R. Gates Vice President Rabobank Nederland North America	S	212/808-2531	212/808-2578
Mr. Clark Gates President Union Capital Advisors (San Diego)	B	619/230-4700	619/230-4391
Ms. Rosanne Gatta A.V.P. & Treasurer Provident Mutual Life Insurance Company	B	215/636-5212	215/636-8322
Mr. Alan Gayle Sr. Vice President & Director Capitoline Investment Services, Inc. (Washington, DC)	B	202/879-6075	202/879-6073
Ms. Lynne Gehling Evangelical Lutheran Church-Board of Pensions	B	612/334-5358	612/334-5307
Mr. Jeffrey Geller Managing Director BEA Associates	B	212/832-2626	212/355-1545
Mr. James C. Gerber Vice President & Manager The Bank of New York (Dealer)	S	212/804-2222	212/495-1017
Mr. Karl D. Gerhart C.F.O. & Treasuer Sovereign Bank, A Federal Savings Bank	B	610/320-8400	610/320-8448
Mr. Elbridge T. Gerry Partner Brown Brothers Harriman & Co. (Investments)	B	212/826-1571	212/493-8526
Mr. Gregory T. Geswein Treasurer The Mead Corporation	B	513/495-5155	513/461-2424
Mr. Geoffrey C. Getman Senior Vice President Falcon Asset Management, Inc.	B	410/547-3398	410/234-2365
Mr. Carl Geuther Chief Financial Officer Great Western Bank, a Federal Savings Bank (Treasury)	B	818/775-3436	818/775-3333
Mr. Stephen Gianoli Senior Vice President Norwest Investment Management (Minnesota)	B	612/667-5856	612/667-0127
Mr. Michael Giarla Principal Smith, Breeden Associates (Chapel Hill)	B	919/967-7221	919/933-3157
Mr. Anthony Gibbons Senior Vice President Daiwa Securities America, Inc.	S	212/612-6594	212/612-7100
Mr. Thomas P. Gibbons Senior Vice President The Bank of New York Company, Inc.	B/S	212/804-2006	212/815-4023
Mr. Paul Gibson Bankers Trust — New York Corporation (Portfolio)	B	212/250-5754	212/775-2487
Mr. William D. Giese Senior Vice President Peregrine Capital Management	B	612/343-7607	612/343-7636

Contact/Firm	Buyside/Sellside	Telephone	Fax
Mr. Walter Giles The Ford Foundation	B	212/573-4737	212/599-4584
Mr. James H. Gill, Jr. Manager — Structured Securities Bank of America NT & SA — Capital Markets	S	415/953-5306	415/622-4386
Ms. Ruth M. Gillis Sr. Vice President & C.F.O. American National Corporation	B	312/661-5000	312/661-6417
Mr. John R. Gilmore Partner Goldman Sachs & Company (Chicago)	S	312/655-4720	312/655-4552
Mr. Robert J. Giordano Managing Director Canadian Imperial Bank of Commerce (U.S.A.)	S	212/856-4600	212/856-6699
Mr. Vincent R. Giordano Senior Vice President Merrill Lynch Asset Management Inc.	B	609/282-2101	609/282-3055
Mr. William Giovanni First Bank, N.A. (Omaha) (Trust)	B	402/348-6000	402/348-7819
Mr. Darrell Girton Vice President Dauphin Deposit Bank & Trust Company (Trust)	B	717/255-2317	717/255-2073
Mr. David Gittings Managing Director BT Securities Corporation	S	212/775-2043	212/250-7071
Mr. Theodore P. Giuliano General Partner Neuberger & Berman Management Inc.	B	212/476-5523	212/476-5535
Mr. Boyd E. Givan Senior Vice President & C.F.O. The Boeing Company	B	206/655-2121	206/655-1177
Mr. Richard J. Glasier S.V.P. & C.F.O. Royal Caribbean Cruises Ltd.	B	305/539-6000	305/539-0562
Mr. Gary A. Glass S.V.P. & Treasurer Federal Home Loan Bank of Atlanta	B	404/888-8181	404/897-1846
Mr. James L. Gleaves Vice President & Treasurer American General Corporation	B	713/831-1222	713/831-6218
Mr. Seth M. Glickenhaus Glickenhaus & Company (Investments)	B	212/953-7877	212/599-2537
Mr. Gary A. Glynn President U.S. Steel & Carnegie Pension Fund	B	212/826-8420	212/826-8443
Mr. Thomas J. Glynn Vice President Bayerische Vereinsbank AG (New York)	S	212/210-0302	212/210-0330
Mr. Thomas Godlasky American Mutual Life Insurance Company	B	515/283-2371	515/242-4670

Contact/Firm	Buyside/Sellside	Telephone	Fax
Mr. Almond G. Goduti, Jr. Vice President The Boston Company Asset Management	B	617/722-7822	617/722-7250
Mr. Jon F. Goebel SouthTrust Bank of Alabama, N.A. (Trust)	B	205/254-5477	205/254-5989
Mr. E. Christian Goetz Senior Vice President Virtus Capital Management	B	804/771-7987	804/775-3948
Mr. John H. Goff, Jr. Senior Vice President AmSouth Bank N.A. (Trust)	B	205/326-5434	205/581-7433
Mr. Thomas C. Goggins Senior Vice President John Hancock Advisers, Inc.	B	617/375-1579	617/375-1831
Mr. Joseph L. Gogola Senior Investment Officer Century Investment Management Co. (CIMCO)	B	608/231-7104	608/238-2316
Mr. Jacob D. Goldfield Partner Goldman Sachs & Company	S	212/902-0388	212/902-1512
Mr. John Goldfield Banque Paribas Ltd. Corporation	S	212/841-2400	212/841-2146
Mr. Duncan Goldie-Morrison Global Manager NationsBanc — CRT	S	312/234-2540	312/234-3089
Mr. Alan R. Goldman Senior Vice President Comerica Bank (Funds Management)	B	313/222-7200	313/222-9825
Mr. Irvin J. Goldman Managing Director CS First Boston Corporation	S	212/909-2854	212/479-0145
Mr. Abner D. Goldstine Senior Vice President Capital Research & Management Company	B	310/996-6118	310/996-6200
Mr. Robert Goldwasser Vice President Westpac Banking Corporation	S	212/818-1578	212/818-1499
Mr. Ben Golub Managing Director BlackRock Financial Management L.P.	B	212/754-5560	212/754-8790
Mr. Charles A. Gomer Vice President Thompson, Siegel & Walmsley, Inc.	B	804/353-4500	804/353-9914
Mr. Paul Gooding MIMLIC Asset Management Company	B	612/298-3840	612/223-5959
Mr. Eric B. Goodman Director Providian Corporation	B	502/560-2960	502/560-3080
Mr. William B. Goodwin Senior Managing Director MONY Financial Services	B	212/708-2666	212/708-2491

Contact/Firm	Buyside/Sellside	Telephone	Fax
Mr. Henry E. Gooss The Portfolio Group, Inc.	B	212/332-4200	212/332-4296
Mr. Herbert M. Gordon Treasurer Regents of the University of California	B	510/987-9620	510/987-9617
Mr. M. Scott Gordon Executive Vice President Mitsubishi Financial Futures Inc.	S	312/930-2301	312/930-2320
Mr. Marc W. Gordon Principal Morgan Stanley & Co., Incorporated (NYC Branch)	S	212/296-5098	212/764-7490
Mr. Richard Gordon Assistant Vice President SunFinancial Group	B	617/237-6030 Ext. 7171	617/431-7521
Mr. Scott Gordon President — Capital Markets ING Barings	S	212/446-0399	212/644-0428
Mr. David S. Gottesman Managing Director First Manhattan Capital Management	B	212/756-3300	212/223-4175
Mr. Christophe Gouelo Vice President Banque Nationale de Paris (New York)	S	212/415-9751	212/415-9798
Mr. Eric W. Gould Assistant Treasurer The Merchants Bank of New York	B	212/973-6372	212/966-4813
Mr. William R. Graber Vice President & C.F.O. The Mead Corporation	B	513/495-3996	513/461-2424
Mr. Robert E. Grady, Jr. Senior Vice President Kennedy Associates Inc.	B	206/624-9640	206/624-8515
Mr. Ladell Graham President Smith, Graham & Co. Asset Managers	B	713/227-1100	713/739-8436
Mr. Troy Grande Assistant Treasurer Fremont General Corporation	B	310/315-5520	310/315-5593
Mr. Remy Grandury Vice President HSBC Markets	S	212/658-1282	212/658-1905
Ms. Janet Grangaard Lutheran Brotherhood	B	612/340-5779	612/340-8328
Mr. John G. Grant Vice President Security Life of Denver Insurance Co.	B	303/860-2618	303/860-2049
Ms. Linda Grant Vice President & Treasurer SCOR Reinsurance Company	B	212/390-5200	212/488-8608
Mr. Jeremy Grantham Senior Partner Grantham, Mayo, Van Otterloo & Company	B	617/346-7610	617/439-0457

Contact/Firm	Buyside/Sellside	Telephone	Fax
Mr. Raymond P. Granville Senior Vice President People's Bank (Investment)	B	203/338-7443	203/338-4927
Mr. Russell Graves Collective Bank	B	609/625-6103	609/625-9149
Mr. Anthony R. Gray Chairman STI Capital Management	B	407/237-4369	407/237-4285
Mr. Michael S. Gray Vice President Fidelity Management & Research Company	B	617/563-2520	617/476-9743
Mr. David Greenberg Associate Director BZW/Barclays Bank	S	212/412-6859	212/412-1768
Mr. Jack M. Greenberg Vice Chairman & C.F.O. McDonald's Corporation	B	708/575-3000	708/575-6941
Mr. Boyce I. Greer Senior Vice President Fidelity Management & Research Company	B	617/563-2552	617/723-9637
Mr. Joseph M. Gregory Managing Director Lehman Brothers, Inc.	S	212/526-8625	212/528-6786
Mr. Andrew Greig Masco Corporation	B	313/274-7400	313/374-6666
Mr. Peter G. Greig Vice President Financial Counselors, Inc.	B	816/751-5215	816/751-5265
Ms. Johanna Griffin Vice President PaineWebber Incorporated	S	212/713-6135	212/713-1303
Mr. Patrick Griffin Vice President Dresdner Securities (USA) Inc.	S	212/429-4100	212/429-4496
Mr. William Griffin Vice President Transamerica Investment Services Inc.	B	213/742-4161	213/742-4150
Mr. Robert E. Griffith Director CS First Boston Corporation	S	212/909-3525	212/318-1226
Mr. Edward B. Grimball Exec. Vice President & C.F.O. Whitney National Bank (Portfolio)	B	504/586-7272	504/586-7383
Mr. Leo Grohowski Managing Director HSBC Asset Management Americas Inc.	B	212/503-6918	212/503-6808
Mr. William H. Gross Managing Director Pacific Investment Management Co. (PIMCO)	B	714/640-3317	714/640-3419
Mr. Blake Grossman Sr. Vice President & Manager BZW Barclays Global Investors	B	415/597-2138	415/597-2011

Contact/Firm	Buyside/Sellside	Telephone	Fax
Mr. Edgar H. Grubb Exec. Vice President & C.F.O. The Transamerica Corporation	B	415/983-4000	415/983-4888
Mr. Michael Grudzien Vice President Charter One Bank, F.S.B.	B	216/566-5300	216/566-5308
Mr. Harold Guardiola Vice President Bank of Montreal (New York)	S	212/702-1284	212/702-1193
Mr. Juan Guerrero Senior Vice President Banco Popular of Puerto Rico (Portfolio)	B	809/765-9800	809/753-9240
Mr. Herbert Gullquist General Partner Lazard Freres Asset Management	B	212/632-6419	212/632-6060
Mr. Thomas Gunderson MIMLIC Asset Management Company	B	612/298-3845	612/223-5959
Mr. John A. Gunn President Dodge & Cox Inc.	B	415/981-1710	415/986-5471
Mr. Rajesh K. Gupta Dean Witter InterCapital Inc.	B	212/392-1655	212/392-3836
Mr. William Gust Vice President Citicorp Global Derivatives	S	312/993-3797	312/993-6830
Mr. Steven Guterman Managing Director Salomon Brothers Asset Management Inc. (U.S.A.)	B	212/783-7000	212/783-4014
Mr. Jerry Guthrie Assistant Treasurer BellSouth Corporation	B	404/249-3300	404/249-5597
Mr. Albert J. Gutierrez Senior Vice President Conseco Capital Management	B	317/817-2741	317/817-6161
Mr. Eric N. Gutterson Vice President Back Bay Advisors, L.P.	B	617/578-1725	617/424-8665
Ms. Margaret D. Hadzima Managing Director Scudder Stevens & Clark, Inc. (Boston)	B	617/728-9260	617/295-1111
Mr. Barry Hagan Treasurer Bank of America Texas, N.A.	B	214/444-5437	214/444-5460
Mr. David Hall Director-Portfolio Management ITT Hartford Life Insurance Company	B	203/843-8003	203/843-6457
Mr. John S. Hall V.P. & Trust Invt. Officer Hibernia National Bank (Trust)	B	504/533-5638	504/533-0153
Mr. Scott Hall Nike Securities (UIT Management)	B	708/241-4141	708/241-8727

Contact/Firm	Buyside/Sellside	Telephone	Fax
Mr. Theodore G. Hall Director — Investments Ohio Police & Firemen's Disability & Pension Fund	B	614/228-4076	614/228-0451
Mr. Ralph Hallenborg Managing Director Smith Barney, Inc. (Greenwich Street)	S	212/723-5815	212/723-8764
Mr. Donald U. Hallman Senior Vice President & C.F.O. Equifax, Inc.	B	404/885-8000	404/885-5452
Mr. Matthew C. Halperin Derivatives Manager Allstate Insurance Company	B	708/402-7309	708/402-0164
Mr. Philip Halpern Washington State Investment Board	B	360/664-8900	360/664-8912
Mr. K. Hamahashi Senior Vice President Union Bank — Los Angeles	B	213/236-5007	213/236-7983
Mr. Carl C. Hamann Fischer, Francis, Trees and Watts, Inc.	B	212/681-3000	212/681-3250
Mr. Anthony Hamer Vice President Chase Securities Inc.	S	212/552-2752	212/425-1404
Mr. Mark Hamilton Sanford C. Bernstein & Co., Inc.	B	212/756-4623	212/756-4550
Mr. Jeffrey Hammer Vice President Dean Witter Reynolds Inc.	S	212/392-8302	212/392-0188
Mr. Susumu Hanada President & C.E.O. Mitsubishi Capital Markets Services	S	212/667-3358	212/667-3560
Ms. Stephany Hanbury-Brown Managing Director J.P. Morgan Securities Inc.	S	212/826-1465	212/648-5253
Mr. Peter Hancock Managing Director J.P. Morgan Securities Inc.	S	212/648-2200	212/648-5925
Mr. George Handjinicolaou Managing Director UBS Securities, Inc.	S	212/821-5069	212/821-5062
Mr. Mark Haney Evangelical Lutheran Church-Board of Pensions	B	612/333-7651	612/334-5307
Mr. Charles W. Hanks Assistant Vice President Twentieth Century Insurance Company	B	818/704-3166	818/704-2989
Mr. Bryant M. Hanley, Jr. President, Secretary/Treasurer Barrow, Hanley, Mewhinney & Strauss, Inc.	B	214/665-1900	214/665-1965
Mr. Wendell J. Hanna Vice President BR Associates	S	908/771-7452	908/771-7452

Contact/Firm	Buyside/Sellside	Telephone	Fax
Mr. Philip S. Hannifan Director — Fixed Income American Family Insurance Group	B	608/242-4100 Ext. 30954	608/243-4923
Mr. Eugene W. Hansen Chairman Seaboard Investment Advisers Inc.	B	804/622-7300	804/622-0918
Mr. Michael Hansen Nebraska State Investment Council	B	402/471-2043	402/471-2498
Ms. Debra Hanson Principal Scudder Stevens & Clark, Inc. (Los Angeles)	B	213/628-1144	213/626-1005
Mr. Jay Harbeck Merrill Lynch Asset Management Inc.	B	609/282-2818	609/282-3055
Mr. David Harbison Vice President Fuji Bank Ltd.	S	212/898-2330	212/321-9408
Mr. Wayne Hardenbrook Meridian Bank (Portfolio)	B	610/655-2788	610/655-3916
Mr. James D. Hardesty Executive Vice President Mercantile — Safe Deposit & Trust Co. (Trust)	B	410/237-5557	410/237-5380
Mr. Stephen R. Hardis Vice Chairman & C.F.O. Eaton Corporation	B	216/523-5000	216/523-4787
Mr. William Hardis Vice President The Bank of New York (Dealer)	S	212/804-2108	212/495-1014
Mr. Jerry Harms Norwest Bank Indiana, N.A.	B	219/461-6473	219/461-6678
Mr. Lawrence S. Harris Senior Managing Director CIGNA Investments, Inc.	B	203/726-7722	203/726-8137
Mr. Michael H. Harris Loomis, Sayles & Company L.P. (Bloomfield Hills)	B	810/646-2100	810/646-2592
Mr. Alfred Harrison Alliance Capital Management (Minneapolis)	B	612/332-1544	612/342-2149
Ms. Lisa Harrison Seaboard Investment Advisers Inc.	B	804/622-7300	804/622-0918
Mr. Michael A. Hart Farmers Insurance Group of Companies	B	213/932-3565	213/549-4410
Mr. Thomas P. Hart Vice President PaineWebber Incorporated	S	212/713-3582	212/713-1303
Mr. Christopher Harvey Managing Director J.P. Morgan Securities Inc.	S	212/648-2121	212/648-5253
Mr. John L. Haseltine Head — Fixed Income Salomon Brothers Inc.	S	212/783-3216	212/783-2284

Contact/Firm	Buyside/Sellside	Telephone	Fax
Mr. Geoff Hauck Vice President National City Bank of Akron	B	216/375-8433	216/375-8434
Mr. Harold Haugli Treasurer Christiana Bank, New York Branch	S	212/827-4850	212/827-4888
Mr. W. Kurt Hauser President Wentworth, Hauser & Violich, Inc.	B	415/981-6911	415/788-7281
Ms. Theresa A. Havell Director Neuberger & Berman Management Inc.	B	212/476-9000	212/476-5535
Mr. Richard Havey Vice President Norwest Investments & Trust Services	B	303/863-4760	303/863-4879
Mr. Ian Hawkins Vice President Westdeutsche Landesbank Girozentrale — New York Branch	S	212/597-8571	212/852-6300
Ms. Marian Hayden Vice President Chase Securities Inc.	S	212/552-0754	212/425-1404
Mr. D. Lee Hayes Managing Director Lehman Brothers, Inc.	S	212/528-1313	212/528-0821
Mr. Daniel K. Hayes Vice President — Research Calvert Asset Management Company, Inc.	B	301/951-4800	301/657-1982
Mr. R. F. Haygood Treasurer Equifax, Inc.	B	404/885-8000	404/885-5452
Mr. Michael Haylon Senior Vice President Phoenix Duff & Phelps Investment Management Co. (Hartford)	B	203/275-5835	203/275-5509
Mr. Jonathan C. Headrick Executive Vice President Ameritas Investment Advisors Inc.	B	402/467-6957	402/467-6970
Mr. Raymond Healy Senior Investment Advisor Pension Boards — United Church of Christ	B	212/870-2777	212/870-2877
Mr. Charles E. Heath Vice President Employers Reinsurance Corporation	B	913/676-5445	913/676-5221
Mr. John R. Hecht Sr. Vice President & C.F.O. AMCORE Financial, Inc.	B	815/968-2241	815/961-7749
Mr. Douglas P. Hedberg Senior Vice President Washington Square Advisers Inc.	B	612/372-5220	612/342-7541
Mr. Charles E. Heeren Vice President Lutheran Brotherhood	B	612/340-7316	612/340-6497

Contact/Firm	Buyside/Sellside	Telephone	Fax
Mr. Peter W. Hegel Executive Vice President Van Kampen American Capital Investment Advisory Corp.	B	708/684-6290	708/684-6270
Mr. P. Joseph Hegener Managing Director The Toronto-Dominion Bank (New York — Dealer)	S	212/468-0375	212/262-1949
Mr. George Heilliwell Millipore Corporation	B	617/275-9200	617/275-5550
Mr. James Held Senior Managing Director Bear, Stearns & Company Inc.	S	212/272-5136	212/272-6291
Ms. Sandra L. Helton S.V.P. & Treasurer Corning Incorporated	B	607/974-9000	607/974-8150
Mr. W. David Hemingway Executive Vice President Zions First National Bank (Portfolio)	B	801/524-4640	801/524-4664
Mr. Charles F. Henderson CTT Investment Management Group	B	312/223-2735	312/223-5170
Mr. Jeremy Henderson First V.P. & Director Societe Generale Securities Corporation	S	212/278-7100	212/278-7195
Mr. Jon L. Henderson Senior Vice President Magna Group, Inc.	B	314/963-3014	314/963-2691
Ms. Nancy Henderson Vice President Bayerische Vereinsbank AG (New York)	S	212/210-0303	212/210-0330
Ms. Maureen A. Hendricks Managing Director J.P. Morgan Securities Inc.	S	212/648-2500	212/648-5253
Mr. John D. Hendrickson Assistant Vice President Credit Lyonnais Bank	S	212/261-7953	212/261-7969
Mr. Darrell J. Hendrix Director Bank of Boston Corporation	S	617/434-8074	617/434-8330
Mr. Frederick L. Henning, Jr. Managing Director Fidelity Management & Research Company	B	617/563-2122	617/723-9637
Mr. Mark Henrici Trader NationsBanc — CRT	S	312/234-2613	312/234-3089
Mr. Timothy P. Henry Assistant Vice President Provident Mutual Life Insurance Company	B	215/636-8147	215/636-8322
Mr. Colton Heppe Vice President Euro Brokers Maxcor, Inc.	S	212/748-7100	212/748-7050
Mr. Lee Herdle Vice President — Investments Paul Revere Investment Management Corp.	B	508/751-7224	508/751-7240

Contact/Firm	Buyside/Sellside	Telephone	Fax
Mr. Laszlo Heredy Vice President Farmers Insurance Group of Companies	B	213/932-3061	213/930-3101
Mr. Thomas V. Herlihy Vice President Oppenheimer & Co., Inc.	S	212/667-5263	212/667-2302
Mr. Matthew G. Herries Vice President Roosevelt Bank, A Federal Savings Bank	B	314/532-6200	314/532-6358
Mr. Henry J. Herrmann Executive Vice President Waddell & Reed Investment Management Co.	B	913/236-1750	913/236-1885
Mr. Ronald M. Hersch Managing Director Bear, Stearns & Company Inc.	S	212/272-9866	212/272-6291
Mr. David Hershey Lotsoff Capital Management	B	312/368-1442	312/750-1131
Mr. Lester Hess Manager — Domestic Finance The Mead Corporation	B	513/495-3020	513/228-5555
Mr. Dennis L. Hesse Managing Partner Brinson Partners, Inc.	B	312/220-7100	312/220-7199
Mr. Gary Hickerson First National Bank of Commerce (Investment)	B	504/561-1351	504/561-1923
Mr. David Hickey Vice President Citicorp Securities, Inc.	S	212/559-5236	212/425-3857
Mr. John L. Hickey Senior Vice President Merita Bank	B	212/318-9300	212/421-4420
Mr. Robert J. Hickey Vice President Van Kampen American Capital Investment Advisory Corp.	B	708/684-6296	708/684-6270
Mr. Howard B. Hill Managing Director Deutsche Morgan Grenfell	S	212/469-6706	212/474-8212
Mr. Lawrence R. Hill Executive Vice President Investment Advisers, Inc.	B	612/376-2770	612/376-2616
Mr. Randy Himelfarb Vice President Rabobank Nederland North America	S	212/808-2520	212/808-2574
Mr. Charles B. Hintz Managing Director — Treasury Morgan Stanley Asset Management, Inc.	B	212/723-7178	212/296-7289
Mr. Craig F. Hintze Principal Olympic Capital Management, Inc.	B	206/447-9399	206/624-3871
Mr. William Hirschberg Managing Director BT Securities Corporation	S	212/775-5611	212/250-7071

Contact/Firm	Buyside/Sellside	Telephone	Fax
Ms. Laurie Hirt Erie Insurance Group	B	814/870-2098	814/870-3126
Mr. Vincent Hitchcock Associate Investment Analyst Allstate Insurance Company	B	708/402-8256	708/402-0164
Mr. Bruce Hitchman Vice President California Federal Bank, A Federal Savings Bank	B	213/932-2070	213/930-6272
Mr. William M. Hjerpe Vice President & C.F.O. Honeywell, Inc.	B	612/951-0142	612/951-3070
Mr. Daniel Ho Vice President General Re Securities Corporation	S	212/307-2327	212/307-2320
Mr. James K. Ho Senior Vice President John Hancock Advisers, Inc.	B	617/375-1981	617/375-1831
Mr. Stuart C. Hochberger Senior Vice President Fiduciary Trust Company International	B	212/466-4100 Ext. 2430	212/839-6403
Mr. Brian Hodgson Vice President Branch Banking & Trust Company (BB&T-NC) (Portfolio)	B	910/733-2146	910/733-2238
Mr. Ralph Hodgson President & C.E.O. General Re Securities Corporation	S	212/307-2321	212/307-2320
Mr. Thomas W. Hodson Sr. Vice President & C.F.O. Caremark International Inc.	B	708/559-4700	708/559-4648
Mr. Richard Hoerner PNC Institutional Management Corp.	B	302/791-1700	302/791-2467
Mr. Joseph W. Hoff Vice President — Finance Household International, Inc.	B	708/564-7973	708/564-6110
Ms. Marjorie E. Hogan Director Bear, Stearns & Company Inc.	S	212/272-3666	212/272-6291
Mr. James Hohorst Treasurer American Express Bank Ltd.	B	212/640-1834	212/619-9872
Mr. Van R. Hoisington, Sr. President Hoisington Investment Management Co.	B	512/327-7200	512/327-8646
Mr. Robert W. Holland Vice President — Fixed Income J.P. Morgan Investment Management, Inc. (U.S.A.)	B	212/837-2096	212/575-0392
Mr. Robert W. Holland Executive Director University of Texas System — Office of Investments	B	512/499-4317	512/499-4429
Mr. Robert W. Holle Treasurer & Asst. Secretary Mark Twain Bank (Portfolio)	B	314/727-1000	314/746-2609

Contact/Firm	Buyside/Sellside	Telephone	Fax
Ms. Marie N. Hollein Vice President Citicorp Global Derivatives	S	312/993-3733	312/993-6830
Mr. Mark A. Holles Vice President Chevy Chase Federal Savings Bank	B	301/986-7222	301/986-7002
Mr. Barry Hollis Assistant Vice President National City Bank of Akron	B	216/375-8433	216/375-8434
Mr. Mark Holmlund Assistant Vice President Pacific Mutual Life Insurance Company	B	714/640-3011	714/640-3199
Mr. Rex W. Holsapple State Investment Officer Nebraska State Investment Council	B	402/471-2043	402/471-2498
Mr. Kevin D. Holt Vice President Scudder Stevens & Clark, Inc. (Chicago)	B	312/861-2743	312/861-1472
Mr. Richard A. Holt Managing Director Scudder Stevens & Clark, Inc. (Chicago)	B	312/861-2718	312/861-1472
Mr. Robert M. Holt, Jr. Vice President Luther King Capital Management	B	817/332-3235	817/332-4630
Mr. Timothy A. Holt Vice President Aetna Life & Casualty (Portfolio Management Group)	B	203/275-2585	203/275-4798
Ms. Celia Holtzberg Vice President New York Life Insurance Company (U.S.A)	B	212/576-4837	212/447-4166
Mr. Jan H. M. Hommen Exec. Vice President & C.F.O. Alcoa	B	412/553-4545	412/553-4498
Mr. Steven T. Honda S.V.P. & C.F.O. Federal Home Loan Bank of San Francisco	B	415/616-1000	415/616-2626
Mr. E. Murray Hood Vice President E.D. & F. Man International Securities Corp.	S	212/902-6170	212/566-9456
Mr. Mark Hood Bond Portfolio Manager Federated Group	B	507/455-5200 Ext. 8460	507/455-5199
Mr. Andrew Hopkins Assistant Vice President Wilmington Trust Company (Fixed Income)	B	302/651-8698	302/651-1758
Mr. Mark Horrell Liberty Bank and Trust Co. (Oklahoma City) (Portfolio)	B	405/231-6000	405/231-6758
Mr. Terrence Horton Director Texas County & District Retirement System	B	512/469-9668	512/479-8114

Contact/Firm	Buyside/Sellside	Telephone	Fax
Mr. Gerard Host Senior Vice President Trustmark National Bank (Portfolio)	B	601/949-6651	601/949-2382
Mr. John F. Hotchkis Hotchkis and Wiley	B	213/362-8888	213/623-7880
Mr. John S. Hottinger Senior Vice President Prebon Yamane (U.S.A.)	S	201/557-5270	201/557-5941
Mr. Peter D. Houchin S.V.P., Treasurer & C.F.O. W.R. Grace & Company	B	407/362-1955	407/362-2193
Mr. Thomas T. Houghton NationsBank (Charlotte) (Funds Management)	B	704/388-2375	704/339-6490
Mr. Laurence O. Howard, Jr. Group V.P. & Sr. Inv. Officer First National Bank Gainesville (Portfolio)	B	770/503-2150	770/503-2706
Mr. Timothy Howard Exec. Vice President & C.F.O. Federal National Mortgage Association	B	202/752-7140	202/752-4447
Mr. Wayne Howe Vice President Westpac Banking Corporation	S	212/850-7821	212/818-1499
Mr. David J. Howell SouthTrust Bank of Alabama, N.A. (Trust)	B	205/254-6780	205/254-5989
Ms. Jean E. Hoysradt Senior Vice President New York Life Insurance Company (U.S.A)	B	212/576-4965	212/576-8163
Mr. Barry G. Hoyt Partner & C.I.O. Asset Allocation & Management Company	B	312/263-2900	312/263-1193
Ms. Susan Huang Vice President Chase Manhattan Private Bank Investment Management	B	212/789-5846	212/398-1872
Ms. Kristen M. Hudak Senior E.V.P. & C.F.O. AmSouth Bank N.A. (Portfolio)	B	205/326-5120	205/326-5572
Mr. Daryl L. Hudson Chairman Consistent Asset Management Company	B	610/558-3000	610/558-3002
Mr. Howard Hudson Senior Vice President Fortis Asset Management	B	212/859-7084	212/775-9773
Mr. John Hughes Trader NationsBanc — CRT	S	312/234-5437	312/234-3089
Mr. Rodney Hughes Branch Banking & Trust Company (BB&T-NC) (Portfolio)	B	910/733-2147	910/733-2238

Contact/Firm	Buyside/Sellside	Telephone	Fax
Mr. T. J. Hughes Managing Director Bank of Boston Corporation	S	617/434-4884	617/434-8330
Mr. Raymond Humiston Executive Vice President Greenwich Capital Markets, Inc.	S	203/625-2818	203/629-8743
Ms. Nancy Humphreys Managing Director Citicorp Securities, Inc.	S	212/291-7120	212/425-3857
Ms. Elaine Hunt Senior Vice President Atlantic Asset Management Partners Inc.	B	203/425-3519	203/363-5110
Mr. Thomas Hunt Assistant Vice President Boatmen's Trust Company of Texas	B	713/952-9100	713/952-9141
Mr. Robert Hunter Vice President Crestar Bank (Portfolio)	B	804/782-7837	804/782-5100
Mr. James L. Huntzinger Senior Vice President BancOklahoma Trust Company	B	918/588-6317	918/588-6939
Mr. Taylor Hurst Managing Director BA Futures Inc.	S	312/269-4552	312/987-0644
Mr. Richard S. Huson The Crabbe-Huson Group, Inc.	B	503/295-0111	503/295-2939
Mr. Michael T. Hutchins Managing Director Salomon Brothers Inc.	S	212/783-2849	212/783-2318
Mr. B. Craig Hutson Partner Brinson Partners, Inc.	B	312/220-7100	312/220-7808
Mr. Michael S. Hyland President Salomon Brothers Asset Management Inc. (U.S.A.)	B	212/783-7416	212/783-4014
Mr. Richard F. Hyland Treasurer The Vanguard Group, Inc.	B	610/669-1000	610/640-6894
Mr. Harry Hyslop Southern Farm Bureau Casualty Insurance Co.	B	601/957-7777	601/957-4329
Mr. John Ignaszak Assistant Vice President Dresdner Securities (USA) Inc.	S	212/429-4100	212/429-4496
Mr. Hideaki Ikeuchi Vice President Dai-Ichi Kangyo Bank Ltd. (New York)	S	212/466-5271	212/912-0915
Mr. Joe Ince President Boatmen's Trust Company of Texas	B	713/952-9100	713/952-9141
Mr. Edmund F. Ingalls, Jr. Vice President INVESCO Management and Research, Inc.	B	617/345-8246	617/261-4560

Contact/Firm	Buyside/Sellside	Telephone	Fax
Ms. Martha J. Ingraham Vice President Commander Corporation	S	814/724-5078	No fax
Mr. Kevin Ingram Vice President Goldman Sachs & Company	S	212/902-8362	212/902-1512
Mr. Koichi Ino Vice President DKB Financial Products, Inc.	S	212/313-0530	212/432-8464
Mr. Masami Inoue Senior Vice President Dai-Ichi Kangyo Bank Ltd. (New York)	S	212/466-5270	212/912-0915
Mr. Yohisuke Inoue Assistant Vice President Sanwa Bank	S	212/339-6531	212/750-3284
Mr. Glen T. Insley S.V.P. & Director First Union National Bank of North Carolina — Funds Mgmt.	B	704/383-7682	704/374-6902
Ms. Susan Ip Managing Director General Re Securities Corporation	S	212/307-2299	212/307-2320
Mr. Lee Irving E.V.P. & Treasurer KeyCorp	B	216/689-0234	216/689-5115
Mr. John P. Isaacson Executive Vice President Payden & Rygel Investment Counsel	B	213/625-1900	213/628-8488
Mr. Curtis D. Ishii Principal Investment Officer California Public Employees' Retirement System	B	916/326-3425	916/326-3363
Mr. Takayuki Ishikawa Assistant Vice President The Tokai Bank Ltd.	S	212/339-1267	212/754-2174
Mr. Marko Issever Managing Director Sakura Global Capital, Inc.	S	212/486-8269	212/355-4271
Mr. Sham Ito Manager Fuji Bank Ltd.	S	212/898-2324	212/321-9408
Mr. James Ivey Sr. Vice President-Investments Dana Investment Advisors, Inc.	B	414/782-2907	414/782-0581
Mr. Kiyo Izutsu Vice President Yamaichi International (America), Inc.	S	212/524-8282	212/912-0172
Mr. James E. Jack Exec. Vice President & C.F.O. Associates Corporation of North America	B	214/541-4566	214/541-4629
Mr. James Jackson Northwestern Mutual Life Insurance Co.	B	414/299-3340	414/299-7124

Contact/Firm	Buyside/Sellside	Telephone	Fax
Mr. Charles E. Jacobs Chairman C.S. McKee & Company, Inc.	B	412/566-1234 Ext. 218	412/566-1548
Mr. Cris W. Jacobs Managing Director CIGNA Investments, Inc.	B	203/726-7591	203/726-8137
Mr. Douglas L. Jacobs Exec. V.P. & Treasurer Fleet Financial Group	B	617/346-1165	617/346-0130
Mr. Joshua Jacobs Manager Exco Noonan Inc.	S	201/200-4960	201/200-5069
Mr. Matthew Jacobs Managing Director Lehman Brothers, Inc.	S	212/526-6610	212/528-7920
Mr. Robert B. Jacobs Managing Director & Co-Head PaineWebber Incorporated	S	212/713-2740	212/713-6051
Mr. Paul F. Jacobson Managing Director Deutsche Morgan Grenfell	S	212/469-6708	212/474-8212
Mr. David W. Jacus Vice President The Boatmen's National Bank of St. Louis (Portfolio)	B	314/466-8318	314/466-8480
Mr. David A. Jaeger Vice President & Treasurer The Boeing Company	B	206/655-2121	206/655-1177
Mr. Petter Jahnsen Vice President Alaska Permanent Capital Management Company	B	907/272-7575	907/272-7574
Mr. Kevin Jaklin Associated Bank Green Bay, N.A.	B	414/433-7737	414/433-4381
Mr. Ronald Jampel Vice President Euro Brokers Maxcor, Inc.	S	212/748-7080	212/748-7050
Mr. Harry M. Jansen Kraemer, Jr. Sr. Vice President & C.F.O. Baxter International Inc.	B	847/948-2000	847/948-3948
Mr. Theodore Janulis Managing Director Lehman Brothers, Inc.	S	212/526-7406	212/528-8955
Mr. Michael J. Januzik Vice President Quantilogic Asset Management	B	415/434-1130	415/434-1139
Ms. Barbara L. Jarriel Chief Investment Officer Florida State Board of Administration	B	904/488-3061	904/921-2131
Mr. Jorge Jasson Senior Vice President Chase Securities Inc.	S	212/552-1475	212/552-6163
Mr. Mark Javurek Great Western Bank, a Federal Savings Bank (Treasury)	B	818/775-2800	818/775-2811

Contact/Firm	Buyside/Sellside	Telephone	Fax
Mr. Timothy W. Jay Managing Director Lehman Brothers, Inc.	S	212/526-6420	212/528-6786
Ms. Cherie Jeffries Brown Brothers Harriman & Co. (Investments) (Chicago)	B	312/781-7111	312/368-1287
Mr. Ralph H. Jenkins INVESCO MIM Inc.	B	404/892-0896	404/607-2192
Mr. John R. Jenks State Investment Officer Alaska Retirement Systems	B	907/465-4399	907/465-4397
Mr. John Jenney Head of Fixed Income Smith Affiliated Capital Corporation	B	212/644-9440	212/644-1979
Mr. Joseph A. Jennings III Central Fidelity National Bank (Richmond) (Portfolio)	B	804/697-6921	804/783-8335
Mr. Timothy J. Jennings Director The Toronto-Dominion Bank (New York — Dealer)	S	212/468-0377	212/262-1949
Mr. Michael Jensen U.S. West, Inc.	B	303/649-4509	303/649-4520
Mr. Oscar Jensen BR Investment Associates	B	908/771-7452	908/771-7452
Mr. Christopher Johansen Vice President The Tokai Bank Ltd.	S	212/339-1268	212/754-2174
Mr. Charles B. Johnson Senior Vice President Liberty Bank and Trust Co. (Oklahoma City) (Trust)	B	405/231-6453	405/231-6725
Ms. Cynthia Johnson Vice President Canadian Imperial Bank of Commerce (U.S.A.)	S	212/856-6601	212/856-6699
Ms. Debra J. Johnson Partner Brinson Partners, Inc.	B	312/220-7100	312/220-7199
Mr. Gary P. Johnson Managing Director Scudder Stevens & Clark, Inc. (Boston)	B	617/728-9319	617/295-1111
Mr. Robert T. Johnson Senior Vice President Prudential Securities Inc.	S	212/778-6165	212/778-6154
Dr. Timothy E. Johnson President Johnson Investment Counsel Incorporated	B	513/385-4001	513/385-8947
Mr. Thomas J. Johnston Group Senior Vice President ABN AMRO Securities (USA) Inc.	S	312/904-7001	312/781-8167
Mr. Alistair Johnstone Executive Vice President Euro Brokers Maxcor, Inc.	S	212/748-7012	212/748-7329

Contact/Firm	Buyside/Sellside	Telephone	Fax
Mr. James D. Jolley Executive Vice President Magna Group, Inc.	B	314/963-3012	314/963-2691
Ms. Judith Jonas Dimensional Fund Advisors, Inc.	B	310/395-7603	310/395-6140
Mr. Stanley Jonas Manager FIMAT Futures U.S.A., Inc.	S	212/759-2626	212/759-2898
Mr. Drayton Jones Senior Vice President Key Trust Company (Syracuse)	B	315/470-5213	315/470-5283
Dr. Frank J. Jones Exec. Vice President & C.I.O. Guardian Life Insurance Co. of America	B	212/598-8232	212/777-6715
Mr. Laurance G. Jones Exec. V.P., Treasurer & C.F.O. One Valley Bancorp of West Virginia	B	304/348-7062	304/348-7315
Mr. Martin L. Jones Managing Director-Fixed Income First Asset Management	B	612/973-0174	612/973-0200
Mr. Michael Jones Commonwealth Investment Counsel	B	804/782-3207	804/782-3759
Mr. Thomas E. Jones E.V.P. — Financial Control Citicorp	B	212/291-2542	212/291-4007
Ms. Shirley P. Jordan Executive Vice President Presidential Life Insurance Company	B	914/358-2300 Ext. 220	914/358-2818
Mr. Robert H. Joseph, Jr. Sr. Vice President & C.F.O. Alliance Capital Management L.P.	B	212/969-2384	212/969-2284
Mr. Robert Jostes Director Allstate Insurance Company	B	708/402-5294	708/402-0164
Mr. Michael T. Kabat Assistant Vice President PriMerit Bank, A Federal Savings Bank	B	702/365-3458	702/365-3477
Mr. Thomas L. Kalaris Managing Director J.P. Morgan Securities Inc.	S	212/648-0925	212/648-5181
Mr. John H. Kallis Senior Vice President State Street Research & Management Co.	B	617/357-1200	617/542-7753
Mr. Yoichi Kambara S.V.P. & General Manager The Bank of California, N.A.	B	415/765-0400	415/765-2788
Mr. Koudou Kamimura Assistant Vice President Sanwa Bank	S	212/339-6516	212/750-3284
Mr. Mitsuo Kamimura Assistant Vice President Sanwa Bank	S	212/339-6533	212/750-3284

Contact/Firm	Buyside/Sellside	Telephone	Fax
Mr. Charles A. Kaminski Vice President — Investments GNA Capital Management Inc.	B	206/625-1755	206/516-4998
Mr. William J. Kamperman President & C.E.O. Acorn Derivatives Management Corp.	B	914/949-3516	914/949-3521
Mr. Stephen M. Kane Hotchkis and Wiley	B	213/362-8888	213/623-7880
Mr. Thomas G. Kane Vice President The Bank of New York (Dealer)	S	212/804-2179	212/495-1019
Mr. John Kapanke President Evangelical Lutheran Church-Board of Pensions	B	612/333-7651	612/334-5307
Mr. Robert S. Kapito Vice Chairman BlackRock Financial Management L.P.	B	212/754-5330	212/754-8790
Mr. Peter Kaplan Merganser Capital Management Corporation	B	617/494-1000	617/494-1899
Ms. Janet Kappenberg Senior Vice President Atlantic Asset Management Partners Inc.	B	203/425-3517	203/425-3542
Mr. A. J. Karanikolas Vice President HSBC Markets	S	212/658-5690	212/658-1905
Mr. Peter F. Karches Managing Director Morgan Stanley & Co., Incorporated (NYC Branch)	S	212/296-6502	212/296-5256
Dr. Denis S. Karnosky Partner Brinson Partners, Inc.	B	312/220-7100	312/220-7199
Mr. James A. Karpowicz Vice President — Investments MGIC Investment Corporation	B	414/347-2569	414/347-6382
Ms. Kimberly Kassin Vice President Westdeutsche Landesbank Girozentrale — New York Branch	S	212/597-8500	212/852-6300
Mr. Yoshimi Kato Assistant Treasurer The Tokai Bank Ltd.	S	212/339-1286	212/754-2174
Mr. Mark Katzelnick Vice President ING Barings	S	212/446-0905	212/688-0582
Mr. Henry Kaufman President Henry Kaufman & Company, Inc.	B	212/755-3040	212/755-4090
Mr. M. Scot Kaufman Chief Financial Officer MBNA Corporation	B	302/456-8588	302/456-8541
Mr. Brian Kaye Chairman FIMAT Futures U.S.A., Inc.	S	212/527-8101	212/759-2898

Contact/Firm	Buyside/Sellside	Telephone	Fax
Mr. Richard J. Kaye Sanford C. Bernstein & Co., Inc.	B	212/756-4127	212/756-4550
Mr. Bruce Kaz Vice President Marine Midland Bank, N.A. (Trust)	B	716/841-7345	716/841-4244
Mr. Hideo Kazusa The Bank of Tokyo Trust Company (Securities & Investments)	B	212/782-6705	212/782-6426
Mr. Daniel L. Keating Senior Managing Director Bear, Stearns & Company Inc.	S	212/272-4911	212/272-6291
Mr. Joseph T. Keating Senior Vice President Old Kent Bank & Trust Company (Trust)	B	616/771-5875	616/771-4640
Mr. James Keefer Ford Motor Company	B	313/322-1480	313/390-2106
Mr. John D. Keenan Vice President Euro Brokers Maxcor, Inc.	S	212/748-7080	212/748-7088
Mr. George Kegler Senior Vice President Sanwa Securities (USA) Co., L.P.	S	212/527-2450	212/486-1279
Mr. Garnett Keith Prudential Capital Management	B	201/802-8126	201/802-8845
Mr. Sean Kelleher Director Nomura Securities International, Inc.	S	212/667-2240	212/667-1006
Mr. Charles E. Keller President Richmond Capital Management, Inc.	B	804/379-8285	804/379-9362
Mr. Ronald E. Keller Principal Mutual Life Insurance Company	B	515/247-5192	515/248-8486
Mr. James Kellerman Nicholas-Applegate Capital Management (Houston)	B	713/963-5250	713/963-5280
Mr. Steven Kellner Vice President Prudential Capital Management	B	201/802-4762	201/802-7021
Mr. James P. Kelly First Vice President Dean Witter Reynolds Inc.	S	212/392-3770	212/392-0188
Mr. Michael W. Kelly Managing Director AMBAC Financial Services, L.P.	B	203/341-2303	203/341-2351
Mr. James M. Kelso Director Prudential Securities Inc.	S	212/778-7860	212/776-3463
Mr. Duff Kennedy President & C.E.O. Kennedy Associates Inc.	B	206/624-9640	206/624-8515

Contact/Firm	Buyside/Sellside	Telephone	Fax
Ms. Mary Eileen Kennedy Sr. Vice President & Treasurer First Chicago/NBD Corporation	B	312/732-1581	312/732-3366
Mr. James Kenny Manager Exco Noonan Inc.	S	201/200-4950	201/200-5069
Mr. William Kenny Vice President Merrill Lynch Capital Markets	S	212/449-5911	212/449-2805
Mr. Donald Kenst Senior Portfolio Manager Integra Financial Corporation	B	412/644-7910	412/261-7279
Ms. Linda A. Kent Partner Brinson Partners, Inc.	B	312/220-7100	312/220-7199
Mr. Timothy B. Kerr First Vice President NBD Bank, N.A. (Trust)	B	313/225-1064	313/225-1038
Mr. Frederick C. Kessell Chief Investment Officer Providian Corporation	B	502/560-2393	502/560-3080
Mr. James Kestner V.P.-Securities Research Provident Mutual Life Insurance Company	B	215/636-5291	215/636-5036
Mr. Wolfgang Ketzer Assistant Vice President Westdeutsche Landesbank Girozentrale — New York Branch	S	212/852-6026	212/852-6300
Mr. Robert Khanna Vice President Citicorp Securities, Inc.	S	212/291-2155	212/425-3857
Ms. Leslie Khosravani First of America Bank Corporation	B	616/376-7463	616/376-7484
Mr. Sanjeev Khullar Director Nomura Securities International, Inc.	S	212/667-2334	212/667-1058
Mr. Peter Kiely Director — Research Eaton Vance Management, Inc.	B	617/482-8260	617/451-0642
Mr. Gregory Kiernan Managing Director PaineWebber Incorporated	S	212/713-2344	212/713-1303
Mr. Gary Killian Managing Director Lehman Brothers, Inc.	S	212/528-6027	212/528-7891
Mr. John Y. Kim Managing Director Aetna Life & Casualty (Portfolio Management Group)	B	203/273-4936	203/275-4846
Mr. Christopher King Assistant Vice President Dresdner Securities (USA) Inc.	S	212/429-4120	212/429-4496
Mr. Creston A. King III United Services Advisors Inc.	B	210/308-1234	210/308-1270

Contact/Firm	Buyside/Sellside	Telephone	Fax
Mr. J. Luther King President Luther King Capital Management	B	817/332-3235	817/332-4630
Mr. Randall C. King S.V.P. & Treasurer PNC Bank — Asset Liability (Portfolio)	B	412/762-8235	412/762-4167
Mr. Scott A. King Executive Vice President Payden & Rygel Investment Counsel	B	213/625-1900	213/628-8488
Mr. Thomas S. King Vice President American Family Insurance Group	B	608/242-4100 Ext. 30373	608/243-4923
Mr. M. G. Kingford Vice President BR Investment Associates	B	908/771-7452	908/771-7452
Mr. Daniel J. Kingston Portfolio Manager Stanford Management Company	B	415/926-0228	415/854-9188
Mr. Thomas Kinnally Manager — Repos Euro Brokers Maxcor, Inc.	S	212/748-7180	212/748-7343
Mr. Jerry L. Kirby Chairman & President Citizens Federal Bank, F.S.B.	B	513/223-4234	513/228-5510
Mr. Walter G. Kirkland Vice President Eastbridge Capital, Inc.	B	212/756-7263	212/756-7270
Mr. Stanley Kirtman President Nikko Capital Management (U.S.A.)	B	212/559-4631	212/599-4640
Mr. William Kistler Integra Financial Corporation	B	412/644-6032	412/261-7279
Mr. Robert E. Kline Vice President & Manager NatWest Securities Corporation	S	212/602-1880	212/602-4939
Ms. Patricia Klink President Advisers Capital Management Inc.	B	212/514-5110	212/514-5780
Mr. Martin L. Klopping President Rodney Square Management Corporation	B	302/651-1923	302/651-1507
Mr. Edward Klungele Chief Financial Officer Staten Island Savings Bank	B	718/447-7900	718/727-3794
Mr. Michael J. Klyce Vice President & Treasurer Torchmark Corporation	B	205/325-2051	205/325-4157
Mr. Craig Knebel Vice President HSBC Markets	S	212/658-2217	212/658-1905

Contact/Firm	Buyside/Sellside	Telephone	Fax
Mr. Michael C. Knebel Vice President SAFECO Insurance Companies	B	206/545-3129	206/545-3446
Ms. Linda K. Knight S.V.P. & Treasurer Federal National Mortgage Association	B	202/752-6113	202/752-4447
Mr. Paul D. Knudsvig Vice President Alliance Capital Management L.P.	B	212/969-2496	212/969-1162
Mr. Daniel Knytych Account Executive BA Futures Inc.	S	312/269-4510	312/987-0644
Mr. James E. Koenig S.V.P., Treasurer & C.F.O. WMX Technologies, Inc.	B	708/572-8800	708/572-3094
Mr. Mark Koenigsberg Vice President Citicorp Securities, Inc.	S	212/559-5902	212/425-3857
Mr. Kenneth Kolber Vice President Banco Santander of New York (Dealer)	S	212/756-9200	212/350-3535
Mr. Reto Koller Vice President Winterthur Swiss Group	B	212/416-5855	212/524-6839
Mr. Michael L. Kolodner Managing Director Bear, Stearns & Company Inc.	S	212/272-4936	212/272-6291
Mr. William Koski Vice President GNA Capital Management Inc.	B	206/625-2854	206/583-5606
Mr. John Kottmeyer Treasurer AmSouth Bank N.A. (Portfolio)	B	205/326-5120	205/326-5572
Mr. Scott D. Krase Vice President Oak Hill Partners	B	212/326-1500	212/593-3596
Mr. Arthur B. Krause Exec. Vice President & C.F.O. Sprint Corporation	B	913/624-3000	913/624-3281
Mr. Richard Krause Senior Dealer BZW/Barclays Bank	S	212/693-4070	212/412-1768
Ms. Katherine Kreig Gibraltar Advisors	B	212/415-5833	212/415-5814
Ms. Gail Kreitman Vice President Prudential Securities Inc.	S	212/778-2166	212/776-3463
Mr. Konrad Krill Dean Witter InterCapital Inc.	B	212/392-1818	212/392-4282
Mr. Jeffrey W. Kronthal Managing Director Merrill Lynch Capital Markets	S	212/449-1635	212/449-6639

Contact/Firm	Buyside/Sellside	Telephone	Fax
Mr. David Kroon Nicholas-Applegate Capital Management (Houston)	B	713/963-5243	713/963-5280
Mr. Douglas W. Kroske President Liberty Capital Advisors, Inc.	B	803/268-8303	803/292-4097
Mr. Joseph E. Krul Senior Vice President & C.F.O. Standard Federal Bank	B	810/637-2530	810/643-0329
Mr. Adam Kugler Senior Vice President Manufacturers & Traders Trust Company (Portfolio)	B	212/350-2486	212/350-2166
Mr. Frank Kuhlman Nike Securities (UIT Management)	B	708/241-8637	708/241-8727
Mr. John Kuhn Trader NationsBanc — CRT	S	312/234-2585	312/234-3089
Mr. Michael Kukanza Trader NationsBanc — CRT	S	312/234-2349	312/234-3089
Ms. Jeanette Kulka Assistant Vice President Bank Julius Baer & Co., Ltd.	S	212/297-1911	212/297-1935
Mr. Birenda Kumar S.V.P. & Treasurer Dean Witter, Discover & Co.	B	212/392-2222	212/392-8405
Mr. David M. Kuplic American Express Financial Advisors	B	612/671-2227	612/671-6314
Mr. Keith Kursner Senior Vice President Oppenheimer & Co., Inc.	S	212/667-5328	212/667-5302
Ms. Kim B. Kurtz BR Investment Associates	B	908/771-7452	908/771-7452
Mr. James LaBelle Senior Vice President Mercantile Banks of St. Louis, N.A.	B	314/425-1341	314/425-2727
Mr. Edward Labenski, Jr. President IDS Fixed Income Advisors	B	612/671-3227	612/671-2733
Mr. Simon Lack Managing Director Chemical Securities Incorporated	S	212/834-4445	212/834-6527
Mr. Alan J. Lacy E.V.P. & C.F.O. Sears Roebuck and Company	B	312/875-2500	312/875-8351
Mr. Matt Lagman Commander Investment Corporation	B	814/724-5078	No fax
Mr. David Lahorgue C.I.O.-Investment Strategy BZW Barclays Global Investors	B	415/597-2106	415/597-2011

Contact/Firm	Buyside/Sellside	Telephone	Fax
Mr. Clifford E. Lai Managing Director Hyperion Capital Management, Inc.	B	212/980-8400	212/593-4906
Mr. Gary Lakritz Vice President The Tokai Bank Ltd.	S	212/339-1288	212/754-2174
Mr. Alexander Lamb General Manager FIMAT Futures U.S.A. Inc. (Chicago)	S	312/578-5201	312/578-5277
Mr. Mark Lamb Director Providian Corporation	B	502/560-3202	502/560-3080
Mr. Thomas W. Lambert Exec. Vice President & C.F.O. First of America Bank Corporation	B	616/376-7004	616/376-7484
Mr. Hugh R. Lamle Executive Vice President M.D. Sass Investors Services, Inc.	B	212/730-2000 Ext. 2112	212/764-0381
Mr. Laird Landmann Hotchkis and Wiley	B	213/362-8888	213/623-7880
Mr. Andrew D. Langerman Managing Director Bear, Stearns & Company, Inc.	S	212/272-6459	212/272-6291
Mr. Michael G. Landreville A.V.P.-Derivative Management Lutheran Brotherhood	B	612/340-8505	612/340-6497
Mr. John Lane Chief Financial Officer Pennsylvania Public School Employees' Retirement System	B	717/783-5613	717/783-9424
Mr. Herbert J. Lanese Exec. Vice President & C.F.O. McDonnell Douglas Corporation	B	314/232-0232	314/234-3826
Mr. Nicholas Lang Investments Officer Federal Home Loan Bank of Boston	B	617/542-0150	617/292-9645
Mr. Rudolph E. Lang, Jr. Chief Financial Officer Litton Industries, Inc.	B	310/859-5000	310/859-5940
Ms. Sara C. Lange V.P. — Portfolio Management Provident Mutual Life Insurance Company	B	215/636-5326	215/636-8322
Mr. Ralph Langenbourg Vice President Bankers Trust Global Investment Management	B	212/250-6087	212/250-9857
Ms. Susan Lansel Vice President Bay View Federal Bank, A Federal Savings Bank	B	415/312-7268	415/573-1028
Mr. James A. Laphen President & C.O.O. Commercial Federal Corporation	B	402/554-9200	402/390-5143

Contact/Firm	Buyside/Sellside	Telephone	Fax
Mr. Donald LaPiana United Missouri Bank, N.A. (Portfolio)	B	816/860-7200	816/860-4829
Mr. Jean Pierre Lardy First Vice President Societe Generale Securities Corporation	S	212/278-7100	212/278-7195
Mr. Jeffrey R. Larsen Managing Director Chemical Securities Incorporated	S	212/834-5240	212/834-6527
Mr. Thomas Latta Vice President Templeton Global Bond Managers, Inc.	B	954/527-7434	954/462-2504
Mr. Richard N. Latzer Sr. Vice President & C.I.O. The Transamerica Corporation	B	415/983-4000	415/983-4888
Ms. Constance H. Lau Treasurer Hawaiian Electric Industries, Inc.	B	808/543-7384	808/543-7966
Mr. Russell Lau Vice President First Chicago Capital Markets, Inc.	S	312/732-8378	312/732-8733
Mr. Brendon Lavelle Vice President Fuji Bank Ltd.	S	212/898-2805	212/321-9408
Mr. Robert J. Lavin Vice President-Investments Sallie Mae	B	202/298-2668	202/965-7085
Ms. Veronique Lavorel Director The World Bank	B	202/458-0040	202/477-8589
Mr. Thomas Lawler Senior Vice President Federal National Mortgage Association	B	202/752-6785	202/752-4447
Mr. David N. Lawrence Managing Director Westdeutsche Landesbank Girozentrale — New York Branch	S	212/852-6362	212/852-6140
Mr. Gary L. Lazarini Executive Vice President National Bank of Commerce (Portfolio)	B	901/523-3797	901/523-3910
Mr. Steven Lazarus Director Credit Suisse Financial Products	S	212/322-5960	212/238-5332
Mr. Walter Lazuka Senior Vice President LaSalle National Bank (Portfolio)	B	312/781-8349	312/781-8026
Mr. Timothy Leach Qualivest Capital Management, Inc.	B	503/275-6806	503/274-0405
Mr. William F. Ledwin President Fort Washington Investment Advisors Inc.	B	513/629-1170	513/629-1047
Mr. Boon Chai Lee Director Merrill Lynch Capital Markets	S	212/449-6177	212/449-2805

Contact/Firm	Buyside/Sellside	Telephone	Fax
Mr. J. Daniel Lee, Jr. Executive Vice President Teachers Insurance & Annuity Association	B	212/916-4300	212/916-6690
Ms. Kim Lee Derivatives Manager First of America Bank Corporation	B	616/376-7460	616/376-7484
Mr. Ned Lee Vice President Norwest Bank Indiana, N.A.	B	219/461-6000	219/461-6678
Mr. Raymond J. Lee Senior Vice President Pacific Mutual Life Insurance Company	B	714/640-3011	714/640-3199
Mr. Robert E. Lee President South Boston Savings Bank	B	617/268-2500	617/269-5354
Mr. Tong Lee Vice President General Re Securities Corporation	S	212/307-2341	212/307-2320
Mr. William Lee American Express Financial Advisors	B	612/671-2169	612/671-6314
Mr. S. Kenneth Leech Director-Portfolio Management Western Asset Management Company	B	818/584-4300 Ext. 368	818/584-4390
Mr. Louis LeGoullon President Madison Scottsdale	B	602/596-3338	602/596-3303
Mr. Martin Leibowitz Vice Chairman & C.I.O. Teachers Insurance & Annuity Association	B	212/916-4010	212/916-6690
Mr. Alan Leiderman Senior Vice President Oppenheimer & Co., Inc.	S	212/667-5430	212/667-5302
Mr. Raymond Lemanski Managing Director Prudential Securities Inc.	S	212/778-5500	212/778-5297
Ms. Denise LeMay Calamos Asset Management, Inc.	B	708/245-7200	708/245-7531
Mr. John D. Lemery President Paul Revere Investment Management Corp.	B	508/751-7220	508/751-7240
Mr. William LePard Director Bank of Boston Corporation	S	617/434-7129	617/434-8330
Mr. Randall Lert Frank Russell Investment Management Co.	B	206/627-7001	206/596-3120
Mr. David Lessing Senior Vice President Euro Brokers Maxcor, Inc.	S	212/748-7100	212/748-7050
Mr. William O. Leszinske President Harris Investment Management, Inc.	B	312/461-7699	312/765-8160

Contact/Firm	Buyside/Sellside	Telephone	Fax
Mr. William Leugers Executive Vice President Gradison-McDonald Asset Management	B	513/579-5098	513/579-5080
Mr. Kenneth M. Levine Executive Vice President MONY Financial Services	B	212/708-2907	212/708-2491
Mr. Robert R. Levine Vice President & Treasurer Sallie Mae	B	202/298-2632	202/298-2726
Mr. Martin Levion First V.P. & Manager Societe Generale Securities Corporation	S	212/278-7100	212/278-7195
Mr. Michael Levy Vice President Commerz Financial Products	S	212/266-7515	212/266-7567
Mr. Dean Lewallen Dreyfus Management	B	212/922-6239	212/715-6014
Mr. Yves Leyson Director Credit Suisse Financial Products	S	212/322-5900	212/238-5332
Mr. Hartmut Liebel Director — Financial Risk Mgmt W.R. Grace & Company	B	407/362-1962	407/362-2193
Mr. Stephen A. Lieber Chairman & Co-C.E.O. Evergreen Asset Management Corp. (New York)	B	914/694-2020	914/641-2279
Mr. Martin J. Liebgott Senior Vice President I.B.J.-Schroder Bank & Trust Co. (Trust)	B	212/858-2385	212/514-9279
Mr. John Light Banque Paribas Ltd. Corporation	S	212/841-2425	212/841-2146
Ms. Denise Lilien Trader NationsBanc — CRT	S	312/234-3545	312/234-3089
Mr. Steven H. Lim Vice President Rabobank Nederland North America	S	212/808-2531	212/808-2578
Mr. Robert J. Limage Senior Investment Officer New York State & Local Retirement Systems	B	518/474-6035	518/473-6755
Mr. Curt Lin Vice President Smith Barney, Inc. (Greenwich Street)	S	212/723-7585	212/723-8792
Mr. Robert R. Lindberg Vice President & Treasurer The Transamerica Corporation	B	415/983-4000	415/983-4888
Mr. Arthur Lindenauer E.V.P. — Finance & C.F.O. Schlumberger, Ltd.	B	212/350-9400	212/350-9564
Mr. S. Craig Lindner President American Money Management Corporation	B	513/579-2529	513/579-2915

Contact/Firm	Buyside/Sellside	Telephone	Fax
Mr. James F. Link Treasurer Texaco Inc.	B	914/253-4000	914/253-7753
Mr. Michael J. Link Senior Vice President Gradison-McDonald Asset Management	B	513/579-5860	513/579-5080
Ms. Kristine Lino Manager — Global Investments PanAgora Asset Management, Inc. (U.S.A.)	B	617/439-6300	617/439-6302
Ms. Patricia Lipton Executive Director State of Wisconsin Investment Board	B	608/266-9451	608/266-2436
Mr. Richard J. Litchfield Assistant Vice President Allmerica Asset Management, Inc.	B	508/855-2461	508/855-6508
Mr. Donald Lloyd Chief Trader Bank of Montreal (Chicago)	S	312/845-4060	312/845-4198
Ms. Elaine Lloyd Managing Director Morgan Stanley & Co., Incorporated (NYC Branch)	S	212/761-2700	212/764-7490
Ms. Joan LoCascio Vice President Lehman Brothers, Inc.	S	212/528-0656	212/526-3738
Mr. Hans P. Lochmeier Senior Vice President Union Bank of Switzerland Private Banking	B	212/715-3730	212/715-3498
Mr. Ralf Lochmüller LGT Asset Management	B	415/392-6181	415/956-5617
Mr. Roland Lochoff Senior Mgr.-U.S. Fixed Income PanAgora Asset Management, Inc. (U.S.A.)	B	617/439-6300	617/439-6302
Mr. Howard Lodge Lincoln National Investment Management Co.	B	219/455-6492	219/455-1475
Mr. Leon Loewenstine Scudder Stevens & Clark, Inc. (Cincinnati)	B	513/621-2733	513/621-5081
Mr. Paul Loffredo First Vice President Dresdner Securities (USA) Inc.	S	212/429-4140	212/429-4496
Mr. Anthony L. Longi, Jr. Executive Vice President Pacholder Associates, Inc.	B	513/985-3200	513/985-3217
Mr. Nicholas Lopardo Chairman & C.E.O. State Street Global Advisors	B	617/654-3312	617/654-6176
Mr. Seymour N. Lotsoff Lotsoff Capital Management	B	312/368-1442	312/750-1131
Mr. Robert B. Lowe, Jr. Vice President United Jersey Bank (Princeton) (Trust)	B	609/987-3688	609/921-2474
Mr. Joseph M. Lowery Synovus Financial Corporation	B	706/649-4424	706/649-2479

Contact/Firm	Buyside/Sellside	Telephone	Fax
Mr. Chad Loweth Senior Vice President NatWest Securities Corporation	S	212/602-4880	212/495-5803
Ms. Terry Ludwig Director CS First Boston Corporation	S	212/909-3700	212/308-1187
Mr. Steven P. Luetger Vice President & Principal Stein Roe & Farnham Incorporated	B	312/368-7645	312/368-8103
Mr. James H. Lukens Manager — Fixed Income Minnesota State Board of Investment	B	612/296-3328	612/296-9572
Ms. Su Lum Vice President Westdeutsche Landesbank Girozentrale — New York Branch	S	212/597-8500	212/852-6300
Mr. Kevin Lund Provident Life & Accident Insurance Co.	B	615/755-8931	615/755-1671
Mr. Michael Lundquist Vice President Commerzbank Capital Markets	S	212/266-7559	212/266-7797
Ms. Barbara Luttich Managing Director Chase Securities Inc.	S	212/834-4440	212/425-1404
Mr. Brendan Lynch Vice President Republic New York Securities Corporation	S	212/525-8611	212/525-6958
Mr. Patrick Q. Lynch Executive Vice President Yamaichi International (America), Inc.	S	212/524-6585	212/912-0172
Mr. Thomas R. Lynett, Jr. Managing Director & C.O.O. Merrill Lynch Capital Markets	S	212/449-5843	212/449-6673
Mr. Edward Lynn Trader PaineWebber Incorporated	S	212/713-4498	212/713-1303
Ms. Patricia Lynott-Bonan Managing Director Chase Securities Inc.	S	212/552-1401	212/552-0630
Mr. Kevin T. Lyons Director The Toronto-Dominion Bank (New York — Dealer)	S	212/468-0375	212/262-1949
Mr. Jeffrey H. MacArthur Vice President The Fifth Third Bank of Northwestern Ohio	B	419/259-6951	419/259-6939
Ms. Bridget Macaskill President & C.E.O. & C.O.O. Oppenheimer Management Corporation	B	212/323-0200	212/323-0558
Mr. Malcolm S. Macdonald Treasurer Ford Motor Company	B	313/322-3000	313/390-2106

Contact/Firm	Buyside/Sellside	Telephone	Fax
Mr. Patrick MacDonald Executive Director Swiss Bank Corporation (SBC Warburg)	S	212/335-1331	212/335-1389
Mr. G. David MacEwen Benham Capital Management Group	B	415/967-9787	415/965-4902
Mr. Roland Machold New Jersey Division of Investments	B	609/292-5106	609/396-1073
Mr. James M. MacIver Vice President Capitoline Investment Services, Inc. (Washington, DC)	B	202/879-6284	202/879-6333
Mr. Christopher Mackenzie Senior Vice President NatWest Securities Corporation	S	212/602-4357	212/602-4939
Mr. George MacKenzie Vice President & Treasurer Hercules Incorporated	B	302/597-5175	302/594-5405
Mr. Ian A. MacKinnon Senior Vice President The Vanguard Group, Inc.	B	610/669-6340	610/640-6894
Mr. Craig A. MacPherson Vice President Commerce Bank Investment Management Group	B	816/234-2415	816/234-2545
Mr. David Madden Vice President Citicorp Securities, Inc.	S	212/291-7452	212/425-3857
Mr. J. Thomas Madden Senior Vice President Federated Investors	B	412/288-1932	412/288-7560
Mr. Ronald E. Madey Bridgewater Associates Inc.	B	203/762-8511	203/762-2615
Mr. Gerald Madigan Executive Vice President Smith, Breeden Associates (Boulder)	B	303/440-5151	303/440-5131
Mr. Anthony Magdowski Comerica Bank (Funds Management)	B	313/222-0058	313/222-9825
Mr. John L. Maginn United of Omaha Life Insurance Company	B	402/351-2530	402/351-2913
Mr. John P. Maguire Vice President Fiduciary Asset Management	B	314/726-5533	314/863-4360
Mr. Christopher Mahabir Director-Derivative Strategies Fidelity Management & Research Company	B	617/563-2512	617/479-9743
Mr. Richard Mahany Senior Vice President Integra Financial Corporation	B	412/644-8116	412/261-7279
Mr. Robert Mahany Treasurer The Rochester Community Savings Bank	B	716/238-8862	716/423-7210

Contact/Firm	Buyside/Sellside	Telephone	Fax
Mr. John Mahoney Director CS First Boston Corporation	S	212/909-2730	212/308-1187
Mr. Peter Mahoney Director — Fixed Income Bear, Stearns Asset Management Inc.	B	212/272-6027	212/272-3107
Mr. Vache Mahseredjian Managing Director National Mutual Funds Management Inc.	B	310/557-1500	310/286-2314
Mr. Timothy Maimone American Savings Bank, F.A.	B	714/252-6858	714/252-6884
Mr. Douglas L. Maine Chief Financial Officer MCI Communications Corporation	B	202/872-1600	202/887-2443
Mr. Mark Maissonneuf Heber Fuger Wendin Incorporated	B	810/258-6866	810/258-9295
Mr. Francisco J. Maldonado Officer Investment Division Banco Popular of Puerto Rico (Portfolio)	B	809/753-1400	809/754-9290
Ms. Kathleen Mallon Treasurer North Side Savings Bank	B	516/488-6900	516/488-6546
Mr. William Malone Vice President Oppenheimer & Co., Inc.	S	212/667-5430	212/667-5488
Mr. John Maloney Back Bay Advisors, L.P.	B	617/578-1770	617/424-8665
Ms. Christine Mandell Senior Vice President Bank of America NT & SA — Capital Markets (New York)	S	212/836-5500	212/836-5390
Mr. Paul J. Mangus First NH Investment Services	B	603/634-6160	603/224-9405
Mr. Andreas Mann Chief Dealer Commerzbank Capital Markets	S	212/266-7414	212/266-7797
Mr. William Manning Manning & Napier Advisors Inc.	B	716/325-6880	716/325-1992
Mr. William Mansfield Vice President Nomura Securities International, Inc.	S	212/667-1480	212/667-9000
Mr. Thomas E. Mara E.V.P. & Treasurer Leucadia National Corporation	B	212/460-1981	212/598-4869
Mr. James R. Marbach Director — Fixed Income Ark Asset Management Company, Inc.	B	212/668-5640	212/668-6198
Mr. Jerry Marer Senior Vice President Republic New York Securities Corporation	S	212/525-6736	212/525-6958

Contact/Firm	Buyside/Sellside	Telephone	Fax
Mr. Robert S. Marjan S.V.P. & Treasurer American National Corporation	B	312/661-5000	312/661-6417
Mr. Alan D. Marks Executive Vice President Smith Barney, Inc. (Greenwich Street)	S	212/723-5671	212/723-8792
Mr. David P. Marks President Allianz Investment Corporation	B	203/221-8525	203/221-8529
Mr. Morris D. Marley Treasurer Branch Banking & Trust Company (BB&T-NC) (Portfolio)	B	910/733-2288	910/733-2238
Mr. John Marow Bank of Oklahoma, N.A. (Portfolio)	B	918/588-6000	918/588-6510
Mr. Howard D. Marsh Managing Director Smith Barney, Inc. (Greenwich Street)	S	212/723-7097	212/723-8951
Mr. Thomas Marthaler Vice President CTT Investment Management Group	B	312/223-2612	312/223-5170
Mr. Joseph Martin Senior Vice President United Farm Bureau Life Insurance Co.	B	317/692-7504	317/692-7525
Mr. Robert J. Martin III Vice President Continental Asset Management	B	212/440-7544	212/440-7518
Mr. Mark S. Martini Vice President — Investments Leader Federal Bank for Savings	B	901/578-2452	901/524-5715
Mr. Reno Martini Chief Investment Officer Calvert Asset Management Company, Inc.	B	301/951-4800	301/657-1982
Mr. Martin Marx Executive Vice President Smith Barney, Inc. (Greenwich Street)	S	212/723-7250	212/723-8792
Ms. Zelda Marzec President & C.E.O. Bradford & Marzec, Inc.	B	213/687-9170	213/687-9189
Mr. Anthony Mason Los Angeles County Treasurer	B	213/974-2191	213/625-2249
Mr. John Mason Roosevelt Bank, A Federal Savings Bank	B	314/532-6200	314/532-6358
Ms. Sara Mason Coast Federal Bank, Federal Savings Bank (Administration)	B	818/316-8000 Ext. 8635	818/368-4767
Mr. T. J. Masonius Vice President Euro Brokers Maxcor, Inc.	S	212/748-7160	212/748-7050
Mr. Andrew H. Massie, Jr. Warburg, Pincus Counsellors, Inc.	B	212/878-0600	212/878-9351

Contact/Firm	Buyside/Sellside	Telephone	Fax
Mr. Koichi Masuda Senior Vice President The Sakura Bank Ltd. (New York)	S	212/756-6900	212/644-9565
Mr. James Mather Vice President Bank of Boston Corporation	S	212/415-9743	617/434-8330
Mr. Steven Matsuo Vice President First National Bank of Chicago (Dealer)	S	312/732-9090	312/732-4840
Mr. Donald Mattersdorf Vice President LGT Asset Management	B	415/399-5444	415/956-5617
Mr. Anthony Matthews Assistant Vice President Westpac Banking Corporation	S	212/818-1578	212/818-1499
Mr. Brian W. Matthews Vice President Payden & Rygel Investment Counsel	B	213/625-1900	213/628-8488
Mr. Tuulikki Matthews Vice President NatWest Securities Corporation	S	212/602-4050	212/602-4939
Mr. Earle Mauldin Exec. Vice President & C.F.O. BellSouth Corporation	B	404/249-4030	404/249-5597
Mr. Anthony R. Mauro Vice President Greenwich Capital Markets, Inc.	S	203/625-2828	203/629-2513
Mr. Benjamin Mayer Senior Portfolio Manager AMR Investment Services, Inc.	B	817/967-0824	817/967-9721
Mr. Peter Mayers Assistant Vice President Bank Julius Baer & Co., Ltd.	S	212/297-1979	212/297-1935
Mr. Joseph Mazon CIGNA Investment Management (U.S.A.)	B	203/726-7423	203/726-8530
Mr. Luke C. Mazur MERUS Capital Management	B	415/291-7468	415/296-6472
Mr. Lloyd McAdams Chairman Pacific Income Advisers	B	310/393-1039	310/393-0714
Mr. Joseph J. McAlinden Managing Director Dean Witter InterCapital Inc.	B	212/392-0770	212/392-4282
Mr. Kenneth J. McAlley E.V.P./Head-Fixed Inc. Invsts. United States Trust Company of New York (Portfolio)	B	212/852-3374	212/635-3580
Mr. James McAuliffe Vice President The Bank of New York (Dealer)	S	212/804-2137	212/495-1014
Mr. Tom McAvity V.P.-Quantitative Research Lincoln National Investment Management Co.	B	219/455-5118	219/455-1475

Contact/Firm	Buyside/Sellside	Telephone	Fax
Mr. Gerald P. McBride E.V.P. & National Manager Prudential Securities Inc.	S	212/778-3688	212/778-7137
Mr. James E. McCabe Vice President-Fixed Income Benefit Capital Management Corporation	B	203/794-5938	203/794-2693
Ms. Tracey McCabe Vice President J. Aron & Company	S	212/902-7850	212/346-2687
Mr. Thomas D. McCaffery Managing Director Westdeutsche Landesbank Girozentrale — New York Branch	S	212/852-6036	212/852-6140
Mr. James R. McCall President Keystone Custodian Funds, Inc.	B	617/338-3462	617/338-3351
Mr. Leonard H. McCandless Vice President Rittenhouse Financial Services Inc.	B	610/971-9300	610/293-2444
Mr. James McCarthy, Jr. Director Merrill Lynch Capital Markets	S	212/449-5578	212/449-2805
Mr. John McCarthy Vice President ING Barings	S	212/446-1553	212/644-0428
Mr. William M. McCarthy Sr. Vice President & Manager INVESCO Management and Research, Inc.	B	617/345-8536	617/261-4560
Mr. Dennis McCauley Mitchell Hutchins Asset Management, Inc.	B	212/713-1842	212/713-1459
Mr. Greg McClaren Assistant Vice President Federal Home Loan Bank of Topeka	B	913/233-0507 Ext. 552	913/234-1796
Ms. Linda W. McCleary Senior Vice President Investment Counselors of Maryland, Inc.	B	410/539-3838	410/783-7321
Mr. Kevin M. McClintock Managing Director The Dreyfus Corporation	B	212/922-6000	212/922-6076
Ms. Aimee McCormack Vice President Rabobank Nederland North America	S	212/808-7900	212/818-0233
Ms. Deborah McCoy Florida State Board of Administration	B	904/488-3061	904/921-2131
Mr. Robert S. McCoy, Jr. Exec. Vice President & C.F.O. Wachovia Corporation	B	910/770-5926	910/770-5959
Mr. William K. McCrackin Vice Chairman & C.F.O. MCN Corporation	B	313/256-5500	313/256-5232
Mr. Bart McDade Managing Director Lehman Brothers, Inc.	S	212/526-7067	212/526-3738

Contact/Firm	Buyside/Sellside	Telephone	Fax
Ms. Lisa McDaniel Investment Officer First Commercial Capital Management	B	501/371-6756	501/371-7487
Mr. Frank L. McDermott Senior Vice President Daiwa Securities America, Inc.	S	212/612-6540	212/612-7100
Mr. Scott McDermott Vice President Goldman Sachs & Company	S	212/902-5052	212/902-1512
Mr. Arlen L. McDonald E.V.P. & C.F.O. Deposit Guaranty Corp.	B	601/354-8211	601/354-8329
Ms. Anne M. McDonley Senior Vice President John Hancock Advisers, Inc.	B	617/375-6253	617/375-1831
Mr. Dennis J. McDonnell President Van Kampen American Capital Investment Advisory Corp.	B	708/684-6330	708/684-6270
Mr. Steve McDougall Director The Toronto-Dominion Bank (New York — Dealer)	S	212/468-0375	212/262-1949
Mr. Michael McEachern V.P. — Fixed-Income Trading American General Corporation	B	713/831-6232	713/831-6218
Mr. Daniel R. McFadden Manager — Foreign Exchange Hercules Incorporated	B	302/594-5452	302/594-5371
Ms. Maureen McFarland Brown Brothers Harriman & Co. (Investments)	B	212/493-8017	212/493-8526
Mr. Kevin McGivern Manager BZW/Barclays Bank	S	212/412-6850	212/412-1768
Ms. Denise McGlone Chief Financial Officer Sallie Mae	B	202/333-8000	202/965-7085
Mr. J. Michael McGonagle Vice President Union Bank — Los Angeles	B	213/236-7484	213/236-7366
Mr. Mark J. McGrew Senior Investment Officer Norwest Bank Iowa, N.A.	B	515/245-3226	515/245-8117
Mr. James B. McGuire Vice President Fort Washington Investment Advisors Inc. (Cincinnati)	B	513/361-7600	513/361-7699
Mr. Peter J. McGuire Senior Vice President Garvin GuyButler Corporation	S	212/732-6900	212/815-6587
Mr. Neil F. McKay Executive Vice President Capitol Federal Savings & Loan Association	B	913/235-1341	913/231-6361
Ms. Gypsy A. McKenzie Branch Banking & Trust Company (BB&T-NC) (Portfolio)	B	910/733-2143	910/733-2238

Contact/Firm	Buyside/Sellside	Telephone	Fax
Mr. Thomas McKernan VP-Hedging & Derivatives U.S. National Bank of Oregon (Portfolio)	B	503/275-3686	503/275-5032
Mr. Timothy McKessy Assistant Vice President Dresdner Securities (USA) Inc.	S	212/429-4120	212/429-4496
Mr. Richard McLaughlin Integra Financial Corporation	B	412/644-8758	412/261-7279
Mr. Gary McLoughlin Senior Managing Director Bear, Stearns & Company Inc.	S	212/272-5514	212/272-6247
Mr. Philip R. McLoughlin Executive Vice President Phoenix Duff & Phelps Investment Management Co. (Hartford)	B	203/275-5365	203/275-5543
Mr. Brian J. McMahon Managing Director Thornburg Management Company, Inc.	B	505/984-0200	505/984-0310
Mr. David McMahon Branch Banking & Trust Company (Trust)	B	919/831-4350	919/831-4397
Mr. H. Thomas McMeekin President & C.I.O. Lincoln National Investment Management Co.	B	219/455-2000	219/455-1475
Mr. Michael McMennamin Exec. Vice President-Finance BANC ONE Corporation	B	614/248-5944	614/248-9344
Mr. Daniel J. McMorrow Senior Vice President Garvin GuyButler Corporation	S	212/732-6900	212/815-6587
Ms. Carol C. McMurtrie Managing Partner Loomis, Sayles & Company L.P. (Pasadena)	B	818/793-8989	818/584-1197
Mr. Eugene M. McQuade Exec. Vice President & C.F.O. Fleet Financial Group	B	617/346-2000	617/346-0130
Ms. Mary McQuillen American Express Financial Advisors	B	612/671-2998	612/671-2733
Mr. Michael T. McRee Investek Capital Management	B	601/949-3105	601/949-3177
Mr. John McVey Vice President — Sales Daiwa Securities America, Inc.	S	212/612-6500	212/612-7100
Mr. Richard McVey Managing Director J.P. Morgan Futures Inc. (Chicago)	S	312/541-3344	312/541-3381
Mr. Timothy McWalters Vice President Banque Nationale de Paris (New York)	S	212/415-9755	212/415-9798
Mr. David Mead Harris Trust & Savings (Personal Trust)	B	312/461-7756	312/461-7142

Contact/Firm	Buyside/Sellside	Telephone	Fax
Mr. George Mead Executive Vice President The Frost National Bank (Portfolio)	B	210/220-4936	210/220-4619
Mr. Thomas M. Meade Laidlaw Capital Management, Inc.	B	212/949-5400	212/233-7784
Mr. Donald S. Mears Vice President Norwest Bank Iowa, N.A.	B	515/245-3233	515/245-8117
Mr. George R. Meiling Treasurer BANC ONE Corporation	B	614/248-5944	614/248-9344
Ms. Elizabeth Meitzler National City Bank, Indiana	B	317/267-6283	317/267-6112
Mr. Azza Meleik Co-Manager FIMAT Futures U.S.A. Inc. (Chicago)	S	312/578-5212	312/578-5277
Mr. Thomas Merfeld Director — Asset Liability Century Investment Management Co. (CIMCO)	B	608/231-8597	608/238-2316
Mr. Randall Merk Vice President Benham Capital Management Group	B	415/967-9792	415/965-1446
Mr. Mark R. Mershon Vice President PNC Bank — Asset Liability (Portfolio)	B	412/762-8402	412/762-4167
Mr. Robert B. Mersky President Peregrine Capital Management	B	612/343-7602	612/343-7636
Mr. Jack R. Meyer President & C.E.O. Harvard Management Company	B	617/523-4400	617/523-1283
Mr. Allan J. Meyers V.P. & Director — Fixed Income Old Kent Bank & Trust Company (Trust)	B	616/771-5219	616/771-4640
Mr. Gary Meyerson Vice President Morgan Stanley & Co., Incorporated (NYC Branch)	S	212/761-2433	212/764-7490
Ms. Kim I. Michalski V.P./Director-T/E Fixed Income BofA Capital Management Inc. (Los Angeles)	B	213/229-1404	213/626-2162
Mr. Michael Middleton Vice President First National Bank of Commerce (Investment)	B	504/561-1388	504/561-1923
Mr. Glenn Migliozzi Managing Director-Fixed Income Fleet Investment Advisors (Boston)	B	617/346-2221	617/292-2061
Mr. Tony Miliote Dean Witter Reynolds Inc.	S	212/392-4472	212/392-0188
Mr. Bruce T. Miller Managing Director Credit Suisse Financial Products	S	212/322-5960	212/238-5332

Contact/Firm	Buyside/Sellside	Telephone	Fax
Mr. Don L. Miller Woodmen of the World Life Insurance Society	B	402/342-1890	402/342-5136
Mr. Eric Miller Director BZW/Barclays Bank	S	212/412-1768	212/412-1768
Ms. Heidi G. Miller Chief Financial Officer Travelers Group	B	212/816-8000	212/816-8912
Mr. Keith Miller S.V.P. — Finance & C.F.O. Mark Twain Bank (Portfolio)	B	314/889-0799	314/889-0784
Mr. Lawrence R. Miller Senior Executive Director AON Advisors Incorporated	B	312/701-3918	312/701-3900
Ms. Margo Miller Vice President Crestar Bank (Portfolio)	B	804/782-7391	804/782-5100
Mr. Michael I. Miller Vice President & Treasurer Owens-Corning Fiberglass Corporation	B	419/248-8000	419/248-6227
Mr. Paul S. Miller Principal Morgan Stanley & Co., Incorporated (NYC Branch)	S	212/761-2328	212/764-7490
Mr. Richard W. Miller Sr. E.V.P. & C.F.O. AT&T	B	212/387-5400	212/226-4935
Mr. Steve Miller VP-Investment Derivatives United of Omaha Life Insurance Company	B	402/351-3004	402/351-2913
Mr. Thomas J. Miller Investment Officer New York State & Local Retirement Systems	B	518/473-4558	518/473-6755
Mr. William D. Miller Vice President-Capital Markets Federal Home Loan Bank of Chicago	B	312/565-6924	312/565-5823
Mr. William P. Miller Director General Motors Investment Management Corp.	B	212/418-6327	212/418-3665
Mr. Scott Millimet Executive Vice President Back Bay Advisors, L.P.	B	617/578-1767	617/424-8665
Mr. Wallace B. Millner III Sr. Vice President & C.F.O. Signet Banking Corporation	B	804/747-2000	804/771-7599
Mr. Andrew B. Mills V.P.-Investment Svcs & Systems Federal Home Loan Bank of Atlanta	B	404/888-8187	404/897-1846
Ms. Lynne M. Mills Vice President MIMLIC Asset Management Company	B	612/223-4434	612/223-5959

Contact/Firm	Buyside/Sellside	Telephone	Fax
Mr. Frank Minard Managing Director Bankers Trust Global Investment Management	B	212/250-3870	212/250-9857
Mr. B. Scott Minerd Managing Director CS First Boston Corporation	S	212/909-3728	212/318-1354
Mr. Lee W. Minton, Jr. President Minton Investment Management	B	610/940-0695	610/940-0696
Ms. Elaine Mintzer Sanford C. Bernstein & Co., Inc.	B	212/756-4131	212/486-8329
Mr. Azam Mistry Vice President HSBC Markets	S	212/658-1047	212/658-1905
Ms. E. T. Mitchell Vice President BR Associates	S	908/771-7452	908/771-7452
Mr. Patrick Mitchell Chief-Fixed Income & Equities California State Teachers' Retirement System	B	916/229-3723	916/387-9585
Mr. David R. Mittelman S.V.P. & Director-Fixed Income Harvard Management Company	B	617/523-4400	617/523-5308
Mr. David Moffett Chief Financial Officer Star Bank, N.A. (Cincinnati) (Portfolio)	B	513/632-4534	513/632-4653
Mr. Joseph H. Moglia Managing Director Merrill Lynch Capital Markets	S	212/449-5730	212/449-3774
Mr. Kenneth Mokray Director Public Employees Retirement Association of Colorado	B	303/832-9550 Ext. 572	303/831-8521
Mr. Thomas G. Moles Managing Director J & W Seligman & Co., Incorporated	B	212/850-1467	212/922-5747
Mr. Lawrence Mollner Executive Vice President Dean Witter Reynolds Institutional Futures	S	312/984-4205	312/641-0463
Mr. Michael P. Monaco E.V.P., Treasurer & C.F.O. American Express Company	B	212/640-2000	212/611-9802
Mr. Joseph T. Monagle Senior Vice President Merrill Lynch Asset Management Inc.	B	609/282-2070	609/282-3360
Mr. Edward W. Moneypenny S.V.P. — Finance & C.F.O. Oryx Energy Company	B	214/715/8950	214/715-3311
Mr. Dennis Monroe Senior Vice President Wachovia Bank Capital Management	B	910/732-6317	910/770-6630

Contact/Firm	Buyside/Sellside	Telephone	Fax
Mr. Thomas K. Montag Partner Goldman Sachs & Company	S	212/902-8285	212/902-1512
Mr. E. Jack Montgomery MERUS Capital Management	B	415/296-6820	415/552-7880
Mr. Philip Moody Senior Vice President Garvin GuyButler Corporation	S	212/732-6900	212/815-6587
Mr. Brian Mooney Vice President Goldman Sachs & Company	S	212/902-8366	212/902-1512
Ms. Jacqueline R. Moore PNC Bank Ohio (Trust)	B	513/651-8484	513/651-7156
Mr. Johnson Moore Vice President Mellon Bank, N.A. (Portfolio)	B	412/234-8604	412/234-7834
Mr. Michael Moore Federal Home Loan Bank of Chicago	B	312/565-5797	312/565-5823
Mr. Robert J. Moore Managing Director BEA Associates	B	212/832-2626 Ext. 204	212/355-1662
Mr. Robert J. Moore Senior Vice President Phoenix Duff & Phelps Investment Management Co. (Chicago)	B	312/368-5500	312/368-5512
Mr. Roderick Moore Vice President Southern Farm Bureau Casualty Insurance Co.	B	601/957-7777	601/957-4329
Mr. Theodore Moran ITT Hartford Life Insurance Company	B	203/547-5000	203/843-6457
Mr. Timothy Moran Managing Director & Treasurer The Putnam Management Company Inc.	B	617/292-1776	617/292-1713
Mr. Michael E. Morandi Vice President Citicorp Securities, Inc.	S	212/291-2954	212/425-3857
Ms. Regina Morellino Vice President Chemical Securities Incorporated	S	212/834-5062	212/834-6527
Mr. George Morgan President Bloom Staloff Brokerage Services Inc.	S	215/568-9311	215/569-3377
Mr. William J. Morgan President Pacholder Associates, Inc.	B	513/985-3200	513/985-3217
Mr. Takahiro Moriguchi Vice Chairman & C.F.O. Union Bank — Los Angeles	B	213/236-5000	213/236-7983
Mr. Lee Moriwaki Bank of Hawaii (Investments)	B	808/537-8347	808/538-4471

Contact/Firm	Buyside/Sellside	Telephone	Fax
Ms. Donna Morlack Vice President Bank of Montreal (Chicago)	S	312/845-5020	312/845-4198
Mr. George Morris Vice Chairman General Accident Group	B	215/625-1021	215/625-2103
Mr. J. Gary Morris Senior Portfolio Manager Harleysville Mutual Insurance Company	B	215/256-5029	215/256-5601
Mr. Timothy J. Morris Sr. E.V.P.& Chief Inv. Officer Bessemer Trust Company, N.A.	B	212/708-9100	212/265-5826
Mr. George W. Morriss Exec. Vice President & C.F.O. People's Bank	B	203/338-7171	203/338-2502
Ms. Dolores J. Morrissey Executive Vice President Mutual of America Capital Management Corporation	B	212/224-1939	212/224-2539
Mr. Richard Morton Managing Director First Chicago Capital Markets, Inc.	S	312/732-4440	312/732-5442
Mr. Warren B. Mosler President & C.E.O. Adams, Viner & Mosler	B	407/655-4900	407/655-3059
Mr. E. T. Moss Vice President Commander Corporation	S	814/724-5078	No fax
Ms. Sharmin Mossavar-Rahmani Goldman Sachs Asset Management (U.S.A.)	B	212/902-2300	212/902-9100
Mr. Jack Moswich Sr. Partner & Mgr.- Analytics Harris Investment Management, Inc.	B	312/461-3233	312/765-8160
Mr. John Moubayed Vice President CS First Boston Corporation	S	212/909-3180	212/308-1187
Mr. Robert F. Mougeot Financial Vice Pres. & C.F.O. Hawaiian Electric Industries, Inc.	B	808/543-7750	808/543-7966
Mr. James R. Mulally Senior Vice President Capital Guardian Trust Company	B	310/996-6109	310/996-6200
Mr. Michael Mullan Inter-American Development Bank	B	202/623-2320	202/623-3096
Mr. Steven Mullaney Vice President Fuji Bank Ltd.	S	212/898-2810	212/321-9408
Mr. John Mullen Managing Director J.P. Morgan Securities Inc.	S	212/648-0743	212/648-5953
Mr. Douglas Muller Vice President Chase Securities Inc.	S	212/552-5183	212/425-1404

Contact/Firm	Buyside/Sellside	Telephone	Fax
Ms. Laura Mulpagano Hotchkis and Wiley	B	213/362-8888	213/623-7880
Mr. James Mulvey Senior Vice President Smith Barney, Inc. (Greenwich Street)	S	212/723-7001	212/723-8792
Mr. Donald B. Murphy Partner Brown Brothers Harriman & Co. (Investments)	B	212/483-1818	212/493-8526
Mr. Gregory E. Murphy Sr. Vice President — Finance Selective Insurance of America	B	201/948-1292	201/948-6709
Mr. John Murphy Vice President Citicorp Global Derivatives	S	312/993-3868	312/993-6830
Mr. John J. Murphy Vice President Skandia Investment Management Inc. (U.S.A.)	B	212/978-2806	212/385-2169
Mr. John W. Murphy, Jr. Managing Director First Asset Management	B	612/973-0180	612/973-0200
Mr. Patrick Murphy Chairman & C.E.O. First NH Bank	B	603/634-7145	603/634-7189
Mr. Robert C. Murray Vice President & C.F.O. Public Service Enterprise Group Incorporated	B	201/430-7000	201/430-5845
Mr. Timothy Murray Managing Director Bear, Stearns & Company Inc.	S	212/272-5138	212/272-6291
Mr. Albert F. Myers Vice President & Treasurer Northrop Grumman Corporation	B	310/553-6262	310/201-3023
Mr. Stephen R. Myers State Investment Officer South Dakota Investment Council	B	605/367-5850	605/367-5863
Mr. Peter A. Nadosy President Morgan Stanley Asset Management, Inc.	B	212/296-7115	212/296-7289
Mr. Jorge Nagel Director Deutsche Morgan Grenfell	S	212/469-8046	212/474-8212
Mr. Lynn A. Nagorske E.V.P., Treasurer & C.F.O. TCF Bank Minnesota fsb	B	612/661-6500	612/376-9089
Mr. David Nahor Vice President Christiana Bank, New York Branch	S	212/827-4852	212/827-4888
Ms. Ruth Nail Regions Financial Corporation (Investments)	B	205/326-7016	205/326-7775
Mr. Hiroshi Nakazawa Assistant Vice President The Sakura Bank Ltd. (New York)	S	212/756-6931	212/644-9565

Contact/Firm	Buyside/Sellside	Telephone	Fax
Mr. Leslie J. Nanberg Managing Director Massachusetts Financial Services Company	B	617/954-5860	617/954-6603
Mr. David T. Napoli Senior Vice President Merrill Lynch Capital Markets	S	212/449-5841	212/449-2805
Ms. Joy J. Narzisi Treasurer Commercial Federal Corporation	B	402/390-5132	402/390-5143
Mr. John Nasti Director BZW/Barclays Bank	S	212/693-4070	212/412-1768
Mr. Roger G. Nastou Vice President John Hancock Mutual Life Insurance Company	B	617/572-9615	617/572-1605
Mr. Harold Nathan Senior Portfolio Manager GMG/Seneca Capital Management	B	415/677-1550	415/677-1692
Mr. W. Dayle Nattress President & C.E.O. AMBAC Financial Services, L.P.	B	203/222-9691	203/341-2351
Ms. Maryann E. Navin John Hancock Mutual Life Insurance Company	B	617/572-4249	617/572-9560
Mr. Jacob Navon Columbus Circle Investors	B	203/353-5776	203/353-6041
Ms. Marilyn Needleman Director Dean Witter Reynolds Inc.	S	212/392-2950	212/392-0188
Mr. Hector Negroni Vice President Societe Generale Securities Corporation	S	212/278-7106	212/278-7195
Mr. Bradley Nelson UBS Asset Management, Inc. (U.S.A.)	B	212/789-7100	212/789-7237
Mr. Christopher L. Nelson South Dakota Investment Council	B	605/367-5850	605/335-5832
Mr. Matthew J. Nelson Vice President General Re Securities Corporation	S	212/307-2327	212/307-2320
Mr. Paul R. Nelson Michigan Department of Treasury	B	517/373-9151	517/335-2164
Mr. Edward Neminski Vice President Nomura Securities International, Inc.	S	212/667-2174	212/667-1058
Mr. Michael Nesseler Vice President Westdeutsche Landesbank Girozentrale — New York Branch	S	212/597-8500	212/852-6300
Mr. Richard W. Neu Exec. Vice President & C.F.O. Charter One Bank, F.S.B.	B	216/566-5337	216/566-5308
Mr. Robert W. Neu, Jr. Vice President The Provident Bank (Portfolio)	B	513/579-2075	513/579-2233

Contact/Firm	Buyside/Sellside	Telephone	Fax
Mr. Gary F. Neubeck Managing Director Prudential Capital Management	B	201/802-6279	201/802-9272
Mr. Thomas Nevin President PNC Institutional Management Corp.	B	302/791-1728	302/791-2467
Ms. Nancy S. Newcomb Senior Officer — Treasury Citicorp	B	212/291-2542	212/291-4007
Ms. Kathryn A. Newell Trader Chemical Futures & Options Inc.	S	215/561-0880	215/561-3027
Mr. Mark E. Newlin Senior Partner & Manager Harris Investment Management, Inc.	B	312/461-5521	312/765-8160
Mr. Charles W. Newman Chief Financial Officer Barnett Banks, Inc.	B	904/791-7500	904/791-7185
Mr. Frank Newman President & C.E.O. Bankers Trust — New York Corporation (Portfolio)	B	212/250-2500	212/775-2487
Mr. Kent P. Newmark Managing Partner Loomis, Sayles & Company Inc. (San Francisco)	B	415/956-2424	415/956-1052
Mr. Paul H. Newmark Manager — Investments Teledyne Inc.	B	310/551-4240	310/551-4225
Mr. Arthur Nicholas Partner Nicholas-Applegate Capital Management	B	619/687-8000	619/687-8040
Mr. Will Nichols Senior Vice President Garvin GuyButler Corporation	S	212/732-6900	212/815-6587
Mr. Kenneth F. Nimmer Vice President & Manager Associated Bank Green Bay, N.A.	B	414/433-3105	414/433-4381
Mr. Stephen Nix Smith, Breeden Associates (Dallas)	B	214/871-2575	214/871-1329
Mr. William Noah Director-Asset Mix Management General Motors Investment Management Corp.	B	212/418-6100	212/418-3665
Mr. John R. Noles First Citizens Bank & Trust Co.	B	919/755-7324	919/755-7545
Mr. Richard Noone Mellon Private Asset Management Group	B	617/722-7619	617/722-7250
Ms. Maria Nordone Vice President J. Aron & Company	S	212/902-7850	212/346-2687
Mr. Kelvin Norman Vice President NatWest Securities Corporation	S	212/602-4060	212/602-4939

Contact/Firm	Buyside/Sellside	Telephone	Fax
Mr. Michael Normile Managing Director Merrill Lynch Capital Markets	S	212/449-5835	212/449-9015
Mr. Peter D. Norris Executive Vice President The Equitable Companies Incorporated	B	212/554-1234	212/554-2320
Ms. Ellen Nose Banque Paribas Ltd. Corporation	S	212/841-3442	212/841-2146
Mr. Seth Novatt Managing Director Oppenheimer & Co., Inc.	S	212/667-7365	212/667-5514
Mr. George W. Noyes President Standish, Ayer & Wood Inc.	B	617/457-7312	617/350-7520
Ms. Nancy Noyes Director-Asset Management Salomon Brothers Asset Management Inc. (U.S.A.)	B	212/783-6315	212/783-4014
Mr. Philip Nucomb Director Morgan Stanley & Co., Incorporated (NYC Branch)	S	212/761-2840	212/764-7490
Mr. John Nunley Senior Vice President Allmerica Asset Management, Inc.	B	508/855-2170	508/852-6935
Ms. Susan C. Nustra Vice President — Treasury WMX Technologies, Inc.	B	708/572-8800	708/572-3094
Mr. Reed Nuttall Securities Analyst Farmers Insurance Group of Companies	B	213/932-3213	213/930-3101
Mr. Jonathan H. Nye Vice President Alliance Capital Management L.P.	B	212/969-2483	212/969-2285
Mr. John Nyhoff Vice President Mitsubishi Financial Futures Inc.	S	312/930-2310	312/930-2320
Mr. David A. O'Brien Vice President & Treasurer Federal Home Loan Bank of San Francisco	B	415/616-2570	415/616-2626
Ms. Maryann O'Brien Vice President Citicorp Global Derivatives	S	312/993-3165	312/993-6830
Mr. Ralph M. O'Brien Senior Vice President AEGON U.S.A. Investment Management (Cedar Rapids)	B	319/398-8529	319/369-2009
Mr. David O'Clair Vice President Berkshire Life Insurance Co.	B	413/499-4321 Ext. 468	413/443-9397
Mr. Michael F. O'Connell Managing Director Anhalt/O'Connell, Inc.	B	213/622-0066	213/613-0805

Contact/Firm	Buyside/Sellside	Telephone	Fax
Mr. Richard S. O'Connell, Jr. Senior Vice President Enhance Financial Services Group Inc.	B	212/983-3100	212/682-5377
Mr. John O'Connor First Vice President Societe Generale Securities Corporation	S	212/278-6739	212/278-7195
Mr. Kevin O'Connor Senior Vice President North Fork Bank (Portfolio)	B	516/298-5000	516/298-5769
Mr. Thomas E. O'Connor Managing General Partner Gabelli-O'Connor Fixed Income Management Co.	B	203/655-1999	203/655-7719
Mr. David Oda C.H. Dean Investment Associates	B	513/222-9531 Ext. 394	513/227-9313
Mr. James O'Donnell Trader NationsBanc — CRT	S	312/234-2585	312/234-3089
Mr. Morris W. Offit Chairman, President & C.E.O. OFFITBANK	B	212/350-3800	212/486-6957
Mr. Andrew O'Flaherty Managing Director Deutsche Morgan Grenfell	S	212/469-6715	212/474-8212
Mr. Atsuo Ogaki Second Vice President Chase Securities Inc.	S	212/552-5222	212/425-1404
Mr. Robert Ohanesian President MBIA Securities Corporation	B	914/273-3370	914/765-3375
Mr. Nobuaki Ohmura President & C.O.O. Daiwa Securities America, Inc.	S	212/612-6660	212/612-7100
Mr. Masao Okada Vice President Dai-Ichi Kangyo Bank Ltd. (New York)	S	212/466-6656	212/912-0915
Mr. William B. O'Keefe Managing Director Morgan Stanley & Co., Incorporated (NYC Branch)	S	212/296-7654	212/719-3141
Mr. Jiro J. Okochi Vice President Westdeutsche Landesbank Girozentrale — New York Branch	S	212/597-8500	212/852-6300
Ms. Susan A. Ollila Director — Fixed-Income The Ford Foundation	B	212/573-4757	212/599-4584
Mr. James Olney Senior Vice President FIMAT Futures U.S.A. Inc. (Chicago)	S	312/578-5201	312/578-5277
Mr. Walter J. Olson III Vice President Southern Farm Bureau Life Insurance Co.	B	601/981-7422	601/981-3605

Contact/Firm	Buyside/Sellside	Telephone	Fax
Mr. Brian S. O'Neil Exec. Vice President & C.I.O. The Equitable Companies Incorporated	B	212/554-1234	212/554-2320
Mr. Thomas M. O'Neill Chief Investment Officer Fleet Investment Advisors (Boston)	B	617/346-2201	617/292-2061
Mr. Michael O'Reilly Chief Investment Officer The Chubb Corporation	B	908/903-3764	908/580-3775
Mr. Howard G. Orelek BR Investment Associates	B	908/771-7452	908/771-7452
Mr. Christopher Orndorff Vice President Payden & Rygel Investment Counsel	B	213/625-1900	213/628-8488
Ms. Sandy Orr Executive Vice President Coastal Banc ssb	B	713/623-2600	713/960-9864
Mr. Anthony Ortiaga Assistant Treasurer Commerzbank Capital Markets	S	212/266-7414	212/266-7797
Mr. Jose Ortiz Assistant Vice President Dean Witter Reynolds Inc. (Philadelphia)	S	215/665-1481	215/665-1486
Ms. Karen R. Osar Vice President & Treasurer Tenneco Inc.	B	713/757-2131	713/757-4257
Mr. Richard J. Osborne Vice President & C.F.O. Duke Power Company	B	704/382-5159	704/382-7363
Ms. Tammy V. Otten South Dakota Investment Council	B	605/367-5850	605/367-5863
Mr. Gunnar S. Overstrom Vice Chairman Fleet Investment Advisors (Boston)	B	617/346-5686	617/292-2061
Mr. Dennis Owczarski Treasurer Caremark International Inc.	B	708/559-4700	708/559-4648
Mr. Robert J. Oxenburgh Manager — Risk Management Bank of America NT & SA — Capital Markets	S	415/953-5310	415/622-4386
Mr. Kent Oz Banque Paribas Ltd. Corporation	S	212/841-3740	212/841-2146
Mr. Alan Pabst Treasurer Wells Fargo Bank, N.A. (Treasury)	B	415/396-6264	415/989-3851
Dr. Asher Pacholder Chairman Pacholder Associates, Inc.	B	713/784-2350	513/985-3217
Mr. John T. Packard Scudder Stevens & Clark, Inc. (San Francisco)	B	415/403-0715	415/403-0784

Contact/Firm	Buyside/Sellside	Telephone	Fax
Mr. Ralph K. Packard Chief Financial Officer The Vanguard Group, Inc.	B	610/669-1000	610/640-6894
Mr. Christopher S. Page Vice President American National Bank & Trust (Chicago) (Trust)	B	312/661-5282	312/661-5341
Mr. Louis Paglia S.V.P. & Treasurer TIG Holdings Inc.	B	212/446-2708	212/371-8360
Mr. James F. Palmer Vice President — Treasurer McDonnell Douglas Corporation	B	314/232-0232	314/234-3826
Mr. Timothy A. Palmer Senior Vice President Investment Advisers, Inc.	B	612/376-2773	612/376-2616
Mr. John H. Pankratz Vice President & Director Reliance Insurance Company	B	212/909-1320	212/909-1844
Mr. Jeffrey A. Pantages Senior Vice President Security Benefit Life Insurance Co. of Kansas	B	913/295-3184	913/295-3099
Mr. Demitri Papacostas Vice President Chase Securities Inc.	S	212/552-5222	212/425-1404
Mr. Deno D. Papageorge Sr. Exec. Vice President & CFO The Bank of New York Company, Inc.	B	212/495-1427	212/815-4023
Mr. Thomas L. Pappas Vice President Wellington Management Company	B	617/951-5037	617/951-5250
Ms. Jennifer Paquette Public Employees Retirement Association of Colorado	B	303/832-9550 Ext. 568	303/863-3753
Mr. Mark J. Paris Director Merrill Lynch Capital Markets	S	212/449-0679	212/449-2805
Mr. William H. Park Exec. Vice President & C.F.O. United Asset Management Corporation	B	617/330-8900	617/330-1133
Mr. James A. Parke Sr. Vice President — Finance General Electric Capital Corporation	B	203/357-4304	203/357-6791
Mr. Timothy Parker Senior Portfolio Manager Florida State Board of Administration	B	904/488-3061	904/921-2131
Mr. W. Harold Parker, Jr. S.V.P. & Controller Central Carolina Bank & Trust Co. (Portfolio)	B	919/683-7777	919/682-3870
Mr. R. Ponder Parks Senior Vice President SouthTrust Bank of Alabama, N.A. (Trust)	B	205/254-5428	205/254-5839

Contact/Firm	Buyside/Sellside	Telephone	Fax
Mr. Eric E. Parsons Vice President — Investments Standard Insurance Company	B	503/321-8616	503/321-8431
Ms. Lois A. Pasquale CTT Investment Management Group	B	312/223-2767	312/223-5170
Mr. Paul E. Passman Manager Commander Corporation	S	814/724-5078	No fax
Mr. Joseph B. Patterson President The Patterson Capital Corporation	B	310/556-2496	310/553-3605
Mr. Timothy Patton New Jersey Division of Investments	B	609/292-5025	609/396-1073
Mr. James W. Paulsen Senior Managing Director Investors Management Group, Ltd. (IMG)	B	515/244-5426	515/244-2353
Mr. David G. Paulson Integra Financial Corporation	B	412/644-8210	412/261-7279
Mr. Lawrence J. Pavelec V.P./Director-Fixed Income M & I Investment Management Corp.	B	414/287-8785	414/287-8730
Mr. Bernard Pawloski Vice President Charter One Bank, F.S.B. (Michigan)	B	313/965-5902	313/965-5936
Ms. Joan A. Payden President Payden & Rygel Investment Counsel	B	213/625-1900	213/628-8488
Mr. Glen Payne Capital Guardian Trust Company	B	310/996-6113	310/996-6200
Mr. George Paz Treasurer Life Partners Group	B	303/779-1111	303/796-7576
Mr. Robert C. Peck, Jr. Senior Vice President Van Kampen American Capital Management & Research	B	713/993-4167	713/966-7411
Mr. Stephen M. Peet Executive Vice President Greenwich Capital Markets, Inc.	S	203/625-2712	203/629-1686
Mr. Joseph C. Pellegrino V.P. — Pension Fund Invts. Alcoa	B	412/553-4545	412/553-4498
Mr. John Pender Aid Association for Lutherans (AAL)	B	414/730-2606	414/730-3752
Mr. Edward G. Pendergast Vice President — Fixed Income The St. Paul Companies Inc.	B	612/221-7903	612/221-8439
Mr. Scott Peng BlackRock Financial Management L.P.	B	212/754-5560	212/754-8790

Contact/Firm	Buyside/Sellside	Telephone	Fax
Mr. Mitchell S. Penn Portfolio Manager Aetna Life & Casualty (Portfolio Management Group)	B	203/275-3405	203/275-4496
Mr. James R. Penner Chief Investment Officer Montana Board of Investments	B	406/444-0578	406/449-6579
Mr. Martin Penstein Senior Vice President LaSalle National Bank (Portfolio)	B	312/904-7805	312/750-6244
Mr. John T. Percy, Jr. Corporate Exec. Vice President Central Fidelity National Bank (Richmond) (Portfolio)	B	804/697-6766	804/783-8335
Mr. Donald Perdue The Central Trust Bank	B	314/634-1234	314/634-7813
Mr. William E. Peressini Treasurer Pacificorp	B	503/731-2000	503/731-2136
Mr. William Perfit Manager Merrill Lynch Capital Markets	S	212/449-5578	212/449-2805
Mr. Timothy Perman Boeing Employee Credit Union	B	206/439-5952	206/439-5806
Mr. Kyle A. Permut Managing Director Oppenheimer & Co., Inc.	S	212/667-5634	212/667-5995
Mr. Perry R. Pero Sr. Exec. V.P. & C.F.O. Northern Trust Corporation	B	312/630-6000	312/444-7843
Mr. Ronald E. Perry Managing Director Greenwich Street Advisors Municipal Management	B	212/816-5711	212/816-5117
Mr. Anthony Pertile Senior Vice President Bank of America Illinois (Institutional Trust)	B	312/828-7530	312/987-0500
Mr. Anthony Pesco Managing Director Santander Financial Products	S	212/407-2975	212/350-3535
Mr. Edgar E. Peters Chief Investment Strategist PanAgora Asset Management, Inc. (U.S.A.)	B	617/439-6300	617/439-6302
Ms. Helen F. Peters S.V.P. & Director Colonial Management Associates	B	617/772-3730	617/737-0358
Mr. Jerry Peters Pennsylvania Public School Employees' Retirement System	B	717/720-4715	717/783-9424
Mr. Phillip E. Peters E.V.P. & Managing Director The Boatmen's National Bank of St. Louis (Portfolio)	B	314/466-6000	314/466-8480
Mr. Bruce Petersen Vice President Goldman Sachs & Company	S	212/902-8228	212/902-1512

Contact/Firm	Buyside/Sellside	Telephone	Fax
Ms. Alice M. Peterson Vice President & Treasurer Sears Roebuck and Company	B	312/875-2500	312/875-8351
Ms. Ann T. Peterson Research Associate Colonial Management Associates	B	617/772-3773	617/737-0358
Ms. Susan Peterson Assistant Vice President Alliance Capital Management (Minneapolis)	B	612/332-1544	612/342-2149
Mr. Daniel Petrula Vice President The Zenith Insurance Company	B	818/594-5266	818/713-0177
Mr. Christopher Phelan Vice President Nomura Securities International, Inc.	S	212/667-1489	212/667-1058
Mr. Bruce Phelps Portfolio Manager Ark Asset Management Company, Inc.	B	212/668-5672	212/668-6198
Mr. George M. Philip Executive Director New York State Teachers' Retirement System	B	518/447-2666	518/447-2630
Mr. Christopher Phillips State Investment Officer Alaska Retirement Systems	B	907/465-4399	907/465-4397
Mr. Craig S. Phillips Managing Director Morgan Stanley & Co., Incorporated (NYC Branch)	S	212/296-4311	212/921-5861
Mr. Kenneth D. Phillips Vice President Lehman Brothers, Inc.	S	212/528-0656	212/526-3738
Mr. Robert Phillips President ASB Capital Management, Inc.	B	202/383-6379	202/347-8389
Mr. James Phoenix Vice President Canadian Imperial Bank of Commerce (U.S.A.)	S	212/856-6647	212/856-6699
Mr. Robert C. Pickett Chairman & President Commercial Union Investment Management	B	617/725-6445	617/725-6702
Mr. Christian Picot Banque Paribas Ltd. Corporation	S	212/841-3670	212/841-2146
Mr. David Pierce-Jones Director Credit Suisse Financial Products	S	212/322-5960	212/238-5332
Mr. Mario J. Pierro Managing Director Deutsche Morgan Grenfell	S	212/469-7194	212/474-8212
Mr. Thomas Piersanti Vice President Mitsui T & B Futures Inc.	S	312/362-2244	312/362-4568

Contact/Firm	Buyside/Sellside	Telephone	Fax
Ms. Elizabeth S. Pierson Vice President AMCORE Bank, N.A. Rockford	B	815/961-7126	815/961-7746
Mr. W. Terrence Pigott Senior Vice President Daiwa Securities America, Inc.	S	212/612-6566	212/612-7100
Mr. William H. Pike Managing Director Chemical Securities Incorporated	S	212/834-4500	212/834-6024
Ms. Christine Pilat Fixed Income Specialist Harris Associates, L.P.	B	312/621-0373	312/621-0372
Mr. Michael Pillari Prudential Securities Inc.	S	212/214-1000	212/776-3463
Mr. Shaiy Pilpel Managing Director Canadian Imperial Bank of Commerce (U.S.A.)	S	212/856-4233	212/856-6699
Mr. Thomas Pindelski Chief Financial Officer Nicholas-Applegate Capital Management	B	619/687-8000	619/687-8040
Mr. John B. Pinkham V.P. — Franklin Group of Funds Franklin Resources, Inc.	B	203/866-8575	203/866-9961
Mr. Michael Piper ITT Hartford Life Insurance Company	B	203/547-5000	203/843-6457
Mr. Guy Piserchia Vice President Merrill Lynch Capital Markets	S	212/449-5578	212/449-2805
Mr. Frederick Pitone Key Trust Company (Albany)	B	518/488-5841	518/488-5846
Mr. Paul Plesser Vice President Chemical Securities Incorporated	S	212/834-4610	212/834-6527
Mr. Theodor K. Plomgren Managing Director Chemical Securities Incorporated	S	212/834-4567	212/834-6521
Ms. Elaine Pochtar Vice President Morgan Stanley & Co., Incorporated (NYC Branch)	S	212/761-2324	212/719-3141
Mr. Steven Poling Chief Financial Officer Fortis Advisers, Inc.	B	612/544-1531	612/544-6363
Mr. Ira Polk Executive Vice President E.D. & F. Man International Securities Corp.	S	212/566-9008	212/566-9456
Mr. Gary R. Pollack Vice President Bankers Trust Global Investment Management	B	212/250-9640	212/250-9857
Mr. Dale W. Polley Vice Chairman & President First American Corporation	B	615/748-2000	615/541-6372

Contact/Firm	Buyside/Sellside	Telephone	Fax
Ms. Lisa Polsky Managing Director BT Securities Corporation	S	212/775-3418	212/250-7071
Mr. C. Lee Ponder President Ponder Investment Company	B	817/354-8282	817/354-1437
Mr. Vijay Popat Vice President Goldman Sachs & Company	S	212/902-4402	212/902-1512
Mr. Charles Porten Senior Vice President I.B.J.-Schroder Bank & Trust Co. (Trust)	B	212/858-2278	212/514-9279
Mr. Timothy Porter The Bank of North Dakota	B	701/328-5600	701/328-5820
Mr. Dennis Porterfield Executive Vice President United Jersey Bank (Portfolio)	B	201/646-5208	201/489-7909
Ms. Helen Potter Quantilogic Asset Management	B	415/434-1130	415/434-1139
Mr. Joseph Powell Treasurer Deposit Guaranty National Bank (Portfolio)	B	601/354-8018	601/354-8361
Mr. Thomas Powell Senior Vice President Old Kent Bank & Trust Company (Portfolio)	B	616/771-1957	616/771-4317
Mr. John Power Senior Vice President Baring Asset Management Company	B	617/951-0052	617/951-1432
Mr. Jerome Powers GNA Capital Management Inc.	B	206/625-2799	206/583-5606
Mr. Robert Powers Vice President HSBC Markets	S	212/658-6710	212/658-1905
Mr. Richard Prager Managing Director ING Barings	S	212/446-1961	212/935-3811
Mr. Salvatore Pramas V.P. — Global Fixed Income Pioneering Management Corporation	B	617/422-4812	617/422-4281
Mr. Anil Prasad Vice President Citicorp Securities, Inc.	S	212/291-7120	212/425-3857
Mr. Narayan Prasad Managing Director Citicorp Securities, Inc.	S	212/559-4971	212/425-3857
Mr. S. Lawrence Prendergast Vice President & Treasurer AT&T	B	212/387-5400	212/226-4935
Mr. Lawrence B. Prescott Vice President U.S. National Bank of Oregon (Portfolio)	B	503/275-5006	503/275-5032

Contact/Firm	Buyside/Sellside	Telephone	Fax
Ms. Sheryl Pressler Chief Investment Officer California Public Employees' Retirement System	B	916/326-3400	916/326-3363
Mr. Perry D. Preusch Vice President Transamerica Investment Services Inc.	B	213/742-3556	213/742-4150
Mr. Donald Price Sr. Vice President — Finance Alfa Corporation	B	334/288-3900	334/288-0905
Mr. Michael F. Price President Heine Securities Corporation	B	201/912-2010	201/912-0147
Mr. C. James Prieur Vice President — Investments Ext. 1139 SunFinancial Group	B	617/237-6030	617/431-7521
Mr. Timothy Prister Vice President General Re Securities Corporation	S	212/307-2327	212/307-2320
Mr. David Prochaska First Bank System (Portfolio)	B	612/973-2297	612/973-0965
Mr. Robert E. Pruyne Managing Director Scudder Stevens & Clark, Inc. (Boston)	B	617/295-1000	617/295-1111
Mr. David Pryde Managing Director J.P. Morgan Securities Inc.	S	212/648-9307	212/648-5253
Mr. L. Wayne Purdy Ferguson, Wellman, Rudd, Purdy & Van Winkle, Inc.	B	503/226-1444	503/226-3647
Mr. Michael Purdy Assistant Vice President Commerzbank Capital Markets	S	212/266-7417	212/266-7797
Mr. James Purnell Vice President Westdeutsche Landesbank Girozentrale — New York Branch	S	212/597-8500	212/852-6300
Mr. David Puth Managing Director Chemical Securities Incorporated	S	212/834-5060	212/834-6527
Mr. C. Lee Quaintance Managing Director CS First Boston Corporation	S	212/909-4166	212/318-1226
Mr. James A. Quale Senior Vice President State Street Bank & Trust (Trust)	B	617/664-5301	617/654-4449
Mr. See Yeng Quek Second Vice President Conseco Capital Management	B	317/817-6725	317/817-6347
Ms. Christine A. Quigley Vice President The Long Island Savings Bank, F.S.B.	B	516/547-3072	516/547-3029
Mr. David Quinn Senior Vice President United States Trust Company of New York (Portfolio)	B	212/852-3151	212/635-3580

Contact/Firm	Buyside/Sellside	Telephone	Fax
Mr. George J. Quinn Executive Vice President Prebon Yamane (U.S.A.)	S	201/557-5210	201/557-5920
Mr. William F. Quinn President AMR Investment Services, Inc.	B	817/967-1525	817/967-9721
Mr. William F. Quinn Principal Smith, Breeden Associates	B	913/451-1566	913/451-6313
Mr. Mark E. Raaberg Senior Portfolio Strategist RCM Capital Management	B	415/954-5419	415/954-8200
Mr. Dale H. Rabiner Director — Fixed Income Bartlett & Co.	B	513/621-4612	513/621-6462
Mr. Frank B. Rabinowitz Managing Director Pacific Investment Management Co. (PIMCO)	B	714/640-3843	714/640-3419
Mr. William Rachal, Jr. Sallie Mae	B	202/333-8000	202/965-7085
Mr. Stephen A. Radez President Essex Radez Company	S	312/362-2916	No fax
Mr. Peter Rading Manager NatWest Securities Corporation	S	212/602-4265	212/602-4939
Mr. Mathew F. Raftree Executive Vice President Investors Savings Bank	B	201/376-5100 Ext. 285	201/376-5243
Mr. Suresh Raghavan Vice President CIGNA Investment Management (U.S.A.)	B	203/726-5757	203/726-8530
Mr. Shaun N. Rai Vice President Canadian Imperial Bank of Commerce (U.S.A.)	S	212/648-6502	212/856-6099
Mr. Donald L. Raiff Senior Vice President The Northern Trust Company (Treasury)	B	312/630-6000	312/444-5666
Mr. Eugene C. Rainis Partner & Director Brown Brothers Harriman & Co. (Investments)	B	212/493-7830	212/493-8526
Ms. Tazmeen Rajwani Vice President The Bank of New York (Dealer)	S	212/804-2142	212/495-1014
Mr. James Ramsay V.P. — M.B.S. & Derivatives Provident Life & Accident Insurance Co.	B	615/755-8341	615/755-1671
Mr. Joseph Randazzo Senior Vice President Republic New York Securities Corporation	S	212/525-6734	212/525-6958

Contact/Firm	Buyside/Sellside	Telephone	Fax
Mr. Guy Randolph Principal Morgan Stanley & Co., Incorporated (NYC Branch)	S	212/761-2700	212/764-7490
Mr. Robert M. Raney Managing Director United States Trust Co. of California., N.A.	B	213/488-4011	213/488-4029
Mr. V. K. Ranganadhan Manager Bank of America NT & SA — Capital Markets (New York)	S	212/836-5585	212/836-5390
Mr. Robert P. Rank Sr. Vice President & C.I.O. Selective Insurance of America	B	201/948-3000	201/948-6709
Mr. William Rappolt Executive Vice President Manufacturers & Traders Trust Company (Portfolio)	B	212/350-2403	212/350-2166
Mr. Ralph J. Rasmussen General Manager-Invt. Services The Bank of California, N.A.	B	415/765-0400	415/765-2788
Mr. Dipak K. Rastogi Managing Director Citicorp Securities, Inc.	S	212/291-6121	212/291-3158
Mr. Robert Ray Senior Vice President First National Bank of Maryland (Portfolio)	B	410/244-4676	410/244-4477
Mr. Mark Razzano Vice President Prudential Securities Inc.	S	212/778-3988	212/776-3463
Mr. Andrew Readinger Vice President J.P. Morgan Securities Inc.	S	212/648-2429	212/648-5253
Mr. Frederick W. Reams President Reams Asset Management Company Inc.	B	812/372-6606	812/376-3137
Mr. Stanley R. Reber Executive Vice President Provident Mutual Life Insurance Company	B	215/636-5215	215/636-8322
Mr. Richard J. Redick Director — Finance Barnett Banks, Inc.	B	904/791-7500	904/791-7185
Mr. Daniel Redmond Vice President UNUM Life Insurance Company	B	207/770-4108	207/770-4152
Mr. David L. Redo President & C.E.O. Fremont Investment Advisors Inc.	B	415/768-6959	415/284-8122
Mr. Edgar M. Reed Executive Vice President Back Bay Advisors, L.P.	B	617/578-1748	617/424-8665
Mr. Lawrence Reed Treasurer First Nationwide Bank, A Federal Savings Bank	B	415/904-1348	415/904-0149

Contact/Firm	Buyside/Sellside	Telephone	Fax
Mr. Russell Reed Vice President Oppenheimer Management Corporation	B	212/323-0588	212/323-0558
Mr. Scott E. Reed Sr. Exec. V.P. & C.F.O. Branch Banking & Trust Company (BB&T-NC) (Portfolio)	B	910/733-3088	910/733-2238
Mr. W. Allen Reed President & C.E.O. General Motors Investment Management Corp.	B	212/418-3585	212/418-3665
Mr. Arthur C. Reeds III President CIGNA Investments, Inc.	B	203/726-7559	203/726-8137
Mr. Douglas R. Rees Senior Director Merck & Co., Inc.	B	908/423-7958	908/735-1275
Ms. Ann N. Reese S.V.P. & Treasurer ITT Corporation	B	212/258-1000	212/489-3596
Mr. Michael Reger General Partner Adams, Viner & Mosler	B	407/655-4900	407/655-3059
Mr. Boyce G. Reid Director Capitoline Investment Services, Inc. (Richmond)	B	804/782-7921	804/782-5839
Mr. Beat Reinhart Assistant Vice President Commerzbank Capital Markets	S	212/266/7575	212/266-7797
Mr. Alan H. Resnick Vice President & Treasurer Bausch & Lomb Incorporated	B	716/338-6045	716/338-6007
Mr. John W. Ressner Vice President Capital Research & Management Company (New York)	B	212/649-1577	212/649-1533
Mr. Anthony Rettino S.V.P./Financial Risk Manager AON Advisors Incorporated	B	312/701-3909	312/701-3900
Mr. John Reynolds S.V.P.-Investments Marine Midland Bank, N.A. (Trust)	B	716/841-7800	716/841-4244
Mr. Richard I. Reynolds Vice President & C.F.O. Libby, Inc.	B	419/727-2100	419/727-2585
Mr. William T. Reynolds Mng. Director-Municipal Bonds T. Rowe Price Associates, Inc.	B	410/547-5703	410/659-0965
Mr. J. Douglas Rhoten Managing Director Garvin GuyButler Corporation	S	212/732-6900	212/815-6587
Mr. Frank J. Riccardi Senior Vice President Society Asset Management, Inc.	B	216/689-9838	216/689-7083

Contact/Firm	Buyside/Sellside	Telephone	Fax
Mr. Michael Ricciardi Managing Director Citicorp Securities, Inc.	S	212/291-6407	212/291-3454
Mr. William C. Rice Senior Vice President AmSouth Bank N.A. (Portfolio)	B	205/326-5645	205/801-0109
Mr. Bruce J. Richards Managing Director Smith Barney, Inc. (Greenwich Street)	S	212/723-5287	212/723-8764
Mr. Jack Richards Vice President Westpac Banking Corporation	S	212/818-1578	212/818-1499
Mr. John Richards Vice President Bank of America NT & SA — Capital Markets (New York)	S	212/836-5572	212/836-5390
Mr. B. Phil Richardson Vice President & Treasurer Alfa Corporation	B	334/288-3900	334/288-0905
Mr. Mark R. Richardson Senior Vice President Chase Manhattan Private Bank Investment Management	B	212/789-5193	212/398-1872
Mr. Gregory P. Richter Managing Director Prudential Securities Inc.	S	212/778-2741	212/778-1905
Mr. David Ricketts Manager Canadian Imperial Bank of Commerce (U.S.A.)	S	212/856-6602	212/856-6699
Ms. Susan Riechel Vice President First Interstate Bank of California (Trust)	B	213/614-2990	213/614-2468
Mr. Francis J. Riepl Treasurer Public Service Enterprise Group Incorporated	B	201/430-7000	201/430-5845
Mr. Bruce Rigione Managing Director Chase Securities Inc.	S	212/552-2716	212/552-4907
Ms. Terrie Ringwalt Vice President First Bank, N.A. (Omaha) (Trust)	B	402/348-6042	402/348-7819
Ms. Susan Ripley Vice President Washington Square Advisers Inc.	B	612/372-5595	612/342-7541
Mr. James F. Rippey President Columbia Management Company	B	503/222-3600	503/243-5052
Mr. Tad Rivelle Hotchkis and Wiley	B	213/362-8888	213/623-8905
Mr. Richard Robb Chief Trader DKB Financial Products, Inc.	S	212/313-0530	212/432-8464

Contact/Firm	Buyside/Sellside	Telephone	Fax
Mr. Sadakichi B. Robbins Assistant Vice President First Federal Savings and Loan Association of Rochester	B	716/238-2119	716/238-2056
Mr. Daniel C. Roberts Managing Director UBS Asset Management, Inc. (U.S.A.)	B	212/789-7100	212/789-7237
Mr. Enoch G. Roberts Director of Administration Kentucky National Insurance Co.	B	606/253-5200	606/253-5203
Mr. Philip R. Roberts Executive Vice President Mellon Bank, N.A. (Trust)	B	412/234-1685	412/236-0648
Mr. Richard B. Roberts E.V.P. & Treasurer Wachovia Corporation	B	910/732-4554	910/770-6667
Mr. Linwood R. Robertson Vice President & Treasurer Dominion Resources, Inc.	B	804/775-5895	804/775-5819
Mr. Randy B. Robertson Director-Investments Barnett Banks, Inc.	B	904/791-7621	904/791-7185
Mr. Richard S. Robertson E.V.P. — Risk Management Lincoln National Corporation	B	219/455-2000	219/455-2301
Mr. E.A. Robinson Vice President & Treasurer Exxon Corporation	B	214/444-1000	214/444-1348
Mr. James C. Robinson Director — Fixed Income Munder Capital Management, Inc.	B	810/647-9200	810/647-5931
Mr. Kevin J. Roche V.P. — Finance & C.F.O. Dow Jones & Company, Inc.	B	212/416-2000	212/416-2655
Mr. Stephen A. Roell Vice President & C.F.O. Johnson Controls, Inc.	B	414/228-1200	414/228-2302
Mr. Max A. Roesler Treasurer Lincoln National Corporation	B	219/455-2000	219/455-2301
Mr. Jonathan Rogers Assistant Vice President Trustmark National Bank (Portfolio)	B	601/961-6561	601/949-2382
Ms. Marian Rogers Commander Investment Corporation	B	814/724-5078	No fax
Ms. Alicia Rojo Santander National Bank	B	809/740-4444	809/798-4480
Mr. Gary U. Rolle Executive Vice President Transamerica Investment Services Inc.	B	213/742-3551	213/742-4150
Mr. David A. Rose Chairman & C.E.O. Alaska Permanent Capital Management Company	B	907/272-7575	907/272-7574

Contact/Firm	Buyside/Sellside	Telephone	Fax
Mr. David W. Rose Vice President General Re Securities Corporation	S	212/307-2327	212/307-2320
Mr. Scott Rosebrook V.P. & Manager Bank of America NT & SA — Capital Markets	S	415/622-9182	415/622-5901
Mr. Michael S. Rosen Vice President Fielding Management Company, Inc.	B	716/383-1300	716/383-0914
Mr. David A. Rosenberg Vice President Oppenheimer Management Corporation	B	212/323-0584	212/323-0558
Mr. Mark Rosenberg President RXR Capital Management, Inc.	B	203/323-5015	203/325-5999
Mr. Robert M. Rosenberg Exec. Vice President & C.F.O. Enhance Financial Services Group Inc.	B	212/983-3100	212/682-5377
Mr. Ronald Rosenberg Managing Director Merrill Lynch Capital Markets	S	212/449-5390	212/449-2805
Mr. Robert A. Rosholt Exec. Vice President & C.F.O. First Chicago/NBD Corporation	B	312/732-3209	312/732-3366
Mr. Howard Rosof NatWest Bank, N.A. (Portfolio)	B	201/547-7000	201/547-2979
Mr. James Ross Executive Vice President AEGON U.S.A. Investment Management (Cedar Rapids)	B	319/398-7821	319/369-2009
Mr. Simon Ross Associate BT Securities Corporation	S	212/775-4937	212/250-7071
Mr. David W. Rossmiller Vice President Bankers Trust Global Investment Management	B	212/250-8521	212/250-9857
Mr. Alfred G. Roth Senior Managing Director First Chicago Capital Markets, Inc.	S	312/732-4401	312/732-4239
Mr. Peter F. Rotondo Executive Vice President Exco Noonan Inc.	S	201/200-4610	201/200-5069
Mr. Bryan R. Roub Senior Vice President & C.F.O. Harris Corporation	B	407/727-9100	407/727-9344
Mr. Ramine Rouhani CDC Investment Management Corp. (CIMCO)	B	212/891-6170	212/891-6294
Mr. Emmanuel Rousseau Trader — Hybrid Derivatives Bear, Stearns & Company, Inc.	S	212/272-5135	212/272-6291
Mr. Sumit Roy Vice President Salomon Brothers Inc.	S	212/783-2917	212/783-2284

Contact/Firm	Buyside/Sellside	Telephone	Fax
Mr. Leonard M. Rubenstein Executive Vice President General American Investment Management Company (GAIMCO)	B	314/444-0624	314/444-0486
Mr. James Rudd Chief Executive Officer Ferguson, Wellman, Rudd, Purdy & Van Winkle, Inc.	B	503/226-1444	503/226-3647
Mr. Edward C. Ruff Sr. Vice President & C.F.O. Interstate/Johnson Lane, Inc.	B	704/379-9119	704/379-9122
Mr. Michael Rulle Executive Managing Director Canadian Imperial Bank of Commerce (U.S.A.)	S	212/856-6050	212/856-6699
Mr. Derek Rummel First of America Investment Corporation	B	616/385-0222	616/385-0227
Mr. Robert R. Rupp Managing Director Chemical Securities Incorporated	S	212/834-5305	212/834-6539
Ms. Elizabeth Ruskin Senior Portfolio Manager Sanford C. Bernstein & Co., Inc.	B	212/756-4135	212/756-4550
Mr. Sherman B. Russ Vice President Pioneering Management Corporation	B	617/422-4830	617/422-4281
Ms. Elana D. Russell Chief Executive Officer Evergreen Asset Management, Inc. (Washington)	B	206/224-9914	206/382-0950
Mr. Sheldon Rutstein Senior Vice President & C.F.O. Raytheon Company	B	617/862-6600	617/860-2172
Mr. Charles E. Ryan Vice President The Bank of Tokyo Trust Company (Pension & Investments)	B	212/766-8683	212/571-5150
Mr. Larry Ryan Manager-Investments & Funding AgriBank, FCB	B	612/282-8472	612/282-8666
Mr. Patrick G. Ryan President & C.I.O. AON Advisors Incorporated	B	312/701-3000	312/701-3900
Mr. Robert C. Ryan Vice President The Bank of New York (Dealer)	S	212/804-2165	212/495-1014
Mr. Robert Ryan Manager of Trading Delphi Capital Management, Inc.	B	212/838-7000	212/838-7598
Mr. Daniel Ryczek Vice President Loomis, Sayles & Company Inc. (Washington, D.C.)	B	202/463-6200	202/293-8264
Mr. David Sacherman The Patterson Capital Corporation	B	310/556-2496	310/553-3605
Ms. Ellen B. Safir Managing Director-Investments Howard Hughes Medical Institute	B	301/215-8687	301/215-8691

Contact/Firm	Buyside/Sellside	Telephone	Fax
Mr. Edward M. Safran President Merganser Capital Management Corporation	B	617/494-1000	617/494-1899
Ms. Jonelle St. John Treasurer MCI Communications Corporation	B	202/872-1600	202/887-2443
Mr. Paul N. Saleh Vice President & Treasurer Honeywell, Inc.	B	612/951-1000	612/951-3070
Mr. A. R. Sales Treasurer Arvin Industries, Inc.	B	812/379-3000	812/379-3688
Mr. Kenneth Sallade Executive Vice President Dauphin Deposit Bank & Trust Company (Portfolio)	B	717/255-2131	717/255-2135
Mr. Bruce D. Salvog Director Piper Capital Management Inc.	B	612/342-1155	612/342-6992
Mr. Ronald E. Samford, Jr. E.V.P. & Controller Hibernia Corporation	B	504/586-5552	504/586-5841
Mr. Paul R. Samuelson Chief Investment Officer PanAgora Asset Management, Inc. (U.S.A.)	B	617/439-6300	617/439-6302
Mr. Jonathan Sandelman Managing Director Salomon Brothers Inc.	S	212/783-3180	212/783-2284
Mr. Charles C. Sanders, Jr. Sr. Assistant State Treasurer South Carolina Retirement System	B	803/734-2114	803/734-2039
Mr. Ivan Sands First Vice President Credit Lyonnais Bank	S	212/261-7979	212/459-3170
Mr. Stephen Santangelo Assistant Vice President Continental Asset Management	B	212/440-7515	212/440-7518
Mr. Robert Santora Executive Vice President Dean Witter Reynolds Inc.	S	212/392-1922	212/392-2887
Mr. Ronald L. Saper Exec. Vice President & C.F.O. Washington Federal Savings & Loan Association	B	206/624-7930	206/467-0524
Mr. George D. Sapp Senior Vice President-Invsts. American United Life Insurance Company	B	317/263-1823	317/263-1225
Mr. Bruce D. Sargent Chairman & C.E.O. Smith Barney, Inc. (Capital Management)	B	212/816-2233	212/816-6167
Mr. Martin D. Sass President Ext. 2115 M.D. Sass Investors Services, Inc.	B	212/730-2000	212/764-0381
Mr. Michael T. Sauer Vice President Citizens Federal Bank, F.S.B.	B	513/229-8352	513/228-5510

Contact/Firm	Buyside/Sellside	Telephone	Fax
Ms. Cathleen Saylor Vice President-Fixed Income Dauphin Deposit Bank & Trust Company (Trust)	B	717/255-2318	717/255-2073
Mr. Michael Sbabo Vice President Citicorp Securities, Inc.	S	212/291-2782	212/425-3857
Mr. Anthony Scamardolla Vice President Westdeutsche Landesbank Girozentrale — New York Branch	S	212/852-6052	212/852-6300
Ms. Joy Schaefer Vice President & C.O.O. Western Financial Savings Bank, Fsb	B	714/727-1000	714/727-2306
Mr. Mark Schaefer Dealer BZW/Barclays Bank	S	212/693-4070	212/412-1768
Mr. Keith M. Schappert President & C.E.O. J.P. Morgan Investment Management, Inc. (U.S.A.)	B	212/837-2300	212/575-0392
Ms. Lois Scheirer Senior Vice President BayBank Boston, N.A. (Dealer)	S	617/556-6996	617/556-6650
Mr. Phillip Schemel Vice President & Director Societe Generale Securities Corporation	S	212/278-7105	212/278-7195
Mr. Daniel G. Scherman Assistant Vice President Massachusetts Financial Services Company	B	617/954-5860	617/954-6603
Ms. Patricia Scheuer National Western Asset Management, Inc.	B	512/836-1010	512/835-2729
Mr. Craig Schiffer Managing Director Lehman Brothers, Inc.	S	212/526-4445	212/526-3738
Mr. Kevin Schildt Vice President General Accident Group	B	215/625-2064	215/625-2103
Mr. Paul R. Schlaack President & C.E.O. Equitable Investment Services, Inc.	B	515/282-0323	515/282-9538
Mr. Richard A. Schlanger Vice President Pioneering Management Corporation	B	617/422-4835	617/422-4281
Mr. Timothy A. Schlindlwein Chairman Stein Roe & Farnham Incorporated	B	312/368-7678	312/368-8103
Ms. Kathy Schmidt Director Sakura Global Capital, Inc.	S	212/486-8716	212/355-4271
Mr. Ken Schmidt V.P. & Senior Trader The Dime Savings Bank of New York, FSB	B	212/326-6951	212/326-6907

Contact/Firm	Buyside/Sellside	Telephone	Fax
Mr. Joseph Schmuckler Executive Managing Director Nomura Securities International, Inc.	S	212/667-2099	212/667-1058
Mr. Thomas C. Schneider Exec. Vice President & C.F.O. Dean Witter, Discover & Co.	B	212/392-2222	212/392-8405
Mr. Charles Schoenig Vice President CDC Investment Management Corp. (CIMCO)	B	212/891-6169	212/891-6294
Mr. David Schoenthal Senior Managing Director Bear, Stearns & Company Inc.	S	212/272-7683	212/272-6291
Mr. Garret A. Scholz Vice President — Finance McKesson Corporation	B	415/983-8639	415/983-7160
Ms. Suzanne Schonman Vice President FIMAT Futures U.S.A., Inc.	S	212/527-8115	212/759-2898
Mr. George Schott Co-Head — Global Derivatives ING Barings	S	212/446-0403	212/644-0428
Mr. Douglas R. Schrank Vice President & C.F.O. M.A. Hanna Company	B	216/589-4000	216/589-4200
Mr. Gary W. Schreyer Principal RCM Capital Management	B	415/954-5400	415/954-5304
Mr. Ronald T. Schroeder Managing Director J & W Seligman & Co., Incorporated	B	212/850-1351	212/922-5747
Mr. W. L. Schroeder Shell Oil Company	B	713/241-2847	713/241-2341
Mr. James Schrott Integra Financial Corporation	B	412/644-8513	412/261-7279
Mr. Kirk Schubert Senior Vice President DKB Financial Products, Inc.	S	212/313-0480	212/432-8464
Mr. Ivor Schucking Pacific Investment Management Co. (PIMCO)	B	714/640-3507	714/720-1376
Mr. Mark O. Schultz Vice President Yamaichi International (America), Inc.	S	212/524-1160	212/524-1159
Mr. Ronald Schultz Investment Manager Texas County & District Retirement System	B	512/479-6021	512/479-8114
Mr. David W. Schulz President M & I Investment Management Corp.	B	414/287-8755	414/287-8730
Mr. Bernard Schumacher Senior Vice President Webster Bank	B	203/578-2446	203/573-8301

Contact/Firm	Buyside/Sellside	Telephone	Fax
Mr. Michael Schwartz Senior Vice President Oppenheimer & Co., Inc.	S	212/667-7130	212/667-5302
Mr. Robert Schwartz President Republic New York Securities Corporation	S	212/525-6837	212/525-6958
Mr. Ronald H. Schwartz Senior Vice President STI Capital Management	B	407/237-4176	407/237-4285
Mr. Simeon Schwartz Vice President UBS Securities, Inc.	S	212/821-4131	212/821-5871
Mr. Joel Schweitzer Vice President Citicorp Global Derivatives	S	312/993-3796	312/993-6830
Mr. Steven Schwimmer Senior Vice President PaineWebber Incorporated	S	212/713-8700	212/713-1303
Mr. Alexander K. Scott Senior Vice President Crestar Bank (Portfolio)	B	804/782-5697	804/782-5100
Mr. Robert Q. Scott Director Merrill Lynch Capital Markets	S	212/449-6177	212/449-2805
Mr. Stephen Scott Investment Counselors of Maryland, Inc.	B	410/539-3838	410/783-7321
Mr. Richard J. Seaman C.F.O. & Treasurer Independent Bank Corp.	B	617/878-6100	617/982-6591
Mr. Robert P. Seass S.V.P. & Controller Dean Witter, Discover & Co.	B	212/392-2222	212/392-8405
Mr. Paul Secord Farmers Insurance Group of Companies	B	213/932-3200	213/930-3101
Mr. Verne O. Sedlacek Exec. Vice President & C.F.O. Harvard Management Company	B	617/523-4400	617/523-1283
Mr. Jeffrey Seel S.V.P. & Managing Director Security Life of Denver Insurance Co.	B	303/860-2041	303/860-2049
Ms. Margarita M. Seeley Assistant Vice President Federal Home Loan Bank of Seattle	B	206/340-2300	206/340-2485
Ms. Donna Seferian Vice President Bank Julius Baer & Co., Ltd.	S	212/297-1981	212/297-1935
Mr. Mark Seidner Standish, Ayer & Wood Inc.	B	617/457-5025	617/350-7520
Mr. Wolfgang Seiler Chief Financial Officer LGT Asset Management	B	415/392-6181	415/956-5617

Contact/Firm	Buyside/Sellside	Telephone	Fax
Mr. Gerald Seizert Munder Capital Management, Inc.	B	810/647-9200	810/647-5931
Mr. Paul Selian Aetna Life & Casualty (Portfolio Management Group)	B	203/275-3410	203/275-4846
Mr. Ronald W. Sellers President & C.E.O. Atlantic Asset Management Partners Inc.	B	203/363-5100	203/363-5110
Ms. Gail P. Seneca GMG/Seneca Capital Management	B	415/677-1550	415/677-1692
Mr. Andrew Serotta Vice President Columbus Circle Investors	B	203/353-5693	203/353-6041
Ms. Roseann Sezcik Life Insurance Company of the Southwest	B	214/638-9243	214/638-9393
Mr. Daniel Shackelford Vice President Investment Counselors of Maryland, Inc.	B	410/539-3838	410/783-7321
Mr. Alan Shaffran Vice President Salomon Brothers Inc.	S	212/783-2693	212/783-2284
Mr. Shahriar Shahida Banque Paribas Ltd. Corporation	S	212/841-3900	212/841-2146
Mr. Joel Shaiman BlackRock Financial Management L.P.	B	212/754-5540	212/754-8777
Mr. Wayne H. Shaner Vice President Martin Marietta Corporation	B	301/897-6000	301/897-6929
Mr. Brian Shannahan Bank of Boston (Treasury)	B	617/434-6851	617/434-6795
Mr. Michael E. Shannon Vice Chairman, C.F.O. & C.A.O. Ecolab Inc.	B	612/293-2233	612/293-2471
Mr. Peter Shapiro Senior Vice President Euro Brokers Maxcor, Inc.	S	212/748-7416	212/748-7050
Mr. Farhan Sharaff Vice President and C.I.O. Citibank Private Banking Investment Division	B	212/559-4478	212/527-2099
Mr. Lawrence Sharley Comerica Bank (Funds Management)	B	313/222-7201	313/222-9825
Mr. Srikane Sharma Manager The Toronto-Dominion Bank (New York — Dealer)	S	212/468-0375	212/262-1949
Mr. Thomas Sharpe Manager The Sakura Bank Ltd. (New York)	S	212/756-6931	212/644-9565
Mr. David P. Shaw Central Carolina Bank & Trust Co. (Portfolio)	B	919/683-7608	919/682-1191

Contact/Firm	Buyside/Sellside	Telephone	Fax
Mr. Greg Shaw Senior Vice President South Boston Savings Bank	B	617/268-2500	617/269-5354
Mr. Rodger D. Shay, Sr. President & C.E.O. Shay Assets Management Co.	B	312/938-2586	312/938-2548
Mr. Patrick Sheehan Vice President Greenwich Street Advisors	B	212/816-5700	212/816-6006
Mr. Thomas Sheehan Integra Financial Corporation	B	412/644-8469	412/261-7279
Mr. Clifford A. Sheets Executive Vice President AEGON U.S.A. Investment Management (Cedar Rapids)	B	319/369-2351	319/369-2009
Ms. Jennifer Sheppard Investment Officer Back Bay Advisors, L.P.	B	617/578-1627	617/424-8665
Mr. David Sherman Vice President Leucadia National Corporation	B	212/460-1935	212/598-4869
Mr. B. P. Sherwood III Vice Chairman & Treasurer Old Kent Bank & Trust Company (Portfolio)	B	616/771-5589	616/771-4317
Mr. James Shiel President — Investments Berkley Dean & Co.	B	203/629-2880	203/629-4359
Mr. Hitoshi Shimamura V.P. & Manager — Capital Mkts. The Tokai Bank Ltd.	S	212/339-1282	212/754-2174
Mr. Donald Shiner Vice President The Tokai Bank Ltd.	S	212/339-1276	212/754-2174
Mr. Thomas A. Shively Senior Vice President State Street Research & Management Co.	B	617/357-1256	617/542-7753
Ms. Janet Showers Managing Director Salomon Brothers Inc.	S	212/783-6612	212/783-2284
Mr. Randolph W. Sides Managing Director Chase Securities Inc.	S	212/552-3081	212/552-7955
Mr. John T. Siegel President & Treasurer Thompson, Siegel & Walmsley, Inc.	B	804/353-4500	804/353-0925
Mr. Mark K. Silverstein Senior Vice President BEA Associates	B	212/310-0305	212/355-1545
Mr. Joseph Simanek Treasurer Bluebonnet Savings Bank Fsb	B	214/443-9000 Ext. 3336	214/443-4376

Contact/Firm	Buyside/Sellside	Telephone	Fax
Mr. Mark L. Simenstad Vice President Investment Advisers, Inc.	B	612/376-2667	612/376-2616
Mr. Daniel P. Simet Household International, Inc.	B	708/564-5000	708/564-6110
Mr. Clay Simmons Chief Financial Officer First Federal Savings and Loan Association of Rochester	B	716/238-2426	716/238-2056
Mr. Jonathan Simmons Banque Paribas Ltd. Corporation	S	212/841-2400	212/841-2146
Mr. Robert C. Simmons Federal Home Loan Bank of Boston	B	617/542-0150	617/292-9645
Mr. Richard Simon Assistant Vice President NatWest Securities Corporation	S	212/602-4050	212/602-4939
Mr. Walter Simon Vice President Bank Julius Baer & Co., Ltd.	S	212/808-9392	212/297-1935
Mr. Robert M. Simonson Managing Director Merrill Lynch Capital Markets	S	212/449-5693	212/449-8896
Mr. Steven Sinacore Managing Director J.P. Morgan Securities Inc.	S	212/648-2333	212/648-5253
Mr. Joseph Sindelar Vice President New York Life Insurance Company (U.S.A)	B	212/576-4257	212/576-8163
Mr. Nathaniel R. Singer Senior Managing Director Bear, Stearns & Company Inc.	S	212/272-5630	212/272-6291
Mr. W. Douglas Singer Executive Vice President The Long Island Savings Bank, F.S.B.	B	516/547-3070	516/547-3029
Mr. Vinayek Singh Vice President Dresdner Securities (USA) Inc.	S	212/429-0437	212/429-4496
Mr. Rex A. Sinquefield Chairman & C.I.O. Dimensional Fund Advisors, Inc.	B	310/395-8005	310/395-6140
Ms. Debra A. Sit Vice President Sit Investment Fixed Income Advisors Inc.	B	612/332-3223	612/342-2018
Mr. John A. Sitek Vice President Wilmington Trust Company (Portfolio)	B	302/651-1862	302/651-1187
Mr. Dennis P. Slattery Manager Smith Affiliated Capital Corporation	B	212/644-9440	212/644-1979
Mr. Thomas J. Slefinger First Vice President Van Kampen American Capital Investment Advisory Corp.	B	708/684-6295	708/684-6270

Contact/Firm	Buyside/Sellside	Telephone	Fax
Mr. Maceo K. Sloan Chairman, President & C.E.O. NCM Capital Management Group, Inc.	B	919/688-0620	919/688-5333
Mr. Gregory C. Smalis Group Vice President The FINOVA Group Inc.	B	602/207-4900	602/207-5543
Mr. William Smethurst President & C.I.O. Schroder Wertheim Investment Services	B	212/641-3900	212/641-3985
Mr. Bradley Smith Assistant Vice President Employers Reinsurance Corporation	B	913/676-5200	913/676-5221
Mr. Craig A. Smith Vice President AIM Advisors, Inc.	B	713/626-1919	713/626-0642
Mr. Damon P. Smith III Managing Director J.P. Morgan Securities Inc.	S	212/648-0916	212/648-5916
Mr. Derrick Smith Vice President Goldman Sachs & Company	S	212/902-8366	212/902-1512
Mr. Gerald Smith Chairman & C.E.O. Smith, Graham & Co. Asset Managers	B	713/227-1100	713/227-0912
Mr. Gregory P. Smith Partner Brinson Partners, Inc.	B	312/220-7253	312/220-7266
Mr. Harold C. Smith President YMCA Retirement Fund	B	212/766-4173	212/766-4178
Mr. Henley L. Smith Sr. Portfolio Mgr.-Money Mkt. Gabelli-O'Connor Fixed Income Management Co.	B	203/655-1999	203/655-7719
Mr. Herbert R. Smith Chairman & C.E.O. Herbert R. Smith, Inc.	B	817/723-5565	817/322-3887
Mr. Irwin F. Smith Chairman & C.E.O. Columbus Circle Investors	B	203/353-6010	203/353-6041
Mr. Joseph W. Smith, Jr. Sr. Vice President & C.I.O. American Family Life Assurance Company (AFLAC)	B	706/323-3431	706/323-1838
Ms. Kathleen Smith Vice President Chase Securities Inc.	S	212/552-6318	212/425-1404
Mr. Matthew R. Smith Lotsoff Capital Management	B	312/368-1442	312/750-1131
Mr. Richard A. Smith Vice President & C.F.O. Arvin Industries, Inc.	B	812/379-3000	812/379-3688

Contact/Firm	Buyside/Sellside	Telephone	Fax
Mr. Robert G. Smith, Sr. President & C.E.O. Smith Affiliated Capital Corporation	B	212/644-9440	212/644-1979
Mr. Robert M. Smith Principal Morgan Stanley Asset Management, Inc.	B	212/296-7087	212/296-7289
Ms. Sheilah R. Smith Florida State Board of Administration	B	904/488-3061	904/921-2131
Mr. William B. Smith III President William B. Smith & Company Inc.	B	508/741-4933	617/289-9555
Mr. Winthrop A. Smith Executive Vice President Merrill Lynch Capital Markets	S	212/449-6349	212/449-2805
Mr. Douglas Smith-Petersen Fiduciary Trust Company of Massachusetts	B	617/482-5270	617/482-3774
Mr. Jack W. Smock, Jr. Principal Scudder Stevens & Clark, Inc. (Los Angeles)	B	213/229-0260	213/626-1005
Mr. Gene Smolenski The Greater New York Savings Bank	B	212/613-4000	212/613-4117
Mr. Michael Snow Senior Managing Director UBS Securities, Inc.	S	212/821-3100	212/821-5846
Mr. James W. Snyder American Express Financial Advisors	B	612/671-3701	612/671-5514
Mr. Arvind Sodhani Vice President — Treasurer Intel Corporation	B	408/765-8080	408/765-1821
Mr. Terrence J. Soffera Senior Portfolio Manager Meridian Investment Company	B	610/251-7991	610/251-5985
Mr. Michael Sollott Falcon Asset Management, Inc.	B	410/547-3545	410/547-3582
Mr. Edward Somekh Managing Director Merrill Lynch Capital Markets	S	212/449-7860	212/449-2805
Mr. K. Brent Somers Sr. Exec. V.P. & C.F.O. KeyCorp	B	216/689-0234	216/689-5115
Mr. Joseph Soprani Delaware Management Company Inc.	B	215/255-2984	215/988-1005
Mr. Peter Sorrentino Vice President Bank One, Dayton, N.A.	B	513/449-4820	513/449-7199
Mr. Craig Sosey First Nationwide Bank, A Federal Savings Bank	B	415/904-1349	415/904-1325
Mr. Theodore T. Sotir Goldman Sachs Asset Management (U.S.A.)	B	212/357-1221	212/902-9100

Contact/Firm	Buyside/Sellside	Telephone	Fax
Mr. Michel Soublin Vice President & Treasurer Schlumberger, Ltd.	B	212/350-9400	212/350-9564
Ms. Mary Lynn Soulas Trader PaineWebber Incorporated	S	212/713-1101	212/713-1303
Mr. David E. Sparks Vice Chairman & C.F.O. Meridian Bancorp, Inc.	B	610/655-2000	610/655-2428
Mr. Wesley Sparks Managing Director Merrill Lynch Capital Markets	S	212/449-5003	212/449-6339
Mr. Ronald L. Spaulding SAFECO Insurance Companies	B	206/545-5734	206/545-3446
Mr. Warren J. Spector Senior Managing Director Bear, Stearns & Company Inc.	S	212/272-5719	212/272-6291
Mr. Matthew Spelker Vice President NatWest Securities Corporation	S	212/602-4060	212/602-4939
Mr. Robert Spicer Senior Vice President Dauphin Deposit Bank & Trust Company (Trust)	B	717/255-2315	717/255-2073
Mr. Marc Spilker Vice President J. Aron & Company	S	212/902-7746	212/346-2687
Mr. Bernard Spilko Managing Director Bank Julius Baer & Co., Ltd.	S	212/297-3939	212/297-1935
Mr. David A. Spina Vice Chairman State Street Boston Corporation	B	617/786-3000	617/664-5377
Ms. Susan Spinner Director Bank of Montreal (Chicago)	S	312/845-5020	312/845-4198
Ms. Ellen Spiro Assistant Vice President Westdeutsche Landesbank Girozentrale — New York Branch	S	212/597-8500	212/852-6300
Mr. Charles L. Stafford Vice President General Re Securities Corporation	S	212/307-2327	212/307-2320
Mr. Per Stahlkrantz Assistant Treasurer NYNEX Corporation	B	914/644-7300	914/644-6287
Mr. Mark E. Stalnecker Chief Investment Officer CoreStates Investment Advisers, Inc.	B	215/786-7566	215/973-3460
Mr. B. Clark Stamper Executive Vice President Davis Selected Advisers, L.P.	B	505/820-1000	505/820-1222

Contact/Firm	Buyside/Sellside	Telephone	Fax
Mr. Roger Stamper Managing Director First of America Investment Corporation	B	616/385-0200	616/385-0227
Mr. Kenneth R. Stancliff S.V.P. & Treasurer First Union Corporation	B	704/374-6161	704/374-4609
Mr. Martin D. Standish Vice President Union Capital Advisors (San Diego)	B	619/230-3344	619/230-3480
Ms. M. Jeannine Standjord Sr. Vice President & Treasurer Sprint Corporation	B	913/624-3000	913/624-3281
Mr. Richard W. Stanley Manager — Investment Research First Asset Management	B	612/973-0027	612/973-0200
Ms. Elizabeth Stanners Vice President Bank of America NT & SA — Capital Markets	S	415/622-8965	415/622-5901
Mr. Gregory Staples Managing Director MONY Financial Services	B	212/708-2643	212/708-2491
Mr. Robert Stapleton President & C.I.O. Independence One Capital Management Corp.	B	810/473-2615	810/473-3094
Mr. Ronald J. Stapleton Manager — Fixed Income Shell Oil Company	B	713/241-0285	713/241-2341
Mr. James M. Stark Vice President First Union National Bank (Pennsylvania) (Instl. Trust)	B	215/985-6424	215/985-6441
Mr. Wendell M. Starke President INVESCO MIM Inc.	B	404/892-0896	404/892-3204
Mr. Raymond Starrett S.V.P. & Treasurer Franklin Federal Bancorp, A Federal Savings Bank	B	512/477-5000	512/479-3498
Mr. David Steck Investment Officer Massachusetts Financial Services Company	B	617/954-5860	617/954-6603
Mr. Michael Steed S.V.P. — Investments Union Labor Life Insurance Co. (ULLICO)	B	202/682-0900	202/682-7932
Mr. Gary L. Stegman S.V.P. & Assistant C.F.O. American Family Life Assurance Company (AFLAC)	B	706/323-3431	706/323-1838
Mr. Orest Stelmach Chief Investment Officer TIG Holdings Inc.	B	212/446-2717	212/371-8360
Mr. Peter Stephenson S.V.P. — Finance Bausch & Lomb Incorporated	B	716/338-6000	716/338-6007

Contact/Firm	Buyside/Sellside	Telephone	Fax
Mr. Ronald C. Stephonic Assistant Treasurer Westfield Companies	B	330/887-0411	330/887-0840
Mr. Merrick L. Sterling E.V.P. — Portfolio Risk Union Bank — Los Angeles	B	213/236-5000	213/236-7983
Mr. Barry L. Stevens Director Michigan Department of Treasury	B	517/373-3140	517/335-2164
Mr. Glenn Stevens Chief Director Merrill Lynch Capital Markets	S	212/449-5578	212/449-2805
Mr. Thomas Stevens Senior Vice President Minnesota State Board of Investment	B	612/296-3328	612/296-9572
Mr. Thomas B. Stevens Vice President Denver Investment Advisors Inc.	B	303/312-5062	303/312-4900
Mr. Wayne C. Stevens President Phoenix Duff & Phelps Investment Management Co. (Chicago)	B	312/368-5540	312/368-5512
Mr. Brian D. Stewart Vice President BayBank Boston, N.A.	B/S	617/556-6717	617/556-6650
Mr. Ian Stewart Vice President Westpac Banking Corporation	S	212/850-7821	212/818-1499
Mr. Scott Stewart Fidelity Management Trust Company	B	617/563-7706	617/476-3834
Mr. Geoffrey Stiff Chief Investment Officer GNA Capital Management Inc.	B	206/625-1755	206/583-5606
Mr. Thomas B. Stiles Chairman Greenwich Street Advisors	B	212/816-5723	212/816-6006
Mr. Peter Stimes Vice President Flaherty & Crumrine, Inc.	B	818/795-7300	818/795-0269
Mr. Jordan Stitzer Vice President The Travelers Insurance Company	B	203-277-3992	203/277-3667
Mr. Clifford W. Stober V.P. & Senior Portfolio Mgr. Nikko Capital Management (U.S.A.)	B	212/559-4632	212/599-4640
Mr. John Stodden ANB Investment Management & Trust Co. of Chicago	B	312/661-6840	312/661-5054
Mr. Gary Stoefen Modern Woodmen of America	B	309/793-5560	309/786-1701
Mr. Timothy Stokes Assistant Vice President Deposit Guaranty National Bank (Portfolio)	B	601/354-8517	601/354-8361

Contact/Firm	Buyside/Sellside	Telephone	Fax
Mr. Howard Stolar Trader NationsBanc — CRT	S	312/234-5437	312/234-3089
Mr. Andrew Stone Managing Director CS First Boston Corporation	S	212/909-2131	212/308-1187
Mr. Samuel G. Stone Sr. Vice President & Treasurer First of America Bank Corporation	B	616/376-7008	616/376-7484
Mr. Robert D. Storer Alaska Retirement Systems	B	907/465-4399	907/465-4397
Mr. Will M. Storey E.V.P., Treasurer & C.F.O. American President Companies, Ltd.	B	510/272-7000	510/272-7941
Mr. Howard J. Stover Vice President E.D. & F. Man International Securities Corp.	S	212/902-6170	212/566-9456
Mr. Edward J. Strafaci Managing Director Lipper & Company, L.P.	B	212/883-2301	212/883-8701
Mr. Kevin J. Straine Dealer Morgan Stanley & Co., Incorporated (NYC Branch)	S	212/761-1786	212/764-7490
Mr. Michael Straine First Vice President Societe Generale Securities Corporation	S	212/278-5316	212/278-7195
Mr. Robert Stricker Vice President Citibank Private Banking Investment Division	B	212/559-5029	212/527-2099
Mr. Gregory Stroik Vice President/Asst. Treasurer Federated Group	B	507/455-5200 Ext. 5229	507/455-5199
Mr. Paul Strong Kiewit Investment Management	B	402/271-2896	402/271-2918
Mr. Richard S. Strong Strong Capital Management Inc.	B	414/359-3600	414/359-3460
Mr. David Strouse Partner Brinson Partners, Inc.	B	312/220-7100	312/220-7199
Ms. Linda B. Strumpf Vice President The Ford Foundation	B	212/573-5052	212/599-4584
Mr. Richard Stuckey Managing Director Salomon Brothers Inc.	S	212/783-2693	212/783-2284
Mr. Jaime Suarez Vice President Banco Santander of New York (Dealer)	S	212/756-9222	212/350-3579
Mr. Peter Succoso Vice President Wilmington Trust Company (Fixed Income)	B	302/651-8784	302/651-1758

Contact/Firm	Buyside/Sellside	Telephone	Fax
Mr. Paul E. Suckow Senior Vice President Delaware Management Company Inc.	B	215/255-2310	215/988-1325
Mr. William Suliburk Vice President First Commercial Corporation	B	501/371-7108	501/371-7413
Mr. Barry M. Sullivan Vice President & Treasurer Harsco Corporation	B	717/763-7064	717/763-6424
Mr. John Sullivan Assistant Vice President Peregrine Derivatives Ltd.	S	212/593-5920	212/593-5932
Mr. Michael J. Sullivan Vice President Prudential Securities Inc.	S	212/778-3399	212/778-2279
Mr. Michael T. Sullivan Scudder Stevens & Clark, Inc. (Boston)	B	617/295-2522	617/295-1111
Mr. Terrence Sullivan Vice President Banque Worms Capital Corporation	S	212/826-5463	212/593-4854
Mr. Thomas A. Sullivan President Delphi Capital Management, Inc.	B	212/838-7000	212/838-7598
Mr. Thomas K. Sullivan RXR Capital Management, Inc.	B	203/323-5015	203/325-5999
Mr. Shelly Sussman Vice President General Re Securities Corporation	S	212/307-2327	212/307-2320
Mr. Steven R. Sutermeister Vice President Carillon Advisers, Inc.	B	513/595-2745	513/595-2843
Ms. Judith M. Swain Manager — Treasury Operations PACCAR Incorporated	B	206/455-7400	206/453-4900
Mr. Russell Swansen President PPM America Inc.	B	312/634-2500	312/634-0050
Mr. Joel R. Swanson President National Mutual Funds Management Inc.	B	310/557-1500	310/286-2314
Mr. Christian Swantek Vice President First of America Investment Corporation	B	616/385-0297	616/385-0227
Mr. James E. Sweeney President — Futures Division Republic New York Securities Corporation	S	212/525-6117	212/525-6958
Mr. John Sweeney Senior Vice President Falcon Asset Management, Inc.	B	410/547-3662	410/547-3582
Mr. Sherif Sweillam Associate Director Fuji Bank Ltd.	S	212/898-2827	212/321-9408

Contact/Firm	Buyside/Sellside	Telephone	Fax
Mr. L. Britt Swofford Senior Vice President First National Bank of Chicago (Dealer)	S	312/732-7029	312/732-4840
Mr. Casey J. Sylla Senior Vice President Allstate Insurance Company	B	708/402-5000	708/402-4347
Mr. Ichiro Tago The Bank of Tokyo Trust Company (Securities & Investments)	B	212/782-6705	212/782-6426
Ms. Shakun Tahiliani Assistant State Treasurer South Carolina Retirement System	B	803/734-2641	803/737-6810
Ms. Terri Tanaka Vice President General American Investment Management Company (GAIMCO)	B	314/444-0781	314/444-0726
Mr. Oscar Tang President Reich & Tang L.P.	B	212/830-5200	212/830-5350
Mr. Bradley C. Tank Principal Strong Capital Management Inc.	B	414/359-3861	414/359-3745
Mr. Gordon Tanner Vice President Salomon Brothers Inc.	S	212/783-2917	212/783-2284
Mr. Gary Taratunio Vice President UBS Securities, Inc.	S	212/821-3580	212/821-5805
Mr. Friench S. Tarkington S.V.P./Trust Invt. Officer Victoria Bank & Trust Company (Trust)	B	512/574-5869	512/574-5669
Mr. Frederick B. Taylor Vice Chairman United States Trust Company of New York (Trust)	B	212/852-3756	212/852-3370
Mr. Terry Taylor V.P. Inv. Products Risk Mgmt. KeyCorp	B	216/689-4875	216/689-5115
Mr. Leonard Teifeld Senior Vice President Lehman Brothers, Inc. (Chicago)	S	312/609-4007	312/609-8562
Mr. Frank W. Terrizzi Managing Director Renaissance Investment Management Inc.	B	513/723-4500	513/723-4512
Mr. Paul Tezak Vice President & Treasurer Smith's Food & Drug Centers Inc.	B	801/974-1400	801/974-1662
Mr. Steven Thatcher Vice President Citicorp Securities, Inc.	S	212/559-5292	212/425-3857
Mr. Jeffrey J. Theodorou Managing Director Prudential Securities Inc.	S	212/778-7444	212/778-4516

Contact/Firm	Buyside/Sellside	Telephone	Fax
Mr. Carl S. Thigpen Second V.P. — Investments Protective Life Corporation	B	205/868-3620	205/868-3609
Mr. Lee Thomas, III Sr. Portfolio Manager Pacific Investment Management Co. (PIMCO)	B	714/640-3031	714/720-1376
Mr. Parker W. Thomas, Jr. SunTrust Bank, Nashville, N.A. (Trust)	B	615/748-5154	615/255-2804
Mr. Robert Thomason Vice President & C.F.O. The Quaker Oats Company	B	312/222-7111	312/222-8323
Mr. David H. Thompson Director — Fixed Income Funds The Private Bank of Bank of Boston	B	617/434-2559	617/434-6311
Mr. J. Victor Thompson, Jr. Principal State Street Global Advisors	B	617/654-3271	617/654-4338
Mr. James C. Thompson, Jr. Divisional E.V.P. Ext. 7200 United Missouri Bank, N.A. (Portfolio)	B	816/860-7200	816/860-4829
Mr. John M. Thompson Vice President & Treasurer Fleming Companies, Inc.	B	405/841-8170	405/841-8149
Ms. Lynn H. Thompson Senior Portfolio Manager Florida State Board of Administration	B	904/488-4061	904/921-2131
Mr. Mark A. Thompson Director Credit Lyonnais Bank	S	212/261-7932	212/261-3641
Mr. Mark I. Thompson Vice President Wachovia Bank Capital Management	B	910/732-5915	910/770-6630
Mr. Matthew G. Thompson Managing Director Thompson, Siegel & Walmsley, Inc.	B	804/353-4500	804/353-0925
Mr. Raymond Thompson Senior Vice President Deposit Guaranty National Bank (Portfolio)	B	601/354-8494	601/354-8361
Mr. Todd C. Thompson Ohio Public Employees' Retirement System	B	614/466-7320	614/469-8276
Mr. Thomas L. Thomsen Vice President — Bonds Columbia Management Company	B	503/222-3600	503/243-2928
Mr. Frederick G. Thorne Chairman Harbor Capital Management Company, Inc.	B	617/478-7216	617/439-9789
Mr. Randall Thornton Vice President First National Bank of Ohio	B	216/384-7354	216/253-1849
Mr. Gerald E. Thunelius Portfolio Manager The Dreyfus Corporation	B	212/922-6496	212/922-6076

Contact/Firm	Buyside/Sellside	Telephone	Fax
Mr. Brett Tidland Trader NationsBanc — CRT	S	312/234-5437	312/234-3089
Mr. Frank Tiernan Vice President & C.F.O. Federal Home Loan Bank of Topeka	B	913/233-0507 Ext. 224	913/234-1796
Ms. Hilary Till The Putnam Management Company Inc.	B	617/292-1633	617/292-1713
Mr. Stephen B. Timbers Chairman & C.E.O. Zurich-Kemper Investments, Inc.	B	312/499-1984	312/499-1001
Mr. Lawrence Tint BZW Barclays Global Investors	B	415/597-2000	415/597-2011
Mr. David Todani Bank of Hawaii (Investments)	B	808/538-4637	808/538-4007
Mr. Bosworth M. Todd, Jr. Chairman Todd Investment Advisors Inc.	B	502/585-3121	502/585-4203
Ms. Hey Ran Toh Vice President Dresdner Securities (USA) Inc.	S	212/429-4120	212/429-4171
Mr. Edward T. Tokar Vice President — Investments Allied-Signal Inc.	B	201/455-2000	201/455-4807
Ms. Diane Tolby Federated Investors	B	412/288-1925	412/288-6425
Mr. Vincent Tomasi Senior Vice President NatWest Securities Corporation	S	212/602-4377	212/602-4547
Mr. John Tormondsen Senior Vice President Goldman Sachs & Company	S	212/902-8340	212/902-1512
Ms. Judith M. Tornese V.P. — Risk Management The Transamerica Corporation	B	415/983-4000	415/983-4888
Mr. Marc Tourangeau Vice President First of America Investment Corporation	B	616/385-0221	616/385-0227
Ms. Karen Towler Senior Vice President Garvin GuyButler Corporation	S	212/732-6900	212/815-6587
Mr. J. R. Tracy Executive Director Swiss Bank Corporation (SBC Warburg)	S	212/574-6088	212/335-1389
Mr. Francis H. Trainer, Jr. Director — Fixed Income Sanford C. Bernstein & Co., Inc.	B	212/756-4138	212/756-4550
Ms. Virginia H. Tranchik Managing Director UBS Securities, Inc.	S	212/821-3500	212/821-4815

Contact/Firm	Buyside/Sellside	Telephone	Fax
Mr. Stephen Traynor Assistant Treasurer Federal Home Loan Bank of San Francisco	B	415/616-1000	415/616-2626
Ms. Anne M. Tremmel Partner Brinson Partners, Inc.	B	312/220-7100	312/220-7199
Mr. Clayton J. Trible, Jr. S.V.P. & Treasurer Standard Federal Bank	B	810/643-2508	810/643-0329
Mr. Steven Trimble Trader Bear, Stearns Securities Corp.	S	312/474-4726	312/474-4690
Ms. Ann K. Tripp Vice President Allmerica Asset Management, Inc.	B	508/855-3856	508/853-6332
Mr. David D. Tripple President Pioneering Management Corporation	B	617/742-8810	617/422-4281
Mr. Keith Trotman Senior Vice President The Zenith Insurance Company	B	818/594-5590	818/713-0177
Mr. Dean Trotzuk Vice President Nomura Securities International, Inc.	S	212/667-2331	212/667-1058
Mr. Patrick Trozzo Senior Vice President Westdeutsche Landesbank Girozentrale — New York Branch	S	212/597-8545	212/852-6300
Mr. Theodore Tsao Banque Paribas Ltd. Corporation	S	212/841-3716	212/841-2146
Mr. Jay S. Tucker Manager CS First Boston Corporation	S	212/909-3180	212/308-1187
Mr. Alan J. Tulp Principal Morgan Stanley & Co., Incorporated (NYC Branch)	S	212/761-7640	212/719-3141
Mr. William Tunis S.V.P.-Treasurer-Secretary Pekin Insurance Company	B	309/346-1161	309/346-8512
Mr. Steven J. Turi Vice President Daiwa Securities America, Inc.	S	212/612-6607	212/612-7100
Ms. Kimberley Turner Vice President BT Securities Corporation	S	212/250-7616	212/250-7071
Mr. Mark Turner Managing Director CDC Investment Management Corp. (CIMCO)	B	212/891-6100	212/891-6294
Mr. Terry Turner S.V.P.-Risk Management First Union National Bank of North Carolina — Funds Mgmt.	B	704/383-1815	704/374-6902

Contact/Firm	Buyside/Sellside	Telephone	Fax
Mr. Richard S. Turney Vice President Bank of America NT & SA — Capital Markets	S	415/622-3007	415/622-4386
Mr. Peter V. Tuters Sr. Vice President & C.I.O. American General Corporation	B	713/831-1935	713/831-1366
Mr. Kevin M. Twomey Exec. Vice President & C.F.O. H.F. Ahmanson & Company	B	818/960-6311	818/962-9679
Dr. David A. Tyson Vice President The Travelers Insurance Company	B	203/954-2041	203/954-4278
Mr. Daniel Ukkestad Vice President Golden Eagle Insurance Company	B	619/463-5800 Ext. 1315	619/460-3820
Mr. Joseph M. Ulrey First Asset Management	B	612/973-0196	612/973-0200
Mr. Richard W. Ulrich Senior Vice President Associates Corporation of North America	B	214/541-6307	214/541-4629
Mr. Kenneth Umezaki Senior Vice President Lehman Brothers, Inc.	S	212/526-6570	212/528-7920
Mr. Gerald Untermann President GEM Capital Management, Inc.	B	212/753-0700	212/753-0735
Mr. William S. Unverzagt Senior Investment Officer Oregon State Treasury Investment Division — Fixed Income	B	503/378-4113	503/378-6772
Mr. David Urben Union Capital Advisors (San Diego)	B	619/230-4712	619/230-4391
Mr. Oka Usi Managing Director BZW/Barclays Bank	S	212/492-6900	212/412-1768
Mr. James R. Vaccacio Manager Glickenhaus & Company (Investments)	B	212/953-7563	212/599-2537
Mr. Samuel Valenti III Vice President — Investments Masco Corporation	B	313/274-7400	313/374-6666
Mr. John Randall Valentine President One Valley Bancorp of West Virginia	B	304/348-7258	304/348-7315
Mr. Latchmi Vandari Vice President Warburg, Pincus Counsellors, Inc.	B	212/878-9366	212/878-9351
Mr. Michael Vandenboffshe First of America Investment Corporation	B	616/385-0206	616/385-0227

Contact/Firm	Buyside/Sellside	Telephone	Fax
Mr. Jeffrey A. Vanderbeek Managing Director Lehman Brothers, Inc.	S	212/526-0770	212/528-6187
Mr. Paul Van Kampen S.V.P. & Dir. — Fixed Income NCM Capital Management Group, Inc.	B	919/688-0620	919/682-0414
Mr. Stephen N. VanOrder Asst.Mgr.-Portfolio Investment Calvert Asset Management Company, Inc.	B	301/951-4800	301/657-1982
Mr. Robert VanParidon Treasurer ABN AMRO Securities (USA) Inc.	S	312/904-5510	312/781-8167
Mr. Nicholas Van Steenberg First Vice President The Laredo National Bank	B	210/723-1151	210/723-0260
Mr. Srinivasa Varathan Banque Paribas Ltd. Corporation	S	212/841-3750	212/841-2146
Mr. Philip Vasan Director CS First Boston Corporation	S	212/909-4222	212/308-1187
Mr. Eugene H. Vaughan President & C.E.O. Vaughan, Nelson, Scarborough & McConnell Inc.	B	713/224-2545	713/247-9534
Mr. Richard C. Vaughan Exec. Vice President & C.F.O. Lincoln National Corporation	B	219/455-2000	219/455-2301
Mr. Jack Veffer First Vice President Credit Lyonnais Bank	S	212/261-7981	212/459-3152
Mr. Mark S. Venezia Vice President Eaton Vance Management, Inc.	B	617/482-8260 Ext. 563	617/482-1572
Mr. Gopal Verdahan Director Deutsche Morgan Grenfell	S	212/469-7401	212/474-8212
Mr. Bert F. Verdicchio Vice President PaineWebber Incorporated	S	212/713-2548	212/713-1303
Mr. George Vere-Laurie Banque Paribas Ltd. Corporation	S	212/841-3433	212/841-2146
Mr. David Viar Citizens National Bank of Evansville (Portfolio)	B	812/464-3400	812/464-3496
Mr. David I. Vickers V.P., Treasurer & C.F.O. Pioneer Financial Services, Inc.	B	708/995-0400	708/413-7192
Mr. Perry J. Vieth Fleet Investment Advisors (Boston)	B	617/346-5709	617/292-2061
Mr. David Vincent Vice President E.D. & F. Man International Inc. (Chicago)	S	312/663-7503	312/663-7710

Contact/Firm	Buyside/Sellside	Telephone	Fax
Mr. Clifford Viner General Partner Adams, Viner & Mosler	B	407/655-4900	407/655-3059
Mr. Puru Voruganti Director Deutsche Morgan Grenfell	S	212/469-7231	212/474-8212
Mr. Daniel Vrabac Vice President Waddell & Reed Investment Management Co.	B	913/236-1834	913/236-1885
Mr. Dung Vukhas Senior Vice President CoreStates Investment Advisers, Inc.	B	215/973-3745	215/973-3589
Mr. Robert S. Waas Colonial Management Associates	B	617/772-3191	617/737-0358
Mr. David Wadlington Leader Federal Bank for Savings	B	901/578-2410	901/524-5715
Mr. Clark D. Wagner Vice President First Investors Management Co., Inc.	B	212/858-8094	212/858-8078
Mr. David E. Wagner Director Canadian Imperial Bank of Commerce (U.S.A.)	S	212/856-6513	212/856-6699
Mr. David J. Wagner President & C.E.O. Old Kent Bank & Trust Company (Portfolio)	B	616/771-5899	616/771-4317
Mr. Henry C. Wagner III CIGNA Investments, Inc.	B	203/726-2793	203/726-8137
Mr. Bert Wagnon Vice President-Investments Alaska Permanent Capital Management Company	B	907/272-7575	907/272-7574
Mr. John J. Wagoneer Treasurer PACCAR Incorporated	B	206/455-7400	206/453-4900
Mr. Richard K. Wagoner Executive Vice President First Union National Bank of North Carolina — Funds Mgmt.	B	704-374-4549	704/374-6902
Mr. David Wald Co-Director NatWest Securities Corporation	S	212/602-5651	212/602-4939
Mr. Charles C. Walden Senior Vice President Knights of Columbus	B	203/865-1710 Ext. 331	203/772-0037
Mr. Allan J. Waldron Principal Vaughan, Nelson, Scarborough & McConnell Inc.	B	713/224-2545	713/247-9534
Mr. David Wales Director Bank of Montreal (Chicago)	S	312/845-5020	312/845-4198
Ms. Kimberly Wales Trader BR Associates	S	908/771-7452	908/771-7452

Contact/Firm	Buyside/Sellside	Telephone	Fax
Mr. David Walker Director-Liability Risk Mgmt. General Motors Acceptance Corporation	B	313/974-1222	313/974-1244
Ms. Barbara Wall Grantham, Mayo, Van Otterloo & Company	B	617/346-7610	617/439-0457
Mr. Douglas Wallace Senior Vice President Crestar Bank (Portfolio)	B	804/782-5696	804/782-5100
Mr. H. Peter Wallace Director — Fixed Income Heritage Asset Management, Inc.	B	813/573-8320	813/573-8334
Mr. Richard Walsh Director Intercapital Securities Inc.	S	212/888-5242	212/319-4001
Mr. Ronald Walter Director — Investments Citibank, N.A. (Portfolio)	B	212/559-4393	212/527-2737
Mr. Kelly Walters Deputy Manager/Head-Fixed Inc. Brown Brothers Harriman & Co. (Investments) (Chicago)	B	312/781-7118	312/368-1287
Mr. Kenneth E. Walters Israel Discount Bank of New York	B	212/551-8820	212/370-9623
Mr. Timothy Walz Vice President Banque Worms Capital Corporation	S	212/826-5464	212/593-4854
Mr. Ian R. Ward Vice President Auto-Owners Insurance Company	B	517/323-1487	517/323-8796
Mr. Jeff Ward State Street Research & Management Co.	B	617/357-1270	617/542-7753
Mr. Stephen Ward Charles Schwab Investment Management	B	415/974-7613	415/974-7660
Mr. Richard H. Warden American Express Financial Advisors	B	612/671-3131	612/671-2733
Mr. Craig M. Wardlaw Executive Vice President NationsBank (Charlotte) (Funds Management)	B	704/386-7696	704/388-0602
Mr. Scott Warman Vice President Manufacturers & Traders Trust Company (Treasury)	B	716/842-5813	716/842-5823
Ms. Ann L. Warner Senior Vice President Lincoln National Investment Management Co.	B	219/455-3204	219/455-1441
Mr. Bradford H. Warner Treasurer Bank of Boston (Treasury)	B	617/434-2200	617/434-6795
Mr. Brian Warner Associate BZW/Barclays Bank	S	212/412-6850	212/412-1768

Contact/Firm	Buyside/Sellside	Telephone	Fax
Mr. Timothy Warner President Berkeley Capital Management	B	415/393-0300	415/393-0392
Mr. Douglas Warren Vice President Citicorp Securities, Inc.	S	212/291-4783	212/425-3857
Mr. Timothy Wartman Manager — Investments United Air Lines Employees Credit Union	B	708/952-6600	708/952-6593
Mr. Robert A. Wasilewski Managing Director ASB Capital Management, Inc.	B	202/383-6286	202/347-8389
Mr. David S. Wasserman Vice President — Treasurer Harris Corporation	B	407/727-9100	407/727-9344
Mr. Zach Wasson Vice President & Treasury Mgr. Trustmark National Bank (Portfolio)	B	601/949-6816	601/949-2382
Mr. Phillip M. Waterman Sr. Executive Vice President Smith Barney, Inc. (Greenwich Street)	S	212/723-5888	212/723-8792
Mr. Stuart Waters President & C.E.O. Pillar Point Capital Management Inc.	B	415/377-3900	415/573-0672
Ms. Catherine Waterworth Managing Director Continental Asset Management	B	212/440-7753	212/440-7518
Mr. Thomas Watjen Chief Financial Officer Provident Life & Accident Insurance Co.	B	615/755-1011	615/755-1671
Mr. Charles Watson Brundage, Story and Rose	B	212/269-3050	212/425-4286
Mr. John H. Watts Chairman Fischer, Francis, Trees and Watts, Inc.	B	212/681-3000	212/681-3250
Mr. Richard B. Waugh Vice President & C.F.O. Northrop Grumman Corporation	B	310/553-6262	310/201-3023
Mr. Alexander Webb III Vice Chairman The Boston Company Asset Management	B	617/722-7779	617/722-7250
Mr. Charles H. Webb Chief Investment Officer Tennessee Consolidated Retirement System	B	615/532-1157	615/741-1061
Mr. Christopher Webb Vice President J. Aron & Company	S	212/902-7747	212/346-2687
Mr. Thomas Webber Vice President Fulton Bank (Trust)	B	717/291-2556	717/291-2695
Mr. Kenneth L. Weddle The Medical Protective Company	B	219/485-9622	219/486-0415

Contact/Firm	Buyside/Sellside	Telephone	Fax
Mr. Anthony Wegener Vice President Merrill Lynch Capital Markets	S	212/449-5578	212/449-2805
Mr. Thomas E. Weiford Senior Vice President Commerce Bank Investment Management Group	B	816/234-2579	816/234-2545
Ms. Melissa Weiler Trust Company of the West (TCW) (High Yield Dept.)	B	310/575-9700	310/575-1997
Mr. Marc Weill Senior Vice President The Travelers Insurance Company	B	203/954-8423	203/277-3667
Mr. Matthew Weinberg Managing Director Smith Barney, Inc. (Greenwich Street)	S	212/723-7414	212/723-8846
Mr. Eric Weinstein Executive Director Swiss Bank Corporation (SBC Warburg)	S	212/574-6042	212/335-1389
Mr. Allen F. Weisbeck Investment Department Manager The Bank of North Dakota	B	701/328-5678	701/328-5632
Mr. Frank E. Weise III Senior Vice President & C.F.O. Campbell Soup Company	B	609/342-4800	609/342-3878
Mr. Kenneth Weisman Vice President Dresdner Securities (USA) Inc.	S	212/429-4120	212/429-4496
Ms. Carol A. Weisner Vice President & Treasurer Litton Industries, Inc.	B	310/859-5000	310/859-5940
Mr. Karl Weiss Managing Director Bank United of Texas, FSB	B	713/543-6500	713/543-7927
Mr. Leigh Weiss Vice President United States Trust Company of New York (Trust)	B	212/852-3578	212/852-3370
Mr. Lawrence Weithers Trader NationsBanc — CRT	S	312/234-3110	312/234-3089
Mr. Wayne P. Weitz Director — Corporate Finance Equifax, Inc.	B	404/885-8575	404/885-8121
Ms. Dina M. Welch Assistant Vice President Provident Mutual Life Insurance Company	B	215/636-5597	215/636-8322
Mr. James S. Welch Vice President Back Bay Advisors, L.P.	B	617/578-1755	617/424-8665
Mr. Michael Welcome Executive Vice President Yamaichi International (America), Inc.	S	212/524-8260	212/390-8815

Contact/Firm	Buyside/Sellside	Telephone	Fax
Mr. Keith Welden Vice President The Boatmen's National Bank of St. Louis (Portfolio)	B	314/466-8317	314/466-8480
Mr. Roy O. Wellington III Tennessee Consolidated Retirement System	B	615/532-1151	615/741-1061
Ms. Cynthia Welton Vice President Old Kent Bank & Trust Company (Portfolio)	B	616/771-5230	616/771-4317
Mr. Gary E. Wendlandt Executive Vice President Massachusetts Mutual Life Insurance Co.	B	413/744-6060	413/744-6127
Mr. Allan P. Wentworth Treasurer Wentworth, Hauser & Violich, Inc.	B	415/981-6911	415/788-7281
Mr. Nathaniel R. Wentworth Vice President Back Bay Advisors, L.P.	B	617/578-1703	617/424-8665
Mr. Jeffrey S. Werner Vice President & Treasurer General Electric Capital Corporation	B	203/357-4963	203/357-6791
Mr. James W. Wert Chief Investment Officer KeyCorp	B	216/689-5850	216/689-7827
Mr. Paul D. Werts Vice President Anhalt/O'Connell, Inc.	B	213/622-0066	213/613-0805
Mr. David D. Wesselimk Vice President & Treasurer Household International, Inc.	B	708/564-5000	708/564-6110
Mr. Steven Wesselkamper Gradison-McDonald Asset Management	B	513/579-5074	513/579-5947
Mr. Hance West Jr. Commonwealth Investment Counsel	B	804/782-3742	804/782-3629
Mr. Benjamin Weston Managing Director Credit Suisse Financial Products	S	212/322-5998	212/318-0730
Mr. Martin H. Wexler President Stacey Braun Associates Incorporated	B	212/226-7707	212/941-0759
Mr. Lee A. Whatcott Asst. Vice President & C.F.O. Western Financial Savings Bank, Fsb	B	714/727-1000	714/727-2306
Mr. Allan R. White III Managing Director Salomon Brothers Asset Management Inc. (U.S.A.)	B	212/783-7413	212/783-4014
Mr. Andrew S. White Vice President — Securities Ext. 415 The Acacia Group	B	202/628-4506	202/638-0345
Mr. Charles M. White Managing Director Avatar Investors Associates	B	212/753-7710	212/644-0332

Contact/Firm	Buyside/Sellside	Telephone	Fax
Mr. Gerald L. White Senior Vice President Deposit Guaranty National Bank (Trust)	B	601/354-8129	601/354-8143
Mr. James A. White Exec. Vice President & C.F.O. Bank of Oklahoma, N.A. (Portfolio)	B	918/588-6416	918/588-6510
Mr. Bruce A. Whiteford Vice President Chase Manhattan Private Bank Investment Management	B	212/789-5569	212/789-5589
Ms. Elizabeth W. Whitehead Director — Public Finance BayBank Boston, N.A. (Dealer)	S	617/556-6990	617/556-6650
Mr. Gregory Whiteley Continental Asset Management	B	212/440-7522	212/440-7518
Mr. Steven Whiting Vice President ING Barings	S	212/446-1555	212/935-3811
Ms. Lisa Y. Whitley Vice President Bear, Stearns & Company Inc.	S	212/272-5631	212/272-6291
Mr. Peter M. Whitman, Jr. President Dewey Square Investors Corporation	B	617/434-6229	617/526-1337
Mr. Cyrus Whitney Vice President Commerzbank Capital Markets	S	212/266-7412	212/266-7797
Mr. Christian Wignall LGT Asset Management	B	415/392-6181	415/956-5617
Mr. Roland Wikstrom Assistant Vice President Bank of Montreal (Chicago)	S	312/845-5021	312/845-4198
Mr. Jonathan Wilcox Vice President Societe Generale Securities Corporation	S	212/278-7105	212/278-7195
Mr. Peter Wild Senior Vice President Bank Julius Baer & Co., Ltd.	S	212/297-1950	212/297-1935
Mr. George Wiley Hotchkis and Wiley	B	213/362-8888	213/623-7880
Mr. Randy J. Wiley Vice President OnBank, Inc. (Portfolio)	B	315/424-4559	315/424-4439
Mr. Kenneth G. Wilkes Vice President & Treasurer Libby, Inc.	B	419/727-2100	419/727-2585
Mr. Christopher Wilkinson Assistant Vice President NatWest Securities Corporation	S	212/602-4060	212/602-4939
Mr. Thomas Wilkinson Vice President Templeton Global Bond Managers, Inc.	B	954/527-7442	954/462-2504

Contact/Firm	Buyside/Sellside	Telephone	Fax
Mr. Peter F. Willard Vice President Westdeutsche Landesbank Girozentrale — New York Branch	S	212/597-8550	212/852-6300
Ms. Victoria Willard Director — Fixed Income Maryland State Retirement & Pension System	B	410/225-1025	410/523-8133
Mr. David M. Willey Sr. Vice President & Treasurer Capital One Financial Corporation	B	703/205-1000	703/205-1755
Mr. A. Steve Williams III Sr. Vice President-Investments Protective Life Corporation	B	205/868-3600	205/868-3609
Mr. Frederic Williams Chairman Williams, Jones & Associates Inc.	B	212/935-8750	212/753-3072
Mr. Gerald R. Williams Exec. Vice President & C.F.O. Huntington Bancshares, Incorporated	B	614/480-8300	614/480-3761
Mr. John S. Williams Principal Barrow, Hanley, Mewhinney & Strauss, Inc.	B	214/665-1900	214/871-5309
Mr. Mark Williams President Heber Fuger Wendin Incorporated	B	810/258-6866	810/258-9295
Ms. Marsha C. Williams Treasurer Amoco Corporation	B	312/856-6111	312/856-2454
Mr. P. Greggory Williams Kiewit Investment Management	B	402/342-3665	402/271-2918
Mr. Charles Williamson Bank of Oklahoma, N.A. (Portfolio)	B	918/588-6000	918/588-6510
Mr. Stanley Willie Director — Trust Invt. Mgmt. U.S. West, Inc.	B	303/649-4514	303/649-4520
Mr. James F. Willison Senior Vice President Dean Witter InterCapital Inc.	B	212/392-1659	212/392-4282
Mr. Donald Wilson Treasurer Marshall & Ilsley Corporation	B	414/765-8043	414/765-7645
Ms. Mary E. Wilson Vice President Massachusetts Mutual Life Insurance Co.	B	413/788-8411	413/744-8798
Ms. Mary M. Wilson Partner Brinson Partners, Inc.	B	312/220-7100	312/220-7199
Mr. Thomas J. Wilson Chief Financial Officer Allstate Insurance Company	B	708/402-5000	708/402-4347
Mr. Kenneth Windheim President Strategic Fixed Income L.P.	B	703/812-8300	703/812-9554

Contact/Firm	Buyside/Sellside	Telephone	Fax
Mr. Jay Windsor Principal Mutual Life Insurance Company	B	515/248-9621	515/248-8486
Mr. Jeffrey L. Winter Managing Director Quantilogic Asset Management	B	415/434-1130	415/434-1139
Mr. Kevin Winter Investment Officer California Public Employees' Retirement System	B	916/326-3394	916/326-3363
Mr. H. Vernon Winters Boston Safe Deposit and Trust Company	B	617/722-7000	617/722-7807
Mr. Jack Winters Lehman Brothers Global Asset Management, Inc. (New York)	B	212/526-7850	212/528-6300
Mr. Thomas J. Winters, Sr. Ryan Labs, Inc.	B	212/635-2300	212/635-2309
Ms. Mary Ann B. Wirts V.P. & Director — Fixed Income The Glenmede Trust Company	B	215/419-6037	215/419-6197
Mr. Keith Wirtz Senior Vice President BofA Capital Management Inc. (Los Angeles)	B	213/229-1928	213/626-2162
Ms. Roseanne M. Witmer Senior Vice President The Bank of New York Company, Inc.	B	212/495-1784	212/815-4023
Mr. Richard A. Witt Sr. Vice President & Manager United of Omaha Life Insurance Company	B	402/351-2503	402/351-2913
Mr. Spencer Witty Chairman The Merchants Bank of New York	B	212/973-6666	212/966-4813
Mr. William Wivel V.P. & Trust Officer Riggs Investment Management Corporation	B	202/835-6879	202/835-6806
Ms. Mary Wladkowski Investment Manager National Bank of Alaska	B	907/265-2975	907/265-2139
Mr. William Wogstad Treasurer & C.I.O. Ext. 2238 St. Paul Federal Bank for Savings	B	312/804-2110	312/804-2285
Mr. Michael Wohl Managing Director BT Securities Corporation	S	212/250-7602	212/250-7071
Mr. H. Jerry Wolf President & Principal Wolf, Webb, Burk & Campbell Inc.	B	215/735-5910	215/735-7892
Mr. Pierre Wolf Managing Director FIMAT Futures U.S.A., Inc.	S	212/759-2626	212/759-2898
Mr. Richard A. Wolf President First of America Investment Corporation	B	616/385-0202	616/385-0227
Mr. Lavern R. Wolfanger Vice President Beneficial Insurance Group, Inc.	B	908/781-4246	908/781-4479

Contact/Firm	Buyside/Sellside	Telephone	Fax
Mr. Carter Wolfe Vice President Howard Hughes Medical Institute	B	301/215-8686	301/215-8691
Mr. William Wolfe Treasurer AgriBank, FCB	B	612/282-8734	612/282-8666
Mr. Elliot K. Wolk Senior Managing Director Bear, Stearns & Company Inc.	S	212/272-4806	212/272-6291
Mr. Benjamin Wolkowitz Managing Director Morgan Stanley & Co., Incorporated (NYC Branch)	S	212/761-1700	212/764-7490
Mr. John Womble Senior Vice President National Bank of Commerce (Portfolio)	B	901/523-3271	901/523-3879
Mr. Elwyn Wong Managing Director Sakura Global Capital, Inc.	S	212/486-5193	212/355-4271
Ms. Diane E. Wood Executive Vice President Allmerica Asset Management, Inc.	B	508/855-3593	508/853-6332
Mr. James R. Wood President & C.F.O. STI Capital Management	B	407/237-4472	407/237-4285
Mr. Richard S. Wood Executive Vice President Standish International Management Co., L.P.	B	617/350-6100	617/350-7520
Mr. Stephen D. Wood Managing Director Ark Asset Management Company, Inc.	B	212/668-7611	212/668-6196
Mr. Richard B. Woodbury Principal Berkeley Capital Management	B	415/393-0354	415/393-0391
Ms. Dea Woodham V.P. & Sr. Trust Officer Compass Bank (Trust)	B	205/558-6308	205/558-6754
Mr. Martin Woodhams Managing Director Bear, Stearns & Company Inc.	S	212/272-4518	212/272-6291
Mr. Trevor Woodland Vice President Bank of Montreal (Chicago)	S	312/845-4080	312/461-7385
Mr. James Woods Sr. Vice President & Treasurer Security Benefit Life Insurance Co. of Kansas	B	913/295-3131	913/295-3099
Mr. Robert Woodward Nationwide Financial Services	B	614/249-7111	614/249-4698
Mr. Harold S. Woolley Senior Vice President Bessemer Trust Company, N.A.	B	212/708-9293	212/586-2806
Mr. Michael Wootton Assistant Vice President The Bank of New York (Dealer)	S	212/804-2109	212/495-1014

Contact/Firm	Buyside/Sellside	Telephone	Fax
Mr. Glenn G. Wozniak Partner Brinson Partners, Inc.	B	312/220-7100	312/220-7266
Mr. William Wraith Executive Managing Director Nomura Securities International, Inc.	S	212/667-1355	212/667-1058
Mr. Neil Wright ANB Investment Management & Trust Co. of Chicago	B	312/661-6009	312/661-5054
Mr. Richard W. Wroten Exec. Vice President & C.F.O. Old Kent Bank & Trust Company (Portfolio)	B	616/771-5808	616/771-4317
Mr. John K. Wulff Vice President Union Carbide Corporation	B	203/794-2000	203/794-3334
Ms. Jane M. Wyatt Chief Investment Officer Voyageur Fund Managers	B	612/376-7063	612/341-2818
Mr. James E. Yacobucci S.V.P. — Investments Reliance Insurance Company	B	212/909-1850	212/909-1864
Mr. Gary Yalen President Fortis Asset Management	B	212/859-7062	212/859-7202
Mr. Yoshiaka Yamaka Senior Vice President Dai-Ichi Kangyo Bank Ltd. (New York)	S	212/432-6670	212/912-0915
Mr. Yifeng Yang Assistant Director General Re Asset Management, Inc.	B	203/328-5000	203/328-6504
Mr. James Yealin First of America Bank Corporation	B	616/376-7460	616/376-7484
Mr. Arlen G. Yokley Vice President & Treasurer BellSouth Corporation	B	404/249-3400	404/249-5597
Mr. Kevin York Vice President Euro Brokers Maxcor, Inc.	S	212/748-7220	212/748-7050
Mr. Hajime Yoshida Executive Managing Director Nomura Securities International, Inc.	S	212/667-2335	212/667-9000
Mr. Hideshu Yoshimura Vice President Sanwa Bank	S	212/339-6512	212/750-3284
Mr. William Yost I.B.J.-Schroder Bank & Trust Co. (Trust)	B	212/858-2402	212/514-9279
Mr. Austin P. Young Sr. Vice President & C.F.O. American General Corporation	B	713/831-1094	713/831-6218
Mr. Douglas S. Young Vice President WESTAMERICA Bank	B	415/257-8047	415/257-8127

Contact/Firm	Buyside/Sellside	Telephone	Fax
Mr. Gregory Young Senior Vice President Santander Financial Products	S	212/407-7821	212/350-3535
Mr. John E. Young Teachers' Retirement System of Texas	B	512/397-6460	512/370-0519
Mr. Alvin M. Younger, Jr. Managing Director & Treasurer T. Rowe Price Associates, Inc.	B	410/547-2000	410/659-0965
Mr. Gregory A. Yovan Vice President Comerica Bank (Funds Management)	B	313/222-7202	313/222-9825
Mr. Mario Yrun Director Credit Lyonnais Bank	S	212/459-3065	212/459-3170
Mr. Richard Zackroff Fixed-Income Co-Dept. Head Cashman, Farrell and Associates	B	610/889-1500	610/889-1665
Mr. David Zagorski Portfolio Manager The Dreyfus Corporation	B	212/922-6207	212/922-6076
Mr. M. G. Zappia Commander Investment Corporation	B	814/724-5078	No fax
Mr. Michael Zazzarino Eastbridge Capital, Inc.	B	212/756-7264	212/756-7160
Mr. Arthur H. Zeikel Senior Vice President Merrill Lynch Asset Management Inc.	B	609/282-2012	609/282-3055
Ms. Cynthia Zeltwanger General Manager FIMAT Futures U.S.A., Inc.	S	212/527-8125	212/759-2898
Mr. Edouard Ziecina Desk Manager FIMAT Futures U.S.A. Inc. (Chicago)	S	312/578-5250	312/578-5277
Mr. Douglas F. Ziegler Sr. Vice President & Treasurer Erie Insurance Group	B	814/870-2038	814/870-3126
Mr. James M. Zinn Sr. Vice President & C.F.O. Capital One Financial Corporation	B	703/205-1000	703/205-1755
Mr. Brian R. Zipp Managing Director Lehman Brothers, Inc.	S	212/526-8817	212/528-8955
Mr. Edward J. Zore Senior Vice President Northwestern Mutual Life Insurance Co.	B	414/299-7339	414/299-7124
Mr. Mark Zurack Partner Goldman Sachs & Company	S	212/902-8654	212/902-1512
Mr. John Zwadzich Investment Director State of Wisconsin Investment Board	B	608/266-2047	608/266-2436

Advertising Index

What is included in the Derivatives Desk Reference?

Complete the application on the reverse side to be included in our publication.

Derivatives Contact Data

- Name
- Title
- Direct Phone & Fax
- Job Function

Derivatives Firm Data

- Company Name
- Location
- Phone & Fax Numbers
- Firm Type
- Notional Amount Indicator
- Investment Profile
- Derivatives Use
- Regions of Activity
- Currencies
- Derivatives Activities
- Counterparty Rating Requirements

Derivatives Firm Types

- Buyside Firms
  - Banks and S&Ls
  - Corporations
  - Insurance Companies
  - Investment Managers
  - Mutual Fund Managers
  - Pension Fund Managers
- Sellside Firms

Would you like to be included in the Derivatives Desk Reference?

If you would like to be included in the next *Derivatives Desk Reference*, please complete and return this form, and we will send you a profile application.

(PLEASE PRINT)

NAME:

TITLE:

COMPANY:

TYPE OF BUSINESS:

ADDRESS:

CITY:

STATE: ZIP:

PHONE:

FAX:

For immediate attention, call Capital Access at 800/866-5987 or fax this information to:

Capital Access Corporation
Fax: 908/771-0330